Bank Street

Early Childhood Education

LEARNING TOGETHER

Virginia Casper
Bank Street College of Education

Rachel Theilheimer
Borough of Manhattan Community College

Mc Graw Hill

Connect
Learn
Succeed™

McGraw-Hill Higher Education
    A Division of The McGraw-Hill Companies

1 2 3 4 5 6 7 8 9 0 QPD / QPD 0 9

ISBN: 978-0-07-337848-0
MHID: 0-07-337848-8

Vice President Editorial: Michael Ryan
Editorial Director: Beth Mejia
Publisher: David S. Patterson
Senior Sponsoring Editor: Allison McNamara
Executive Marketing Manager: James Headley
Marketing Manager: Yasuko Okada
Executive Market Development Manager: Sheryl Adams
Director of Development: Dawn Groundwater
Market Development Coordinator: Emory Davis
Editorial Coordinator: Sarah Kiefer
Senior Production Editor: Catherine Morris
Manuscript Editor: Beverley DeWitt
Design Manager: Andrei Pasternak
Text Designer: Lisa Buckley
Cover Designer: Andrei Pasternak/Lisa Buckley
Art Editor: Sonia Brown
Senior Photo Research Coordinator: Nora Agbayani
Photo Researcher: Toni Michaels
Production Supervisor: Louis Swaim
Composition: 11/13 Arno Pro Regular, by Thompson Type
Printing: 45# New Era Matte Plus Recycle, World Color Press Inc.

Cover: Martin Barraud/OJO Images/Getty Images

Credits: The credits section for this book begins on page 506 and is considered an extension of the copyright page.

Library of Congress Cataloging-in-Publication Data

Casper, Virginia.
  Early childhood education : learning together / Virginia Casper, Rachel Theilheimer. — 1st ed.
     p. cm.
  Includes bibliographical references and index.
  ISBN-13: 978-0-07-337848-0 (alk. paper)
  ISBN-10: 0-07-337848-8 (alk. paper)
  1. Early childhood education. I. Theilheimer, Rachel. II. Title.
  LB1139.23.C388 2010
  372.21—dc22
                                                                2009034037

www.mhhe.com

Brief Contents

Contents

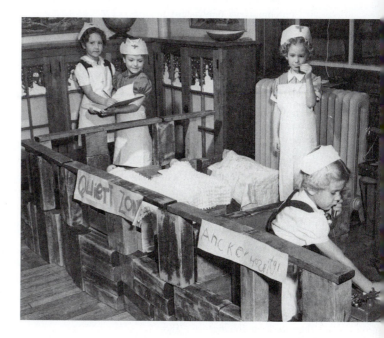

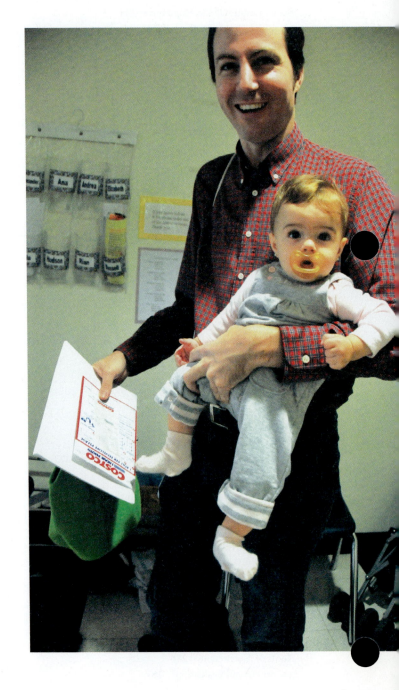

We Listen.

Students tell us they need:

- material that is grounded in the real world of the early childhood profession.
- a good value in their course materials.
- an engaging presentation that helps them read and review.
- a text that helps them explore their interest in the field and perhaps discover a new profession or career.

These needs shape every aspect of *Early Childhood Education*. From the real cases and NAEYC standards, to the graphs and tables for easy reference and student review, we bring together the best research and the most effective practices in Early Childhood.

We also understand that college can be a financial challenge for students.

Because of this, *Early Childhood Education* is half the price of comparable introductory texts.

Developed with leaders in the field. Priced with students in mind.

As an emerging professional, we hope you will come to

- believe in and respect young children's agency, integrity, and wisdom;
- demonstrate creativity and thoughtfulness; and
- embrace a willingness to listen to and learn from young children.

Developed in conjunction with the Bank Street College of Education, *Early Childhood Education: Learning Together* guides future professionals to think critically about the issues involved in the early care and education of young children. Early childhood education is not a one-size-fits-all proposition, so this text encourages you in multiple ways to reflect on why you do what you do. It also helps you to develop the skills, knowledge, and dispositions desirable in early childhood educators through real-life, practical examples and case material, presentation of evidence-based research, and equips you with tools to guide your learning.

Learning Together and Thinking Critically

College students typically enroll in an introductory early childhood class eager to learn about children and commit to working with them. With *Early Childhood Education: Learning Together*, we create a parallel process. As you learn about children's learning, you also learn about yourself. You will see that working with children involves more than just "being good with children" or "loving kids." It takes a lot of thought. The lens of **developmental interaction**—finding and creating environments in which children can grow and learn to their full potential—provides a frame for thinking about the kind of teacher you want to become. You will learn to create environments where children learn skills and concepts through investigations of the world, engage in collaborative learning, and stand up for what is fair and just.

Increasing numbers of young children from diverse ethnic, cultural, language, socioeconomic, and family backgrounds are entering the full range of early childhood programs. In this text, you will read and think about children and families in many contexts, including poverty, homelessness, and other challenging conditions. To be able to respond to a broad swath of populations, *Early Childhood Education: Learning Together* probes the role of culture and how your personal and educational experiences can affect your understanding of others. This book addresses values as an inherent aspect of teaching. You will read about what some of the best educators believe, articulate your own beliefs about teaching, and anticipate the role they will play in your teaching.

Children learn through relationships—and this book takes an integrated view of children's social, cognitive, and physical development and focuses on the role of relationships in enhancing children's capacities to learn. We introduce these concepts in Chapter 3: Children Learning about the World through Relationships to provide the basis for understanding self-regulation, communication, attachment, and related neuroscience concepts that thread throughout other chapters. These ideas serve as a foundation for future teachers aspiring to meaningfully guide the behaviors of children at different points in their early years.

Thinking critically about early care and education. *Early Childhood Education: Learning Together* uses developmental interaction as a frame for thinking critically about questions in early care and education instead of providing readers with single solutions. We use **Case Material**—stories about teachers, children, and families that thread throughout each chapter—to introduce you to dilemmas of practice. Not only does such Case Material integrate theory and practice, it prepares you to deal with the variety of situations you will face in your future career and provides fertile soil for rich discussions inside and beyond your college classroom. To encourage you to think about *why* you will do everything you do with children as a future educator, we use **Thought Questions** that ask you to reflect on what you are reading and apply it to what you already know. Each chapter includes five to ten Thought Questions that raise thorny issues, connect what you are reading to your own experience, and relate ideas across chapters.

THOUGHT QUESTION Consider your own culture and upbringing. How were children disciplined in your family? What role did children play during family gatherings? Why are your early family experiences important for you as a teacher?

Real-Life Examples and Cases

REAL VOICES Elaine Chu, *New York, New York*

As teachers, we are not supposed to have favorite students; we are expected to see each child for his or her strengths and abilities. Of course, there are always the "difficult" students—those with whom we struggle because they present behavior that makes it hard for us to do our jobs. Perhaps worse than categorizing students as problematic would be to have a "least favorite" student—someone who, for personal reasons, one simply dislikes. What can you do about someone who just rubs you the wrong way?

I have such a student. She is not one of the attention-demanding ones, nor is she a struggling student. Victoria is a quiet child who follows directions, works well independently, and meets grade-level academic standards. Yet, while I have forged a connection with almost all my students, I cannot seem to find any endearing qualities in Victoria.

What is perhaps most surprising about my reaction is that Victoria comes from a background very similar to my own. In fact, Victoria is the student whose background most resembles mine: she is American-born Chinese. The way Victoria performs well on tasks that demand right answers but loses confidence in open-ended activities, her quiet competitiveness when interacting with peers, the way her parents seem concerned only about the standardized tests, the fact that she plays violin—all this feels so familiar to me.

the one we're playing, I think "selfish." Victoria's conduct calls to mind my own childhood behaviors that were labeled selfish and stubborn, so much so that I, too, now see them this way.

When I finally realized that what made Americans truly American was an independence of thought and action, I began to actively cultivate this quality. I still remember the day in high school when a friend asked me why I alway agreed with what everyone said. It was embarrassing to be confronted so directly, but it gave me the determination to change this "defect of character," which happens to be a respected trait in many Eastern societies. It probably wasn't until college—when I learned to think critically and to engage in

Elaine Chu

Each chapter includes a first-person account—a **Real Voice**—written by a student, educator, or parent that relates a problem or situation that taught the essayist something important. In Chapter 7's Real Voice, for example, Alexis Harper reveals the dilemmas of a new teacher. She elaborates on her values and goals as she describes her experience in a less-than-ideal setting. She struggles with her desire to work in a high-quality center and to create one of her own. These informative and often moving personal stories provide insight into and context for the path on which you are embarking.

The integrated **Case Material** (identified with a ✕ icon) links theory to practice by giving students a real-world context for what they are reading. Chapter 6, for example, describes a staff meeting at which a teacher raises questions about young Michael's increased aggressive behavior. Throughout the chapter, you return to Michael's story to consider how various theories help to explain his actions.

Evidence-Based Practice

Early Childhood Education: Learning Together infuses classic and current research to invite you into the field as a practitioner and scholar. We hope that you will read and use others' research along with your own experience and practice to broaden the scope of your teaching. Teaching that is based on current, peer-reviewed studies about children and the experience of teachers and families will bring integrity to your work. We present research with a critical eye and try to avoid objectifying children or concentrating too heavily on predictions of later behavior instead of focusing on who the child is now.

Tools to Guide Learning

Early Childhood Education: Learning Together equips you with tools to guide your learning. **Learning goals** focus on key information you need to know. Each chapter begins with a preview of its major topics of focus. Next, within the text narrative, each main heading is followed by that section's key learning goal. And finally, the end-of-chapter summaries restate the learning goals and review the key take-away information section by section.

Located at the end of each chapter, **activities linked to *National Association for the Education of Young Children (NAEYC) Professional Preparation Standards*** help you connect learning in class to broader early childhood education standards. Such activities document your growing competence and allow you to generate material for portfolios. A correlation guide to the NAEYC Standards can be found on the inside front cover.

Organization

As an introductory overview of early childhood education (birth through age 8), this book is organized into 15 chapters to simplify access and to align with syllabi and the number of semester weeks. It provides a flexible approach to the central topics so that instructors can assign the chapters in whatever order they choose.

Beginning with a discussion of children and the societal context in which they and their families live, the text addresses theoretical and practical foundational issues, including identity and personal development as a teacher; children and self-regulation; and the history, theories, and range of early childhood programs. In the chapters that follow, explanations and examples focus on understanding, observing, and developing curriculum for all children in the three age groups within early childhood. These chapters address the world of early childhood: social studies, emergent literacy, art and music, math and scientific inquiry, and uses of technology. The book closes with a section on families and the community, including an overview of policy issues and ways to advocate for children and social change in children's interests.

Our Collaboration

Our partnership unites college teaching expertise from early childhood professionals at a large institution and a small one, a public university and a private college, and undergraduate and graduate institutions. Both Bank Street College of Education and Borough of Manhattan Community College faculty participated in this project in a variety of ways, and students from both schools provided valuable feedback. Because undergraduates are the main audience for this book, we are especially grateful for the help, feedback, and opinions of the education students at Borough of Manhattan Community College. This book is truly a collaborative effort, one that we hope will appeal to a wide and eager audience of students aspiring to become teachers and educators.

—Virginia Casper, Graduate Faculty,
Bank Street College of Education, New York, New York

—Rachel Theilheimer, Professor, Teacher Education Department,
Borough of Manhattan Community College/City University of New York

Teaching and Learning Resources Program

Online Learning Center for Instructors

This password-protected website contains the Test Bank, Instructor's Manual, Power-Point presentations, and Image Gallery, as well as access to the entire student side of the website. To access these resources, please go to www.mhhe.com/casper1e.

Instructor's Manual

Created by Tracey Bennet, Vance Granville Community College

This guide provides the key components for teaching early childhood education. Each chapter includes the learning objectives and key terms from the text, a chapter outline, classroom activities, discussion suggestions, journal entry topics, websites, and video resources. The *Instructor's Manual* can be accessed on the text's Online Learning Center for instructors.

Test Bank

Created by Tara Newman, Stephen F. Austin State University

Each chapter of the test bank offers 80 questions, including multiple choice, true/false, fill-in-the-blank, and short answer/essay questions. These test items are available on the instructor's Online Learning Center as Word files and in EZ Test, an easy-to-use electronic test bank that allows instructors to easily edit and add their own questions.

PowerPoint Presentations

Created by Jeanne Barker, Tallahassee Community College

Available on the Online Learning Center, these slides cover the key points of the chapter and can be used as-is or modified to support individual instructors' lectures. Digital versions of many images and figures from the textbook are also available in the Image Gallery.

Online Learning Center for Students

Prepared by Carla Ahmann, Waubonsee Community College

The students' online learning center includes multiple choice, true/false, and fill-in-the-blank practice quizzes to help the students prepare for exams. To access these resources please go to www.mhhe.com/casper1e.

For information on any component of the teaching and learning package, instructors should contact their McGraw-Hill representative.

Acknowledgments

We are tremendously grateful to the following individuals whose insightful contributions during the book's development improved it immeasurably.

CONTRIBUTING WRITERS

Joan Almon
Nancy Balaban, Bank Street College
Betsy Blachly, Bank Street College
Todd Boressoff
Sue Carbary, Bank Street College
Leslie Craigo, Borough of Manhattan Community College/City University of New York
Harriet Cuffaro
Alika Hope Despotopoulos, Borough of Manhattan Community College/City University of New York
Joanne Frantz, School for Young Children, Columbus, OH
Celia Genishi, Teachers College, Columbia University
Sheila Hanna, Westchester Community College
Alexis Harper
Min Hong
Joe Kleinman, Bank Street College
Lesley Koplow, Bank Street College
Faith Lamb-Parker, Mailman School of Public Health, Columbia University
Judy Lesch, Bank Street College
Meredith Lewis, Bank Street College
Nancy Nager, Bank Street College
Susan Ochshorn, New York City Professional Development Institute/City University of New York
Toni Porter, Bank Street College
Victoria Puig
Stephanie Rottmayer , School for Young Children, Columbus, OH
Cristian Solarza, Bank Street College
Barbara Stern, Bank Street College
Charlotte Stetson
Elizabeth Tingley, Bank Street College
Sal Vascellaro, Bank Street College
Ellen Wahl
Jan Waters, School for Young Children, Columbus, OH
Karen Weiss, Bank Street College

EDITORIAL ASSISTANTS

Alexis Harper, Bellingham, WA
Anna Kotelchuck, New York, NY

OTHER CONTRIBUTORS

Maria Arcurio, Bloomingdale Family Program Head Start
Nancy Barnwell, Manchester, CT
Jonathan Beard, New York, NY
Sadie Bragg, Borough of Manhattan Community College/City University of New York
Kathy Brown, Roosevelt Early Childhood Center, St. Cloud, MN
Mary Dooley Burns, Frogtown Family Resource Center, St. Paul, MN
Betsy Cahill, New Mexico State University
Evan Casper-Futterman, New Orleans, LA
Christina D'Aiello, Bank Street College
Jackie Davidson and New Hampshire Estates Elementary School
Michelle DeMarmels, Arthur R. Ware Elementary School, Staunton, VA
Joyce Dye, Bloomingdale Family Program Head Start
Amy Flynn and the staff of the Bank Street Family Center
Jonathan Fribley, St. Cloud, MN
Marjorie Goldsmith and the staff of Rockefeller University Child and Family Center
Yvonne Gutierrez, Borough of Manhattan Community College Early Childhood Education Center
Alyse Hachey, Borough of Manhattan Community College
Mary Hauser, National Louis University
Judy Jablon, South Orange, NJ
Elisabeth Jakab, Bank Street College of Education
Danielle Kaminsky, Murfreesboro Public School System, TN
Marie Ellen Larcada, Teachers College Press
Doua Lee, Frogtown Family Resource Center, St. Paul, MN
Patricia Lent, New York, NY
Hedi Levine, New York, NY

Joy Lundeen, Bank Street College of Education
Kathy Marte, John Jay College of Criminal Justice/CUNY
Jeff McCartney, Bank Street College
Peggy McNamara, Bank Street College
Linda McNelly, Roosevelt Early Childhood Center,
    St. Cloud, MN
Liege Motta, Bank Street College
Megan O'Sullivan, Chicago, IL
Dena Oneal, Murfreesboro Public School System, TN
Antonio Perez, Borough of Manhattan Community
    College/City University of New York
Carla Poole, Los Angeles, CA
Kate Puckett, New Mexico State University
Ryan Ratajski, Camden, NJ
Barbara Rawlings, Frances Starms Child Development
    Center, Milwaukee, WI
Stuart Reifel, University of Texas, Austin
Rena Rice, Bank Street College
Tracy Rich, Leech Lake Head Start, MN
Rachel Rippy, New York, NY
Harolyn Rousso, New York, NY
Kim St. John, Leech Lake Head Start, MN
Cecilia Scott-Croff, Borough of Manhattan Community
    College ECE Center
Marilyn Scudder-Barnwell, Bloomington Family Center
Jonathan Silin, Toronto, Canada
Arhondus Simmons, Frogtown Family Resource Center,
    St. Paul, MN
Jon Snyder, Bank Street College of Education
Matt Sullivan, Bozeman, MT
Maureen Sullivan, Woodlands School, Milwaukee
Meg Sullivan, University of Chicago
Catherine Thomas, Lawrenceville, NJ
Vera Thompson, Mississippi County Head Start,
    Arkansas
Indira Vann, Borough of Manhattan Community College
Jose Velilla, Bloomingdale Family Program Head Start
Martha Wheeler-Fair, Frances Starms Child Develop-
    ment Center, Milwaukee, WI
Anna Zabriskie, Murfreesboro Public School System, TN
Karen Zabriskie, Affect Plus, Woodbury, TN
Marika Zaslow, Bank Street College of Education

ADVISORS

Barbara Abel, University of Illinois, Chicago
Nancy Balaban, Bank Street College of Education
Nilda Bayron-Resnick, Bank Street College of Education
Todd Boressoff, independent consultant

Takiema Bunche-Smith, independent consultant
Nancy Cardwell, Bank Street College of Education
Leslie Craigo, Borough of Manhattan Community
    College
Harriet Cuffaro, independent consultant
Helen Friedus, Bank Street College of Education
Marjorie Goldsmith, City College/CUNY
Betsy Grob, Bank Street College of Education
Nancy Gropper, Bank Street College of Education
Margot Hammond, Bank Street College of Education
Sheila Hanna, Westchester Community College
Mary Hauser, National Louis University
Judy Jablon, independent consultant
Laura Kates, Kingsboro Community College/CUNY
Kira Kingren, Bank Street College of Education
Lesley Koplow, Bank Street College of Education
Judy Lesch, Bank Street College of Education
Meredith Lewis, Bank Street College of Education
Tracey Lee Lucas, Bank Street College of Education
Diana-Elena Matsoukas, Bank Street College
    of Education
Peggy McNamara, Bank Street College of Education
Yolanda (Jolie) Medina, Borough of Manhattan
    Community College
Nancy Nager, Bank Street College of Education
Susan Ochshorn, CUNY
Lillian Oxtoby, independent consultant
Jean Plaisir, Borough of Manhattan Community College
Carla Poole, Bank Street College of Education
Toni Porter, Bank Street College of Education
Denise Prince, Bank Street College of Education
Ruby Richardson, Borough of Manhattan
    Community College
Harolyn Rousso, independent consultant
Sharon Ryan, Rutgers University
Marilyn Scudder-Barnwell, Borough of Manhattan
    Community College
Cristian Solorza, Bank Street College of Education
Barbara Stern, Bank Street College of Education
Elizabeth Tingley, Bank Street College of Education
Joseph Tobin, Arizona State University
Sal Vascellaro, Bank Street College of Education
Karen Weiss, Bank Street College of Education
Sara Wilford, Sarah Lawrence College
Gay Wilgus, City College of New York/CUNY
Donna Wright, Medgar Evers/CUNY
Ahmed Zaman, Borough of Manhattan
    Community College

STUDENT CONTRIBUTORS

We wish to thank former students for their written contributions:

Jane Andris
Chelsea Baptiste
Gwen Brown-Murray
Paige Callaghan
Nicole Ciorciari
Natasha Forde
Lindsay Freedman
Sarah Gilbert
Thea Gunhouse
Samantha Hay
Dafna Izcovich
Terri Machtiger
Micaela Morse
Dorothy O'Connell
Eva Peck
Becky Plattus
Nishanna Ramoutar
Leela Sarathy
Sara Seigel
Margaret Sullivan

REVIEWERS

Manuscript Reviewers

Sally Adler, Washtenaw Community College
Carla Ahmann, Waubonsee Community College
Katherine Allen, Blue Ridge Community College
Linda Anderson, Northwestern Michigan College
Nicole Andrews, University of Houston
Larry Ashley, Mercy College–Dobbs Ferry
Jeanne Barker, Tallahassee Community College
Tracey Bennett, Vance-Granville Community College
Teresa L. Bridger, Prince George's Community College
Shelly Moss Brooks, Oakland Community College
Carolynn Bush, KCTCS Hazard Community and
    Technical College
Karen Callahan, Central Piedmont Community College
Tara Chaumont, McNeese State University
Angela Cockrell, Northern Virginia Community
    College–Manassas
Mary Cordell, Navarro College
Leda M. Cott, Collin County Community College
Margi Coxwell, Minot State University
Nancy T. Cupolo, Hudson Valley Community College
Susan Davies, Ivy Tech Community College

Linda DeMoe, Chippewa Valley Technical College
Patricia A. Dickmann, Ivy Tech Community College
Ann Oden Disque, East Tennessee State University
Claude Endfield, Northland Pioneer College
Deirdre Englehart, University of Central Florida
Grace Essex, Ohio University–Athens
Colleen Fawcett, Palm Beach Community College
Ellen Firestone, Wilkes Community College
Teresa Frazier, Thomas Nelson Community College
Priscilla Garcia, Laredo Community College
Connie Gassner, Ivy Tech Community College
Sabine Gerhardt, University of Akron
Carla Goble, Tulsa Community College
Gail Gottschling, Indiana State University
Marilyn Haller, Oklahoma Baptist University
Ginger Harris-Pike, Central Carolina
    Community College
Celia Billescas Hilber, Jacksonville State University
Jane Hildenbrand, Ivy Tech Community College
Sharon Hirschy, Collin County Community College
Grace Hively, Lone Star College
Jeannie Ho, Montgomery College
Christy Hopkins, Stanly Community College
Luis Huerta-Charles, New Mexico State University
Jennifer M. Johnson, Vance-Granville
    Community College
Traci A. Johnston, Pulaski Technical College
Malinda E. Jones, Metropolitan State College of Denver
Gertrude Keiper, Concordia University
Elisabeth Kyle, Central New Mexico Community College
Colleen Lemhouse, Lower Columbia College
Sharon F. Libby, Owens Community College
Amanda Barche Lindberg, Ivy Tech Community College
Michelle List, Herkimer County Community College
Julia Lorenz, Chippewa Valley Technical College
Linda H. Lowman, San Antonio College
Kathleen Ludlow, Northern Virginia Community
    College–Manassas
Katherine MacTavish, Oregon State University
Catherine McLaughlin, Corning Community College
Patricia Merritt, University of Alaska–Fairbanks
Donda Miller, Saint Louis Community College
Mark Mills, Florida Community College
Cindy Moseman, Ashland University
Rebecca Sue Moyer, Fayetteville Tech
    Community College
Dawn S. Munson, Elgin Community College
Tara A. Newman, Angelina College
Barbie Norvell, Coastal Carolina University

Lucia Obregon, Miami Dade College
Glenn Olsen, University of North Dakota
Cynthia Osborne, Stanly Community College
Erica Otiono, Cosumnes River College
Susan Peet, Bowling Green State University
Elizabeth A. Persons, Pensacola Junior College
Mary Jo Pollman, Metropolitan State College of Denver
Robin Rackley, Texas A&M University
Brenda Ragle, Ivy Tech Community College
Gordia Ross, Miami Dade College
Christine Schull, Northern Virginia Community
    College–Manassas
Barbara Payne Shelton, Towson University
Darlene Shumate, Wilkes Community College
Jane Spruill, Pensacola Junior College
Dolores Stegelin, Clemson University
Kathryn J. Stuckey, State College of Florida, Manatee
James P. Sullivan, Miami Dade College
Sheila R. Thomas, Albany Technical College

Connie Unger, Moravian College
Linn Violett, Cosumnes River College
Elaine Washburn, Kansas City Kansas
    Community College
Patsy F. Washington, Towson University
Patricia Weaver, Fayetteville Tech Community College
Barbara Weiserbs, Kingsborough Community College
Elaine Wilkinson, Collin County Community
    College–Plano
Julie Williams, Pulaski Technical College
Wanda York, Montgomery College
Benita Yowe, Albany Technical College

Design Reviewers
Anne Oden Disque, East Tennessee State University
Sabine Gerhardt, University of Akron
Kathleen Ludlow, Northern Virginia Community
    College–Manassas
Julie Williams, Pulaski Technical College

Virginia Casper is a developmental psychologist and teacher educator who has worked for over thirty years with children and families in early intervention and research. She is on the graduate faculty at Bank Street College of Education, where she directed the Infant and Family Development and Early Intervention Program and served as Associate Dean for Academic Affairs in the Graduate School from 2002–2007. Virginia has also worked internationally, for the past decade, in South Africa. Her current work there involves a community-based, participatory research and curriculum development model that includes community training in HIV/AIDS prevention and infant/toddler group care and advocacy. Her work on attachment, gender, and teacher-parent relations has been published in Teacher's College Record, The Harvard Education Review and Zero to Three. She co-authored a previous book entitled *Gay Parents/Straight Schools: Building Communication and Trust* (1999). She and her partner, Donna Futterman, are the parents of an adult son.

Rachel Theilheimer has worked with young children, their families, and teachers in public school, private and public child care, Head Start, and parent groups. She has been a teacher, a group leader, a director, and an educational consultant. For the past twenty-five years, she has taught adults at the pre-GED, community college, bachelors, and graduate levels and conducted numerous professional development workshops. She is professor of early childhood education at Borough of Manhattan Community College where she chairs the Teacher Education Department. She has published articles and book chapters about teacher education, social justice issues, and infant care.

This book would not have been possible without the many students we have taught over the years. We would also like to acknowledge our colleagues, friends, and families, with special appreciation to our Bank Street College colleagues in Publications and Media, Jeffrey McCartney and Elisabeth Jakab. We would like to especially thank our partners, Jonathan Beard (Rachel) and Donna Futterman (Virginia), for their support over the past three years while this book was a work in progress.

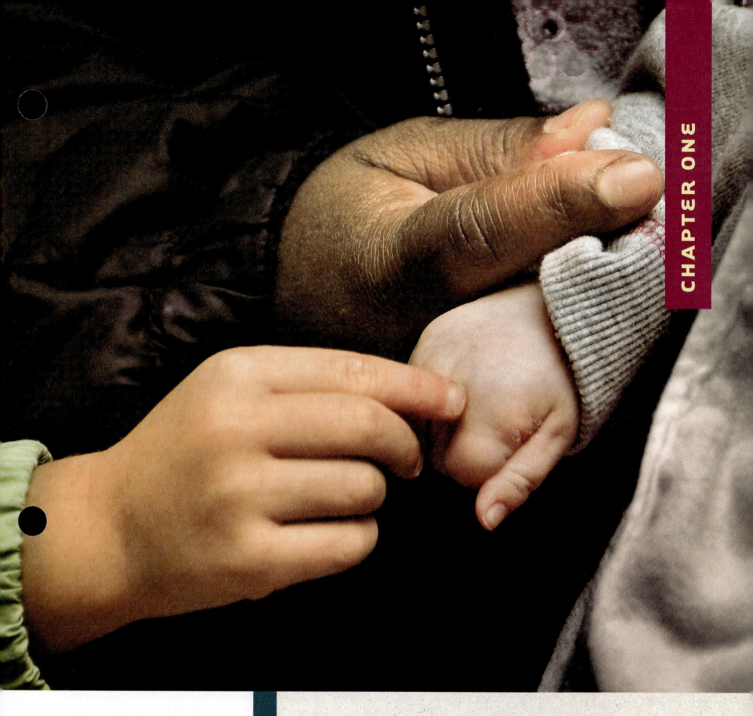

Working with Young Children

Neither children nor teachers can have a truly good life unless both have it. Indeed, the essence of a good life for either children or teachers is that they live it together.

Lucy Sprague Mitchell

What does it mean for children and the adults who care for and educate them to have a "good life" together? What are the ingredients that contribute to that good life that they live together?

In this chapter we begin to address these questions as we think about what it means to care for and educate young children. We look at what makes work with children of high quality and how adults prepare for it and continue to learn about it as professionals. You will read about some essential personal qualities teachers have, jobs and career options in the field of early childhood education, and the qualifications you'll need for them.

EARLY CARE AND EDUCATION

What is involved in caring for and educating young children?

The National Association for the Education of Young Children (NAEYC), the largest organization of early childhood educators in the United States, defines early childhood as the years from birth to eight. What else can we say to describe young children? Only that every child is the result of many combining influences and is continually growing and changing. Who children are—the personal preferences and nature with which they are born—interacts with the people, places, and circumstances of their lives.

We, the adults in children's lives, are part of the environment that shapes them. Children, in turn, change us as we care for them and educate them. In this section, we discuss what it means to care for and educate children and some of the purposes for early care and education.

> Caring for young children involves both feeling and acting. We grow to care *about* them as we care *for* them.

THOUGHT QUESTION Caring can bring people together; but it also can set the one doing the caring apart from the people receiving the care. Consider these situations:

- A mother enters the infant center to pick up her son. She gathers his belongings but can't find his mittens. Glaring at the caregiver, the mother demands to know where the mittens are.
- Another mother enters an infant center to pick up her son. As she gathers his belongings, a caregiver glances at her and says, "You *must* bring his mittens. It's too cold to go out without them."

Who seems to have the power in each of these stories? What information does the caregiver need from the mother in each of these situations? What could the caregiver do before answering, if the mother's response made her angry?

What Is Care?

Although most people associate caring with feelings, caring is also an intellectual activity (McNamee, Mercurio, and Peloso 2007). Even diapering an infant is an opportunity to pay close attention, gather information, and come up with new ideas. Picture the adult who engages the baby and follows her gaze as he changes her diaper.

Caring is a way of feeling *and* a set of actions (Tronto 2001). We feel strongly about ourselves, others, places, and things; we care about them. We also take care of ourselves, others, places, and things, and that kind of caring involves action. Caring for young children involves both feeling and acting. We grow to care *about* them as we care *for* them.

Tronto (2001) names four elements of care:

- *Attentiveness:* Caring people are fully present and observe children to understand them.
- *Responsibility:* Caring people are responsible for the physical, intellectual, and emotional well-being of the children in their care.
- *Competence:* Caring people need the knowledge, skills, and attitudes for the job.
- *Responsiveness:* Caring people listen carefully to children to understand their perspectives and communicate with them, whether or not those children speak the educator's language—or speak at all.

What kind of caring do you think took place behind the scenes to enable these children to work together and then sit back and admire their construction?

Although all people need to care to retain their humanity (Jones 2007), many people consider caring activities to be women's work. Work that involves caring, whether for children or elders, is often underpaid. We believe that men *and* women can and should become qualified to care for young children and that they deserve fair pay for this important work.

At the foundation of early care and education are the relationships that grow and develop among the children and between them and the adults who care for them and teach them. These relationships are the basis for young children's learning. Intimacy derives from spending hours together, from getting to know each other well, and from sharing everyday events as well as special achievements. Commitment to each other and to shared projects cements relationships within the group. We hope you will cultivate intimacy, commitment, and passion (Goldstein 1997) in the early childhood classrooms in which you teach.

What Is Education?

What do you picture when you hear the word *education*? Do you see children at desks? Or are they outside collecting plants for a science project or sprawled across the floor writing in their journals? Do you visualize an infant mouthing a toy or snuggling into a caring adult? All of these experiences can be part of a young child's education.

Deborah Ball and Francesca Forzani (2008, 530) define education as "the deliberate activity of helping learners to develop understanding and skills." They say that education is not just teaching and not just learning. Education is the *interaction* of teaching, learning, content, and the environment that leads learners to make meaning from or interpret what they are learning. Thus, your teaching is important, but what children bring to education is equally important. Imagine the infant's attention to/interest in a ray of light, the toddler's focus while repeatedly transferring water from one container to another, the preschooler's determination to complete a puzzle, and the early elementary child's dedication to building an exact replica of a bridge, and you can envision the child's motivation to struggle and persist. Children

Education is not just teaching and learning. Education is the *interaction* of teaching, learning, content, and the environment that leads learners to make meaning from or interpret what they are learning.

THOUGHT QUESTION Jot down some of the reasons *you* think a society should educate its children. Your responses will bring your beliefs about children, families, and education into focus and help you move beyond acting on instinct or repeating what you've always done. As you interact with children, we hope you will also take their families' values into consideration.

have interests, focus, determination, and dedication. These are essential for the successful learner, as is persistence, because learning is not always easy.

Thus, education is not simply a matter of having an idea of what to teach and carrying out that idea. It is a constant exploration for the teacher and an ongoing opportunity to learn about content, about the children and their families, and about the contexts in which they live. Education requires pacing the learning activities according to the cues children give you, while at the same time holding expectations that stretch them beyond where they are at any given moment.

Some Purposes of Early Care and Education

Children, families, and teachers have expectations of the school experience. A three-year-old who has visited his new school may envision a play area. Meanwhile, his mother may anticipate his preparation for kindergarten and first grade, and his teacher may think about the community of learners that will develop during the year. As you read about the purposes of early education and care, consider the perspectives of children, families, and teachers along with those of administrators and policymakers, the public, and politicians, all of whom influence care and education for young children in this country.

A society educates young children for the sake of the child and for what the child can and will contribute to the larger community to which that child belongs (Hodgkinson 2006, 2). Education provides children with the tools to live fulfilling lives and equips children to care for themselves and others. Education necessarily looks to the future, but it does children a disservice if it does not also attend to who they are in the present.

Education transmits the ways of the society in which children live and the roles different people play in it. According to its website (http://www.ed.gov/about/landing.jhtml), the mission of the U.S. Department of Education is "to promote student achievement and preparation for global competitiveness by fostering educational excellence and ensuring equal access." The United States has a history of concern for global competitiveness. When the Soviets launched Sputnik in 1957, we reexamined children's education. When it became evident that Asian students were surpassing U.S. students in math and science skills, we took another close look. In 2002, to increase every student's achievement, Congress funded the No Child Left Behind (NCLB) Act of 2001, which, as you will read in Chapter 15, exerted an overarching influence on education in the first decade of the twenty-first century.

Education necessarily looks to the future, but it does children a disservice if it does not also attend to who they are in the present.

QUALITY OF EARLY CARE AND EDUCATION

What issues do discussions of the quality of early care and education raise, and why are early childhood educators having those discussions now?

In the 1930s, many young children helped around the house and played outdoors with other children. By the 1950s, some nursery schools had sprung up, but child care and its quality were not part of a national conversation. By 1965, though, with the advent of Head Start, early education entered the national consciousness. In

TABLE 1.1	NAEYC's Efforts to Improve Early Education Quality
YEAR	**INITIATIVE**
1985	Voluntary accreditation program for centers and schools
1986	*Developmentally Appropriate Practice*
1989	Initial Code of Ethical Conduct
1997	Revision of *Developmentally Appropriate Practice*
2001–2003	Standards for early childhood professional preparation for: initial licensure programs (2001), advanced programs (2002), and associate degree programs (2003)
2003	Code of Ethical Conduct for teacher educators
2005	Revision of *Early Childhood Program Standards and Accreditation Criteria*
2009	Revision of *Developmentally Appropriate Practice*

1971, President Nixon vetoed legislation to provide child care to all (Cohen 2001), and by the 1970s, child care was a national issue.

Today, quality-of-care issues are often in the news. Over the past thirty years, the number of mothers of children under six in the workforce has doubled. In 2005, about 61 percent of U.S. children between birth and six spent at least part of their day in nonparental care (www.childtrendsdatabank.org/indicators/21ChildCare .cfm). Moreover, research (e.g., Peisner-Feinberg et al. 2000) indicates that the quality of an early childhood setting makes a huge difference to children educationally and socially. Such research, and early childhood educators' efforts to educate the public about it, has convinced citizens and lawmakers alike of the importance of children's early experiences.

In the 1980s, NAEYC instituted a number of initiatives to improve the quality of early care and education. Table 1.1 outlines the organization's early efforts and those that followed them. As you can see, on the national level, early childhood educators have talked broadly about quality for the past several decades. These efforts have been collaborative, and NAEYC leaders revisit them periodically to revise them.

Applying Child Development Principles

According to NAEYC, quality early childhood education promotes children's development and learning. With *Developmentally Appropriate Practice* (Bredekamp 1986; Bredekamp and Copple 1997; Copple and Bredekamp 2009) and the standards for program accreditation (introduced in 1985 and 2005; see http://www .naeyc.org/academy/standards/), NAEYC aimed to create guidelines for interactions, curriculum, and assessment that would do just that. *Developmentally Appropriate Practice* (Bredekamp 1986), which quickly became known as *DAP*, provides teachers with

- a framework for making decisions;
- a set of developmental and learning principles; and
- explanations, examples, and charts to help teachers understand how to apply the framework.

Recognizing that children and their cultures are constantly in flux, *DAP* asks early childhood professionals to base developmentally appropriate decisions on the following three interrelated dimensions (Bredekamp and Copple 1997):

1. *Knowledge of child development and learning*—what they know about children in general, based on research and observations about children
2. *Knowledge of the individual child's strengths, interests, and abilities*—what they know based on observation of and interaction with a specific child and information from families
3. *Knowledge of the social and cultural contexts in which the child lives*—what they know about the family's practices

In response to criticism that the first version of *DAP* suggested only one way of working with children, the 1997 version featured a discussion of "both/and" thinking (Bredekamp and Copple 1997, 23). Imagine a parent helping in the classroom who draws pictures for the children. The staff believes that when adults draw for children, they discourage children's creativity. Instead of forcing a choice between the two points of view, both/and thinking could lead the parent to explain that she didn't want to refuse children's requests and that her older siblings had shown her how to draw. The staff might say that, because children draw differently from adults, they may try to copy the adult's style or give up altogether. Both/and thinking opens up the possibility of listening to and learning from each other.

Despite the discussion of both/and thinking in the second version of *DAP*, however, the publication contrasted examples of appropriate and inappropriate practices as if choices were clear-cut. As they prepared the third version of *DAP* for publication, Carol Copple and Sue Bredekamp (2008, 55) cautioned instead, "The effectiveness of many practices tends to depend on their purpose and the context in which they are used." They urged early childhood educators to talk to each other and to families to become clear themselves and to communicate articulately about "practices we believe serve children best."

This child experiments and makes many decisions about his work.

PART 1 An Introduction to Early Childhood

NAEYC also seeks to help teachers behave as responsive and responsible professionals. An NAEYC task force arrived at core values for early childhood educators and developed a **code of ethical conduct,** a statement of NAEYC's position on teacher roles and responsibilities.

Workplace issues, compensation, and number of children per adult in the room affect even the most well prepared and responsive teachers; they also affect the quality of education and care for children. As you read in the quote at the beginning of this chapter, when early childhood educators are underpaid or overworked, children do not get the care and education they deserve.

THOUGHT QUESTION Read through the *Code of Ethical Conduct* in Appendix A to see if you agree with the ideals. Do the principles outline your responsibilities as you imagine them? Try this again at the end of the semester. Have your ideas changed?

The pay for early childhood teachers is low, especially for those working in community-based rather than school-based programs (Kagan, Kauerz, and Tarrant 2008). Furthermore, early childhood educators are less likely than other professionals to have adequate health and retirement benefits. The low pay and poor benefits affect **staff turnover,** as teachers leave to find better-paying work. Children then experience many different adults instead of **continuity of care.** As you will read throughout this book, consistency of adults over time helps children develop trusting relationships. Fortunately, the United States is in the midst of professionalizing early childhood education, with rising certification requirements and calls for making preschool teachers' pay equal to that of elementary teachers and other helping professionals.

Early childhood systems

In recent years, researchers and early childhood organizations have looked for ways to create systems that enable joint efforts. Such a **systemic approach** to the **compensation, quality, affordability tri-lemma**—the problem that paying adequate salaries to ensure higher quality costs more than families can afford—can also address the inadequate supply of quality early childhood settings.

As states begin to implement **universal prekindergarten (UPK)**—an effort to make free early childhood education available to every family—they find that public schools cannot provide enough classrooms. Some states have turned to the private sector and to public child care and Head Start programs to provide UPK classrooms with public funding, creating a new system of public-private partnerships in early childhood education.

Standards without standardization

Early learning standards help to define expectations for children's care and education. They are meant to guide early childhood educators so that more children experience more consistent, high-quality early childhood education.

But standards, once written, seem rigid and inflexible, while early childhood curriculum should bend and grow with the children, accommodating their interests, prior experiences, and abilities. The challenge, then, is to uphold the standards and at the same time develop curriculum with and for the children with whom you work and whom you know best.

You can meet your state's standards or expectations of what children will learn in your group when you set up an environment and develop a curriculum that includes children's play and investigations (Gronlund 2006). Look back at the end of each day to compare children's experiences to the state learning standards. This requires familiarizing yourself with the standards and paying close attention to what children do and say throughout the day. You can also plan play settings and creative and thought-provoking experiences that you know will address specific standards.

Standards and the pressure to meet them can lead administrators at the school, district, state, or federal level to mandate specific curricula. If your school requires you to use a set curriculum, evaluate it and use it in the way that best fits your children and families. You may see ways to deepen it or to address it quickly, to leave time to pursue children's interests. Marjorie Siegel and Stephanie Lukas (2008) describe a kindergarten's in-depth studies of plants and animals. Children began by telling each other what they already knew about plants and gardens—their **prior knowledge**—from their experience in the city and in the countries from which they had emigrated. Their stories, the books they read, and the experiments they did with soil, seeds, and water enabled them to cover the mandated curriculum and expand far beyond it. Throughout, they "combine[d] the mandated with the magical" (34).

Reconceptualizing Early Childhood Education

"Quality means good teachers and good schools" (Kirp 2007, 7), but what you consider good is probably different from what someone else thinks "good" means, and "good" may depend on the situation. How people define quality early childhood education depends on their goals for children (Consultative Group on Early Childhood Care and Development 1996).

Instead of establishing specific definitions of quality, Joseph Tobin suggests that everyone involved negotiate with each other to create a high-quality setting that fits that group of individuals (Bernard van Leer Foundation 2007). Often, those involved align themselves behind two opposing choices, or **dichotomies.** Early childhood reconceptualizers urge early childhood educators to view things from multiple perspectives and avoid dichotomies.

Reconceptualizers look analytically and critically at issues facing young children, their teachers, and their families. They question *DAP*'s reliance on psychological theories that can lead early childhood educators to make assumptions about children. Instead, reconceptualizers turn to anthropology, philosophy, sociology, history, literature, the arts, and popular culture, along with psychology, to think about early childhood practices that have meaning for specific children in a given setting, rather than what is (more abstractly) "appropriate."

Literacy education is mandated, but something magical is happening here, too.

Reconceptualizers use a family of theories called critical theory (Ryan and Grieshaber 2004) to examine power relations between adults and children and among children, as well as to question and understand more about who is marginalized and who is privileged in classrooms as well as in society. Throughout this book we, too, raise questions that ask you to think critically about children, families, and teachers. We invite you to reconceptualize early childhood education as you learn about it.

EARLY CHILDHOOD EDUCATORS

What are the characteristics of a professional early childhood educator?

Teachers of young children are "thoughtful individuals with biographies" (Ryan, Ochsner, and Genishi 2001, 51) who know themselves and live with the uncertainties that come with teaching and learning. Your biography—your past experiences that differ from anyone else's—frames your work in early care and education. Your thoughtfulness and your ability to reflect on what you see, say, and do, along with your self-knowledge, are essential qualities for adults who work with children in any capacity.

Work with young children demands complete engagement. Being fully present with children and families means

- paying attention to what children do,
- concentrating to understand what they and their families say, and
- trying to put aside distracting worries and joys.

You will find it easier to throw yourself into your work with children if that work captures your imagination. Finding the right early childhood setting and, for that matter, continually assessing if early childhood is the right career are part of an ongoing and necessary process.

Diverse Biographies and Cultural Identities

According to 2007 data from the National Bureau of Labor Statistics, 94.6 percent of the 1,341,000 child care workers in the United States were women, 16 percent of

A diverse workforce enriches a community of learning in which professionals can take risks, care, and dream together.

We draw on
autobiographical
stories when we
face big choices
in our lives:
choosing a partner,
taking a job, or
turning down
an opportunity.

the child care workforce were black or African-American, 2.7 percent were Asian, and 16.8 percent were Hispanic or Latino (Figure 1.1). These statistics do not identify percentages of early childhood educators by age or with disabilities, although we know teachers are diverse in those ways, too. Our personal characteristics, experiences, and the sense we make of them contribute to the kind of person each of us is with children and families.

Who you are before you become a teacher shapes who you become as an educator. Your personal characteristics can be part of your teaching, as was the case for Sam:

Sam, an early childhood student who is blind, did his first field placement at the child care program at his college. The children gravitated to Sam and learned not to play with Coal, Sam's Seeing Eye dog, who lay near the door while Sam worked with the children. When the teacher first introduced Sam to the children, Sam explained, "When you talk to me, describe what you're talking about. Please don't show things to me, because I can't see them." Sam's disability made it necessary for the children to use colorful and specific language, an academic goal their teacher had for them.

Teachers can feel vulnerable when they put their private selves forward in a public way. Parker Palmer writes that the good teacher must stand where public and private meet, which he describes as feeling as if you are on foot crossing the freeway (Palmer 1998, 17). By confronting the scary or vulnerable part of teaching head-on, Palmer argues, we become good teachers.

Telling your story: autobiography and narratives

For centuries, human societies have told stories to explain natural and social phenomena and to communicate morals to their members. Stories organize our experiences, enable us to present ourselves in different ways (Dyson and Genishi 1994), and over time, even serve an integrative function for our brains (Siegel 1999). Human beings think and remember through story.

People tell their stories in many ways: in late-night talks with friends, on YouTube, in hip-hop, and in personal and political blogs. When teachers tell stories at workshops or staff meetings, classroom issues become clearer. The experiences and the meanings that they have for the teller enter a common space that provides some distance from the experience. Then the teacher can reframe the experiences and reflect upon them and interpretations of them. We implicitly draw on autobiographical stories when we face big choices in our lives: choosing a partner, taking a job, or turning down an opportunity (Carey 2007). Sometimes we use our autobiography to move against the "story" of who we are—to recreate ourselves in some way.

Teachers' stories have particular value (Jones 1994) and can let us see, not only our own routes and pathways, but also those of others. As D. Jean Clandinin and F. Michael Connelly (1995, 12) point out, teachers not only tell stories, they are "characters in their own stories of teaching, which they author."

Telling, reading, and writing our stories help us become aware of our identities—our ideas about who we are. Each of us has an

of a total of 1,341,000 workers

1.1 *Child Care Worker Profile*
National Bureau of Labor Statistics 2007

THOUGHT QUESTION List as many characteristics as you can that make you who you are. You can include your gender, ethnicity, religion, geographic location, abilities, interests, position in your family, professional experiences, and lots of other qualities. Sketch and label a graphic that illustrates your identity and that shows how your identity changes. How do the people around you affect who you are and how you act? What else influences you?

identity made up of many parts. We belong to families that have ways of doing and being that are easy to take for granted.

Identity is socially constructed—that means people of a particular place and time create it. Who you are shifts as you undergo experiences, read, and meet and get to know people who influence you, your beliefs, and how you behave. Yet some aspects of our identities remain stable and help us function. Your identity tells you who you are.

In the course of shaping your identity as an early childhood educator you may, among other things:

- Spend time in classrooms to learn about how you interact with children.
- Talk with people who have been in the field for a long time.
- Argue with family members who believe you should go into a more lucrative field.
- Compare yourself to colleagues, including those who teach older or younger children.
- Read about early childhood educators.
- Anticipate your life ten years from now.

Confronting biases

Everyone has **biases**—tendencies or preferences that can affect behavior. Biases are not always negative, though often they are prejudices that we have even though we wish we didn't. If we don't acknowledge biases, we can't understand them and work through them. Thinking together about bias can be an illuminating experience, as it was for Dina.

Some families want their child to have a primary caregiver and others do not. When discussing such issues, staff examine their personal and professional biases and what they know about the child and family.

> As a visitor observed, Dina played a cleanup game with two-year-old Holly, who put the red and then the blue blocks into a basket. Holly had played with the blocks for five minutes, unlike the four boys who had used them for forty minutes a bit earlier. Meanwhile, the boys sat on a bench and waited to have their shoes tied before going outside.

When the visitor described what she'd observed, Dina saw how she had unwittingly supported stereotypical roles and expectations. Because the observer acknowledged that Dina did not intend to perpetuate stereotypes of docile girls and feisty boys, Dina said she didn't feel threatened and, instead, would try to be more aware and alert in the future, to overcome an ingrained bias.

A team of early childhood educators examining their practice can unearth bias in unexpected ways, too. When a mother enrolled her baby in the infant room, she knew about the center's **primary caregiving system,** which meant her child would have one caregiver who would get to know her and her child very well. Nonetheless, the mom resisted the system. As a single mother living in a dangerous housing project, she never knew what misfortune might befall the family next. She didn't want her baby to have a primary caregiver because she believed that her baby needed to learn to be with multiple caregivers at an early age.

As Fran Stott points out, "We pay lip service to context, yet when parents, students and others have different ideas from those

THOUGHT QUESTION What are the roots of a bias for or against primary caregiving? Should this baby have a primary caregiver like all the other babies? Would you be in favor of the mother's request, or would you support the center's primary caregiving policy? What other alternatives do you see?

My story overlaps and encircles me. As a child, I had a special kindergarten experience at the Creative Learning Center in Albuquerque, and I've come to realize through the years that teachers and students often develop memorable relationships. I never forgot my teacher, and evidently she never forgot me. In my first college classroom, I realized the instructor was my former kindergarten teacher. I approached her after class, and she recognized me as well. Years later, when I entered an early childhood program, I found her across the nation, where she was happy to respond to a research question. My first son was in the first class I had as a preschool teacher. Basing my pedagogical foundation on life experiences and mutual respect, my professional and personal lives have intertwined again and again.

I am an artist who never planned on being a teacher, and wound up in a Reggio-based preschool program. My role was teacher-assistant and to develop as an *atelierista* due to my background in art. And so, I got into early education for the money—needing to be a provider—but not for big bucks.

Art found its place early on in my study of education. Studying art had taught me the skills I needed to decipher, dissect, and discuss something new or foreign. Through this process, I developed understandings and constructed knowledge about education just as I had about art. Once you learn the language, be it of clay or ions, carburetors or pedagogy, your exposure and experience (in essence, who you are and the perspective you bring with you) guide your interpretations of the world and subsequent responses and expressions to it. So another lesson came back around to me, that to communicate or learn, you must first learn the language.

The two- and three-year-olds in my class explore everything, and each exploration radiates with wonder through their expressions. They share with me and repeat over and over their new discoveries. Children are each individuals, and what they do amazes and teaches me how unique we truly are. One very cold day we were outside playing. A boy in a small foot-powered car just sat there staring. I asked him if he was cold. He looked up and said, "No, I'm in the car, and I have the heater on." When they play, children are very serious about their play, and the worlds that contain it. Play, like art, lends itself to thinking outside the box, outside our own worlds, and to exploring others.

As a teacher, I've had to get outside my own boxes. I remember when I first began teaching, I pushed a child in a swing—not that hard—and the child fell out. I was doing something so "ordinary" I didn't even think about it, but for the child swinging was a new experience. That terrifying moment helped me gain a child's perspective. I saw that we don't all have the same understandings and how easily we can take this for granted.

Efrén Michael Léon

Once a child called me "Mom." Wow! As a man, that was something I never thought I'd hear! On reflection, I realized that a mom is someone you care about, have strong feelings about. It felt good to be called "Mom" and to think the child cared about me. These relationships helped form my foundation.

The values I grew up with influence me as a preschool teacher: Respect people, be attentive, and live in the moment. If children are to learn from you, they must respect you, and you earn this by respecting them, their culture, and their context. For example, when I met the mother of a student from the Middle East, I wanted to shake her hand, but she looked at me funny. A colleague later told me that in the family's culture, unrelated men and women do not touch. That changed me professionally. I always aimed to respect other people's language and customs, but now I was prompted to learn more, with and for the families, as well as for my own understanding.

So, I keep learning more through my work with children, and at the same time rely on the skills and talents collected throughout my life. I give children opportunity with art—that is, opportunity to be creative, to experience and express themselves free without boundaries. No matter the medium, two dimensions or three, they can express something's essence, a cat, for example. They express what a cat is to them through paint or clay, or by getting on the floor and being a cat. Art is everywhere. It's a personal perspective, and children have their own perspectives. I try to be open to what they're saying.

Besides working with individuals, I do art with groups of children. We were in a university building that had few windows, but we did have a great view of the playground. The children created life-size windows out of paper and gave them to the people in the building who had offices that needed windows. They all loved their new windows.

Like life, art is everywhere, and it is process. You take things in, and then respond. The responding is art; art is not just a product. It's the same with learning. As Dewey said, experience is education. We learn from experience right from the start.

suggested by formal knowledge of theory and research, they are often summarily dismissed as uninformed" (1997, 7). In the course of your teaching, values will collide in new and unanticipated ways. Sometimes there are no "just-right" solutions that please everyone. This is the ambiguity of everyday work in the early childhood field.

Our prior experiences can lead us to have misconceptions or to assume, sometimes unconsciously, that others share our experiences or take the same meaning from experiences. Balancing your experience with that of others is a professional's constant challenge. What can help?

- Share stories about your background with children, parents, and coworkers.
- Spend time getting to know others informally so that you learn about them and don't have to rely on guesses and assumptions.
- Be honest about differences, and don't pretend to agree when you don't.
- Let others know you are willing to work on possible solutions but that these take time and effort and the results may not be apparent for a while.

If you can understand your own perspectives and the biases that may lie under their surface, it can be easier to hear other people's points of view, recognize their biases, and build relationships that enable you to work together.

Some people are keenly aware of their culture; others don't think they have one at all. A student wrote, "'Ethnic identity?' asked my mother. 'I didn't know that you had one.' I felt about the same. Ethnics were people who were different from you" (Derman-Sparks and Phillips 1997, 54). This student's writing implies that her background is the norm and anyone who is different from her is "other." We all have a culture that influences our attitudes toward children, families, and colleagues and our expectations of ourselves and others. Everyone is "other" to someone.

All teachers work more empathically with children when they know more about themselves. White teachers, in particular, improve their practice when they recognize the often-hidden privileges they enjoy.

Your leanings toward music, physical outdoor activity, or cooking are also part of who you are, and you can pursue them in the classroom once you see that the children share your interests. At the same time, you will want or need to do activities with children that you may never have imagined doing. For example, not all adults are equally comfortable with art materials. They may dislike the potential messiness, lack experience with materials, or have had negative experiences in school that inhibit their enjoyment of expressive materials. Also, art materials take time to set up and clean up even when children are part of the process. But children's joy and sense of accomplishment make overcoming a bias against art activities worthwhile. This is clear when watching twos and threes derive pleasure and a sense of mastery from guiding the paint down the page and catching the drips. Later, children revel in their ability to represent their experiences with increasing realism.

Becoming comfortable with different types of activities is the first step in overcoming a bias against them. Communicating with teachers who specialize in art, music, science, or math can help you. Moreover, taking some time to play with materials when the children are not around can help you discover their potential.

> In teaching, values will collide in new and unanticipated ways. Sometimes there are no "just-right" solutions that please everyone. This is the ambiguity of everyday work in the early childhood field.

THOUGHT QUESTION Rita and her co-teacher respect each other's work. Rita has noticed, though, that the director of the center seems to assume Rita will work well with children, but that the director closely supervises Rita's co-teacher who, unlike Rita, is a person of color. What can Rita do or say?

Thoughtful Individuals

Teachers make decisions all the time: simple ones, such as whether the group should go outside when it might rain, and complicated ones, such as how to talk to children about race and exclusion. Sometimes teachers make decisions so quickly that they have no time to register them, for example, when a child is in danger. Such split-second decisions usually rest on past experiences. Most of the time, though, thoughtful decision making and critical reflection are crucial to the quality of a teacher's work, take time, and cannot be rushed.

How do you feel about constant thought and reflection or about contending with situations where no choice seems right? You may welcome the ongoing challenge and only sometimes think "Enough! My brain needs a break," as everyone's does. Perhaps, on the other hand, just the thought of reviewing your actions and mulling over the behaviors of a child or a family member makes you tired. If so, you may want to reconsider whether this field makes sense for you. Early childhood is not for everyone.

In our work with children, our learning and our thoughtful selves combine with other aspects of our being to make us humane and insightful. Early childhood educators play multiple roles. Individuals enact them in their own ways, and a teacher's many professional identities can contradict one another (Ryan and Grieshaber 2005).

Teachers need to experience materials to gain a deep understanding of children's play.

Engaging in critical reflection

Leah Levinger (1987, 25) says that at moments when you can't take the time to think about what a situation means or what caused it, later on you

> . . . must be able to reexamine it and learn from it what the next steps may be. This will never be an easy task but over the years people may become firmer in the balance between theory and practice.

As you reflect on your work, you combine thinking and doing. Your deepening understanding of your beliefs informs your practice, and your practice provides many questions to investigate.

Some reflection takes place internally—on the way home, while doing dishes, or while writing in a journal. It is "a uniquely individual and personal process" (Weigand et al. 2007, 17). Some happens with others, a "professional use of self in an interpersonal context" (Eggbeer, Mann, and Seibel 2007, 5). Some happens in a portfolio that you prepare as an early childhood student or as a teacher and can show to anyone you wish. When

We all have a culture that influences our attitudes toward children, families, colleagues, and our expectations of ourselves and others.

THOUGHT QUESTION Think of as many adjectives as you can to describe an early childhood educator you admire. What attributes seem contradictory? How will you reconcile all the aspects of your own professional identity?

we share ideas, we have opportunities to include new perspectives, shape a goal for action, or summon the nerve to try a new idea in the classroom or with a family. Collaborative reflection gives us courage and keeps us honest.

According to Donald Schön (1983, 1996), reflective practice has three components. It involves:

- thoughtfully considering your past experiences,
- applying knowledge that you gain from thinking and reading to your practice, and
- being coached by someone who has more experience than you do.

The National Board for Professional Teaching Standards maintains that teachers must be able to think systematically about their practice and learn from experience. They must be able to "critically examine their practice, seek the advice of others, and draw on educational research to deepen their knowledge, sharpen their judgment, and adapt their teaching to new findings and ideas" (National Commission on Teaching and America's Future 1996, 75). Critically examining practice probes what a behavior means, how it fits into the situation in which it occurred, and who benefits from it.

The progressive educator and philosopher John Dewey (1910/1933) looked closely at reflection, experience, and education. For Dewey, an experience is an *interaction* between oneself and the world that is followed by a thinking process to conceptualize or reorganize the experience for that person and others. Simply having an experience is not enough: an experience gains meaning and we arrive at a more complex level of engagement with ideas when we think critically about and express our reactions to the experience. According to Dewey, reflection

- comprises *systematic rigorous thinking*
- followed by *action*
- conducted *with others* who share the goal of personal and intellectual growth. (cited in Rogers 2002)

Through his work over the first part of the twentieth century, Dewey refined his ideas about reflection, ultimately coming up with six phases that are a part of it:

1. The experience
2. Spontaneous interpretations of the experience
3. Naming the problem or the questions that arise out of the experience
4. Generating possible explanations for the problems or questions posed
5. Shaping the explanations into a hypothesis
6. Acting in a way that experiments with or tests the hypothesis

Simply having an experience is not enough: an experience gains meaning and we arrive at a more complex level of engagement with ideas when we think critically about and express our reactions to the experience.

THOUGHT QUESTION Many college students prepare **teaching portfolios** to document their learning about children. A portfolio is a physical or an electronic assemblage of work and reflections and usually includes a statement of your personal philosophy. It also may contain your resume, a record of your fieldwork, and evaluations of your work. While the assignments you include in your portfolio are important, the reflection you do on that work is crucial. What are you learning that surprises you? What helps you learn? What questions do your assignments, your observations, and your fieldwork raise for you? How are you answering them?

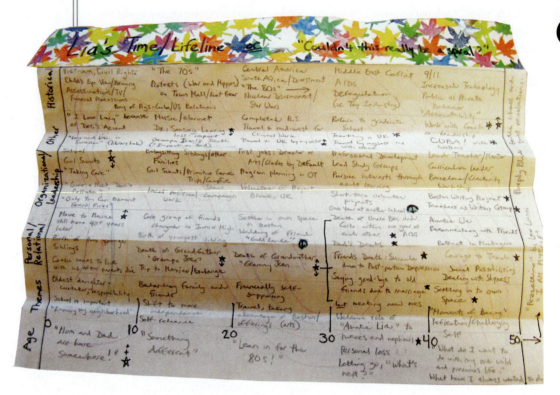

The teacher who developed this lifeline used it to reflect on her past experiences and on patterns of behavior that influence her current practice with children.

A fours teacher, Roberta, used Dewey's phases when an epidemic of "marriages" erupted about halfway through the school year. At first she was thrilled with the rich dramatic play and learning. Some children said girls could marry girls if they loved each other, and others said no, only a boy and a girl could marry. In discussions at meeting time, children described what a law meant and read books about children raised by lesbian mothers and gay fathers who could not officially marry in their state. But as the "marrying" activity progressed, it became more frantic, and Roberta became anxious about it. It was taking over the classroom with less play and more talk. At their weekly team meeting, Roberta and the other teachers realized that the children were using "marriage" to include and exclude classmates, with outbursts, tears, and exclamations of "I'm *not* going to marry you!" Now the marriages were interfering with learning and the group's ability to function as a community.

Here is how Roberta used Dewey's framework to assist her with this challenge:

1. *The experience:* Children marrying each other in dramatic play.
2. *Spontaneous interpretations:* Rich material for children to pursue in other areas of the curriculum—group discussion, literature, social studies, and the arts.
3. *Naming the problem:* Now children are obsessing about "marriage" and using it to exclude others. Parents encourage the marriage play, finding it cute.
4. *Generating possible explanations:* Marriage means something different to the children than to the teachers. Parents don't see that the marriage play is excluding children.

5. *Shaping the explanations into a hypothesis:* Children, families, and teachers need to clarify what the marriage play means. Everyone needs to think about friendship.

6. *The action they took:* The teachers wrote a letter home, asking parents to have conversations to help their children understand that, under the guise of "marriage," they were including and excluding various children and hurting some.

In a few days there was a snowstorm, and building snow caves and snow people captivated the children. The teachers removed the dress-up dresses and shoes for a few weeks, and the children resumed a range of play scenarios they had used before the wedding extravaganzas. Discussions continued about what it means to be a friend, about what makes a family, and about laws that say whom someone can marry.

Dewey's framework is not a checklist for reflection; it is a coherent model that emphasizes thinking processes. Dewey possessed a complex sense of the rigorous intellectual and emotional work involved in a teacher's reflective practice (Rogers 2002).

Dealing with raw emotions

When you work with young children and families, raw emotions are in the air all day and can follow you home at night. You live with the children's emotions and bring yours with you as well. Understanding your reactions to children, to their families, to your colleagues, and to the stress of your work life helps you take care of yourself, enjoy your work, and be a better teacher.

A student new to working with young children described the toddlers in her group as "emotions on two legs" (Carol Zeavin, personal communication, 1996). The primacy of young children's needs and their swings from pensive to explosive expression enter our conscious and unconscious selves. Our experience of children's emotional turmoil can bring up feelings from our pasts. Our vulnerabilities are part of our humanity, so dismissing children's emotions isn't the answer. Instead, we need to consider our daily experiences with children and be alert to how their emotions and behaviors affect us. As you can see with Dahlia, when teachers put the effect that children's emotions have on them into perspective, they lessen the chances of getting stuck in them.

When teachers experience children's strong emotions they may confront emotions from their past.

As Dahlia told the story, it was a dramatic face-off with a determined two-year-old who wouldn't bring the play dough back to the table, as Dahlia repeatedly requested. The room became quiet, and the teachers watched how she (the novice student teacher) would resolve the adult-child conflict. While the two-year-old's determination was intimidating, Dahlia stood her ground and twice guided the child back to the table. Later, Dahlia talked about being scared. Expressing her vulnerability to her college supervisor and telling her she was scared was this student teacher's way of managing her anxiety. Only then could she think about what she was so afraid of. Was it fear of the child's becoming angry and having a temper tantrum or Dahlia as a student teacher becoming angry or losing face? (adapted from Poole and Casper 2006)

When we understand our own feelings, we can understand children more easily and also feel more comfortable in our own shoes.

Raw emotions in the early childhood setting don't always originate with the children. Many, if not most, early childhood educators start their careers with a deep-seated desire for the children to like them. You may want to spend the whole day with the child who scrambles onto your lap or leads you by the hand to the water table.

She's angry. How would you react if you were her teacher?

While it is natural to want to be liked, you may find that these feelings complicate your relationships with the children—for example, when you want them to do something they don't want to do.

Some students and new teachers can sum up their delight in teaching children with, "They like me." While it is natural to want to be liked, you may find that these feelings complicate your relationships with the children—for example, when you want them to do something they don't want to do. Try focusing on the children themselves, on their abilities and interests. Take children seriously and listen hard to their verbal and nonverbal communication. You may find that this helps you grow from someone who just wants to be liked to someone who is also a partner in a teaching-learning-caring relationship.

Work with children can provoke a variety of other feelings as you integrate your personal and work selves. For instance, teachers who have raised children, read various theories, and continue to learn about children every day may have regrets about ways in which they related to their own children.

Emotions can be frightening, and sometimes people steer away from situations that could evoke them, especially if they could result in a conflict or at least a disagreement. Conflict—or the prospect of it—is particularly hard for most women to handle because they have been socialized to avoid it. Fear of conflict is easier to address when you look at how you feel about anger. Is it okay to get angry? Or is anger terrifying? If you can face your own anger instead of suppressing it, you will have an easier time discussing the content of the conflict with others. Once again, figuring out how you feel and what to do about how you feel will help you in your relationships with children, families, and colleagues.

Work with young children can be stressful. As emotions fly around the room, supervisors and families place demands, and the daily routine proceeds at a hectic pace, you may find yourself wearing thin. How do you protect yourself from **burnout**, that is, from getting to the point where you can take no more? Here are some suggestions for managing some of the factors that contribute to burnout:

- *Pacing:* Although you have a lot to do as an early childhood educator, try to plan ahead so that you accomplish a lot without constantly rushing.
- *Efficacy:* Think about what makes you feel effective as an early childhood educator, and seek and create situations that make you feel that way.
- *Support:* Figure out who can support you and help you as you determine how to respond to everyday situations.
- *Appreciation:* Let the people around you show you how valuable you are. You might, for example, consider asking for a raise.

Professional Development

During your career you may have different roles—for example, assistant teacher, teacher, and then director—and you can grow and develop in your work, whatever your jobs are. Since the late 1970s, theorists of early childhood teacher development have conceptualized that development in a variety of ways.

Linear Path or an Interactive Experience Network?

Theories about stages of teacher development trace a teacher's growth from beginner to someone with experience. Linear progressions, they describe how teachers move from one stage of development to the next.

Lilian Katz (1977), for example, describes a teacher's progression

- from daily survival—during the first year of teaching, just getting through each day is the teacher's primary goal;
- to consolidation of what the teacher knows about children—soon, the teacher can relax enough to process experiences with children;
- to an urge for renewal—after about five years, the teacher is ready for new input;
- to maturity—when the teacher can mentor and teach others about teaching.

Katz's theory describes teachers at different points in their careers in ways many teachers agree are accurate. The theory recommends professional development activities based on the characteristics that these descriptions ascribe to teachers at each stage.

As you can see, in this model the teacher begins as someone who needs help and develops into someone who offers help to others. Such stage models can be useful because you can picture yourself at a specific point on your career trajectory. They can be limiting, though, because no one fits perfectly into descriptive slots.

More recent theoretical models take an open-ended approach. They emphasize teachers' voice and agency, their empowerment, and their development in the context of the programs in which they work. These models take into consideration teachers' cultures and the children, families, and communities with whom they work. These models do not describe teachers who progress from stage to stage. Rather, they show teachers as reflecting on a variety of experiences and interactions that can change their practices.

Alma Fleet and Catherine Patterson (2001), for example, describe a process of professional development that acknowledges that new teachers bring prior knowledge and experience to their work. They "recognize staff as empowered learners who build their working knowledge through spirals of engagement with many aspects of early childhood philosophy and practice over time." This means that professional development is more like a network of roads than a single path. You may wind back and forth as you turn to various people, theories, and communities with whom you engage for learning purposes. You are likely to feel unsure of yourself as a teacher periodically, as you confront new challenges, and then more confident as you make new discoveries about yourself, about children, and about your work.

Meaningful performance appraisals or teacher evaluations can help you chart the course of your professional development. Evaluations can be more or less formal. You may set goals and evaluate how close you've come to meeting them. You may do another kind of self-evaluation, perhaps using a checklist or writing a bit about your work. In either case, you will probably discuss these evaluations with your supervisor or with colleagues. They may observe your work with children and talk to you about what they saw, or they may fill in a form or write a report about your work. Evaluation is most helpful when everyone involved takes an honest and open look at your work, when the evaluation of it is based on your **job description**—what you are hired to do—and when the evaluation is specific and detailed. Some people dread observations and evaluations, perhaps because they don't want to be judged and fear negative feedback. These feelings are real, but, at the same time, you deserve clear feedback that helps you grow as a teacher.

Evaluation is most helpful when everyone involved takes an honest and open look at your work, when the evaluation is based on your job description, and when the evaluation is specific and detailed.

A spirit of inquiry

Working with young children involves learning constantly. Observing with an open mind and discussing your observations with colleagues, supervisors, and children's family members are among the best ways to continue learning. Professional journals and books; websites of early childhood organizations; and local, national, and even international organizations offer new ideas about children and families. Your constant learning communicates your interest and care to families and lets children know how much you value learning for them and for yourself.

Moreover, early childhood educators constantly need information. Suddenly, you want to know more about trucks, dinosaurs, and fish than you ever thought imaginable because these are the topics that fascinate the children in your preschool class. You gain that knowledge from children's books; the Internet; specialists whom you meet, interview, or read; and observation that is sharper thanks to your inquiry. When the opportunity arises to use robotics or another new technology with the children, you have to learn about it yourself. In many instances, you learn alongside the children, illustrating your commitment to learning and your willingness to be fallible as a learner.

In addition to the curiosity and inquiry necessary to constantly gain content and process knowledge, early childhood educators are learning about children all the time. Every day raises questions for adults who work with children. An informal process recurs: wanting to know; figuring out how to find out; observing, reading, and discussing to learn; guessing at possible answers; and gathering more information to test those guesses (Figure 1.2).

Some early childhood educators formalize that process on their own or in research groups. They conduct teacher research and systematically

- frame a question or questions,
- read about what others have discovered that relates to the question,
- plan a method for investigating the question,
- carry out their plans,
- analyze what they've found, and
- consider the implications of that analysis and come up with ideas for more teacher research.

While teacher research may not be the norm in early childhood settings, early childhood classrooms "have great potential for sustained inquiry" (Meier and Henderson 2007, 6). For instance, Vivian Gussin Paley (e.g., 1979, 1981, 1993) tape-recorded children in her classrooms, listened to the tapes again and again, and wrote thought-provoking books about her findings. She provides a model of early childhood teacher research. Karen Gallas (1994, 1995, 1997, 2003), Sylvia Ashton-Warner (1963), and other teachers of young children who have written books and

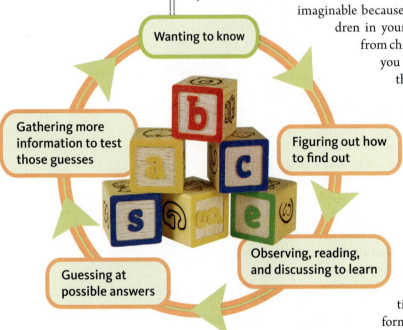

Wanting to know

Gathering more information to test those guesses

Figuring out how to find out

Guessing at possible answers

Observing, reading, and discussing to learn

1.2 *The Educator's Informal Learning Process*

articles about their work offer you engaging reading along with ideas for a research agenda of your own. Plus, their work helps you rethink teaching in the context of real classrooms.

Knowledge utilization

Teachers need lots of different kinds of knowledge. You've read here about knowing and continuing to know yourself. In addition, everything you and the children do is rooted in the history, social issues, politics, economics, and culture that you are part of and that surround you all. **Content knowledge,** the subjects people study in high school and college, is crucial to understanding these factors that, in turn, offer a range of perspectives on what happens in the classroom. In addition, knowledge of human development and how people learn and behave individually and in groups enables teachers to think about classroom interactions in different ways. Knowing the individual children and how they think, feel, and understand the world, as well as knowing as much as possible about their families and communities, enables teachers to apply general knowledge to the specifics of their classrooms. Of course, teachers know about curriculum and learning environments, too, and they must look beneath the surface at hidden curriculum—the unspoken agendas for each child that teachers communicate by how they treat children and what they show children is important to them (Ayers 2004).

Although what teachers know is important, what counts is what they can do with what they know. **Knowledge utilization,** which refers to how any of us generates and uses knowledge (Buysse and Wesley 2006), can help us understand how we develop as teachers. Does knowledge just sit with us, like a shelved book you mean to read someday, or does it get put into practice and tried out, like a new dish you've tasted and then make for yourself?

Workshops and conferences are great resources for gaining new knowledge and for networking, but only if you apply what you've learned when you return. If you attend with coworkers, you can meet while at the conference, share ideas, and make plans for follow-up once you return. However, even after you change your practice, new ideas may not stick, perhaps because of changes in personnel; lack of resources, such as time to convey the ideas or strategies to others; or lack of ongoing support (Berman and McLaughlin 1978). Most often, real change takes time.

How do the people at a program or school use knowledge best? Some say that it makes sense to generate knowledge near where it will be used, so the ideas can be more easily translated into the local context. For example, in addition to individual teacher conferences with the director each week and weekly team meetings for each classroom, one child care center has monthly meetings or workshops for the whole school. One meeting was devoted to generating ideas for successful parent conferences; at another, a mother who was a singer presented a workshop on music; and, as part of a yearlong study, the staff read and talked about racism at yet another. Pam Winton (2006) describes this as a kind of constructivist process: one where learners are active participants and construct their own learning with others on site, based on issues that are relevant to *their* practice.

It can be hard to create and implement knowledge on your own, or even to bring an idea back to your classroom from a workshop or from your own reading. To create knowledge that makes sense for your setting means working with others on-site. Together, you can, for example, look closely at your practice by using video and then discuss and analyze what you see with a colleague, group of colleagues, supervisor, or staff developer (Finn 2002; Goetz-Haver 2002; Sherin 2000).

> Does knowledge just sit with us, like a shelved book you mean to read someday, or does it get put into practice and tried out, like a new dish you've tasted and then make for yourself?

When Early Head Start assistant teachers participated in the videotaping of their room, they became highly motivated to observe, learn, and assess their work (Healy 2002, 33) because they could see and feel what was happening in the classroom.

> Jeanette realized that no matter what you were watching on the video, her voice came across very loudly, even when she wasn't visible. . . . "I learned that I had to lower my voice because it was carrying over the whole room."

Watching the tape, the teachers discovered that they were competing for the children's interest rather than working together to plan and do activities. Their supervisor believed that they had to see themselves on tape to understand and analyze the dynamic in their room.

New cheaper, user-friendly video tools are increasingly available for classroom use. However, if you do not have access to video, try telling stories of your practice regularly to a small group of keen listeners who care about you and your work.

Career directions

Given your biography, your cultural identity, and everything else that contributes to who you are, where will you work, and on what aspect of early childhood will you focus? Take some time to explore possibilities. Since early care and education offers many choices, you can have a variety of experiences over the course of your career.

The early childhood **career lattice**—a system of professional roles that goes in all directions—offers you the chance to do a range of jobs. Early childhood educators often move from substituting in a classroom for a teacher who is ill or away to becoming an assistant teacher. Assistant teachers who gain experience and education can become lead teachers, and some lead teachers choose to become directors or principals. With classroom experience to draw upon, some early childhood educators become educational consultants who regulate programs. Some design and conduct professional development, perhaps teaching at the college level. Yet others take less direct routes to jobs with and for children. The image of a lattice (Figure 1.3), rather than a ladder, allows room for the variety of places from which early childhood educators come and the variety of positions that they take via a variety of educational routes.

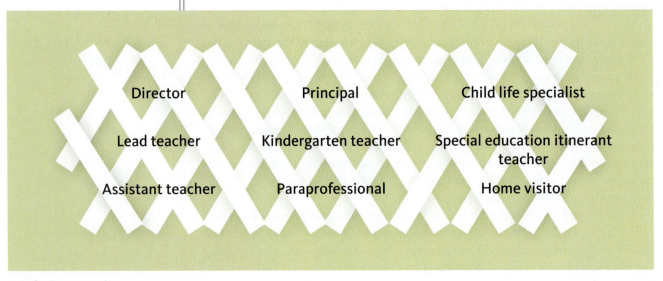

Director   Principal   Child life specialist

Lead teacher   Kindergarten teacher   Special education itinerant teacher

Assistant teacher   Paraprofessional   Home visitor

1.3 *The Career Lattice*

Perhaps you want to teach and already know which age group or groups you prefer. If you keep your options open and observe and try different age groups, however, you may surprise yourself. Every age has its own delights. Those who work with infants will learn to interpret their cues, witness their dramatic changes, and become a primary person in children's lives. Working with toddlers or twos, you'll be swept up in the intensity of their emotions, their passion to figure out how things work, and the intriguing process of their developing language. With threes and fours, you'll facilitate their interactions with each other and their independent work with materials. In a kindergarten, you'll be part of a community of children who are increasingly able to plan and execute projects, notice details, make discoveries, and take in information. Or you can orchestrate experiences for first graders, whose literacy and mathematical skills grow significantly as they explore social and scientific ideas. Or you might teach second or third grade and plan for children to apply basic skills and research topics in depth. The range of ages within early childhood offers many possibilities. Consider what draws you to each age.

THOUGHT QUESTION You may choose to work in a public or a private program. You may look for a program that includes children with and without disabilities. Think about why you want to work with children whose backgrounds are similar to or different from your own. What do you want to do that is like or unlike what you experienced as a child? What do you hope to learn about children and about yourself?

Not all early childhood educators work in center or school settings, and, even if they do, they may not be classroom teachers. Nannies work in other people's homes; family child care providers usually work in their own homes. Some early childhood special educators work at a program with individual children, either in the child's classroom or outside of the class to support the child's development. Other early childhood educators work in hospitals, clinics, or libraries.

An early childhood educator may decide not to work directly with children. Some focus on policy issues that affect children and families. They may do research and publish their findings. They may work with legislators and, through their speaking

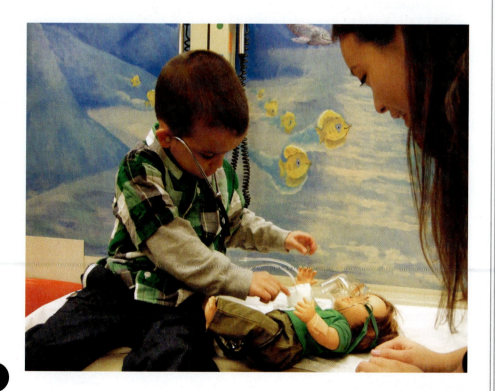

Medical play, supported by a child life specialist, helps children use medical tools to calm and master their fears about medical procedures.

TABLE 1.2	Some Early Childhood Professional Roles	
WORK WITH CHILDREN	**WORK FOR CHILDREN**
Nanny	Policy analyst
Infant caregiver	Researcher and writer
Toddler teacher	Advocate
Preschool teacher	College professor
Kindergarten teacher	Parent group leader
Early elementary teacher	Children's health specialist
Early interventionist/ special educator	Children's media producer or developer
Child life specialist	Toy creator
Home visitor	Children's book writer or illustrator

and writing, mobilize others to speak out on behalf of children. Others may prefer to work with families, supporting their parenting in individual or group sessions. Early childhood educators may focus on children's health issues, children's media, or toys. And, of course, you could write and/or illustrate a children's book. As you see, you have many possibilities (Table 1.2).

The work you want to do with children may require certification. Teacher certification requirements differ from state to state, determined by each state's department of education. Please check the website of your state's department of education (Table 1.3) to find out its requirements.

Often, students graduating with a bachelor's degree in early childhood education also need to pass certification exams and gather other documentation to become certified. Students at community colleges can transfer into baccalaureate programs that offer certification, and when their community college has an **articulation agreement** with a four-year program, credits from the community college count toward the bachelor's degree and teacher certification.

Some states certify early childhood teachers separately from elementary school teachers. This certification acknowledges that early childhood education is a different body of knowledge from elementary education and that early childhood educators need specific preparation to work with young children. Some colleges offer routes to **dual certification** in early childhood and special education, so teachers will be prepared to teach all young children.

NAEYC has written standards for initial licensure in early childhood education that the National Council for the Accreditation of Teacher Education (NCATE) approved in 2001. You will encounter these standards throughout this book; we refer to them in the Further Activities at the end of each chapter. Colleges use these standards to ensure that their programs help students meet national standards for early childhood teachers. While NCATE does not accredit community colleges, community colleges can use the NAEYC standards to prepare their students for transfer. In addition, NAEYC offers community college early childhood programs the option of voluntary accreditation.

EDUCATOR RELATIONSHIPS WITH OTHER ADULTS

What are the key elements of successful collaborations with other adults?

Adults who work well together feed each other's minds and spirits; they create a climate that makes children and adults alike want to be there. In contrast, tension with other adults can sap your energy and, over time, lead to burnout and even to your leaving the field prematurely. Even more important, regardless of how subtle you think the tensions are, young children pick up the tone of interactions between adults and react accordingly.

NAEYC has written standards for initial licensure in early childhood education that the National Council for the Accreditation of Teacher Education (NCATE) approved in 2001. You will encounter these standards throughout this book; we refer to them in the Further Activities at the end of each chapter.

TABLE 1.3 State Department of Education Websites

Alabama	http://www.alsde.edu/html/home.asp	Montana	http://www.opi.mt.gov/
Alaska	http://www.eed.state.ak.us/	Nebraska	http://www.nde.state.ne.us/
Arizona	http://www.ade.az.gov/	Nevada	http://www.doe.nv.gov/
Arkansas	http://arkansased.org/	New Hampshire	http://www.ed.state.nh.us/
California	http://www.cde.ca.gov/	New Jersey	http://www.state.nj.us/education/
Colorado	http://www.cde.state.co.us/	New Mexico	http://www.ped.state.nm.us/
Connecticut	http://www.sde.ct.gov/	New York	http://www.nysed.gov/
Delaware	http://www.doe.state.de.us/	North Carolina	http://www.ncpublicschools.org/
D.C.	http://www.k12.dc.us/	North Dakota	http://www.dpi.state.nd.us/
Florida	http://www.fldoe.org/	Ohio	http://www.ode.state.oh.us/
Georgia	http://public.doe.k12.ga.us/index.aspx	Oklahoma	http://sde.state.ok.us/
Hawaii	http://doe.k12.hi.us/	Oregon	http://www.ode.state.or.us/
Idaho	http://www.sde.state.id.us/dept/	Pennsylvania	http://www.pde.state.pa.us/
Illinois	http://www.isbe.net/	Rhode Island	http://www.ridoe.net/
Indiana	http://www.doe.state.in.us/	South Carolina	http://ed.sc.gov/
Iowa	http://www.iowa.gov/educate	South Dakota	http://doe.sd.gov/
Kansas	http://www.ksde.org/	Tennessee	http://www.state.tn.us/education/
Kentucky	http://www.education.ky.gov/	Texas	http://www.tea.state.tx.us/
Louisiana	http://www.louisianaschools.net/	Utah	http://www.schools.utah.gov/
Maine	http://www.maine.gov/portal/education/	Vermont	http://www.education.vermont.gov/
Maryland	http://www.marylandpublicschools.org/MSDE	Virginia	http://www.doe.virginia.gov/
Massachusetts	http://www.doe.mass.edu/	Washington	http://www.k12.wa.us/
Michigan	http://www.michigan.gov/mde/	West Virginia	http://wvde.state.wv.us/
Minnesota	http://education.state.mn.us/mde/index.html	Wisconsin	http://dpi.wi.gov/
Mississippi	http://www.mde.k12.ms.us/	Wyoming	http://www.k12.wy.us/index.asp
Missouri	http://dese.mo.gov/		

Working as Part of a Classroom Team

The mayor of a major city once asked a gathering of hundreds of early childhood educators what he thought was a rhetorical question: What would they prefer, smaller class sizes or two teachers in a kindergarten class? To his surprise, the attendees all said they wanted to be part of a team. Two or more adults in a room can share their perspectives on what's happening for individual children and with the group. They can put their heads together to develop curriculum and plan for individual children. They can bounce ideas off each other and join forces when difficult situations arise.

Teachers who work well together develop verbal and nonverbal language. A lifted eyebrow and tilt of the head alert another teacher to observe a child as he struggles to dress a doll. An exchanged glance, and one teacher moves to the block area just before a crisis. When the team includes men and women of diverse backgrounds, it shows children how people who are different from each other can relate.

Collaboration requires communication, and that takes time, space, and a willingness to listen to each other.

A classroom team can function as a hierarchy or a collaboration. In a hierarchy, the leader tells the others what to do, and the other teachers may follow the leader's instructions without taking initiative themselves. In a collaboration, which can exist among people of different roles, the teachers exchange information and take on tasks as equals.

Collaboration includes conflict. Teams don't work if people pretend to agree when they don't. At a productive team meeting, people with differing opinions present their points of view, listen carefully to each other, argue their points, and try to understand all perspectives—but don't necessarily end up agreeing. The process takes time and does not offer quick fixes. Team members may agree to try a suggestion without agreeing with the suggestion itself. Once they see what happens, they return to the group for an honest discussion of what occurred.

People in collaborative teams need a shared commitment to young children and their families. In addition, team members must be willing and able to

- work hard;
- voice their ideas and opinions;
- seek, accept, and give criticism;
- be open to new ideas;
- admit mistakes; and
- take joy and learn from other people's strengths as well as from their own. (Jalongo 2002)

Sometimes when a new person enters a room that works collaboratively, he or she is not accepted right away as a team member. Teachers have preconceptions about roles, too, and may treat a fieldwork student, for example, differently from the way they treat each other.

Your first job is likely to be as an assistant teacher, working with a group teacher who has more responsibility for the class. In some public schools, assistants are called paraprofessionals, or teaching or educational assistants, or aides. Whatever the title, you are a member of the classroom team, interacting with children and families, planning, and keeping observational records. How much your team expects of you depends on the program and your coworkers. If you assist in a class with a teacher you admire, you may adopt habits you will prize in the future. Assisting someone you don't respect is challenging, as is working with someone with whom you don't get along. Do what you can, perhaps with your director's, principal's, or another's help, to develop a good working relationship. If the match really doesn't work, do what you can to change it.

Often assistant teachers share class and/or cultural backgrounds with the children and families in their class and have an insider's

THOUGHT QUESTION Jermaine, a fieldwork student who started three weeks ago, was annoyed because the lead teacher in his room always asked him to clean the tables instead of letting him sit with the children at meeting. He didn't mind the dirty work and was glad to do it occasionally, but he preferred being with the children, would have welcomed the chance to lead meeting sometimes, and thought the teachers should take turns cleaning up. If you were Jermaine, how would you begin a conversation with the other teachers about your concerns?

knowledge of the community. When such assistants remain in the same position for some time, others at the school may overlook their expertise. A group of assistant teachers in Newark, New Jersey, met with a staff developer, who taped their conversation as part of a professional development session. Once, when the developer stopped them to turn over the tape, the assistant teachers kept talking. Joking about continuing to talk, one of them "asserted proudly, 'Nobody ever asked me to tell my story before, and I like telling it'" (Hammond 2003, 130). They had fun telling their stories, but the experience proved much deeper than that. As the assistant teachers and the staff developer exchanged information, all of them learned about themselves and about teaching in their community.

Some teachers choose to remain assistants. They don't want the responsibility of the classroom or else decide not to pursue more education. Many, though, use the assistant teacher position as a stepping stone and a learning opportunity for becoming a confident lead teacher.

Working with Supervisors

Someone will supervise you, and you will supervise others. As an assistant teacher, for example, you will supervise a substitute teacher who covers when the lead teacher is out. If you think about what you want from supervision both as the supervisee and the supervisor, you can make sure you receive the support you need, if not from your immediate supervisor, then from one or more people in the program, someone at your college, or another mentor. Sam, the student who is blind whom you met earlier in this chapter, formed a close relationship with his early childhood professor but also spoke often with a teacher who is blind and could coach him based on her experiences.

The teacher-supervisor relationship and the teacher-child relationship are similar in various respects. As in relationships with children, trust lays the foundation for serious thinking with other adults. Strength-based, collaborative interactions without judgments make others feel worthy of trust. We have bad days, and mistakes do happen, but everyone *can* move forward from a negative occurrence.

When something upsetting happens in the classroom, as you saw with Dahlia's face-off with a two-year-old earlier in this chapter, the supervision relationship provides a place to release the emotions and reflect on the situation. Sometimes, however, especially early in your professional development, you may not realize that there is anything to examine or reflect upon. The pace of a classroom day is not always conducive to stepping back and considering a situation from another perspective. Here is what happened with Jake, a new student teacher in a preschool classroom:

> At the play dough table with a small group of three-year-olds, Jake rolled out the dough, using a mini rolling pin. He kept his eye on the children as he cut out a circle, poked in facial features, and made small rolls for hair. The children stopped using their play dough and asked Jake questions about his face. Then, one by one, they left the table.
>
>
>
> Malvina, Jake's cooperating teacher, did not say anything to him until they met for a supervision session two days later. She began by asking him to retell what happened at the play dough table. When he did, she asked why he thought the children had left the table. "Maybe they were finished?" he suggested. "Maybe they were," she said, "but can you think of anything else?" He paused for a minute and responded, "They seemed interested in the face I made. Do you think I shouldn't have done that?" "What do you think?"

The teacher-supervisor relationship and the teacher-child relationship are similar. As in relationships with children, trust lays the foundation for serious thinking with other adults.

Malvina asked. Jake answered, "Do you think my play dough face made them give up on what they were doing?" "I don't know for sure," Malvina said, "but that happens sometimes. They probably don't think they can make a face the way you did."

Malvina asked him what he'd do differently next time, and Jake said thoughtfully, "I think I'll just watch them and then do whatever they do with the dough. I'll get ideas from them instead of giving them ideas." Malvina suggested that he try that and continued, "Please let me know what you find out. I really don't know myself for sure."

Just as in an authentic conversation with children, Malvina didn't know the answers to the questions she asked, although she knew what she believed about interacting with children while they use materials. Her goal was to support Jake's thinking so they could learn together.

Ideally, people involved in a supervisory process engage in learning together, using stories the supervisee tells about the work experience. The reflective supervisory relationship helps the early childhood educator think about experiences from different points of view. Most important, much as a teacher does with children and families, the supervisor "holds" the early childhood educator's experiences and aspirations in mind, thus providing a trusting space where learning can occur (Pawl 1995).

When an early childhood educator and a supervisor collaborate to learn together, they

- share a common focus and a desire to learn;
- find ways to talk to each other when they disagree or don't like what the other person is doing with the children;
- discover the other person's strengths, to learn from and bolster those capabilities;
- are open and honest.

Learning to work with a supervisor is part of the process of becoming a professional. Agree upon ground rules for the supervisory process, so you can discuss your impressions even when you are scared or not pleased with your own or another's response to a classroom event, as was the case for Kara (see Thought Question below).

THOUGHT QUESTION Kara is a fieldwork student in Pat and Elaine's fours room. Kara thinks both teachers speak too abruptly to the children. Pat told Kara not to cuddle the children, even though they come to her for hugs each morning. Kara's faculty supervisor told her that she should have a reflective conversation with Pat and Elaine. How could Kara begin that conversation?

Students who work in classrooms commonly worry about telling their cooperating or supervisory teacher what they believe. They may fear that the teacher will think ill of them or hold their ideas against them. Of course, how one raises an issue can determine the tone of the discussion. Openness and honesty must be mutual.

Working with Others to Support Inclusion

Laws, research, families' determination, and early childhood educators' commitment all promote the inclusion of young children who have disabilities. You will read more about inclusive classrooms throughout this book, especially in Chapters 8 and 15. In an inclusive setting:

- Children who have and do not have known disabilities participate in activities together throughout the day.

- Children develop relationships with each other.
- Every child's strengths are celebrated and everyone's dignity is respected.

Work in an inclusive setting means collaborating with a range of professionals in addition to your classroom team. A child who has a disability may be assigned an aide who assists the child but does not take the place of the teacher. Ideally, the aide becomes a member of the class and works with the child together with other children. Specialists support the particular needs and strengths of children who have disabilities. Just as these children are part of the classroom, so, too, are the part-timers in their support team. Sue is a special education itinerant teacher (SEIT) who writes:

> One aspect of my job is being respectful of the classroom routine, curriculum, and philosophy. I always remember that I am entering someone else's room and I keep in mind the definition of "itinerant." I work from place to place; consequently I need to be able to fit in. I do this by trying my best to articulate my work, my philosophy, my expectations for the child, and I seek information from teachers and directors that will help me collaborate in the school, in the classroom. I ask about what their expectations are for me in their room. I offer my help with common classroom duties, cleaning tables, for example, as I want to be helpful and accepted.
>
> I find it important to be accepted as a peer, and in that way I can be heard when talking about the work I need to do with respect to the child's special needs. In the spirit of collaboration I ask for a time to meet, to share our observations and expectations. I continually find that thinking of SEIT work as service helps me find the tone for collaboration. I am experienced in my work, but I am not the expert. I respect that the classroom teacher has expertise that will benefit my work, and this professional collaboration will ultimately benefit the child receiving the SEIT services. Collaboration improves my practice, and it is a stronger foundation for lasting improvement in a child's ability.

Through meetings with and without the child's family, informal conversations, notes to each other, and shared readings, all the professionals involved can develop relationships with each other to make inclusion work.

Collaborating with Family Members

In addition to working with children and colleagues, much of your work will involve the children's families. In Chapter 14, you will learn about various approaches to working with families that strive toward mutual understanding and respect. Once again, different values, goals, and beliefs can be a source of conflict between teachers and families. Teachers, for example, can blame parents for being what they consider too tough or not tough enough. Sometimes we look only at the parents' behaviors and don't recognize the parents' goals for their children (LeVine 1974). All families have these goals whether or not they are aware of them or can articulate them.

We discover families' goals for their children by getting to know family members, with the aim of creating a trusting relationship. Involving families in curriculum, writing notes home, and informal and formal conversations with families are the main vehicles toward this end. When teachers are fair, thoughtfully honest, and demonstrate that they have been thinking about the family, most parenting adults respond in kind.

"I am experienced in my work, but I am not the expert. I respect that the classroom teacher has expertise that will benefit . . . our collaboration will ultimately benefit the child receiving the SEIT services."

Families and teachers can join together in a variety of ways, including at meetings such as this one.

SUMMARY

EARLY CARE AND EDUCATION

What is involved in caring for and educating young children?

In early childhood education, care and education go hand-in-hand. Caring relationships form the foundation of early childhood education. Care involves attentiveness, responsibility, competence, and responsiveness. Education, too, has four components. It is the *interaction* of teaching, learning, content, and the environment that leads learners to make meaning from or interpret what they are learning.

QUALITY OF EARLY CARE AND EDUCATION

What issues do discussions of the quality of early care and education raise, and why are early childhood educators having those discussions now?

NAEYC, the National Association for the Education of Young Children, has worked over time to increase the professionalism of early childhood educators and the quality of early care and education for children. However, the definition of quality is not clear-cut, as questions that reconceptualizers raise about early childhood issues indicate. We invite you to question and reconceptualize early care and education as you learn about it.

EARLY CHILDHOOD EDUCATORS

What are the characteristics of a professional early childhood educator?

Work with young children is complex, in part because early childhood educators bring their respective identities to the roles they play. They can make sense of their work by being reflective, telling their stories, confronting their biases, and facing their emotions. If they embody a spirit of inquiry, they are motivated to keep learning, use knowledge well, and develop as teachers. Careers in early childhood education take many directions, from assistant teacher to director, and including jobs outside of the classroom.

EDUCATOR RELATIONSHIPS WITH OTHER ADULTS

What are the key elements of successful collaborations with other adults?
Working with other adults as well as with children can be fulfilling and challenging. Collaboration demands open communication that builds trust relationships along with a willingness to look at yourself honestly and the flexibility to learn from and with others.

FURTHER ACTIVITIES

1. How would you resolve the ethical dilemma that arises when a child is tired and her parent does not want her to nap at school? Write your response, supporting it with points from the Code of Ethical Conduct. State what you would tell the parent. In your conclusion, discuss in what way the Code of Ethical Conduct was or was not helpful, and why. (**NAEYC Standard 2: Building Family and Community Relationships**)

2. Draw a picture of an early childhood teacher. Then look through a professional journal for photographs of early childhood educators. Categorize your drawing and the photographs by ethnicity, gender, types of clothing depicted, any language or labeling included, and evidence of intellectual qualities. In a short paper, discuss your findings and what they mean about your own and others' perceptions of early childhood educators. (**NAEYC Standard 6: Becoming a Professional**)

3. Write a professional development plan for yourself. What ages and settings interest you most? Why? Where do you see yourself in two years? In five years? In ten years? Explain the reasons for your aspirations. How do you learn best? What helps you learn about children and families? What will you do to learn as much as you can about children and families? (**NAEYC Standard 6: Becoming a Professional**)

I am powerful

JCDecaux

CHAPTER TWO

Children and the Worlds They Inhabit

"Everyone from everywhere is in my class now!"

A teacher education student

Chapter Outline

Our Rapidly Changing World

What Can We Provide for
    Young Children?

Social Justice

fter her first week, a student teacher told her university mentor, "Everyone from everywhere is in my class now!" (quoted in Levine 2000). The student was referring to the diversity of learners and their many backgrounds. If you haven't yet worked with children from diverse cultures, backgrounds, and learning styles, you are likely to do so at some time in your career. How can we as teachers know about all the places and cultures from which the children we teach originate? How can we come to understand and use such knowledge in a positive way? What do social scientists tell us about children that can be useful for those who work with them? The answers to these questions and discussion of these issues form the bedrock of this chapter.

OUR RAPIDLY CHANGING WORLD

How might your awareness of globalization, culture, and ecological theories influence your work with young children?

Even before it was a nation, the United States was composed of diverse cultural groups. Then and now, Native Americans represent many subgroups (Maschinot 2008). They came to North America, crossing the Bering Strait. Immigrants began coming again as early as the sixteenth century. Now, in the twenty-first century, the growth of immigrant, or "newcomer," families is surging. As of 2005, 25 percent of young children in this country lived in immigrant families (Hernandez, Denton and Macartney 2008). Figure 2.1 shows concentrations of immigrant children by state. Early care and education services are among the first institutional entry points for all children, whether born in the United States or newcomers from different countries.

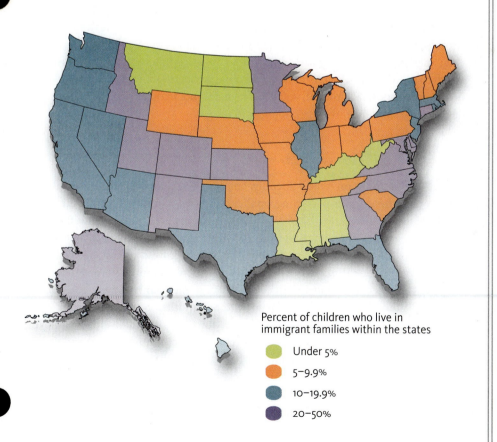

2.1 *Percentage of Children Living in Immigrant Families, by State*
From Hernandez, Denton, and Macartney 2008, 6

Percent of children who live in immigrant families within the states

- Under 5%
- 5–9.9%
- 10–19.9%
- 20–50%

This child helps adults during a robotics workshop for teachers.

If your class is more homogeneous, with children from seemingly similar backgrounds and cultures, consider that diversity takes many forms. People are different from each other in many ways. Children not only reflect diversity, but, with your help, they can also think about diversity.

We do not teach a universal child, but a specific child in a particular context, and contexts continually change. In this section, we introduce a thread that weaves throughout this book: how do changes in society affect our work with young children and families, and how can educators adapt to best meet these changes? Given children's individual differences, what do children know about the adult world, and how do they know it? How will you decide what topics to include in your curriculum and how to handle them?

Globalization and Education

The word **globalization** is used liberally, but there is no one definition. Certainly we can say that the world is becoming smaller at a rapid pace, with "accelerated compression" (Epstein in Gutek 2006, 99). Most people are aware that we live in a world that is increasingly interconnected (Hytten and Bettez 2008). Throughout history, cultures have had contact with each other and have borrowed and learned from each other; but with global markets and the worldwide economic interdependence of the twenty-first century, more than ever, events in one country affect many others.

For example, low-paid workers in other countries provide goods at cheap prices. The United States can compete either by paying its workers less or by purchasing goods from abroad and preparing U.S. children for higher paid jobs that require more education (National Center on Education and the Economy 2007).

The Internet and other technological advances contribute to what feels like a smaller world. Even in developing nations, many people can communicate easily to almost anywhere in the world.

THOUGHT QUESTION How do you experience "accelerated compression"? How might the smallness of today's world affect your work with young children and their families?

For example, a South African couple noticed that their three-year-old son, Big Boy, flapped his arms and did not make eye contact. Big Boy's grandparents assumed he was possessed by demons. Although Big Boy's parents wanted him to see a Western physician, the grandparents insisted on an indigenous healer, or *nyanga*. After observing Big Boy for two days, the *nyanga* said that the boy showed signs of **autism,** a disorder marked by challenges to interpersonal communication and a restricted repertoire of repeated behaviors. How did the *nyanga* know? He had read about autism on the Internet (Grinker 2008). This *nyanga* is not alone. Millions of professionals and parents all over the world are now in touch with each other and sharing information.

In an effort to protect children in all parts of the world, in 1990 the General Assembly of the United Nations adopted the **Convention on the Rights of the Child** (CRC). Countries that signed the CRC agree to guarantee basic human rights for all children—including the right to be protected from harm, develop to their fullest potential, and participate in all aspects of family and community life (*Early Childhood Matters* 2001).

The movement of greater numbers of people from one country to another reflects another aspect of globalization. Throughout the United States, there are young children who have emigrated from other countries and those who **transmigrate,** that is, live in more than one country or, perhaps, go back and forth between their homeland and the United States. Other children have recently relocated from other areas of the United States or have been adopted from other countries. With this kind of diversity in many schools, no teacher can ever be an expert on every child's background. For this reason, teachers are better off learning about a family's cultural background directly from the children and their family than from reading about the practices of a particular group. Throughout this book, you will learn ways to work collaboratively with families to build a curriculum that reflects the best of the worlds of home and school, and builds connections between them (González, Moll, and Amanti 2005).

Culture

Each child lives in a nest of societal contexts. Early care and education, too, exists within the larger society's goals and interactions. As a teacher, you will encounter children and families from many different cultures. But just what is **culture**? We use the following definition: "an intricate dynamic process that shapes and is shaped by how people live and experience their everyday realities" (Williams and Norton 2008, 104). Regardless of what definition of culture you use, we *all* have a culture or cultures that are at the root of who we are. Culture is not something exotic or different from us. Rather, it is the ways we learn to be, to be understood, and to understand one another. As the definition states, culture is dynamic; that is, like a busy intersection (Rosaldo 1989), it doesn't stay still. We cause culture to change, and, in turn, culture changes us. Here is an example:

> Hillary, a first-time mother, joined a mother's group in her middle-class neighborhood soon after Jenny was born. The mothers were interested in a parenting movement based on principles of attachment (www.attachmentparenting.org). Hillary was intrigued, and soon Jenny was sleeping in the family bed with her parents. Hillary carried Jenny close to her body in a sling until she was too heavy, and breastfed her until she was close to three years old.

The caregiving practices Hillary's group embraced go back to a period of early human existence and continue in most parts of the developing world today to ensure survival (co-sleeping for safety, warmth, and proximity), birth control (as a result

Culture is not something exotic or different from us. Rather, it is the ways we learn to be, to be understood, and to understand one another.

of extended breastfeeding), and the ability to work (carrying babies so they are safe *and* the mother's hands are free). These practices reflect a world in which everyone is more **interdependent** than in dominant U.S. cultures. People who value interdependence help each other, expect others to need their help, and count on help from others. You can see how this differs from a value of independence.

The practices these mothers adopted may not fit the goals of independence and autonomy that predominate in the United States, but they were a closer fit to what these mothers wanted for themselves and their children. If their practices affect other mothers, the dynamic cycle of a changing culture continues.

Knowing how our own cultural practices shape our values and beliefs helps us be clearer about our behaviors and roles with children. Then we are better prepared to learn about the cultures of the children we teach without enforcing our judgments and biases—including those ideas we acquire as we study early childhood education—on them and their families.

The following example of Priscilla and Sasha illustrates how early childhood educators can learn about a family's culture while the family learns about early childhood education.

Priscilla and her husband are from Jamaica. They send their four-year-old daughter Michele to a child-centered private preschool where most, but not all, of the children and teachers are European American, including the director, Sasha. Priscilla told Sasha that she understood the value of all the children's books in the room and appreciated the charts recording children's ideas, but, she said, "In Jamaica, where we were raised, children attend school as soon as they can use the toilet, learn nursery rhymes, and by age three are writing their names. Other parents here may not worry about their children learning to read and write. They know their children will make it, but lots of children who look like our kids don't make it. We need a guarantee that our children will learn." Although Sasha was dedicated to developing children's literacy without direct instruction, she listened and took in what Priscilla said.

Sasha then spoke to the staff, and they decided to learn more about Priscilla's perspective. They wanted a mix of approaches to serve all the children in their program. They began to encourage the children, especially Michele, to write their names when they could and were more explicit about literacy instruction, but without compromising their deep-seated beliefs about play as a vehicle for learning. They continued to rethink their curriculum throughout the year.

Priscilla's story cautions us not to generalize about cultures and children but to listen closely to individuals who tell us about themselves and what they want for their children. It also reminds us not to take the culture of early childhood education and developmentally appropriate practice for granted but, rather, to explain our thinking to families and others. Surprisingly, within-group differences—generational differences, various stages of **acculturation** (the degree to which people adopt beliefs and practices other than their own), and seemingly minor variations in dialect—can often be more significant than across-group differences. The staff did not assume that Priscilla spoke for all Jamaican families but instead listened to Priscilla as one individual.

Ecological Theories

Ecological theories can help us think about Priscilla and the questions she raised for Sasha and the staff. Throughout this book we consider how **theories**—well-developed ideas that attempt to explain phenomena—relate to situations with children and their families. Ecological theories propose that to understand people you need to know about the contexts in which they live. Moreover, they maintain that these contexts influence each other. Theorists who have studied people and their contexts have found helpful ways to describe these systems.

Ecological Systems Theory

The renowned American psychologist Urie Bronfenbrenner (1917–2005), best known for his Ecological Systems Theory, introduced new ideas about the contexts in which children develop (Bronfenbrenner 1979). As you can see in Figure 2.2, Bronfenbrenner viewed the child's world as nested and interacting systems. The core unit is the **microsystem,** the setting in which children live—for example, their family and all the immediate and daily experiences that take place in the preschool, playground, grocery store, or religious institution they attend. The **mesosystem** reflects the interconnections between the people and organizations in the microsystem, such as those between school and home.

Thus, Priscilla's interaction with Michele's preschool is an example of the mesosystem at work. When the norms and customs of the preschool conflicted with those of the family, the interactive sparks that followed were in the mesosystem. Priscilla, the teachers, and the school's director voiced their different beliefs and ideologies about what it means for young children to learn. Here we see how the effects are mutual— how two microsystems were interactive. Priscilla and staff at Michele's school listened to each other. This drama played itself out within larger contexts as well—in the **exosystem,** which includes Michele's extended family and neighbors and the services her family receives occasionally, along with the mass media. Michele and her family were also affected by the **macrosystem,** wherein the values of the larger culture reside. Because Michele's family is new to the United States, their macrosystem, especially for Priscilla, has changed from the one they knew in Jamaica. Finally, all these interconnected systems are like a slowly moving ball, rolling on through a sociopolitical context that changes over time. Bronfenbrenner called this the **chronosystem.**

2.2 *Bronfenbrenner's Ecological Systems*

Developmental niche

By definition, we take our cultural beliefs for granted. How you talk to your baby, the implements with which you eat, and how you say hello to a friend are behaviors you just do. Only when we consciously reflect on them or observe different practices do we think about the "how" of our daily actions. Building on Bronfenbrenner's work, two anthropologists, Charles Super and Sara Harkness, developed an informal framework to examine how cultures organize children's environments and thus influence their development.

Every child grows up in an environment that establishes "how we do things here." Super and Harkness (1986) had this in mind when they came up with the **developmental niche** theoretical framework to help understand the "cultural regulation of the microenvironment of the child" from the child's point of view (p. 552). Super and Harkness define the three components of the niche that interact and support each other:

- The physical and social setting in which the child lives
- The customs of child care and child rearing
- The psychology of the caretakers

In the story that follows, Felipe Orozco (2008) reflects on how the niche of his own childhood birthday parties compares with that of the children in his first grade class.

I always celebrated my birthday with my family and friends in either the comfort of my house or at a fairy-tale, child-friendly party hall that my mother hired for the day. You can imagine my face when the mother of one of my students came to ask me, "Around what time should I bring the cake tomorrow?"

Students celebrate a classmate's birthday in school.

The public school in which I teach is located in an urban setting, with a class of children from widely diverse backgrounds and ethnicities and with many different stories. Parents in this community rely on school for all sorts of extracurricular activities, including the celebration of their children's birthdays. Even though parents provide the cake, drinks, and utensils, on most occasions the teacher is in charge of distributing food and provides the customary songs and games.

My first classroom birthday party experience was both surprising and humbling. It made me realize the contrast between my students' experiences and mine and helped me understand what is at the core: a parent trying to provide entertainment and joy to his or her child even with very limited resources.

I do not think any of the students who celebrated their birthdays in my classroom will miss the gimmicks, clowns, or expensive toys that a privileged child may have. On the contrary, my children will always remember their moms working that extra shift so they could celebrate their birthday in the company of their friends . . . and teacher. At the end of the day, both party narratives, mine and theirs, carry the same weight: extraordinary efforts in order to celebrate the fact that we are alive and well one more year and a culturally transforming experience that will remain with us through adulthood.

THOUGHT QUESTION Describe some aspect of your developmental niche to a classmate. Compare it to those of the young children with whom you work or whom you've observed. What meaning could the similarities and/or differences have for you as their teacher?

What Children Know and How

The adult world is part of young children's lives, whether or not we think, or like to think, that it is. Children overhear what adults say in person and in the media. Most know, for example, about wars and tragedies that are depicted on the news. They also pick up adults' emotions even when grownups are trying to hide them. A family may think their five-year-old doesn't know that a new baby is on the way, or they may believe that their young son is unaware of the tensions between his parents because the frequent arguments occur after he is asleep. Probably, though, these children know something is going on.

How and when you introduce emotionally charged topics or subjects that are considered to be adult territory depends in part on how you think children learn. Do you think children's development makes them unable to understand complex ideas and emotions? Or do you think they can understand certain complex ideas and emotions that are personally interesting or relevant to them?

You will read later about Jean Piaget, who held to the first way of thinking, with some exceptions. He believed that children internalize increasingly complex thoughts only when they are cognitively ready. Lev Vygotsky, about whom you will also learn more, believed that children "tug" at ideas and grow into them over time. Clearly, experience, not just a child's personal predilections and interests, plays a large role regardless of your point of view.

In previous generations, child development texts advised parents and teachers to wait until a child asked a question to make sure not to go beyond the child's comfort zone and cognitive level. Today, many educators and teacher educators (Silin 1995; Derman-Sparks and Ramsey 2006) believe that children can stretch into new concepts and that this is preferable to their trying to figure out difficult topics on their own or only with each other. What should you do?

- Find out the policies of your school.
- Think about your own comfort level, and consider challenging yourself.
- Talk with families about how comfortable they are with sensitive conversations.
- Think about the areas in which children demonstrate interest.
- Let children know that you and their families will do everything to keep them safe and healthy.

And sometimes, it makes sense to take a risk.

WHAT CAN WE PROVIDE FOR YOUNG CHILDREN?

How might you provide children with consistency and predictability, support for good health practices, and respect and equal access?

First and foremost, young children need to be safe and feel secure. While this may seem to contradict the preceding discussion, it does not. As a teacher, you cannot protect children from reality, provide all the basic necessities for them, nor provide immediate "fixes" for them. You can, however, lend a sense of security and develop trusting relationships that will allow them to learn to trust others and fully engage in learning. Children need to feel that they are "known," that someone understands who they are and what their needs are. This is something that adults, especially teachers and parents, can provide. Once children are known, it becomes a bit easier for the people who know them well to tailor learning experiences to their individual differences (Brazelton and Greenspan 2000).

A family may think their five-year-old doesn't know that a new baby is on the way, or they may believe that their young son is unaware of the tensions between his parents because the frequent arguments occur after he is asleep.

THOUGHT QUESTION Think of children you know who are between four and eight years old. Have you had any conversations with them in which the topics surprised you? Do you believe topics such as politics, religion, or war can be part of a young child's repertoire? Why or why not?

Children need adults to "know" them.

Consistency and Predictability

Like adults, children are vulnerable to **acute,** or one-time, **stressors,** as well as to ongoing **chronic stressors** (Sapolsky 1998). The stress may be physical or emotional or both, with significantly different long-term effects for children and adults. Sometimes, humans create stress for themselves by anticipating bad events that they imagine or predict will occur, whether or not those things actually transpire. Whatever the reason, in response, our bodies go on "automatic pilot," and special hormones that are always in our bodies, especially **cortisol,** flood our systems. This **stress response** allows us to mobilize our energy, focus our attention, feel pain less intensely, and take on whatever challenge we face. The stress response is an important feature of our evolution and, ultimately, our survival. In order to function, however, the stress system borrows from long-term growth and repair functions such as our digestive or immune systems. Then, when the stress system is finally turned down again, we can eat, sleep, and have other experiences that restore our bodily functions (Gilkerson and Klein 2008).

However, because they are in the process of developing, children are more vulnerable to chronic stressors than are adults. Long-term stress can seriously inhibit growth and repair functions that don't get replenished. Children lose precious energy for functions that are necessary for future development. Repeated insults to a developing child's system make it more difficult for the child to spring back. For example, children who had experienced trauma before 9/11 and who then experienced the 9/11 trauma were more likely to feel the effects of the 9/11 trauma a few years later. Children for whom 9/11 was the first trauma seemed to fare better overall (Carey 2008).

At the same time, children have stores of **resilience**—the ability to thrive despite adversity—although some children have more

After observing the events of 9/11, a child drew this picture of a plane flying into New York City's World Trade Center towers.

resilience than others. A trustworthy adult can enable a child to draw upon her inner resources and the protective factors of the environment (Werner 1990, Bowman 2006). For example, a supportive teacher-child relationship can help a child cope when his mother is hospitalized. *Responsive, consistent,* and *predictable* caregiving is protective of all children's development, but it especially protects those suffering from trauma and stress (Gunnar and Quevedo 2007). The stresses we discuss below are but some of those young children can face. You will read about others throughout this book. What you as an educator can do is to recognize stress when it occurs and respond to a stressed child in an empathic and helpful way while knowing that you can probably not eradicate or fix the source of the stress itself.

Addressing homelessness

In the United States today, approximately 1.35 million children experience homelessness during a given year. Too many of these children—42 percent—are under the age of six (see http://www.familyhomelessness.org/pdf/fact_children.pdf). Some of them temporarily have a roof over their head but live in a large and/or impersonal shelter that makes forming routines difficult. Having more than a few simple possessions becomes impossible. A child who is homeless may be in your classroom for three months and then disappear with an untraceable family that may have moved to a new shelter or gone to stay with family members in another state. Working with children who move often or live in impromptu settings is a challenge that requires considerable thought as to the child's needs, along with a desire to reach out to the child's family to learn more about them and their child.

Detecting and preventing child abuse

More than three million children are reported as maltreated to child welfare agencies every year (Child Welfare League of America n.d.). According to MedlinePlus, a service of the National Library of Medicine and the National Institutes of Health:

> Child abuse is doing something or failing to do something that results in harm to a child or puts a child at risk of harm. Child abuse can be physical, sexual or emotional. Neglect, or not providing for a child's needs, is also a form of abuse.

As an educator, you are a **mandated reporter.** Having this mandate means that, unlike a friend or neighbor who suspects abuse or neglect, you *must* contact your local child protective agency or state hotline if you think a child is being mistreated. Search the Web to find information about your state's child abuse regulations and how to report in your area.

To report accurately, you must know the signs of abuse and neglect. Danger signals include unexplained marks on the child's body, obvious lack of physical care, and explanations from the parent or child that either keep changing or do not make sense. If a child's behavior changes suddenly or if the child is withdrawn, doesn't want to go home, or is on the alert as if she expects something bad to happen to her, your suspicions should be aroused.

A single sign does not prove child abuse, but a combination of signs or repeated events are cause for alarm. For example, many children do not want to leave school when their parents arrive at the end of the day, perhaps because they don't want to stop what they are doing or because they are angry at their parents for having been left all day. But when a child does not want to leave your class with the parent *and* you have other reasons for concern, those end-of-day protests take on a more ominous significance. Discuss signs you observe with other teachers and your supervisor. However, if you suspect abuse, even if others at your job do not, you *must* report it.

Because they are in the process of developing, children are more vulnerable to chronic stressors than are adults. Long-term stress can seriously inhibit growth and repair functions.

A single sign does not prove child abuse, but a combination of signs or repeated events are cause for alarm. If you suspect abuse, even if others at your job do not, you *must* report it.

Children can learn healthy habits in school, but it takes planning on the part of the adults.

Practice That Supports Health

Parents are young children's first line of defense for their health. Parents plan and cook meals, keep pediatric appointments for immunizations and checkups, and help children learn self-care habits like brushing their teeth. However, in the early years, especially, young children's teachers play a special role in supporting healthy habits.

Opportunities for reinforcing good health habits arise throughout the day. For instance, some programs make toothbrushing part of their dental health routine. Toothbrushes should be uncontaminated and separate from one another, and toothbrushing should not interrupt children's play. Although routines are important, they do not take precedence over children's thinking and learning.

If a child becomes ill while in your care, do whatever you can to make her comfortable, but isolate her from the other children in case she is contagious. Alert families when a child in your group has a contagious illness. Then everyone will know what to look for to head off anything serious. Children with a disease such as conjunctivitis should return to school only after a physician prescribes treatment and confirms that their condition is no longer contagious. The more you know about childhood diseases, the better you will be able to detect them right away and support families when their children become ill. Access to knowledgeable medical personnel, books, articles, and online resources will help you recognize children's illnesses and discuss them accurately with families.

Preventing illnesses—from serious ones to the everyday cold—is a crucial part of the job for anyone working with children. For example, although no one knows the exact causes of sudden infant death syndrome (SIDS), infant caregivers are aware of the need to place children on their backs when they put them to sleep, while remembering to provide plenty of **tummy time,** where babies lie on their tummies, during the day, to allow for complementary muscle development. Teachers can prevent run-of-the-mill sickness by washing their hands often throughout the day and teaching children to do the same. Figure 2.3 contains some important information about handwashing.

Contending with illness and chronic conditions

We know that many things can challenge a child's developing system. While still in the womb, babies can experience strokes, infections, and developmental abnormali-

Facts about Handwashing

Did you know that . . .

• More than 100 years ago, Dr. Ignaz Semmelweis showed that routine handwashing prevents disease from spreading.

• Germs can live on surfaces for two or more hours.

• A study of 305 Detroit schoolchildren found that children who washed their hands four times a day had 24 percent fewer sick days due to respiratory illness and 51 percent fewer sick days because of stomach upset.

What can we do?

• Wash your hands for as long as it takes to sing the Happy Birthday song twice.

• Teach children and ask adults to wash their hands with soap and warm water after each time they use the toilet, before and after they eat, after they blow their noses, when they enter from outdoors, before and after messy activities, and after touching pets.

• Teach children to sneeze and cough into the crook of their elbow to keep germs away from their hands.

• Encourage them to keep their hands away from their eyes and noses.

For more information about handwashing, see these government-sponsored Web sources:

http://www.cdc.gov/od/oc/media/pressrel/r2k0306c.htm
http://www.cdc.gov/germstopper/home_work_school.htm
http://www.foodsafety.gov/~dms/fsehandw.html

2.3 *Facts about Handwashing*

ties; and problems during delivery can cause other forms of disability. Infants born prematurely or with very low birth weights are susceptible to a variety of later learning problems, as are those who are exposed to toxins, alcohol, drugs, or cigarette smoke.

Chronic illness is another problem for many families and children. When children are sick, the energy they ordinarily would use to learn and grow is diverted. They need that energy to overcome pain and fear, deal with medication, adjust to hospitalization, and heal. Most children are resilient and recover quickly from short-term illnesses, but chronic illnesses are ongoing, with long-term effects. While all children's illnesses affect the family, chronic illnesses such as cancer, HIV, sickle cell anemia, and neurological conditions such as epilepsy are particularly traumatic for families. Child life workers and other early childhood specialists may work with terminally ill children. Other children who have chronic diseases or conditions may attend school with other children. When a child is hospitalized, a visit from the teacher (with the family's permission) is usually a positive experience for the child and serves to link home and school.

Two conditions that are especially prevalent in young children in the United States today are asthma and lead poisoning. Both are related to environmental conditions that adults can work to improve.

Nearly nine million children in the United States have asthma, a chronic disease that makes breathing difficult. Many factors contribute to asthma, including second-hand smoke, mold, and other airborne irritants to which the child may be allergic (see MedlinePlus at http://www.nlm.nih.gov/medlineplus/asthmainchildren.html).

> Two conditions that are especially prevalent in young children in the United States today are asthma and lead poisoning. Both are related to environmental conditions that adults can work to improve.

How is this child benefiting from running and playing outside?

According to the Centers for Disease Control and Prevention website (http://www.cdc.gov/nceh/lead/faq/about.htm), approximately 310,000 children in the United States have lead poisoning. Unlike asthma, lead poisoning does not have obvious symptoms, but it can cause learning disabilities or behavioral problems and, at high levels, can threaten a child's life. Lead-based paint is the main source of lead poisoning in children, but other sources of lead may also contribute.

Children in the United States today are also increasingly at risk for obesity and related health problems such as diabetes. One of every three children in the United States is overweight (10–15 percent over optimum body weight) or obese (Ludwig 2007). Researchers recommend that children eat a nutritious diet—which is costly for families on a limited budget—and engage in at least an hour of vigorous daily exercise.

Exercise

Fresh air and exercise are essential to good health, yet, for many reasons, greater numbers of children are spending more time indoors, often in front of television or other electronic screens. In early care and education, especially in the elementary grades, children are indoors much more than outside, but they can put more effort into activities requiring intense concentration if they also participate in activities they find relaxing and energizing. Dramatic play during outdoor time enhances children's language and imaginations as it cements social relationships. Many children are more independent outdoors than at any other time, and, outside, teachers can get to know children in a new way.

Concerned that children will not perform well enough on tests, some principals have cut back recess to use that time for academics instead (NAECS/SDE 2007). However, the National Association of Early Childhood Specialists in State Departments of Education (NAECS/SDE) asserts that recess supports children's emotional, social, and even intellectual growth and should not be sacrificed. NAEYC's 1998 Position Statement on The Value of School Recess and Outdoor Play puts it this way:

> Our society has become increasingly complex, but there remains a need for every child to feel the sun and wind on his cheek and engage in self-paced play. Children's attempts to make their way across monkey bars, negotiate the hopscotch course, play jacks, or toss a football require intricate behaviors of planning, balance, and strength—traits we want to encourage in children. Ignoring the developmental functions of unstructured outdoor play denies children the opportunity to expand their imaginations beyond the constraints of the classroom. (NAEYC 1998)

Nutrition

Good eating habits begin early. Breastfeeding is a natural way to supply children with good nutrition and protection from disease while supporting their immune systems. Some centers for infants and toddlers have spaces for mothers to breastfeed in comfort. They encourage mothers to visit throughout the day to nurse their children.

THOUGHT QUESTION What you eat at school provides an opportunity to teach about nutrition. Children will notice when you serve them healthy foods and encourage them to eat them—but put none on your own plate. What will you do? How will you promote good eating habits among the children and be a model for good nutrition?

Respect and Equal Access

Respect for each child is a personal matter and one that takes on societal proportions. Every day, adults who work with children demonstrate respect for them when they listen carefully to them, come to know them, and take them seriously. On a larger scale, early childhood educators show their respect for all people by understanding race, class, linguistic background, and gender—all of which are ways in which groups of people are similar and different—and what those similarities and differences mean about equal access to the benefits our society has to offer.

"Race" and ethnicity

Race is one of many categories we use to describe people, but the concept of race is a cultural construction, not a biological reality (Mukhopadhyay, Henze, and Moses 2007). The term itself is a relatively recent one in English, coined in the Middle Ages. The Illusion of Race website debunks a number of myths about race:

> There is less—and more—to race than meets the eye:
> - Race has no genetic basis. Not one characteristic, trait, or even gene distinguishes all the members of one race from all the members of another race.
> - Unlike many animals, modern humans simply haven't been around long enough or isolated enough to evolve into separate subspecies or races. Despite surface differences, we are one of the most similar of all species.
> - Skin color really is only skin deep. Most traits are inherited independently of one another. The genes influencing skin color have nothing to do with the genes influencing hair form, eye shape, blood type, musical talent, athletic ability, or forms of intelligence.
> - Slavery predates the idea of race. Throughout much of human history, societies have enslaved others, often as a result of conquest or war, even debt, but not because of their physical characteristics or a belief in natural inferiority. Due to a unique set of historical circumstances, ours was the first slave system where all the slaves shared similar physical characteristics.
> - Race justified social inequalities as "natural." As the race idea evolved, white superiority became "common sense" in the United States. It validated not only slavery but the extermination of Indians, the exclusion of Asian immigrants, and the taking of Mexican lands by a nation that professed a belief in democracy. Racial practices were institutionalized within U.S. government, laws, and society.
> - Racism is real. Race is a powerful social idea that gives certain people, and not others, access to opportunities and resources. Our government and social institutions have created advantages that disproportionately channel wealth, power, and resources to white people.
> - Colorblindness will not end racism. Pretending difference doesn't exist is not the same as creating equality. Race is more than stereotypes and individual prejudice. To combat racism, we need to identify and remedy social and institutional policies and practices that advantage some groups at the expense of others. (Adapted from http://www.pbs.org/race/000 _About/002_04-background-01-x.htm)

Children pick up ideas about physical differences of all kinds from the adults around them, but they also construct their own ideas about race and various physical characteristics. Debra Van Ausdale and Joe Feagin (2001) found that young children have complex reasons for identifying a particular skin color as similar to

Some centers for infants and toddlers have spaces for mothers to breastfeed in comfort. They encourage mothers to visit throughout the day to nurse their children.

I am an enrolled member of the White Earth Band of Ojibwe. My parents did not graduate from high school, but both highly valued education. I earned a bachelor's degree in elementary education from the University of North Dakota (UND) in the Northern Plains Indian Teacher Corps in 1974. I began my career as a teaching intern for fifth and sixth grades in a remote town on the western edge of the Turtle Mountain Reservation. I was supposed to observe a veteran teacher and slowly begin to teach, but when I arrived, the school was short two teachers. I was nineteen years old and relied on my memory of what it was like to be in elementary school to teach.

This was during the second historical event at Wounded Knee, South Dakota, and at the height of the American Indian Movement (AIM). The schools then, as now, provided little knowledge or background for us to understand our history. Social studies curricula kept perpetuating stereotypes, having kindergarten teachers reenact the Thanksgiving myth with children portraying Indians wearing butcher-paper ponchos and paper headbands with feathers. I helped students question bias in our texts and pushed for the acceptance of our culture in the school.

At my first real job, I worked for a month at Eagle Feather Day Care Center on the UND campus, which served children of American Indian students. I was assigned the three-year-old group with only my elementary degree as preparation, and no training or mentoring. I realized during my first minutes of group time that I knew nothing about three-year-olds. I was expected to keep them at a table for twenty minutes, just like the four- and five-year-olds. That first day, we sat in silence for a couple of minutes, staring at each other. Then I said, "Let's get out of here." We walked across campus to a stream, where we studied nature and developed math, language, and social skills.

Many American Indian parents at the university taught their children to introduce themselves proudly and to identify with their heritage. But in recent years, I've seen students act out stereotypes from TV cartoons, saying, "Teacher, look, I'm an Indian!" patting their mouths to make whoops.

One day, an instructor from the Early Childhood Department at UND stopped by to invite me to take an early childhood class at the university. Maurice Lucas became my mentor, advisor, and teacher. He modeled the Child Development Associate (CDA) advisor role at the center. He taught creative art, the value of play, and developmentally appropriate education.

In 1984, I started at an innovative Minnesota early childhood initiative, Early Childhood Family Education (ECFE). Parents and children (birth through age four) attended class together and participated in activities, and parents attended a parent education class. On my first day I felt uncomfortable with all the parents in the room. But I soon realized I could provide a wide variety of activities and that each child had an adult at his/her side. Parents said they enjoyed the uninterrupted time with their children and especially liked the messy activities. Many reported that initially they came for their children but then recognized the

Joan Bibeau

value of parent education, which is especially meaningful in rural communities.

In 1987, I went to the Leech Lake Reservation to teach at the small and remote Eagleview Elementary School. I had a multiage class including kindergarten, Head Start, School Readiness (the Minnesota state Early Childhood program for three- to four-year-olds), and ECFE. This model made it possible for all the children in the community to attend school. Eagleview is a nurturing environment: for example, all students, staff, and often parents and community members eat lunch together. Family and community involvement has increased due to staff-initiated outreach programs and efforts. We discuss increasing the Ojibwe culture and language curriculum and addressing health issues that impact American Indian people, such as lack of physical activity and diabetes prevention.

Retention, relevance, and engagement are crucial issues for American Indian students. Today, only 50 percent of them graduate high school. Many begin talking about dropping out of school in fourth grade due to a lack of motivation to participate and learn. At an American Indian Education conference, someone asked, "Why are our children who are only three years old already behind?" As an early childhood educator, I have given this question much thought. What are the values and practices of American Indian families and child care providers? How do these contribute to our children's not performing on developmental assessments that are supposed to be nonbiased? What needs to be changed to help prekindergarten American Indian students succeed?

their own. They also found that adults too often misunderstand children's remarks about race. In Van Ausdale and Feagin's ethnographic study, for example, an African American child chose the color pink to make her handprint in a class activity, but she did not think of herself as white. Instead, she had observed that her palms and those of some other black people are pink, not black.

As you have just read, race has no genetic basis, but children are aware of differences early on, and racism exists in classrooms and society. It takes time, thought, and collaboration to actively work against it. Throughout this book, you will have opportunities to consider racism in your own life.

Ethnicity refers to one's ancestry and country of origin. Young children can learn about distinct ethnic heritages whether or not differences are apparent in your class. Books, trips, and visits from parents and community members can introduce children to people from different backgrounds.

> Habiba's father brought Afghani music to school to play for the four-year-olds. Many of them found it unusual, and Tory even asked the teacher to turn it off. "Listen to it for a while," the teacher urged. "Give it a chance. It's just different from what you know." A few days later, Tory approached the teacher to say, "You know what? I like Afghani music."

Young children may resist what's new, but, as with Tory, teachers can help children to learn flexibility in the face of difference.

Young children can be keen observers of the world around them. From what they see of power relations at home, at school, in the neighborhood, and in the media, they construct ideas about people and how they interact with each other (Van Ausdale and Feagin 2001). The Anti-Bias Curriculum (Sparks et al. 1989), aspects of which are displayed in Figure 2.4, describes an active approach to helping children counter stereotypes and learn about fair ways of behaving toward others.

Various curricular approaches expose children to ethnic and cultural diversities. Be careful, however, that an approach that makes difference exotic (Derman-Sparks and Ramsey 2006) doesn't backfire. If children categorize *more* than they did before the curriculum—as evidenced in such comments as, "We learned that African women carry things on their heads. Why don't you?"—reconsider the approach.

An African American child chose the color pink to make her handprint in a class activity, but she did not think of herself as white. Instead, she had observed that her palms and those of some other black people are pink, not black.

Children represent how they see their skin tones.

Aspects of the Anti-Bias Curriculum

- The environment has materials that represent a wide variety of people engaged in non–stereotypical activities.

- Stories and language—for example, using the word *firefighter* instead of *fireman*—counter stereotypes.

- Teachers address children's discomfort or misconceptions directly and honestly.

- Teachers and children explore questions as they arise (and teachers seek opportunities to raise questions even when they do not arise).

- Teachers support children whom others exclude and teach children how to include others in natural ways.

- Teachers and families create opportunities for children to join community activities that promote fairness.

Children whose families have more resources and social support are also likely to have learning opportunities that provide advantages in school.

Class

Class, or the stratification of people by their socioeconomic status, shapes a young child's day-to-day life. Wearing a worn winter coat and having no money for a coveted toy sets one child apart from another one who does not face those challenges. Mark, for example, is always at school when his second-grade teacher arrives. He is hungry, his teacher discovers, and wants to be first on the breakfast line. At the other end of the spectrum is Hally, a three-year-old from an upper-middle-class family who, like Mark, has two working parents. A live-in helper serves Hally breakfast every morning. Her parents work late most nights, however, and when they don't, they bring work home with them. A few nights a week, Hally, who has a television in her room, falls asleep, remote in hand.

Not all low-income children arrive at school hungry, nor are all wealthy children neglected at bedtime, but Mark and Hally illustrate some ways in which class might shape children's lives. Children whose families have more resources and social support are also likely to have learning opportunities that provide advantages in school. Children of highly educated mothers, for example, tend to do better academically throughout their schooling than do children whose mothers are less well educated (Lareau 2003).

THOUGHT QUESTION Will you pay as much attention to a child who tells you about his backyard soccer game as you might to the child who shows you her trophy from a tournament? Will one child's trip to a nearby city to see relatives evoke as much interest as another child's vacation to a foreign country? How will you attempt to remove class biases from your repertoire?

Language and English-language learning

Students who speak another language and are learning English but cannot yet participate meaningfully in a school program in English are generally identified as **English language learners (ELLs)** (U.S. Department of Education 2008). Some researchers now use the term **emergent bilinguals** to describe these students (García, Kleifgen, and Falchi 2008) because the term validates the child's native language while explaining the second-language acquisition process. No term, however, encapsulates the diversity of ELLs. Some ELLs have recently moved to the United States from a war-torn country; others have lived in a U.S. city their entire lives. As with all children, ELLs "vary significantly in their socioeconomic status, cultural traditions, family literacy rates, prior schooling, English proficiency and other factors" (Crawford and Krashen 2007, 12).

ELLs are the fastest growing group of students in the nation, increasing from about three million in 1994–1995 to about five million in 2004–2005 (NCELA 2006). The increasing ELL population presents challenges for teachers, who need to be prepared to provide meaningful educational experiences for all children.

Depending on where you work, ELL students may not be evenly distributed across your community. In some communities, about three-quarters of your newly arrived ELL students and their parents will speak Spanish. If you speak Spanish, you will be able to communicate with them. But how do you communicate with students and families who speak Cantonese, Hmong, or Russian? How do you teach these children the academic content of first through third grades if they cannot understand, speak, read, or write in English? How do you help young children trust a new environment when they do not understand its language?

Four-year-old Siru recently moved to San Francisco with her mother from Taipei, Taiwan. She and her mother speak Mandarin and Taiwanese. Her mother understands a little English. Siru misses her father, grandmother, grandfather, and many aunties, uncles, and cousins back home.

Siru's eyes welled up with tears whenever her mother left her to go to work. She found solace in the block corner. She learned to balance heavy rectangular blocks to create towering walls. She even draped her structures with colorful strips of cloth. Teachers conjectured that her buildings surrounded and protected her from a new world she experienced as overwhelming. Her teachers photographed her structures and created a big book of Siru's architectural feats.

Siru soon made friends. She played like any child would but communicated nonverbally. She even made a best friend who helped her learn the classroom rituals.

One morning, the teachers showed Siru's mother the big book of her block work. Once she had studied each of her daughter's impressive architectural structures, Siru's mother motioned that she wanted to add captions in Chinese to describe each of the pictures. The teachers asked her to read the captions in the big book aloud to the children during the morning meeting. The children sat motionless as they listened to the sounds. When they reached the end, Siru described the last picture. After a month in school, Siru had spoken her first words. The children shouted, "Siru is talking! She's speaking Chinese!"

What did it take for Siru to speak? First and foremost, the teachers valued Siru and her mother's native Mandarin instead of viewing their inability to speak English as a deficiency. They knew that Siru's language skills in Mandarin would help her eventually tell stories in English. Although her teachers wondered when she would speak her first English words, they knew she was going through her **silent period,** the first stage of second-language acquisition, which can last from several days to several months (Samway and McKeon 2007), in which a child absorbs the new language without expressing it. They understood that Siru was quietly adapting to a new culture, new faces, and a new set of rules. Each meaningful activity and interaction with peers helped create the context and motivation for learning the rules and uses of English. They saw that Siru was ready to take risks with her friends and soon would express her needs and opinions in English.

Teachers can support a child's cultural identity and language by providing experiences, resources, and services that value the child's linguistic and cultural heritage. Most importantly, to provide each child with an equitable education, teachers need

Teachers can make it clear that no language is better or worse than another.

to reflect on and evaluate their personal biases and prejudices. Racism and discrimination against languages of ethnic minorities have no place in the classroom. For example, bias can lead an educator to mistakenly refer emergent bilingual students for special education services. With self-awareness, teachers can avoid such misjudgments. They also can make it clear that no language is better or worse than another (Zentella 2005). Many believe that if language learners feel anxious, develop low self-esteem, and do not consider themselves valued members in the community, they will not be receptive to learning the new language or new concepts (Krashen, 2003).

Gender

The first and second graders are discussing the pet bunny in their class who is pregnant and about to give birth. Their teacher asks, "Will we be able to tell if the babies are male or female?"

Clive answers, "Boy bunnies will run around. Girl bunnies will sit still."

Erika responds immediately, "Clive, you're new [she rolls her eyes slightly] . . . that's not the way we do it here."

THOUGHT QUESTION Watch a children's TV show. How are girls and boys portrayed? Compare what you found with the observations of your classmates who watched different shows. What are children learning about boys and girls and men and women? How do you think children of different ages incorporate media messages about gender with what they learn from their families and school?

When Erika says, "that's not the way we do it here" she means, "this is our culture." Her ideas about **gender,** about what it means to be male or female, are different from Clive's. So far, these two children appear to have been socialized differently regarding gender expectations.

Since the 1970s in the United States and more recently in many other places (Veneman 2007), educators have been concerned about girls and boys having **gender equity,** that is, support for comparable educational opportunities. Gender bias exists throughout society—in the media and in the children's toy market, to name only two significant forces.

Often, teachers are unaware that they base their behaviors on gender-related stereotypes and not individual characteristics. Some teachers:

- monitor all boys, wherever they are in the room, but respond to girls only when they are nearby
- unwittingly compliment girls on the neatness of their written work instead of on its content
- make sure *everyone* learns penmanship and reading but do not worry when girls don't do blocks or science

These are only a few pitfalls to avoid, to ensure that the way you treat children is not based on their gender. Sometimes we also have to rethink what are gender-related behaviors and what are not.

Zeny, a college student, sat on the floor of a kindergarten during free-play, doing an observation for her child development class. She described how Tom built a corral-like enclosure using long unit blocks and how he gently placed horses inside the corral while quietly humming to himself. She then thought about the part of the assignment that asked students to connect their observation to theories they were studying. Zeny remembered that Erik Erikson wrote about how boys build up and girls build round enclosed spaces, representing their physical and emotional differences. In her notes, she reflected, "I guess the world really does affect how and what children do with materials! The world is different from when Erikson wrote about blockbuilding."

We need to compare our theories to what we observe in children's behaviors.

Sometimes we have to rethink what are gender-related behaviors and what are not.

Children of all ages make choices that demonstrate their clothing preferences.

We have to keep comparing theories to our observations and vice versa to better understand children's behaviors. The two four-year-olds in the photograph on the next page took the marriage play to another level, continuing their pretend play into "pregnancy." Their ideas of what being pregnant means came from many sources in the world around them. These two offer a clear example of gender-related roles that children are trying on for size.

Are there any ways in which most girls and boys do differ? In general, boys tend to lag slightly behind girls in their social and small motor development but tend to grow taller than girls. Boys' ability to self-regulate is generally less well developed than is girls' (Eisenberg, Martin, and Fabes 1996). Boys also tend to be somewhat more active than girls, although you can probably think of children who are exceptions to this generalization, too.

Especially in the elementary years, as academic demands and the requirement to sit still longer increase, many boys find school to be a stressor. Boys *and* girls need

Children show us what they know through their dramatic play.

time to move, and, when schools do away with recess, active children can get in trouble for aggressive or disruptive behavior.

Francesca, an urban first-grade teacher whose children do not have recess and who is mandated to have hour-and-a-half literacy blocks, slips in ways to keep children active throughout that time. Every so often, for ten minutes, the children act out what they are reading. Francesca leads them in calisthenics, too, and has taught them to rub their earlobes when they get sleepy, a technique to bring back one's attention. Using these approaches, Francesca helps both boys and girls cope with an academic schedule that is beyond their years.

THOUGHT QUESTION Some people believe that repression of sexual urges causes children to feel guilty or anxious. Others say children should learn to control those urges. What do you think? How do you feel when children are curious about the bodies of their playmates and play "doctor"? How will you react if a seven-month-old has an erection while you are changing his diaper? What about when a four-year-old girl masturbates during naptime?

Gender and sexuality are separate topics, but they become intertwined in daily practice, especially when children's behavior does not conform to gender stereotypes. You can serve the children in your care more equitably if you reflect on how you were socialized about these issues. With that self-awareness, you are likely to be more conscious of, and avoid giving, gendered messages to children. Marge, the lead teacher in a toddler room, objects when the assistant teacher Sherry says, "Come on, Steven! Your girlfriend Clara's waiting for you" as the toddlers get ready to go outside. Marge worries that Sherry is imposing an adult sensibility on very young children and giving them an implicit message that everyone is heterosexual.

Sexuality is part of every child's developing identity, and children need adults to consider this aspect of their growth and development carefully. More than a century ago, talking about children's sexual feelings and interests was taboo, but today we have scientific evidence that even infants have sexual urges (Haroian 2000). Yet, in today's far more sexually liberated society, many are still hesitant to mention sexuality and young children in the same sentence. Joseph Tobin (2004) notes a generally open attitude throughout the twentieth century until the 1980s. He argues that one reason for the change was the panic in the 1980s about sexual abuse of children in child care settings that was spread by sensational, largely unsubstantiated media reports.

Gender-typical and gender-atypical behaviors are a daily topic of discussion across this country, from infant-toddler programs through graduate school. Many people conflate gender nonconformity with homosexuality. And even as homosexuality has become more accepted in the United States, **homophobia**—fear of homosexuality—related to young children is still strong.

When boys act like girls, some people fear that they will be homosexual. A child in your class may already be feeling such a "difference," as some gay adults confirm retrospectively. Yet other children may experience "difference" for other reasons, including those who believe they are of a different gender, or **transsexual.** Regardless of the reasons, all of which have complex roots, children have a right to develop in accordance with their desires, so teachers need to find ways to support children and their families. One helpful route for families in conflict about gender-atypical behavior is to join a group of other families who also wish to discuss these issues (Menville and Tuerk 2002).

Inclusion of Those with Disabilities and Special Needs

In the past twenty years, many more children with a range of disabilities or special needs (the terms are often used interchangeably) have been included in classrooms than ever before. Parents of children with special needs pushed for federal legislation, which, over time, has allowed for early childhood inclusion principles. Parallel federal legislation was created for children birth to age three. Figure 2.5 displays NAEYC and DEC's proposed joint position statement on early childhood inclusion (2008).

THOUGHT QUESTION Nora, not yet five, brings lip gloss to preschool every day. Does she bring it because it is from home and reminds her of her mother, because it is an object of female adornment, or both? If Ned brought lip gloss to school, why might some teachers be concerned about his effeminate behavior? If Nora brought a dump truck to school every day, why might some teachers be less concerned about that than about Ned's lip gloss? What would you tell these teachers?

One helpful route for families in conflict about gender-atypical behavior is to join a group of other families who also wish to discuss these issues.

2.5 *NAEYC and DEC's Proposed Joint Statement on Early Childhood Inclusion*
From NAEYC 2008

Early childhood inclusion embodies the values, policies, and practices that support the right of every infant and young child and his or her family, regardless of ability, to participate in a broad range of activities and contexts as members of families, communities, and society. The desired results of inclusive experiences for children with disabilities and their families include a sense of belonging and membership, positive social relationships and friendships, and development of learning to reach their full potential. The defining features that can be used to identify high quality early childhood programs and services include: 1. access, 2. participation, and 3. supports.

NAEYC & DEC Statement

These children's school makes it possible for all of them to participate fully in their own ways.

A truly individualized program requires that a continuum of settings and services—from inclusive classrooms to self-contained special education classes—be available to meet each child's needs.

What does inclusion look like in everyday life? **Full inclusion** means that children with special needs receive all their education in a general education classroom. There, special educators often co-teach with general educators. **Partial inclusion** means that children receive **"push-in services"** from special educators in their regular classrooms or that they are **"pulled out"** to receive these services in resource rooms or other settings where they may work one-on-one with a specialist or special education teacher.

A truly individualized program requires that a **continuum of settings and services**—from inclusive classrooms to self-contained special education classes—be available to meet each child's needs. The Council for Exceptional Children (CEC) promotes this policy. For example, some children with significant special needs function best in self-contained classrooms that have fewer children and more specific and ongoing educational support.

When you walk into a special education classroom or when you count the number of children receiving special education services in a school, you may notice that the percentage of children from a given demographic group is not the same as the percentage that group represents within the general population. This is known as **disproportionate representation,** and it may occur because of discrimination or lack of understanding of cultural differences. As a result, schools may misclassify children and/or withhold services from children who need them.

Children are classified by race and ethnicity. Nationwide, black children comprise 14.8 percent of the population, yet 20.2 percent of the children in special education are black. Children of Asian/Pacific Islander descent comprise 3.8 percent of the population yet only 1.7 percent of the special education population. More boys receive special education services than girls (EMSTAC 2007). With an eye toward ending disproportionate representation, we must understand cultural variations and gender differences.

Lack of agreement on specific diagnoses can complicate efforts to understand the distribution of disabilities. States have differing recording procedures, and there is some under- and overreporting. For children six years and younger, the most common disabilities are communication disorders, which are known as **high-incidence**

disabilities. For older children, the most common disabilities are specific learning disabilities. Developmental disabilities, mental retardation, emotional disorders, and health impairments are somewhat less common and are therefore known as **low-incidence disabilities.** Autism affects between 2 and 3 percent of the population, although there is evidence that the incidence of children with an autism diagnosis is increasing. Many people believe that autism is diagnosed more frequently today because diagnostic criteria have improved, but there are other theories as well, including complex interactions between the environment and biological processes (Pessah 2006). Hearing impairments, visual impairments, orthopedic impairments, traumatic brain injury, and multiple disabilities all occur in less than 3 percent of the population. Children with these low-incidence disabilities require trained professionals and appropriate services, just as do children with more common high-incidence disabilities.

Work Against Poverty and Racism

In the United States, 20 percent of children under six live in poverty, but that percentage is deceptive. The poverty level has not been adjusted to the financial demands families face today, and 39 percent of the nation's children live in families that cannot make ends meet (Fass and Cauthen 2007).

Poverty and low incomes affect families and children in multiple ways, including:

- poor nutrition
- environmental hazards, such as lead paint and fumes
- lack of affordable or healthy housing
- lack of health coverage or poor medical care
- frequent uprooting
- unsafe neighborhoods
- parental job instability

According to the American Academy of Pediatrics, after infancy, most risks to young children's health and safety are preventable (http://brightfutures.aap.org/). We could eradicate environmental toxins—beginning with screening for lead paint, especially in poor neighborhoods—and provide immunizations and routine screening for developmental delays for all children. But we haven't. Your careful observation of children can provide information that helps families and medical professionals rule out or diagnose a health condition.

Adults transmit their anxiety to children when they have too few resources. Poverty directly affects early brain development, particularly language and memory (Cookson 2008). Early childhood programs can help children's growth, development, and learning but are hard-pressed to overcome the odds that children face from before birth.

The number of children living in poverty increased by 11 percent from 2000 to 2006 (Fass and Cauthen 2007). Although more poor children are European American than any other group, African American and Latino children are twice as likely, percentage-wise, to live in poverty. Thirty-three percent of African American children live in poverty, as do 27 percent of Latino children and 40 percent of Native American children.

These numbers show that a disproportionate percentage of children of color are poor. The million-and-a-half children with parents incarcerated in state or federal prisons further illustrate **institutionalized racism** at work. Almost half of all

Poverty directly affects early brain development, particularly language and memory.

prisoners are African American, 29 percent are European American, and 9 percent are Hispanic (Mumola 2000).

Racism and other forms of discrimination work against the escape from poverty. **Racism** is:

> . . . an institutionalized system of power. It encompasses a web of economic, political, social, and cultural structures, actions, and beliefs that systemize and ensure an unequal distribution of privilege, resources and power in favor of the dominant racial group and at the expense of all other racial groups (Derman-Sparks and Phillips 1997, 9).

Children and families can experience racism interwoven with prejudice against their class, ethnicity, language and dialect, sexual orientation, or disability (Connolly 1998).

Given the complexity of racism, how can we consider its effects on young children's learning and on the well-being of their families, schools, and communities? First, think about how racism works on the individual and the societal level. Racism can be overt—out in the open, as in a racist remark. It can also be covert, hidden, and difficult to pinpoint—invisible to others, in one's thoughts or assumptions (Derman-Sparks and Phillips 1997).

Second, everyone is part of a racist society and internalizes racism early on. As an educator, your covert and overt attitudes about race will influence children's thinking and, in turn, how they experience race. In Chapter 1, you read about reflecting, alone and with colleagues, and articulating a rationale for your interactions with children and families. Such reflection is a helpful way to approach personal attitudes about race.

Third, "race" constructs an "us" and "them" psychology. People *are* different from each other, but it is possible to uproot racism by examining societal structures without pitting people against each other.

Anti-bias approaches go beyond just appreciating cultural diversity to begin to untangle the messy knot of personal and institutional racism. Critical thinking is essential to comprehend all the forces of bias at work (Derman-Sparks and Ramsey 2006).

SOCIAL JUSTICE

What does social justice have to do with early care and education?

The U.S. Department of Education's website states that "ensuring equal access" is part of its mission. Education has and continues to be touted as the road to equality for all. Unfortunately this view overlooks the societal inequities for which education cannot compensate (Mishel and Rothstein 2007). For example, **resegregation**, the comeback of segregated schools, is on the rise due to neighborhood segregation and fewer legal mandates for integrated schools (Orfield and Lee 2007). Children in poor communities are more likely to attend schools in poorer districts, which have a smaller tax base and fewer educational resources. Wealthier communities have deeper pockets from which to support their public schools, and parents often raise additional funds for programs in the arts, for example, or specialized sports equipment. Furthermore, **privatization**—private groups taking charge of public

THOUGHT QUESTION A European American kindergarten teacher works in a public school where 99 percent of the children are African American. Reflecting on her first year of teaching, she admitted that she had lower expectations for the children she was teaching than she'd had for the European American children she worked with as a student teacher. What supports and resources could help this young teacher as she tries to overcome racist assumptions about the children?

Anti-bias approaches go beyond just appreciating cultural diversity to begin to untangle the messy knot of personal and institutional racism. Critical thinking is essential to comprehend bias at work.

services—is on the rise, including wealthy segregated neighborhoods that incorporate as new towns to create exclusive schools (Klein 2007).

These large forces may seem separate from your work in the classroom, but really, they are not. Having a point of view about social inequality puts you into the equation for making change. Maxine Greene (2000) writes about "wide-awakeness," a quality in teachers and in children that she links to imagination and the ability to speculate about what might be possible. Teachers who are wide awake, in Greene's (1978) sense, are interested in and attentive to the world around them. They are engaged enough in their surroundings to question how things are and to think about how to improve them. They challenge what might be taken for granted. Instead of saying, "We do it this way because we've always done it this way," they ask, "What do we notice about the children when we do it this way? How else could we do it, and what would happen then?"

The Developmental-Interaction Approach

One way to enact social justice is through classroom curriculum and direct work with children. The developmental-interaction approach provides one framework for thinking in ways that can promote this kind of work. Having a voice and using it to speak out and advocate on behalf of children is another way to take a stand. As a professional, you can also join with others to create a stronger voice.

> David is five years old. He has been diagnosed as autistic and is a member of an inclusive and mixed-age class in child care. He towers over the other children as, with his hands on the child in front of him, he and the rest of the group pretend to get on the "train to the zoo" and move toward the lunch tables. Allowing physical contact and pretending with others is a recent achievement for David.
>
> A state licensing official has come to inspect the center and joins the children at lunch. David mucks about in his food and drags his hand, which is covered with chili, across his forehead and down into his eyes. He sniffles quietly, using his hand to shield himself from the eyes of the stranger. The inspector stares and asks the teacher, as though David and the other children were not present, "What's wrong with him?" Tamika, who is nearly four, leans forward with a chili and milk mustache and declares, "Ain't nothin' wrong with him, Mister. Takes him longer. He's gettin' there."

Tamika based her defense of David on her knowledge of him as a member of her group. Her comment was tied to democratic ideas about their classroom community. It illustrates how young children think about how we are similar to, yet different from, one another and how children give moral meaning to their experiences and behaviors (Paley 2000). As Tamika's comment demonstrates, children are connected to the political context in which they live (Grieshaber and Canella 2001).

Having a curriculum that helps children consider social justice requires thinking about how to create equity within the classroom. That means thinking about what is going on in the classroom at any given moment and figuring out how to help children create links from their interactions to larger principles, as is developmentally meaningful. Teachers can listen to children and value their thoughts and feelings and, at the same time, help children become aware of others.

The children in David's classroom got to know him well through their daily life together, in which their teachers demonstrated respect and caring for him and

Having a curriculum that helps children consider social justice requires thinking about what is going on in the classroom and figuring out how to help children create links from their interactions to larger principles, as is developmentally meaningful.

Seven-year-olds created pictures like this of their vision of a better society.

Everyone should have the right to have a warm and safe home.

everyone else. But how can you introduce concepts that are not so close to children's experiences? If all the children in your class have consistent and safe housing, for example, how do they react to seeing homeless people on the street? What might their understanding of homelessness be? A social studies curriculum can support and further develop children's thinking about such topics that are important to us all. In one public-school first-through-third-grade class, curriculum that strove for a sense of social justice grew out of a brief conversation between a few children about what it means to throw away your unfinished snacks or lunch when some people are homeless and have little to eat. No child in this class was homeless at this point in time.

The next morning the teacher, Ms. Lin, wrote on the board, "What is homelessness?" Jamar began, "I think it means when you're by yourself or something." Colin offered, "Means you're all alone and probably poor." Reuben said he could not trust people who are homeless because he does not know them. Then Kevin asked to tell a story about a homeless man he saw on the street. "Not to be nasty or nothing; he really had to go. He didn't have a home or nothing or a toilet."

Ms. Lin suggested that the children draw their ideas about homelessness. Once they settled into their work, they engaged in

THOUGHT QUESTION How do you feel about Colin's comment? What might have contributed to this seven-year-old's acute sense of another's feelings?

quiet dialogue. Colin sat, arms folded across his chest, pouting. He was not drawing and responded to his teacher's raised eyebrows in an irate tone, "I don't think it's nice to do this, to draw the homeless. How would you like it if you was homeless and someone made you?"

The following day, Ms. Lin read the class *Broken Umbrellas* (Spohn 1994), a story about a homeless woman. Kira said, "You know what? When your clothes don't fit you, you can give them to the homeless people. I did that once."

Drawing, reading *Broken Umbrellas,* and talking to each other made a difference to many of the children. What was abstract became more human. The unfamiliar became familiar. Their ideas fell into themes. They seemed to understand something about the economics, about the cause and effect between the lack of jobs and drugs, and about loneliness. Through this kind of social studies, children take on new perspectives and come to notice the details of social issues as they go about their daily lives. After these discussions, the children decided to take action: they baked cookies, sold them, and gave the proceeds to a nearby shelter.

The ways of thinking about education that we have just presented fit with the **developmental-interaction approach** (DIA) to education. DIA is a philosophy associated with Bank Street College of Education, but many educational settings can and do apply its principles and practices. Developmental interaction can inform your teaching and help you think about teaching, but it does not provide a prescription for how to teach. It is, instead, an ever-changing set of ideas, values, and beliefs about the learner, learning, and teaching (Nager and Shapiro 2000).

Developmental interaction originated in the early years of the twentieth century at the time of the Progressive movement, which held that education provides an opportunity to engage in and create a more equitable democratic society. The possibility that teaching can make the world a better place influences teachers' choices about what and how to teach and about the social and physical environment.

> A yearlong study of their city had culminated with second graders creating their own "crate city" out of small wooden wine crates. They worked individually on their apartment buildings, libraries, and stores and made decisions together about how the city would function and who would make up the families. For example, they unanimously decreed, "No babysitters in our city!"
>
> Although children had spent considerable time discussing their own family structures, the teacher, Cleo, noticed that the cardboard families the children created did not come close to reflecting the diversity of their own families. She raised this with them at a morning meeting. In response to this single probe from Cleo, children began discussing what they did and didn't understand about various family configurations. They went back to their cities and created a more diverse and representative population of families there.

Here we see how children were freed to think differently and subsequently participated in a richer curriculum because of Cleo's awareness of their development—she knew what they understood about families—and their interaction with their environment—she established a forum for discussion and provided time, space, and materials for them to work out their ideas. The term *developmental interaction* highlights these key concepts. "Developmental" implies changing patterns of growth. As children develop, they come to understandings about and respond to their environments. "Interaction" has dual meanings. It refers to the ways in which thought

Through this kind of social studies, children take on new perspectives and come to notice the details of social issues as they go about their daily lives.

The developmental interaction approach maintains that teaching can create a more equitable and democratic world. This possibility influences teachers' choices about what and how to teach and about the social and physical environment.

Contemporary
brain research
provides evidence
that emotions
drive learning.

THOUGHT QUESTION Think about yourself
as a learner. What do your experiences and
feelings have to do with what and how you
think? How do your experiences and feelings influence your ability to think about
biology, anthropology, or even the previous
paragraphs on developmental interaction?

and emotion connect to one another. In fact, contemporary brain research provides evidence that emotions drive learning (Brazel-ton and Greenspan 2000). At the same time, "interaction" speaks to the child's engagement with the world of people, materials, and ideas. As with the "crate city" curriculum, engagement is more than "learning by doing"; it includes reflective follow-up to process the experience. The developmental-interaction approach under-stands children as makers of meaning, individuals who are curious about the world in which they live and who actively engage with the physical and social world to make sense of it.

Having a Voice

Early childhood educators interact with individual children, groups of children, and their families, but your impact can be much broader than that. As you gain an in-creasingly better sense of yourself, we hope you will feel surer about saying what you believe. Then, you can tap into your reflective practice and use what you know about children, families, care, and education to join with others and speak out on behalf of many more children and families than are in your classroom.

You can make your voice heard in a number of ways in a variety of settings:

- Speak up at staff meetings. What you have to say is as important as what others contribute.
- Represent your program in the community. Go to meetings, and say what you believe about children and families.
- Meet with politicians in your area.
- Go to the state capital to discuss children's issues with lawmakers.
- Keep in touch with policymakers through email, or send them letters.

THOUGHT QUESTION What can you say
when someone makes a discriminatory
remark? The challenge is to answer respectfully while letting the person know that you
don't agree and why. Practice with a friend
or classmate, and ask your partner to let
you know how what you say makes her feel.
Would she change her views as a result of
your statement?

Joining with Others

Your voice gains power when combined with other voices. When you become a member of an early childhood organization, you can network with others who have similar interests, keep up with new ideas in the field through journals and online publications, and attend annual professional meetings where you can present your own work and learn about others' work. Many of the national or-ganizations listed here also have state and local affiliate organiza-tions, which you can join through one national membership. They all have policy arms that work to keep practitioners, families, and politicians up-to-date with the latest information concerning chil-dren's well-being.

The National Association for the Education of Young Children (NAEYC) is the largest of these organizations, but you may wish to join other groups as well, groups that address your particular interests—for instance, if you work with infants and toddlers or with children with disabilities. Some organizations are listed below, along with their websites:

- Association for Childhood Education International (ACEI)
  http://www.acei.org

ACEI's journal, *Childhood Education,* reports on issues affecting children from birth to early adolescence.

- Council for Exceptional Children–Division of Early Childhood (CEC-DEC)
http://www.dec-sped.org/
DEC promotes policies and advances evidence-based practices that support families and enhance the optimal development of young children who have or are at risk for developmental delays and disabilities. The organization publishes two journals, *Journal of Early Intervention* and *Young Exceptional Children.*

- National Association for the Education of Young Children (NAEYC)
http://www.naeyc.org/
NAEYC's print journal, *Young Children,* is offered to members. NAEYC also has an online journal, *Beyond the Journal,* available at http://journal.naeyc.org/btj/.

- National Association for Family Child Care (NAFCC)
www.nafcc.org
NAFCC's mission is to strengthen the profession of family child care.

- National Head Start Association (NHSA)
http://www.nhsa.org/
Members can read NHSA's journal, *Children and Families,* online.

- Society for Research in Child Development (SRCD)
www.srcd.org
The purposes of SRCD are to promote multidisciplinary research in the field of human development, to foster the exchange of information among scientists and other professionals of various disciplines, and to encourage applications of research findings.

- Zero to Three (0–3)
http://zerotothree.org
0–3 is the national organization that specializes in children from birth to age three and their families. The organization publishes a journal called *Zero to Three.*

Speaking Out for Children and Families

Your job is first and foremost with the children in your program, but your program functions in the context of your community, your state, and national policies that affect young children and their families. You have to focus beyond the program itself to ensure that legislation, regulations, and other policies support the children and families with whom you work. This makes you an advocate.

You'll read about advocacy and policy in Chapter 15. For now, think about what being an advocate means:

- Reading the newspaper and joining electronic discussion lists to stay abreast of current issues.

- Joining local organizations active on behalf of children to learn about issues in your community. These organizations may include training and technical assistance groups, child care councils, child and maternal health councils, and school boards.

- Sharing information with your colleagues and the children's families about pending legislation, demonstrations, lobbying opportunities, opportunities to sign up for health care, and other news related to children and families.

The national organizations listed here have policy arms that work to keep practitioners, families, and politicians up-to-date with the latest information concerning children's well-being.

- Speaking up when an issue—maybe something as immediate as getting the city to clean up a nearby playground—is of importance to you and the children.
- Writing letters or visit legislators yourself, and you'll organize others to go with you.

Advocacy can sound daunting, so start small. Read the newsletters and websites that your local groups publish, and you will quickly become informed about your community's issues. Go to a local group's meetings, and develop collegial friendships as you join forces on issues about which you all care. Chat with others about what you are learning.

Advocacy work is professionalizing. You will recognize yourself as someone who is making change happen.

SUMMARY

OUR RAPIDLY CHANGING WORLD

How might your awareness of globalization, culture, and ecological theories influence your work with young children?

With dramatic technological changes, people all over the world are increasingly in touch with and influenced by each other. In your work with young children, you are likely to come in contact with people from many parts of the globe. Teachers who understand what culture is will find it easier to establish relationships with children and families that support children's learning and development. Ecological systems theories help early childhood educators think about the range of cultural contexts in which children, families, and early childhood educators themselves live. A developmental niche describes a child's context and the accepted ways of functioning in it, which can enable early childhood educators to further understand children and their families.

WHAT CAN WE PROVIDE FOR YOUNG CHILDREN?

How might you provide children with consistency and predictability, support for good health practices, and respect and equal access?

Children need to be safe, secure, and "known" by the adults in their lives. They are particularly vulnerable to both one-time and ongoing stressors, such as illness and other trauma, because they are in the process of developing. As early childhood educators, we can offer children and families support and resources and can work together with them to overcome societal ills. We can be alert to child abuse and report it as mandated by state regulations. We can reinforce children's good health habits and nutrition throughout the day: handwashing is one of the best ways to prevent disease from spreading. Moreover, we can advocate that exercise and outdoor activity be part of our programs.

Respect for each child is a personal matter that takes on societal proportions. While "race" is a cultural construction that is not based on physical reality, racism is real. Ethnicity, on the other hand, refers to one's ancestry and country of origin, and teachers can learn about a variety of ethnicities so that they can introduce children to different heritages. They can work with children who come to a program speaking languages other than English by giving them time to adapt and take in the new language and by recognizing that the child's first language forms a stepping-stone to learning English. Teachers who respect children will also watch out for gender bias and will try to understand their own socialization about sexuality. They will make sure that children with disabilities receive the services they need in the least restrictive environment and will work against institutionalized racism.

What does social justice have to do with early care and education?

Where we live and where we are from has great bearing on who we are. These are the kinds of things that adults need to know about the children and families with whom they work. The developmental-interaction approach that we use throughout this book recognizes the child as an individual with feelings and intellect who lives and learns with others. Educating the whole child, every child, and addressing inequities are among the purposes of early care and education for social justice.

Even our best efforts, however, cannot negate the stressors some children face. Yet, as you will continue to read, infant-toddler, preschool, and early elementary school experiences can change the way children will live and learn for the rest of their lives. Adults working in these programs can join together to learn more about the children with whom they work and to advocate for the early care and education the children deserve.

FURTHER ACTIVITIES

1. Write a four-page paper that tells a story about your first experience with race and racism directed at you or at someone else. How did adults help you understand your experience then or at a later time? Describe your feelings, and analyze the event. How has this first experience with race and racism become a part of who you are? (**NAEYC Standard 1: Promoting Child Development and Learning**)

2. Choose an experience for children from the Anti-bias Curriculum (Figure 2.4) or another curriculum resource for equitable education. Find a child or small group of children, and try the experience with them. Write up what you tried, what you thought would happen, and what actually occurred. Analyze the outcome, describing what each child did, how each child reacted, and what you think each child gained or did not gain from the experience. (**NAEYC Standard 3: Observing, Documenting, and Assessing to Support Young Children and Families**)

3. Start developing a philosophy statement by completing these sentences in as many different ways as you can: "I believe that children . . . ," "I believe that families . . . ," and "I believe the community. . . ." Then write several paragraphs that describe how you see children, your role with them, and what that means about your relationship with their families. To fully develop your philosophy about working with children and their families, add to this statement as you read the rest of this book and as you continue to take early childhood education courses. (**NAEYC Standard 6: Becoming a Professional**)

CHAPTER THREE

Children Learning about the World through Relationships

Interpersonal experience . . . plays a special organizing role in determining the development of brain structure early in life and the ongoing emergence of brain function throughout the lifespan.

—Daniel Siegel

Chapter Outline

Human beings are wired from before birth to be social: we literally are built to form relationships. Here, we look at the roles emotions, relationships, and self-regulation play in young children's lives. You will read how our emotions are the foundation for our learning, not separate from our ability to learn. We also examine the processes through which the brain takes in and organizes experiences. With an understanding of these processes, you will have a framework for providing trustworthy relationships, creating authentic experiences, and guiding children's growth in a learning community.

The infant comes to know the world through her first relationships with one or more caregivers. The adult helps the infant's immature brain stabilize until it can organize its own processes, at first, by providing the infant with more regulation—for example, by rocking and singing to an infant to calm him. Adults continue to play an organizing role with children throughout early childhood but do so to a lesser and different extent as children increasingly become able to monitor, pace, and control their own emotions and needs—that is, as they **self-regulate.**

EARLY EXPERIENCE

How does children's early experience contribute to who they become?

Children process their experience and make meaning from it first through the senses, then by using symbols to speak, sing, play, write, and paint. Our role, as teachers, is to guide children and offer experiences that hold their interest, in which they find meaning, and that foster new learning.

Brain Development: The Neuroscience of Experience

Each human brain is wired and organized in a slightly different way, yet the *process* of brain development is similar for most of us. We take in the world through our senses, and our brains interpret the information. We act on that information and affect the world around us, and this process repeats constantly as we interact with our environments—we continually shape them and are shaped by them. Although the brain changes most rapidly during developmental spurts such as infancy and adolescence, in actuality our brains keep changing all through life. Research shows that humans thrive on **novelty of experience**—the unfamiliar—but not-too-much and not-too-little newness is best for learning (Jensen 1998). Teachers need to create learning opportunities that draw on children's previous experiences but also allow them to investigate what is new.

The human brain develops in utero from a hollow ball of cells filled with DNA (the genetic code that provides instructions for our development and functioning). Neurons, the cells that make up the brain, go through a series of stages of rapid **growth, migration,** and **differentiation** (Figure 3.1). That is, the cells grow, then move to those parts of the brain where they will specialize. Maternal exposure to toxins (such as liquor, strong drugs, cigarette smoking, or radiation) is especially harmful at various stages, depending on whether a particular toxin interferes with the production, migration, or differentiation of neurons. Once the neurons are in place, they begin to form **synapses,** extensions that connect to other cells. This process of cells connecting to each other continues throughout life, but during pregnancy and the first few months of life, these connections are so plentiful that this time is called a period of **synaptic exuberance**!

> Teachers need to create learning opportunities that draw on children's previous experiences but also allow them to investigate what is new.

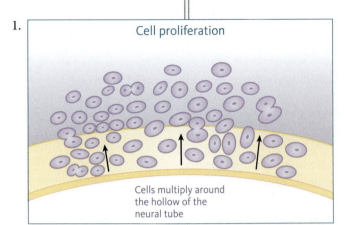

1. **Cell proliferation**

Cells multiply around the hollow of the neural tube

Copyright © 2008 ZERO TO THREE.

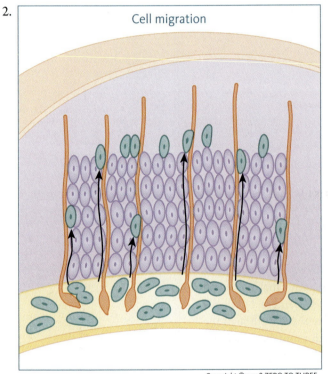

2. **Cell migration**

Copyright © 2008 ZERO TO THREE.

3.1 *Four Stages of Cell Maturation*

3. **Cell differentiation**

Skin

Retina

Spinal cord

Cortex

Cerebellum

Thalamus

Copyright © 2008 ZERO TO THREE.

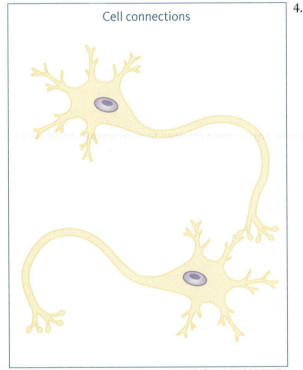

4. **Cell connections**

Copyright © 2008 ZERO TO THREE.

After birth, the child's brain grows in three important ways:

- Neural connections are created in response to experience.
- When certain experiences are repeated, the connections used by the brain in those experiences gain in strength and complexity (Figure 3.2).
- Communication between cells becomes more rapid as nerve pathways become **myelinated,** that is, as a type of fatty insulation surrounds them.

Pathways that are essential for the person's survival myelinate earlier; those that are not, do so later. For example, the nerves communicating to the anal sphincter do not myelinate until around eighteen to twenty-four months, which explains increased toileting success *after* a child's second birthday.

PART 1   An Introduction to Early Childhood

Just as with neural pathways, when no one walks on a path, it becomes overgrown.

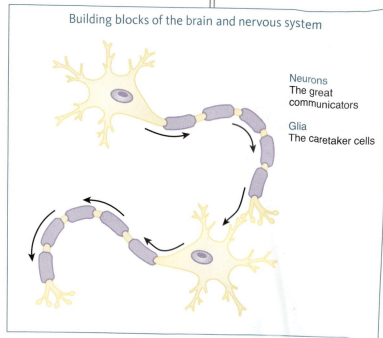

Building blocks of the brain and nervous system

Neurons
The great communicators

Glia
The caretaker cells

Copyright © 2008 ZERO TO THREE.

3.2 *Neural Connections*

Meanwhile, the synapses, or connections, between cells that are not used fall away. This is often referred to as **pruning** (Shore 1997). This is like cutting away the dead branches of a tree to help the rest of the tree thrive. Another way to think about how experience affects our brains is to imagine a neural connection as a dirt path. The more people walk on it, the more defined it becomes. If no one walks on it, it becomes overgrown, and eventually disappears.

Our experiences and our genetic makeup collaborate to make us who we are. But what children experience, or do not experience, in their early life is hardly the last word in long-term development. The back-and-forth between their biological inheritance and their experience continues to shape them throughout life. What is different about the early years is that our brains and nervous system are in the process of formation. That is why people often refer to the way early experience shapes the brain as creating the **architecture** of the brain. This has major implications for the person we become. The "use it or lose it" of brain development sounds harsh, but the brain does become less flexible and malleable with time. Neurologists cite age eight—the official end of early childhood, according to NAEYC—as the cutoff point where the brain loses its maximal degree of plasticity. The stories of Yin and Brad exemplify how the interaction between our brain and our experiences significantly shapes who we become.

Yin's and Brad's Early Experiences

Meet the Cooper family—Tom and Marcia and their children, Yin and Brad. For years, Tom and Marcia tried in vain to conceive a child, then finally adopted Yin, a sixteen-month-old girl, from a Chinese orphanage. When Yin came home with the Coopers, her physical development was delayed, and she spoke no words either in English or in Chinese. She was quiet and cautious—almost vigilant—in her careful observation of everyone and everything. The three of them were not an instant

The back-and-forth between our biological inheritance and our experience continues to shape us throughout life. What is different about the early years is tha̶ us brains o͏͏ of syst͏

67

As you read about these few moments in Yin's and Brad's lives, think about how each brain would take in these experiences if they were repeated daily in one form or another. What expectations would each of these infants develop over time?

family, but slowly they grew closer, and, with early intervention and much parental attention, Yin began to catch up with her peers.

Two years after adopting Yin, the Coopers were amazed to discover that Marcia was pregnant! Now Yin is seven years old, in second grade, and her three-year-old brother, Brad, attends a neighborhood child care center. From birth, Brad was an energetic and rambunctious child who required much parental energy, albeit a different kind than his sister elicited. We'll follow Yin's and Brad's development and education to see how their experiences and relationships contribute to who they are and how they learn.

Despite individual and cultural differences, all humans require a certain amount of sensory intake in the first few years of life; without it, their development suffers. Here is a glimpse of what Yin, at eight months, experienced at a Chinese orphanage before being transferred to a larger, more responsible agency:

> Yin, sleeping **supine** (on her back) hears loud noises and wakes to see a bare ceiling. It is cold; she shivers and begins to whimper. She looks to one side and sees the metal bars of the crib, and more bars beyond those. She looks to the other side and sees a similar landscape of bars. She feels two kinds of cold—one on her arms and one where a wet diaper soaks her skin. She lies on her back whimpering for a half hour until a nurse comes by to check on her, change her diaper, and feed her.

Now, think about Brad at eight months.

> Brad is napping in a playpen in the Coopers' living room. The doorbell rings, and Shadow, the family's German shepherd, barks. These noises permeate Brad's consciousness, and he opens an eye but closes it again. He then hears the clicking of Shadow's toenails on the floor close by. When Brad next opens his eyes, Shadow's snout is a few inches away from his face, and the dog is wagging his tail. Brad twists his body up from a **prone** (on his belly) position by leaning his weight on one side and pushing with his right arm. From a sitting position, he grabs the netting and pulls himself up, holding on to the playpen railing where Shadow's cold, wet nose pushes through the netting to touch his face. Brad cries out a short "ahhhhhh." Yin pops her head over the couch to see the exchange and yells out, "Mama, Braddie is up!" She and her mother come over, laughing at seeing Brad and Shadow cheek to cheek. Marcia picks up Brad, nuzzles his face, and asks, "How was your sleep, Mr. Cooper? I bet you're ready for a diaper change. Let's go see."

No one in Yin's current life knows what her first orphanage was really like, but it is very probable that Yin had considerably fewer interactions and less environmental stimulation than her brother in the early months of life. Brad experiences Shadow's bark, the dog up close, the motivation to pull to stand, and most of all, a cheering section of beloved family members to greet him when he wakes from a nap—with slight variations, again and again, every day. Rich language, with lilting and sing-song sounds from Yin and a distinctly different voice from his mother, the clanging and knocking of pots and pans, and the smell of food being prepared: all of this comes through Brad's senses to his central nervous system and brain. Those pathways in the brain that these interactions and sensory moments use become part of the brain's circuitry, creating a richly embedded brain structure for Brad's further development. Yin, by comparison, at the same point in her development had far fewer rich experiences and less motivation for exploration. At eight months, a pau-

Brad an

city of experience resulted in weaker neural connections being made in Yin's brain than in Brad's at the same age. Keep this in mind as you watch Yin develop in new and more interactive environments.

Just before Yin was nine months, she was transferred to another orphanage in a city far from her first placement. This orphanage was divided into "houses," with primary caregivers assigned to a few babies. Yin came to expect the smell and voice of her caregiver, Lei-Lei. By chance, she was moved to a crib by a window. At ten months, she began to sit up and could see people pass by outside with carts and on bicycles. An old woman came by the window twice a day to talk to her. Most important, Yin was spending more time out of her crib, playing with Lei-Lei and a few other babies and toddlers.

Yin's transfer to a humane and socially responsive institution and her subsequent adoption by the Coopers a few months later clearly allowed her inborn capabilities (nature) a chance to flourish with input from caring people and an interesting environment (nurture). Although earlier is better, Yin began to enjoy rich and varied experiences that allowed her to have relationships with caring others that, in turn, enabled her brain to grow and develop in productive ways. This is reflected in the literature that compares children's development when they are raised in or out of orphanages (Nelson and Zeanah 2007).

Attachment refers to a deep emotional tie with a specific person that endures over time and space. Attachments follow us throughout life and guide many of our behaviors.

ATTACHMENT, RELATIONSHIPS, AND EXPERIENCE

Why is attachment important, and how do teachers and caregivers support it?

Attachment refers to a deep emotional tie with a specific person that endures over time and space. Attachments follow us throughout life and guide many of our behaviors. According to the grandparents of attachment theory, John Bowlby (1982) and Mary Ainsworth et al. (1978), these are its main tenets:

1. A child's secure early relationships promote greater independence and social-emotional competence later on, in accordance with the quality of the child's ongoing attachment relationships and life experiences (Thompson 2000).
2. Sensitive and responsive care early in life promotes secure attachments.
3. Children with secure attachments are able to use adults as a secure base for exploration or to return to when sick, fatigued, or threatened.

An Evolutionary Theory in Cultural Context

Attachment theory is based on human evolution over thousands and thousands of years. It is a primal system that applies to humans of all ages. If you have ever been in an accident or a dangerous situation, your first response, once you

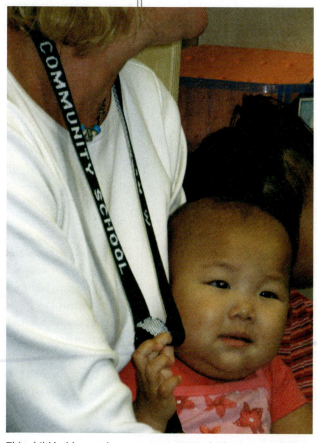

This child holds onto her caregiver's ID cord. Their connection is physical as well as emotional.

were out of harm's way, was probably to connect with someone you love, because to you that person represents a feeling of safety and belonging. Now think about how an infant or a young child might experience such a fright, with fewer of the mental capabilities you have as an adult.

John Bowlby, a British psychoanalyst, theorized that originally the attachment system primed infants to seek physical closeness to their caregivers, especially when in danger or need. In very young infants, this system is automatic and relies on basic reflexes, such as looking, grasping, and crying, to gain the caregiver's attention. In the first year of life, attachment behaviors, such as locomotion and intentional smiling and crying, become more purposeful and sophisticated. As infants develop, they become interested in exploring but also wary of danger. Primary attachment figures provide a **secure base,** or safe place, from which junior toddlers can venture to explore, moving on from their lap-baby status. When startled, scared, or just weary, children tend to "check in" with their loved one, or physically return for support and comfort (Mahler, Pine, and Bergman 1975; Lieberman 1993).

Most attachment theory and research indicate that security with caregivers early on promotes (but does not ensure) curiosity, autonomy, self-esteem, and social-emotional connectedness with peers in the later preschool and elementary years (Cassidy and Shaver 1999). But in some cultures, autonomy and curiosity are not as valued as they are in Western ones, which have set the attachment research agenda. Other research shows that while the attachment system exists in all humans, attachment behaviors can look different across cultures, depending on a society's values regarding approaches to caregiving (Harwood, Miller, and Izizarry 1995; van Ijzendoorn and Sagi 1999). In addition, the field is becoming more aware of how children's thoughts and feelings about loved ones both stay constant and change over time (Thompson 2000). At this point, though, attachment theory is Western culture's "most influential theory of relatedness" (Rothbaum et al. 2000).

Relationship History = Attachment Quality

What does attachment actually feel like to a baby? We can't really know for sure, although we know attachments begin as feelings and sensations of "being with" another that build over time and experience (Stern 1985).

Although infants actually have excellent memories, they aren't like adults' or even three-year-olds' memories because infants don't possess a **symbolic representation** (a picture in their minds) of their caregivers. What they *do* experience are the qualities of that special person and all that they do together. They have a *sense* of the feelings, smells, and ways of being carried that link them to their special person or persons. Infants encode those experiences over time as *expectations*. If parents almost always comfort their baby soon after he cries, the baby comes to expect that. If parents don't comfort their baby soon after he cries, or sometimes do and sometimes don't, the baby must adapt. According to attachment theory, over time that need to adapt leads to avoidance of or ambivalence toward those caregivers. Recall Yin in the first orphanage waiting for care in a wet diaper.

Bowlby theorized that even though infants don't have symbolic representation, all the ways they take in their experiences with different caregivers might nevertheless give them a sensory **internal working model.** Once children can symbolically represent their loved ones as well as the accompanying feelings and experiences, they can call up those internal working models, not only in a sensory way, whenever they want or need that feeling of security. *Bye, Mis' Lela,* a children's book by Doro-

John Bowlby theorized that even though infants don't have symbolic representation, all the ways they take in their experiences with different caregivers might nevertheless give them a sensory internal working model.

thy Carter, illustrates how a child's internal working model becomes representational and how working models can bring humans great pleasure and solace.

Mis' Lela, a young child's beloved grandmother figure, cared for the child while her mother worked. When Mis'Lela dies:

> I grew bigger and went to school.
> When I walked by Mis' Lela's house, I said, "Hi," same as she was there sayin' to me, "Study your lessons, Sugar Plum, and mind your manners."
> I said "Yes ma'am, Bye, Mis' Lela." (Carter 1998)

This child had a working model of Mis' Lela—who was very much alive in the child's mind and spirit. We can also see the self-regulating role Mis' Lela continued to play for this child, even after her death.

Classifying Attachment

In the 1970s, Mary Ainsworth and her colleagues observed middle-class Caucasian infants and mothers in their homes. From the data, they constructed patterns of interaction that included all of Bowlby's essential behavioral components of attachment. Ainsworth then created a laboratory procedure for young toddlers (thirteen to eighteen months old) that calls the attachment system into play. Separations and reunions between mother/father, toddler, and a stranger—the **Strange Situation** procedure—give a complex picture of emotional connection between toddler and parent.

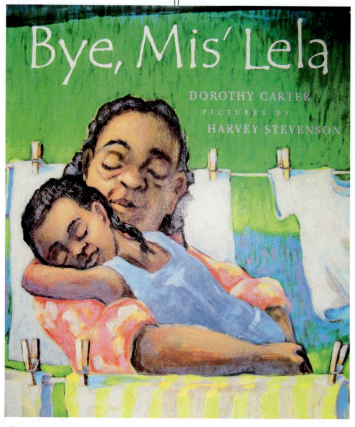

This young girl has an internal working model of her relationship with Mis' Lela.

This Strange Situation procedure is mostly used for research purposes. It assesses the *quality* of the relationship to *one* caregiver. A child can be judged to be securely attached to her father, for example, but insecurely to her mother. These categories do *not* tell you about the child's personality, or whether he is secure or insecure overall, nor about the strength of the attachment. Sometimes, a child can have a strong yet insecure attachment to a caregiver. An extreme example can be seen when children neglected or abused by a parent still cling to the adult. Clinging to an attachment figure can occur for very different reasons, however.

Ainsworth based her study on a stable sample of mother-infant dyads. Of the three categories shown in Figure 3.3, none are pathological. Instead, they show early **defenses,** that is, the child's psychological responses to her relationship with an important caregiver during her first year of life. At a later point, a fourth category, "D," or disorganized, was added that *does* have neurological and/or pathological implications, but the pattern is not considered common.

What kinds of interactions *do* promote a secure attachment? And who can provide this for children? Teachers, as well as parents and other caregivers, certainly can. As you read in Chapter 2, caregiving that is *responsive, reliable,* and *predictable* sets the stage for secure relationships in which children draw strength from caregivers and use them as a secure base from which to explore the environment. Predictability lets

Caregiving that is responsive, reliable, and predictable sets the stage for secure relationships in which children draw strength from caregivers and use them as a secure base from which to explore the environment.

Internal Working Models and Their Attachments

Secure Attachments or "B" category	• Caregivers are trustworthy and reliable • I am worthwhile and lovable • My world is safe and offers pleasure • I deserve to have my needs met
Ambivalent Attachments or "C" category	• Caregivers are unpredictable—they may be nurturing and protective or hostile and rejecting • I never know what to expect and I am always anxious and angry • I cannot leave and become autonomous—I may miss nurturing time • If I can figure out how to get my parent in a giving mood, I will be nurtured and protected
Avoidant Attachments or "A" category	• Caregivers are rejecting and punitive • I have to be vigilant to protect myself • If I deny my needs for nurturing and closeness, I will not be hurt and rejected • If I comply with the needs and demands of my caregiver, I will not be punished and rejected • If I deny my needs and take care of my caregiver, I will be loved

children know what to expect. Examples of caring interactions are portrayed here and throughout the chapter:

> When Mr. and Mrs. Cooper first held Yin on their laps, Yin did not turn in to them, as most toddlers would. Her body felt limp, that is, without **muscle tone.** Soon they also realized that Yin didn't seem to have many preferences for touch, communication, or eating. But because her new parents were consistently responsive to her needs, over time she exhibited more energy and began to develop some preferences. She gurgled when she sat in her father's lap to be read to and turned to look at books across the room. That was how her parents began to understand that she wanted to hear a story.

The Coopers were patient, listened and looked for clues, and were warmly assertive in their approach so that Yin would know they were there for her. Yin's new experiences helped her development move forward. The brain *expects* some basic experiences, such as human interaction and touch. Had Yin stayed in the first orphanage, her chances for a normal development would have been slim because touch and human interaction are so necessary early in life. In contrast, children can learn other things later on, such as a second language or to play a musical instrument (although learning is usually easier the earlier it occurs).

Being Known

Part of attachment relationships is a feeling of being "known" by another person. The desire to be known begins early, and when children feel known by caregivers, they respond in kind.

> Brad (2.3 years) is out for a walk with Pablo (1.3 years) and Julie, their caregiver, on a crisp and bright fall afternoon. Julie points out bright red leaves on a tree. Suddenly, a light breeze blows some leaves off the tree. Brad points excitedly and cries out, "Bubbles?"

Julie smiles and wonders if Brad is making a connection to the way soap bubbles (blowing them is his favorite activity) also float gently on breezes. She says, "It *does* float like a bubble, doesn't it?"

As they are talking, Pablo looks up, seeing the light and shadows moving across a building on the other side of the street. He pulls Julie's arm and points to the light, babbling some sounds with a questioning intonation. Julie asks, "What do you see, Pablo? Do you see the sunshine on the building?"

On the next block, Brad stops at the wheel of a parked car—its top is just at his chest level. Pointing to one hubcap, he says, "Happy." Julie thinks he is responding to the round, swervy contours. She says, "The wheel looks happy?" Brad looks up at Julie smiling, and nods affirmatively.

When the wind picks up, Brad looks at Julie and tucks his chin into his chest, while Pablo snuggles against her leg. Brad says, "It's windy." Julie replies, "Yes, it's windy and chilly. Let's go back inside." (adapted from Anderson 1994)

Do these hubcaps communicate emotions to you? They might to a two-year-old.

Young children may take in the same stimuli as adults, but they process them differently because their brains are structurally and functionally different from adults' brains. The children's associations might not be the same ones that came to Julie, but she listened to their comments and carefully read their body language. When Brad says "Happy" and points to a hubcap, Julie imagines he is experiencing the movement and feelings the hubcap shape elicits in him. Children can wax poetic about events and can see human emotion expressed in aspects of nature and in objects that adults often find mundane (Werner 1940).

With older children in a classroom setting, responsive practice may look a little different, but respect for children's bodies, intellect, and emotions still remains at the core. Here's an exchange in Yin's first grade classroom:

THOUGHT QUESTION Adults are capable of perceptions similar to those you have just read about, when a child brings them to our attention or when we are engaged in musical or artistic pursuits, for example. Look at the hubcaps on this page. Do any of them evoke a particular mood for you?

The children gathered on the rug and listened to Ms. Jennings read *Stone Soup* aloud. When the story was over, Ms. Jennings asked, "What was one special ingredient in the soup?" Alex said, "Carrots." Olivia said, "Onions." Yin tentatively raised her hand, and Ms. Jennings called on her right away. "The rock," Yin said. After each child spoke, Ms. Jennings asked what made that ingredient so special. She listened intently as each child spoke and followed each child's logic. Her interest gave Yin the chance to elaborate. "The rock was special," Yin said, "because you don't usually put rocks in soup." Later, Yin told her friend Jody, "Ms. Jennings likes us. She always wants to know what we think."

Just as Julie knew Brad and Pablo well, Ms. Jennings was aware of Yin's shyness and called on her immediately. Ms. Jennings probed to find out what each child meant and learned that Alex loved carrots and that Olivia's grandmother believes soup isn't soup without onions. Yin experienced Ms. Jennings' attention as an acknowledgement, not just of her thinking, but of her entire self.

As an English as a second language (ESL) teacher in a public school in Alabama, I try to place myself in the mind of a six-year-old who does not understand English and enters a U.S. classroom for the first time. How would it feel to have new experiences with new people who speak a language you don't understand? To develop a relationship with that child, I talk to his parents or caregivers about his personality and preferences. Communication with the child and parents in their home language during the first days and weeks helps develop the child's trust and willingness to become part of the classroom's social group.

Reflecting on my experience learning Spanish helps me imagine the experiences of the English language learners (ELLs). When I began teaching ESL in a public school setting in Alabama, my knowledge of Spanish became a valuable asset. However, even though others considered me fluent, I often felt nervous during my Spanish conversations and completely exhausted afterward. Now I am much more comfortable with that type of translation, but I want to remember how it felt when it was hard and tiring. That is how ELLs feel every day at school. They are bombarded with demands to listen, speak, read, and write in English all day. If they are fortunate enough to have a friend who speaks their home language, they can communicate with that person during the school day. But if not, they must remain silent until they are comfortable enough (or pressured enough) to begin to speak English.

Children who are overwhelmed with novel experiences may have difficulty self-regulating. They may cry for prolonged periods, refuse to move, hide under a table, hit or bite other students or adults, or wet themselves. I try not to form fixed opinions about children's personalities until they have had sufficient time to adjust to their new environment. During this period of adjustment, becoming known and welcomed into a classroom group is vital.

I remember a first grader I will call Yuki, the only Japanese child in her class. Yuki would not smile at me or say hello. I attempted to engage her in small talk as we walked in the hall, but she walked about five paces directly behind me.

I tried to keep our time together playful and stress free. I did not demand that Yuki reply orally. We played games and drew pictures together, and she responded nonverbally to my questions by pointing or drawing. After about a month, Yuki began responding to some of my prompts with single words. When I spoke to Yuki's teacher, she told me that Yuki had many friends. She didn't speak, but the other children didn't find that a problem. Yuki's teacher intuitively accepted Yuki's reluctance to speak. Yuki's experiences in the classroom allowed her to trust the teacher and her classmates and form secure attachments within the group. Yuki demonstrated a growing awareness of English over time and participated with enjoyment in the classroom activities.

One day after the winter holidays, as Yuki and I worked together, I asked her about a *Sesame Street* picture, "What does Big Bird have?" and she responded with, "He have red ball." She was ready to speak, and, from that point on, Yuki chattered away with me, her teacher, and her classmates.

Meg Gillette

Yuki's brother, whom I will call Ko, was friendly and talkative when I first met him. Unlike Yuki, he had previously had some English instruction. Throughout that year, Ko showed steady progress. However, when I arrived to pick him up for our sessions, I saw that he sat apart from the other students working on material from his teacher that was not related to the work the other students were doing. Ko kept a cheerful demeanor in spite of his isolation. At the end of the year, however, the results of the two approaches to integrating (or not) Yuki and Ko into their classes became apparent. Because of the spontaneous support of her classroom teacher, Yuki far outstripped Ko in her ability to speak English and in her command of basic English vocabulary.

Ko may have experienced what Stephen Krashen (1994) calls the affective filter, a mental block resulting from anxiety, low self-esteem, self-consciousness, or a lack of confidence in language use. In contrast, when children focus on an activity and forget about consciously using English, the affective filter is lowered, and they are able to acquire language.

I designed many of the activities in our ESL class to strengthen the students' confidence using English and to help them use English with their classroom teachers and peers. Choral responses, for example, create a safe space to practice English for a child not ready to speak independently. This year, with a first grade group, we practiced greetings chorally every morning. After several weeks, I asked the students to greet their classroom teachers. By the end of the third week, the classroom teachers reported with delight that all their students had greeted them when they arrived in the morning.

Relationships such as the ones we develop in our ESL groups are instrumental to learning. ELLs have the same need to trust and be known as any other child. If they feel safe and secure, as Yuki did, learning will be as natural as breathing. If they feel isolated or different, as Ko must certainly have felt, learning may occur, but it will not be easy or optimal.

EMOTIONS AND SELF-REGULATION

What contributes to children's developing emotions and the ability to self-regulate?

Emotions help our brains engage with what is meaningful to us, like a "heads-up" about what is important. In fact, emotions are behind three key cognitive functions (Jensen 1998):

- focusing our attention
- creating meaning
- utilizing our memory

Almost immediately after birth, our emotions and learning become intertwined. Teachers who consider the emotional content and relevance of curriculum can help children engage in the learning process. As researchers show, the emotional climate of the classroom is related to children's academic achievement (Pianta and Stuhlman 2004). Rather than being separate from learning, our emotions drive our learning.

The Development of Emotions

Within the protective cocoon caregivers provide in the first weeks of life, child and caregiver form a bond, begin to communicate, and learn about the subtle messages to which each can respond. Early communication is based on shifts in posture and movement, fleeting facial expressions, and awareness of social cues. The baby smiles, the parent responds, and two-way affection and responsiveness begin to develop. Long before verbal language emerges, the baby and caregiver imitate each other and expand upon what the other does. This complex interplay helps the baby move into the social world of family and community.

By the second half of the first year of life, infants and their adults have moments of **intersubjectivity,** a feeling of mutual understanding people experience when they share their attention and adapt their behavior in order to communicate (Gauvain 2001). Early intersubjectivity with a loving caregiver helps infants direct their attention to social cues and begin to coordinate their actions and interests with another person. Intersubjectivity continues to develop throughout the life span, taking different forms at different times. At these powerful moments, both parties feel "known" by the other. Intersubjectivity has been shown to play a key role in preschoolers' ability to cooperate and play together (Gonçu 1993).

In the last quarter of the first year, the capacity for intersubjectivity broadens to allow child and adult to focus on a "common reference, which may be an object, person, or event, and to monitor another's attention to this outside entity" (Gauvain 2001, 86). You can see this **joint attention** in the photograph on the next page. Joint attention is different from an adult's shaking a rattle in front of a three-month-old because the older child has *dual awareness* of the object itself and of the object as a shared experience with the adult.

During the first year of life, infants express happiness, distress, pleasure, and excitement through facial expressions and body movements. Caregivers around the world struggle to interpret infants' nonverbal signals and try to alleviate babies' distress, even if they aren't sure what caused the problem.

Rather than being separate from learning, our emotions drive it, and the emotional climate of the classroom is related to children's academic achievement.

Development of intersubjectivity, joint attention, social referencing, and empathy in the first few years of life is crucial to healthy social-emotional development. These capacities are precursors to more complex learning with and through others throughout life.

This grandfather and child share joint attention: they are looking at something together. Joint attention continues to be important as children progress in school and focus on learning tasks with their teachers and peers.

Most toddlers in their second year begin to recognize emotions in themselves and in family members, especially if their adults name and discuss emotions. Even earlier in their lives, they began to check the caregiver's or other children's facial expressions to judge the emotional meaning of a situation. This is known as **social referencing.** Humans thus learn to read each other's **affect,** "the outward facial and postural expression of one's feeling state" (Koplow 2007, 21). They become increasingly concerned about other children's distress, demonstrating expressions of **empathy** (identification with and appreciation for another's situation and feelings) and often trying to comfort the child in distress (Saarni 1999). All of these early abilities are precursors to learning with and through others.

Regulating Emotions

Self-regulation is a core ability that enables us to pace and control our feelings and behaviors. It begins late in the third trimester of pregnancy via reactions to intrauterine arousal and becomes more apparent during the first two months of life (Cole, Cole, and Lightfoot 2005), when babies usually "settle in" and begin to be more awake during the day and asleep at night. By around twelve months, young toddlers notice a stern "No!" even if they don't comply. Older toddlers and two-year-olds begin to wrestle with impulse control and continue to refine these struggles as self-regulation becomes more sophisticated in the preschool and early elementary years (Bronson 2000).

In some cultures, infants and young children learn to use a variety of self-soothing methods to help them through stressful times. Some use pacifiers or suck their thumbs; others hold soft blankets or favorite toys. In cultures where children remain in close proximity to caregivers, being carried during the day and sleeping in the same bed at night, they often require fewer soothing objects. As their cognitive skills, including memory, develop, children's ability to regulate the intensity of their emotional states increases. For example, a child can remember that there were *other* times when Mommy went away and he felt sad, but Mommy came back just as she said she would.

Like all development, self-regulation is a "whole-child" capability. One cannot look at these abilities without considering the child's age, culture, family, and life demands, as well as the child's basic behavioral style, or **temperament.** Temperament, which is inherent, plays a role in self-regulation; unlike temperament, however, some aspects of self-regulation can be learned. Yet a difficult temperament can make the process of learning to self-regulate emotions harder for some children than for others.

Brad, now three, has been in a preschool classroom for a few rocky weeks. Having previously been in a small infant-toddler room, Brad balked at the many new rules, especially regarding naptime, when he insisted he wasn't tired. Missing a nap made his behavior in the afternoon even more difficult for everyone, including him.

One day, his teacher, Cora, handed him a plastic man as he grudgingly made his way to his cot. The next day, he took the figure on his own and added the mother figure. By the end of the week, Brad had a whole family in his cot with him and fell asleep more easily. Cora heard him whispering to the "family" using **private speech,** or speech for self, before sleep overcame him.

Cora had wanted to understand Brad better and tracked when in the day Brad seemed to have the most trouble. She brought her observations to team meeting, and together the teachers decided that Brad, like many children, missed his parents most at naptime, when he was tired and more vulnerable to feelings of loss. Brad didn't have a **transitional object** or favorite comfort toy to use for self-soothing (and never did), yet these plastic people were short-lived interesting objects for him. There was no guarantee that Cora's idea of giving Brad the plastic man would work, but she tried it and it helped. Once he began to nap, his afternoon outbursts lessened.

Brad's teacher brought her observations to team meeting, and together the teachers decided that Brad, like many children, missed his parents most at naptime, when he was tired and more vulnerable to feelings of loss.

Here we see how a small intervention can affect the child's total adjustment to child care. This way of thinking uses a **systems approach,** which you will learn more about in Chapter 6.

During the toddler and preschool years, children develop a sense of themselves as unique individuals. They come to realize they are separate from others and begin forming a sense of individual identity, although they express this "identity" in simple ways, such as deciding on favorite colors and animals. With this knowledge, the children begin to experience more complex emotions such as pride, shame, guilt, and jealousy. How adults and other children around them respond contributes to their identity's continuing development as well as their feelings of self-esteem. Figure 3.4 outlines the typical emotional development continuum for children from birth through age six.

Theory of Mind

At age three or four, children are more able to understand others' thinking, as well as their own. They gain an important component of emotional knowledge called

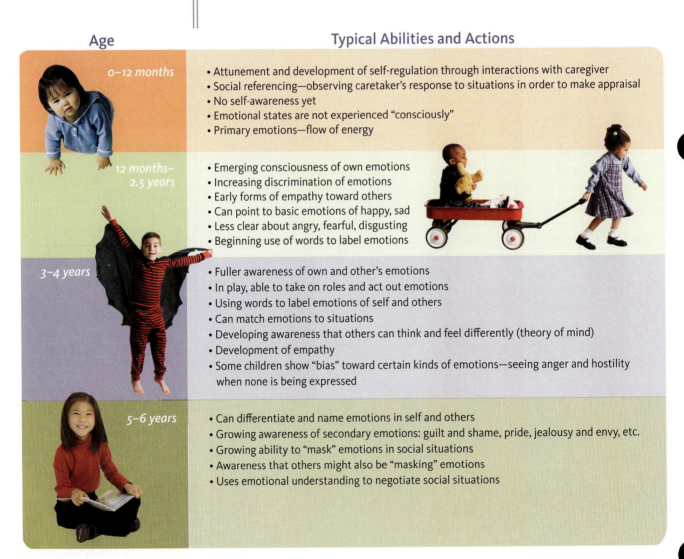

Age	Typical Abilities and Actions
0–12 months	• Attunement and development of self-regulation through interactions with caregiver • Social referencing—observing caretaker's response to situations in order to make appraisal • No self-awareness yet • Emotional states are not experienced "consciously" • Primary emotions—flow of energy
12 months–2.5 years	• Emerging consciousness of own emotions • Increasing discrimination of emotions • Early forms of empathy toward others • Can point to basic emotions of happy, sad • Less clear about angry, fearful, disgusting • Beginning use of words to label emotions
3–4 years	• Fuller awareness of own and other's emotions • In play, able to take on roles and act out emotions • Using words to label emotions of self and others • Can match emotions to situations • Developing awareness that others can think and feel differently (theory of mind) • Development of empathy • Some children show "bias" toward certain kinds of emotions—seeing anger and hostility when none is being expressed
5–6 years	• Can differentiate and name emotions in self and others • Growing awareness of secondary emotions: guilt and shame, pride, jealousy and envy, etc. • Growing ability to "mask" emotions in social situations • Awareness that others might also be "masking" emotions • Uses emotional understanding to negotiate social situations

3.4 *Typical Emotional Development, Birth through Six*
Based on Saarni 1999

	Developmental Precursors to Theory of Mind
AGE	**CHILD'S BEHAVIOR**
birth	Prefers human face and voice to other shapes and sounds
4 months	Looks at faces, smiles
6 months	Can distinguish between different emotional expressions of caretaker
9 months	Looks at a common object together with caretaker—"joint attention"
10 months	Looks to caretaker for emotional response to new experience—"social referencing"
12 months	Points to objects, shows objects, gives objects to caretaker. Knows that actions result from other person's intentions
18–24 months	Engages in pretend play—beginning of symbolic use of objects and actions to represent mental states of others
3 years	Can distinguish physical and mental states, perceptions, and desires in others
4–5 years	Can think about their own mental state and can distinguish their own thoughts and desires from those of others

3.5 *Developmental Precursors to Theory of Mind*
Based on Cole, Cole, and Lightfoot 2005

theory of mind—the ability to think about one's own and other people's thinking (Bjorklund 2005). Many children and adults on the autistic spectrum have difficulty attending to and appreciating what others think and feel because these abilities do not develop naturally for them as they do for other children (Baron-Cohen 1995). Figure 3.5 profiles how children learn the behaviors that lead to the development of theory of mind.

In any social group, people need a theory of mind to anticipate (sometimes making an informed guess about) what others might or might not be thinking and feeling and what might be motivating their behavior. Young children also slowly develop the ability to realize that another person can have *different* thoughts and feelings from their own.

APPLICATIONS TO CLASSROOM PRACTICE

How can teachers and caregivers use knowledge of emotional development?

You have read about some of the foundations of children's emotional development. In this section, we use those ideas to consider what emotionally responsive classrooms look like. We regard attachment relationships as a bona fide aspect of teaching responsibilities and describe some ways classroom adults can use attachment theory to enrich relationships with children.

Throughout infancy, touch continues to be the most primal way we let children know we are there for them. Children, in turn, express their touch preferences to us, and we must attend to their messages! Touch in particular appears to help stimulate or block particular hormones and naturally occurring neurochemicals that influence how we feel, think, and behave. For example, babies who are massaged and held, especially ones born prematurely, gain weight and mature faster than those kept in their incubators with minimal touch (Field et al. 2004).

A few weeks before Brad turned two and Marcia began looking for child care centers for him, she picked up a parenting magazine in the doctor's office and read an

Between ages three and six, children gain an important component of emotional knowledge called theory of mind—the ability to think about one's own and other people's thinking.

What do you know about your own reactions to touch? Which tendencies are inborn and which have familial or cultural roots? For example, does your family always kiss hello or use other forms of greeting? How might (or might not) your own touch tendencies influence your work with young children and their families?

article entitled "Your Spirited Child." The article's recommendations plus her own observations and reflections told her that touch helped Brad calm down and become more organized whenever he was overstimulated. Marcia and her husband chose a center for Brad where these needs would be honored.

Not all children respond to touch the way Brad does. For some children, even a hand on the shoulder is overwhelming and intrusive. To discover what each child needs is part of the challenge of teaching. Observing, talking to parents, and conferring with special education specialists are the best ways to learn about the sensory needs of each child.

Creating **prosocial** and reciprocal relationships—ones in which children get along and are able to negotiate with each other—is a base for all classroom work (Kochanska 1995). As teachers, we also look for strategies to quiet repeated disturbances and outbursts, but these depend on a relational approach. What does a reciprocal relationship look like in an early childhood classroom?

In Yin's second-grade class, an eight-year-old named Rebecca who was repeating the grade had trouble focusing on her work. She went from table to table and struck up conversations. Ms. Bryant asked Rebecca to bring her lunch to the classroom to eat with her on Tuesdays. After their second lunch, Rebecca arrived at the classroom early and asked to help Ms. Bryant set up for the afternoon. Ms. Bryant gave her one task to do at a time, such as putting markers on each table, and pointed out to Rebecca how organized she could be when she had a framework for her activity.

Ms. Bryant successfully created and maintained the trust that propels a child toward relationships and learning.

Researchers' classroom observations show that teachers have more positive interactions with children who are securely attached to them (Goosen and van Ijzendoorn 1990; Howes 1999). Sensitive and caring interactions in the classroom can positively influence relationships lacking in trust (Howes and Ritchie 2002). Children preoccupied with their relationship to their teacher and worried about what the teacher will do next cannot focus on their work or play as well. But even trusting relationships take continual work. Relationships aren't static; each day, our interactions shape and reshape them.

What does responsive care look like in classrooms from the child-parent vantage point? In his first weeks of child care, Brad watched his mother or father wave good-bye every morning from a window of his classroom. They waved even if they were running late. The reliability of the wave became a signal for Brad to start his day. One day when it was raining hard, his mother said, "Brad, it's pouring out! I'm giving you two extra hugs and kisses so I don't stand outside and get wet." Brad could handle the change because Marcia forewarned him and he could rely on her previous consistency. This simple routine is an example of a self-regulatory experience that becomes the bedrock of a child's everyday life in a preschool classroom.

> Children preoccupied with their relationship to their teacher and worried about what the teacher will do next cannot focus on their work or play as well. But even trusting relationships take continual work.

Self-Regulation in Classrooms

Think about what you do to keep yourself going throughout a day at work or in school. As an adult, you already know your inclinations and preferences—when you need to eat and with whom you must control immediate responses. Children

are just acquiring these abilities; they are in the process of becoming themselves and learning about the person they are becoming. One great challenge is functioning simultaneously as an individual and as a contributing member of a group. This includes learning what is expected, how to recognize one's emotions and those of others, and how to communicate so others will respond prosocially. Often, when children hum or talk to themselves about their play or work, they are self-regulating their behaviors through private speech.

Behavioral demands of school

What behavioral demands do young children face as they enter school? Teachers ask them to wait, to delay gratification, and to transition from active physical activities to ones requiring focused attention. Children have to settle disputes when there are too few resources or too many children want the same tool or toy. Eventually, they must do homework, a different kind of school-home transition and adjustment. To meet these demands, children learn to regulate their behavior. Teachers and others can help them internalize these regulatory processes.

This example from Yin's kindergarten class shows how different children respond to sitting for a period of time, and how they monitor their behavior:

> "Crisscross applesauce" were Mrs. Johnson's first words as she gathered the group together for a morning meeting during the first week of school. Yin immediately crossed her legs and looked down to check that her legs and arms were within the square mat on which she sat. Within a few minutes, Ralph, a lanky classmate, was sprawled across the floor, looking off in another direction. "Square check," Mrs. Johnson appealed soon after, followed by a rustle of legs and arms drawn back within each mat. Ralph sat up, but before the group got through a discussion about the weather, he had returned to his more comfortable position.

Understanding how to support children to better self-regulate requires knowing each child well.

Strategies to Develop Focus and Attention in Young Children

Focused engagement helps preschool and prekindergarten children develop stronger and longer attention spans. When play activities and projects are developed around young children's interests, children are motivated and are able to pay attention for longer periods.

• Select and read a story on a topic of particular interest to a child. Such books help children develop focused listening skills and motivate them to expand their attention span. In-depth reading also provides children with opportunities to refine language comprehension skills, exercise visual focus, and build basic knowledge. Increasingly choose longer, more detailed text to further expand the child's attention span.

• Provide unusual combinations of simple play materials to stimulate children to think about old ideas in new ways. They will see, hear, touch, explore, create, and spend longer periods of time engaged in creative thinking and in refining small motor, social, and language abilities as they connect new play schemes to old ones.

• Provide physical and musical games, dress-up, and outdoor play as outlets for children's natural energy. In such activities, children integrate large and small motor skills, develop hand-eye coordination, organize ideas, and practice social and language skills. A young child who gets plenty of exercise is better able to focus attention on other activities. Over the course of an early childhood program, combine increasing periods of mental focus with decreasing periods of large muscle activity to help children become used to mentally focusing for longer periods of time.

• Play quiet background music during art projects and listening games to help children develop the ability to screen out distractions in the environment.

THOUGHT QUESTION As you observe various classes, consider whether you think that children are being asked to sit still for longer than they are developmentally ready to do.

Figure 3.6 offers some strategies to help both you and the children make more out of your time together.

As children learn to self-regulate, they become more reliant on themselves and their peers instead of on the teacher. Understanding how to support children to better self-regulate requires knowing each child well. Consider what happened when Yin asked her second grade teacher, Ms. Bryant, where to find more book response sheets:

Ms. Bryant gave each child two book response sheets and said that anyone who had read more than two books should get more sheets. Yin had read four books but could not remember where Ms. Bryant said the sheets were kept. Yin stewed about it for a day and then garnered all her courage to ask Ms. Bryant where they were. Ms. Bryant said, "Yin, I already told the class where they are kept. Please ask one of your tablemates." Yin was taken aback by Ms. Bryant's response but accepted it. But Yin had used up her nerve for the week and decided it was too hard to ask her tablemates. She later told her mother that she had solved the problem: she wouldn't read any more books!

Yin loves to do things right, but her **executive functions**—the part of the brain that helps us plan and organizes other parts of the brain for various tasks—are still developing. Consequently she couldn't remember and couldn't easily process the information about where the extra sheets were.

In this observation from Harriet Cuffaro, a master teacher guides a painting child, helps him regulate himself through a creative process, and leads him to determine for himself what constitutes a finished product:

> Mitch . . . was busily mixing many colors and energetically placing dabs of the colors in different directions. At one point he announced, "I'm finished." Lois knelt and commented on the various colors, their placement, and the movement in Mitch's painting. She then held up the painting and asked, "Are you finished?" Mitch scanned the painting slowly and carefully and said, "No." . . . Mitch dipped his brush in three colors and . . . placed large dabs of the mixed color on the top right-hand corner of his painting. He looked at his painting and said, "Finished." Lois held it up again and asked, "Are you finished?" Without hesitation, he nodded his head and said, "Yes." Carefully, he lifted the painting from the middle of the sides of the paper so that no paint would drip and took it out to the hall to dry. As he did so, his face and body reflected a sense of accomplishment, of satisfaction and completion. (Cuffaro 1995, 77)

Lois respectfully modeled a relaxed and thoughtful way to approach any endeavor. She communicated that Mitch's work mattered and that he was the master of his creation. Also, she helped Mitch learn to trust and regulate himself in his work. Lois achieved a difficult balance: she avoided under- or overinvolvement in this young child's artistic process.

In addition to teachers and peers, including older children in your class activities can teach children about regulating their behaviors. Opportunities for relationships between children of different ages provide some of the benefits of mixed-age grouping. They promote children's awareness of different ways of being and behaving with various people in a range of situations. When you invite an older group to read to your class, for example, the younger children can picture themselves as one day being able to read as well as the second graders, and they attend to their mentors. The older children, in turn, monitor themselves to be responsible models for the younger children.

Teasing and bullying

Researchers have studied teasing and bullying more often in older elementary, middle, and high school than in early childhood settings, but awareness of the problem is growing in early childhood circles (Gropper and Froschl 2000). **Bullying** is

> repeated, negative acts committed by one or more children against another. These negative acts may be physical or verbal in nature. . . . Implicit in this definition is an imbalance in real or perceived power between the bully and victim. (Limber and Nation 1998)

Children are increasingly aware of the classifications of "bully" and "victim." This is helpful, but how can teachers avoid identifying or stereotyping children in either role, so children can take on other personae (Davies 1998)? See the example of Jahnathan in Chapter 13, in which, over time, a child who bullies is able to adopt a cooperative stance with the thoughtful interventions of his teacher and a group of forgiving classmates.

Intervening early can make a difference. When a child "gets away with" bullying, the implicit message is that it's okay. However a teacher chooses to intervene,

THOUGHT QUESTION Knowing what you already do about self-regulation; executive functions; and Yin's temperament, personality, and abilities, how else might you have handled her question about the book response sheets?

Mitch's teacher, Lois, helped Mitch learn to trust and regulate himself by communicating to him that he was the master of his creation. Lois achieved a difficult balance: she avoided under- or overinvolvement in this young child's artistic process.

everyone agrees that she or he should address both bully and victim and help all children be clear and assertive about their bodies, possessions, and feelings. Children who cannot say what they feel, need, and want may resort to bullying behavior. Children who are bullied can learn to voice their wishes as early as their second year—as soon as they can make a hand motion or say "No!" NAEYC recommends the strategies in Figure 3.7 to encourage clear communication so that children can resist bullying and work out transgressions with each other.

Self-regulation has to do with one's abilities to use selective attention and modulate one's emotions and behaviors. When children develop more internal control, the tone and the mood of the group as a whole is affected. First and foremost, classroom management is about working with children's self-regulatory abilities. They spend more time learning "how to" rather than "don't."

Social and Emotional Development in Classrooms

Social development and emotional development are often discussed in the same breath, but they are not the same. "Social" implies interactions with others, whereas "emotions" are an internal phenomenon that may or may not be expressed in affec-

3.7 *How to Teach Children Assertiveness Skills*
NAEYC 1996

How to Teach Children Assertiveness Skills

- Demonstrate assertive behavior (e.g., saying "No" to another child's unacceptable demands) and contrast aggressive or submissive responses through demonstrations. Let children role-play with puppets or dolls.

- Intervene when interactions seem headed for trouble, and suggest ways for children to compromise or to express their feelings in a productive way.

- Teach children to seek help when confronted by the abuse of power (physical abuse, sexual abuse, or other) by other children or adults.

- Remind children to ignore routine teasing by turning their heads or walking away. Not all provocative behavior must be acknowledged.

- Teach children to ask for things directly and respond directly to each other. Friendly suggestions are taken more readily than bossy demands. Teach children to ask nicely, and to respond appropriately to polite requests.

- After a conflict between children, ask those involved to replay the scene. Show children how to resolve problems firmly and fairly.

- Show children how to tell bullies to stop hurtful acts and to stand up for themselves when they are being treated unfairly.

- Encourage children not to give up objects or territory to bullies (e.g., say, "I'm using this toy now."). Preventing bullies from getting what they want will discourage aggressive behavior.

- Identify acts of aggression, bossiness, or discrimination for children and teach them not to accept them (e.g., say, "Girls are allowed to play that, too.").

- Show children the rewards of personal achievement through standing up for themselves, rather than depending solely on the approval of others.

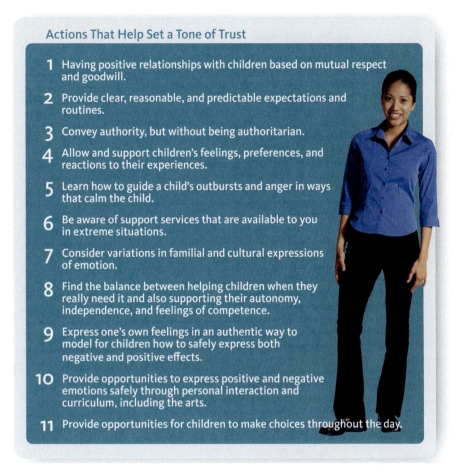

Actions That Help Set a Tone of Trust

1 Having positive relationships with children based on mutual respect and goodwill.

2 Provide clear, reasonable, and predictable expectations and routines.

3 Convey authority, but without being authoritarian.

4 Allow and support children's feelings, preferences, and reactions to their experiences.

5 Learn how to guide a child's outbursts and anger in ways that calm the child.

6 Be aware of support services that are available to you in extreme situations.

7 Consider variations in familial and cultural expressions of emotion.

8 Find the balance between helping children when they really need it and also supporting their autonomy, independence, and feelings of competence.

9 Express one's own feelings in an authentic way to model for children how to safely express both negative and positive effects.

10 Provide opportunities to express positive and negative emotions safely through personal interaction and curriculum, including the arts.

11 Provide opportunities for children to make choices throughout the day.

3.8 *Actions That Help Set a Tone of Trust*
Adapted from Project New Beginnings 2000

tive or interactive terms. When teachers model social behaviors, they set a tone of trust (Figure 3.8) that helps to create an environment in which children can understand their feelings and relate better to each other.

Understanding emotions

A key aspect of an early childhood teacher's job is to help young children become aware of their emotions, identify them, and learn how to express them prosocially. Children are still in the midst of understanding themselves, how they feel, and what they can do about those feelings.

The day in school is a long one for most young children, and proximity to many other people, along with hard work and play, can bring emotions closer to the surface. Those struggles will differ depending, not only on the children, their families, their ages, and even the time of day, but also on the ways the cultures represented in your classroom express and modulate

3.9 *Guidance for Self-regulation*

Child is in a situation that provokes an emotional response.

Teacher helps the child become aware of emotions, identify them, and express them prosocially.

Child begins to internalize new ways of responding to situations.

emotions. You face the challenge of intuiting how children feel and recognizing different modes of expression, as did the student teacher at Brad's preschool:

> Brad sat at lunch on his fourth day of preschool. He was finished eating, although some food remained on his plate. "Yah, yah, yah," he chanted loudly. Some adults might have found the sound annoying, but Shannon, the student teacher at his table, turned to him, and said, "It sounds as if you've enjoyed your lunch, Brad. Is that true?" Brad lowered his chin and peered out at Shannon as a small smile crossed his face.

We have two words of caution, however. One is that adults can get a child's emotion wrong, and we must be wary of assuming we know what a child is thinking or feeling. We cannot be sure, although, over time, we can get to know individual children and an age group well enough to make solid hunches. Second, children do need outlets to *resist* adult power (Schultz 2005), and we have to consider what forms of resistance we can tolerate and what forms are too dangerous to allow. In one preschool backyard, as drizzle turned to rain, Sarah, the teacher, called the children back to the classroom. Once inside, the children protested. They were having so much fun! They chanted: "We love rain! We love rain!" Sarah then led them back outside in a quick double circle around the yard. They returned to class, laughing, and dried each other off with towels. While they waited for lunch, the children drew pictures of themselves running in the rain.

THOUGHT QUESTION Brad seemed to appreciate that a teacher tried to interpret his noises instead of telling him to stop. What did Shannon need to know to respond this way instead of telling Brad to be quiet or just directing him to go scrape his plate?

> Children need outlets to *resist* adult power. We have to consider what forms of resistance we can tolerate and what forms are too dangerous to allow.

Conflict resolution: Rupture and repair

A basic human skill is the ability to repair ruptures in relationships. Research on infant-parent interactions demonstrates that most of them do not go smoothly; it is the *repairing* of the mismatches that develops the relationship (Tronick and Gianino 1986). Different interventions teach children of various ages and stages to solve problems. Two- and three-year-olds, for example, have strong ideas about what they want and object to infringements on their territory or appropriations of what they believe are their objects. Through modeling and coaching, they learn to face each other and work it out.

> The first time Brad's group of threes went outside, Brad's teacher, Cora, told him to hold his partner's hand. His response was clear: "No!" and he wriggled away from his classmate, Cleo. Cora moved them up to the front of the line. She bent down, made eye contact, and told Brad and Cleo together that having a partner and holding hands was necessary to keep children safe outside. She offered a compromise, suggesting that Brad hold onto her with one hand and onto Cleo with the other. When Brad began to cry, she gave him a hug and said, "I bet it is hard to get used to all the new rules here. Is there something you can bring with you that will make you feel better?" Brad looked around and took a ball of play dough he had just made, and wiped his eyes with his jacket sleeve. "Let's go," said Cora, "I want to learn what you like to do at the park."

Four-year-olds can get mad at and "make up" with their "best friend" more than once a day. Emotions can run high because so much of the work of this age is about making and continuing social connections. Folktales, along with books about friends and emotions of all kind, help children this age acquire other models besides their teacher. And preschoolers often can negotiate solutions to problems with each other. For example:

> In the yard, David and Jonathan tugged at the wagon handle. Their teacher approached and asked what the problem was. "I had it first," screamed Jonathan. "No, I did," yelled David, "and I want it!" "Please let me hold the wagon handle while we talk about this," said their teacher. "Now, please tell me what happened." They did, and she responded, "From what I hear, you both want the wagon. How can you solve that problem?" "I know!" Jonathan exclaimed, "David can use the wagon, and then I can use it after him." David looked puzzled. "No," he protested, "Let's use it together," and off they went.

All children don't solve disagreements this easily. These two played together often and had practice negotiating. Yet most children learn to listen to each other and think of solutions when a teacher listens to them with respect. Figure 3.10 offers guidance for helping children resolve conflicts.

Verbal and nonverbal language

How will you address your students? Will you call them together on the rug with "Children!" or "Class" or "Friends"? Each word has implications. Are all the children truly friends? Or is using the word a euphemism? Or is it something for them to aspire to? Does "class" sound too formal for four-year olds? The "Boys and Girls" group name is problematic for many teachers because it calls unnecessary attention to gender difference multiple times a day. All of a sudden, it doesn't seem so easy to choose, does it? Yet choose you will, and we hope that you will think about your choice and adopt a term that has meaning for you and the children.

A Guide to Steps in Conflict Resolution

1. Approach calmly, stopping any hurtful actions.
2. Acknowledge children's feelings.
3. Gather information.
4. Restate the problem.
5. Ask for ideas for solutions and choose one together.
6. Be prepared to give follow-up support.

3.10 *A Guide to Steps in Conflict Resolution*
From http://www.highscope.org/Content.asp?ContentId=284

At times, some teachers use soft and cozy words, but is "Honey" an endearment that communicates love and caring or a word that dismisses children and makes them anonymous? Yin heard Ms. Bryant call Patricia "Honey" and wondered why Ms. Bryant hadn't ever called *her* "Honey."

When communicating an important message to a young child:

- Get down to the child's level.
- Use a culturally friendly approach (which may or may not include eye contact).
- Use concrete language that communicates a simple message.
- Ask if the child has understood, especially if you have explained the consequences of certain actions.

Sometimes nonverbal communication works best. Even facial expressions—a look, a wink, an exaggerated sad face—can send a child your message before greater intervention is necessary.

Becoming part of a group

If you reflect on your own group memberships as an adult and the challenges they bring, you may understand why a child's group experiences can be overwhelming.

Whole-group times can be difficult for some young children. They require children to focus their attention on something often not of their own choosing and to remain still in a small space.

Those experiences, however, lay the foundation for all the group experiences in that child's future.

How a teacher structures group time contributes to that foundation. First, try to know the children well and apply developmental principles to what you observe. Second, think in advance about the rules in your classroom, who makes them, and when and how they are made. Third, think about all the individuals who make up the group. How can you anticipate a child's outbursts so that an adult can shadow the child's movements over a morning? Fourth, consider how you will help children create community.

Whole-group times can be difficult for some young children. They require children to focus their attention on something often not of their own choosing and to remain relatively still in a small space. For young threes, meeting can be a challenge; for example, Leslie creeps away from the circle, and Max pinches Josie's arm. The younger the child, the shorter you may want to make the circle time, or meeting; but some older children also have difficulty with long meetings. Teachers sometimes send a disruptive child away from the meeting space, but "time-out" from the group doesn't help the child learn how to manage *in* the group. The problem may not lie with the child but with the meeting. Decide whether a meeting is the best place for that content or if children could learn it another way.

Electronic Screens: A Relationship?

We have already noted that human beings are wired to be social. What does that mean for generations also connected electronically? Here we will consider the effects of television on young children. The term *electronic screen* refers, not only to television and computers, but also to electronic toy screens. (See Chapter 12 for ideas on how to use computers with young children in thoughtful ways.)

Television

Preschool children have been watching television for decades, and the earliest programs—*Captain Kangaroo, Sesame Street, Mr. Rogers' Neighborhood*—were created for children older than two years (Anderson and Tempek 2005). Since the mid-1990s, however, producers of children's videos and television series have directed programs specifically to the under-two-year-old audience; by the turn of the century, these programs were already mainstream, and thus open to study by child development experts. Research in this area is relatively new, so while findings are not well established, they are important for educators to know about so that teachers can serve as an informed resource for families.

When people leave the television on in the background of homes, young children are exposed to many more hours of total television viewing than their families and caregivers may be aware. At least some of the content of this background television is aimed at older audiences and is often unsuitable for children.

Because television is ubiquitous for most children in life outside of care and education and because of the research findings we discuss next, we strongly advise against its use in infant/toddler programs. For preschoolers, a short video clip may enrich the curriculum, or an animation of a tale you have read them may enhance their experience of the book. For early-elementary-school-age children, too, video

THOUGHT QUESTION The mother of a seven-month-old in your infant/toddler group is about to take her first trip away from her son. Anxiously, she asks if you think she should make a video of herself that the family could play to remind the boy of her. You don't think the baby will process his mother's image on the screen the way an older child or adult would. How would you respond to this mother, and why?

sequences may relate to an area of study and convey information children cannot experience any other way. Nonetheless, television should be a rare occurrence in school.

The neuroscience of young brains and electronic screens

In 1999, the American Academy of Pediatrics recommended that children younger than two not be exposed to television because programmed viewing can never take the place of real interactions with people and things. Also, some evidence indicates that children younger than eighteen months cannot make sense of what are, in effect, moving representational images; that is, the people and objects represented are not real but *represent* living people and real things (Anderson and Tempek 2005).

What about preschool children? Television aimed at them tends to be more developmentally appropriate, because children over two *can* make some representational meaning from screen images. *Sesame Street* is a prime example of such programming: for more than 30 years it has helped children learn letters and concepts that prepare them for school. A number of other programs that serve as "teacher" have joined the array of children's programming (Singer and Singer 2005). Yet as adults we need to remember that even preschoolers' grasp on reality is still fluid.

Long hours of viewing or using television to get to sleep (Figure 3.12) are not good for children. More than an hour a day reduces a child's availability for exercise, reading books, or interactive social contact with peers and family members. And at night, children need to learn how to regulate themselves without relying on television to get to sleep.

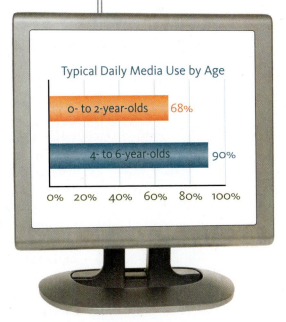

3.11 *Children's Screen Media Use, by Age*
From Rideout, Vandewater, and Wartella 2003

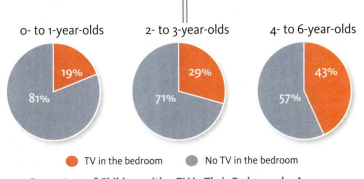

3.12 *Percentage of Children with a TV in Their Bedroom, by Age*
From Rideout, Vandewater, and Wartella 2003

Effects of electronic screens in the classroom

Television viewing at home has multiple effects on young children while they are in school. In an experimental study done in a classroom setting, Dorothy and Jerome Singer (2005) found that children who viewed television during an in-class session exhibited less imaginative play immediately afterward. Children who did not have a television session *and* had a supportive adult present played with greater imaginative content.

The Singer study provides evidence of what teachers of young children have known for years: characters from television and video find their way into children's play in often-inflexible ways that may close off richer intellectual and imaginative experiences. Children who watch many programs usually reintroduce them as (often stereotypic) content for use on the playground and during any free playtime. Characters from television allow some of these children to build friendships based on common television interests that have the *potential* to move in creative directions, but they are not as open-ended as characters children invent in their play.

THOUGHT QUESTION When television characters are entrenched in children's play, what can teachers do to help them elaborate their play in creative and open-ended ways?

DIFFICULT EXPERIENCES AND CHALLENGING CONVERSATIONS

How can teachers help children with difficult experiences?

When illness, death, divorce, or other issues arise in the early childhood classroom, be honest and clear with children, and allow them an opportunity to express themselves. Sometimes, however, the most difficult conversations tend to occur when you least expect them. To prepare, do some thinking well in advance about a whole range of difficult topics and how you might handle discussions about them when children bring them up. You also can bring up these topics before children do. These two ways of proceeding represent different approaches; you need to decide which is best for a particular situation.

Teachers are not therapists, and school is not therapy. Nevertheless, moments occur when school can and should be therapeutic. It is also crucial to know when you should ask for help from a school mental health consultant or arrange for someone to function in that role. Likewise, when children reveal new behaviors that show sadness or anger or become withdrawn, bring in others (including parents, of course) to determine the behaviors' origins.

Illness and Death

Because preschoolers' thinking is still tied to their perceptions, their understanding of death can be transient. They grasp aspects of death at some moments but come up with comments that contradict that knowledge at other times.

Because young children often bring things back to themselves, they may feel responsible for, or guilty about, a death. Reassure them that illness and death do not occur because of something they did. But because children's **"magical thinking"**— that is, their own often unrealistic perceptions of causality—often trump logical explanations, convincing them can be harder than it sounds. Figure 3.13 lists some general guidelines for communicating at times when children experience death.

Just because children aren't talking about illness or death doesn't mean they aren't thinking about it. A child may ask a question days, weeks, or even months later, at home or in school. The important message to convey is that illness and death are subjects that we can talk about. For a letter to parents containing a transcript of one preschool group's discussion after Oreo, their pet rabbit, died, see Figure 3.14.

When a child or a child's parent experiences serious illness or dies, use the same approach of honest delivery of the facts. When a child is ill, communicate with the child and the family about classroom activities. Letters and pictures going back and forth to a sick child maintain the child's prior identity as a healthy and active member of a community. With the family's permission, teachers can visit a child in the hospital to keep the classroom-family connection alive during a stressful period. Filter your understanding about the serious illness or death of a parent directly through the family, with care and attention paid to their wishes. Once again, your clarity and relative comfort with the topic make a huge difference in how children hear this kind of information and the way they think about it from that point onward.

Communicating with Children about Death

- Provide clear and concrete information about death (see Figure 3.14).

- Never use words such as "sleep" or "sick" to refer to the concept of death.

- Give children short responses to their questions. Allow children to slowly process information about death, giving them time and space to formulate their own inquiries.

- Let children know that it is okay to cry and feel sadness and anger about death. Avoid hiding your sadness or telling children, "Don't cry. You are okay."

- Reassure children that they are safe and cared for. For example, you might say, "Usually doctors are able to make you better when you get hurt."

- Have a goodbye or memorial ceremony.

- Show children ways to help cope with the loss. For example, you can make a book about the animal or person with photographs and writing about the things he or she enjoyed doing.

- Provide children with materials to play out their interpretations and feelings about death, such as doctor's kits, baby dolls, puppets, paper and crayons, and vehicles.

- Relate death to the life cycle. Do planting with children, and study the process of the plants: beginning, middle, and end of life.

Divorce

As early as the second year of life, children are aware they are a part of a family unit. Parents' destructive relationships, separations, or divorce disrupt a child's identity as part of a family and threaten the secure base that the family represents to the child (Lieberman 1993). Children's worlds crash in on them, and they are at risk of becoming worried, scared, and/or overwhelmed. Young children can feel responsible for the break and can **regress,** going back to earlier behaviors or seeming to lose newly acquired ones, be they simple activities of daily living or loss of language. School-age children tend to show their sadness and grief, and wish their parents would reunite. They seem less confused by the situation itself than by expectations of loyalty to one or the other parent (Wallerstein and Kelly 1996). These are difficult pressures for a child to live with. Demonstrating support to families as well as to their children helps everyone feel less judged.

Teachers are a secondary secure base for children. In a family curriculum, teachers can emphasize that there are many kinds of families and that although everyone does not always get along, we can do our best to communicate and be fair. Teachers can understand, too, that the anxiety or aggression or depression they see may be a child's reaction to the loss of the family as she knew it. Dismissing the effects of any family loss is not fair to children, regardless of how many children in your group come from divorced homes.

Just because children aren't talking about illness or death doesn't mean they aren't thinking about it. The important message to convey is that illness and death are subjects that can be discussed.

Dear Families,

This morning we shared some sad news with the threes and fours in the Purple Room: Oreo, our rabbit, died yesterday afternoon. In the morning, Emily arrived and noticed that Oreo did not greet her with his usual enthusiasm. When she investigated further, she noticed that his eye looked cloudy. Later in the afternoon he passed away. Judi took Oreo to the veterinarian who buried Oreo in a special place where he buries animals. During circle time, we shared the news with the children. Here is how the conversation went and how we responded:

> *Teacher: Oreo has died and his body has stopped working, medicine will not work anymore.*
> *Evan: Oh man, how about some medicine?*
> *Henry: Is he in his cage?*
> *Teacher: No.*
> *Henry: Maybe we should get a new Oreo.*
> *Karen: Maybe we should get a parrot.*

We talked about the caterpillars and watching them change into butterflies. The children asked whether we could put them into Oreo's cage.

> *Aviva: Where is Oreo get digged?*
> *Teacher: The veterinarian put him in a box and then buried him in the ground in the special place.*
> *Jim: Why is it sad news?*
> *Teacher: It means that we will not be able to see Oreo any more, feed him, play with him or pet him. I will miss him.*
> *Aviva: That means we won't have the job to feed Oreo. Keeping the cage would remind us of Oreo, we could hug it.*
> *Teacher: We can also print out some pictures of Oreo and hang them up in the classroom. Children can also draw pictures, and we can hang them up in the classroom.*
> *Aviva: Can we go to the veterinarian and see Oreo?*
> *Teacher: The veterinarian is near my house and that would be too far a trip for us.*
> *Karen: Let's bring pictures of Oreo to the vet.*
> *Marcia: Can I go see his cage?*

We brought the cage over to the rug so that all the children could look inside.

> *Seth: Hey, Oreo's not in there.*
> *Jim: Tabitha died too.*
> *Teacher: I remember when your cat died, that was a sad time for your family.*
> *Sam (pointing to Oreo's house): He used to sleep in that house.*
> *Henry: Where's Oreo? Poor Oreo.*
> *Sam: I'm sad I'm not going to see him anymore.*
> *Aviva: Why did he die? Did he eat something that made him sick?*
> *Teacher: We don't know why Oreo got sick or why he died.*
> *Aviva: Maybe he rubbed his eye too much.*
> *Teacher: Animals and people don't die from rubbing their eyes.*
> *Aviva: That's good because I rub my eyes too much sometimes.*
> *Jim: I miss feeding Oreo the green part of the strawberries.*
> *Aviva: At least it wasn't one of us.*
> *Teacher: While it is sad that Oreo died because we won't get to play with him anymore, it is good to know that the children and teachers are safe and okay.*

At the end of circle time, we decided that next week we would decide on a new job for the job chart and that we would hang the old job symbol "Feed the Pet" on the wall next to the pictures of Oreo. The children asked if we could leave the cage up for while, so we will. We will also continue to address the children's questions, concerns, and feelings about being sad or missing Oreo as they arise.

Talking about death, separation, and saying goodbye with young chidlren is often hard and can bring up powerful emotions for adults. Please let us know if you have any questions or concerns. We want to talk about these issues with families. We would also love to know what the children are asking or saying at home about Oreo. Thanks, Purple Room Teachers.

3.14 *A Discussion about Death*
Permission granted by Judith Gentry, Children's Programs, Bank Street College of Education, New York

SUMMARY

This chapter examined why our experiences, emotions, and relationships are at the core of early childhood practice.

EARLY EXPERIENCE
How does children's early experience contribute to who they become?
Children's early experience works hand in hand with their genetic makeup to shape them. Yin's and Brad's stories and neuroscientific findings illustrate how early experiences, especially relationships with others, can set the central nervous systems and brains of young children on a good path for development.

ATTACHMENT, RELATIONSHIPS, AND EXPERIENCE
Why is attachment important, and how do teachers and caregivers support it?
We are born ready to engage with our loved ones, and we immediately, too, have raw emotions that our special people help us modulate. Over time, these attachments to special individuals—family members and caregivers/teachers—are what help young children find meaning in their experiences and learn to regulate their emotions and behaviors as they grow and develop.

EMOTIONS AND SELF-REGULATION
What contributes to children's developing emotions and ability to self-regulate?
From the beginning of life, a complex interplay helps the baby move into the social world of family and community. Babies and their caregivers share feelings and experiences, and gradually children come to recognize and even name their own emotions and those of others. The ability to self-regulate starts in the womb and develops throughout the early childhood years as babies settle in to their own routines and toddlers and older children wrestle with impulse control. Children's temperaments and growing cognitive abilities, along with cultural and classroom practices, contribute to their ability to manage their emotions and regulate themselves. Developing theory of mind enables children to put themselves in someone else's shoes and distinguish someone else's thoughts from their own.

APPLICATIONS TO CLASSROOM PRACTICE
How can teachers and caregivers use knowledge of emotional development?
Adults can provide children with experiences that guide them toward becoming part of communities in healthy and open ways that excite them about learning with others. They can behave responsively toward children, teaching them about prosocial and reciprocal relationships. Classrooms pose challenges as children work together, follow rules, and solve problems with each other. How we are with children and families every day and over time makes a difference. Using our most human selves makes it easier to be a teacher who does make a difference.

DIFFICULT EXPERIENCES AND CHALLENGING CONVERSATIONS
How can teachers help children with difficult experiences?
When illness, death, divorce, or some other difficult experience occurs, it usually surfaces in the classroom sooner or later. Children benefit from teachers' honesty, clarity, and willingness to face the situation. Teachers who are knowledgeable about the children with whom they work may anticipate, for example, that children might feel responsible for their parents' separation. They listen closely to check what children understand and how they are interpreting events.

Your clarity and relative comfort with the topic make a huge difference in how children hear this kind of information and the way they think about it from that point onward.

FURTHER ACTIVITIES

1. *Part A:* Write a three- to four-page paper describing the role of self-regulation in your early life, in your family of origin. Think about the routines around sleeping, eating, physical movement, and activity level. What were the contributions of your family, culture(s), and community to those routines? What were your own temperamental contributions?

   Part B: Write another page in which you respond to the following questions: As a teacher, what is the value of looking at your own self-regulatory processes? What are the implications of understanding your own patterns of temperament and self-regulation for your work with children and families? How might some of your patterns of self-regulation help or hinder your development as a teacher? (**NAEYC Standard 1: Promoting Child Development and Learning**)

2. Observe group time at two centers or schools. Take careful notes at each school, paying special attention to the interactions between the adults and children. Whenever possible, capture language verbatim. Read and reread your notes to find all the similarities and differences in the ways in which adults interacted with the children. Chart the similarities and differences. In a page or two, discuss the merits of what you observed in each place, what you might do differently, and why. (**NAEYC Standard 3: Observing, Documenting, and Assessing to Support Young Children and Families**)

3. In a short paper, describe an incidence of bullying you have seen, in which you were involved, or about which you have heard or read. Using the Internet, journals, and books, research bullying. Discuss the incident you described with reference to what you learned from your research. Conclude with an explanation of how you would develop a relationship with a child in your group who bullied another child and with the victim of the bullying. (**NAEYC Standard 4: Using Developmentally Effective Approaches to Connect with Children and Families**)

CHAPTER FOUR

Children Understanding the World through Play

Play is the answer to the question, how does anything new ever come about?

Jean Piaget

Play serves many purposes in a child's development, and, as Jean Piaget suggests, invention is one of them. Play helps children figure out the physical and social worlds, as well as how to express and manage their feelings.

Here, we examine how children learn and develop through play and consider the ways children of different ages play. We look at play's characteristics and at how some theorists have thought about play. Finally, we consider play in relation to the individual, classrooms, and the larger society. We begin with a story of two four-year-olds at their local playground.

Ana comes to this playground every day after school. Michael doesn't go to school yet. His elderly aunt, who is caring for him while his parents are deployed abroad in the National Guard, has brought him.

Ana uses a stick to draw a circle around her sand pile. She fashions the pile into a mountain with a pointy top and sticks a leaf into the top. "That's my flag!" she says proudly. Michael has watched Ana with interest. "Can I play?" he asks. "I have a helicopter." He shows Ana a small plastic helicopter. "Okay," she agrees hesitantly. Michael flies his helicopter over Ana's mountain. "Don't knock it down," she warns. "I won't," he assures her. "This is a rescue helicopter. It comes to take you to a different country." Ana shakes her head. "They don't want to go," she says. She points to pebbles implanted in the sand on the side of the mountain. "My people don't want to."

"My people do," says Michael. "See?" He grabs some pebbles from a path beside the sandbox. He carefully puts them on Ana's mountain near the flag. "The helicopter can spot them if they stand right there. Get on! Get on! Hurry up!" he commands the pebbles. "The bad guys might come! Go home to find the babies!"

Ana watches Michael put his pebbles into the window of the helicopter. They fit in, but many fall out again through the window on the other side. "Put your hand like this," she says, indicating he should cover the other window with his palm. He does and loads the people on board. "Good," Ana says with satisfaction. "Now go get the babies." She looks around. "There!" she says, pointing to some sticks. "Those are the babies. Mama! Mama!" Michael lands the helicopter near the sticks, and the rescued parents have a reunion with their babies.

THOUGHT QUESTION How does Ana's play differ from Michael's? How is it similar? What enables them to play together? Think of two children you know who are different from each other in some important way. How does their play differ? How is it similar?

THE INTEGRATIVE ROLE OF PLAY

How does play enable children to make sense of their experiences?

To a casual observer, there may be nothing remarkable about these two children "just playing." But to an early childhood professional, the children are using play to make sense of their world. Open-ended, imaginative play, such as the scenario Ana and Michael created, allows children to meaningfully **integrate** (or bring together) and master their experiences. They use their imaginations, communicate meaning to themselves and others, actually transform their thinking, and solve problems.

Imagination

To play **symbolically,** children have to go beyond the obvious attributes and qualities of the available playthings. They have to *imagine* attributes and qualities so that the plaything can represent something more, and often something different. Both Ana and Michael imagined the pebbles were people. Imagination allowed both children to transcend the limitations of the available items (leaves and pebbles) and use found objects in a sophisticated way.

Strangers when their play began, the two children became playmates by the scenario's end. Their imaginations led them to common ground. Each child's developmental issues and life-experience concerns motivated his or her play. The invitation to imagine the world that the other child created expanded Ana and Michael's **conceptual parameters**—that is, it pushed the boundaries of their thinking—and enriched their play.

Communication of Meaning

Neither child could have articulated the underlying issues motivating their emergent **play themes** (the main ideas they developed as they played). Play allowed them to communicate complex ideas and concerns that came from their perceptions, life experiences, and developmental preoccupations. Each invented **play symbols** (ways to make one thing stand for another) as the play went on. For example, a leaf symbolized a flag, a symbol holding meaning for both children. Therefore, play became a shared language, and communication was fluent.

Ana and Michael were attracted to the play for different reasons. Ana loved to discover things and own them and often had a hard time sharing objects at school. Defining and marking her territory with a flag that identified her mountain made her feel empowered. Once, stormy weather made Ana's parents late picking her up at school. Now, she often worries that they will forget to come altogether. That was why she didn't like the idea of sending her people far away to another country in Michael's helicopter.

However, Michael's parents *were* far away, and he needed to express his fears and fight his feeling of helplessness. He struggled to remain identified with them while also worrying about their safety. He saw Ana's flag as a safety zone marker, where his make-believe parents could rescue others from bad guys or be rescued themselves. He used his helicopter to identify with his parents' strength and courage. He expanded Ana's scenario to facilitate a story theme ending with the reunion of endangered parents and their children. Although Ana's parents were safe at home, she loved the idea of airlifting missing parents to their children because it gave her a way to address her fears of being separated from her parents.

Transformation of Thought

Theories about play can give you insight into children's play. Jean Piaget, for example, wrote extensively about, and spent much of his professional life observing, young children at play. He believed the appearance of symbolic play in young children signified "the transition from representation in action to internal representation or thought" (Piaget and Inhelder 1972, 57). Referring to play as the "language of childhood," Piaget argued that in order to *think* things through, children needed to *play* things through, just as an adult might talk something through in order to sort it out. In this way, play both facilitates and transforms the young child's thought processes.

Lev Vygotsky, a Russian developmental theorist who believed in play's importance to the developmental process, thought that make-believe play leads development in the direction of **abstract thinking,** that is, thinking independent of a child's

> To play symbolically, children have to go beyond the obvious attributes and qualities of the available playthings. They have to *imagine* attributes and qualities so that the plaything can represent something more, and often something different.

Pretend play helps young children think before they act and, ultimately, leads them in the direction of abstract thinking.

here-and-now experience (Vygotsky 1986). Jan Drucker (1994) suggests that play helps young children begin to think before they act, instead of acting solely on impulse.

When Ana and Michael played in the sandbox, they introduced play symbols that went beyond Ana's initially less-elaborate theme and brought the play to a new level. As the children played out the new themes, they were increasingly invested in ideas of safety, rescue, and reunion. They were drawn to one another, too, and were thus unlikely to behave impulsively, as children that age tend to do—for example, throwing or eating sand—because their play themes were so important to them. Their play transformed their thinking and enabled them to elaborate and deepen their ideas.

Problem Solving

When they play, children solve problems and experience themselves as competent, masterful, and able to discover and invent solutions to challenges. In Ana and Michael's play, Ana solved the problem of defining her territory by drawing a circle around it. She helped Michael avoid losing his pebbles by showing him how to hold his helicopter when loading it, a strategy she discovered playing at her school. Michael worked on his feelings of powerlessness about his parents' safety with his symbolic helicopter rescue mission. Although Michael could not change the events that took his parents away and placed them in danger, through play he became a powerful figure who could bring children and parents together.

Caroline Pratt, Lucy Sprague Mitchell, and Harriet Johnson, founders of the developmental-interaction approach at Bank Street, also believed that children use play to solve problems as well as to express themselves (Franklin 2000). With this in mind, they sought materials children could use in many ways and that provided a range of problems for them to solve. Through group projects and cooperative work on such problems, children joined together to inquire and investigate. Other early childhood educational approaches, including Project High/Scope and Reggio Emilia (see Chapter 7), also value play as a problem-solving medium.

PLAY IN THE LIVES OF CHILDREN

How do children of different ages play?

From the very beginning of life, children explore the world through play. Infants and toddlers use their senses and movements. For preschoolers, play is their arena to construct knowledge, develop intellectual abilities, build social skills, and begin to understand and integrate emotions that the world around them evokes. In the primary grades, play includes more games with rules, dramatic enactment of stories children read or write themselves, and scientific experimentation. Thus, throughout the early years, play is a route to learning.

The Roots of Play

Infants and toddlers must be able to trust their environment in order to have the freedom to explore it through play.

For infants and toddlers, play develops out of their sensory-motor explorations of the environment and is nurtured, protected, and given life within the interaction of **primary attachment relationships,** children's most important personal connections. For infants or toddlers to explore, they must experience their environment as safe, well protected, and allowing for freedom of expression. That is, they must be able to *trust* the environment in order to have the freedom to explore it.

PART 1   An Introduction to Early Childhood

Infants receive sensory feedback from playing with toys and other objects. They mouth toys, bang them, wave them around, watch them move, and shake them. They delight in these sensory explorations and become increasingly motivated to use their developing motor skills to impact their environment. Babies love to roll through a room of soft blocks, push musical toys to make them sing, and punch buttons to cause a hidden person or animal to jump up. As toddlers, using new motor skills that expand their access to the environment, their explorations become more elaborate. They stimulate and challenge their developing brains as they discover the world anew.

Many parent-child play routines in infancy are highly interactive and reciprocal. Babies make sounds their parents repeat. Parents make sounds their babies repeat. Children and parents with secure relationships typically build on each other's actions and sounds to create an early play dialogue. This dialogue invites the baby to imitate **affects** (expressions of feeling, observable signs of emotion), sounds, and motions coming from the parent and invites the parent to imitate affects, sounds, and motions coming from the baby. Between twelve and twenty-four months, a toddler's play begins to include the imitation of actual **motoric routines,** that is, a series of familiar actions. For example, he may hold a cup as if drinking or put a spoon to his mouth as if eating. By copying what he has seen, he shows that he "knows about" eating and drinking and is not frustrated that no food or drink is actually present. These **imitative play schemes** serve as a bridge from physical play that provides actual sensory gratification to play that creates satisfaction through symbols.

Play in the Preschool Years

Three- to five-year-olds want to create play symbols and engage with other children in play. Thus play becomes a **social motivator:** it stimulates children to interact and brings them into a social world that requires them to negotiate, tolerate frustration, and cooperate—all brand-new skills in the early years.

The quality of play in the preschool years is distinctive from toddlers' play. These older children can go beyond imitating familiar motor routines to create play symbols that hold personal meaning for them. They can also engage in dramatic play with other children and create play themes meaningful to all of them. Their spontaneous play contains:

- fantasy- as well as reality-based scenarios,
- complex verbal dialogues as well as play with agreed-upon wordless actions, and
- a cast of many children or a sole player.

By playing with toys, enacting scenarios, or constructing a miniature world of their own design, young children have experiences that answer many questions, including ones with a scientific focus, such as: "How much sand do I need to fill this bucket?" "What if I pour water into my castle's dungeon?" "How can I make a bridge over the moat?" Play gives children the experiential building blocks to generate questions and to discover answers at their developmental level.

Play also offers young children a way to make sense of and integrate confusing and overwhelming emotional experiences. Imagine children on the way to school who see firefighters

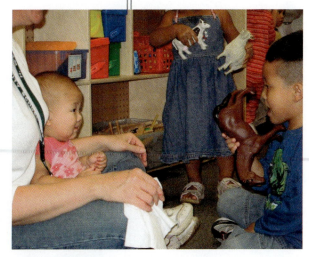

Children of different ages find ways to connect through play.

School-age children need outdoor play just as younger children do.

THOUGHT QUESTION Imagine that your first grade is involved in a half-year-long study of fruit and vegetable markets. How could children's play be woven into the market curriculum?

The children built and operated a market with tags for every job, including for the manager whom you see here.

battling a blaze and hear the cries of frightened people. In class, they can play out this terrifying scenario to assimilate that experience and feel less threatened by it. They can also use play to help resolve lingering developmental issues. The kindergarten child afraid of the dark can make-believe he has superpowers at night and can protect sleeping children.

When young children enter a program, they bring along their motivation to play and their emerging social, emotional, and cognitive capacities for constructive and dramatic play. To be a growth-promoting place, the classroom must meet children's need for the kind of play that organizes their experiences and social interactions.

Play in the Primary Grades

Children in the primary grades use play to structure interactions with one another. They are also concerned about rules of play that they experience as fair, although initially they struggle with the limitations rules impose. Competition becomes a motivating force, and more structured, rule-bound games (such as kickball, soccer, tag, and hopscotch) gain popularity, as do competitive computer and video games and board games (such as checkers, chess, and Monopoly). These games challenge children to improve their skills and to tolerate losing. They also have the chance to enjoy winning and feeling masterful. Children's competence at outdoor recess games may predict their social competence and general adjustment to school in the early grades (Pellegrini and Galda 2001). Such outdoor play also has been found to improve the primary-school child's attention to academic tasks that follow the recess period (Pellegrini and Holmes 2006).

But children in the primary grades still enjoy creative and symbolic play. The school's performing and language arts curricula, as well as extracurricular activities (such as drama club), are their main opportunities for such play. When a teacher integrates drama

with literacy and social studies curricula, children imagine life in other times and places, activities that support their ongoing interest in trying out other identities. Creative construction as part of art, woodshop, and science gives them valuable ways to keep using play as a vehicle for learning and experimenting.

Play can enter the elementary school in another, perhaps unexpected, way. If children understand and engage with language, mathematical concepts, or social or scientific issues, they can play with ideas, just as scholars and professionals do. This kind of play requires an "intellectual emancipation" (Featherstone 2000, 4), the freedom to mess about with ideas and go beyond learning only what the teacher has planned. As with other kinds of play, children who play with ideas create goals and rules for themselves and invite others to play with them. A playful approach leads to submersion in a subject, with children more likely to own the content and invent new ways of thinking about it.

QUALITIES OF PLAY

What makes it play?

What makes play *play*? For one thing, play is fun, and children do it naturally. Play also possesses qualities essential to children's intellectual, emotional, and social development. When educators know what to look for, they can recognize the inherent growth-promoting qualities of spontaneous play and discuss it with colleagues and children's families.

Intrinsic Motivation

Play is **intrinsically motivating** for young children—the urge to play comes from within the child. Play offers opportunities for pleasure, self-expression, and mastery of developmental issues and day-to-day experience. Children play because they want to, not for any external rewards. For them, play *is* the reward.

Lilian Katz (1985) helps us understand the role of intrinsic motivation in learning. She found that when external rewards were the only motivation for learning, the children were less eager to take on new challenges than were those whose early educational experiences were child centered and intrinsically motivated. Intrinsically motivating curricula that valued and incorporated play made the young learners more receptive to later learning challenges. Early learning that lacked an active play component but rewarded children with treats ultimately distracted them from the content of what they were learning as they became overly focused on the prospect of getting, or not getting, the treat.

Attention to Means over End

When children play, they are free to improvise the script as the play unfolds. Whether they play house or build in the block area, they may not be conscious of a goal or particular outcome. Children

Outdoor pretend play takes many forms.

> Children use play to help resolve lingering developmental issues. At night, the young child afraid of the dark can pretend he has superpowers that protect sleeping children.

> Children play because they want to, not for any external rewards. For them, play *is* the reward.

Children's spontaneous play typically unfolds without the structure of adult-imposed rules. Children invent both structure and rules.

are generally more interested in the process of playing than in the outcome, although this is less true for games with rules at which they hope to win.

This **means-over-end** quality—concern with the process of playing instead of an end goal—can make it difficult for an adult to follow a child's thought processes or locate an immediate outcome. That is one reason some adults may not see the educational value of play. It can seem that children are "just playing," and nothing more is occurring than what the adult overhears or sees. But play is more than meets the eye. This very quality of attention to means over end paves the way for emergent themes, conceptual discoveries, and social connections. In this way, children's play parallels the play-with-ideas and innovative and flexible thinking or "adaptive expertise" (Bransford 2001) that adults often need to invent solutions in the workplace. Consider the following example:

> Three-year-old Xang squeezes and pounds his play dough. It changes in his hand and responds to the force of his pounding. Suddenly, with glowing eyes, he whispers, "Turtle." Xang carefully makes a rock for the turtle to rest on "like the turtle in the zoo." His friend asks for a turn with the Play-Doh hammer to make a turtle, too. Xang leans over his Play-Doh to pass the hammer—and squashes his creation so the red of his turtle merges with the white of his rock. He examines the Play-Doh for several seconds. Then he pushes his finger into the Play-Doh and the colors blend more thoroughly. "Pink!" Xang says with excitement.

Xang's focus on means over ends lets him be open to new learning opportunities that arise as he plays and motivated to learn more. Once he notices the turtle shape, the turtle theme informs his play until his play leads him to color mixing.

Freedom from Externally Imposed Rules

Adults often teach children to use materials in ways that promote safety, maintain order, and facilitate their effective use. For example, when adults teach children to cut, they show them the proper way both to hold the scissors and to hand them to another child. These rules set the stage for successful cutting and ensure the children's safety.

In contrast, children's spontaneous play typically unfolds without the structure of adult-imposed rules. Children invent both structure and rules. Just as adults have unspoken rules called **norms** that determine acceptable or unacceptable behavior, children have play rules about which they tacitly agree. In a group of playing children, you will hear their voices change depending on who they are at the moment. Everyone seems to know what voice the baby uses. She sounds nothing like the mommy. You will also hear children negotiating rules ("But what about the hospital?" "They don't need that no more. See? They are stronger than Superman from eating the food."). This agreed-upon or yet-to-be-agreed-upon "shared repertoire of play moves" (Franklin 2000, 66) makes it possible for everyone to play together.

As children make Play-Doh change form and color, they learn concepts, what they can do with a material, and about the properties of that material.

Children are motivated to keep their play going as long as possible, but sometimes it breaks down. As they interact and experiment with play activities, children discover what causes the breakdown, and make rules to avoid it. For instance, it is fun to see who can throw the balloon up in the air the highest, but not if the balloon goes so high that it gets stuck in a tree. It is fun to play tug-of-war with Bruce's jacket, but it stops being fun, at least for Bruce, when the jacket rips and Bruce falls backward into a mud puddle.

Observant adults usually can figure out the underlying and often-unspoken rules of young children's play. This spontaneous group activity can teach them about the children involved in it, and about human interaction, emotions, and thought as well.

Self-Expression through Symbol and Metaphor

Play allows children to use symbols to code their experiences and create metaphors that hold meaning for them. A **symbol** can be defined as "something that represents a meaningful action or idea" (Drucker 1994, 66). Typically, two or more people must agree on what the symbol stands for. A **metaphor** means literally to "transfer" meaning from one thing to another that shares both similarities and differences. In play, a metaphor is a theme. As you saw earlier, Ana and Michael used symbols, such as a leaf for the flag, and metaphors. When the helicopter rescued the people, the play theme was a metaphor for the safety both children craved for themselves and their parents. Symbols and metaphors a child creates have an unlimited capacity to represent that child's experience of the world, and a group of children's symbolic contributions can expand the meaning of any individual child's play symbols into a shared metaphor for the group. A scenario that appears to be about something insignificant can hold meaning of great significance. Here is an example:

> A metaphor means literally to "transfer" meaning from one thing to another that shares both similarities and differences. In play, a metaphor can be thought of as a theme.

This young girl makes up her own rules and dialogue as she feeds her doll.

One day near the end of the school year, five-year-old Lilah was playing on the grass near her kindergarten class play yard and found a fuzzy dandelion top that was detached from its stem. She removed the bandana from her hair and wrapped it around the dandelion, and then approached her kindergarten teacher, Ms. Jasper. "This is a caterpillar," she said, moving the bandana so the teacher could see the "caterpillar."

"Will it come out as a butterfly soon?" Ms. Jasper asked.

"No," Lilah answered. "He likes being a caterpillar in a cocoon." She took her "caterpillar" and placed it under a tree where two classmates were playing a hand-clapping game.

Lilah made the dandelion symbolize a caterpillar and a bandana symbolize a cocoon. She had told her teacher many times that she was "not ready" to go to first grade yet. Ms. Jasper saw Lilah's cocoon play as a metaphor for not feeling ready to move on and wanting to stay where she was. She wondered if Lilah was using play to create a metaphor for her ambivalence about leaving kindergarten and moving on to first grade. If so, the use of metaphor gave Lilah a way to express her feelings about separation and to move toward resolving them without becoming overwhelmed by sadness or anxiety about leaving.

Once Lilah's cocoon was in a protected spot under the tree, she joined the two girls playing the clapping games. "Can I play? I wanna do 'When Suzy Was a Baby!'"

"Okay," Michelle said. "Start when she was a baby and go to when she was six. I'm turning six next week. Since it's my birthday, I wanna say the words about what Suzy does when she's six."

"I want to say the teenager part," said Jessica, "because when I get to be a teenager, I can wear high heels."

Lilah looked at Jessica with interest. She loved dressing in her mom's high heels. "Let's do all the ages," Lilah concluded. The girls nodded and began their game.

THOUGHT QUESTION Think of something you enjoy doing and are motivated to do in your spare time. Compare it to what you have read here about play. What qualities of play does your activity have?

In this example, all the children face the same challenge of separating from their kindergarten class, and all have the capacity and motivation to use play metaphors to explore their feelings about it. The theme of the hand-clapping game becomes another way of addressing their experience of getting bigger and looking at the coming change. It helps them sort out their feelings "out of the moment" itself and to gain distance from the problem of leaving kindergarten. Through play, they explore their emotions and avoid acting out or feeling powerless.

CATEGORIES OF PLAY

How have child developmentalists categorized children's play?

Child development experts have categorized children's play along the developmental continuum. About eighty years ago, psychologist Mildred Parten (1932), for example, described six stages of children's social play, which continue to be used by educators and psychologists today:

1. *Unoccupied play:* The child apparently is not doing anything.
2. *Solitary play:* The child plays alone.
3. *Onlooker play:* The child watches other children at play and does not actively participate.
4. *Parallel play:* The child plays next to, but not with, another child or children.
5. *Associative play:* Children move in and out of play together but without a common focus.
6. *Cooperative play:* Children play together in an organized way of their common design according to their shared purpose.

Another way to consider play is to think about the type of experience the child has doing different activities. Developmental psychologist Sara Smilansky (1968) identified four types of play: functional play, constructive play, dramatic play, and games with rules, which we discuss next.

Functional Play

Infants and toddlers play by moving parts of their bodies and objects. They experience how the movements feel, and then repeat them. Infants lie on their back and kick their feet, smile, become energized from the pleasure of moving, then kick their feet again. Six-month-olds bat at a colorful wheel on an infant toy. The wheel turns. They laugh and bat the wheel again. Smilansky calls this type of play **functional play:** play that involves actions and the body.

Such sensorimotor play is a large part of what waking infants do. They move and something happens. At first they may enjoy that process without realizing they have made something happen or that they can repeat the action to make it happen again. After repeated actions, though, they realize with delight that they are the actors. By four months, infants' movements are no longer just **volitional** (able to move independently without a specific objective) but begin to have **intentionality** (having an objective, the beginning of purposeful behavior).

While functional play may look aimless to an outsider, infant/toddler caregivers observe it closely to see the child's developing intentionality and, at times, to interact with the child to help the process along.

It is raining hard outside. Instead of going out, three toddlers and their caregiver, Claire, take empty miniature shopping carts into the lobby of the building that houses their center. Under a large skylight in the center of the lobby grows a two-story tree, with circular seating around it. Within moments, the children are pushing the carts around the tree, skipping and calling to one another. They imitate the noise the carts make on the tiled floors and giggle when a cart gets stuck in a crack, falling down themselves, as if to dramatize the situation. Sometimes three across, sometimes single file, the children vary their cart-pushing seemingly endlessly. There is no supermarket play, just repeated joyful circling around the tree.

To sum up: Functional play occurs when children of any age explore the world on a sensory level and are motivated to use their emerging physical capacities in a way that gives them sensory feedback. When this play is intentional, they control their actions and use them to explore or communicate. The children in Claire's group, for example, purposely fall on the floor when the carts get stuck, which becomes a mini-routine during their twenty minutes of play.

Constructive Play

According to Smilansky, **constructive play** begins in middle to late toddlerhood when children become motivated to combine and arrange objects to construct something new. A sixteen-month-old loves to play with large plastic beads he joins together in a long strand. The girl next to him delights in stacking square blocks to make a tower and then knocks them apart and rebuilds. The boy next to them is connecting train tracks. The children in the three-year-old

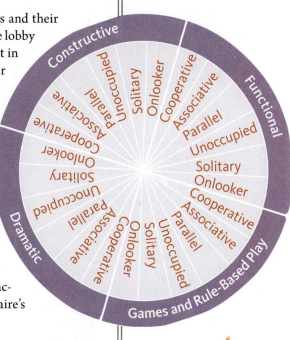

4.1 *Types of Play*

Doctor play is a favorite preschool activity in which children experience the power of hurting and healing (doctors do both). Here, a mother volunteering in the classroom facilitates their play.

classroom next door use the same materials to build long roads and garages for the toy cars. They dress up in the dramatic play corner and string beads together to make necklaces to enhance their outfits. Constructive play begins early and lasts through-out childhood. It motivates the five-year-old building a city with unit blocks as well as the eight-year-old constructing a working robot she connects to the computer.

Dramatic Play

Dramatic play is an interactive and open-ended process in which children invent symbols for ideas, feelings, and issues. Unlike constructive play, dramatic play is not goal oriented. Rather, children develop and improvise play scenarios that allow them to express and explore the material their play generates.

When dramatic play involves a social group, Smilansky calls it **sociodramatic** play. Children engaging in it may agree on a joint vision ("Let's play that I'm the doc-tor and you're sick."), but as they assume roles and narratives emerge, new directions evolve. The play process weaves a story that transcends the specific topic chosen and has layers of meaning for the players.

Here is an illustration of dramatic play:

In the dramatic play area of their pre-K classroom, Juana, Annique, and Sage gather the baby dolls. Marcus inspects the supply of play food in the cupboard. Danny wanders the area and sits down on the doll bed, looking lost. He has special needs and is not **well related**—that is, Danny does not reach out to other children or respond to them in ways they expect.

Juana: Come on! Get the babies ready. We're taking them to the hospital. [Annique and Sage wrap their babies in blankets and scarves.]

Annique: He [pointing at Danny] can be the baby, too. [She hands Danny a baby toy he happily accepts.]

Marcus: Wait! I'm making lunch. They might have to wait a long time in the emergency room. They might be hungry.

Sage: They can put some quarters in [the vending machine] and get chips.

Marcus: They don't got enough quarters. See? I made a picnic for them! [He holds up a basket overflowing with play food.]

Annique: They can't go on a picnic 'cause they're sick.

Marcus: No. They can go because they don't have chicken pox. Look. No spots. They can go on a picnic if they just have a cough. Then they can go to the hospital later.

Sage: Yeah! My baby has a cough.

Annique: My baby has a cough too, and he [Danny] does too.

Marcus: Let's go.

Sage: Where is the picnic?

Marcus: Here, where I put the blanket. Put your babies down.

Annique: Danny! Come! You're a baby. Sit on the blanket. [Danny jumps up and down and flaps his hands. Then he lies down on the blanket.]

Annique: He's tired. He doesn't care about lunch.

[Sage and Annique feed their baby dolls with the food Marcus provided. Danny rolls around on the blanket, which then partially covers one of Annique's dolls.]

Annique: Hey!

Marcus: Oh, look! Your baby is like Superman! [The blanket looks like a cape.] It's a superbaby! Let's pretend the babies are not sick no more. They ate the food and that made them stronger. Put those napkins on their back like this.

Sage: Yeah! Superbaby!

Annique: But what about the hospital?

Marcus: They don't need that no more. See? They are stronger than Superman from eating the food.

Annique [looking doubtful]: Wait! First I have to put this [a cup] over my baby's mouth for her asthma. She can go with you in ten minutes.

Sage: Okay. Let the baby take the asthma machine first. Then she can be superbaby with mine. Danny will wait for her.

With her baby in her arms, Annique develops her own ideas and incorporates them into her friends' play themes.

Here, as in many dramatic play scenes, the theme evolves as the players interact. While the initial goal was to "play hospital," Marcus's suggestion to have a picnic on the way allowed the play to go in an unanticipated direction. When Danny rolled on the blanket, he gave Marcus an idea for a superhero theme. The other children could

THOUGHT QUESTION If you were the teacher observing this scenario, how would you help Danny find other meaningful ways to play within the group?

connect to Marcus's idea because superhero themes are compelling for children this age, who are struggling to feel as powerful as they wish they were. The play weaves elements of fantasy and reality into a narrative. The adult observer gleans information about what each child knows and has experienced, as well as information about developmental issues that are compelling to each child.

For example, Marcus knows something about the limits of social activity placed on children with chicken pox. Annique knows about treatment for asthma attacks. They all assume Danny is well suited for the role of the baby because he doesn't talk yet.

In Smilansky's conceptual framework, constructive play initially occurs at the same time as the earliest stages of symbolic (or dramatic) play, but they differ in a few important ways. Constructive play accomplishes a goal or creates a product, whereas dramatic play is open-ended (Smilansky and Shefatya 2004). In addition, for a child engaged in constructive play, the *quality* of the materials determines her activity because, for example, sand, water, and clay each have different qualities. In symbolic (or dramatic) play, *the child shapes* how the materials are used, what they represent, and what themes she will explore. Smilansky notes that sometimes constructive play leads to dramatic play and the child develops a theme with the product she constructed.

> In constructive play, the *quality* of the materials shapes the child's activity because, for example, sand, water, and clay each have different qualities.

Games with Rules

In the early school grades, children begin to play more games with rules. Board games, sports, and card games are favorites beginning around age five. Children use games with rules to practice game-playing routines such as turn taking, waiting, and use of strategy, as well as skills called for by the particular game.

These games provide an outlet for children's competitive energy but demand cooperation, too. In a schoolyard kickball game, teams compete against each other, but members of a team cooperate with each other. A player runs after the ball and throws it to a teammate who has a better chance than the first player of tagging out an opposing team member. Furthermore, for the game to work, the teams must cooperate with each other. For example, they agree to the rules that three "outs" mean it is the other team's turn to be "up." Whether a child wins or loses, games with rules can help him learn to cooperate as part of a team.

THOUGHT QUESTION Smilansky created four categories of play that can overlap in real life. When have you observed play that you think could fall into more than one category?

Following rules can be difficult for children just beginning to play games. They may want to change the rules ("Now the green card means you skip all the green spaces") to make it easier to win. Or they may collapse into tears when they lose. Gradually, they grasp the fixed nature of rules and understand that rules apply to all players. They come to terms with winning sometimes and losing other times.

Winning at games with rules typically involves a combination of skill and luck. As they play, children learn to master the experience of losing without becoming devastated. They eventually realize that at times they will have good luck and do well with their skills and at other times they will have bad luck and experience difficulties. Over time, games with rules help children use their connection to peers to provide support to friends struggling with some of the difficult aspects of competition, such as losing a game.

AFFECTIVE COMPONENTS

How does play help children express, explore, and integrate their emotions?

Despite the young child's emerging self-image as someone becoming increasingly autonomous and masterful, he often feels emotionally vulnerable. Picture the three- to five-year-old struggling to regulate, express, and integrate complex and intense emotions. In play, that child can express powerful positive and negative affects and use symbols and metaphors to explore the themes that accompany them (Fein 1989).

Communicating and Integrating Emotions

The young child's spontaneous play is in part driven by a need to express and master emotional experience. While children certainly express pleasure and happiness through play, teachers often worry about the predominance of negative affects also expressed. They note that, for example, such play often includes themes involving conflict: "good guys" and "bad guys," ghosts, guns, pirates, and poisonous plots. Indeed, these themes thrive in young children's dramatic play and give them a way of expressing and integrating negative affects often not welcome in other areas of their lives.

As you saw with Lilah's "cocoon" and hand-clapping game, through play, children explore aggressive, anxious, and fearful feelings at a distance from what is actually upsetting them. This allows them to accept and integrate negative affects without becoming overwhelmed. Thus, play is a form of preventive mental health intervention, offering children a social outlet for sharing feelings that might otherwise stay isolated within them, putting them at risk for future depression and antisocial behavior.

Self-regulation

Vygotsky highlighted the way make-believe play helps young children with **self-regulation**—their ability to modulate impulses, exert self-control, delay gratification, and follow routines and social rules even if they don't feel like it (Vygotsky 1935/1978). He asserted that pretend play gave children essential practice in self-regulating. Those behaving according to a play scheme stay within their make-believe roles even when a compelling experience in the here and now tempts them to act differently. For instance, a child playing the role of police officer must keep standing guard by the make-believe jail. She can't join her friend, the make-believe prisoner hiding under the table with his stolen treasures.

Vygotsky's theories are compatible with recent brain research indicating that self-regulation doesn't develop on its own once a child reaches a certain point, that its development depends on supportive experiences (Cheah, Nelson, and Rubin 2001; Thompson 2000). Dramatic play is likely to be one of those experiences (Berk, Mann, and Ogan 2006).

Children typically generate their own play, are invested in it, and have energy for it. When they enter into play half-heartedly, without sustained interest or genuine involvement, we wonder if they are tired or not feeling well. While a range of affects is expressed in the play scenario, healthy play has a joyful quality, even when adults consider the substance of the play negative. Children delight in creating a world of "bad guys" as much as in creating one about finding lost kitties in the forest. Although their play metaphors may represent internal conflicts or confusing emotional experience, dramatic play is integrative and **reparative** (healing) and feels good to the children playing.

Traumatic play

Children who have suffered traumatic life experiences and not been able to recover from them play differently from their nontraumatized peers. Play originating from traumatic experience, or **traumatic play,** does not include the joyful affects of typical play. It is more often grim and businesslike, with an urgent quality that contains the disturbing affects of fear, rage, and helplessness the traumatizing event evoked. Healthy play that includes negative metaphors tends to be compelling to children and draws them in, but traumatic play tends to be off-putting. The intensity of the negative affect expressed overwhelms and frightens other children, and they may no longer want to participate. Then, too, the child engaged in traumatic play may lose the boundaries between the present classroom setting and his troubling past experience, which also disturbs other children.

> A group of preschool children play on the rug with vehicles, including cars, trucks, and airplanes. Jonas is flying the airplane over the cars and trucks that Robin and Eli are "driving." Suddenly he shouts, "All passengers! Prepare for an emergency landing!"
>
> Robin and Eli look up and answer, "Land right here! We made room for you!"
>
> Jonas doesn't respond. "Put your oxygen mask on, Mommy!" he says in a panicky voice. "Cover your eyes, Baby! This plane might be crashing!" No longer holding the airplane, Jonas covers his eyes and crouches down on the floor.
>
> "I don't want to play airplane," Eli says. He moves into a corner with his cars and trucks, and Robin follows. Jonas doesn't seem to notice.

Traumatic play indicates that a child has not been able to use play to resolve his traumatic experience on his own and requires help. Teachers concerned about the traumatic quality of a young child's play can consult the school psychologist or social worker or engage a consultant to observe the child's play. Play therapy may be indicated for children who engage in traumatic play in the classroom setting. In play therapy the therapist uses the child's play to help her make sense of the traumatic experiences underlying her play. As the therapist engages with the child and her play, the child is no longer alone with her traumatic affects.

Many teachers are concerned about gun play in the classroom. Because four- and five-year-olds are interested in being powerful, gun play often comes up in their play to symbolize power. Teachers may want to make rules about gun play, emphasizing that the classroom is a peaceful environment. For instance, most schools do not allow children to bring toy guns into the building.

Yet teachers notice some children play with "guns" anyway, by using a marker to represent a gun or by making a gun shape out of a piece of toast! Children often play happily with this symbol of power and danger. However, when children have had traumatic experiences that involved guns, physical violence, war, or other dangers, gun play may seem too real and too frightening. Teachers may need to help children understand that pretending with guns can be exciting, but that real guns are dangerous and scary. For some children, gun play is too frightening and makes the classroom feel unsafe.

Identity and Mastery

As young children are engaged in discovering themselves, identity issues often motivate their play, interests, and conversation. By taking roles in dramatic play, chil-

> Traumatic play does not include the joyful affects of typical play. It is more often grim and businesslike, with an urgent quality that contains the disturbing affects of fear, rage, and helplessness.

dren try out a number of identities to help develop and solidify their sense of self and to find ways to resolve non-traumatic issues and fears. "Who am I?" "Who will I be like when I'm big?" and "How would it feel to be something else?" are pressing questions for this age group and inspire play scenarios. The child who acts the role of "daddy" tries out being in charge and being "like" his parent. His friend who decides to be the doggie frees himself from the obligation to behave calmly and instead playfully jumps on his "owner." The child who crawls onto the doll bed and says "Goo, goo" connects with an earlier version of herself, one that may be particularly comforting after the birth of a baby brother. Any child can try out any roles because play identities are flexible and temporary.

Repetition—filling the trucks over and over—leads to mastery.

Thus, play allows children to work on their identity issues in prosocial ways.

The mastery of specific abilities is a key part of the young child's developing sense of self. School-age children practice skills through games. Younger children can practice mastery through pretend play.

> Three-year-old Roberto is at his swim lesson at camp, but, as on previous days, he refuses to go into the water. As the children wait for their counselor to take them back to their day bunk, Roberto "swims" across the gymnasium, covering considerable distance, even as his elbows knock against the hard floor.

Roberto is practicing for mastery. Through play, he does what he is not yet ready to do in reality.

Sometimes adults worry about the identities children try on in their play. For example, a father tells a teacher he does not want his son to wear dresses or heels while playing in the housekeeping area. The boy loves to put on gauzy skirts and clomp around in heels every day. The teacher listens to and acknowledges the father's concerns and what he believes are their cultural foundations. She also explains why she wants children to explore identities that are comfortable and interesting to them. Teacher and parent talk about play and the freedom it gives children to try on different personae. The teacher points out that we do not know how or even whether the boy's play is related to his future identity, but that, in any case, the classroom has a philosophy of respect for all ways of being.

Play materials help children investigate their identities, and a teacher's classroom decisions can help or hinder a child with identity work. A three-year-old African American boy approached the doll crib with a dilemma. He looked at the anatomically correct doll. It was pink. He looked at the brown doll. It had no genitals. His teachers saw him look from one doll to the other and made a note to order an anatomically correct brown male doll.

Play engages children so thoroughly that it helps them figure out who they are and what they can do. Sanjeev is a master block builder, and the children in his preschool know that. They approach him for advice on their buildings. Being a skilled builder

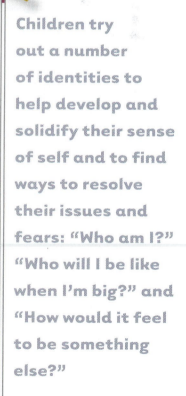

Children try out a number of identities to help develop and solidify their sense of self and to find ways to resolve their issues and fears: "Who am I?" "Who will I be like when I'm big?" and "How would it feel to be something else?"

becomes part of Sanjeev's self-image. Melissa thought she couldn't slide down the pole in the yard, but after playing outside day after day and trying to slide down the pole again and again, she learns that she can do it! She is a competent person.

Playing for and about Power

Power versus powerlessness is a core developmental issue for four- to six-year-olds (Koplow 2002). Children play for and about power in a variety of ways. Whom they play with and how raise questions of power. Their symbolic play is rife with scenarios related to the power issues on their minds.

Children may create games that give them power over whom to include and whom to exclude, often causing distress in the peer group. Children also compete for power when they play together. These informal competitive ventures can be in the form of races or other demonstrations of skill that show them to be "best." This competitive energy infuses classroom routines and makes the question of "who gets to be first" a challenge that precedes every activity.

In addition to power relationships that arise among children, the dramatic play area of every early childhood classroom is home to many scenarios symbolizing power. Children at this age become aware that they are relatively powerless compared with adults, and they often struggle to compensate for that powerlessness by identifying with powerful figures and assuming powerful roles. Dinosaurs and superheroes, princesses and police officers, and, of course, parents become subjects of play.

Play that symbolizes power issues allows children to experience feeling powerful without becoming **disorganized,** or unfocused, by their competitive energy or defeated by their feelings of powerlessness. Here's a scenario familiar to many a teacher:

"I'm a superhero. Do you want to play 'bad guys'?" five-year-old Gerad asks Timmy.

"I wanna play superheroes too. I'm a superhero. My name is Rock Man," responds Timmy.

"Rock Man?" asks Gerad, giggling. "Then my name is Sock Man! I sock the bad guys right in the face!" Both boys collapse in laughter. "Come on! Let's put on capes!"

Jenny has been eying the boys and listening to their conversation. "I will be Rock *Girl*!" she says with conviction.

"Well," says Gillian. "Daria and I are the princess and the queen, and we own this castle. You got to go to the forest and find magic rocks to give you your power. Then come back to the castle."

"I already have my magic rock because I am Rock Man!" said Timmy. "But it's invisible."

"Well, then put it in the invisible treasure chest!" Gillian points to the place where the invisible treasure chest is kept.

"The bad guys don't have the keys!" Gerad says with satisfaction as Timmy approaches the invisible chest.

This play scene quickly ignites the players' passion about power and inspires them to create symbols and metaphors that express power themes. Each child finds a way to identify as powerful and to have power over others without causing power struggles.

THOUGHT QUESTION When and how much do you think an adult should intervene when children exclude other children from their play?

Preschoolers become aware that they are relatively powerless compared with adults, and they often struggle to compensate for that powerlessness by identifying with powerful figures and assuming powerful roles.

PLAY AND DIFFERENCE

How does awareness of gender, culture, class, and disability issues help teachers support children's play?

Children differ in many ways. While play can bridge those differences, it can also emphasize them. Boys' and girls' play, for example, has similarities and glaring differences. Play can be a "social bridge" (Roopnarine and Johnson 2001, 298) among children from different cultures, but it can also be a social barrier between parents and teachers, or among teachers. Children with disabilities may be more similar to other children than different from them. Moreover, we cannot assume they will need our help or help from the other children, but they may.

Play and Gender

Often, the developmental issues that inform play themes are the same for boys and girls, but the metaphors they choose to express them differ. The children in the earlier scenario identified with powerful figures, but the boys chose superheroes to symbolize their power theme and two of the three girls chose royalty metaphors. The play may be gender specific, but the underlying theme of power is the same for boys and girls.

Boys often gravitate to the block area. How will you involve the girls?

Young children in the process of developing their gender identity often seem hyperconnected to play symbols traditionally considered to be "only for girls" or "only for boys." This is true if the culture of home or school defines what is appropriate along gender lines, but it often occurs even in environments that strive to be nonstereotypical. As children become more aware of defining themselves through gender identity, they often use play to "own" their developing gender identity in an all-or-nothing way. For example, girls may concentrate on doll play; boys may become inseparable from toy trucks.

Children thrive in play environments that allow them to explore gender themes in an open-ended way. Teachers set the stage for inviting open-ended, non-gender-specific play when they communicate that all areas of the classroom have equal value for boys and girls. Some teachers who notice that children choose gender-specific play may orchestrate opportunities for them to play where they normally do not. For example, a fours teacher no longer makes the block area a choice on Mondays but pairs off the entire class, and every pair builds at the same time. Throughout the week, some children remain engaged with the material and return to change the blocks or to play with them.

Teachers, like parents, may wonder about both children who cross stereotypical gender lines and those who adhere closely to those stereotypes. Should teachers "allow" boys to dress up in girl's clothing? Should they let girls play "princess" day after day? When children can choose how to represent themselves in play, their play provides them with an important avenue for expressing and integrating gender identification. At the same time, teachers can consider how to help children whose energy goes into one kind of play to the exclusion of others.

Teachers set the stage for inviting open-ended, non-gender-specific play when they communicate that all areas of the classroom have equal value for boys and girls.

THOUGHT QUESTION What is your reaction to children who play in gender-stereotypical ways? What about children who play in ways that differ from the gender stereotype? What do you think your role is in either of these children's play? Why?

Play and Culture

Children of all cultures play, but the time spent on play varies depending on adults' other expectations of children. Such expectations include the degree to which children contribute to the household's survival activities (Lancy 2002), for example, by working alongside adults at a market. Not all cultural groups in all contexts believe play indicates or promotes educational or developmental competence. Thus, various cultural factors influence young children's play choices and the content of that play. Some adults worry about children's safety and remain near them as they play, but others feel children can assess dangers for themselves and that playtime is an opportunity for them to be on their own. Adults have different attitudes about gender roles. Some encourage all children to wear sturdy, androgynous play clothes, while others love the look of girls in dresses and party shoes and boys in jackets and ties.

Children's cultures affect the degree of cooperation and competition in their play. Those growing up within a cultural tradition of cooperation are less likely to compete with their peers and more likely to help them. In Japan, for example, teachers often begin the year with many toys and gradually decrease the amount because they want children to learn to share. In cultures that favor competition, children learn to do their personal best as they play.

Some research indicates that children from families at higher socioeconomic levels are able to use dramatic play more elaborately, and with more developed play narratives, than are those from families in lower socioeconomic brackets (Smilansky 1968; Nicolopoulou, McDowell, and Brockmeyer 2006; Bellin and Singer 2006). Many reasons can explain this discrepancy, including less exposure to verbal narratives and to symbolic play materials among children who have fewer economic advantages. D. W. Winnicott, a child psychoanalyst who used play as a therapeutic tool with young children, noted that children need to trust in the environment, that is, to feel secure and safe in it, to be able to devote energy to play (Winnicott 1971/2005). The risks and dangers poor children are more likely to face may cause them to be less able to put energy into any behaviors that do not safeguard their survival.

To include all children in play opportunities, teachers reach out to children from all socioeconomic and cultural backgrounds and take into account the families' conceptions of play and the children's prior play experiences. Ethnically diverse classrooms abound with examples of culturally relevant themes and activities children generate themselves. A Mexican child rolls out Play-Doh and announces she is making "tortillas for lunch." Her French friend says her Play-Doh will be "crepes for the baby." A boy whose family has just come from Puerto Rico is playing with the puppets and telling a story about the *Cuko* (boogie man) who will take the boy if he doesn't listen to his mama. A new child from India does not venture into the dramatic play area or participate in baking muffins. He does not find such play activities comfortable. He quietly plays on his own with pattern blocks, making complex and colorful designs on the pattern cards. When it's time to go outside, he becomes animated and engaged with the other boys running around in the yard, much more at home in this more culturally familiar way of playing.

Early childhood teachers have the opportunity to learn about the many cultures children bring with them. As we get to know the children and their families, we can learn about the play themes,

THOUGHT QUESTION In your first-grade class, you sit near children as they play. You chat with the block builders and photograph their work. You ask them probing questions and listen to their play themes to get curriculum ideas. Jane's mother is unfamiliar with play as a way to learn. You want to communicate why you put so much of your time into observing and facilitating play. What would you say to Jane's mother, and what would you want to learn from her?

symbols, and interactive styles they find comfortable. We can help children lessen cultural gaps by reading stories, displaying artwork, and using music and cooking projects that involve elements familiar to them. We can help the children build bridges between their familiar play patterns and the many options for play available in the classroom setting. We can put artifacts in the dramatic play and constructive play areas that invite children to use play to generate culturally relevant play symbols and themes, increasing their comfort level with new ways of playing.

Play and Special Needs

Children's abilities and needs differ widely. A child with a walker needs space for it near where she's working and room to stretch out as she builds with blocks. A child who can't see well needs play materials organized so he can locate them. The hearing-impaired child needs a way to follow the play theme. As their teacher, you will find ways to help all children participate in play as fully as possible.

Some children who have special needs may have difficulty generating and organizing their play on the same level as their more typically developing peers. In an earlier scenario, the children gave the baby role to a child with special needs who was nonverbal. Such inclusion settings offer children with special needs a way to connect with group play and an opportunity to see play unfolding at various levels. Their teachers face the challenge of finding ways for these children to be more active partners in the play that develops, so that their experiences can be more meaningful to them. Mixed-age groups are often helpful because these children may sometimes be able to play at their developmental level with the younger children and at other times follow the play schemes of some of the older children.

When children are disorganized in play, seem at a loss, or are unable to sustain play because they cannot regulate their emotional responses to others, teachers may be tempted to plan teacher-directed activities instead of open-ended play time. However, fostering play skills has beneficial effects. It not only increases children's play repertoire but also promotes their overall development (Greenspan 1993). Meaningful play routines strengthen the architecture of the developing brain (National Scientific Council on the Developing Child 2005; Greenspan 1993). Thus, teachers do well to support the child's relationships and capacity to create symbols in play. When a child with special needs circles a train around the track again and again, the teacher who joins the play and puts a passenger in the station makes an evolving theme possible. In this case, the interruption of repetitive play and elaboration of the play theme also helps the child make cognitive connections as he reacts to the presence of something new.

Some children need specific therapies to thrive in the early childhood setting; teachers can collaborate with specialists and

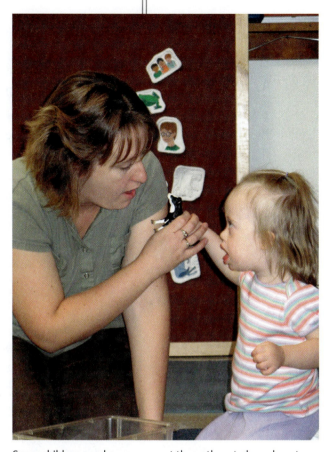

Some children need more support than others to learn how to play symbolically.

THOUGHT QUESTION Teresa uses an assistive listening device. She sits next to Jeff in her second grade class. When they play a board game, Jeff moves Teresa's piece for her before she can even read her card. You know they are friends and that he is trying to help her, but you also know she can play the game unaided. What might you do or say?

When children are disorganized in play, seem at a loss, or are unable to sustain play because they cannot regulate their emotional responses to others, teachers may be tempted to plan teacher-directed activities instead of open-ended play time. However, fostering play skills has beneficial effects, such as increasing abilities to create symbols in play.

consultants to find ways to support their play. However, these children are, above all, children. Like all children, they require time and opportunity for joyful exploration and playful interaction without specific goals or prescribed outcomes.

Glenda Mac Naughton (2003, 199) suggests that teachers consider the following five questions to help ensure inclusive play:

- Do the everyday objects we use reflect the languages and cultures of the children?
- Do we have everyday objects from diverse cultures?
- Do the materials respect and celebrate cultural and racial diversity?
- Do the materials challenge traditional sex-role stereotypes and understandings?
- To what extent do the materials support and respect diverse abilities and ways of being?

PLAY RELATIONSHIPS IN THE CLASSROOM

What can teachers do to promote children's play?

Although children do play alone, relationships are an important aspect of play. Think back to your earliest play experiences. Do you remember the children you played with? What did adults do while you played? While many of us remember the adults in our lives watching from afar while we played, as a teacher of young children, you have a role in their play.

Play and Peer Relationships

Children in early childhood classrooms interact with each other most and best when their teachers support their play. For children, play is the language of connection. By creating their own play routines and themes, they develop a repertoire of symbols with shared meaning and build a common experience that makes them feel included as important members of the group. Often the "requirement" for this "group membership" is the ability to play. "Can I play?" are the magic words that open the door to the peer group.

When children play together day after day, they get to know each other's preferences, vulnerabilities, and interests and discover their own as well. Three-year-olds tend to be absorbed in themes they generate or in the exploration of cause and effect, next to their peers but not necessarily interacting with them. Four- and five-year-olds are increasingly motivated to make friends and play with one another. Friendships in the early grades are considered a primary factor in adjusting to the school setting (Pellegrini and Holmes 2006). If the opportunity for different categories of play occurs during the school day, children will be able to move in and out of social groups to collaborate with different play partners, thereby expanding their capacity to communicate within various peer dyads and peer groups. They can address many of the conflicts and issues of exclusion that occur, and the attuned teacher can use curriculum and group process to help them.

Play and Teacher-Child Relationships

In Chapter 3, you read that young children's attachment relationships organize their development. We also saw that a growing body of research has looked at the power of teacher-child attachment to promote social-emotional well-being and receptivity to learning in early childhood (National Scientific Council 2005). Just as the parent-child attachment relationship provides children a way to feel secure, strong teacher-child relationships can help them use the classroom as a **psychological home base,** that is, an emotionally safe place. These relationships can also inspire the invention of symbols that hold meaning for both child and teacher. Here is an example:

> Lebna, a three-year-old whose family had emigrated recently from Ethiopia, sat frozen at a table during play period each morning, sometimes fingering mancala stones from the game on the shelf. He wept when his mother left for work, and his teacher held him on her lap to comfort him. Lebna knew no English, and no one in the classroom spoke his language. Although he had started to take comfort from his teacher's lap, she felt as if she had no way to communicate with him after the day got underway and she had to share her attention with the other children.
>
> One afternoon his teacher took the glass mancala stones off the shelf, put them on the little table, and sat with Lebna. She pretended her fingers were walking toward the stones, and, when they got close, they quickly snatched a stone and hid it under an empty cup. Lebna hid a smile. The teacher repeated the play routine a second time. This time Lebna really did smile. The teacher sat and waited. Lebna looked up at her with anticipation. Again, his teacher played at sneaking up on a stone, snatching it, and then hiding it under the cup. This time, the little boy did what his teacher did. He made his fingers walk to the stones, snatched one, and hid it under the cup. The teacher and he smiled at one another. Then she took a tissue and covered a couple of stones with it, so you could still see color peeking out. She made a "shhhh" sign with her finger as though she had just put the stones to sleep. Lebna laughed and looked delighted.
>
> The next day during the play period, Lebna went to the shelf and brought the mancala stones to the table, where he arranged them in a circle. Then he put a tiny plastic rabbit in the center and covered it up with a tissue. He was beaming. His teacher photographed it. It was his first self-initiated play at school.

Thus, nurturing and attentive teacher-child interaction can support the birth of symbol in the early childhood classroom. With symbolic play as part of the dialogue, Lebna can expand his ability to communicate more complex ideas and feelings to his peers as well as his teachers.

Respect for play

Teachers communicate their respect for play when they observe, facilitate, scaffold, and validate it. Teachers *observe* play to figure out what it might mean, to get ideas for expanding it, and to determine how to build curriculum based on children's play themes. To *facilitate* children's play—to make it easier for children to play—teachers create time, space, and materials for play and interact with children in ways that make play more likely to occur. *Scaffolding* is a term Vygotsky used to describe what happens when a more experienced person coaches someone in the process of learning. Teachers scaffold children's play when they enable children to play together or otherwise provide an environment that allows children to do more than they could without help. Teachers *validate* children's play when they recognize its importance (for example, by planning for it) and when they speak to families and colleagues about it.

> Strong teacher-child relationships can help children use the classroom as a psychological home base. These relationships can also inspire the invention of symbols that hold meaning for both child and teacher.

The teacher plans to invite every child to work on vocabulary but does not interrupt children building a spaceship. Instead, he waits until a child is in transition between self-selected play activities and then invites her to join him.

Observation and documentation of children's play helps teachers get to the heart of what is important to children. Over time, teachers see patterns, learn with whom children play most productively, and recognize which play themes persist. Children's play also reveals children's social skills and ability with language and thought. Teachers can help children extend and elaborate their play or can introduce curriculum based on what they observe.

Children need enough time and space for open-ended play. The classroom teacher who provides this time and space, along with play materials, "sets the stage" for play to occur.

Teachers scaffold young children's play when they invite children to build on their ideas, elaborate their play schemes, and make connections between one discovery or theme and another. Teachers can provide scaffolding for such components of play as these:

- *Social components:* "Maybe Sammy wants to be a doggie, too."
- *Emotional components:* "It looks as if you feel frustrated when the puzzle piece won't fit just right. Maybe it would help if I sit with you while you try."
- *Conceptual components:* "I wonder if there is a way to use the blocks to connect your two buildings."

Such attuned interventions help children extend their play but do not attempt to control it or change its themes, passions, or metaphors.

How teachers refer to children's play communicates the extent to which they value it, as do their respectful interactions with children at play. For example, as children play in all the areas of the kindergarten, their teacher asks individuals to circle a favorite word on the morning message chart and play word games with him in relation to it. The teacher plans to invite every child to work on vocabulary but does not interrupt children building a spaceship. Instead, he waits until a child is in transition between self-selected play activities and then invites her to join him.

Adult involvement in play

Many factors determine the adult's role during play, including the children's age and developmental needs, the category of play being supported, and the school's philosophy about the play process. For example, an infant/toddler caregiver playing with a child imitates the baby's actions, and eventually toddlers use play to imitate the world around them. A fours teacher sits near the dramatic play or family area and takes notes that she reads back to the children later that morning. A third grade teacher plays a math game with the whole class.

Many teachers consider dramatic play and constructive play to be children's domains and leave projects and themes entirely up to them. Others give children models for their constructive play to direct more specific use of play materials or set up the dramatic play areas for certain themes. For example, props that suggest a post office will result in play being in part organized around that theme. As you will read in Chapter 13, a class of second and third graders used blocks open-endedly at the beginning of the year but, by midyear,

Children need time and space for open-ended play. This young boy's teacher is giving him time to think.

had used every block to replicate a bridge they visited, observed, and studied as part of their class's social studies curriculum.

Many schools encourage some coaching from teachers to ensure that games with rules are successful for inexperienced players. Other programs prefer children to invent their own rules through exploration of the game and consensus about what is fair (DeVries and Kohlberg 1987; Fein 1989; Gonçu and Klein 2001).

Specialized interventions

According to Artin Gonçu and Elisa Klein (2001), play is the foundation for literacy and socialization in the early childhood classroom. Several research studies point to a positive correlation between social dramatic-play experience and an array of other developmental outcomes including

- increased vocabulary and use of language (Shore 1997; Dickinson and Tabors 2001),
- better story comprehension, communication of meaning in story telling, and development of literacy skills (Christie 1991, 1998; Neuman and Roskos 1998; Dickinson and Tabors 2001), and
- better problem solving, social competence, and peer integration (Singer and Singer 2005; Robinson et al. 2003).

Because of these and similar findings, some early childhood professionals recommend teachers take a more active role in facilitating play with children whose play repertoire is limited.

Smilansky worked with Israeli children who played in limited ways and attempted to foster their progress on a hierarchy of dramatic-play skills. She focused dramatic-play sessions around the peer group's common experiences, including the doctor's office and grocery store. She encouraged children to develop their themes, extend their play narrative, and make symbolic bridges between ideas. Studies in America using her approach yielded similar results: children who participated in the facilitated play experience improved their capacity to generate elaborate dramatic play scenarios and simultaneously showed improvements in school-related areas, which included verbal comprehension, speech, organization, thinking, and sequential activities (Smilansky 1968; Dansky 1980).

Stanley Greenspan uses his "floortime" technique to teach parents and teachers to sit on the floor beside a playing child, become a partner in her play routine, and respond to and engage her in an attuned and playful way. Through this reciprocal activity, the child extends the play and enables others to play with her (Greenspan 1993). Greenspan developed this technique for children on the autistic spectrum and has evidence that this play-based intervention stimulates brain development for many.

Story and the role of the adult

Vivian Paley (1991, 1993, 2004) writes about her work in early childhood classrooms where she encouraged children to dictate stories and then collaborate with peers to act them out. This technique promoted positive socialization, symbolic play skills, and motivation for literacy for the developmentally diverse children in her classes. It has been shown to be effective in classrooms across the country with children of diverse socioeconomic status (Groth and Darling 2001; Nicolopoulou, McDowell, and Brockmeyer 2006). Head Start children who participated in this storytelling and story-acting technique produced more sophisticated drawing and story narratives in their daily journals than before (Nicolopoulou, McDowell, and Brockmeyer 2006).

Through reciprocal and attuned exchanges with adult partners in play, children learn to extend and elaborate play, enabling others to play with them. Stanley Greenspan developed this technique for young children on the autistic spectrum.

In *A Child's Work: The Importance of Fantasy Play* (2004), Paley describes Simon, who paces and circles the classroom, crawls under a table, and plays by himself with zoo animals. As other children dictate stories and play in various areas, he weaves in and out and around the room. But when it is time to act out Holly's story, Simon bursts onto the stage. Holly, who explains that "Simon is different," incorporates him into the enactment of her story. Later that day, when the room is empty, Simon brings his zoo animals to the stage. Paley offers gentle prompts to extend his story line but primarily follows his lead, and the two of them craft a story that goes, "Walk, walk, walk. The bear walks over the hill." The story grows as Simon introduces additional animals. The next day, to Paley's surprise, Simon appears suddenly at the story-writing table and performs his story for the children there, who join in. With the help of a skillful facilitator, Simon, a solitary player, found a way to share his play through story.

THE ROLE OF PLAY IN A DEMOCRATIC SOCIETY

How does play help children to become part of a democratic society?

Freedom is a quality of both democracy and play. Playing in childhood provides children with what will become a mental and spiritual memory of the freedom that comes with play. When we ride a bike as adults, we may feel the exhilaration of past experience as well as of the present one. Yet play is endangered as American children become more entranced with technological toys and their adults become more entrenched in longer workdays.

Even so, work for increasing numbers of Americans requires a creative process that generates new ideas. Memorization is less necessary as technology makes facts readily available to everyone. To be competent in a workforce now conceptually and

These children are collaborating as they work with chalk together.

creatively motivated and to be contributing members of society, children need an education that supports conceptual and creative learning (Singer, Golinkoff, and Hirsh-Pasek 2006). Play is a creative and concept-building process.

Play, Imagination, and Social Change

Think about how else play and imagination relate to democracy. Imagination enables people to envision what is possible, and to create anything new. Imagination lets us understand other people's perspectives and helps us make sense of our experience (Egan 2007). In a democracy, citizens must work together for what each believes will be best for the society. When citizens understand each other's points of view, a democracy functions better and can meet the demands of its times.

For children to grow up to become active, prosocial citizens, we can invite them continually to make choices, express preferences, and share their emerging opinions. Play offers many opportunities to practice these expressive skills and allows children the experience of creating social microcosms. Those who play together negotiate, make rules, and collaborate as well as challenge and compete. In this way, play gives children experience with the democratic process (Jones and Cooper 2006).

But play alone will not move children toward socially just actions. As you read earlier, teachers decide the degree to which they shape children's play in that direction. There are games that lead children to cooperate rather than compete. We can talk to children about their play in ways that lead to inclusion—or in ways that may not. When we talk about play for social change, we have in mind teachers who put considerable effort into an anti-bias curriculum that includes play. Years ago, the work of Louise Derman-Sparks and the Anti-Bias Task Force showed us that kindness and fairness are necessary but not enough. It takes action on our part to make the world change in the direction of a more just society (Derman-Sparks 1989).

Debates about Play

Debates about the definition, practice, and value of play in the early childhood classroom can be confusing to the beginning teacher. Some teachers believe play distracts children from learning; others believe, as we do, that play is an essential avenue for learning. Teachers refer to play in different ways. You will see a daily schedule describing "Free Play Time," and another with "Choice Time" or "Work Time." Some professionals refer to play as "the work of children." Yet when we refer to adults "at work," we usually describe effort toward a particular goal, often with a predetermined outcome and a reward. As you read in this chapter, children's play, unlike work, is spontaneous, joyful, and creates emergent themes that change and evolve as the play develops. The experience of play is its own reward.

In recent years, an unprecedented push toward academic performance in early childhood has resulted in the marginalization of play in thousands of classrooms across the United States. Although child development studies, brain research, and early childhood educators' own experiences do not support this performance-driven practice, political policy has made it increasingly difficult for teachers to act according to their knowledge and values regarding play in the early childhood classroom. If the political motive for performance-driven early education is truly to give children a foundation for becoming intellectually and emotionally strong learners,

> Imagination lets us understand other people's perspectives and helps us make sense of our experience.

> **THOUGHT QUESTION** What have you seen in children's play that prepares them to work for social change?

> If the political motive for performance-driven early education is truly to give children a foundation for becoming intellectually and emotionally strong learners, a mandate for play will have to be included in educational policy along with academic standards.

My first year of teaching brought many challenges. Managing children's behavior was not the biggest one. Rather, it involved defending my belief that my pre-K class needed at least an hour of free play each day.

As a new teacher, I struggled to articulate the exact reasons why play was important. I only could say it felt natural and that I was teaching from the heart. For my first three years, the children continued to play in areas such as blocks, free drawing, housekeeping (with various themes such as beauty parlor or veterinary clinic), and math manipulatives. They cared for classroom pets and sometimes incorporated them into their play. Throughout this time, I faced questioning and doubts from visitors about my classroom structure, and still had no "official" reasons to offer. Only in my fourth year, when Sammy entered my classroom, did I finally have the confidence and evidence to explain my teaching practices to my principal, parents, and other teachers.

The day Sammy arrived, I could tell he was different from the rest of my students, with advanced language and knowledge as well as a high energy level. He forced me to change the way I looked at my teaching practices, to make the most of what he brought into the classroom environment. The extent of his playful imagination is the main feature that set him apart. During free play, for example, he sets up chairs in the dramatic play area to be an airplane or car and invited friends to join him to travel around the world. Not only did they pretend to go somewhere, he also set up scenarios for when they arrived at their destination. During his play, he used many areas at one time to completely engage his and his classmates' imaginations. He brought crayons and paper into the block and housekeeping areas and carried in books as entertainment for the passengers. Outside, he extended play beyond the allocated boundaries of the playscape (but still in my sight) because, as he told me, "We're on an archaeological dig, and that's where the dinosaur bones are." Other teachers were concerned. I constantly heard, "Sammy's out by the fence again." But I knew he was learning more from his imaginary play than if I guided him back onto the assigned part of the playground.

Sammy's play and imagination continued to increase as the year progressed. Because he was completely engaged in play and involved his classmates thoroughly in meaningful learning experiences, I used care when I approached their play. At times I tried to add materials to their play or become an active player but was turned away: their thoughts were more important to them than mine. I could see their thinking and their total engagement with the ideas they were creating and exploring. At the end of the year, another pre-K teacher mentioned how lucky Sammy was to have me as a teacher because I allowed him to

explore in ways other teachers would not have permitted. After the year with Sammy in my classroom, I never doubted myself as a supporter of play.

Melissa Dubick

Unfortunately, adults visiting my classroom still could not fully understand how play worked to increase children's academic knowledge. I continued to defend my teaching practices by answering questions such as why didn't I have nameplates for each child on tables, why didn't I use ditto copies, and was I sure I wanted to call it "play" and not "learning"? While others prepare their classrooms with seatwork, my preparations include figuring out how to increase the children's level of engagement in play and how to make the classroom a place where children can safely explore.

Reading about inquiry into children's play and talking with experts have increased my confidence and helped me explain why play has such a presence in my classroom. Early childhood authors, Vivian Paley (*You Can't Say You Can't Play* [1993] and *A Child's Work: The Importance of Fantasy Play* [2005]), among others, helped me see I can trust my students, not only to lead their own learning, but to engage themselves without my being or appearing to be "in control." Giving children the choice of where and with whom to play and whether to continue to play or engage in a teacher oriented project makes their educational experience that much more powerful and personal.

Thanks to Sammy and the research I studied, I can finally say that I am a good teacher. I know I am enriching children's educational and social awareness because I give them opportunities to learn about themselves and their environment within a play-rich classroom. While letting go of control as a teacher is difficult, I trust children to engage in activities that support their individuality. I see that those activities are more advantageous than anything I could present.

a mandate for play will have to be included in educational policy along with academic standards. If you, the teacher, believe in and can explain the importance of play, you can advocate for its importance in the learning process.

SUMMARY

THE INTEGRATIVE ROLE OF PLAY

How does play enable children to make sense of their experiences?

Open-ended play allows children to consolidate and master their experiences. When children play, they have to imagine the attributes and qualities of the objects with which they play and go beyond the limits of the objects themselves. In play, children solve problems creatively. They express themselves to others and clarify their thinking, and they develop ideas together as plots or play themes emerge.

PLAY IN THE LIVES OF CHILDREN

How do children of different ages play?

Children of all ages play, but they play differently at different ages. The youngest children receive sensory feedback from their play with objects. In the second year of life, toddlers begin to imitate familiar actions, moving from physical play to play with symbols. From ages three to five, children are more likely to play with each other and create play symbols that hold personal meaning for them. In the primary grades, children continue to play, although they are more likely to play games with rules. They also thrive on drama, art, and constructive play in the service of curriculum and are motivated to learn as they play with ideas. Whether children use their bodies to explore, materials to build, symbols to express meanings, or rules to frame their games, they deepen their understanding of and participation in the world through play.

QUALITIES OF PLAY

What makes it play?

Children play because they want to—and it is the process of playing that counts. The rules come from the children themselves. Play is rich in symbol and metaphor, helping children to figure out the affective world as well as the physical and social worlds. Through play, children learn about themselves and who they are in relation to others.

CATEGORIES OF PLAY

How have child developmentalists categorized children's play?

Mildred Parten (1932) described six types of play that range from unoccupied, solitary, and onlooker play, in which children play alone; to parallel and associative play, in which they are aware of each other as they play; to cooperative play, in which they truly play together. Sara Smilansky (1968) categorized play in terms of what children do when they play. Functional play involves action and the body; children use it to explore their environment. Constructive play involves arranging materials to create something new. Dramatic play is interactive and is the means for children to improvise play scenarios in which they explore ideas, feelings, and issues.

THOUGHT QUESTION What role do you believe play should have in the early childhood curriculum? What do you think will make children intellectually and emotionally strong learners? How would you combine a mandate for play with a mandate for standards? See www.naeyc.org for position papers that can help you articulate your perspective.

Smilansky's fourth category, games with rules, refers to board games, card games, and sports that provide an outlet for children's energy, an opportunity to practice and demonstrate skill and strategic thinking, and a venue for cooperation as well as competition.

AFFECTIVE COMPONENTS

How does play help children express, explore, and integrate their emotions?

Through play, with guidance and support, children can learn self-regulation and communication skills to help them improve social relations with others as they grow into adulthood. Play motivates children to regulate themselves to sustain the play. The pleasure of playing with others makes it worthwhile for children to develop their communication and social skills. Play therapy may be indicated for children who have suffered a trauma and who play differently from others, without exhibiting the joy that characterizes play. Through therapeutic play interactions, the child is no longer alone with traumatic effects.

PLAY AND DIFFERENCE

How does awareness of gender, culture, class, and disability issues help teachers support children's play?

Children differ in many ways. While play can bridge those differences, it can also emphasize them. Boys' and girls' play, for example, has similarities and glaring differences that challenge the teacher to extend children's horizons as they acknowledge their preferences.

Play can be a "social bridge" (Roopnarine and Johnson 2001, 298) among children from different cultures, since all children play. Culture influences both how children approach play and how their adults see play. Play can be a social barrier between parents and teachers, or among teachers.

Children who have disabilities may be more similar to other children than different from them. Some, however, may need physical accommodations to reach their potential for play. Others may benefit from adult support and coaching. Importantly, neither teachers nor other children can assume that children who have a disability will need help from a teacher or the other children, but they may.

PLAY RELATIONSHIPS IN THE CLASSROOM

What can teachers do to promote children's play?

Play calls the adult's role into question. In classrooms that value play, teachers support children's play interactions with each other, for example, helping children verbalize feelings that arise in play. Teachers help children invite others into their play and coach children on how to ask to play. Yet, as children wield power, struggle to solve problems, and use their imaginations in play, teachers confront the question of how much to intervene.

Teachers who are available and observant can help to make their room a safe place for children's play. When they respect children's play, they facilitate it and scaffold children's increasingly complex use of symbol and narrative. They provide language for and ask probing questions about concepts that children explore through their play. Teachers plan time for play and speak to families and colleagues about what children are learning from their play. Play opens a window of possibility for communicating with children, with those who have disabilities as well as those who do not.

THE ROLE OF PLAY IN A DEMOCRATIC SOCIETY

How does play help children to become part of a democratic society?

Both play and democracy depend on freedom. A democratic society requires imagination and creativity—and imagination is integral to play, while creativity is its natural outcome. Play offers children expressive opportunities that prepare them for democracy and for making the world a better place. Still, not everyone agrees about play, and pressure is on early childhood educators to reduce the amount that children play. The more you think about what you believe about play and why you think it is important, the readier you will be to work with young children who, most of the time, will greet you eager to play.

FURTHER ACTIVITIES

1. Take digital photos or video at a playground in a school or park in your area. Assemble the photos or use the video in a way that you can annotate. Consider what you know about young children's characteristics and needs and about multiple interacting influences on children's development and learning. Annotate the images, stating what makes the environment healthy, respectful, supportive, and challenging for all children (or not). **(NAEYC Standard 3: Observing, Documenting, and Assessing to Support Young Children and Families)**

2. Read Lillian Katz's articles on "Dispositions as Educational Goals" (http://www.ericdigests.org/1994/goals.htm) and "Another Look at What Young Children Should Be Learning" (http://www.ericdigests.org/2000-1/look.html). Form two teams with your classmates to debate the value of play. Argue your case using Katz's findings and conclusions. **(NAEYC Standard 4: Using Developmentally Effective Approaches to Connect with Children and Families)**

3. Listen to and observe one or more children to find out their interests. Research a topic related to the children's interests to learn more about it. Create an annotated list of resources (children's books, websites, print materials, videos) that could help you provide materials and experiences to enrich these children's play. **(NAEYC Standard 5: Using Content Knowledge to Build Meaningful Curriculum)**

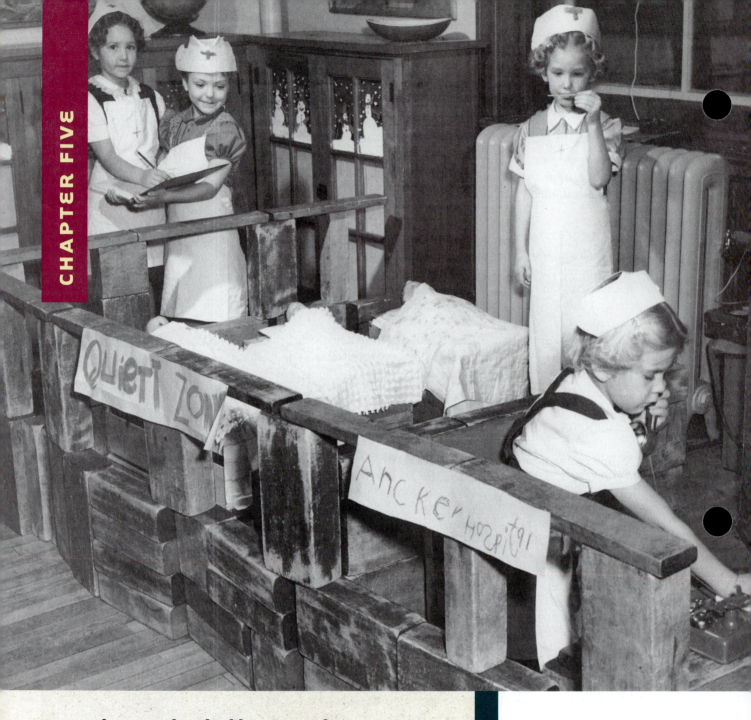

CHAPTER FIVE

Early Childhood Perspectives: Then and Now, Near and Far

The two fundamental notions of history . . . are no longer *time* and the *past* but *change* and the *event*.

Michel Foucault (emphasis in original)

Chapter Outline

Early Childhood around the World

Views of Childhood in Western History

Mid-Twentieth-Century America to Present Times

Although educating occurs in the present, it is also intrinsically connected to the future. What we do in the classroom today influences and speaks to the learner's tomorrow. Yet everyone who enters a classroom, both children and adults, also comes with a "yesterday"—that is, the events and relationships we have experienced, the stories we have been told, the attitudes and preferences we have developed and acquired all have a sociohistorical context. As we look at the history of the education of young children, several questions will guide our exploration:

- What were the goals of educators in other historical periods?
- Was education available to all children?
- What knowledge was considered important to learn?
- What developmental theories from the past inform our teaching practices today?

Exploring different historical periods in different places gives us an opportunity to reflect and to question, to consider the issues and events that have influenced the "what," "how," "when," and "why" of education over time. Doing so places education in the larger societal environments in which it developed. Take, for example, the children from the early 1950s on the previous page who are playing polio hospital. This approach takes us beyond merely acquiring a collection of names and information about the past.

Throughout the history of education, as is true of any history, society rethinks the answer to the question, "What is worth knowing?" Tension runs high between those who want to conserve the old order and those who want to institute new ideas. Change for change's sake is not a goal for educators, but staying open to new ideas is crucial. It is also key to ask, "What kind of educational development does this society want?"

> Throughout the history of education, as is true of any history, society rethinks the answer to the question, "What is worth knowing?"

EARLY CHILDHOOD AROUND THE WORLD

How do the sociopolitical and historical contexts of South Africa, India, and China influence early childhood education in those countries?

Multiple influences shape children's development. In the same way, various philosophers and the times and places in which they lived have shaped countries' early childhood practice, as Figure 5.1 illustrates.

Today, globalization has many implications for education. Families are likely to be influenced by other cultures from abroad and within their country. Centuries-old child care practices, for example, may sit beside other options, creating choice and ambiguity where once there was certainty (Barbarin & Richter 2001). Thus, how people in many times and places have thought about children has a bearing on today's children and families.

With this in mind, we begin this chapter with short histories of education in three parts of the world that together comprise half the world's population. These summaries in no way attempt to speak for all children in these countries; we hope only to offer a glimpse of ways in which early childhood in various cultures is both similar and different. We then continue with the history of early childhood education in the Western world, concluding with some current events in education that will become tomorrow's history.

This photograph of a child in New Delhi, India, could have been taken in many other parts of the world.

1. Society has a responsibility to all its members.
2. Societies should strive for excellence.
3. Education can develop a person's rational thought.
4. Education can build a fair and just society and is a vehicle for reform.
5. Education can lead to spiritual harmony.
6. Education can teach moral responsibility.
7. People are connected and responsible for each other.
8. Children learn through active participation in experiences.
9. Children learn when learning is enjoyable and they follow their interests.
10. Children thrive in a loving environment.
11. Development unfolds and can be observed.

Early Education in South Africa

At the Umanyano Educare Centre in a township in South Africa, forty children, ages three to five, sit in a circle in their new cement classroom. They have just sung a song in their native Xhosa about a father who doesn't believe it when his children say that he snores. After much snoring imitation, the teacher quiets the children and asks if anyone has a story to share.

Five-year-old Siyabulela jumps up and begins: "There is a man who is needing gas for his car. He asks his neighbor, who says no, he also has no gas. Then the man goes off to find gas. When he finally returns with the gas, the tires of the car are all flat! He drives off anyway! Ha Ha Ha Ha!"

The boy's laughter is so contagious and enthusiastic that soon the whole room erupts with laughter and giggles.

A rich oral storytelling and song history fills in for lack of materials in South Africa, and many early childhood teachers make creative use of used plastic and cardboard to create manipulatives and blocks.

This scenario reflects a collaborative and festive spirit that can be seen in many South African early childhood programs. This spirit exists in spite of life's many trials—trials these children are aware of early on.

South Africa is both similar to and different from other parts of Africa (Shutte 1995). Two differences are its multicultural population, with eleven official languages, and its postcolonial history.

European settlers first came to Southern Africa in 1652 with the arrival of the Dutch. They were joined around 1800 by the British, who instituted a British-style educational system that survives to a great extent today. While South Africa achieved independence from Great Britain in the early 1900s, earlier than most countries in Africa, the white governing elite instituted policies collectively called **apartheid**, aimed at controlling its black African population, which lasted from the 1940s until 1994. Apartheid mandated an all-encompassing system of race-based discrimination; it governed voting rights, where you could live and work, whom you could marry, and which bench you could sit on. Black African families—the vast majority of the population—were relegated to so-called homelands and to settlements and townships designated for blacks only. Most black African men had to leave their homes to work in cities or in mines but were not allowed to bring their families with them. Education was of very poor quality or nonexistent—a powerful weapon that the architects of apartheid used to control South Africans of color.

Today, South Africa is desperately in need of economic development to address overwhelming under- and unemployment, and poverty. Social challenges include reining in the spread of HIV/AIDS, malnutrition, and community violence. The government is also working to strengthen community support of orphans instead of supporting orphanages that separate children from their extended families and communities (Seleti 2007).

Ubuntu is at the core of the African spirit. The word derives from an old Xhosa proverb that means, "A person is a person because of another person."

For example, family, friend, and neighbor care is the most common form of child care for the youngest children in most of Africa. Many poor South African mothers receive a small payment for taking in other mothers' children while they work. If and when a mother loses her job, she usually continues to bring her children to be cared for while she looks for another job. To provide unquestioning support for other women, whether or not they can pay, is *ubuntu*, yet this practice leaves the child care provider with a lower and less stable income.

Early childhood educational programs, especially in informal settlements, tend to have larger numbers of children in groups than are common by Western standards. A rich oral storytelling and song history fills in for lack of materials, and many teachers make creative use of used plastic and cardboard to create manipulatives and blocks. Weather permitting, much time is spent outdoors in informal care settings.

In 2000, the government created an early care and education program for all five-year-olds called the Reception Year (similar to Western kindergarten), with training provided for their teachers. In 2008, the government released standards of care for children

A South African caregiver in an informal child care setting brings her baby to work with her.

THOUGHT QUESTION The literal translation of *ubuntu* alludes to deep human connections, not just between individuals, but between individuals and the group (Shutte 1995). As you read and hear about the concepts "development of the self" or "self-esteem," consider what it would mean if your basic definition of self included others.

Rural South African preschoolers have few materials but use them inventively.

aged birth to four. Now, training for the caregivers of infants and toddlers in informal settings is beginning to bring babies and toddlers better programming.

Early Education in India

Vasuda teaches four-year-olds in New Delhi, India. Values that underlie Indian society also ground the hopes she has for the children (Gupta 2006, 77):

> There are so many values . . . loving and caring not just for humans but for animals, for every little thing that is around them—sharing with their friends, sharing with everyone around, then hospitality, honesty, socializing, justice, mercy, discipline . . . good manners towards their adults, respect for the elders . . . taking care of . . . all living things, living as well as non-living things—cleanliness.

Although India, with more than a billion people, is multilingual and has many different religious groups, its Hindu traditions affect everyone. Five-thousand-year-old sacred texts set out the values, beliefs, rituals, and traditions of Hindu culture and govern Indians' behavior and outlooks today.

Such Indian traditions intersected with invading forces and European colonialism and continue beyond them in the present. For example, between 1000 CE and the 1700s, Muslim domination resulted in Islamic schools. After the British fully colonized India in the 1850s, they introduced Protestantism, European scientific methods, and English as the language of instruction. The British aimed to acculturate the indigenous population, that is, to make them take on the culture of their colonial rulers. Schools prepared students to participate in the lower levels of colonial activity.

India's caste system, which categorizes each family with a hereditary label, also has a bearing on education. It has less influence today than in earlier times but continues to pose a "multicultural educational challenge" (Gutek 2006, 391) to Indian society, much as racism and other forms of discrimination do in the United States. Unlike with class distinctions, individuals cannot change caste because their birth determines it.

In India today, "different developmental milestones and skills in children [are] given more significance and importance" (Gupta 2006, 5) than they are in the United States. For example, Indian early childhood education teaches children "to know the self" (Gupta 2006, 23). However, knowing oneself is bound up in interactions with others and how one fulfills one's obligations toward other people, animals, spirits, and gods. Each person fits into a larger scheme such that his or her *dharma* (morality or righteousness) contributes to rightness within the universe. Teachers are expected to guide, since they are adults and, thus, more experienced. Where a Western educator might step back to make sure children discover on their own, the Indian educator might intervene. However, since the purpose of knowledge is to open up the child's mind and to serve a moral function, the Indian early childhood educator's goal is for the child to comprehend, not simply learn by rote.

The role of educational materials and sensory play differs, too. Gupta (2006) suggests two possible explanations. With so many children to teach—and with scarce funding, materials, space, reliable electricity, or water—early childhood educators do not have the resources to provide children experiences with paint, clay, water, and sand. Gupta points out, though, that early educators could use free, natural, or inexpensive materials. However, she adds, it is likely that the concept of *maya*, the idea that the physical world is an illusion, greatly influences Indian early childhood edu-

Indian teachers are expected to guide, since they are adults and, thus, more experienced. The purpose of knowledge is to open up the child's mind and to serve a moral function.

Indian preschools emphasize shared values and academic success.

cation by emphasizing the intellectual realm of ideas—even for young children—in place of concrete, exploratory play.

The extended family plays a large role in children's earliest care and education, especially in rural areas. In urban areas, where more women work outside the home, nannies are becoming more prevalent; more early childhood programs exist, in particular, in urban housing developments; and kindergarten has become part of the urban school system (Gutek 2006), yet only about 25 percent of children under six attend early childhood programs. These programs face the challenge of blending an ancient culture with new economic and social needs, creating early childhood education and care that is uniquely Indian.

Early Education in the People's Republic of China

Nowadays, the living conditions in our country are far better than in the old days, when the younger teachers who work here now were just children. They have not experienced the hardship that we experienced. It is our job to remind them constantly of the good traditions and to instill collective pride among the younger teachers so that they will never lose that spirit. (Ms. Wang, founding director of Daguan Preschool, quoted in Tobin, Hsueh, and Karasawa 2009)

Today's China promotes children's independence more than in previous eras. The government advocates more opportunities for free-play and self-expression, and a more child-centered and constructivist curriculum, one that sees children as able to invent and discover. These approaches are more prevalent in the urban areas. In some parts of rural China, the old guiding ways may still exist. However, China, a global giant with a population of more than two billion people and a rapidly growing market economy, is in a defining moment as it struggles to fuse the best of Western early childhood philosophies with its own deep-seated cultural traditions and unbridled economic changes (Tobin, Hsueh, and Karasawa 2009).

In today's China, the government advocates more opportunities for free-play and self-expression, and a more child-centered and constructivist curriculum, one that sees children as able to invent and discover.

Chinese children exercise at a
kindergarten in Shanghai.

Chinese history often begins with Confucius (551–448 BCE). His secular philosophy emphasized a life of physical and emotional harmony; its deep and far-reaching effects continue in China today. After Confucius, China settled into a feudal or semi-feudal social organization for nearly twenty-five hundred years; children were taught what they had to know within their families. Europe had a much shorter feudal period, multiple revolutions, and many cultural shifts. China entered the modern era almost directly from feudalism, a time during which "little was learned and nothing forgotten" (Belden 1949, 116). As China began to interact with the West during the nineteenth century, it displayed an intermittent interest in incorporating new educational ideas—an ambivalence that continues.

During the early days of the People's Republic of China (from 1949), educators worked in practical ways to create forms of early education that would reach, not just young children, but the vast majority of adult peasants, who were illiterate. As the new government came to power in 1949, a socialist education administrator said, "John Dewey says 'Education is life; school is society.' But we say: 'Life is education; society is a school'" (Belden 1949, 136). Life was indeed the schoolhouse during the early days of the People's Republic. Whether in the farms or cities, illiterate adults first learned Chinese characters and words connected with their work on the job, as they worked, often with children helping them.

Joseph Tobin, David Wu, and Dana Davidson (1989) gathered data in the mid-1980s from visits to China's urban preschools, interviews, and videotaping. Tobin, Yeh Hsueh, and Mayumi Karasawa returned in the early years of the twenty-first century to investigate changes during the intervening years. They paint a complex picture of a diverse China now grappling with competing educational philosophies and their implications for children (Tobin, Hsueh, and Karasawa 2009).

In the 1980s and 1990s, because of China's one-child rule initiated to control population growth, many worried that children would become spoiled and not fulfill long-term needs to work hard, contribute to the country's future, and provide for their elderly parents. Today, there is still some worry over children's moral codes,

PART 2 Foundations of Early Childhood Education

but the materialism of urban China, at least, seems to have spread to parents, not just children. Weekday boarding schools, for example, were popular with working-class families before the 1980s, when parents had many children and worked long hours. Today, Tobin writes, it is urban professional parents who are more likely to have their child in weekday boarding school so that they can fulfill their professional commitments and lead busy adult lives.

While Western influences have played a significant role in China's early childhood educational philosophy at various times, the current period may prove to be more of a tipping point, one where China blends a range of approaches to fit its shifting needs. At the beginning of this chapter, we suggested that education reflects what societies want for their children. China is a particularly apt example, as it tries to determine the attitudes and skills children need to best prepare them for the China of the future. Tobin, Hsueh, and Karasawa (2009) suggest that soon China may be where the early childhood community in the United States and elsewhere looks for inspiration and fresh ideas.

VIEWS OF CHILDHOOD IN WESTERN HISTORY

What ideas developed over the ages that influence early childhood education today?

Here we examine how many of the views of children and early childhood education that ground U.S. early care and education evolved. As we discuss the history of education in Europe and the United States, reflect on what you have just read about current-day South Africa, India, and China and how ideas from civilizations around the world do, or do not, influence our thinking about young children. We begin with Greco-Roman civilization (1200 BCE–500 CE).

Ancient Greece and Rome

Many historians trace the roots of modern Western education to the great thinkers of ancient Greece, who contributed significantly to what we teach as well as how we teach. Greek life centered on full participation in the community, or **polis,** which played a critical role in educating Greek citizens, almost exclusively men. The Greeks were a male-dominated society that valued a broad, inclusive education and saw it as key to the development of all free men (Gutek 1995).

Socrates (ca. 469–399 BCE), first in the series of major philosopher-teachers, sought to demonstrate that a **universal morality,** a code of ethics that applies to everyone, exists to guide one's actions and choices (Gutek 1995, 40).

Socrates believed in a world of absolutes, universal ideal standards toward which all humans strive. He proposed that knowledge comes from within, not from teachers or external experience. The teacher's role is to bring this knowledge to the student's consciousness by asking stimulating questions to help him contemplate and eventually uncover the truth (Gutek 1995).

THOUGHT QUESTION Can an educational idea be right for everyone? Think of an educational idea, and explain why it could or could not apply to everyone everywhere.

A student of Socrates, *Plato* (ca. 427–347 BCE) developed a philosophy built on Socratic beliefs but focused more on teachers helping to develop students' ability to reason and control their emotions. To this end, Plato proposed that for the first six years, children be raised in state-run nurseries, away from their parents and

THOUGHT QUESTION Have you seen young children learn or share an aspect of their family's history as a part of their school's curriculum? How was this implemented, and how were families involved in the curriculum planning process?

The medical model, an approach that treats symptoms instead of the whole person and has since come to influence the field of disability, first appeared in ancient Greece and Rome.

everyday-life experience. That way, educators could help them form proper habits and develop emotional stability (Gutek 1997).

Teachers used stories, music, sports, and drama to assist in forming a good character that reflected high ideals (Weber 1984). Immersing oneself in art and literature was as important as developing the power of pure reasoning.

The realism of *Aristotle* (384–322 BCE) stands in contrast to Plato's idealism. Aristotle believed the goal of life was to use reason well and to make moderate, sensible choices so as to live a harmonious life. He also believed in perfecting the intellect through study, inquiry, and observation. The purpose of education was to promote human excellence; to advance this goal, Aristotle recommended compulsory formal public education (Gutek 1997). All three philosophers focused only on men as thinkers, which reflected the gender views of the time.

Roman society adapted Greek principles and concepts to support its own beliefs and values. Rome was also male dominated, and although wealthy girls and women could be educated, only male children of the aristocracy would become citizens and transmit Roman traditions and values. In addition to reading and writing, learning one's family history and traditions was a key part of boys' primary education (Gutek 1995, 58).

The Roman educator *Quintilian* (ca. 35–ca. 100 CE) was one of the first to develop a rudimentary theory of child development. From birth to seven, he wrote, children were impulsive and needed guidance. He advised that during the early years, learning should be enjoyable, with subjects taught gradually and without the use of corporal punishment. Also, Quintilian suggested that teachers use **didactic,** or instructive, materials to teach literacy skills, for example, having children trace ivory letters to learn to write (Gutek 1995).

Because Greece and Rome considered being a citizen central to life, they cultivated the strong and ignored or dispensed with the weak. Infanticide was practiced by some, but not all, cities as a way to weed out those believed to be incapable of serving the society.

The **medical model,** an approach that treats symptoms instead of the whole person and has since come to influence the field of disability, first appeared in ancient Greece and Rome. *Hippocrates* (460–377 BCE), the Greek physician known as the "father of medicine" (and author of the Hippocratic oath, still taken by physicians today), developed treatments for those with visual and auditory impairment, epilepsy, and mental retardation (Winzer 1993). Hippocrates also believed that each of the four fluids, called humors—blood, lymph, yellow bile, and black bile—characterized a basic human quality. The humors can be seen as a precursor of our notions of individual temperament.

Europe in Medieval Times

During the Middle Ages (600–1100 CE), forces of continuity and change slowly worked together to alter the way people lived. In the feudal system that emerged after the fragmentation of the Roman Empire, local landowners became lords and vassals to kings who granted, or were forced to grant, local rule. Peasants, who had been free, were downgraded to serfs and became little better than slaves. Medieval civilization became a localized, male-dominated, and hierarchical society in which the Catholic Church emerged as the most powerful institution in the West and controlled most schools—all of them for males. Only a few educational opportunities existed for wealthy women, who could enter convents and nunneries to study (Gutek 1995).

People with disabilities were also cloistered from the external world, with few attempts for their care or cure. In addition, numerous impairments we now consider biological or neurological, such as epilepsy, mental retardation, and mental illness, were seen as the work of witches, and thousands of individuals with disabilities, mostly women, were executed.

Throughout the Middle Ages, as social divisions sharpened, literacy became the defining mark of the clergy. Moreover, as class distinctions hardened into "free" and "servile," literacy became associated with freedom (Moore 1998).

John Amos Comenius (1592–1670)

Seventeenth- and Eighteenth-Century Europe

During the historical period called the Protestant *Reformation* (1517–1648), tensions between religious and secular trends reflected and spearheaded political, economic, and social upheaval (MacCulloch 2005) that led to reforms in all areas of life. The German theologian *Martin Luther* (1483–1546), whose challenge to the Catholic Church initiated the Reformation, insisted that all people needed to read and understand scripture in order to work toward salvation. This meant that schools had to be established to teach children to read in their native languages, not only in Latin, the language of the Catholic Church.

John Amos Comenius

Amid the chaos and wars of the Reformation, leaders of some of the new religious groups strove to promote peace and understanding. *John Amos Comenius* (1592–1670), a Moravian Protestant bishop, was one. Comenius's educational philosophy was based on a belief in education for everyone. Ignorance, he claimed, was responsible for violence and intolerance. Greater knowledge, asserted Comenius, would end the prejudice and discrimination against so many people in Europe, including Comenius himself (Gutek 1997).

Comenius drew from his experience as an educator, scientist, and theorist to propose a developmental approach to learning. Having observed that plants and animals had their own timetables for development, he suggested that children also matured at individual rates. Comenius believed that children needed to be psychologically ready to learn and that for the first six years, they should be educated at home by their mothers. He authored the first picture book for children, *Orbis Pictus* ("The World in Pictures") as a way for children to learn the names of objects. Also significant, Comenius recognized the value of play and sensory experiences for young children's learning. His belief in the importance of creating a loving, secure environment from birth to age six to foster growth and independence foreshadows the twentieth-century ideas of theorists Erik Erikson and John Bowlby. Likewise, Comenius's appreciation of the role senses play in all learning is a notion that educators use in their work every day.

> Comenius drew from his experience as an educator, scientist, and theorist to propose a developmental approach: that children, like plants and animals, had their own timetables for development and also matured at individual rates.

THOUGHT QUESTION The idea of knowledge or education as a means to a better world with greater equality is also at the foundation of our democratic way of life in the United States. Think of an example from your experience that illustrates this idea.

John Locke asked, "Whence has [the mind] all the materials of reason and knowledge? To this I answer in one word, from *experience. . . .*"

Rousseau disagreed with Locke's contention that the child was a blank slate to be written upon. Instead, he believed that everyone is born with innate qualities of goodness, abilities, and traits.

John Locke

According to *John Locke* (1632–1704), all that we become is the result of our experience with the environment. The experiences we acquire through our senses, and our reflections on those experiences, is the source of all our ideas and knowledge.

It was Locke who coined the term **tabula rasa,** meaning a blank slate onto which the environment writes. Up to this time, children were often thought to be born evil, and it was society's task to redeem them. Locke, however, argued that children were born *neutral* and that society shaped them. His philosophy formed the basis for the subsequent eighteenth-century intellectual movement known as the *Enlightenment.* Its proponents believed that the world is a rational place that can be known and perfected. Knowledge can be broken down, analyzed, confirmed, and discounted according to one's experiences. This concept became the basis of an extreme environmentalism: the belief that the environment determines everything.

Much has been made of Locke's views as mechanistic, that is, simple and automatic, and as a forerunner to modern behavioral theory, in which the child is seen as passive and malleable. Yet Locke did not think everyone should be molded in the same way (Beatty 1995). He felt that a child's capacities, aptitudes, and temperaments should govern his learning (Gay 1964), and that learning, above all, should be enjoyable. He also emphasized play's importance in the education and growth of the child. Finally, Locke thought girls should be educated similarly to boys, but with less rigorous physical education. Unfortunately, his call for education reform did not include education for poor children. Nonetheless, his ideas broke with traditions of his time and had a strong impact on subsequent educators.

Jean-Jacques Rousseau: The Enlightenment

Like many Enlightenment thinkers, *Jean-Jacques Rousseau* (1712–1778) believed that individuals and society could be perfected. Unlike earlier Enlightenment philosophers who thought civilization was advancing, Rousseau argued that civilization was leading human beings in harmful directions, away from their natural goodness. Only what he called a "natural" education, or **naturalism,** including a new moral outlook, could repair how governments, religion, and superstition had negatively affected humans. He wanted people to connect to themselves and to each other in authentic ways (Edwards 1972).

In his novel, *Emile,* Rousseau explained what he thought an ideal education should be and accomplish. Emile grew and developed through his experiences with nature, people, and things, which Rousseau believed to be the basis of a rich education.

Rousseau disagreed with Locke's contention that the child was a blank slate to be written upon (Gutek 1997, 126). Instead, he believed that everyone is born with innate qualities of goodness, abilities, and traits. To develop these natural qualities, Rousseau envisioned a learning environment that protected children from the corruption of civilization and guided them to remain pure and good.

Rousseau believed that observing children was the key to understanding all stages of human development. A child's developmental readiness signaled that the child was ripe for learning. Believing that humans are basically self-motivated, Rousseau reasoned that self-control, discipline, attention, and perseverance unfolded from within individuals who were given the chance to explore the environment, utilize their senses, and reason on their own (Weber 1984). Thus, through a combination of children's biological capacities and interaction with people and objects in the environment, *children construct their knowledge* rather than passively making mental copies of ideas and experiences received from the outside world (Watson 2002). You can see the seeds of constructivist learning taking root here.

Rousseau's insights and ideas helped form a basis for future progressive educational thought and practice. In addition, his ideas about the importance of maturational readiness helped pave the way for theorists like Arnold Gesell, about whom you will read in Chapter 6. Examples of Rousseau's beliefs that are integral to early childhood practice today include a child-centered curriculum based on cognitive development, direct exploration of the environment, and consideration of the whole child.

Disability and the Enlightenment

Before the mid-1700s in Europe, few people respected variations in human abilities or considered someone who had a disability as a person with human dignity just like anyone else (Winzer 1999). With the growth of **empiricism,** or scientific thought, some earlier ideas about disability—for example, that it had demonic origins—began to fade. While philosophers and educators of this period did not create significant learning interventions for children with disabilities, their writings introduced the world to the idea of increased rights for individuals with disabilities.

An exception occurred just before the turn of the nineteenth century. A feral (or wild) child, known thereafter as "Victor, the wild child," was discovered living with wolves in the woods of southern France. A physician named *Jean-Marc Gaspard Itard,* who had just begun to study deafness, became intrigued with the boy (after many captures and escapes) and worked to try to "educate" him. Here was an opportunity to put the theories of the Enlightenment to work. Was the child thrown out to fend for himself because he was lacking in cognitive abilities? Or, as Itard presumed, was the boy the way he was because he had *not* grown up with humans and lacked education (Itard 1962)?

Victor improved in some very basic areas such as standing up but never really progressed to the point of joining human society. However, Itard's methods laid the foundation for later innovations in educating individuals with disabilities by such future educators as Eduard Seguin and Maria Montessori.

Nineteenth-Century Europe and the United States

The nineteenth century was an era of transition, during which sociopolitical and historical events again served to shape early childhood education. Three ideas from this period changed life in the Western hemisphere and influenced education as well.

The *Industrial Revolution* was an era when factories full of manufacturing machines—and the people to tend them—spread across the Western world. This revolution began in Great Britain and reached the United States by about 1780, transforming the nature of work, altering class structure, and changing international relations. While it provided new jobs for men and women that enabled them to enjoy a higher standard of living, for many workers factory life was brutal, with long hours and sometimes dangerous and unhealthy work environments. Children as young

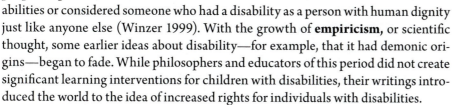

Victor, the Wild Child

Rousseau said, "With our false ideas of [childhood] the more we do, the more we blunder. The wisest people are so concerned with what grown ups should know that they never consider what children are capable of learning. They keep looking for the man in the child, not thinking of what he is before he becomes a man."

as six could be found working in factories during this time. Industrialization dehumanized people and devalued nature at the same time as it made new goods and opportunities available.

Nationalism was a new idea at this time: nationalists believed (as Rousseau did about individuals) that every nation had the right to be free and independent, and that such independence would promote harmony and unity among all peoples. While this idea was originally a liberating force, it gradually fostered or worsened conflicts between nations. Nationalism pitted countries against one another; as a philosophy, it underlies the root of conflicts that continue today.

Another new idea of this time was *Romanticism,* a revolt against the Enlightenment's immersion in rational thought. Romanticists believed that human creativity was the result of emotional intensity, imagination, and spontaneity, not only in art, but also in everyday life. European progressive educators, working and writing at different times during the Industrial Revolution, attempted to establish educational philosophies and practices that would create a natural, caring environment in an increasingly depersonalized world (McKay, Hill, Buckler, and Ebry 2004).

Johann Heinrich Pestalozzi

Influenced by both Rousseau and the ideas of the Enlightenment, *Johann Heinrich Pestalozzi* (1746–1827), an Italian-Swiss teacher, championed poor and orphaned children, believing that providing universal education (education for all) would restore meaning to lives that had been negatively affected by industrialization. Education, he believed, would allow these children to develop into moral, economically productive, and socially responsible adults.

Several assumptions underlie Pestalozzi's educational theory. First, using the metaphor of a developing plant, Pestalozzi devised a theory of child development grounded in his basic belief in a child's innate goodness. Second, Pestalozzi claimed that education could occur only in an environment in which a child experienced being loved. This begins with a loving mother who fosters the child's feelings of trust and emotional security. This idea foreshadows twentieth-century attachment theory. With time, the child connects this feeling of love to others, which in Pestalozzi's view leads to the formation of religious values and the concepts of duty and justice. Thus, education produces a responsible moral person connected to others, creating a just society (Gutek 1968). Pestalozzi also was a strong believer in multiage, or "family," groupings, another precursor to educational ideas that hold currency today.

Third, Pestalozzi believed that the aim of education is to stimulate the child from within, not impose from without. A teacher should carefully observe the stages of the child's development to be able to offer experiences to enhance that child's innate intellectual, moral, and physical capacities in a meaningful way. Harmonious growth requires paying attention to the whole child, not just to one domain, or area, of development.

To Pestalozzi, learning was active and interactive. As we take in the world through our senses, we gather data about it. Then, with a growing consciousness of what we have perceived, we act to translate the sensorial into forms and mental images that fit with our previous learning. In this way, we begin to understand concepts. To accomplish this, children need to interact with objects, explore them, name them, and number them.

Pestalozzi's contribution to education had wide-reaching effects. His approach, which stressed the need to consider the cognitive, emotional, and physical needs of the child, led to reforms in elementary and teacher education. It also laid the foundation

Pestalozzi said, "Teaching is like the art of the gardener under whose care a thousand trees blossom and grow. He contributes nothing to their actual growth; the principle of growth lies in the trees themselves. He plants and waters, but God gives the increase."

THOUGHT QUESTION Pestalozzi compared teaching to gardening. What is your metaphor for teaching? Explain why you think your metaphor makes sense.

PART 2 Foundations of Early Childhood Education

for the nineteenth- and early twentieth-century progressive education movement, which embraced child-centered, experiential learning and curriculum based on developmental stages (Gutek 1968), as well as the use of manipulative materials.

Robert Owen

As a result of industrialization, by the early nineteenth century, work had moved from the house to the factory, and many women now also worked outside the home. *Robert Owen*, a Scottish industrialist, felt that these workers' children needed to be in a safe and secure environment while their parents were at work. Consequently, he began the first Infant School in New Lanark, Scotland, in 1816 (Williams and Fromberg 1992) in what was known as a **utopian** community, that is, one built on a vision for a new and ideal society. The term *infant* in the school's name referred to preschool and early elementary-aged children, not infants.

Owen's school deemphasized punishment; and, like Pestolozzi, Owen incorporated song, play, physical exercise, and exploration of nature as part of the curriculum (Williams and Fromberg 1992). Owen's goal was to promote social interaction (Guthrie 2003). While a few infant schools were started in the United States during the 1820s in response to Owen's utopian experiment—notably, in New Harmony, Indiana (1824)—all of them were shut down by 1830 (Williams 1992) with the collapse of New Harmony. However, the idea of education for children aged two to five inspired subsequent educators to found similar schools during the twentieth century.

Friedrich Froebel

In many ways, *Friedrich Froebel* (1782–1852), with his creation of the kindergarten and his ideas about play, gave birth to the field of early childhood education. The deeply religious Froebel's educational work grew out of his belief that all things have their origin in God and that God lives in all things. As a result, he maintained, a spiritual unity binds everything in nature, and the aim of life is to realize our divine essence.

In line with his spiritual philosophy, Froebel devised an educational program—the **kindergarten** (in German, "child's garden")—for which he created a variety of materials and activities. Early childhood development was an unfolding of the divine essence within, personified in the child's innocent, open, and active exploration. The teacher's job was to help the child's inner self engage with the outer world. One of the most powerful ways to do this was through play (Weber 1984).

The materials Froebel used, or **gifts** as he called them, enabled children to understand the principles of harmony, unity, and diversity. When they used the gifts, which they did in a clearly specified way, children experienced and intuited mathematical ideas and principles and focused on contrasts, opposites, relationships, and differentiation. The gifts also awakened a sense of beauty, offering a means for creative expression of the inner life (Weber 1984).

Froebel believed that songs and stories enriched a child's life. Nursery rhymes sung by the mother and stories she told about the family developed language, which helped connect the child to objects and experiences in the environment. Froebel's program also incorporated the visual arts because he felt that painting and drawing promote an unfolding of one's inner life (Weber 1984).

In addition, Froebel's kindergarten included **occupations,** physical activities such as sewing, weaving, and gardening. In the ideal kindergarten, each child worked her own plot as well as a common one (Weber 1984).

Froebel established his kindergarten during a time when forces such as nationalism and romanticism were sweeping through Europe, threatening established

For Froebel, early childhood development was an unfolding of the divine essence within, personified in the child's innocent, open, and active exploration. The teacher's job was to help the child's inner self engage with the outer world.

These are examples of three of the eight Froebelian gifts.

social and political structures and resulting in uprisings and revolts. Given what it considered to be the radical nature of Froebel's beliefs, the Prussian government closed his school in 1852. Despite this, Froebel's educational philosophy spread throughout Europe and reached the United States in the mid-1800s.

The proliferation of the kindergarten

By the 1840s, what we know as Germany was only a loose federation of states. An uprising of nationalists—those who wanted a unified Germany with more freedoms—did not succeed, forcing many German advocates of the Froebelian kindergarten to flee. *Margarethe Schurz* (1832–1876), a follower of Froebel, left Europe and settled in Watertown, Wisconsin, where she started a small Froebelian German-speaking kindergarten in 1856. Schurz soon met *Elizabeth Palmer Peabody* (1804–1894), a Boston intellectual who had been involved in educational reform movements, and introduced her to the work of Froebel.

Peabody was particularly taken with Froebelian spiritualism and, in 1860, started the first Froebelian kindergarten for English-speaking children. Although the number of such kindergartens increased dramatically as a result of her efforts (from ten in 1870 to four thousand in 1890), Peabody's strict interpretation of Froebel's program led to criticism from the late nineteenth- and early twentieth-century American progressives.

Susan Blow (1843–1916), another kindergarten advocate, persuaded St. Louis's superintendent of schools, William Harris, to open the first public kindergarten in the United States in 1873. Like Peabody, Blow believed in the goal of moral perfection and that the only path to it was a strict adherence to Froebelian practice, regardless of any cultural or geographic differences.

In the late nineteenth and early twentieth centuries, there were few kindergartens for African American children, and in them vocational training prevailed. A 1901 survey found that no public kindergartens existed in the South, where most African Americans lived (Beatty 1995). White supporters of kindergartens for blacks argued that they were needed to train blacks for domestic work. Given the alternative of no kindergartens, some African Americans agreed. At the Hampton Institute—founded in 1868 for the education of former slaves—the free kindergarten curriculum consisted of dusting, washing clothes, ironing, janitorial work for the boys, and agricultural work such as planting and making farm tools (Beatty 1995).

The birth of special education

By the nineteenth century, *Eduard Seguin* (1812–1880) and other European educators were basing their theories on humane, egalitarian, and optimistic philosophies. Seguin understood that learning could be achieved by stimulating alternate senses that complemented the diminished ones in deaf and visually impaired individuals. Schools for the deaf appeared in France, along with manual and oral systems of communication. Seguin also developed a multilayered approach for people with mental retardation that became known as the "physiological method," in which his students were challenged by cognitive and physical tasks that fostered a sense of independence. His approach, which owes much to Itard's earlier efforts, laid the groundwork for contemporary special education principles (Winzer 1999).

Following this work in Europe, institutions for the disabled, such as Boston's Perkins Institute for the Blind (1829), sprang up in North America as well. These institutions raised the level of care and introduced more educational programs for those with disabilities. Social reformers also pushed for disabled individuals to be accepted as equal members of society (Winzer 1999). *Helen Keller* (1880–1968), who became deaf and blind by age two, contributed to this acceptance. A special relationship grew between Keller and her teacher, *Anne Sullivan* (1866–1936). Their work led the way for new communication possibilities, learning techniques, and rights for deaf and visually impaired individuals.

Twentieth-Century Europe and the United States

From the start of the twentieth century, education built upon the innovations of the previous century. As you read about the ideas in this section, reflect on some of their precursors.

Maria Montessori

While Froebel's work grew out of the Romantic era, *Maria Montessori* (1870–1952) began her work with children during the late nineteenth and early twentieth centuries. Italy, where Montessori was raised, was ruled by a monarchy and had an inflexible and fixed class system and rigid gender distinctions. Despite these constraints, Montessori became the country's first woman doctor.

After her graduation, Montessori educated developmentally disabled children. While working in a psychiatric clinic at the

> By the nineteenth century, Seguin and other educators understood that learning could be achieved by stimulating alternate senses that complemented the diminished ones in deaf and visually impaired individuals.

Helen Keller when she was eight years old, left, holding hands with her teacher, Anne Sullivan, during a summer vacation in Brewster, Massachusetts, Cape Cod in 1888. Keller became deaf and blind before the age of two.

University of Rome, she learned of the work of Itard and Seguin and became interested in the connection between child development and education. Desiring to put her wide-ranging knowledge and ideas into practice, in 1907 Montessori opened the *Casa dei Bambini* ("Children's House") in the slums of Rome for the young children of working mothers.

Bringing a clinical and scientific approach to her educational efforts, Montessori, like Froebel, placed the child as learner at the center of the educational environment. Her experience with developmentally challenged children had convinced her that, with the right educational approaches, all children could learn and grow. To Montessori, dignity and self-respect could be acquired and maintained through mastery in work, independence, and responsibility.

Montessori considered development as a natural process that unfolded according to a biological pattern at different rates in different children, so that schoolwork had to be adapted to the individual child. We see here the seeds of what has today become **differentiated instruction,** flexible teaching that offers children a range of ways to learn that suit their needs.

In addition, Montessori emphasized the close connection between motor and sensory functions and the development of a child's physical and mental abilities. To promote these abilities, Montessori devised **self-correcting materials,** for example, puzzles in which a child can figure out if a response is correct without a teacher. Some materials were designed to be introduced in a particular sequence, to prepare children's senses for more formalized skills such as reading and writing. Other materials and activities promoted **practical life skills,** such as getting dressed, pouring juice, and washing dishes.

Montessori designed child-sized furniture for the classroom and placed materials where children could reach them. She believed that children tend toward movement, order, and exploration of their environment; that they need to classify and clarify the random impressions they receive; and that, given proper tasks, a struc-

Many Montessori teachers keep Maria Montessori close to their hearts and minds.

ture for behavior, and freedom to work uninterrupted for as long as they like, they develop self-direction and concentration. This demands from the teacher a solid understanding of child development and close observation to discover children's "sensitive" periods of learning. The teacher then prepares the classroom for these sensitive periods, introduces the materials, and allows the children to take responsibility for their learning.

During the Fascist era in Italy (1922–1943), the government became increasingly hostile to the Montessori schools, and they were closed by 1936, once again demonstrating the relationship between schools and the dictates of a society. Montessori schools made a comeback in the United States in the 1950s (Roopnarine and Johnson 2005), and her approach continues to make key contributions to early childhood education today. Montessori's application of child psychology to educational practice; her notion of individual instruction in which all children, including those with disabilities, proceed at their own pace; and the active participation of young children in their own learning have had an immense impact on early childhood educational theory and practice (Kramer 1988).

Rudolf Steiner and Waldorf Education

In the aftermath of World War I (1914–1918), Europe was in a shambles physically, socially, and economically. *Rudolf Steiner,* a German scientist, educator, and spiritual philosopher, described a new way of organizing societies. In his view, a "threefold social order"—in which the integrity of the individual would be nurtured through education, religion, and the arts and everyone would be treated equally under the law—was needed. Workers unions, consumer unions, environmental groups, and manufacturers would work together to address multiple needs, not only immediate profit.

In 1919, Steiner described these ideas in a speech before the workers of the Waldorf Astoria Cigarette Factory in Stuttgart, Germany. They were inspired when he said that education should help individuals develop all of their capacities, not just those needed in the workplace. The next day the workers, as well as the factory owner, asked Steiner to start a school for the workers' children. Six months later, the first Waldorf school—later also called Steiner schools—opened. In a few years, Waldorf schools were educating nearly a thousand children from kindergarten to grade twelve. Waldorf Education expanded throughout Europe until the rise of Nazism in the 1930s, when the Nazis closed the schools. After World War II (1939–1945), the Waldorf schools reopened; their philosophy of education spread widely and continues to thrive in many parts of the world.

The Progressive Movement, 1890—1930

In the United States, the early years of the twentieth century saw an unleashing of major societal forces and energies working to organize labor, capital, and agriculture. A women's movement arose, representing different ethnic groups and social classes. And a new middle class sought to bring about greater social justice among the poor (Antler 1987).

Educators of the late nineteenth and early twentieth centuries, who came to be called *progressives,* held several basic values in common that they applied to educational institutions. Qualities drawn from their Protestant roots, including a sense of moral duty and reform, merged with the promise of knowledge through the application of natural and social scientific principles. The harsh realities of industrial life led many progressives to fear the new concentration of power in the hands of major

Montessori said ". . . the origins of development lie within. The child does not grow because he is nourished, because he breathes . . . he grows because the potential life within him develops, making itself visible."

THOUGHT QUESTION Kindergartens spread like wildfire in the late nineteenth and early twentieth centuries. Can you think of early childhood programs in the twentieth and twenty-first centuries that spread that as rapidly? As you read further, see if any come to mind.

By the 1870s, public schools existed throughout the United States; and, because of new child labor laws, by 1918, all states had some form of compulsory school attendance.

capitalists. Others wished to bring modern ideas of efficiency and organization into schools, an approach that became known as the *efficiency movement*. Some, seeking government intervention to address anxieties about moral laxity, campaigned against alcoholism, divorce, and prostitution. Still others, worried about the breakdown of traditional community, focused on restoring social cohesion through social reform. Overall, a widespread desire for change existed along with optimism that a better society could be created.

By the 1870s, public schools existed throughout the United States. Progressives advocated for, and the government passed, a *child labor law;* by 1918, all states had some form of compulsory school attendance (Foner and Garraty 1991). As a result of these laws and of ever-rising immigration, between 1890 and 1930, there was an enormous increase in the number of students attending public schools. At that time, the schools were extended both upward, to the secondary level, and downward, to kindergarten.

The *child study movement* emerged during the Progressive Era, promoted by the National Education Association (NEA) and individual advocates, such as the prominent psychologist *G. Stanley Hall* (1844–1924), who founded the *American Psychological Association*. As part of this movement, two disciplines that continue to sustain early childhood practice—education and psychology—began to work together with a joint focus on children's growth and development. Many institutions, such as the Gesell Institute, originated during this period, along with Bank Street's Bureau of Educational Experiments.

However, not all was progressive during the Progressive Era. Amid ever-increasing waves of immigration, white Americans who had lived in the United States for longer than the immigrants—sometimes not by much—became fearful and mistrustful of those who were different from them. Adherents of *eugenics* (a movement to

THE FIRST STEP

American-born social planners often regarded immigrants as ignorant.

increase the number of people supposed to have superior genetic makeup) created **taxonomies,** that is, hierarchical categories of intelligence, which became popular and were used to justify their prejudices.

By 1912, psychologists like *Lewis Termin* were introducing IQ (intelligence quotient) tests to school systems. Such testing was promoted in the name of democracy because it presumably measured a person's native intelligence. In fact, IQ tests drew upon funds of knowledge that, like subject matter tests, favored those who could afford excellent schools or were better prepared at home. Based on the results of these tests, children of immigrant families were often assigned to the school's lower tracks, with less rigorous expectations and teaching, while middle-class children, who invariably scored higher, were placed in the upper tracks, thus reinforcing the notion that middle-class Protestant values were superior. Some progressives, concerned about the social impact of rapid immigration on American society and relying on their faith in science, were drawn to such tests because, theoretically, they helped educators to better understand children's learning needs. Others, though not drawn into the testing rage, did little to protest it.

Paradoxically, at the same time that human differences were highlighted in the name of science, the U.S. government was sending Native American children to be educated at *Bureau of Indian Affairs'* boarding schools, far away from their families, language, and culture. This practice tapered off in the 1930s, and now Native American families have more school options, including tribal schools on the reservation.

John Dewey

The most influential force behind the Progressive movement was *John Dewey* (1859–1952), who rejected Froebel's spiritual notions of unity and imitative use of materials. Rather, Dewey applied the philosophical tradition of pragmatism to educational reform. *Pragmatism* proposed that truth can be found in experience, not in the abstract; and Dewey argued that education is built on experience. Influenced in part by Rousseau, Dewey also stressed that when children follow their interests, they learn language, science, art, and history. He also maintained that since society changes constantly, children had to learn to navigate the dynamic social environment.

Dewey addressed the depth and essence of democracy, not just its surface appearance (Cuffaro 1995). He believed the purpose of education was to enable students to participate eventually in the continual experiment of a more democratic society, and he challenged educators to decide what knowledge and experiences lead learners to understand the meaning and responsibilities of democracy.

Dewey observed that traditional education separated the social classes, school and society, leisure and labor, mind and body, and thought and action. It isolated subject matter, precluding integrated understanding. Only an education rooted in experience, he believed, could solve life's problems and restore meaning in people's lives.

Offering no set curriculum, Dewey left specific content, and when to teach it, up to the teacher. He questioned the trend of relying on testing, standardization, and behavioral theories of learning because of their emphasis on skills acquisition over thinking and creativity (Smith and Smith 1994). Yet in his book *Experience and Education* (1938/1997), Dewey himself seemed to be aware of the potential weaknesses of progressive education. He felt that, in some instances, it had become too centered on freedom and the child's self-expression, and without enough emphasis on subject matter. He warned that progressive education was in danger of becoming just as dogmatic as traditional education.

THOUGHT QUESTION Standardized tests, although not intelligence tests, are used today and continue to have a great impact on children. Some children do better on these tests than others. What can you find out about tests and their impact on children? See http://www.fairtest.org for some issues to consider.

Dewey observed that traditional education separated the social classes, school and society, leisure and labor, mind and body, and thought and action. It isolated subject matter, precluding integrated understanding.

Dewey said, "Since a democratic society repudiates the principle of external authority, it must find a substitute in voluntary disposition and interest: these can be created only by education."

I am the art specialist for children K–8 at an urban elementary school that is influenced by the history of progressive education. The school has 700 students, and 80 percent of them are eligible for free or reduced-cost lunch. Over the years, the school has undergone major reform and is now one of the highest achieving in the city. This reform succeeded, in part, because the school kept social justice and John Dewey's ideas about schools and democracy at the core of its mission.

I am also an artist. One afternoon, when the painting surfaces were too wet and sticky to work on, I was thinking about the meaning I was attempting to create. I turned to Dewey for insights and came across a passage (Dewey 1938/1997, 64) that proved to be a turning point in my career as a teacher and as an artist:

> Natural impulses and desires constitute in any case the starting point. But there is no intellectual growth without some reconstruction, some remaking, of impulse and desires in the form in which they first show themselves.

I understood this passage as permission to be stuck (which I was). According to Dewey, I, like any learner, needed that space to pause, reflect, and further develop.

Having thought about Dewey's words for some time, I came to an understanding. I was the kind of student who could get the right answer but not the way the teacher expected. I think I knew at an early age, even in kindergarten, that my tacit knowledge, or the gut instinct that I had from living a social life, as Dewey would say, was not a kind of knowledge my public school experience embraced. In time, I stopped bothering with tasks that I found held little to no personal meaning. School, for me, was a waste of time.

My experience and feelings about my schooling were validated by another of Dewey's (1915/2001, 46) notions:

> From the standpoint of the child the great waste in the school comes from an inability to utilize the experience he gets outside the school in any completed and free way within the school itself; while, on the other hand, he is unable to apply in daily life what he is learning at school. That is the isolation of the school—the isolation from life.

Not only did these words substantiate my personal experience, but they shifted my thinking from reflecting on myself as artist to myself as teacher. I began to question how my methods are or are not isolating the potential of my students. Was I allowing my students to use their unique social lives at school?

Did the learning in my classroom carry over into the social lives of my students? Moreover, was I providing a place for my students to take pause, think, and question?

I thought of an interaction that I had had during the second year of my career with a parent who showed up one morning in my classroom. He wanted to know if he could watch me with a group of kindergartners.

What is art?

Feeling some-what defensive, I asked why. He responded that he was curious about why his five-year-old daughter repeatedly flushed the toilet the night before while saying the words "Dada" and "Duchamp." She gave him only a few clues, such as "art class," "Dada," "toy horse," "Duchamp," "finding art," "Mutt," and "toilet." Her father was stumped but intrigued, and her words led to an evening of father-daughter Google searches. The father found that his daughter was trying to re-create and further understand her art experience learning about the famous found-object sculpture (urinal) signed R. Mutt by Dada artist Marcel Duchamp. What did it mean, he wondered, for a child this age to be aware of such a movement in art?

I explained that I started the school year by asking the students to talk about what art could be. However, with young children I had to root this conversation in something that they all knew and had experienced. I was mindful that not all of my students would have had an opportunity to go to an art museum or gallery, so the next best thing was to find something from the history of art to which all the children could relate.

The curious father of the five-year-old was my proof that what had occurred in my classroom was carried over into the social life of his child. Her learning in the school was in a real-life context of questioning and exploring and not an environment where children were handed answers to memorize. As teachers, I think many times we let seemingly mundane aspects of real life slip away, as we do not understand them as the source of a potentially powerful experience.

George Counts

Writing in the decades of the Russian Revolution (1917) and the Great Depression (1929–late 1930s), *George Counts* (1889–1974), a younger colleague of Dewey, extended Dewey's criticisms of progressive education and American education in general. Like Dewey, Counts believed that schools did not reflect conditions in the world and were thus isolated from it. He called for *social reconstruction,* or changing the curriculum in schools to address the inequalities among children. He claimed that progressive educators ignored the social injustices facing the nation by taking a politically neutral position and focusing instead on children's self-expression. Thus, he felt, the opportunity for social reconstruction and a more just society was lost (Counts 1978).

Counts also criticized what Lawrence Cremin (1962, 202) called the Romantic Progressives for ignoring social injustices. Embracing the ideas of Rousseau and heavily influenced by psychoanalytic theory (see Chapter 6), this arm of the Progressive movement asserted that children develop naturally and that learning should begin with children's interests. They focused on children's individual physical and social-emotional development, believing that individual growth had to take place before society could change, and that helping children develop an integrated personality was the best way to achieve the larger societal goal (Smith and Smith 1994).

Progressive Women Educators

An important aspect of the social reform that resulted from the Progressive movement was the growth of a women's suffrage movement. Middle- and upper-class women, especially, concentrated on political and social reform to overcome traditional female roles that subjugated them personally and professionally. This was particularly true in the field of progressive education.

Patty Smith Hill (1868–1946) was one of the women who helped shape the future of early childhood education during this period. Once a believer in the Froebelian approach, Hill, director of the Louisville Free Kindergarten Association, began to change her views after she studied with Dewey in Chicago. She advocated the development of kindergartens and nursery schools based on scientific principles and founded the National Committee on Nursery Schools, which became NANE (National Association for Nursery Education) and, in 1966, NAEYC (Williams and Fromberg 1992).

Another leader of the nursery school movement in the United States was *Abigail Eliot* (1892–1992). Unlike other progressives who felt the family hindered the growth of healthy children, Eliot advocated parent involvement. After studying with Arnold Gesell at Yale, she traveled to England to observe nursery education. While she admired the schools there, she realized that class sizes were too large, often with thirty-two two-year-olds in a class.

On her return to Boston in 1922, Eliot took over a nursery school for poor children on Ruggles Street in Roxbury. In addition to decreasing class size and shortening the school day, Eliot invited parents to become involved. Mothers visited, helped in the nursery room, and had informal meetings at school. If parents could not attend,

THOUGHT QUESTION Think about early childhood classrooms that you have worked in or visited. How do you think John Dewey's ideas have influenced them? For example, do teachers follow a set curriculum or create their own based on the interests of the children in their class?

teachers visited the homes. By 1926, the *Ruggles Street School* became a training center for nursery school teachers and offered courses in various Boston colleges (Beatty 1995).

The *MacMillan sisters,* Rachel (1859–1917) and Margaret (1860–1931), were horrified by conditions for poor children who worked in factories in the industrial north of England. In 1914, the sisters began an Open Air Nursery and Training Centre that emphasized hygiene and fresh air in Peckham, an area of London. In the Centre's first six months, only one child became ill, and the illness did not spread. The McMillan sisters' legacy to early childhood education is an emphasis on hygiene and safety and an appreciation of outdoor time as a valuable part of the day.

A particularly influential woman in progressive education was *Lucy Sprague Mitchell* (1878–1967). Excited by Dewey's belief that the goal of education was to foster democratic values and that the curriculum needed to root itself in children's experiences, in 1916 Mitchell founded the *Bureau of Educational Experiments,* which later became *Bank Street College of Education.*

In 1919, Mitchell, along with *Harriet Johnson* (1871–1956), established the Bureau's nursery school, which emphasized teaching to all the domains (or areas) of development. In addition, Mitchell promoted an integrated curriculum that stressed the connections between art and science and the importance of analyzing the larger, diverse social world, especially through the study of geography and social studies. Mitchell and the Bureau's staff also collaborated with public school teachers interested in a more progressive pedagogy. These Public School Workshops paved the way for Bank Street College's participation and leadership during the 1960s in the government's Head Start and Follow Through programs (Roopnarine and Johnson 2005).

The Bureau of Educational Experiments was part of the child study movement, recording and cataloging every aspect of children's physical, cognitive, and psychological life. However, its research went on in the context of the school day, connecting each aspect of children's growth and development to the other aspects and to curriculum (Antler 1987). These educators were, in Mitchell's vision, less involved with testing than in observing natural behaviors in the classroom, as this story illustrates:

> Early child study institutes followed methods of the physical sciences and one institute in Iowa found that children wiggled when they tried to measure them— providing uneven data from one day to the next. The solution for them was to put the children in casts, because wiggling couldn't be measured. Mitchell related this story noting that "Now, we cared, really, more about the wiggle and the emotional strain than about the physical growth." (Antler 1987, 289)

Another colleague of Mitchell's, *Caroline Pratt* (1867–1954), was particularly interested in play and designed the wooden unit blocks that children in most early childhood classrooms use today. Accompanying these blocks were

Lucy Sprague Mitchell, founder of the Bureau of Educational Experiments, which later became Bank Street College of Education.

wooden figures of adults and children, known as the "do withs." Using these blocks and figures, children symbolically represented and reconstructed their experiences to gain a better understanding of themselves and their world (Williams and Fromberg 1992).

In 1914, Pratt founded a private school in New York City called the Play School, which became the City and Country School in 1930. At City and Country School, the curriculum centered around the newly designed blocks and a jobs program for the older children, who helped in the daily functioning of the school. Similar to other progressive thinkers, Pratt thought that children's experience and reflection upon that experience should drive learning and that social studies should be at the core of the curriculum (Weber 1969).

Located next to City and Country School was the nursery school that Harriet Johnson had started. Like Pratt, Johnson emphasized the use of blocks and close observation of children at play, which formed the basis of the nursery school curriculum (Williams and Fromberg 1992).

While Johnson's nursery school was child centered and children were given freedom to create and explore materials, there were rules. Socialization was stressed. Children had to share the materials since they belonged to everyone in the community. Also, children were removed from the group if they resorted to physical or verbal abuse of others (Beatty 1995). Pratt and Johnson—although less so Johnson,

Lucy Sprague Mitchell promoted an integrated curriculum that stressed the connections between art and science and the importance of analyzing the larger, diverse social world, especially through the study of geography and social studies.

These replicas of the original do-withs, made by City and Country School in New York, are plain wood, leaving much to the children's imagination as they use them in their blockbuilding.

Elizabeth Irwin worked with colleagues to bring progressive education to public schools. However, funding dried up during the Great Depression, thwarting these efforts.

True progressive education remains underutilized. If our culture is not interested in social reform or child development and is wary of theories that accord power to the child, education for a more democratic society will continue to fall short.

who was herself a parent—did not fully trust parents, believing that they constrained their children's creativity (Beatty 1995).

Another "dauntless" woman within the Progressive movement was *Elisabeth Irwin* (1880–1942) (Snyder 1972). Also a member of the Dewey circle, Irwin believed in educating the whole child. As a staff psychologist for the Progressive Education Association, Irwin worked with colleagues to bring progressive education to public schools. However, funding dried up during the Great Depression (1929–late 1930s). In response to the possible closing of PS 41, a public school in New York City's Greenwich Village, many parents, along with Irwin, decided to turn the Little Red School House into a private school.

That these progressive public experiments eventually became private schools demonstrates the public funding constraints and class tensions that existed during the Progressive Era. Ironically (since Pratt, for example, originally sought their children's enrollment), working-class parents mistrusted progressive educators, many of whom came from the middle and upper classes. Moreover, progressive education seemed disconnected from the concrete goals of literacy and numeracy skills that working-class parents had for their children.

The Progressive Era in retrospect

By the 1930s, proponents of all three strands of progressive education (those who advocated a more scientific approach; the social reconstructionists such as Dewey and Counts, who saw schools as a way to change society; and the psychological progressives, who cared more about the social-emotional development of the child) had a profound effect on American education and society. Over time, however, their differences and contradictions made it impossible for them to present a coherent program and thus weakened their impact (Weber 1984).

Froebel, Montessori, Mitchell, and Dewey shared a deep respect for the child. Other language, concepts, and materials of the Progressive Era—such as the "whole child," the importance of play, and the use of wooden unit blocks, to name a few—also became central to early childhood education. Yet, true progressive education remains underutilized and seen as a nontraditional approach. If our culture is not interested in social reform or child development and is wary of theories that accord power to the child, education for a more democratic society will continue to fall short.

Susan Isaacs and her influence

Influenced by Dewey's educational philosophy and Sigmund Freud's psychodynamic theory (about which you will read in Chapter 6), British educators such as *Susan Isaacs* (1885–1948) stressed understanding children's social-emotional development and the importance of their play. Isaacs believed that social interactions with adults and peers formed the basis for children's acquisition of knowledge. As director of the Malting House School for Young Children in Cambridge, England, Isaacs promoted **integrated curriculum,** that is, interdisciplinary learning. Children used a multidisciplinary approach to analyze and understand topics. Teachers observed children closely to determine their interests, plan stimulating activities, gather and distribute materials, and bridge home and school (Roopnarine and Johnson 2005; Williams and Fromberg 1992).

After World War II (1939–1945), Isaacs's work and theories took root in Britain. Thanks to postwar prosperity and governmental reforms in health, education, and welfare, a more mobile and democratic society began to emerge in Britain and Europe. In 1967, the British Plowden Report was published. The report, which examined, among other things, concrete experience and learning in the classroom, drew attention to the major thinkers of that time, such as Isaacs, *Jerome Bruner,* and especially the Swiss cognitive psychologist Jean Piaget, as well as to the practices and ideas of Montessori and Dewey. The report encouraged schools to provide an environment in which thinking was considered the core of learning and process was understood to be more important than product. British Infant schools picked up Robert Owen's ideas from a century and a half before.

Like most progressive education, the British Infant schools primarily influenced early childhood education, perhaps because educators have difficulty conceptualizing and implementing active learning for older children. During the 1970s, the British economy slowed, and a need for more technical job training arose, resulting in less educational experimentation throughout all the grades (Gutek 1995).

THOUGHT QUESTION A student at the Wisconsin campus of National Louis University reflected on the history of early childhood education: "Learning about history has been an eye-opening experience for me. . . . If these things make sense, then why are we not practicing them in our classrooms today? Why do we seem to be moving backward instead of forward?"

How would you answer this student?

MID-TWENTIETH-CENTURY AMERICA TO PRESENT TIMES

How have more recent events influenced early childhood education?

Beneath the calm surface of suburban affluence that characterized sectors of U.S. society in the 1950s was a growing restlessness that resulted in tremendous changes during the following decade. The cold war between the United States and its allies and the Communist U.S.S.R. and its adherents that began after World War II led to uncertainty about America's position in the world. Then, too, the increasing visibility and awareness of persistent poverty amid rising affluence also contributed to making the 1960s a turbulent decade. Another influence was the United States' continuing escalation of the conflict in Southeast Asia, prompted by its desire to prevent a communist North Vietnam from winning control of the capitalist South Vietnam.

The strong mid-century civil rights movement that originated with African Americans in the South spurred other groups to advocate for greater voice and societal rights and put pressure on inequitable economic and social structures. Perhaps the most significant legal event of the era was the 1954 *Brown v. Board of Education* Supreme Court decision. Although not the first, and certainly not the last, legal action to challenge segregation by race, this landmark case resulted in the declaration of racial segregation in schools and other public settings as discriminatory and in violation of the Fourteenth Amendment of the Constitution. The decision transcended education. It struck a clear and penetrating blow to all forms of discrimination and separation based on race, with reverberations throughout America and the world.

The Great Society and Head Start

Calls for social justice required a bold response from government. President Lyndon Baines Johnson, in office from 1963 through 1968, proposed a reform known as the Great Society. As part of his vision of a new America, one in which all citizens enjoyed equal rights, Johnson launched a series of programs beginning in 1964 called the War on Poverty. The programs were aimed at eliminating the structural roots of poverty many attributed to a lack of economic and educational opportunity.

The 1954 landmark Brown v. Board of Education *Supreme Court decision resulted in the declaration of racial segregation in schools and other public settings as discriminatory and in violation of the Fourteenth Amendment of the Constitution.*

One program, *Project Head Start,* begun in 1965, focused on improving the education of poor children. In addition to providing early childhood education, Head Start included comprehensive social services, health and nutrition teaching, parent education, and parent involvement. Eligibility was, and still is, based on income. Most Head Start families live below the official federal poverty level. Within a year, half a million children were signed up (Yettick 2003).

While several studies showed that attending Head Start resulted in positive outcomes for children, some people questioned its success, subjecting the program to criticisms from all sides (Zill et al. 2001). Today, Head Start is considered one of the more successful federal antipoverty programs in U.S. history and has widespread public support. Studies continue to indicate positive short-term and long-term effects of preschool programs such as Head Start. The program has served to improve children's health, increase their self-esteem, and help their mothers find jobs and finish schooling (Beatty 1995). But while Congress has continued to reauthorize funding, with 18,865 centers in the United States serving 912,000 children, the percentage of eligible children in Head Start is declining. According to an analysis by the National Head Start Association (2006), only five of ten eligible children actually attend Head Start and only three of one hundred eligible children attend Early Head Start programs. This is due to declining government financial support for Head Start as well as to the increase in the number of children living in poverty.

The connection between parent involvement—a tenet of Head Start—and advocacy made its first impact in the 1970s, as did the second generation of feminism. Once again, the *zeitgeist,* or the spirit of the era, created the milieu for such parallel movements to arise around the same time.

Special Education: From Mainstreaming to Inclusion to Continuum of Services

After years of legal cases and advocacy on the part of parents of children with disabilities, Public Law (PL) 94-142 (now known as the Individuals with Disabilities Education Act, or IDEA) was passed in 1976. It mandated that all children, regardless of their disability, be assured a "free and appropriate public education in the least restrictive environment." This law provided for increased funding for research and new programs, which in turn led to **deinstitutionalization,** the return to their communities of American children and adults who had been kept in institutions. Research had other outcomes: for example, mothers called into question the belief that maternal coldness was the root cause of autism just as early scientific studies emerged demonstrating that some biological factors were involved in the etiology, or cause, of autism (Rutter 1971).

The "least restrictive environment" (LRE) clause in PL 94-124 has been interpreted differently over the years. In the 1970s **least restrictive** usually meant a self-contained classroom for children with disabilities that was housed in a public school. Children with disabilities were then **mainstreamed** into general education classrooms for special classes such as gym or art, or occasionally for socialization or academic subjects if they demonstrated age-appropriate skills in those areas. Later, as the result of lawsuits and shifts in public perceptions of people with disabilities, children with disabilities were "included" full time in general education classes, with the services they needed provided by specialists who came into the classroom or who served the children in "pull-out" programs.

In these inclusive classrooms, socialization was a primary focus, with documented benefits for both children with disabilities and their general education classmates. The government supported the move toward inclusion through the Regular Education Initiative (Reynolds, Wang, and Walberg 1987). It maintained that separate general and special education structures were incompatible with the special education laws. The initiative argued that educational practice needed to be changed to provide an effective education for the range of children for whom a general education classroom would truly be the LRE. As we have seen in this chapter, children with disabilities have made many strides in access to education since the days of ancient Greece and Rome (Figure 5.2).

Standardization, Accountability, and Testing

From the end of World War II in 1945 into the 1980s, Congress and numerous educational think tanks called for increased educational rigor in schools. These calls were prompted by an awareness that U.S. schoolchildren's academic achievements paled in comparison with those of children in other parts of the world—and specifically, in the Soviet Union (now the Russian Federation). These concerns were greatly heightened when the Soviet Union successfully launched its satellite, Sputnik, in 1957—the first human-made object to orbit the Earth. Fears of U.S. inferiority drove federal and state reforms to improve the academic achievement of the nation's youth, especially that of its future scientific workforce (Gutek, 2006).

These concerns persisted in 1983, when *A Nation at Risk* (National Commission on Excellence in Education) was published. This open letter to the American public warned that other countries were equaling and surpassing the educational attainments of U.S. students and adults. The panel of experts who wrote the report called for increasing the quality of U.S. educational systems to move beyond educational "mediocrity." Although these first calls for testing and accountability were focused on the upper grades, it did not take long for them to reach the preschools.

Testing and demands for accountability have resulted in push-down curriculum, so that, for example, expectations of today's kindergartners are similar to those for yesterday's first graders. Head Start is a good example of how vulnerable programs are to such winds of political change. Many Head Start programs have added academic emphasis that devalues their traditionally play-based curricula.

In the 1990s, new technology enabled advances in neuroscientific research on the brains and nervous systems of infants and young children. The results demonstrated both the vulnerabilities and resilience of brain function in this period and gave greater credibility to the promise of early childhood intervention. The nature-versus-nurture question was finally transformed, to most people's satisfaction, into a nature-*and*-nurture framework, with an understanding that there are complex interactions between the two. Relieved of this century-old debate, scientists joined forces with practitioners in determining early childhood research agendas.

All the preceding developments played some role in the bipartisan authorization of the 2001 *No Child Left Behind (NCLB)* law that makes states responsible for

last quarter of the 20th century

IDEA: government regulation mandating free and appropriate education in the least restrictive environment

early 20th century

New communication possibilities, techniques, and rights — Helen Keller and Anne Sullivan

19th century

Education for people with disabilities — Seguin

16th century

Increased rights; realization that disabilities are not demonic — Enlightenment

Ancient Rome

The medical model — Hippocrates

Ancient Greece and Rome

Children with disabilities are not valued as future citizens

5.2 *Attitudes toward Educating Those with Disabilities*

IDEA mandated
that all children,
regardless of
their disability,
be assured
a "free and
appropriate public
education in the
least restrictive
environment."
This law led to
deinstitutionaliza-
tion, the return of
American children
and adults who
had been kept in
institutions to
their communities.

ensuring that *all* U.S. children be proficient in reading and mathematics by 2014, as measured by standardized tests. Testing begins, theoretically, when children move into "childhood" at age eight (or third grade) and continues through eighth grade. Because states create their own standards and tests, state results often differ from the federal test results, in which children are also expected to make adequate annual progress (Ravitch 2007). Schools face strict sanctions when their test scores do not meet expected standards. Critics complain that the tests do not measure children's progress fairly, that extenuating circumstances preclude some children from progressing at the required rates, and that the federal government did not provide enough money to successfully fund the NCLB initiative (Kozol 2007). They also note that fear of school failure has put an undue emphasis on test preparation to the detriment of curriculum.

Finally, although the financial situation at the start of 2009 was grim, the outlook for investing in early childhood seemed brighter with a new government administration. In his campaign for president Barack Obama emphasized the importance of quality early care and education as a way to help the next generation excel.

SUMMARY

EARLY CHILDHOOD AROUND THE WORLD
How do the sociopolitical and historical contexts of South Africa, India, and China influence early childhood education in those countries?
South Africa, India, and China all draw from rich and ancient traditions that influence each country's approach to early childhood education. Each country's history also shapes early childhood education: South Africa experienced both colonial rule and apartheid; India was invaded and colonized; and China underwent a long feudal period. Current contexts—such as poverty; unemployment; and other social challenges, including the spread of HIV/AIDS, malnutrition, community violence facing South Africa, and China's rapidly growing market economy—frame early childhood efforts. In all three countries, the government now provides some programs for young children.

VIEWS OF CHILDHOOD IN WESTERN HISTORY
What ideas developed over the ages that influence early childhood education today?
Beginning with the roots of child-centered education (Socrates) and an emphasis on the arts and athletics as well as reasoning (Plato), the elements of early childhood education as we know it today emerged from the individuals and movements that make up Western history. Quintilian was the first to focus on the early years in ancient Rome. By the seventeenth and eighteenth centuries, important thinkers discussed the value of play (Comenius), experience (Locke), and exploration (Rousseau) for learning. Pestalozzi implemented education that is active and interactive and extended it to children who were not wealthy. Froebel introduced materials and activities specifically designed for children. Owen provided a safe and secure environment for children of working parents, and the MacMillan sisters proved the importance of outdoor play. Attention to individual children and their capabilities (Montessori), the role of the arts in education (Steiner), and the importance of parent involvement (Eliot) came to the fore in the twentieth century. At that time, too,

Dewey and other progressives proposed education as preparation for participation in a democratic society.

People with disabilities were not valued in ancient Greece or Rome or during the Middle Ages. By the Enlightenment, people began to recognize those with disabilities as individuals deserving of rights. It was Seguin in the nineteenth century who challenged students with disabilities with tasks that fostered their independence.

MID-TWENTIETH-CENTURY AMERICA TO PRESENT TIMES

How have more recent events influenced early childhood education?

In the second half of the twentieth century the United States made strides toward more equitable education that positively affected early childhood education. In 1954 *Brown v. Board of Education* successfully challenged segregation by race, declaring it discriminatory and in violation of the Fourteenth Amendment. A decade later, President Johnson's Great Society included Head Start, which began to prepare children from low-income families for kindergarten and has endured as a successful federally funded social program. The following decade saw legal support for the rights of people who have disabilities with the Individuals with Disabilities Education Act, or IDEA.

At the same time, though, pressure to perform in the Sputnik era of the 1950s and 1960s, reports written in the 1980s, and the No Child Left Behind Act of the early twenty-first century have led to an era of standardization, testing, and accountability that has influenced early childhood programming. Early childhood educators are hopeful, though, as support for the nation's youngest inhabitants seems forthcoming.

FURTHER ACTIVITIES

1. Using the Internet and print resources, research the Progressive Era further, and choose one educator to whom you are drawn. Imagine that you are that progressive educator in the early 1930s. Based on what you have learned about the tensions within this movement, describe "your" beliefs and the dilemmas and contradictions that confront you. Explain your rationales. Be prepared to take your position in a role-play with classmates who have chosen different educators of that time. (**NAEYC Standard 1: Promoting Child Development and Learning**)

2. Research the goals for family participation in Head Start that were developed in the 1960s. Then, interview staff and parents from a Head Start center in or near your community to find out how family participation now compares with Head Start's original goals. Write a paper that explains what you found. (**NAEYC Standard 2: Building Family and Community Relationships**)

3. Research American institutions for and treatment of children with disabilities during the nineteenth and twentieth centuries. Compare what you find with what you know or can learn about U.S. history of those times. Visit a program for children with disabilities. Compare what you see to what you have read, and write a short paper describing the program you visited. Link your observations to the history of education for children with disabilities and to U.S. history of the nineteenth and twentieth centuries. (**NAEYC Standard 5: Using Content Knowledge to Build Meaningful Curriculum**)

CHAPTER SIX

Theories of Early Childhood: Explanations, Applications, and Critiques

There is nothing so practical as a good theory.

Kurt Lewin

The early childhood teacher—busy developing curriculum, establishing and sustaining relationships with children and their parents, supervising volunteers and assistant teachers—may not think she has the luxury to stand back and consider her activities from a broader perspective. Despite this common assumption, knowledge of theory is a critical element in early childhood educators' daily decisions about classroom practice.

In this chapter, we weave eleven different child development theories generated over the past hundred years into a story about Michael and his Head Start teacher. You will observe that educators have many different ideas about children and that each theory has various origins and has changed over time. Finally, we explore the relationship between the commonsense ideas of the staff at Michael's Head Start to these formal theories so that you can see how theory can be—and is—used to support children's well-being.

WHAT IS A THEORY?

What are theories, and how do early childhood educators use them?

A **theory** is a set of assumptions or principles that organize, analyze, predict, or explain specific events, behaviors, or processes. In early childhood education, the specifics of each classroom, curriculum, and child are our **data**—they are what we analyze. A theory can organize our thinking—guide us to look for certain data and help us make sense of those data after we collect them. We can think of a theory as a kind of lens we use to view the world. We see and think about different phenomena with different kinds of lenses. For example, a scientist who wants to study cells might use a microscope, whose lens makes visible tiny particles that cannot be seen with the human eye alone. On the other hand, astronomers look at the surface of the moon with a telescope, whose lens makes distant objects appear closer and larger. How a lens is used and positioned affects what you see when you look through it. Consider the separate stars most of us view as the Big Dipper. Those stars can be seen as a completely different image by using another kind of organizing lens, or frame of reference.

You will find that a single theory, or lens, is inadequate for thinking about all aspects of work with young children, although it can guide you to formulate theory that works for you. During the team meeting at Michael's Head Start that you will read about below, we can trace each staff member's suggestions about how to handle Michael's aggression to a point of view based in a given theory. No one can follow all of the team members' suggestions; some even contradict each other. Thus, finding a meaningful application of theory in a practical approach takes time and effort.

> We can think of a theory as a kind of lens we use to view the world.

6.1 *Effect of Frame of Reference*
These stars illustrate how different people can see the same thing differently because they use different organizing lenses.

I was nearing the end of my first year of graduate school, where I was first exposed to theories of child development, as well as my first year as a full-time caregiver in an inclusive infant-toddler/twos' room. I was deeply enmeshed in newly learned theory on the one hand and in the practice of daily life experiences with children on the other. It was from this framework that I began looking at and thinking about the interactions between Donny and Aaron.

Aaron and Donny were 30 and 35 months old, respectively. Donny was a child who the staff thought had a vivid imagination, but he could also be emotional and volatile, as he frequently had temper tantrums and was aggressive with other children, especially if they interrupted his play. Though he was within normal limits in his language development, we were concerned because he rarely used words to communicate his needs. Conversely, Aaron was an extremely verbal child, but he seemed not to engage in pretend play with other children.

I do not expect them to play together. I stopped to watch because I anticipated conflict. Donny was playing with the three-foot-long cylindrical stuffed snake, and Aaron looked is if he wanted to join in the play.

Contrary to my expectations, they seemed to be playing together and with apparent success. I wanted to know how—or why—they were able to get past what I assumed to be their differences and cooperate with each other.

I began to doubt my assumptions about Donny's and Aaron's skills and to look at development with what was for me a new perspective.

I had arrived at this point with assumptions about the way children think and about how they learn. Now, instead of assuming the presence and absence of abilities first and then trying to analyze the children's behavior according to those assumptions, I turned myself around and asked instead, "What are these two doing, and *what does that mean in terms of their development?*" I then began to capture moments when they were together, in order to decipher both their individual skills and the subtle nature of the interactions.

Not surprisingly, my transition from theory to practice was not as smooth as I had anticipated. I thought I could take Donny's and Aaron's ages, match them up to a list of Piagetian stages, and thereby determine what skills they should and should not have. Vygotsky, I thought, would help me out with a nice little explanation of the social context of their development and their play.

But it was when I turned to theory to help me articulate what I observed that the avalanche of questions really began. I realized that I needed to further define the type of interaction I had observed and then define what it was about the interaction that was *specifically* about Aaron and Donny.

I learned that the process was about *integrating* theory with practice, not about applying one to the other. I explained to a fellow teacher that I had to experience the theory on a practical level first—watching

A plush snake toy, two young boys, and getting past differences

children play—before I could really grasp it intellectually. He explained that he had to understand the theory intellectually before he could understand it practically. We came to understand that neither of us was right, we simply went through different processes to get to the same conceptual place.

I felt as if I held in one hand a collection of rational and reasonable theories that did not reflect or capture the nature and quality of the children's behavior. I held in my other hand the boys and their interactions; they were vivid, real, and fascinating, but they needed filtering for me to understand them better. What I eventually came to understand was that it was valuable to think about what stage of development Aaron and Donny were in, but it was just as important and valuable to look at *how* each of them was progressing through that stage. Here is where those missing puzzle pieces began taking shape.

What I came to think of as the most remarkable moment in this episode was that *each child seemed to be using the other's strengths to boost or overcome his own weakness.* They found a common ground on which they could experience the sensation of shared thought, and this experience then prompted further development. It gave each boy the push he needed to pull together various developing skills. By focusing on the process rather than the achievements of development, I began to see each boy—as well as cognitive development itself—in a new, more fascinating, and more comprehensive light.

Michael's Story

Michael is an active three-year-old who has been popular in his Head Start classroom. But in the last couple of months, his teacher, Juanita, has noticed that Michael is fighting with others. Yesterday, Michael got so angry with his friend Freddy that he almost bit him.

Today, Juanita is on the alert, ready to intervene. As she turns to put Kareem's painting on the drying rack, she hears a commotion. Ellen, the assistant teacher, calls to Juanita, with distress in her voice: Michael bit Anthony. Ellen takes Anthony for first aid, and Juanita sits with Michael. Speaking sternly, she describes the incident and tells him that she must call both boys' mothers to tell them what happened.

Michael looks as if he will cry and then yells angrily, "I don't care!" his blue eyes narrowing. When Ellen returns with Anthony, Juanita takes Michael out to the hall. She tells him with some emotion in her voice that he cannot bite and that she thinks he does care. Michael's lower lip quivers, and he whimpers, "I didn't want to hurt him." As Michael sits crying, the cook, Betty, walks by. She stops, looks at Michael and Juanita, and mutters under her breath, "I knew that child would be trouble. His three older brothers and even that sister Angela were bad news. That's just the way that family is." Juanita feels upset hearing this but doesn't know what to say. She doesn't understand what she considers to be the change in Michael.

Juanita is trying to make sense of this child's newfound aggression. What should she examine to understand Michael's experience and to help him with it? As we will see below, different theories lead us to consider different aspects of Michael's behavior.

Theories Arise in Context

As we consider world history, we see that various lenses, or worldviews, help to explain specific events and behaviors in a particular time and place. For example, Sigmund Freud (1856–1939) emphasized the role of sexuality in human development and developed his psychoanalytic theory at a place and time (nineteenth-century Europe) when unacknowledged, or repressed, sexuality troubled his patients. It made sense, then, to put sexuality in the foreground of his theory. With today's greater openness about sexual matters, an emphasis on repressed sexuality is less helpful than it was then. However, as you will soon see, theories evolve over time as new data and new contexts emerge. In addition, theorists' life stories often provide clues to their personalities and perspectives that, in turn, govern the nature of the theories they develop.

To whom do theories belong?

Some educators believe that theory is too grand or abstract to be useful. They think theories can be used by those with power or in elite positions to make others feel that ideas are inaccessible or so complex that the average person is not capable of putting them to use. However, in a democracy, everyone should have access to many ideas. Besides, we all theorize. While we don't always realize that we *are* theorizing, all of us have ideas about how the world works. We hypothesize about the natural

> As we consider world history, we see that various lenses, or worldviews, help to explain specific events and behaviors in a particular time and place.

world—for instance, that our dog gets excited right before a thunderstorm. Does he know it is coming? We might hypothesize that yes, he does! Such natural or commonsense ideas are sometimes referred to as "folk theories." These ideas are not the same as formal theories that guide an experiment to test a hypothesis. However, any explanation for a child's behavior requires some "folk psychology," too, and you will find that most formal theories connect to these commonsense ideas. Consider again, why has Michael begun to bite?

The Team Meeting

Juanita wants to gather ideas about how to help Michael. Betty, the cook, has already stated her opinion! Juanita doesn't find it helpful, though, and goes to a staff meeting to ask for advice.

When the Educational Director, Andrea, asks Juanita to present her concerns about Michael, Juanita describes the changes in his behavior and asks for input. Clarice, the family worker, speaks first.

"Mom says that things are tough at home right now. Michael Senior went back to Northern Ireland, and Mom is having trouble getting the rent together. She didn't say it exactly, but I got the feeling they'd been fighting a lot before he left."

Ned, the assistant teacher in the other threes class, says, "Michael has always needed to toughen up. He's just being a boy; boys at this age learn how to fight. He's got this natural aggression," Ned laughs and adds, "Not that those girls don't."

Jasper, the music teacher, says, "We don't want him to turn into a sissy like Julian. I'd put it more strongly than Ned. He's got to learn to fight. I know his dad feels that way, too."

Clarice says again, "He does have those three older brothers. I am sure he sees them horsing around, and maybe he plays a lot of rough and tumble with them, but biting?"

"He's biting for a reason, that's for sure," adds Sandra, a head teacher in the fours. "What's going on just before he lashes out?"

Ellen, the assistant teacher in Michael's class, speaks up. "It's like he thinks the other children are going to tease him or hurt him. So he goes after them when they are close to him, even when the other kids haven't done anything."

Sandra asks, "So he gets agitated if another child enters his personal space. Maybe he needs someone with him to help him sort out what's going on. Maybe he needs to look at the other children's faces and see that they aren't trying to hurt him. Talk it through with him, so that he thinks through what's really going on."

Ellen joins in. "It's hard, though, for them at this age to tune into what's going on with other children. I've been thinking about working with him to find strategies for those times when he thinks kids are crowding him, like helping him to put his hand out and say 'back off.'"

Juanita inserts, "I have noticed that it is more likely to happen first thing in the morning and at the end of the day."

Nancy says, "What is he like when his mother leaves him?"

Ellen answers, "Oh, he doesn't cry or anything, but he looks really, really tired and is restless right when she goes. His Mom kind of looks the same way. It may be linked to Alex's arrival in the class. Somehow Alex upsets the balance among the kids."

Andrea asks, "What's Alex doing?"

Juanita answers, "Alex is really quiet, but I have started to see that he's a little sneaky. You just don't notice him because he is so quiet." She pauses and asks, "So what should we do to help Michael?"

Carmen, an assistant teacher in the fours, says, "I bet he likes the attention he gets. Something about it is working for Michael. Figure out what that is, and your problem will be solved."

Lucille, the other threes head teacher, tells Juanita, "That boy needs your attention and love. He must be suffering with his Dad gone and his Mom all stressed out. Put him on your lap a lot and give him hugs. As a matter of fact, I'm going into your room and give him a hug myself. Besides, you know he will grow out of it."

Nancy says, "He needs help to express himself, to be actively engaged in working out his feelings. Try to get him to use the expressive materials, like play dough, for pounding, or painting or dramatic play where he can be a superhero."

Sandra says, "He needs structure. He needs to know the consequences of his actions. You better make up a reward chart. Give him a star for every activity period that goes by without any fighting."

Ned adds, "And make sure you do time-outs when he acts up."

Clarice says, "I better call Mom in and get the whole story, so we know if Michael is responding to something more going on at home."

It's about time for the staff meeting to end. Andrea asks Juanita, "Has this been helpful to you?"

Juanita chuckles and says, "You all have given me a lot to think about. No easy answers, though."

Andrea replies, "We know things are stressful at home, and we'll learn more about that when Clarice talks with Mom. Also, things in the peer group have changed because of the new child in the class; Michael seems to be overreacting to other children in his space. And there's probably more. How about I observe Michael, and then we'll talk, you, me, Ellen, and Clarice?"

Juanita nods in agreement. She feels they have the beginnings of a plan that could help Michael.

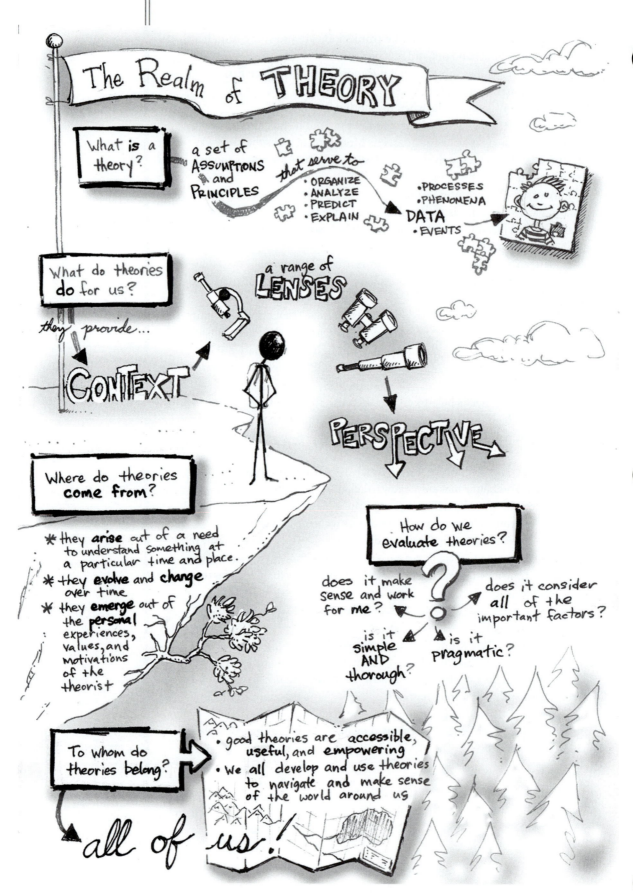

How would you use what you know about theories to explain why Michael has begun to bite?

How theories differ and evaluating differences between them

As you think about theories that might be helpful, consider the nature of the questions or problems you seek to address. If you are concerned about a child's feelings or thoughts, you need a theory that focuses on children's internal world. To understand a sequence of social interaction between two children, a theory that helps you focus on the flow of exchanges between the children may be more useful.

Here are some questions to consider when choosing a theory:

- Does the theory explain all or at least enough of what you see in your data?
- Does the theory unnecessarily complicate or oversimplify your understanding of the data?
- Does the theory focus your attention on aspects of the data that you might have overlooked?
- Does the theory have an optimistic point of view?
- How does this theory relate to your core values and assumptions?
- Does this theory, when applied, work practically to address the issues you seek to explain or change?

Keep these questions in mind as you read about theories. Think, too, about how the different viewpoints represented in the theories can help to answer questions about your practice. Do any of these "lenses" bring into focus the confusing situations you see in classrooms and with children?

PSYCHOANALYTIC AND PSYCHOANALYTICALLY INFORMED THEORIES

How do psychoanalytic and psychoanalytically informed theories explain children's development and learning?

Freudian Theory

The first psychoanalytic theory was that of *Sigmund Freud,* who coined the term *psychoanalysis.* Freud lived in Vienna, Austria, in the late nineteenth and early twentieth centuries, where there was considerable anti-Semitism. As a Jewish physician, Freud was treated as an outsider, and his outsider status allowed him to consider his patients' difficulties in unconventional ways. He came up with the theory that sexuality and aggression were key human motives and that human behavior often is determined by thoughts and wishes of which we are unaware (Gay 1989).

> As you think about theories that might be helpful, consider the nature of the questions or problems you seek to address.

Two aspects of traditional psychoanalytic theory address the nature of early childhood. First, Freud outlined the **psychosexual** stages of development (1974a). He named each stage for the area of the body he thought gave the most pleasure and served as the focal point for contact with the world for children of that age. These psychosexual stages and their meaning are shown in Figure 6.2. As you can see, Freud saw the early childhood period through the lens of specific bodily experiences that he believed shape the child's development.

Second, Freud saw the self as having three parts (1974b). The first is the **superego,** or conscience. Freud observed that by the end of the preschool period children had developed an internal voice that helped them refrain from inappropriate or impulsive, selfish behavior. However, he believed that throughout life the conscience is in conflict with that part of the self he called the **id,** the unsocialized part that tries to do as it pleases and seeks gratification any way it can. Freud's third part, which he called the **ego,** mediates between the id and the superego. This is the mature, adaptive part of the self that weighs any gratification against the social conventions regarding right and wrong that stand in its way. Freud theorized that in the **latency period** (the elementary school years), the id, ego, and superego reach a balance, and the child tends not to be as bothered by inner conflict. This leaves the child freer to focus on learning and schoolwork. Freud also suggested that a key issue in the preschool period is the development of what he considered appropriate gender identity.

Freud's Immediate Successors

Through the years, there have been many additions and changes to Freud's theory. *Erik Erikson* (1902–1994) studied with Freud's daughter, *Anna Freud* (1895–1982) and did his major work in the middle of the twentieth century. Erikson (1963) suggested that in addition to sexuality and individual life experiences shaping development, the **social context**—the interpersonal surroundings—in which each person develops needed to be better understood. He argued that each stage of development created a psychological state or quality with its own set of tensions particular to that

Freud observed that by the end of the preschool period children had developed an internal voice that helped them refrain from inappropriate or impulsive, selfish behavior.

Without a parent's mentalization or reflective function, say Fonagy and Target, the child's early psychological development—emotional, cognitive, and social—suffers. Fonagy and Target's theory of mentalization suggests the importance of early childhood teachers being able to recognize, feel, and empathize with children's thoughts and feelings, but with as few assumptions or personal overlays as possible.

Evaluation of the Psychoanalytic Viewpoint

You have seen how the time, place, culture, and social class of his patients influenced Freud's theories. Today, repressed female sexuality or the nuclear family constellation are not, if they ever were, the universal phenomena Freud considered them to be;

This father is likely to be using reflective functions to think about how his daughter is doing.

nor do they need to be at the center of a theory of childhood. Second, some people find Freud's ideas about sexuality and aggression incompatible with their worldview that human beings are basically good. However, Freud does maintain that with socialization, children learn to self-regulate and can unlearn aggressive behavior. Perhaps most important are Freud's ideas that, in the early childhood period, children are just developing a conscience and must struggle with a wide range of internal conflicts. Finally, most of us would agree with Freud's notion that humans possess unconscious thoughts and feelings that can unknowingly shape our behaviors.

Revisiting Michael's Head Start Using Psychoanalytic and Psychoanalytically Informed Theories

Some advice from the staff fits with psychoanalytic and psychoanalytically informed theories:

- Ned's comment that Michael's aggression is normal relates to the idea that aggression is innate and that children struggle to master their own *aggressive impulses*. Ned's thought that Michael is working out what it means to be a boy relates to psychoanalytic notions of *gender development*.
- Nancy's suggestion that Michael be shown appropriate ways to express his feelings aims to help him *channel his impulses*.
- Juanita recognizes that Michael *faces conflict within himself* over his aggressive actions.
- Lucille's urging of *hugs and support* for Michael reflects a relational theory.
- Ellen, describing Michael at drop-off, notes that his frame of mind is similar to his mother's—an echo of the theory of *mentalization*—and that Michael and his mother might be *tuned into each other emotionally*—that he might *feel his mother's emotional distress.*

THOUGHT QUESTION Which aspects of psychoanalytic and psychoanalytically informed theories resonate with your worldview? Do some of Freud's classic ideas make sense to you? Which ones? Do some of the more recent ideas appeal to you? Why?

Behaviorists believe that we begin as blank slates and the environment fills in what we are to become. In this sense, everyone starts out as equals.

BEHAVIORIST THEORIES

How do behaviorists explain children's development and learning?

Growing out of the **experimental tradition** in medicine and psychology—a tradition based on scientific processes and empirical evidence—**behaviorists** have used the **scientific method,** which includes objective observation of behavior, to explain the development and activity of the mind. In 1913, *John Watson* (1898–1958) wrote what later became known as the "Behaviorist Manifesto," which argued that the goal of psychological study is to *control and predict behavior.*

Behaviorists believe that we begin as blank slates and the environment fills in what we are to become. In this sense, everyone starts out as equals. Individuals and society, therefore, can be changed and improved by shaping the learning environment, an idea that reflects the democratic and egalitarian ethos of the early twentieth century in the United States.

Ivan Pavlov (1849–1936), another pioneer of behaviorism, studied the rate of salivation in dogs by putting food powder in their mouths and measuring the amount of saliva produced (1927/1960). He noticed that the dogs started to salivate before the food powder was put before them. They associated the assistant's preparations with the food they were about to eat. Pavlov came to call this effect **conditioning.** While today it is called **classical conditioning,** it is also known as **learning through association**—that is, the pairing of two stimuli in such a manner that one (food preparation) comes to stand for the other (the food itself). In Pavlov's most famous study, he rang a bell just before he gave the food to the dog. In time, the dog salivated at the sound of the bell. The dog had learned to associate the bell tone with the food.

This principle is often at work in an early childhood classroom. For instance, at transitions between activities some teachers use a signal, like turning off the lights or singing a song. Children in the classroom may learn to associate this stimulus with the next activity—say, cleaning up. Some children will begin to clean up as soon as they see the lights go off or even as they see their teacher crossing to the wall that houses the light switch. Such behaviors speak to one way children learn from predictable routines.

B. F. Skinner is probably the best known of the behaviorists. He developed a set of principles called **operant conditioning,** based on his theory that rewards and punishments explain how behaviors come into being (1979). Rewards, or **reinforcers,** increase the likelihood of a behavior recurring. A punishment decreases the likelihood of the behavior continuing. Using these principles, Skinner was able to teach rats to run mazes and pigeons to play the piano.

Recent behavioral theories have drawn from work in **cognitive science,** a multidisciplinary study of the mind and behavior, and their relationship. Unlike the original behaviorists, these behaviorists now acknowledge that the mind or the brain does play a role in determining behavior. These more contemporary approaches are not considered to be strictly behavioral.

Social Learning Theory

First developed by *Albert Bandura* (b. 1925) in the 1960s, **social learning theory** suggests that children learn through imitation. Bandura (1976) was interested in what caused children to become aggressive. He theorized that they acquire such behavior from aggressive models in the environment. To test this hypothesis, he

Preschool children imitate aggressive behavior in one of Bandura's doll studies.

showed two groups of children two different films: one, a nature film with no violent content; the other, a film with violent content. He then put the children in a room with a punching bag. The children who had seen the nature film did less punching than the children who had seen the violent film. Bandura concluded that some learning occurs through imitation. This work is especially relevant for educators concerned about the amount of violence children see in the mass media or, unfortunately, may see or experience in their daily lives. Moreover, here the teacher can be a role model, as can other adults and peers whom children imitate.

Likewise, some theories of gender-role learning and performing, a key developmental issue in the preschool period, suggest that behavioral principles such as classical and operant conditioning and social learning theory are one explanation for gendered behavior and identity. Young children may associate a common feature of one gender with the gender itself, saying, for example, "You're a boy because you have short hair" or "You're a girl because you are wearing pink." Children also learn to behave according to sex-role stereotypes because adults reinforce that behavior or punish them if they do not act in keeping with those roles. Finally, children imitate what they see. Children learn, as Bandura suggests, from the people around them.

Behavioral principles and social learning theory can be used to explain some aspects of gender-role learning and performing in early childhood.

Cognitive Behavioral Theory

Another behavioral theory relevant to early childhood is the **cognitive behavioral** approach, which suggests that behavior changes as structures of the mind, or **mental representations,** change. The first to use this term was *Aaron Beck* (1976), who worked primarily with adults. He found that depressed adults often had negative thoughts, or "cognitions," about themselves that were inaccurate. He discovered that depressive symptoms decreased when these negative thoughts were challenged and the individual was encouraged to *act as if* they were not true. This suggests that

THOUGHT QUESTION **Time-out** refers to the practice of isolating a child who has behaved inappropriately. Drawn from the behaviorist school of thought, time-out aims to reduce the likelihood that the child will misbehave again by leading the child to associate misbehavior with an unpleasant consequence: time-out. Some early childhood educators ask a child to move away from the group, saying: "You are showing me that you need to be away from the other children for a little while because you were being too wild. I'll come back in a few minutes, and we can talk about what happened." What is the difference between these two approaches to time-out? Do a web search to learn more about time-out for children. Would you use time-out? Why or why not? If you would use it, with what age groups, when, and how?

a strategy for helping young children grow and change might focus first on how children perceive themselves and then on how they can change their behavior, ultimately generating new perceptions. This helps explain research (discussed in Chapter 3) demonstrating that positive experiences and relationships at school can help overcome negative experiences in other parts of a child's life.

Evaluation of Behaviorist Theory

Like psychoanalytic theories, behaviorist theories are not without controversy. First, although they explain particular behavior in specific contexts, they do not explain the acquisition of more complex systems of knowledge such as language. A strictly behavioral account of language learning would show that children are rewarded for learning each sound, word, and sentence in their native tongue. In fact, we know that children do not learn word by word, but rather say novel things they have never heard before. Children seem to have mental rules they use to generate new words, like *see-ed*, instead of *saw*, or *mouse-s* for *mice*. These are not words children have received reinforcement for saying. Second, behaviorists have had difficulty showing that people can generalize behavior they learn through operant conditioning from one context to another.

Another criticism of behaviorist approaches to learning is that they take no notice of underlying motivational states. For instance, children often enjoy an activity for its own sake; they do not need rewards for all behavior. As mentioned in Chapter 4, a system of rewards actually may undermine a child's **intrinsic motivation,** or urge to achieve a goal set by the child herself.

Revisiting Michael's Head Start Using Behaviorist Theories

Again, the staff gave advice that fit with behaviorist theories:

- Sandra asked an important question when she inquired about the *specific events* that set off Michael's aggression. She suggested that a *particular observable event might trigger or reinforce the biting.* Later, Sandra proposed that Michael needed a *system of rewards* for positive, nonaggressive behavior.

- Ned suggested time-outs, a well-known strategy related to punishment, one element of a behavioral approach. According to *operant conditioning*, time-outs would decrease the likelihood of Michael's aggressive behavior.

- Ellen focused on Michael's thoughts about his peers as a cause for his behavior, noting that he seemed to *misperceive the situation* and think other children were trying to hurt him when they got too close.

- Sandra suggested that a teacher stay close to Michael to point out the other children's behavior, facial expressions, and body language when he begins to look as if he is concerned about the other children. The goal here is to *change how Michael sees things,* which in turn will help him to stop biting by taking away his reason for doing so.

MATURATIONAL THEORIES

How do maturational theories explain children's development and learning?

Maturational theory argues that children's development results from the natural unfolding of children's biological potential, and that all children grow and change in directions specified primarily by their own biological makeup, or genetic code. From this point of view, all families, schools, and communities can do is allow children to develop all of their natural potential. Maturational theories typically describe developmental norms. What is it that characterizes children's behavior at different ages across a number of areas—thinking, perceiving, playing, sleeping, and so forth?

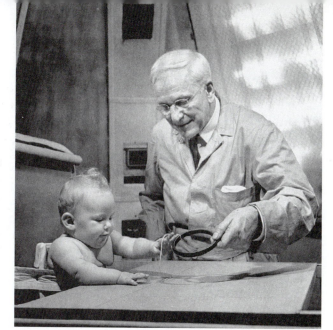

Arnold Gesell

Arnold Gesell (1880–1961) was one of the most important maturational theorists of the twentieth century. In part, Gesell chose his orientation in reaction to the behavioral point of view, where all development is linked to experience, or to what the child learns. Gesell is best known for his pioneering work observing children's behavior in detail and creating specific milestones and behavioral norms for children of different ages. Before Gesell, children had most often been studied for their pathologies. Gesell wanted to know what young children *could* do rather than what they could not.

Like a biologist, Gesell focused his work on cataloging and categorizing behaviors. In looking at children from birth to age ten, Gesell observed more than 500 children. However, like many Western theorists of this era, he observed only middle-class, Northern European children to define what was normal.

Evaluation of Maturational Theories

One doesn't hear much about Gesell in our contemporary early childhood world. Now maturation is assumed to be but one part of the complex interaction that makes up children's development. Few today argue for biology or environment alone because their mutuality has become evident (Shonkoff and Phillips 2000).

Critics of Gesell's maturational approach also point out that he defined "normality" through the observation of one type of child at a certain point in history, turning, in the words of critics, what he found to be "typical into the desirable" (Thelen and Adolph 1992, 374). Given what we know about cultural variation, one set of norms can never be the ideal for everyone. However, Gesell's interest in looking carefully at infants and young children to better understand their competencies remains an important contribution to the early childhood field.

In the classroom, however, the teacher who thinks "He'll grow out of it" is hopeful about children's development but may not take an active role or try curriculum that might help children achieve their potential.

Revisiting Michael's Head Start Using Maturational Theories

- Lucille notes that Michael is sure to grow out of his aggressive behavior, implying that perhaps everyone was making too big a fuss over something temporary. This "*it will all come out in the wash*" attitude recalls Gesell's optimistic theory.

Given what we know about individual and cultural variation, one set of norms can never be the ideal for everyone. However, Gesell's careful work on infants' and young children's competencies remains an important contribution to the early childhood field.

- Betty remarks that Michael comes from a "bad family." Betty may think that the *unfolding of Michael's natural potential* (in this case, a negative potential) would result in aggressive behavior.

As early childhood educators, if nothing else, we can recognize that Betty's point of view is not practical or optimistic; it doesn't lead to any theory of teaching and learning that can help a child grow. On the other hand, Lucille's application of a maturational approach is "positive" because it suggests that teachers need to be tolerant and understanding of children's behavior that may seem inappropriate but that is more prevalent during a certain developmental stage.

CONSTRUCTIVIST THEORIES

How does constructivist theory explain children's development and learning?

Constructivist theory emphasizes the child's active role, that is, that children construct their knowledge primarily through engagement with the world. This engagement reveals how children grow and change. The foremost constructivist theorist was the Swiss *Jean Piaget* (1896–1980). In his adolescence, Piaget became an astute observer of animal behavior. As a young adult, he studied philosophy, which led him to questions about **epistemology,** the nature of knowledge and how it is created. In France, he helped create standardized intelligence tests with *Alfred Binet.* As Piaget asked children the standardized questions on Binet's tests, he noticed that children of the same ages tended to make similar mistakes. This observation prompted him to use clinical interviewing techniques that led children to voice their thinking (1952). Piaget was just as interested in the thinking processes that led to wrong answers as in those that led to the "right" answers.

As Piaget explored children's underlying reasoning, he discovered different systems of logic, or ways of conceptualizing the world, in children of different ages. Through careful dialogue with, and observation of, children, Piaget addressed philosophical questions about the nature of knowledge and its construction. He called himself a **genetic epistemologist**—*genetic* in the sense of seeking the origins of this knowledge, and *epistemologist* because he focused on the nature of knowledge itself. Throughout his life, Piaget interviewed children about their thinking and conducted experiments that revealed children's concepts of the world around them. In addition, he and his wife made detailed observations of their own three children as infants.

Based on these data, Piaget described how children think at different ages and stages. Piaget considered children to be like scientists, always experimenting, exploring, and doing. Through these activities, he believed, children develop different modes of thought at different ages. In the early childhood age range, from birth to age eight, Piaget theorized that there are three stages (Figure 6.3). A fourth stage, formal operations, applies to older children and adults.

Piaget argued that children's development occurs in stages, where (with only few exceptions that he called *décalage,* or out of step), children's capacities in all areas of cognitive development in each stage are **homologous,** or at the same level. Piaget also stated that these stages are universal: all children go through the same ones. He believed that stages are **hierarchical,** that they progress from lower to higher levels, with each new stage being constructed from the prior one. Piaget understood that there are differences in children's responses because he understood emotional

Piaget considered children to be like scientists, always experimenting, exploring, and doing. Through these activities, he believed, children develop different modes of thought at different ages.

development to be a crucial aspect of children's development. However, he did not study these areas, just as Freud, for example, did not analyze the growth of knowledge in children.

Piaget described the mechanisms of learning as a process of **adaptation,** where children learn new ways to relate to the world around them. The components of adaptation are **assimilation** and **accommodation.** In this process, children first take in new information and make it fit with information they already have, thereby *assimilating* it. For example, a child who sees a lion at the zoo might assimilate this new input and call the animal "dog," a four-legged animal he already knows. However, over time, with experiences with different animals, the child will come to realize that there are similarities and differences. Then the child will

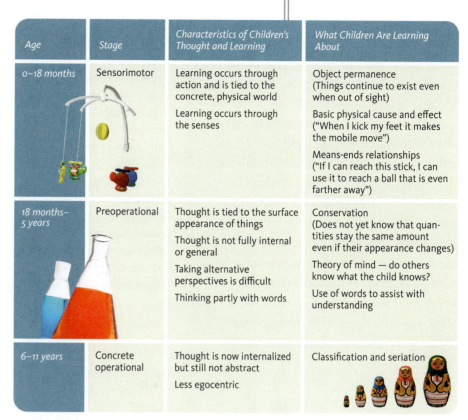

Age	Stage	Characteristics of Children's Thought and Learning	What Children Are Learning About
0–18 months	Sensorimotor	Learning occurs through action and is tied to the concrete, physical world Learning occurs through the senses	Object permanence (Things continue to exist even when out of sight) Basic physical cause and effect ("When I kick my feet it makes the mobile move") Means-ends relationships ("If I can reach this stick, I can use it to reach a ball that is even farther away")
18 months–5 years	Preoperational	Thought is tied to the surface appearance of things Thought is not fully internal or general Taking alternative perspectives is difficult Thinking partly with words	Conservation (Does not yet know that quantities stay the same amount even if their appearance changes) Theory of mind — do others know what the child knows? Use of words to assist with understanding
6–11 years	Concrete operational	Thought is now internalized but still not abstract Less egocentric	Classification and seriation

6.3 *Piagetian Stages of Development*

modify his animal categories to add the class of lion. This modification is called **accommodation.** Through this process, the child becomes better adapted to the world. In this example, the child can distinguish between scary and nonscary animals, learning to pet the dog and to keep his hand away from the lion. Again, none of this knowledge would be possible without the child's active engagement with the environment.

Neo-Piagetian Theories

As they did with other theories, additional thinkers modified and advanced the constructivist point of view. This group, including *Robbie Case, Kurt W. Fischer,* and *Eleanor Duckworth,* is referred to as the neo-Piagetians. They do not focus on grand notions of developmental stages, but on how development happens in context. These theorists continue to believe that children are active agents in their own development, learning through active experience. They maintain that the child's capacity to use different amounts of information at any one point increases over time. Thus, to evaluate the child's development, one must examine how effectively the child combines and integrates information (Case 1991; Fischer 1980; Duckworth 2001). For example, Piaget believed that young children cannot assume the perspective of another person. Yet, when children play with a doll, many of them can articulate what they would be able to see from that doll's position.

Neo-Piagetians do not focus on grand notions of developmental stages, but on how development happens in context.

Evaluation of Piagetian and Neo-Piagetian Theory

Piaget's theory of cognitive development was certainly one of the most influential of the twentieth century. It addressed both details of children's cognitive development and the bigger questions of the nature of development and mechanisms of change.

Many agree that Piaget's work enriches our understanding of how children think, and that he asked important questions about the nature of their thought. However, research over the past twenty years has prompted criticisms of his theory. First, there is evidence that Piaget's stages are not universal; that different experiences and cultures influence children's thinking. Second, since he did not have the benefit of recent research on the abilities of young infants and young children, Piaget probably underestimated their capacities. For example, such research has shown that infants have the beginnings of **object permanence** (the knowledge that things continue to exist when they are out of sight) earlier than Piaget believed. Piaget called preschool children's thinking **egocentric**, maintaining that they do not readily take the perspective of others. However, research has shown that with support and a meaningful context, children can, with certain limitations, understand that others see things differently.

Revisiting Michael's Head Start Using Constructivist Theory

Let's see what it would mean to use constructivist thinking to help staff address their dilemmas with Michael:

- Ellen invoked a Piagetian idea (that *preoperational thinking constrains perspective-taking abilities*) when she said that Michael might not understand his classmates' points of view. She also implied that she should solicit Michael's *active participation* when she suggested he find other ways to respond to his peers.

- Several staff believed that Michael needed to *learn to handle his own aggressive behavior.*

- Nancy recommended giving Michael play dough or other *expressive materials* to work on his feelings.

- Sandra proposed that Michael actively gather information about what his peers were doing so that he could *develop alternative ways of understanding.*

CONTEXTUALIST THEORIES

How do contextualist theories explain children's development and learning?

Contextualist theory emphasizes the role of the environment in child development but does so differently from the behaviorists. It focuses on the dimensions of the child's experiences with other people, the physical environment, and the social-historical context in which the child lives. This approach assumes that development will be different for every child and seeks to explain these variations.

Lev Vygotsky (1896–1934) was a **sociohistorical** theorist who worked in Soviet Russia following the 1917 Revolution. Although he did not live a long life, the social ferment and rise of a Marxist, or **materialist,** philosophy provided a fertile context in which Vygotsky and, later, other psychologists like *A. R. Luria* (1902–1977) produced an important body of thinking and new ways to consider human development. A materialist point of view argues that the social, economic, and political conditions of people's lives determine their psychologies or mental lives. Vygotsky combined as-

> Contextualist theories focus on the dimensions of the child's experiences with other people, the physical environment, and the social-historical context in which the child lives, with the assumption that development will be different for every child.

pects of then-current theories with Marxism to create what he saw as a more coherent view of human development (Wertsch 1985).

For Vygotsky, the individual and the social world are part of an interactive system in which people's mental structures take in and reflect what goes on in the world. Vygotsky believed that the child absorbs what occurs around her, as well as her own interaction with other people or objects. In other words, external experiences become internalized as a part of the child's mental structures (Vygotsky 1934/1978).

For example, the child first hears and learns words from others. Then the child uses **egocentric speech,** Vygotsky's term for when children talk to themselves or to others to rehearse or practice rather than to communicate. Think of children who rhyme words over and over or who play with the sounds in words. Speech, Vygotsky said, then becomes part of the child's mental structure. Put another way, the child begins to think using the categories of his native language. Try to think for thirty seconds without using words. Could you do it? Language structures the ways that we are able to think. Vygotsky also proposed that language and other cultural materials (art, music, social interaction, and broader social institutions or contexts) are "tools" the child uses to develop.

Scaffolding is another important term built on Vygotskian concepts. Vygotsky believed that the adult or another more experienced learner plays an important role in fostering **internalization,** the child's consolidation of what she learns. The experienced learner provides a scaffold, or a platform, that raises the child to a higher level of functioning than she could reach on her own.

Vygotsky created the term **zone of proximal development** as part of his thinking about how children develop. Although it was not a key aspect of his work at the time, it has become a central idea among educators (Chaiklin 2003). The ZPD is what a child can do "through problem solving under adult guidance or in collaboration with more capable peers" (Vygotsky 1978, 89). Imagine the child who, on his

THOUGHT QUESTION How do you think Vygotsky might explain the impact of the technological revolution on how today's four- to eight-year-olds think and learn in comparison with their parents at that age?

> Vygotsky proposed that language and other cultural materials—art, music, social interaction, and broader social institutions or contexts—are "tools" the child uses to develop.

It is likely that an older "experienced other" is nearby to scaffold this three-year-old's juice making. What clues in the photograph help you know this?

Jean Piaget	Lev Vygotsky
Looked at what children did and said with less concern for the context in which it took place.	Believed the child's cultural and social context were important developmental influences.
 Theorized about internalized mental structures or schemata that develop based on a child's active engagement with the world, especially from creating mental relationships between physical objects or phenomena.	Theorized about internalized mental structures that are based on what children take in and make sense of from their world, particularly from the people around them. 
Believed that thought drives language.	Believed that language drives thought.
Regarded egocentric speech as evidence of the child's self-oriented perspective.	Regarded egocentric or private speech as the child's thinking aloud to better understand and self-regulate.
Emphasized the child's internal thinking processes or logico-motor thinking, depending on others primarily for what is impossible to figure out, such as social conventions and the names of things.	Emphasized the role of an experienced other in moving a child's thinking forward through the zone of proximal development.
Believed that development leads learning.	Believed learning leads development.

own, is not yet ready to play with others. But when his teacher sits near him and another child and says, "We would like to play too," the child who could not play with others enters into an interaction. Thus, the ZPD *goes beyond* helping a child accomplish a specific task to actually push development forward. For the best learning conditions and internalization, the adult must determine where the child is developmentally and culturally, and scaffold accordingly. Vygotsky believed that learning leads development, unlike Piaget, who believed that a child's changing cognitive structures (brain development) paved the way for learning. Figure 6.4 compares a number of Piaget's and Vygotsky's ideas about early childhood development.

Contemporary Contextualist Theories

There have been other contextualist developmental theories as well, notably the **ecological model** of development devised by *Urie Bronfenbrenner* (1917–2005), which you read about in Chapter 2, and the work of *Barbara Rogoff,* a contemporary psychologist who articulated a "cultural psychology." These contextual points of view lead us to focus on the broader social context and historical era in which children learn. Rogoff (2003) suggests that different cultures arrange children's experiences in ways that enable them to acquire the skills necessary for competence in their own societies. She calls these activities **guided participation,** because children learn through their involvement in whatever the adults are doing. For instance, Guatemalan children learn to weave as they perform tasks related to the weaving that their adults do. What children know is a function, not of their minds, but of the social-cultural-historical world in which they live. To understand a child's mind, one must understand that world.

Contextualist Theories and Early Childhood Education

Contextualist theories have a great deal of relevance for the early childhood educator. First, they mandate that knowing children should include knowing their individual worlds—their families, their communities, their cultures. To understand what a child brings to the classroom, the early childhood educator needs to open a dialogue with families and other cultural informants and then to listen, with respect, to their goals and understandings. In addition, how the classroom environment is arranged contributes to the room's culture and to how the child learns. About any class, we can ask: What values do classroom practices, routines, and rules embody? Finally, both Vygotsky and Rogoff see an important role for the educator. Vygotsky believed that children actually "tug" at development. When learning engages children deeply and adults provide thoughtful scaffolding, children can grapple with ideas that might otherwise seem too complex for them. Rogoff would add that the teacher is a participant in the classroom culture whose role is to guide children into fuller participation in the social world.

Evaluation of Contextualist Theory

Contextualist theory addresses big questions about development. One of its strengths is that it looks to cultures and subcultures with the explicit understanding that all children are different. A contextualist theory does not aim to impose cultural norms nor decide what is "best" about different child-rearing contexts and values. A contextualist point of view also directs us to the details of development, asking adults to understand minute aspects of the child's learning environment, along with the child's particular set of skills and abilities at each point in time. By considering how various cultures affect children, the contextualist point of view embodies democratic values. However, some educators are not comfortable with the level of adult intervention that Vygotsky's theory suggests.

Revisiting Michael's Head Start Using Contextualist Theory

Several suggestions from the staff of Michael's school implied that what Michael knows is tied to his context, his experiences in the world in which he lives:

- Clarice noted that Michael's behavior was affected by *changes in his family life*. Michael's father may have returned to Northern Ireland for sociopolitical reasons, demonstrating how the larger culture can have an impact on one boy.
- Ellen's thought that a new child in the group had *altered Michael's peer interactions* also considers context.
- Suggestions that Michael needed assistance from adults to develop new understandings and alternative modes of expressing himself were calls for *guided participation*.

> Vygotsky believed that children actually "tug" at development. When learning engages children deeply and adults provide thoughtful scaffolding, children can grapple with ideas that might otherwise seem too complex for them.

Carl Rogers maintained that the creation of a community of learners occurred when the teacher embodied a set of qualities: realness, trust or acceptance of others, empathy, and being fully present.

HUMANIST THEORIES

How do humanist theories explain how children develop and learn?

In the middle of the twentieth century, many people in the United States were experiencing a new optimism about the future, the potential for progress, and human nature. It was a time of growing prosperity in which the U.S. victory in World War II was seen by many as a triumph of good over evil. It was in this context that a specifically humanistic psychology developed, with *Carl Rogers* (1902–1987) as one of its main proponents. In his clinical work with troubled families and children over much of the twentieth century, Rogers (1989) found that a lot of what he thought would be effective was not, in fact, helpful. Instead, he discovered that what was most helpful to those with whom he worked was to align himself with the good in each person through empathy and understanding. He believed that each person had a basically positive direction and that any helping person (including educators) could facilitate the individual's natural growth process by being genuinely "present" with that person. Rogers maintained that the creation of a **community of learners** occurred when the teacher embodied a set of qualities: realness, trust or acceptance of others, empathy, and being fully present. Only in a relationship with others who have these facilitating qualities, he argued, does real learning occur.

Maslow's Hierarchy of Needs

Another humanistic psychologist, *Abraham Maslow* (1908–1970), believed that human beings have a specific hierarchy of needs (Figure 6.5). Maslow (1999) believed that individuals prioritize getting their needs met one level at a time. When they are hungry, their behavior is directed toward meeting that need. Only when all their physical needs are met will individuals move to the next level and strive for safety. The ultimate goal of all people, Maslow believed, was **self-actualization,** or the capacity to reach one's fullest potential.

Humanist Theory and the Early Childhood Educator

Both Rogers's and Maslow's work are relevant to the early childhood teacher. First, Rogers directs the early childhood educator to look for each child's positive potential and highlights how conscious relationships promote learning between teachers and children. Maslow reminds us that a hungry or frightened child will not be able to learn, and that schools and programs for children must address those basic needs before children can explore the world around them.

Evaluation of Humanist Theory

Although Rogers himself did not believe that he was naive, critics point out that his point of view does not directly address the flaws or problems in human nature. However, his theories do imply a certain set of values and orientations valuable to practitioners of early childhood education. Some limitations of Maslow's hierarchy of needs are that it seems to imply there is but one ideal kind of person or only one direction to development—which may not be

Self-actualization

Esteem Needs

Social Needs

Safety Needs

Physiological Needs

6.5 *Maslow's Hierarchy of Needs*

relevant across cultures. Also, the order of Maslow's human needs might be taken to mean that people who don't have adequate food or shelter, for example, are unable to appreciate beauty or the aesthetics of their environment.

Revisiting Michael's Head Start Using Humanist Theory

- Lucille thought that Michael needed positive attention and affection. She wanted to have a genuine relationship with him and believed in the *positive direction* of his development.

- In her rejection of Betty's negative and rather hopeless view of Michael, Juanita, too, took a humanist point of view; namely, that Michael could be helped to change in important ways.

- Clarice understood that Michael's mother was stressed from worrying about paying the rent and putting food on the table. She seemed to be saying that Michael's mother could not respond to her son's social needs *because she was so focused on these basic needs.*

DEVELOPMENTAL SYSTEMS THEORIES

How do developmental systems theories explain how children develop and learn?

Theory-making of the twentieth century aimed to resolve the old question of "nature versus nurture," asking, in effect, which is most important in shaping the child, his biology or his environment? In contrast, all versions of **systems theory** argue that nature and nurture do not operate independently of each other and that a child's development is best understood by looking at how these elements work together. The developmental-interaction approach, first described in Chapter 2, is one early attempt to describe the combined workings of nature and nurture. Both the nature-only and the nurture-only explanations of children's development look at only part of the picture. In Figure 6.6a, you can see that in the nativist view, constitution, or biology, trumps environment; in the nurturist view, the environment controls the outcome. A more complex understanding suggests that the two, nature and nurture, affect each other, as in the bidirectional, or interactional, model in Figure 6.6b.

Transactional Model of Development

Throughout the twentieth century to the present, many theorists have elaborated on and expanded the idea that nothing in human behavior results from simple or single causes. In the mid-1970s, *Arnold J. Sameroff* and *Michael J. Chandler* made a significant contribution when they proposed a developmental systems theory they named the **transactional model of development** (Sameroff 1975; Sameroff and Chandler 1975). This theory goes beyond bidirectional or interactional effects to illustrate the complexity of how multiple effects interact with each other. The transactional

> Maslow reminds us that a hungry or frightened child will not be able to learn, and that schools and programs for children must address those basic needs before children can explore the world around them.

THOUGHT QUESTION Look back on the twentieth-century theories described so far, and place each in a category of arguing more for nature or for nurture.

THOUGHT QUESTION Think of a child you have known well over the course of a few years. How do you think the child's genetic inheritance, the environment, and the child herself work together in what you have observed of the child's development? How does a transactional approach help you to think about development?

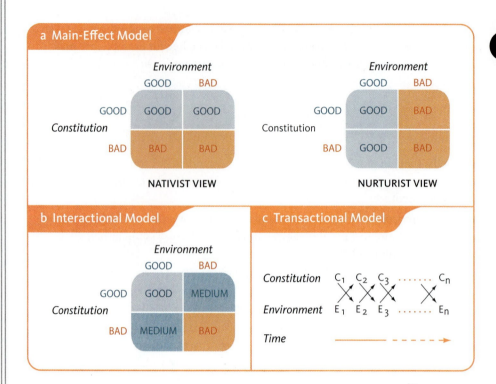

a **Main-Effect Model**

Environment

GOOD   BAD

GOOD | GOOD | GOOD
Constitution
BAD | BAD | BAD

NATIVIST VIEW

Environment

GOOD   BAD

GOOD | GOOD | BAD
Constitution
BAD | GOOD | BAD

NURTURIST VIEW

b **Interactional Model**

Environment

GOOD   BAD

GOOD | GOOD | MEDIUM
Constitution
BAD | MEDIUM | BAD

c **Transactional Model**

Constitution C_1 C_2 C_3 .... C_n

Environment E_1 E_2 E_3 .... E_n

Time

The transactional model of development illustrates the complexity of how multiple effects interact with each other. Over time the child grows and changes because of mutual, or transacting, influences.

model (Figure 6.6c) suggests that *over time* the child grows and changes because of mutual, or **transacting,** influences.

As an example, consider male baldness. In most instances, male baldness is genetically inherited from the mother's side of the family. To know what a man's future hairline will be, look at his maternal grandfather's. However, in rare instances, such as times of extreme shock and stress, any man can lose all his hair suddenly. In such a case, the effects of the environment overrode what biology (constitution) said should happen to this individual's hairline.

Dynamic Systems Theory

The most contemporary developmental systems theory is the **dynamic systems theory of development** articulated by *Esther Thelen.* Thelen (Thelen and Smith 2006) was interested in the problem of motor development in infancy, a field that had long relied on a maturational theory for explanation. Through careful observation, Thelen determined that multiple factors influenced the timing of and variability in infants' growing motor skills and decided that no model completely explained the processes she was seeing. She turned to new ideas in physics that were related to what is popularly known as **chaos theory** (Gleick 1988). Chaos theory suggests that there are always *unpredictable factors* that create change.

Consider the earlier example of how an extreme shock can cause abrupt hair loss. If someone experiences an unexpected trauma, like the death of a loved one in a car accident, we could say that this was a random, chaotic event that no one could have predicted would affect this person. Yet it had a significant effect on the individual's life and development. What Thelen also pointed out, however, was that a system, such as the one described as the transactional model of development, finds a way to reorganize itself

Esther Thelen

after the effects of the unpredictable. In the case of sudden baldness, we could say that, in the face of high levels of stress hormones, the body found a way to adapt or reorganize by shedding hair. This is a more adaptive response than, say, a heart attack, which can also be triggered by high levels of stress. When there are seemingly unpredictable influences on the child's development, the overall system finds a way to right itself, incorporating the changes caused by the unexpected. Self-righting tendencies are another example of an optimistic approach.

IDENTITY THEORIES

How do identity theories explain how children develop and learn?

Identity is about, not only how we become the people we are, but also how we think about who we are. In other parts of this book, we have stated that everyone has more than one identity. Adults can support young children as they wrestle with their identities and gender roles—a fundamental aspect of human growth and development.

Theories about Gender Identity and Gender Roles

By the time children are about two or three years old, they can label themselves and others as male or female. They have developed a **gender identity.** However, ask a three-year-old boy playing "house" if he can be a mother when he grows up, and you may be surprised by his answer because **gender constancy** tends to develop later in the preschool years, especially for boys. See Figure 6.7 to understand these and other terms theorists use to talk about gender identity.

Lawrence Kohlberg (1966), a constructivist theorist, was an early investigator of how young children think about gender. Although when and how children acquire gender constancy differs, research on Kohlberg's stages confirms that children go through a structured sequence in the way they understand gender.

In the early years, most children experiment with gender-typed behaviors and do not rigidly conform to gender norms. As they grow older, however, a biased role rigidity can set in. In other words, one way to adapt to cultural expectations is to take them on with a vengeance. In the following story, a male K–1 teacher in an urban public school demonstrates how a teacher can help children find their voice amid the gender banter in early childhood settings.

[K]ids, usually girls . . . would say to me [in a sing-song tempo] "You have a pony-tail, you have earrings, that's for girls." And my answer was always this very even-tempered, "Well, I have a pony tail and I have earrings, and I'm a boy, so I guess they're for boys too." And my triumph was when I was watching the kids at the sand table. They were pretending that they were making ice cream. One little girl says, "I'm making a double vanilla fudge." And [Ralph] said "Well, I'm going to make a double vanilla fudge too," and the little girl said, "No, only

> Systems theory suggests that there are always unpredictable factors that create change but that human systems are basically self-organizing and can reorganize after unexpected influences.

Gender Constancy
Understanding that one cannot change one's gender by changing one's appearance or behavior

Gender Identity
An internal sense of being male or female

Gender Roles
Cultural and social attitudes and expectations about what constitutes male or female behavior

Sexual Orientation
Patterns of psychological and emotional-erotic attraction to another person; the gender of one's love object in relation to one's own gender

Transgendered
Descriptor for individuals whose gender identity differs from their biological sex

6.7 *Terms Related to Gender Identity*

girls make double vanilla fudge ice cream." And he said, "Well I'm a boy and I'm making a double vanilla fudge ice cream, so I guess boys do it too." (Casper and Schultz 1999, 120)

Theories about gender and gender roles attempt to explain such phenomena. Most theories of gender identity start with the assumption that children's perceptions of themselves as male and female and what that means are tied to **sociocultural norms**—the expectations and behaviors of the people around them—rather than to any underlying biological predispositions. Gender theory also points out that females have been discriminated against and denied access to equal opportunities, a power imbalance that children are well aware of. Being a late twentieth and early twenty-first century point of view, gender identity theories typically imply that equity between the genders can and must be created.

Transgendered individuals

Most children come to feel that they have the identity of their biological sex. However, some do not feel identified with their own sex and instead feel more as if they belong to the opposite sex. Many adults who perceive themselves as **transgendered** remember feeling this way since early preschool. Some believe that this cross-gender identification results from subtle biological differences, perhaps related to prenatal exposure to hormones. The brains of children may be altered from this exposure, and cross-gender identity can be seen as a healthy and normal response to this biological variation. Others suggest that rigid role requirements that some children cannot tolerate serve to create such identifications. To yet others, cross-gender identification is a disorder in which a person feels serious conflict between his or her biological sex and psychological gender.

Clearly, transgender issues were not on the minds of the gender theorists of the last century. But today, not only are children coming forth with feelings of being a different sex or gender, but early childhood classrooms may have young children whose parents change their genders during a school year. In these situations, as young children grapple with the crossing of boundaries that they are still trying to internalize, none of the older classic gender theories may be helpful. This is an area where there is a need for alternative theories.

Gender identity is a complex psychological process that results from a variety of factors interacting and reacting together. As a basic category, gender serves to define much about each individual. Cognitive-developmental change, social learning and operant conditioning processes, and biology probably come together to create children's sense of who they are as a male or female as they grow and develop.

Revisiting Michael's Head Start Using Gender Theory

- Both male staff members suggested that, as a boy, Michael needed to learn to be tough and know how to fight, which points to their concern about gender roles.
- When Jasper stated that it was important that Michael not turn out to be a sissy like another boy in the program, Jasper seemed concerned that otherwise Michael would not be "boy enough." He also implied that to identify as a male, Michael needed to be tough like his father.

Some believe that a deep fear of homosexuality lies at the heart of responses such as Jasper's. Although both gay men and lesbians can have gendered behaviors that are stereotypical or not, many people still believe, even in the absence of supporting data, that gender-atypical behaviors, and gayness itself, can rub off, especially on children. These are complex classroom issues because how we dress, our gender identities, and sexualities—our multiple identities—are influenced by culture, religion, family background, and much more. As we discussed in earlier chapters, it is important to become educated about gender and identity issues and to have a forum where you feel safe talking out these issues and their implications for you as an educator.

Postmodern and Feminist Poststructuralist Theories

A postmodernist might reject the title of theorist altogether, but we discuss this worldview here because of the postmodern idea of multiple and fluid identities. The **postmodern** approach to knowledge and understanding is one of skepticism of all-encompassing theories. Above all, postmodernists don't trust unifying principles or ideas or single explanations. To them, the "big picture," as any of us understand it, is an illusion. For example, Piaget and Freud constructed complex, tightly woven systems that have internal structures—hence, they are **structuralists.** Rather than constructing theories, postmodernists argue that knowledge must be **deconstructed,** that is, taken apart, in order to reveal the hidden power relations, contradictions, and paradoxes of what is often accepted as fact (Butler 2002). Take, for example, a child who ignores a teacher who asks her to go down the slide and who threatens to pinch another child instead of clearing the way for her. A postmodern or critical interpretation might focus on the power relations between the two children and between the ignored teacher and the child who refuses to budge. From a postmodern perspective, the child's behavior might be interpreted as an act of resistance (Schultz 1989). Postmodernism raises questions about what such resistance means to the child and whether a teacher can empower a child or whether the child must take power herself.

Michel Foucault, a French historian, focused on the power structures of social institutions. Foucault's (1988) description of prison guards high up in their towers watching over their inmates conjures up the term *super-vision,* in which he saw parallels to social service personnel, including teachers, at the front of the classroom, watching over their students.

Glenda Mac Naughton (2003) writes about early childhood practices from a feminist poststructuralist perspective, examining assumptions about gender and gender equity. She argues, for example, that changing the stereotypical gendered behavior of preschoolers requires more than allowing children equal access to materials and roles. She suggests that the early childhood professional needs to deconstruct the entire gender **discourse,** or interpretations of meaning, present in early childhood programs and literature before it is possible to meaningfully change inequitable gendered behaviors. This involves analyzing the teacher's assumptions about power and the sexes as well as the assumptions of children, families, and others in the early childhood community. Mac Naughton encourages questions about how we categorize people, including ourselves; about the social practices through which we give meanings to these categories; and about the patterns and emotional meanings we have invested in these categories.

Gender is a complex classroom issue because how we dress, our gender identities, and sexualities—our multiple identities—are influenced by culture, religion, family background, and much more.

Postmodernism and feminist poststructuralism offer the early childhood educator in general, and Juanita, Michael's teacher, in particular (as she figures out how to respond to his aggression), the idea that no single theory explains any phenomenon. Instead, one should understand that multiple and shifting perspectives may be partially valid and often useful. In some sense, the different perspectives at the staff meeting that attempt to explain why Michael is biting, what the biting means, and how to respond to it, suggest a postmodern sensibility. From a postmodern perspective, multiple responses to a situation likely reflect underlying values, including those about the power relations between children and adults. At the same time, we would argue that not every theory is equal and that, therefore, practitioners must examine theories for evidence of their meaning and utility.

Theories of Racial and Ethnic Identity

In the middle of the twentieth century, *Kenneth Clark* and *Mamie Clark* conducted some now-famous experiments about racial identity. They asked African American and European American preschoolers about their preferences for black and white dolls (Clark, Chein, and Cook 1994). They found that as early as preschool, European American and African American children attributed more positive qualities to the white dolls than to the black dolls. Clark and Clark interpreted this to mean that even very young black children had acquired a negative self-image in regard to their skin color. Their work became part of the public record when, in 1954, the Supreme Court of the United States held, in **Brown v. Board of Education,** that segregated education did not provide equal opportunities for all children. Since that time, several theorists have worked to explain the development of racial and ethnic identity. (For a modern-day Clark and Clark experiment, see Davis 2005.)

Like the Clarks, *William Cross* (1991) focused primarily on the development of racial identity among African Americans. Looking at adolescents and adults, he sug-

Mamie Clark and Kenneth Clark

gested that African Americans start their identity formation in what he termed the "pre-encounter" stage, where individuals have essentially absorbed the messages of the dominant white culture, including a sense that it is better to be white. At this stage, however, racial identity is not at the forefront of the individual's consciousness. In the encounter stage, however, African Americans have experiences that cause them to reexamine their own beliefs regarding race, power, and status. The next phase, the immersion/emersion stage, is the stage of change—a period of turmoil where individuals put race into a more central position in their own identity. In the fourth phase, internalization, these individuals are free from negative attitudes toward being black and have reached a level of psychological comfort with the self. In the final phase, which Cross called internalization/commitment, they realize the necessity of making a commitment to social action to create racial equality.

Beverly Tatum (1997), among others, applied Cross's model to childhood. She suggested that children are in the pre-encounter stage, where they are developing attitudes about the self derived from their social contexts, relationships, families, and schools. Tatum suggests that young children are essentially naive to the real effects of racism. Preadolescents or young adolescents are likely to have experiences that lead them to the encounter stage. Tatum also found that young children, before about ages nine or ten, tend to play and relate to each other without regard to race if they are in truly integrated settings. The situation changes as adolescence approaches and the need to develop an identity builds. Others believe that young children do not just reproduce racist comments or ideas they overhear but can also construct them anew (Van Ausdale and Feagin 2001).

Using a cognitive-developmental framework, *Rebecca Bigler* and *Lynn Liben* (1993) found that children's attitudes toward their own race are related to stages in their cognitive development. Young children view race concretely, in binary categories (such as good or bad), and tend to evaluate their own group more positively than other groups. This observation conflicts with the Clarks' original findings that young African American children tend to attribute more positive qualities to whites than to blacks. *Margaret Beale Spencer*'s work also suggests that many young African American children may have good self-esteem yet recognize that the European American "white" culture is dominant in the United States, and thus respond to questions accordingly (Spencer and Markstrom-Adams 1990).

An understanding that even young children are taking in information about group membership and differences related to ethnicity and race is crucial to the early childhood teacher. Teachers need to feel comfortable talking with children honestly about differences related to skin color and to cultural differences and similarities among children's families. Awareness that children's understanding of these categories is influenced by their cognitive developmental capacities is also important, so that teachers will work with children and the way children think without imposing adult conceptions or anxieties about children's perceptions and ideas.

Among the staff at Michael's Head Start there was no direct focus on Michael's ethnicity. However, implied in the mention of Michael's father's return to Northern Ireland is the idea that ethnic heritage and identity play a role in the family dynamics and processes affecting Michael. Racial/ethnic identity theory also suggests that Michael is taking in attitudes toward his own and others' ethnicity, especially as Michael's Head Start appears to be racially and ethnically diverse.

> Tatum found that young children before the ages of nine or ten tend to play and relate to each other without regard to race if they are in truly integrated settings.

THOUGHT QUESTION How could one or more of the theories in this chapter help you respond to a European American four-year old who says she does not want to play with an African American child? What questions would you ask yourself? What would you ask and say to the child?

Intelligence type	Ability/talent	Preferred ways of learning
Linguistic	Words and language	Through talking and reading
Logico-mathematical	Logic and numbers	Through reasoning, quantifying, and thinking
Musical	Music, sounds, rhythms	Through listening, especially to melodies and rhythms/rhymes
Bodily kinesthetic	Body awareness and body control	Through moving
Spatial-visual	Images and space	Through looking
Interpersonal	Understanding others Social skills	Through social interaction and observing others
Intrapersonal	Self-awareness	Through reflecting on and observing self
Existential	Thinking about big life questions, such as, Why are we on earth?	Through reflecting on life and one's experiences
Naturalist	Observing patterns in nature	Through looking and comparing features of the environment

6.8 *Gardner's Multiple Intelligences*
From: Gardner 2006.

THEORIES ABOUT INTELLIGENCE

How do theories about intelligence explain how children develop and learn?

What does it mean to be intelligent? Does it mean to succeed in school? To solve practical problems? To think quickly? To speak articulately and clearly? To solve complicated mathematical problems? What does musical ability have to do with intelligence? Does it require intelligence to build a bridge? When you think about children, what qualities do you consider if you evaluate how "smart" they are?

Intelligence in the Psychological Literature

In the psychological literature, **intelligence** is regarded as one global capacity that typically includes verbal and mathematical abilities and the capacity to learn and to create novel solutions to complex problems. IQ scores are related to reaction time and quickness of response that now can be measured not just by how rapidly an individual performs a task but also by brain waves. However, IQ scores are controversial because some argue that they are culturally biased; certainly, average differences in IQ scores between minority and majority children have been used to attempt to characterize minority groups as less intelligent than majority groups (Jensen 1998; Hernnstein and Murray 1994).

Multiple Intelligences

Howard Gardner (2006) suggests that there are **multiple intelligences,** or capacities, that indicate how intelligent a person is; Figure 6.8 lists and explains Gardner's intelligences. Early childhood educators who recognize different intelligences in children can support these children's diverse abilities and the ways in which they learn best. Gardner is still researching the last two intelligences: existential and naturalist. He now refers to "8½ intelligences"—with existential intelligence being the one that does not quite fit all the criteria that the others do (Gardner 2006). Once again we see how theories continue to evolve.

When the staff discussed Michael, they did not mention intelligence directly, but much of what the staff talked about could be considered "interpersonal intelligence" as well as "intrapersonal intelligence," to use Gardner's terms. The staff members wanted to help Michael understand how to interact with other children, that is, to increase his social skills, or interpersonal intelligence. They also wanted to increase his self-understanding, or intrapersonal in-

THOUGHT QUESTION Think about a time that you learned something significant. Which of Gardner's intelligences did you use?

IDENTITY THEORIES

How do identity theories explain how children develop and learn?

Research on Lawrence Kohlberg's stages confirms that children go through a structured sequence in the way they understand gender, understandings that are influenced by the expectations and behaviors of those around them. Although most children identify with their biological sex, early childhood classrooms may include those whose genders will change. The postmodern approach to identities, in fact, is that they are multiple and fluid; this approach takes a skeptical view of any all-encompassing theories, unifying principles, or single explanations. Postmodernist Michel Foucault's focus on the power structure of institutions has implications for the early childhood classroom, and Glenda Mac Naughton urges teachers to deconstruct classroom gender discourse. Researching racial identity, Kenneth and Mamie Clark found that very young black children had a negative self-image with regard to their skin color. Beverly Tatum applied William Cross's model of racial identity formation to childhood and suggested that children develop attitudes about themselves derived from their social contexts, relationships, families, and schools.

THEORIES ABOUT INTELLIGENCE

How do theories about intelligence explain how children develop and learn?

The psychological literature has measured intelligence with tests of verbal and mathematical abilities and the capacity to learn and create novel solutions to complex problems. Howard Gardner suggests, instead, that there are multiple intelligences and that understanding them can help early childhood educators support children's diverse abilities and the ways in which they learn best. His theory of multiple intelligence is constantly evolving, illustrating how theories can change with new information and insights.

FURTHER ACTIVITIES

1. Choose three theories discussed in this chapter. For each, explain how it
   a. Helps you understand children's characteristics and needs,
   b. Addresses or can address how different factors influence children's development and learning, and
   c. Offers guidance for creating a healthy, respectful, supportive, and challenging environment for all children. (**NAEYC Standard 1: Promoting Child Development and Learning**)

2. Choose a theory from this chapter that you believe helps explain the behavior of a child you have observed often and know well. Draft a letter to the child's family, describing what the theory leads you to believe about the child. Be sure to include examples of the child's behavior that illustrate your points. Discuss your letter with a colleague. (**NAEYC Standard 2: Building Family and Community Relationships**)

3. Describe an experience for children that you have designed or observed and that you believe promotes positive development and learning. Explain how the experience does or does not fit with Vygotskian theory. (**NAEYC Standard 4: Using Developmentally Effective Approaches to Connect with Children and Families**)

CHAPTER SEVEN

Early Childhood Programming

What the best and wisest parent wants for his own child, that must the community want for all of its children.

John Dewey

The community as a whole benefits when all children have the best possible care and education. As you read this chapter about the types of programs and individuals who make up children's care and education experience, think about what distinguishes them from one another and what families might want of each. Understanding programming possibilities can help you decide where to work and can help you suggest alternatives to families. To start, let's consider the people and programs that fit together for Wendy.

Five-year-old Wendy's parents are divorced. Wendy lives with her mom, Judith, a nurse who works three 7:00 a.m. to 7:30 p.m. shifts a week. When she's not working, Judith brings Wendy to kindergarten and picks her up at 3 p.m., except for Tuesdays, when Wendy stays late for after-school karate. On the days Judith works, she wakes Wendy up at 6:15 a.m. and slides her into the car in her pajamas with her school clothes and knapsack. They drive a mile to Grandpa Joe's, and he lets Wendy sleep, then gives her breakfast, gets her dressed, and takes her to school. He picks her up, too, unless Grandma Yvette, a realtor, doesn't have an appointment and can get to the school on time. Wendy's dad is a banquet chef whose hours vary. On the days Wendy sleeps at his house, which are different each week, he takes Wendy to school. If he's not working in the afternoon, he picks her up and brings her back to his house, unless, of course, it's Tuesday, when she stays for karate.

Confused? Wendy has a complicated care and education schedule, but so do many children. The pieces of Wendy's care and education puzzle usually fit together in a way that works. In her case, two programs and four loving individuals contribute to her care.

CARE AND EDUCATION

Why have care and education been treated separately, and why do they go together?

Think about what you read in Chapter 1 about care and education. Can a program or individual offer care but not education? Can programs educate children without caring for them? We think not.

Yet, over the years, U.S. society has behaved as if care and education can be distinct from one another (Kagan and Kauerz 2007). In the nineteenth century, poor women who worked as domestic servants or in factories needed care for their children. Day nurseries sprang up as an alternative to the orphan asylums that mothers paid to board their children (Polakow 2007). They were open long hours, six days a week and took in infants through preschoolers; they even offered after-school care.

Children were eligible for these day nurseries based on financial need; parental employment was not the consideration (Polakow 2007). Instead, the nurseries aimed to Americanize immigrant children and be an uplifting force in the lives of poor children. In contrast, the middle-class black women who ran the African American day nurseries understood that women had to work and regarded their clients more sympathetically.

The day nurseries were grim places, and reformers in the early twentieth century rallied to close them and institute public funding to allow mothers to remain at home with their children (Polakow 2007). The stage was set, though, for care facilities aimed at children from low-income families, while programs for middle-class and wealthy children constituted early education.

THOUGHT QUESTION Put yourself in Wendy's shoes. What would you like about this schedule? What might reassure and comfort you? What might make you anxious? Compare your responses with two classmates' answers. Talk to each other about how Wendy's kindergarten teacher could help Wendy make her schedule work well for her.

Over the years, U.S. society has behaved as if care and education can be distinct from one another.

Middle- and upper-income parents began forming cooperative playgroups for their children as early as 1915 (Hewes 1998) and participated in their children's classrooms. At the University of Chicago, mothers began one of the earliest multipurpose parent cooperatives: they sought parent education for themselves, free time to do other volunteer work (Coontz n.d.), and play opportunities for their children. An increasing number of these parent cooperatives came into being in the 1940s and 1950s. Parent cooperative nursery schools arose according to the need of the families who established them, without a central coordinating force. Nonetheless, these cooperatives shared a belief that children learned through self-directed play (Hewes 1998).

Although today some people still think of child care as separate from education, many preschools extend their days, and child care activities mirror the traditional nursery school. Child care and Head Start centers, along with other programs, help states offer prekindergarten to more children than the public schools alone can serve. Moreover, pressure to "educationalize" (Kagan and Kauerz 2007, 12) all programs for young children—that is, to make all programs positive learning situations—and to create a coherent system of early care and education programs has helped integrate care and education programs.

The Role of Continuity

Continuity of care provides children with stability across their care and education experience over the course of the day and through the years. Instead of a series of unrelated experiences, continuity of care means that children are together with one another and an adult for more than one year (Theilheimer 2006). Programs that ensure continuity of care recognize the importance of the caring and educative relationship and, when possible, do not disrupt those relationships with a transition to a new teacher or classroom. Two program structures that further continuity of care are looping and mixed-age grouping.

With **looping,** children move from class to class or grade to grade with the same teacher or teachers from the previous class or grade. In one infant/toddler program, an infant caregiver becomes a toddler teacher when children are ready to make that switch. A year or two later, she moves with them to the preschool class. They have a number of teacher caregivers, but the caregiver who began with them as infants is a continuous presence in their care and education.

Looping is equally beneficial for older children. Linda's kindergartners know the classroom, its rules, and even its layout. They are still in her class for first grade, and, instead of learning a new classroom, they confront the challenges of new work right away. Linda knows them and their learning styles and does not spend the start of school getting to know a new group.

With looping, teachers get to know children well, and children become comfortable in and knowledgeable about their learning environment. On the other hand, if a child or family's relationship with a teacher is not a good one, looping could prolong an undesirable situation. On the plus side, it could also provide an opportunity to work through tensions.

In **mixed-age grouping,** children of different ages are in the same group or class. For example, an Early Head Start group can include infants, toddlers, and two-year-olds. An elementary school may have a first/second grade classroom instead of separate rooms for each grade.

When children stay with the same teacher or teachers over several years in mixed-age groups, they have the same advantages of continuity of care they would if

With looping, teachers get to know children well, and children become comfortable in and knowledgeable about their learning environment.

they were looping with their teacher. They have the added advantage (or disadvantage) of being in a group with children who are older than they are during the first year, and younger during the second year. The younger children learn from the older ones, as they might from a sibling at home. The older children have the satisfaction of teaching younger children. Nonetheless, some parents worry about older children in a mixed-age group: one fear is that they will adopt babyish behavior; another, that they won't receive the stimulation they need.

One other advantage of mixed-age grouping is that it enables adults to provide materials and experiences that children of various ages can use differently. Then, adults can learn from a range of developmental behaviors. Yet, with all its advantages, mixed-age grouping demands a vigilant and creative teacher who pays careful attention to each child and develops curriculum that is rich enough for exploration from different entry points.

While looping and mixed-age grouping ensure continuity of care, educators look at continuity in other ways, too. Some teachers work together to smooth children's transitions from one class to another. As you'll read later in this chapter, schools that include only prekindergarten through third grade consider the child's total educational experience, so that each grade contributes to a coherent whole. On an even larger scale, educators are trying to fit together a range of early childhood programs, such as Head Start and child care programs, into one system.

THOUGHT QUESTION Why would or wouldn't you want to loop with a group of children? Why would or wouldn't teaching in a mixed-age class appeal to you? What do your preferences suggest that you value (relationships? order and organization? novelty?)? Check your state's licensing requirements to see how local regulators look upon mixed-age grouping.

A Continuum of Care

Take a look at the photograph below of a care provider and the children she cares for. Who is this woman, and what is she doing? Is she providing care for children illegally, with too many children under age three? Does she legally operate a family child care business in her home? Is she a mother or grandmother?

Actually, she could be any of these people. Child care can be viewed as a continuum that extends from parents on one end, to care and education in child care

Whether she is a mother, other family member, friend, neighbor, or family child care provider, the woman in this photo is providing child care that fits along the continuum of care.

centers on the other (Figure 7.1). In between are grandparents, aunts or uncles, and friends or neighbors, along with regulated family child care providers who offer care and education in their own homes (Porter and Rice 2000).

The **child care continuum** contends that any environment where a child spends time—at home with parents, in grandpa's house, at the home of a family child care provider, or in a classroom in a child care center or school—should be safe and healthy for children. The other assumption is that anyone who cares for young children should have the knowledge and skills to support their development and learning.

CARE AND EDUCATION IN THE HOME

What issues do the three types of in-home care and education raise?

Although professionals used to pay it little attention, care and education for children in their own or another home is the most common form of child care for children under five whose parents work. Here we discuss three variations: family member, friend, and neighbor care; family child care; and nannies.

Family, Friend, and Neighbor Care

With good reason, **family, friend, and neighbor (FFN) care** (formerly called kith and kin care) is now accepted as an integral part of the child care system. Nearly half of all young children are in relative child care alone (Boushey and Wright 2004). FFN care also accounts for a significant proportion of the child care arrangements for infants and toddlers (Brandon 2005).

Many parents, especially those with low incomes (Layzer and Goodson 2006), single mothers, and families with more than one child (Snyder and Adelman 2004; Anderson, Ramsburg, and Scott 2005), choose FFN care regardless of any other options. These parents say they want their children, especially their infants and toddlers, cared for by someone they know and trust. They feel their child will be safe and will receive more individual attention; in addition, they feel more comfortable with someone who shares their language and culture. FFN caregivers also are available before 7:00 a.m., after 6:30 p.m., at night, and on weekends—an important consideration for many families who work in retail, health services, or other low-wage jobs (Bromer and Henly 2002). Many of these caregivers, especially relatives, do not charge parents; others ask for fees that are considerably less than the rates charged by regulated family child care providers or centers (Layzer and Goodson 2006).

Care and education for children in their own or another home is the most common form of child care for children under five whose parents work.

How high researchers rate the quality of care in FFN homes seems to depend on the way they measure that care. However, these researchers point to a need for FFN providers to learn about activities they can do with children and about how to engage them in higher-level talk. Such training for FFN care providers is now on the agenda for many states and privately funded agencies.

Family Child Care

Family child care, care and education in the home of an unrelated family, differs from FFN care in that the provider usually does not know the family before the child care arrangement begins, and the provider and the family enter into a business relationship. The family or a public agency pays the provider. Family child care providers must be licensed or registered in some states, but even in states that require licensing, many homes operate without a license. As a result, "fully 82 percent of the roughly one million family-care homes in the United States are unregulated by anyone" (Crittenden 2001, 210).

Family care and education tends to be less expensive than center care and has smaller groups. According to Susan Kontos (1992, 5), the families most likely to use family child care are "families in which mothers are employed part-time and families with children under the age of three." They like the convenience, flexible hours, reliability, and loving environment of family child care (Kontos 1992, Layzer and Goodson 2006). Family child care providers vary in background and education. They may be mothers of young children with no formal background in early childhood, or they may be early childhood educators with master's degrees, like Alexis of this chapter's Real Voice. Family child care providers may perceive themselves more as mothers than as teachers, which may result in more nurturing but less education and stimulation. In fact, in their study, Layzer and Goodson (2006) found that the television was turned *off* in only 28 percent of the homes.

Family child care providers may feel isolated taking care of children for long hours. To combat this isolation and to support quality care and education, family child care networks, often under the auspices of local child care resource and referral agencies, offer providers workshops, individual meetings, opportunities to meet other providers, and toy exchanges. You can read more about these networks on the website of the National Association for Family Child Care, at http://www.nafcc.org/include/default.asp.

Nannies

A **nanny** takes care of children in the family's home. Nanny care is typically the most expensive type of care and education because the family provides the nanny's total income. Nannies often work more than forty hours a week to accommodate parent work schedules, and they also may do household chores to lessen the parents' burden. As with other types of child care, nanny care varies in quality, depending on the nanny's experience, education, disposition, and compensation.

An unequal relationship can develop between nanny and parent because the caregiver's livelihood depends exclusively on the parent. In other child care arrangements, more than one family contributes to the caregiver's wage, or the wages come from a mixture of public funds and tuition. However, some parents report feeling dependent on the nanny because of their urgent need for child care (Cancelmo and Bandini 1999). Thus, a nanny and a parent can have difficulty creating an equal partnership

To combat the isolation that family child care providers may experience and to support quality care and education, family child care networks offer workshops, individual meetings, opportunities to meet other providers, and toy exchanges.

I've been a child care provider for eight years, mostly working with ages three months through three years. I've worked full time in four centers that varied in philosophy, student-teacher ratio, setting, and quality of care. Two centers were part of a larger chain of child care programs owned by one individual, who made a profit. At these for-profit centers, the desire to make money seemed to get in the way of doing what was right. The other two programs were run by a board of directors and were nonprofit. I felt more satisfied in my positions at the nonprofit centers because I thought that decisions at these centers were made with the children in mind first.

So when I moved a few months ago, I knew that I wanted to work in a nonprofit setting. During an Internet search, I came across a program that seemed to be doing everything it could to support children and families. They offer a sliding scale for tuition. The remainder is paid for by a scholarship provided by a large philanthropic organization. This means that almost any family can attend the center, regardless of income.

I applied for a job and was hired into the infant classroom. To my delight, the center paid according to a wage ladder. Since I have a degree in child development, I would be paid a higher wage.

The center partnered with the local Head Start agency to provide all qualifying children with additional services. Two staff members of the partner agency visit the center to do health and hearing screenings, developmental assessments, classroom observations, teacher mentoring, and conferences with the families. Thus, the center ensures that the children and their families receive a wide range of services that it could not provide alone.

But for all of the good this program is doing, I see the same barriers to quality I've seen in each center where I've worked. The group sizes are too large. In the chaotic atmosphere that results from having 12 one-year-olds in the same room, I can barely prevent them from pushing or biting one another, let alone model appropriate behavior and attend to each child's social and emotional needs. Another barrier to quality care is that to remain within its budget, the center must be full at all times. Sometimes children are moved to a new classroom before they are ready, say goodbye prematurely to their beloved teachers, and enter into a new classroom where they are the smallest children and are expected to conform to higher demands.

I felt disempowered and unable to make a difference. While I believe that it is possible to provide good child care, I now realize how complicated it is to provide excellent care and education at a large center.

Letting children be secure and be individuals

I have dreams of working in a program with small groups—say, six children at the most—composed of children of various ages. The children in the group could balance each other's needs. For example, a young baby does not mind if a toddler walks up and takes his toy. Or if a toddler takes a four-year-old's toy, the four-year-old has enough language to say, "That's mine," and enough patience to wait for a teacher's help. I would also like the opportunity to care for kids longer than twelve months without having to send them to the next room just when I've gotten to truly know them.

That is why I'm working toward opening a family child care home. In a home-based child care, I hope to make decisions about the day based on the needs of individual children. If one child wants to carry her blanket around all day, I can let her. If there are puddles outside and the children want to stomp in them, I can let them without worrying that anyone will complain about the mess. If an infant is colicky and just needs to be held, I see myself wrapping him against my body in a baby sling so that he feels cared for and included while I am attending to the other children. I want to be free to give children the type of experiences I believe they deserve.

To make my dream a reality, I researched the Washington State Department of Early Learning website. In Washington State, unlike most other states, individuals who care for children in their home for payment, unless the child is a relative, must be licensed. I eagerly signed up for the first step in becoming licensed and attended a full-day orientation, where I learned the rules and regulations that a licensed program must follow. I've decided to call my program Secure Beginnings, because that is what I believe a child needs most.

to benefit the children. However, when this relationship works well, all benefit; and a sense of family can develop (Cancelmo and Bandini, 1999).

FUNDING

How are early care and education programs funded?

Historically, care and education programs have depended on different funding streams. **Publicly funded** programs, ones receiving monies from the local, state, or federal government, primarily paid for child care for children in families with incomes low enough to be eligible for subsidies. Meanwhile, traditional nursery schools were typically **privately funded,** paid for by parent tuitions and donations and gifts from foundations and corporations.

Public Funding

Today, publicly funded early childhood education falls into three categories: programs for low-income families, programs for families affiliated with an arm of the government, and programs for all children. Head Start, among other programs, is funded for income-eligible families, although children with disabilities are eligible regardless of family income. Military child care is also for a specific population, although it is the family's association with the Department of Defense—not income—that decides their eligibility. Finally, other publicly funded programs, such as public elementary schools and their universal prekindergartens and universal home visiting, are for all children, regardless of income or affiliation with a government agency.

Publicly funded early childhood programs provide free or low-cost care and education and must follow government regulations that do not apply to agencies without government funding. These regulations set program standards and require ongoing evidence that the program meets them.

Head Start and Early Head Start

As you read in Chapter 5, Project Head Start is a comprehensive, federally funded program for low-income families with young children aged three to five. Head Start's founders aimed to offer these children a middle-class nursery school experience to reduce their risk of poverty in adulthood and prevent intergenerational transmission of values and attitudes associated with poverty. When Head Start began, there were different reactions to the plan. Some parents and community action groups challenged what they perceived as Head Start's demeaning view of low-income families' cultures.

Now, Head Start is the longest running federally mandated program for young children in the United States. By 2008, nearly 25 million children had benefited from Head Start. Its founders designed the program to foster children's cognitive, language, social, and emotional development, as well as their health and nutrition. The involvement of parents and other family members is integral to the program.

Head Start's founders designed the program to foster children's cognitive, language, social, and emotional development, as well as their health and nutrition. The involvement of parents and other family members is integral to the program.

Head Start views child development from a whole-child perspective as mandated by the original *Program Performance Standards* of 1975. Although since revised, they still define the features of a quality Head Start program, specifying

- partnering with families and communities—for example, including families in program administration and development;
- services to children with disabilities;
- how the program is run;
- family eligibility and recruitment; and
- staffing.

Nonetheless, the model has the flexibility for local programs to adapt to the diverse needs of their communities and to local leadership and resources. This allows for individual differences in culture, language, type of service delivery, and curriculum choice.

From its inception as a community-driven program, Head Start included

- parenting programs and job skills training,
- home visiting and social supports and referrals,
- English language classes, and
- management skills training for parents and other significant adults in young children's lives.

More than one-third of Head Start staff—from cooks and transportation staff to teachers to management—are parents of current or former Head Start children. Through the Child Development Associate (CDA) credential and other credentialing programs, teachers can move up the educational ladder to acquire bachelor's and master's degrees and become head teachers, educational coordinators, and administrators within Head Start. Sue's story illustrates such a progression:

> Sue and her family lived in town when her oldest daughter began Head Start in their farm community. Whenever they woke up late and missed the bus, Sue walked her daughter to school and observed the activities. She started working there, attended several colleges, acquired degrees, and is now director of the program.

Early Head Start (EHS), a program for infants and toddlers, was instituted when Congress reauthorized the Head Start Act in 1994. The growth of infant child care centers in the private sector and increased awareness of the significant role of early experience on brain development highlighted the need for a federally sponsored program for infants and toddlers. EHS is designed to support families and ensure that they and their very young children have access to comprehensive services that lead to healthy developmental outcomes. EHS's vision is to honor the unique characteristics of the infant/toddler years and to provide warm, loving, learning experiences in full-day and part-day programs. In most ways, EHS resembles Head Start, especially in its cornerstones of child, family, community, and staff development.

Military child care

The Department of Defense regulates and subsidizes **military child care** for 200,000 children (Blades and Rowe-Finkbeiner 2006). Both center and family child care homes meet this demand.

Military child care providers earn as much or more than nonmilitary providers, and the families, who pay according to a sliding scale based on income, spend less than their civilian counterparts. The 1989 Military Child Care Act mandated that child care workers on a military base be paid on a par with other workers on the base with the same levels of education and responsibility (Clarke-Stewart and Allhusen 2005). Not surprisingly, this act resulted in a decrease in staff turnover and an increase in quality in military child care programs.

Universal Prekindergarten

Universal prekindergarten (UPK) aims to provide *all* preschool-aged children with a free, supportive, literacy-rich educational environment prior to kindergarten. However, for pre-K to become universal, states have to create and pass legislation to develop and fund systems. UPK will then provide access for all children to comprehensive early childhood education experiences.

Many longitudinal research studies have reported the benefits of a quality early childhood education, beginning with the Perry Preschool study (Karoly, Kilburn, and Cannon 2005), and this research has helped to convince both Democratic and Republican legislators to support UPK. Money for pre-K initiatives has increased since the start of the twenty-first century, and the number of children served in state-funded pre-K programs has grown rapidly throughout the United States.

In some states, public schools do not have enough pre-K classrooms to serve all four-year-olds. To meet that need, some private and publicly funded centers, Head Start programs, and campus-based child care centers have pre-K classrooms in their programs. Ideally, families can decide to enroll their four-year-old in public school or in a community-based organization based on their family's preference, their need for full-day care, their convenience, and their assessment of the quality of different early childhood settings. As pre-K centers expand throughout the country, agencies that have not worked together in the past are learning to collaborate with each other (Holcomb 2006).

Private Child Care

Private child care can be for profit or not for profit. Funds for both come from private sources, although some private centers can receive targeted government funding, such as for food for low-income children attending a program, from the U.S. Department of Agriculture's Child and Adult Care Food Program.

For-profit, or **proprietary,** child care is a business, run with the assumption that the owner(s) will make money. A company or one or more individuals can run a for-profit center. Child care chains save money by purchasing in bulk and by developing a building design that the company uses in different locations. In contrast, one or more individuals can open a business in a home or other space. Unlike company-run

In some states, public schools do not have enough pre-K classrooms to serve all four-year-olds. To meet that need, some private and publicly funded centers, Head Start programs, and campus-based child care centers have pre-K classrooms in their programs.

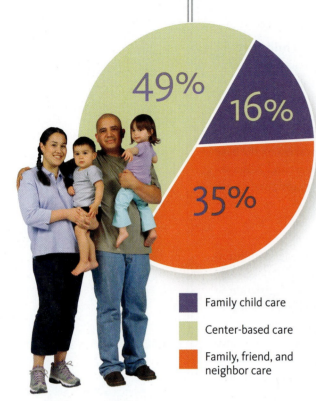

49%

16%

35%

■ Family child care

■ Center-based care

■ Family, friend, and neighbor care

7.2 *Choice of Child Care Program Type (2005)*
From: Human Services Policy Center 2006/2007

THOUGHT QUESTION Why do families make the care and education choices they make? Speak to a young child's family to find out what makes them feel that a particular care and education choice is right for them and their child.

centers, "mom and pop" centers are one-of-a-kind. The owner may make even less money than a salaried employee of a nonprofit program. However, in either a company-run or an individual-run program, any money left after the owners pay operating expenses belongs to them.

A private agency that is not designed for financial profit (generating income beyond the cost of the program) runs a **not-for-profit,** or nonprofit, child care program. An elected board of directors takes responsibility for such a center. Its budget includes salaries and, we hope, benefits for the teachers, director, and other staff, along with all other expenses such as rent, utilities, materials, supplies, and equipment. Tuition and donations pay those expenses. Any leftover money, which is rare, pays for additional center-related expenses. No individual or group keeps that excess.

FULL-DAY CHILD CARE

What characterizes different types of child care?

Centers serve more than 12 million children in the United States (National Association of Child Care Resource and Referral Agencies [NACCRRA] 2007). In 2005 center-based care served almost half the children receiving some type of child care (Figure 7.2). Center-based care and education is the most regulated form of child care.

Individual states and localities grant licenses that enable centers to operate legally, and minimum licensing standards for centers differ dramatically throughout the United States. Child care licensing standards focus on:

- staff-child ratios: how many children there are to one teacher;
- group size requirements: younger children need to be in a smaller group than older children;
- educational requirements for teachers and directors, both preservice and ongoing;
- criminal background check requirements;
- the developmental domains that programs must address;
- health and safety requirements; and
- parent involvement, communication, and access. (NACCRRA 2007)

In a child care center, children interact with many different children and caregivers, which can contribute positively to their emerging social skills (Barnett and Rivers 1996; Clarke-Stewart and Allhusen 2005) as long as the children are able to develop close relationships with one or more program adults. Moreover, many programs provide stimulating, educational experiences (Clarke-Stewart and Allhusen 2005).

Center-Based Infant/Toddler Programs

While some families choose an individual to care for their infants, others prefer their child to be at a center with other children and with teacher caregivers. Since children under three require a great deal of one-on-one attention, the ratio of adults to children in infant/toddler care is higher than for older children. For example, in some areas, centers must have two adults for every eight children younger than two, while requiring only two adults for every 25 five-year-olds.

Families who use center-based infant care often say they feel safer with many adults watching their child and making sure that the care and education is as good as possible. In addition to their interactions with adults, infants who are beginning to crawl and then learning to walk, and toddlers who repeatedly practice and increase their newfound skills, need plenty of space and equipment and materials specifically suited to their interests and abilities.

This infant/toddler child care center is housed in a high school for the children of teen parents. The room has toys on low shelves and space for mobile children to explore.

Faith-Based Programs

Faith-based programs are associated with religious institutions, and "religious principles often inspire their work" (Wright and Montiel 2008, 5), although to differing degrees. Some **nonsectarian** programs have no religious content but, for example, receive financial support from the church in which they operate. If religious organizations apply for federal and state funding for child care, they must accept children of any religion. Within limits, they may give preference to families who are members of their organizations and to job applicants who belong to their institutions (Child Care Bureau n.d.).

Faith-based programs for children have existed for many years, often preceding publicly funded programs in low-income communities (Horn 2002). In 2002, 28 percent of children from birth to age five who attended center-based programs attended faith-based programs. With reductions in public funding for services to communities, people once again rely heavily on their religious institutions (Salling 2007).

Employer Involvement

Employers, too, provide child care and related services. The number of women in the workforce, the long hours many parents work, and concern about staff who are not happy at work and thus likely to switch jobs (Galinsky and Backon 2007) make employers more likely to offer benefits that support families and consequently contribute to family members' productivity in the workplace.

An employer may establish a child care center **on-site** (at the workplace) or off-site and may or may not subsidize children's attendance. At an on-site center, children's parents are nearby, and mothers can nurse their infants during the workday. However, many employer-sponsored centers are at or near hospitals. They also may take different forms: in Dearborn, Michigan, for example, the child care chain Bright Horizons runs the United Auto Workers/Ford Motors center. Stride Rite, a shoe company in Cambridge, Massachusetts, and Lancaster Laboratories in Lancaster, Pennsylvania, provide both child care and elder care, and intergenerational activities help children and elders get to know each other.

Infants who are beginning to crawl and then learning to walk, and toddlers who repeatedly practice and increase their newfound skills, need plenty of space, equipment, and materials specifically suited to their interests and abilities.

Workers are absent less when their employer improves their child care choices, and especially when that employer also offers financial assistance (Connelly, De-Graff, and Willis 2004). Some employers may have a **dependent care assistance plan** that allows employees to pay for various services, including child care, with money deducted from their paychecks before taxes. Others may set up vouchers to pay for child care, may reimburse employees for all or part of their child care expenses, or may contract with a local center for employee discounts. Employers can also support families with

- parent workshops—for example, on balancing work and family responsibilities;
- a contract with a child care resource and referral agency;
- part-time or alternative schedules;
- paid sick days families can use when their children are ill; and
- generous parental leave policies. (Pennsylvania State University 2001)

Under the Family and Medical Leave Act, family members who have worked long enough for a large enough employer are entitled to up to twelve weeks of unpaid leave during any twelve-month period for the birth, adoption, or foster care placement of a child or for their child's serious illness (U.S. Department of Labor 2007). They are guaranteed their job upon return, and their health benefits continue during their leave.

Campus Child Care

Today, almost half of the more than 4,000 two- and four-year higher education institutions in the United States have campus-based early care and education programs

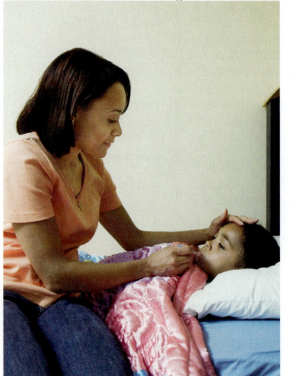

This child is not at home but is nonetheless receiving comfort and care.

(American Council on Education 2007). They range from single classrooms to centers that serve hundreds of children per week. Most are full day, some opening as early as 6:30 a.m. Most enroll the children of student, faculty, staff, and community families (Boswell 2003; Shultz 2004; Thomas n.d.).

Funding sources range from parent fees, student activity fees, and other direct college support to federal Child Care and Development Block Grant Head Start and Higher Education funding. Campus programs care for children while their parents attend college or work. Some serve as early education **lab schools** for the associated college or university, where students and faculty can do research on children and learning, observe, do fieldwork, and student teach.

Short-Term Child Care

Families use back-up child care and drop-in care infrequently. They turn to **backup child care** centers when the primary child care arrangement breaks down, such as when the nanny or the family child care provider is ill or on vacation. Some companies offer center-based backup child care as an employee benefit that reduces absenteeism. Families may also use **drop-in care** services available at a gym or a shopping center, for example, when they wish to use the facilities or do their grocery shopping.

Type of Care and Education	Convenience	Curriculum	Cost
Family, friend, neighbor	In home of family, friend, or neighbor's home	Depends on individual	May be free or low cost; may be paid for with public funds
Nanny	In home	Depends on individual	Total amount of one person's salary
Family Child Care	Often has flexible hours; usually in nearby home	Depends on provider and affiliation with a network	May be publicly funded; individual's salary shared by several families
Head Start and Early Head Start	In the community	Follows Performance Standards; may be accredited	Federally funded
Military Child Care	On military bases	Regulations for staff training; may be accredited	Sliding scale by income
Universal Pre-K	In the community	Depends on school system or center; may be accredited	Pubicly funded
Private Child Care (including Infant Care)	In the community	Follows local licensing rules; may be accredited	Tuition pays for salaries and other costs
Publicly Funded Child Care (including Infant Care)	In the community	Follows local licensing rules; may be accredited	Sliding scale by income; may be free
Faith-based Care	In local churches, synagogues, and mosques	Follows local licensing rules; may be accredited	Could be pubicly or privately funded; religious institution may donate space or funds
Employer-based Care	At the work-site	Follows local licensing rules; may be accredited	Employer may subsidize; could be publicly or privately funded
Campus Child Care	At a college or university	Follows local licensing rules; may be accredited	College may subsidize; government funding may contribute; parents may pay tuition
Short-term Child Care	Location varies	Generally unregulated	Parent fees; some are publicly funded; employers may subsidize

While seriously ill children should be home with their families, a child who is too sick to be in a group with other children but well enough to go out may go to a **sick child care center.** A child with a chronic illness who does not need extensive nursing care may also attend such a program.

A **crisis nursery** provides short-term, round-the-clock care for children whose families ask for help. The crisis nursery staff offers parent education, will make in-home visits, refers families to partner organizations, and can offer medical care while the child is there. **Respite care** gives families a break, for example, from caring for a child with special health or chronic medical needs.

Homeless children may also attend special centers for short periods: one such center offers its services to children whose families are living temporarily in the building that houses the center. When a family finds permanent housing, teachers are happy for the family's good fortune but sad to end the relationship.

While short-term care is convenient for working families and provides support to families in crisis, it poses many challenges to children and teachers. Relationships don't have time to develop when care is sporadic. Children with families in crisis or who are sick may find it hard to part from parents, even for a few hours, in an unknown place with unfamiliar adults. In some programs, like Ronald McDonald Houses, however, children with cancer and their siblings return often over time and build relationships with other children and staff.

ELEMENTARY SCHOOLS

What program options exist for elementary school age children?

Programs in, and associated with, public and private elementary schools differ from the other programs you have read about so far, in part because of the age of the children and also because the programs usually are located within schools. While some families may choose not to enroll their child in many of the programs you have just read about, by the time children are seven years old, every state requires them to attend school or to be homeschooled (Maeroff 2006).

THOUGHT QUESTION Using Figure 7.3 as a resource, consider the types of child care programs you have just read about. Recalling what you learned about quality in Chapter 1, note the characteristics of each program that you think could pose a barrier to quality care and education. How would you address each of these issues? What resources would you tap to make each of these programs a high-quality program?

Kindergarten

Kindergarten is the year between preschool or home and first grade. In Froebel's kindergarten, children developed small motor skills through games and activities and played with the language of chants, songs, and books. When children play in kindergarten, they make discoveries and think through ideas, develop relationships with peers, and use language to negotiate intellectually and socially. They learn about being away from their families and about becoming part of a group. Today, however, a **push-down** of academic curriculum has pressured many kindergarten teachers to teach skills that were once taught only in first grade (Education Commission of the States 2008).

For years, kindergarten was an optional half-day program for five-year-olds. Now, many states offer full-day kindergarten, though nine states do not require districts to offer kindergarten at all (Maeroff 2006). Full-day kindergarten can prepare children to succeed in elementary school, motivate better attendance through the primary grades, help children increase their later gains in literacy and language, and support their social and emotional adjustment to school (WestEd 2005). Opponents of full-day kindergarten contend that a full day is too hard on children, especially when kindergarten is academically oriented and takes time away from play and discovery.

Although some decades ago kindergartners could turn five anytime in the calendar year that they entered school, now in many schools children must turn five by July, August, or September 1. In addition, some families decide to delay their children's entry to kindergarten so that they will be older and possibly more mature than their classmates for the rest of their school years. Some call this practice **redshirting,** a term taken from college sports that means to hold someone back for a time to give the individual a greater advantage. A national redshirting trend in the United States affects boys in particular, since most boys mature more slowly than girls in the early childhood and primary school years.

PK–3 Schools

PK–3 schools serve children from ages three or four through the third grade; these schools consider prekindergarten, kindergarten, and first, second, and third grades as a cohesive unit of learning and developmental experiences. A PK–3 school focuses exclusively on the early childhood years and on what makes them special (Maeroff 2006) and ensures that children continue the gains they make at the early childhood level.

In PK–3 schools, the standards, curriculum, and assessments are **vertically aligned.** Teachers in every grade contribute to a coherent education for a child's entire time in the school "based on research on children's developmental capabilities" (Takanishi and Kauerz 2008, 484). The school offers full-day programs at every age level, and its structure enables teachers to collaborate with each other and develop professionally. Qualified teachers are proficient and familiar with the entire PK–3 spectrum (Foundation for Child Development 2007).

Charter Schools and Vouchers

Charter schools and school vouchers give families a choice about which elementary school their children attend. **Charter schools** are nonsectarian public schools that an individual or group establishes with approval and funding from the state but that do not need to comply with all the regulations that govern public schools. **Vouchers** are like scholarships, enabling families to send their child to either private or public school with money that would otherwise pay for their child's public school education.

According to the Charter Schools website (http://www.charterschoolsusa .com/), more than 3,000 charter schools have opened since the 1990s' state legislation that made them possible. A renewable charter, or contract, describes the school's purpose, how it will operate, and how the school will evaluate its success at educating its children. Although they must demonstrate that they are accomplishing what they intend, charter schools have more freedom than other public schools to develop curriculum and to assess student learning as they see fit. Critics of charter schools note that, under public auspices, they often encourage segregation by class, ethnic background, or religion.

As with charter schools, proponents of vouchers claim that they enable families to opt out of poorly performing local schools. Critics of school vouchers oppose this public financial support—full or partial—of private (and in particular, religious) schools and of public schools that are not subject to the same rules as other public schools. They also maintain that vouchers will not help all parents and children in low-income communities and that it is the government's and the public's responsibility to improve the quality of all schools for all children.

Homeschooling

Some families **homeschool** their children for part or all of their elementary school years and beyond, which means that children learn the school curriculum at home with one or more adults in their family. Families develop curriculum for their children with materials from the school district, the Internet, and the community. People choose to homeschool their children to protect them from the bureaucracy or inadequacies of the formal school options; to imbue them with their own, often religious, values instead of exposing them to the school's values; or because the school

In PK–3 schools, the standards, curriculum, and assessments are vertically aligned. Teachers in every grade contribute to a coherent education for a child's entire time in the school "based on research on children's developmental capabilities."

Homeschooling sometimes offers children learning opportunities they would not have in school.

is far away or inconvenient for the family.

Homeschooling families often enrich the paper-and-pencil work of elementary school with trips into the community, library visits, and hands-on activities of all sorts. Many homeschooled children interact with their peers in chess clubs, dance classes, or local team sports. However, a family might place limits on what they allow the child to learn, and the child may not have social interactions beyond the family.

Out-of-School Programs

It's 3 p.m. on Tuesday at an urban elementary school. The bell rings; and six-year-old Aisha, some of her first grade classmates, and Carla, one of the after-school teachers, go to Room 308. Settling in with fruit and crackers, Aisha talks with friends about the drums they played when the multicultural arts program visited. Carla says they'll be back next month, "but in the meantime, we'll make our own rhythms!" The children and staff push desks aside, and the movement specialist leads the children in African dance steps.

At 4 p.m., small groups of children and staff read poetry aloud, listen to the rhythm of the words, and draw pictures, talking and acting out the poems. Tomorrow they'll write or dictate their own. Thirty minutes later, they move the furniture again to make drums, rainsticks, and maracas. Again, they listen and try different rhythm patterns. The room is noisy, but everyone is engaged.

At 5:30 p.m., they return the furniture to the way it was for the daytime class. Then they gather at the rug and reflect on the rhythms they've heard and created. They head to the cafeteria, where their families and caregivers arrive for a 6 p.m. pickup.

THOUGHT QUESTION What do you think this program adds to Aisha's academic and social experience? Would you make any changes? Why?

A range of organizations—including but not limited to schools; national youth and service organizations; local community agencies; and sports, science, and arts institutions—offer programs before and after school. These may be school based or community based or located in museums and other institutions. They may meet every day or not, and attendance may be required or voluntary.

Several out-of-school models developed in the 1990s contain common elements: a safe environment, qualified and trained staff, and a set of engaging and diverse activities. All the models include academic enrichment, but the question of just how different from, or similar to, in-school experiences these programs should be is under constant discussion.

Federal, state, and local funding for out-of-school programs for school-age children increased a thousandfold between 1992 and 2002. **Universal access,** or after-school for all, has become a greater likelihood; however, at present there is no systematic approach that provides continuity of care, particularly for the youngest children. Programs that work with children from low-income backgrounds generally are free or have minimal cost, thanks to public and private funds. In fee-based, out-of-school programs, families typically choose from skill-building sessions in music, art, hands-on science, cooking, or gymnastics.

Science museums, art museums, children's museums, zoos, and botanical gardens often have a rich array of out-of-school programming for young children. They may provide single or ongoing classes and workshops for children.

SPECIALIZED PROGRAMS FOR INFANTS AND TODDLERS

What do specialized programs offer infants and toddlers and their families?

Early childhood educators need additional skills and certifications in most states to provide caring and competent early intervention and infant mental health services for children between the ages of birth and three. Both types of services may be provided in families' homes, in a community setting, or in a center-based program.

Early Intervention

Every state has some kind of **early intervention** (EI) program that offers a variety of therapeutic and support services to infants, toddlers, and twos with disabilities and to their families. Services include family education and counseling; home visits; and speech and audiology, occupational, and physical therapy. Services can begin before a baby even leaves the hospital; intervening when children are young increases the success rate for remediating the effects of a disability. When a baby is born with an obvious handicap or is significantly premature or is assessed with quantitative measures as having a delay, early intervention remedial services are available for that child's family. Anyone—parent, doctor, caregiver, teacher, or friend—can make a referral by calling a well-advertised phone number, but services themselves require the family's consent.

An EI worker conducts an intake interview with the family, and then professionals from the appropriate disciplines do an assessment or series of assessments of the child. The family and the professionals meet to discuss the results. At this meeting, the family's wishes for their child become an integral part of the initial goal-setting process, resulting in an **Individualized Family Service Plan,** or **IFSP,** that outlines steps for bringing the baby or toddler as far along as possible in his development.

For EI services to be **family centered,** or based on the family's needs, the professionals involved must make sure that families are aware of their rights. Service delivery can take place anywhere that makes sense within the context of a very young child's life: at home, at a center, or in the community. For example, if a child with motor delays can't sit up in a grocery cart, the specialist might go to the store with the mother to show her how to position the child in the cart and to give her

> Universal access, or after-school for all, has become a greater likelihood; however, at present there is no systematic approach that provides continuity of care, particularly for the youngest children.

THOUGHT QUESTION Visit the following websites to learn more about the types of out-of-school programs available. Then search for museum, garden, and zoo listings in your area. What do your local organizations offer, and what do you wish they would offer? How could you work with them?

Museum of Nature and Science, Dallas, TX: http://www.natureandscience.org/kids/default.asp

National Gallery of Art, Washington, DC: http://www.nga.gov/kids/kids.htm

Children's Museum of Indianapolis, Indianapolis, IN: http://www.childrensmuseum.org/index2.htm

Memphis Zoo, Memphis, TN: http://memphiszoo.org/education.aspx?pid=13

Desert Botanical Garden, Phoenix, AZ: http://www.dbg.org/index.php/education/childrensprog

Early intervention service delivery can take place anywhere that makes sense within the context of a very young child's life: at home, at a center, or in the community.

other suggestions for a smooth shopping trip (Educational Development Corporation 2007).

The early interventionist helps family members spend time with their infants and toddlers in ways that are meaningful for the child's development and teaches them parenting approaches that support prosocial behaviors. Early interventionists model interactions, including strategies that enhance babies' development during bathing, eating, and play, that all family members can practice when the specialists are not present.

Since parents from many cultures see professionals as "the expert" and the only one qualified to work with their child, early interventionists need **cultural competence,** or the ability to listen and learn about families' perspectives. Regardless of the coaching and support they receive from professionals, families may believe their child's therapist has a special role and may not want or expect to be involved in their child's therapy. Some change their views over time—as, for example, did the parent who said: "When I first heard we were having a specialist come to our home, I thought, 'Oh good, I'll have an hour free,' but I now see this isn't the case at all . . . [i]t's been great how much I'm involved in these visits. They teach [my child], but really they are teaching me how to work with her" (Educational Development Corporation 2007).

Infant Mental Health Services

Mental health begins before birth and follows us through life. Infant mental health comprises an ever-growing range of research and services to support healthy infant development within the context of the family and community. Families under immediate stress who seek or are referred to an infant mental health program or specialist need concrete services such as food and shelter first. Second comes emotional support, for example, with a sick newborn. Infant mental health specialists also practice **developmental guidance**—not therapy *per se,* but it supports families through their child's ups and downs and helps them become more aware of their child's specific needs. Sometimes developmental guidance might mean offering **anticipatory guidance,** a specific technique where the professional and parent observe the baby with the family, in real time or on video, to notice the baby's cues, discuss meaningful responses, and predict the baby's behaviors over the coming months (Weatherston 2000).

Selma Fraiberg helped establish the field of infant mental health when she began working with mothers and their infants in their homes, often around the kitchen table. She created therapeutic relationships that enabled mothers to reveal some of the fears and worries that stood in the way of their parenting abilities. They discovered "ghosts in the nursery" (Fraiberg 1987)—that is, difficult memories of their own parents that haunted them and affected their relationships with their children. Twenty-five years later, the field is equally interested in how positive representations are communicated intergenerationally, leading to the term "angels in the nursery" (Lieberman et al., 2005).

T. Berry Brazelton (1994) points out that babies experience **touchpoints,** that is, periods of frustration and irritability that precede a new development. Early childhood educators can help families identify these predictable touchpoints to understand their child's mental health and subsequent behavior.

THOUGHT QUESTION If you were an early interventionist, what could help you partner with a family? What could pose difficulties? What could be tricky about working with a team of specialists? What could help you become a productive part of that team?

PROGRAMS FOR FAMILIES

In what kinds of programs are early childhood educators working with families?

Like the programs you have read about so far, those in this section focus on children's emotional and social well-being as well as their intellectual development. However, the primary recipients of these services are families, either along with their children or instead of them.

Parent-Child Programs

Parent-child programs, groups for families and their children, can take many forms. Museums, botanical gardens, and zoos have sessions for adults and children. Nonprofit and profit-making community groups sponsor activities for children and families—for example, music or art activities that children and families do together. Adults and children can attend playgroups together. Parent-child programs in some Head Start centers, for example, bring children and families together at a center-based program one or more times a week for a few hours.

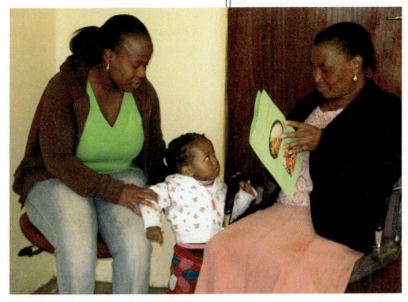

This infant mental health specialist points out the child's special ways of functioning and makes suggestions that help this mother interact productively with her child.

Other parent-child programs offer support to parents while at the same time giving their children a chance to play together. For example, in St. Paul, Minnesota, a group of deaf Hmong parents meet together with a facilitator who signs as she speaks. While the children play with each other and the caregivers, the parents discuss issues that are on their minds.

Formally organized or informally arranged by the families themselves, playgroups give parents an opportunity to chat while their children have a social experience with one another. In some cases, a group leader helps families observe and enjoy their children at play, perhaps providing information about topics of interest and concern to the parents. In others, an early childhood professional leads discussions for family members, sometimes with a topic in mind. Parent classes (for example, in infant massage) also combine the dual purposes of the playgroup: parent education and a worthwhile experience for the child.

Home Visiting

For more than a hundred years, professionals and paraprofessionals have visited families in their homes (Center for Home Visiting 1998). In the past decade, however, **home visits** have increased to more than half a million (Gomby, Culross, and Behrman 1999). Home visitors work primarily with families of children under three, although they also work with the families of preschoolers.

Whether the home visitor is a nurse, an early interventionist, a social worker, or an early childhood educator, she tries to form a close relationship with family members;

> Today the infancy field is interested not just in "ghosts" in the nursery, but in "angels," too: in knowing about how positive representations of parenting are communicated across generations.

to support and develop their strengths; and to provide information, activities, and/or materials that will help them as they parent. With this in mind, instead of interacting directly with the child, most home visitors bring a new toy or suggest a response for a family member to try (Sweet and Appelbaum 2004). In addition to supporting the child's development, programs can have more specialized intervention purposes, such as helping families find employment. While some home visiting programs target families who live in poverty or who have been reported for or suspected of child abuse or neglect, universal home visiting is for any parent of a newborn. Home visiting is a way to deliver services, which vary based on the agency providing them and the families who receive the visits.

Home visitors are often community members. They may be paraprofessionals who have not formally studied early childhood education, or they may have degrees in early childhood, related fields, or nursing. They may work for well-known national programs such as Parents as Teachers, Home Instruction for Parents of Preschool Youngsters (HIPPY), the Parent-Child Home Program, or the Nurse-Family Partnership (Figure 7.4), or they may work for a local program. Many Head Start and Early Head Start programs also have a home visiting component.

Since families receive services in their home and so don't have to travel, they are more likely to feel comfortable. Home visitors can tailor what they do to fit the environment of the home, can involve the entire family, and can gain insights from the visit (Sweet and Appelbaum 2004). One home visitor, for example, visited a toddler and his family in their small mobile home in a snowed-in and remote northern county of her state. She saw how badly the toddler needed room to move, but having seen the family's situation firsthand, she could understand the mother's constraints, too, and could work with her more effectively to find solutions.

Family Literacy Programs

Family literacy programs work with families to help increase the time they read aloud to their children and also help them to play with their children in ways that focus on language and literacy. Research indicates that children who spend more time with their families on such activities tend to have greater academic gains (Grinder et al. 2005).

Federally funded Even Start Family Literacy Programs exist in all fifty states and are directed at low-income families whose members do not have strong literacy skills themselves or who do not know English. A partnership between schools and their communities, Even Start helps family members learn about early childhood education, gain literacy skills themselves, and develop their parenting skills (National Even Start Association 2007).

Since the National Center for Family Literacy was founded in 1989, it has prepared more than 150,000 teachers and thousands of volunteers who have, in turn, worked with more than a million American families. In addition to preparing teachers and volunteers to work with families, family literacy programs typically lend or give children's books to families to read aloud to their children at home. For more

This home visitor is packing toys to use with a child and her family.

Some National Home Visiting Programs

Home instruction for parents of preschool youngsters (HIPPY)	http://www.hippyusa.org/ A parent-involvement school-readiness program that helps parents prepare three-, four-, and five-year-old children at home for success in school and beyond.
Nurse-family partnership	http://www.nursefamilypartnership.org/index.cfm?fuseaction=home A national program with local affiliates that send nurses into the homes of first-time, low-income families to help them succeed as parents.
Parent-child home program	http://www.parent-child.org/index.html A research-based home-visiting program designed to strengthen families' relationships with their children and develop children's literacy and social skills.
Parents as teachers	http://www.parentsasteachers.org/site/pp.asp?c=ekIRLcMZJxE&b=272091 A parent education program based on the belief that parents are children's teachers and that communities can offer parents support for their children's development, for example, through home visits.

information, see the National Center for Family Literacy website at http://www.famlit.org/site/c.gtJWJdMQIsE/b.1205483/k.C84E/About_Us.htm.

Child Care Resource and Referral Agencies

Child care resource and referral (CCR&R) agencies serve families and the larger early childhood community throughout the United States (NACCRRA 2007). In particular, CCR&Rs share their lists of child care centers and criteria for choosing a center with families who contact them.

CCR&Rs also offer assistance to program staff, family child care providers, and FFN providers to improve the quality of their care and education. They conduct sessions specifically for infant/toddler caregivers, for bilingual programs, for new caregivers, or for family child care providers. They teach people within the community how to start a child care program and meet child care standards.

Finally, CCR&Rs play an **advocacy** role within their communities. They contact state and local legislators, briefing them on children's issues. CCR&R staff organize early childhood educators and families to lobby government officials about funding or about state or local regulations that affect children and families.

Child care resource and referral agencies play an advocacy role and offer assistance to program staff, family child care providers, and FFN providers to improve the quality of their care and education.

APPROACHES: EXPLANATION, APPLICATION, AND CRITIQUES

What philosophical approaches do different programs take, and how can you find the right one for you?

Early childhood care and education programs differ in the philosophical stance they take and the curriculum they choose. Here are some of the most prominent approaches.

THOUGHT QUESTION What program intrigues you? How can you find out more about it? What do you know about such programs in your community? What would it take to start a program like that?

Some Early Approaches and Methods

In Chapter 5 and 6, you read about influential figures who formulated approaches that early childhood educators continue to adopt and adapt today. For instance, Maria Montessori's method has been used all over the world since the beginning of the twentieth century. The behaviorists of the mid-twentieth century shaped Direct Instruction. Lucy Sprague Mitchell, Caroline Pratt, and others established the developmental-interaction approach, and Waldorf Education is based on the work of Rudolf Steiner.

The Montessori Method

The **Montessori Method** has influenced many programs that came after it, at least in part. The Montessori classroom provides a **prepared environment** with carefully chosen materials, or "work," for children placed on open shelves in order of increasing difficulty from left to right. Each set of materials for an activity is clearly defined and ready for children to use on their own and then return to the shelf so that the next child can use it in the same way.

Self-correcting materials inform the child whether she has completed a task correctly. For example, each of ten wooden cylinder blocks is longer and wider in diameter than the next. Each cylinder fits in only one spot of a wooden frame. If a child places a small cylinder into a larger hole, she will have a larger cylinder left over and thus will know to try again until every cylinder is in its proper place.

The Montessori teacher is a facilitator who, during limited whole-group time, introduces new work (that is, materials) to the children and shows them how to use it and where it is on the shelves. The teacher also sets up areas for learning about practical life in which children acquire the skills of daily living, such as pouring. In addition, she creates an environment for experiencing sensorial materials, including sand and water, and environments for learning language, math, arts, music, geography, and science (Roopnarine and Johnson 2005). The teacher stresses cooperation over competition.

The Montessori Method combines choice with structure and a sense of order with beauty. Its critics contend that it does not leave room for creativity because many of the materials and activities lead to a single correct answer. They worry, too, that the emphasis on individual work does not provide children with enough social interaction or close relationships.

Two organizations, the Association Montessori Internationale and the American Montessori Society, are primarily responsible for spreading Montessori's ideas. See Figure 7.5 for the organizations' websites, as well as for electronic sources of additional information about the other approaches to early childhood care and education discussed in this section.

Direct Instruction

Direct Instruction was developed in the mid-1960s by *Siegfried Engelmann*

Montessori cylinders are an example of a self-correcting material.

and *Carl Bereiter* as an intervention for pre-schoolers whom they and others considered disadvantaged. Engelmann and Bereiter believed that teachers need to teach vocabulary, general information, and basic skills to preschool children living in poverty, and not expect them to learn such content and skills without explicit instruction. In many programs that adopted direct instruction, math, language, and reading lessons replaced the learning-through-play activities typical of most middle-class preschools (Bereiter 1988).

Faultless instruction, an approach used in Direct Instruction, is designed so that teachers present learning activities in a progressive sequence from easiest to hardest. For the instruction to be consistently "fault-less," as well as to save teachers time and effort, the teaching process is **scripted.** Teachers read from a guide that tells them what to say and do at each point in the lesson. Lessons move at a fast clip but incorporate a lot of repetition to ensure that the children catch on. The script provides the teacher with alternative responses for the range of children's reactions.

Montessori science materials are consciously arranged in this first-through-third-grade inclusive classroom.

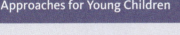

Resources on Care and Education Approaches for Young Children	
American Montessori Society	http://www.amshq.org/
Association Montessori Internationale	http://www.montessori-ami.org/
Developmental Interaction	http://www.bankstreet.edu/sfc/developmental_interaction.html
Direct Instruction	http://www.nifdi.org/index.html#what
High/Scope	http://www.highscope.org/
Reggio Emilia	http://ceep.crc.uiuc.edu/poptopics/reggio.html
Waldorf Education	http://www.rudolfsteinerweb.com/Rudolf_Steiner_and_Waldorf_Education.php
	http://www.steinercollege.org/waldorfed.html

7.5 *Resources on Care and Education Approaches for Young Children*

Enthusiasts of Direct Instruction believe that a preestablished plan will succeed with all children if it is designed properly. Critics, however, maintain that direct instruction dehumanizes children and teachers alike because it does not leave room for them to think or create.

Developmental interaction at Bank Street

Developmental interaction as it was formulated at Bank Street reflects the beliefs that as children grow and develop, their thoughts and emotions work together and that children learn from engaging with the world. The approach informs teachers about children through a theoretical framework, rather than prescribing a particular way to teach. Democratic ideas influence the teacher's decisions about content, practices, and the social and physical environment. Developmental interaction regards the young child as a maker of meaning who is actively engaged in making sense of the world. Teachers help children expand their understanding of themselves and their surroundings through extensive curriculum that builds on the children's questions and concerns. Teachers thoughtfully add their own questions to enrich and deepen the children's inquiry.

Based on principles of development and interaction, school is a place to promote competence in all areas of children's lives and help them both take charge of their learning and work with others. It is an active community connected to the social world, not an isolated place for learning lessons. This means that the school shares responsibility and power with children's families and neighborhood institutions.

Supporters of the developmental-interaction approach appreciate that it serves as a guide rather than a prescription for practice. It is not a curriculum to follow. It demands the teacher's broad understanding of children's learning and developmental needs; a deep knowledge of multiple subject areas; and the ability to create caring, intellectually challenging, and democratic classrooms. Thus, its critics point out that becoming a competent teacher using this approach takes careful preparation and considerable practice. Although critics have questioned whether this approach

These children work together to design and paint a mural for their community.

can succeed in different arenas, it has—including in low-resourced settings such as early childhood classrooms in Newark, New Jersey (Silin and Lippman 2003).

Waldorf Education

Waldorf Education, founded by Rudolf Steiner (1861–1925), aims to develop the head, heart, and hand of the child—that is, his thinking, feeling, and willing. While all three areas grow throughout childhood, Waldorf Education puts an emphasis on different aspects at different stages of life. In early childhood, children learn primarily through hands-on activities, such as open-ended play. In the elementary school years, the emphasis shifts to the development of a rich imagination, so that all subjects are taught through the arts and story telling.

Waldorf early childhood programs serve children from birth until first grade. They range from parent-child groups to half-day classrooms to full-time child care. Waldorf programs nurture warm relations between children and adults, emphasize child-initiated play as a foundation for life and learning, and create environments of simple beauty that are as homelike as possible. Art activities are integrated into the day. Teachers frequently work on life activities such as baking, gardening, woodworking, or sewing while the children play or participate in these activities. Teachers support play and the child's developing imagination with story telling and puppetry, and with songs, verses, and traditional games, often accompanied by movement. During circle time and story time of fifteen to twenty minutes, children focus directly on the teacher.

Waldorf Education envelops children in aesthetics and encourages their imagination. However, its critics worry that it delays elementary school readiness, to which Waldorf educators respond that creative and meaningful activities provide a

THOUGHT QUESTION What are the advantages and disadvantages of developing your own curriculum? What would you like or dislike about following a prepared curriculum? How do you envision yourself combining these two approaches? What other options might you have?

Aesthetics and spiritual development are important in the Waldorf classroom.

foundation for later cognitive development and that young children's brains are not ready for academics before elementary school. Some critics also may question Steiner's inclusion of the spiritual nature of our world in education, as his ideas extend beyond empirical science. To read more about Waldorf Education, see the websites listed in Figure 7.5.

More Recent Approaches

Two other approaches became popular in the United States in the second half of the twentieth century: High/Scope and the Reggio Emilia approach. The first takes its foundation from the work of Piaget; the second makes use of both Piaget's and Vygotsky's ideas.

High/Scope

High/Scope is based on Piaget's ideas about "children as *active learners*" (Roopnarine and Johnson 2005, 235 emphasis in original). In a High/Scope classroom, children make decisions. Classroom adults help them make those choices and aid them in elaborating on and extending their play.

This approach features a predictable daily routine that thoroughly familiarizes each child with the classroom. Firm routines enable children to think about what they want to do and how to do it. A planning period before the children use classroom "interest areas" emphasizes the children's role as decision makers. After children engage in activities, they reflect on what they did with their teachers and each other. High/Scope calls this process **Plan, Do, Review.**

In addition to their use of interest areas, children carry out small-group activities that their teacher designs using the High/Scope key experiences as a guide. These key experiences, based on research about young children, include creative representation, language and literacy, initiative and social relationships, movement, music, and activities that work with concepts of classification, seriation, number, space, and time (Roopnarine and Johnson 2005). Children also participate in a large-group time when they have music and finger plays. High/Scope teachers keep careful notes about children as they play in the classroom and use the Child Observation Record (COR) to measure children's development based on what they observe.

The Perry Preschool Project is one of numerous studies that validate the High/Scope approach. This **longitudinal study** (following the same children over time) gathered information about children who participated in a preschool program that encouraged choices and decision making and contrasted them with a control group. The study found that as young adults the High/Scope children were more likely to finish high school, had fewer arrests, and had fewer unplanned pregnancies than the control group. You can read a follow-up study, *Lifetime Effects: The High/Scope Perry Preschool Study through Age 40* (Schweinhart et al. 2005), or find out more by checking the website in Figure 7.5.

Reggio Emilia approach

In the late 1980s and early 1990s, American educators began to visit and report on the public preschools of Reggio Emilia in the Emilia-Romagna region of Italy. The schools serve infants and toddlers through what we consider kindergarten. Loris Malaguzzi (1920–1994) collaborated with local teachers and families to develop the approach.

The **Reggio Emilia approach** is based on a vision of the child as a strong and capable human being (Edwards, Forman, and Gandini 1996). This respect for children's abilities leads Reggio Emilia educators to study children's interests and develop cur-

The Perry Preschool study found that as young adults the High/Scope children were more likely to finish high school, had fewer arrests, and had fewer unplanned pregnancies than the control group.

riculum projects for small or larger groups of children based on those interests. For example, when a group of children who described their summer vacations discussed the crowds on the beach, Reggio Emilia educators developed a project on crowds. Children drew pictures of crowds and brainstormed together about what crowds are. Using what Malaguzzi termed the **hundred languages of childhood,** or many means of expression, they communicated, revisited, and revised their ideas.

As is the case in several of the other approaches you have read about here, Reggio Emilia educators carefully design the environment for children. These educators refer to the classroom environment as "the third teacher" because children learn so much from the space in which they play and work. In Reggio Emilia, and in an increasing number of Reggio-Emilia-influenced schools in the United States, an

This photograph, taken in an *atelier,* or studio space, demonstrates the influence of Reggio Emilia.

atelier, or studio space, enables children to design and execute products that communicate their ideas about whatever they study.

Teachers collaborate with children, families, and each other. A *pedagogista,* who supports the teachers' work, joins their animated discussions about children and curriculum. An *atelierista,* or teacher-artist, provides materials and instructs children in the skills they need to produce work that expresses their thinking. Teachers and families meet and discuss the children, of course, but they also talk about curriculum. Teachers document the children's projects with photographs showing them at work and also display their products with extensive explanations that keep families and others abreast of the curriculum.

The Reggio Emilia approach is founded on a set of principles that its implementers in Italy and North America advise others to adapt, not adopt. They encourage educators to think about their own communities, about the values and resources there, and about how the Reggio Emilia principles of collaboration and emphasis on children's strengths fit their setting. The creativity and remarkable quality of children's work in Reggio Emilia have inspired innumerable teachers in the United States. Critics note, however, that not everyone is suited to the Reggio Emilia approach. For example, Reggio Emilia educators in Italy encourage argumentative discussion in children and engage in it among themselves and with families. Such interactions are culturally appropriate for them but not for those who may be uncomfortable with openly expressed conflict. See Figure 7.5 for electronic resources about the Reggio Emilia approach.

Making Approaches Your Own

As you have seen, you or the program where you work can consider many approaches and curricula. These approaches are similar in some ways and differ dramatically in others. Many experienced early childhood educators incorporate aspects of different approaches into their classrooms. Sometimes their practice becomes so much a part of them that they do not recognize its various origins.

Implementers of the Reggio Emilia approach advise others to adapt, not just adopt, the approach. They encourage educators to think about the values and resources of their own communities and how the Reggio Emilia principles fit their setting.

THOUGHT QUESTION Which of the approaches you have just read about appeal to you most? What do you especially like about them? How do they fit your personal philosophies and style?

Although teachers experiment with new ideas both to understand them and to see how they might be applied to their work with children, ultimately an eclectic approach that borrows from here and there without a framework will not provide you with a coherent philosophy of teaching.

How can you make sense of all these approaches? The process is similar to the one you used when you considered different theories in Chapter 6. As you think about how to integrate theory and practice, be clear about the different theories and approaches and how they came to be. Consciously observe teachers' approaches to teaching, and look for research on different approaches. What are the short- and long-term implications of the approach on individual and group development? Respectfully challenge your colleagues to articulate why they do what they do, and what they expect the children to gain.

Often, approaches are lodged within a family of theories (Reese and Overton 1970). Drawing from theories within the same family, you can create a coherent framework for yourself: "a quilt of practice"—*your* practice. Rather than snip a practice from here and another from there, consider the *principles* your favorite theories and approaches have in common. Proceeding in this way (and it does take time) allows you to avoid a crazy quilt. Rather, you will construct a quilt with a design structure and color pattern that makes it more coherent and cohesive than a crazy quilt. For example, consider some principles that borrow from the developmental-interaction family of theories and that a teacher might use to frame her approach:

1. Education is a vehicle for creating and promoting social justice and encouraging participation in democratic processes.
2. The teacher has a deep knowledge of subject matter areas and is actively engaged in learning through formal study, direct observation, and participation.
3. Understanding children's learning and development in the context of family, community, and culture is needed for teaching.
4. The teacher continues to grow as a person and as a professional.
5. Teaching requires a philosophy of education—a view of learning and the learner, knowledge and knowing—which informs all elements of teaching. (Nager and Shapiro 2007, 9)

These principles draw from a compatible perspective that values people—children, teachers, and the society as a whole. A teacher who follows another set of principles might value people, too, but might value something else more.

Keeping the principles you value at the forefront will help you to work conscientiously. Although teachers experiment with new ideas both to understand them and to see how they might be applied to their work with children, ultimately an **eclectic approach** that borrows from here and there without a common framework will not provide you with a coherent philosophy of teaching.

Work with children entails decision making throughout the day and also throughout one's career. When you are not sure how to proceed, take stock; develop and test your hypotheses; take note of the results; and, most of all, collaborate with others in a thoughtful way.

SUMMARY

CARE AND EDUCATION
Why have care and education been treated separately, and why do they go together?
Initially, care settings provided services for immigrants and other poor children. Educational programs were only for the enrichment of children whose families could afford them. Yet, all children need and deserve both care and education. At-

tention to children's relationships with peers and adults through such programmatic elements as continuity of care, looping, and mixed-age grouping sets the stage for learning.

CARE AND EDUCATION IN THE HOME
What issues do the three types of in-home care and education raise?
Care and education for children in their own or another home is the most common form of child care for children under five whose parents work. Although families who employ a nanny pay that individual's salary, family, friend, and neighbor care and family child care are often less expensive than center-based care. All three types—FFN, family child care, and nannies—raise issues related to professional preparation and ongoing support for those caring for and educating children in a home. Families often choose home care and education because it gives them scheduling flexibility, is convenient and reliable, and enables them to build close and trusting relationships with the individual caring for their children.

FUNDING
How are early care and education programs funded?
Publicly funded programs receive monies from the local, state, or federal government. Head Start and Early Head Start, for example, are paid for with federal funds, as are programs for children whose families are in the military. State and local funds pay for child care programs based on income eligibility and for universal pre-kindergarten programs. Privately funded programs can be nonprofit, receiving parent tuitions and donations and gifts from foundations and corporations, or for-profit, run by individuals or corporations and also funded by parent tuition.

FULL-DAY CHILD CARE
What characterizes different types of child care?
Center-based care and education is the most regulated form of child care. Infant/toddler child care centers are for children under age three and have a high ratio of adults to children. Faith-based programs are associated with religious institutions and may be nonsectarian or may have religious content. Employers may provide on-site centers or offer related services, such as vouchers to pay for child care and education in the community. Campus child care is located at institutions of higher learning and may serve the children of students, faculty, staff, and the community. Short-term child care can be for children who are too sick to attend their regular program or a respite for families in crisis.

ELEMENTARY SCHOOLS
What program options exist for elementary school age children?
Many states offer public full-day kindergarten, the year between preschool or home and first grade, but not all states require local districts to provide public kindergarten at all. Elementary schools uniquely designed for the early childhood years, called PK–3 schools, consider prekindergarten, kindergarten, and first, second, and third grades as a cohesive unit of learning and developmental experiences. Charter schools and school vouchers give families a choice of which elementary school their children attend, paid by public monies, and homeschooling means that children learn the school curriculum at home. After-school programming extends the school day; may be school based, community based, or located in museums or other institutions; and may meet every day or not, with attendance required or voluntary.

SPECIALIZED PROGRAMS FOR INFANTS AND TODDLERS

What do specialized programs offer infants and toddlers and their families?

Most states provide early intervention programs that offer a variety of therapeutic and support services to infants, toddlers, and twos with disabilities and to their families. Infant mental health comprises an ever-growing range of research and services to families under stress to support healthy infant development within the context of the family and community.

PROGRAMS FOR FAMILIES

In what kinds of programs are early childhood educators working with families?

Early childhood educators who conduct parent-child programs provide activities for families and their children together or offer support to parents while the children play together supervised in a separate space. Home visitors, whether they are nurses, early interventionists, social workers, or early childhood educators, try to form close relationships with family members; to support and develop their strengths; and to provide information, activities, and/or materials that will help them as they parent. Through family literacy programs, early childhood educators work with families to help increase the time they read aloud to their children and also help them to play with their children in ways that focus on language and literacy. Finally, working at child care resource and referral agencies, early childhood educators give families lists of child care centers and criteria for choosing a center; offer assistance to program staff, family child care providers, and FFN providers to improve the quality of their care and education; and play an advocacy role within their communities.

APPROACHES: EXPLANATION, APPLICATION, AND CRITIQUES

What philosophical approaches do different programs take, and how can you find the right one for you?

The Montessori classroom provides a prepared environment with carefully chosen materials, or "work," that are clearly defined and ready for children to use on their own. Using Direct Instruction, teachers explicitly teach vocabulary, general information, and basic skills using a fast-paced script. Developmental interaction, influenced by democratic ideas and a belief that as children grow and develop, their thoughts and emotions work together, involves curriculum that engages children with their world. Waldorf programs nurture warm relations between children and adults, emphasize child-initiated play as a foundation for life and learning, and create environments of simple beauty that are as homelike as possible. In a High/Scope classroom, children make decisions, and adults aid them in elaborating on and extending their play. The Reggio Emilia approach is based on respect for children's abilities that leads Reggio Emilia educators to study children's interests and develop curriculum projects that reflect them. To make approaches your own, take stock; develop and test your hypotheses; take note of the results; and, most of all, collaborate thoughtfully with others.

FURTHER ACTIVITIES

1. Using the Internet, the local CCR&R, or other resources, find out what kinds of children's services your community offers. Create a visual (it could be a grid, a pie chart, or other graphic) that shows the options for part- and full-day, and public and private care and education in your community. (**NAEYC Standard 2: Building Family and Community Relationships**)

2. Imagine that you are working for a CCR&R agency. Recommend one or more types of programs to each family in the scenarios below. In your response, include the approach or approaches discussed in this chapter that you think might suit the family and child best.

   a. Hector is three years old. His mother works at a hospital forty-five minutes from their home. She is looking for an exciting and innovative program for her son. Based on what you know about different program models in early care and education, what would you suggest?

   b. Lisa is eight months old. Her parents are looking for a safe and secure place for her to be while they are in school. Their work and class hours are difficult to juggle: they want as much flexibility as they can find but also want their child to learn from and be cared for by professionals. Based on what you know about different program models in early care and education, what would you suggest?

   c. Daquan is a seven-year-old whose grandmother wants him to have an enriched learning experience but is very serious about his learning all the basic skills. She works until 5 p.m. every day and cannot pick him up in their neighborhood until 5:45 p.m. Based on what you know about different program models in early care and education, what would you suggest? (**NAEYC Standard 2: Building Family and Community Relationships**)

3. Design a one-page flier for your fantasy program. Using the information in this chapter as a guide, include all the services and approaches your program would offer. Specify its location (is it in a community center, school building, private home, religious institution?), and explain how it would be funded. Briefly describe the philosophical approach and illustrate your fantasy program with a drawing or photo. Explain the families' role in your program. (**NAEYC Standard 4: Using Developmentally Effective Approaches to Connect with Children and Families**)

CHAPTER EIGHT

Children, Development, and Culture

There is no such thing as developmental competence outside of a cultural context.

Barbara Bowman

What do teachers need to know about all the children in their classrooms, and how can they know the multiple contexts in which children develop? To begin, teachers need to discover the various ways in which children grow and develop and what their abilities and interests are; then they can create a curriculum that will be both engaging and within the children's reach. It is the teacher's responsibility, with help from other educational specialists, to discover the particular strengths and challenges of each child in the classroom.

In this chapter, you will meet two teachers and some of the children who enter their kindergarten at the beginning of the year. As we follow the teachers' journey to understand and teach their students, you will see how the teachers and other specialists use their knowledge about the children and development to adapt their teaching.

As Lucia entered kindergarten, she felt a bit overwhelmed. At four years and ten months, she had experienced much change in her life. Thinking of her homeland, Guatemala, the three different apartments where the family had lived in her new country, and the familiarity of her Head Start center, Lucia held her mother's hand tightly as she approached the big new school.

Tony is five years and ten months old. Eating Fruit Loops out of a plastic bag and looking down as he spins the wheels of his toy car, he lags behind his mother and father as they pull him into the classroom.

Sagal is five years and three months old. She is excited to be entering kindergarten in the school her older siblings attend. She can't wait to start playing with everything she sees in the classroom.

Amy is six years and six months old. She enters the classroom holding her mother's hand but eagerly seeks out the teachers, smiles at them, and reaches out to them for a hug.

Ms. Scott grew up in a middle-class community among people of European or British ancestry. When Ms. Scott thinks back on her childhood, she doesn't remember any children with disabilities or children of recent immigrants attending her school. She was a successful student and looked forward to becoming a teacher when she grew up. Now she is a certified teacher in early childhood general education.

Mr. Aragona was raised in a working-class Italian neighborhood. He remembers well-defined social and gender roles for children and adults. Mr. Aragona developed a special bond with his cousin, who was considered to be "slow." Motivated by his interactions with his cousin, Mr. Aragona decided to become a teacher with certification in both special and general education.

Ms. Scott and Mr. Aragona co-teach a kindergarten class in Room 205. Lucia, Tony, Sagal, and Amy are but four of the twenty-five children who entered their classroom on this first day of school. Room 205 is an **inclusive classroom,** which means that some of the children have disabilities and receive special education services. Before school began, Ms. Scott and Mr. Aragona planned activities for the children's first school day. When they sat down at the end of the first day, they recalled the tears and tantrums at the door and how hard the children found it to listen to a story in a group. A few children wouldn't participate in any of the activities. As experienced teachers, they know that it takes a while for young children to accommodate to school, yet every year they find themselves taken aback by the intensity of the first few days.

Since Ms. Scott and Mr. Aragona teach kindergarten, they set up activities they knew most five-year-olds could do and would enjoy. Over time, they will learn about the diversity of the children who make up the class and understand each child's individual circumstances and experiences. They know that the more their classroom activities match the specific styles and learning needs of these children, the more successful the teaching and learning will be.

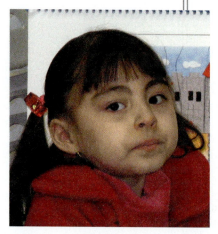

Lucia

Tony

Sagal

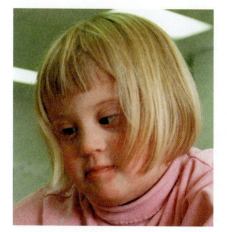

Amy

Ms. Scott

Mr. Aragona

Ms. Scott and Mr. Aragona co-teach in an inclusive classroom of kindergarten students; four of their twenty-five students are shown here.

UNDERSTANDING AND APPLYING CHILD DEVELOPMENT PRINCIPLES

What do teachers need to understand about child development, and how do they apply those understandings?

Every child grows up within a unique combination of family traditions, culture, patterns of language, community and geographical values, and social and political circumstances. But no matter what their situations, all children change and develop along pathways that are in some ways universal for all children and in other ways particular to each child.

Basic Principles of Development

The study of child development seeks to answer a few key questions. How do children develop over time? What causes growth and change? What accounts for individual differences? Our current understanding of development provides four principles to help us answer these questions.

Principle 1: Genetic inheritance and experience are intertwined

Each child has a specific biological and genetic inheritance from his parents. We often refer to these inborn traits and processes as **nature.** However, a child is also born into a family, home, and cultural environment full of objects, events, and people. This **nurture,** the learned experiences of the world outside the child's body, influences the child, too. The inborn biological processes (nature) and the external environment (nurture) are always interacting: even before a child's birth, the environment of the womb shapes the fetus's development.

Development occurs as a result of these intricate interactions. Neither the genetic inheritance from your family nor the environment into which you are born single-handedly determines who you are. Nature *and* nurture together generate the pathway of development for each child (see Chapter 6 on the transactional approach to development).

Principle 2: The sequence of development is predictable and variable

As you read in Chapter 6, Freud, Erikson, and Piaget, among others, thought that children progress through a series of predictable stages. Stage theorists maintain that the sequence of development is essentially the same for all children, but that not all children reach each stage at exactly the same age. Today, we understand that children grow up in different circumstances, and so we are aware of greater variation in development, especially across the **domains,** or areas, of development. For example, a child's social-emotional thinking could be more advanced than her mathematical thinking. This individual unevenness is now thought to be more the rule than the exception and has been documented by neo-Piagetian and non-stage theorists.

We know that development occurs over time, and research on young children indicates that children do not just add new skills and behaviors to old ones. Instead, they undergo shifts, transitions, and periods of **disequilibrium,** times when they may seem fragile and not themselves and when changes may occur suddenly. Some of these changes seem to follow a universal pattern, such as the bio-social behavioral shifts we see in children at two-and-a-half months, nine months, twenty-four months, and during the five- to seven-year-old period (Cole, Cole and Lightfoot, 2005). Other changes appear to be influenced by aspects of an individual child's physical growth, brain maturation, or environmental experience.

The term **developmental milestones** refers to the sequential changes in children's behaviors that correspond to different ages and developmental levels, such as the first time an infant turns over or a toddler says a complete sentence. The term conjures up images of a road along which stones serve as mileposts to indicate how far a traveler has come. This is a helpful analogy because travelers take breaks along the way and celebrate when they reach a particular goal, just as children do. What is different, however, is that travelers usually don't go back, they only move forward. As development progresses, children can **regress**—that is, they can go back to earlier behaviors and abilities or may show evidence of an advanced behavior for a day or two that disappears before reappearing weeks later.

Children reach developmental milestones at various ages, depending on an assortment of factors. First of all, every child is different (Rogoff 2003). Second, all children are increasingly able to adapt their behavior to their own physical capacities and to the world they inhabit. How they *adapt,* and therefore the particular developmental pathway they travel, depends on the complex interactions between the

> **THOUGHT QUESTION** Think of two children you know who are the same age. Write down what you know about them. How are they different? How are they similar?

As development progresses, children can regress or may show evidence of an advanced behavior for a day or two that disappears before reappearing weeks later.

child and the environment. For example, most children learn to stand up and walk, counteracting the force of gravity, in order to explore and gain control over their environment. A child born with **spina bifida** (a congenital malformation of the spinal column) will find another way to move about and explore his world. His developmental pathway will not be like that of a child with an intact spinal cord, but in the end, both children will achieve similar goals: to explore and gain control over their environment. Each child's pathway is purposeful and adaptive.

Principle 3: The course of development can be altered

A child's experiences in infancy and the early childhood years can have an enormous effect on her later development and functioning in society. However, these early experiences are not "set in stone," as many originally thought. We have learned that intensive education and supportive relationships can help a child who has experienced trauma early in life to achieve a more positive outcome. In addition, recent research demonstrates that early intervention is economically beneficial to society (Rolnick and Grunewald 2007) because later interventions are more costly. Educators can help children build **resilience,** that is, the ability to recover from hardship, and set them on a more productive path (National Research Council 2000, 32; Foley and Hochman 2006, 10).

Principle 4: All children have strengths

A child's developmental pathway is not necessarily "good" or "bad." When teachers become familiar with children's particular developmental patterns, they can work more effectively with them in their **zone of proximal development** (see Chapter 6). Vygotsky's work suggests that teachers should adapt activities to each child's current abilities and interests (Vygotsky 1935/1978) and help all children learn from each other. Early childhood educators can be a positive force in a child's life if they identify a child's strengths to gain a deeper understanding of the child (Himley 2000).

Influences on Development

As the teachers of Room 205 reflect on the first day of kindergarten, they begin the process of learning about each child in the classroom. There are so many differences among the children. How can teachers know about all the influences that make children who they are? What are some of the factors that affect a child's development? Here we will describe three of the most powerful and mutually dependent influences on development: culture, temperament, and biological and environmental factors.

Culture

For the major part of the last century, most theorists and researchers looked to only one segment of society in their efforts to explore patterns of human development and establish norms against which to measure all human beings (O'Connor and Fernandez 2006). For example, much of the early research on developmental milestones only studied children from European American backgrounds. The researchers largely ignored the influence of temperament, culture, and language. Such biases made it more likely that children who did not perform according to the stated norms for their age would be seen as deficient.

Consider this example:

Four-year-old Gina is the only child of Asian descent in her class. She has attended preschool near her mother's job for the past week. Gina's teachers have noticed that she only reluctantly eats the food they offer her. They have also noticed that she generally takes longer than the other children to eat.

She does not hold utensils like the other children. The teachers are concerned that Gina could have delayed self-feeding skills.

Here are some facts the teachers did not know: At home Gina feeds herself proficiently using chopsticks. Also, Gina was not familiar with the food her teachers offered her. Until they made a home visit and spent time with Gina and her mother, her teachers could see only what she couldn't do, and judged her accordingly.

People's cultural backgrounds may affect how they view

- independence,
- problem solving,
- competition,
- cooperation,
- the role of adult authority,
- the importance of peer groups, and
- the whole range of human functioning.

Children's cultural experiences interact with their genetic potential to affect their development. A child raised in a child-centered family that values independence and autonomy may be assertive and confident when interacting with adults. One raised in a culture that values peer relations may hesitate when speaking with adults but be able to solve problems with peers. In some cultures, eye contact with adults is a sign of disrespect. In others, adults tell children, "Look at me when I talk to you!" Our thought processes, actions, relationships, and development are shaped by our culture, and that includes the culture of the school or program. Ms. Scott and Mr. Aragona grew up in very different circumstances and have learned to recognize and take into consideration their disparate backgrounds and assumptions as they collaborate in the classroom.

THOUGHT QUESTION Consider your own culture and upbringing. How were children disciplined in your family? What role did children play during family gatherings? Why are your early family experiences important for you as a teacher?

Temperament

Lucia clings to her mother's leg at the kindergarten door and turns her head away from the teacher, who is trying to greet her.

Sagal marches into the classroom without looking back, eager to use the colorful materials on the table. She beckons her mother to follow her, and then waves a quick goodbye when her mother says she has to go to work.

Tony runs around the room with his toy car and bumps into other children and the tables. He throws himself to the ground and cries when a teacher tries to intervene. Tony's mother explains to Mr. Aragona that Tony needs a quiet space with few visual distractions so that he can calm down. Mr. Aragona helps Tony sit at a table away from the other children.

As any parent with more than one child can tell you, every child is born with his own temperament. **Temperament** refers to an individual child's typical patterns of behavior, in particular, the child's emotional reactions and activity level, general persistence, and ability to manage change (Pelco and Reed-Victor 2003; Sturm 2004; Chess and Thomas 1996). Temperament is the *how* of behavior, not the *what* or the *why* of it. Most temperamental differences are inborn, that is, they are part of our biological heritage. In contrast, our personality is more subject to environmental influences and includes our temperament, but also our individual psychological makeup.

Research on temperament has shown that some children are shy and reserved and "slow to warm up," while others are adaptable, good-natured, and "easy." Still others are full of strong emotions, experience wide mood swings, and have been referred to as "difficult" (Chess and Thomas 1996) or as "movers and shakers" (Lerner and Dombro 2000). However, not every child falls squarely into one group or another. Sensitive parenting and changes in the child's school and family environments can sometimes slightly alter some aspects of a child's basic temperament (Kochanska 1995) and can help children of different temperaments adjust to the demands of their particular settings. Yet many characteristics will remain a part of the child's makeup throughout the early years and in some cases throughout life.

Why should Ms. Scott and Mr. Aragona get to know the children's individual temperaments? Educators have learned to understand and respect children's temperamental tendencies in order to create learning situations that best suit each child (Pelco and Reed-Victor 2003). In both classrooms and families, problems occur when the teacher or caregiver expects the child to act in a way that runs counter to the child's temperament. We search for a **goodness of fit** between the child's tendencies and those of the parents or teachers. Goodness of fit does not mean that teacher and child have similar temperaments. Rather, it means that the teacher recognizes and appreciates the child's temperament and can guide the child within the framework of her inborn tendencies. For this to occur, both teachers and parents need to be aware of their own temperamental styles as well as of their notions of the "ideal" temperament in children (Figure 8.1). Temperament is also influenced by culture, gender expectations, and family experiences (Carlson, Feng, and Harwood 2004).

THOUGHT QUESTION Try filling out the questionnaire in Figure 8.1 for yourself and for a child you know well. Comparing the results will help you visualize some of the differences and similarities in your temperaments. Then think about your relationship with the child in light of your new knowledge.

We can use our knowledge of different temperaments as a way of identifying strengths in children (Developmental Principle 4), because each variation has both advantages and disadvantages. The shy and cautious child may be careful and thorough, thoughtfully taking time to watch and learn before attempting a new activity. The dramatic child may be creative and exciting, a charismatic leader, drawing other children into his realm of excitement and interests. The balanced and easy-going nature of an even-tempered child may give her resilience in the face of adversity or may help her become a mediator among other children. Here is an example of how Sagal's preschool teachers helped her parents, Jada and Maurice, understand and come to value her temperamental characteristics:

Sagal entered the world kicking and screaming, ready to live life to the fullest and be heard the loudest. She responded enthusiastically to her older siblings, and they in turn loved her antics. Sagal began saying words at ten months. She walked at eleven months and was into everything. The caregivers at Sagal's day care center also loved Sagal's spirit. Even in the toddler room, she was the leader. Jada was concerned: She thought Sagal was a bit "high strung." She hoped that Sagal would become calmer as she grew older and commented that, in her culture, girls were not so loud and outspoken. The caregivers assured Sagal's mother that her daughter's temperament was healthy and natural. As Sagal moved into the preschool room, artwork, woodwork, and dramatic play became her passion. She used language innovatively and persuasively. One day she convinced her peers that not only should they wash the babies but they should all take a bath. Prompts from her teachers redirected Sagal's activity, and the four-year-olds were dissuaded from climbing into the water table. With continued guidance from her teachers, Sagal

Assessing temperament: Yours or a Child's

1. Sensitivity
Are you aware of and sensitive to noises, temperature changes, taste of food, and the texture of things?

1	2	3	4	5
usually not sensitive				very sensitive

2. Regularity
Do you normally eat, sleep, wake up, eliminate at the same time each day? Do you like things scheduled and in order, or are you more of the disorderly "easy" type?

1	2	3	4	5
regular, orderly				irregular, disorderly

3. Activity
Do you have lots of energy and love to go, go, go? Do you have trouble sitting still and relaxing?

1	2	3	4	5
quiet				active

4. Intensity
Do you have strong dramatic reactions? Do you easily let people know what you're feeling, or are you more reserved and hard to read?

1	2	3	4	5
mild reaction				high intensity/dramatic

5. Approach/withdrawal
What is your first and usual reaction to new people, situations, ideas, or places?

1	2	3	4	5
outgoing				slow to warm up

6. Adaptability
Do you adapt quickly to changes, new places, expectations? Is it difficult for you when there is a new routine or schedule?

1	2	3	4	5
fast adapting				slow adapting

7. Persistence
Do you stick with things even when you are getting frustrated? Can you easily stop an activity even if you are not done?

1	2	3	4	5
get "locked in," persistent				can stop, not persistent

8. Distractibility
Are you very aware of and easily distracted by noises and people around you? Do you forget what you were going to do when something else catches your attention?

1	2	3	4	5
easily distracted and calmed				not easily distracted and calmed

9. Mood
How often do you feel happy and have a positive attitude versus feeling negative or serious?

1	2	3	4	5
usually positive				often negative or serious

8.1 *Assessing Temperament: Yours or a Child's*
Helen F. Neville, based on work by Stella Chase, Alexander Thomas, and James Cameron, with permission from the Kaiser Foundation Health Plan.

Sagal is always up to something.

learned to use her leadership qualities for positive outcomes. By seeing Sagal through her teachers' positive lens, her parents, too, began to appreciate her intelligence and drive, even though her behavior didn't correspond with their cultural expectations for a girl.

Biological and environmental factors

The differences in our journeys through life actually begin before birth. Some are due to genetic variations that cause specific disabilities or other more subtle learning or behavioral changes as we mature. For example, both Amy and Tony have been identified as having **special needs** and require adaptations in their everyday life and learning. Amy is Melissa and Dave's first child. Melissa was twenty-six when Amy was born. She had no prenatal testing and was shocked to find that her infant had **Down syndrome,** a chromosomal disorder. Melissa and Dave learned that Amy's disability came about by chance and that it would affect every aspect of her development. Although her parents and their extended family found the first year of Amy's life difficult in many ways, they grew to adore her. Melissa and Dave began to understand that Amy would grow and develop just like any other child, but on her own timetable. They started to celebrate each new hard-won achievement.

Tony's parents only found out that he was autistic (Figure 8.2) when he began to attend preschool. As an infant, Tony had been difficult to soothe and did not like to be cuddled. He had a hard time developing sleeping routines, but as soon as he was old enough to grasp a toy, he found great delight and comfort in examining the different parts of an object and in turning the wheels on his toy cars. Tony began to speak at two, but instead of using single words to label objects, he repeated strings of words he had heard on TV. His parents wondered whether he was specially gifted because of his memory and distinct interest in certain objects. Tony's preschool teachers talked with his parents about his problems relating to the other children

8.2 *Autism Defined*
From: National Institute of
Neurological Disorders and
Strokes 2006

Autism Defined

Autism is not a disease, but a developmental disorder of brain function. What is often called "classical autism" is the most common of a group of disorders that fall under the heading of autistic spectrum disorders (ASDs).

Austism is characterized by

- impaired social interaction,
- problems with verbal and nonverbal communication and imagination, and
- unusual or severely limited interests and activities.

Symptoms of autism usually appear during the first three years of childhood and continue throughout life. Although there is no cure, appropriate management may foster relatively normal development and reduce undesirable behaviors. Males are four times more likely to have autism than females.

and his difficulty in making transitions. The teachers noted that he was bright—he knew all his letters and numbers at age three—yet his interpersonal issues meant that, among other things, he found it difficult to listen to stories in school and to follow the teachers' directions.

We know that many things can challenge a child's developing system. While still in the womb, babies can experience strokes, infections, and developmental abnormalities; and problems during delivery can cause other forms of disability. Infants born prematurely or with very low birth weights are susceptible to a variety of later learning problems. So are infants who are exposed to toxins, alcohol, drugs, or cigarette smoke.

As we consider the whole child, we want to include the family. Ms. Scott and Mr. Aragona have no way of knowing all the complexities of each child's family circumstances. However, as they observe and interact with the children and their families, they learn how everyone can work together to help the child reach full potential. And, as you have read throughout this book, environmental influences interact with other variables to seriously affect children's health, mental acuity or sharpness, and familial relationships. We examine these mutual influences in the following section.

Mutual influences on development

While we already have described some of the influences on development, we need to keep in mind that none of these exist separately. As you can see in Figure 8.3, the relationships among culture, temperament, biology, and the environment have profound effects on a child's developmental pathways.

Because these influences interact with as well as affect each other (you read about Samaroff's work in Chapter 6), children have many opportunities to overcome early problems and disadvantages (National Research Council 2000; Foley and Hochman 2006). But consistent and reoccurring negative experiences wear down children's tendencies toward resilience. Remembering Developmental Principle 3, however, we want to emphasize that families and teachers can make real differences

> Ms. Scott and Mr. Aragona have no way of knowing all the complexities of each child's family circumstances. However, as they observe and interact with the children and their families, they learn how everyone can work together to help the child reach full potential.

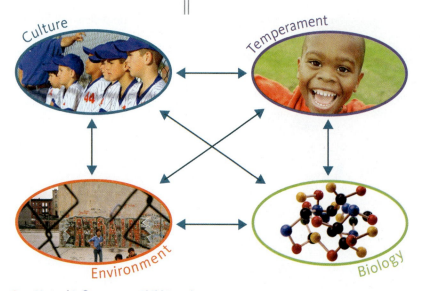

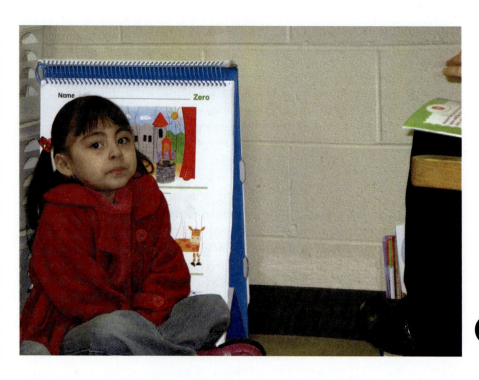

Culture

Temperament

Environment

Biology

8.3 *Mutual Influences on Child Development*

in children's lives, regardless of their difficult circumstances. Below we describe some examples.

Although Lucia grew up in a very poor family in rural Guatemala, her **extended family**—grandparents, aunts, cousins, and neighbors who were considered family—formed a tight support network. Lucia was her parents' first child, and her family gave her a great deal of attention, care, and love. As a result, she thrived and grew, reaching developmental milestones appropriately. Her shy temperament fit well with her family's expectations of behavior for girls. When she was three and her father left for the United States, Lucia helped care for the younger children in her extended family. In Lucia's case, her basic temperament affected the way she interacted with her family, culture, and community. She had many opportunities to learn and to contribute to her community, which set the stage for her developing feelings of efficacy, positive social affiliation, and acceptance.

Tony, on the other hand, upended his family's beliefs about child rearing. Even before they learned of his disability, Tony's stormy temperament and difficulty with transitions caused them to try behavioral strategies they never would have used with their other children. At two, Tony threw tantrums when he had to put on his clothes, have a diaper change, get in his car seat, or alter a familiar routine. His parents learned to give him Fruit Loops to distract him long enough to carry out these daily tasks. Tony's grandparents felt his parents were spoiling him and that

Lucia is a shy child who nonetheless has had many opportunities to play important roles in her family and community.

Tony is a dinosaur expert who is learning social skills with the help of therapists, his teachers, his classmates, and his family.

the entire family was catering to his wants. In this case, Tony's biological and temperamental needs shaped the child-rearing practices of his family, challenging their beliefs and values. Once Tony's parents learned that he had a disability, they worked with his therapists to help him develop more socially acceptable behavioral patterns so that he could participate in his school community. The influences of culture, disability, and temperament propelled Tony forward on his own unique developmental pathway. We can readily imagine how a different set of perhaps less positive mutual influences could have led to a different pathway that would have given Tony fewer options as he grew older.

Understanding these "multiple interacting influences on children's development and learning" (NAEYC Standard 1) can be a challenge for early childhood teachers. Ms. Scott and Mr. Aragona have learned that to grasp the uniqueness of each child they need to form "respectful, reciprocal relationships" (NAEYC Standard 2) with the children and their families. Although teachers can learn a great deal about a child's temperament from observing her in the classroom, information about culture, biology, and environment comes mainly through a trusting, supportive relationship with families and the community. Learning about a child's positive relationships within the family or his experience of early trauma helps teachers comprehend the complex circumstances of each child's life. In Chapter 14, you will discover ways to work with families to learn about a child's strengths and how the expectations of a child's culture and community help shape him or her.

DOMAINS OF DEVELOPMENT

How is knowledge of developmental domains useful to teachers?

Developmental sequences are usually separated into specific **domains,** or areas, such as the ones we use in this chapter: **physical, social-emotional, cognitive,** and **language and literacy.** First, let's examine how separating behavior into these domains can both help and hinder our understanding.

Ms. Scott and Mr. Aragona know about developmental milestones. Understanding how each of the children in Room 205 is progressing on his or her individual pathways will give the teachers more data to use as they organize learning activities. Yet Ms. Scott and Mr. Aragona have learned that sometimes children's behaviors do not break down easily into a defined category. Consider this example:

Three children in a preschool classroom are sitting at a table with markers and paper. The teacher asks them to write some letters they know. Two children pick up markers and attempt to write letters, but the third child sits and looks around the room, not using the markers at all.

What might we hypothesize from this observation? Maybe the third child doesn't know how to write letters. Maybe he doesn't have the physical ability to hold a marker and form letters. Maybe he doesn't understand the directions, either because he doesn't speak the language of this classroom or because of language processing or attentional problems. Maybe he fears making a mistake and therefore isn't willing to try. It also could be that he is so interested in the social interactions around him that he can't—or doesn't want to—focus on the task. Ms. Scott and Mr. Aragona have learned that they need *many* observations of a child before arriving at a conclusion about what his behavior means and which domains of development are affecting his performance. At best, teachers draw from a combination of data from a variety of sources.

The preceding example demonstrates how a child's thinking, language, physical skills, feelings, social interactions, and **prior knowledge** (what a child brings to a learning situation from earlier learning) are intertwined in a given class activity. The younger the child is, the more interrelated these domains are. As long as Ms. Scott and Mr. Aragona remember this, they can organize their observations according to separate domains of development to highlight what they are learning about the children. They make *many* observations before attempting to evaluate the reasons for a child's behavior and deciding which domains affect it. To further their knowledge, they col-

The younger the child, the more interrelated are the domains of development.

Professional Roles

Consultant/itinerant teacher	Provides educational support to regular classroom teachers, suggests modifications to curriculum, assists individual children
Social worker	Coordinates services/resources for families and teachers; provides play therapy, family therapy
Speech and language therapist	Provides therapy to promote increased use of language, understanding of language, oral motor development, and independent feeding skills
Physical therapist	Facilitates functional use of large muscles to develop motor skills, locomotion, balance, and range of motion
Occupational therapist	Promotes coordinated use of small muscles and senses to accomplish the tasks of everyday life: dressing, eating, playing, cutting, writing
School psychologist	Provides play therapy, counseling, behavior management plans
Developmental pediatrician	Provides biomedical supports to promote healthy physical development

8.4 *Professional Roles*

laborate with related service providers, professionals in the school who work with individual children and help teachers plan instruction. Figure 8.4 identifies various types of service providers and their roles.

In the section that follows we look more closely at the physical, social-emotional, cognitive, and language and literacy domains in young children's development and discuss the variations that occur within them.

Physical Growth and Motor Development

As young children's bodies grow and change, they don't simply get bigger and stronger and more coordinated. They change to interact more fully with the world in which they live.

In addition to processing sensory input from vision, hearing, smell, taste, and touch, children (and adults) organize messages from two other sensory systems that are important for movement. The **vestibular system** affects balance, and the **proprioceptive system** relates to body awareness. Input from the vestibular system helps a child orient his eyes and head to what is occurring around him, and helps the child remain upright against the force of gravity. Proprioceptive information from sensors in joints and muscles helps a child "feel" where her body is in space—for example, how to move her arm and hand to reach for a toy. As children get older, proprioception helps them have a sense of their body in space and to "stand in line," for example, or sit in a group without getting too close to other children. Children aren't aware of much of the vestibular and proprioceptive information they take in, yet it is an important component of every action they make.

This girl knows where her body is in space. Her proprioception enables her to slide down the handrail.

Motor development as a dynamic system

How do children acquire all the motor skills they need? How do we grow up to become tennis players, knitters, skateboard riders? Maturationists believed that an invariable inner plan for motor development unfolds as we grow, resulting in familiar milestones such as being able to sit and to walk (Gesell 1940). But dynamic systems theory and other integrative approaches that you read about in Chapter 6 give us another way to think about motor skill development. Thinking of the body as a system in which different elements work together, we can see how a child's new action pattern emerges from the ongoing interplay of four different variables:

THOUGHT QUESTION When children play on swings, the vestibular system is the main processor of their movement. List some other activities that children do, and consider which senses children use to register the sensory input.

1. Central nervous system: ongoing process of brain and nervous system development
2. Movement repertoire: the kinds of movements the child can currently perform
3. Child's intention: the child's action plan, what the child wants to do
4. Current environmental situation: the obstacles and resources the surroundings present

These variables take on different roles at various stages in the child's development (Thelen and Smith 2006).

As an example, imagine a four-month-old lying on her stomach trying to reach a shiny rolling tube. Her brain and muscular system (central nervous system) have matured enough for her to hold her head up to see the shiny tube, and she can reach her arm out toward it while maintaining her balance on her tummy. She wants to feel and explore the tube (intention), but every time she touches it, it rolls away. In this case, what the child is capable of doing (repertoire) is not enough to overcome the immediate constraints (environmental situation) that prevent her from reaching her goal. She will keep trying because she is motivated to explore her world. When she later learns to sit up, she will develop a new set of action patterns to fit that new position and the environmental situation that comes with it.

As we see from this example, and as dynamic systems theory suggests, the physical abilities the child displayed did not develop because of some predetermined biological plan that predicted specific movements appearing at a certain time. Rather, the child's actions were responses to the changing interactions based on her physical growth, the environment, and her developing need and capacity to understand and master the world around her. Understanding this makes us appreciate even more the arguments put forward to allow young children to experience movement (gym, recess, dance, etc.) as part of their school or child care day.

Motor milestones and variability

Because all human infants grow up with some similarities in environmental conditions—all babies experience gravity and motion; and most grow up in a world of sight, color, sound, feeling, and smell—there are many common patterns to motor development. **Movement** makes use of our motor skills; **action** is movement with a purpose, as opposed to the uncoordinated movements of a newborn, for example. We organize motor skills into two main areas.

- **Gross motor development,** which supports actions for moving around in the environment
- **Fine motor development,** which supports the more precise movements of the hand and fingers

Developmental milestones emerge as children learn to coordinate different abilities such as balance, postural stability (the ability to hold oneself steady), muscular strength, and vision. However, as Figure 8.5 shows, children developing in a typical manner do not reach each motor milestone at the same age. This range can be explained, in part, by the fact that at least four variables are at work in different ways in each child. Thus, dynamic systems theory helps us understand why children achieve milestones at different ages—and that such variability is to be expected.

Cultural differences also come into play with motor milestones. In a New Guinean community, children were not allowed to crawl and walk until they were almost two years old, to keep them safe from the dangers on the ground. Then, at two, they learned to "walk well within two or three days" (Rogoff 2003). In many cultures and communities, children as young as three and four sew and weave, prepare and plant a garden, or carry a heavy baby sibling, important household chores requiring motor skills that published Western motor milestones rate as advanced (Rogoff 2003).

Children with disabilities often follow a different motor timeline from that shown in Figure 8.5. When Amy was born with Down syndrome, she seemed floppy. Amy's mother, Melissa, was told that Amy had **hypotonia,** a condition in which a child's joints and muscles are overly flexible and loose. A **physical therapist** (see Figure 8.4) began working with Amy and her mother at home through

THOUGHT QUESTION As you observe children in classrooms, consider which of their behaviors are simply movements and which are goal-directed actions. During what activities or periods of the day might you expect to see more of one than the other?

8.5 *Gross and Fine Motor Development Milestones*
Adapted from: Cole, Cole and Lightfoot 2005; World Health Organization 2006.

Age range within which 90 percent of children achieve skill	Milestone
3 weeks–4 months	Holds head upright
2–7 months	Rolls from back to side
3–9 months	Sits alone
5–13 months	Crawls
8–18 months	Walks alone
9–12 months	Uses thumb and index finger to grasp
10–21 months	Scribbles with crayon
17–30 months	Jumps in place
18–36 months	Imitates circle; vertical, horizontal strokes
36–48 months	Balances on one foot for ten seconds
30–48 months	Throws and catches ball
30–48 months	Cuts with scissors
36–60 months	Imitates letters
36–60 months	Skips
18–60 months	Demonstrates right- or left-handedness

the early intervention program. The therapist showed Melissa how to support Amy's body and head so that she could pay attention to the world around her and could look at Melissa's face. As Amy grew, the physical therapist continued to show Melissa different ways to play with her baby to support Amy's motor development. Even though Amy didn't sit up until she was one and didn't walk until she was more than two, each milestone was another important step on her developmental pathway.

Early childhood educators need familiarity with the timetable for motor milestones, but they also must understand that *how* a child moves is as important as *when* a child is able to do something. Children are not only handling sensory input from vision, hearing, smell, taste, and touch, they are also busy processing messages from other sensory systems that help them with balance and body awareness. Ordinarily children and adults coordinate this complex array of sensory input without thinking about it, but for some children, doing so poses a challenge (Williamson and Anzalone 2001; Bundy, Lane, and Murray 2002).

How will you notice when parts of a child's sensory-motor system are still developing or not working effectively? Sam is an example of a child with sensory-motor challenges:

Early childhood educators need familiarity with the timetable for motor milestones, but they also must understand that *how* a child moves is as important as *when* a child is able to do something.

Amy has Down Syndrome and has gained skills at a different rate from most other children. Yet, as with all children, each milestone she reaches is an important step along her developmental pathway.

During the first weeks of school, Ms. Scott grew increasingly frustrated with Sam, a five-year-old who wiggled and bothered other children during every morning meeting. She reminded him to sit with his legs crossed like the other children, but instead he shifted his body around, lay down, or leaned against the child next to him. The **occupational therapist** (see Figure 8.4) explained that Sam had trouble maintaining his balance in a cross-legged sitting position. Sitting up was something he had to work at all the time. He didn't have the concentration or energy to listen to the story because most of his attention was taken up trying to stay upright like the other children. The occupational therapist suggested that Sam sit with his back against a sturdy bookcase and that he use different sitting positions that were easier for him. She gave him a plastic pillow with bumps on it to use in a chair. These small adaptations helped Sam stay upright, and Ms. Scott soon saw that other children found these supports helpful too, so that Sam did not feel singled out.

All children gain confidence and knowledge when they can move freely and competently in their environments. In spite of their school's heavy emphasis on preparing children to read and write, Mr. Aragona and Ms. Scott are committed to giving the children ample opportunity to spend time on the playground and to enjoy movement and music in the classroom. They work with the occupational and physical therapists to provide **adaptations,** or changes in the environment, for those children still learning how to use their bodies ably.

Social-Emotional Development

Children enter the Room 205 class with rich and varied emotional and social histories. Perhaps more than any other domain of development, the social-emotional one is difficult to observe because it depends on experiences unique to each child. Parents and siblings have already played an important role in developing a child's self-concept.

Now it is the teachers' job to create a classroom community that supports each child's emotional and social development as the basis of further learning. Mr. Aragona and Ms. Scott know that emotional safety and shared expectations can have a profound influence on children's learning (Bransford 2000). Their classroom goals are to:

- Find ways for each child to succeed in school.
- Find the balance between providing support for each child and encouraging independence.
- Promote feelings of competence and **self-efficacy** (that is, feeling capable and able to accomplish goals).
- Develop a sense of community, with emphasis on attitudes of caring, sensitivity to others, and safety.
- Recognize children's strengths and reward their efforts.
- Establish routines that allow learning to flourish.
- Model conflict resolution, problem solving, and kindness.
- Address and redirect limit testing, bullying, and aggression.

As we saw in Chapter 3, from the earliest days of a child's life, emotions and social experiences are woven together. The infant and young child express emotions, learn to regulate them, and come to understand their meaning through social interaction. Along the way, children absorb their culture's expectations for the expression and understanding of emotional states.

An important component of the early childhood years is children's increasing awareness of themselves as unique individuals with a specific identity. Children need to develop a positive sense of their abilities, based on their growing competence and their grasp of family and cultural ideas of "appropriate" behavior. But learning all the new material in school is challenging; children who lack the confidence to attempt new things often have difficulty learning. Experiences that build on their previous learning, at whatever level, are often key to providing children entering school with a positive initial school experience. Teachers also can reassure children that it is okay to make mistakes and that school is a nurturing and supportive place where their accomplishments will be recognized.

As children develop cause-and-effect reasoning, they can become aware of the emotions that different situations evoke, and they can learn to label their own and others' emotions. Their increasing language acquisition further supports their understanding of emotion. Ms. Scott and Mr. Aragona take care to deal with social-emotional learning in their curriculum. They read books aloud, tell stories, and discuss children's television shows that focus on social situations in order to help children understand the complex emotions that are part of everyday life. They focus in these ways because the emotional and social life of their classroom provides the foundation for all the children's subsequent educational accomplishments.

Cognitive Development

What exactly do we mean by **cognition,** that is, intellectual functioning? Its simplest definition is the ability to acquire, store, and make use of information or knowledge (Bjorkland 2005). Cognition involves remembering, symbolic representation, thinking, and intentional control. As with the other domains, these cognitive processes change as a child grows and develops. Infants and young children are incredible learning systems. Their brains are primed to process and absorb all kinds of information about the world of people and things into which they have been born.

> As children develop cause-and-effect reasoning and more sophisticated language, they can become aware of the emotions that different situations evoke and learn to label their own and others' emotions.

Children learn about the physical properties and functions of objects from using them independently and from participating in activities with others (Rogoff 2003; Gauvain 2001). Back in her rural village in Guatemala, Lucia watched and sometimes helped her mother dye fibers and weave cloth. She also learned what was safe and what was dangerous for her younger siblings as she helped care for them in the family courtyard. When Lucia's classmate Sagal was two, she learned how to use markers and look at books by imitating the actions of her older siblings as they did their homework each night. These activities are examples of Developmental Principle 1: children's social environment and culture, interacting with their biological inheritance, can determine what they learn and how and when they learn it.

Memory

Memory is an important component of cognitive development that exists across all cultures. All children get better at remembering as they get older. Children store concepts about objects in their memory even before they possess the language for them: for instance, a child has an early concept of a ball that she developed from nonverbal sensory experiences and action patterns. As children acquire language, they store the names of objects with the matching sensory memories and **elaborate** and **differentiate** the stored underlying concept. That is, they extend and enrich their understanding of the concept (elaborate) and also start to recognize its subtleties and the differences between it and similar things (differentiate). For example, when Sagal was fourteen months old, she learned she could throw anything that was not too heavy for her to pick up. Her mother and father quickly had to teach her that only balls were for throwing and that she was not allowed to throw anything else. They helped her to differentiate, or separate out, the concept of "ball" from all other things that could be thrown but shouldn't be.

Young children, often with an adult, begin to make-believe in the form of a **script,** for example, about going to the grocery, having a birthday party, taking a bath, or going to church. Scripts, or scenarios from everyday life, specify, not only the materials and setting needed for an event, but the social roles people play and the sequence of activities that recurs (Cole, Cole, and Lightfoot 2005). Scripts help children understand an event more fully (Nelson 1996); they also seem to help young children practice, remember, and learn to anticipate recurring events and contribute to children's developing memory for events.

The kinds of things children remember and the way they use their memory in everyday life vary widely. Children's prior knowledge influences what new information they consider important and how well they store it in memory. For example, Tony has always been fascinated by dinosaurs and has learned about them at home from books and videos. All his prior knowledge has made it easier for him to remember the names of new dinosaurs he finds out about and to use that information. He readily classifies meat-eaters and plant-eaters. Tony has become a five-year-old dinosaur

What is a ball? How do children learn concepts?

expert, and everything he knows contributes to his ability to store more information about dinosaurs and to think about them.

Symbolic representation

Over time, children develop the ability to use symbols to represent experience and as tools for thinking (Vygotsky 1978). These different forms of symbolic representation in turn support the children's cognitive development. When very young children look at books with an adult, they use the pictures as symbols to represent objects and animals that are new to them. As you read in Chapter 4, when children pretend, their actions become the symbols. Developing at the same time as play, language itself emerges as a primary symbolic form. Language enhances the development of more complex concepts and paves the way for later abstract thinking.

In spite of Tony's sophisticated knowledge about dinosaurs, he has difficulty using play as a symbolic system. At the age of five, he still doesn't engage in make-believe play with the other children. His lack of imaginative play is characteristic of a child on the autistic spectrum. This affects his ability to recreate social situations in a play environment in order to understand them, as other children do (Rogers and Williams 2006). Although his ability to use symbols such as letters and numbers is advanced, Tony has trouble figuring out the social world and anticipating sequential events. Tony prefers it when life patterns remain the same. He gets upset and confused by changes in his daily routine. Tony also has a hard time understanding why people act the way they do. It is difficult for him to realize how another person feels, an ability you may recall from the "Theory of Mind" section in Chapter 3. Tony's parents tell the teachers that they worry that Tony can often be bluntly honest, for example, telling a teacher, "You're fat," without realizing how those words might make the teacher feel. Ms. Scott and Mr. Aragona help Tony process social information so that he will be able to function better in school.

As we see from Tony's example, symbolic representation can take many forms. Young children also develop their skills symbolically representing their world through drawing and diagrams and, later, through reading and writing. As school-age children develop literacy, they can use symbols to understand and express more abstract ideas that are not necessarily part of the "here and now." Howard Gardner (1983, 1999) reminds us that children can experience deep understanding and acquire knowledge through construction, music and movement, social awareness of self and others, and affinity for the natural world. All of these representational systems are important avenues for different forms of cognition and constitute what Gardner calls forms of **multiple intelligences,** which you read about in Chapter 6.

Intentional control

Young children use symbols and memory to think about their world and to use what they know to meet goals and solve problems. As they grow older, they become more efficient at storing and categorizing information, recognizing cause-and-effect relationships, and applying prior knowledge to new situations. They also become better at planning and at organizing their thinking process itself, as well as at using different mental strategies in different situations. This ability to plan and carry out complex mental and physical actions is called **executive function.** It develops slowly as the brain and nervous system mature and is not fully developed until late adolescence.

Some children have significant problems in developing intentional control of their thinking and actions. **Intentional control** is a complex skill that includes the ability

Lack of imaginative play is characteristic of a child on the autistic spectrum.

Executive function develops slowly as the brain and nervous system mature and is not fully developed until late adolescence.

- to inhibit or control action;
- to direct and continue to pay attention;
- to shift attention, when necessary, to screen out extraneous stimuli; and
- to figure out what aspect of a task is most important. (Barkley 1997, Levine 2002)

Although most children develop the ability to calm themselves and regulate their actions and attention, some children are highly active and are easily distracted by sounds and movement and by visual and tactile stimuli around them. They have trouble stopping or controlling their actions and words. Some children with these characteristics may be diagnosed with **attention deficit hyperactivity disorder (ADHD)** and given special accommodations (in the form of specialized tools or extra time) under the special education or rehabilitation laws. However, not all children who display high levels of activity are showing symptoms of ADHD.

The teachers in Room 205 have noticed that a few children have some trouble with self-regulation but that Dylan is a child who, in spite of their efforts, has serious trouble listening to and following directions. The teachers do not want to label Dylan but believe he will need extra help so that he can learn. On his part, Dylan seems unaware of how his behavior differs from that of most of the other children in his class. If Dylan could tell us how school feels for him, his description might sound like this:

> Every day I come to school and I promise my mom that I will be good. But when I sit down at the morning meeting, I tell everyone about the great idea I had about the block corner. The teachers tell me to raise my hand and wait, but a bird flies by the window and lands on the sill, so I look over there. The teachers tell me to sit up, and I see that Amy is trying to put something up on the calendar, but I know where it should go so I get up and show her. The teachers tell me to sit down, and they sound angry, but I don't know why because I was trying to help her. Then I feel that sticky label on my shirt, and I have to tell Brian next to me that my dog licked my face this morning. Then everyone is getting up and going to the tables, and I'm not sure where to go, and so I go over to the block corner because I want to try out my very good idea, and the teachers come and tell me that it is not block time now. So I run around the room until Ms. Scott takes me by the hand and shows me the chair to sit in. And then I feel so sleepy that I have to put my head down on the table, and then there is a pencil that gets stuck in a crack and I have to get it out. I know I have to do something with the pencil and the paper, but I don't know how to start.

Although Dylan is a capable child, his attentional problems are already interfering with his ability to learn in the classroom. Ms. Scott and Mr. Aragona have a number of strategies they use with Dylan. For example, when one of them gives instructions to the whole class, the other gives Dylan one-on-one directions. They also turn to the support services in their school to gain further insights: the school psychologist and the social worker will contact the family to seek their collaboration in helping Dylan. The teachers know that a successful plan for Dylan must be consistent across both home and school environments.

Language and Literacy

Language is an aspect of cognitive development that is unique to humans. The children entering Room 205 have already become amazingly proficient language users. How does this remarkable accomplishment happen for children who are so young?

Early Language Development Milestones

Age	Milestones
0–5 months	• Responds to familiar voices • Looks and smiles at faces • Coos, babbles
6–12 months	• Expresses pleasure and delight • Shares smiles and facial expressions • Takes turns with adult using sounds, actions, objects • Turns when own name is called (9–12 months) • Uses gestures to show, give, and point to objects • Produces some consonant sounds: dada, baba • Participates in familiar routines with gestures: bye-bye, pat-a-cake
12–18 months	• Uses one to ten words • When asked, can point to familiar objects: ball, shoe, cup • Imitates actions and a few words (although articulation is poor) • Uses jargon to join in conversation or express emotions • Looks to see if caretaker is watching; shares joint attention with caretaker when playing with objects or looking at books
18–24 months	• Expands expressive vocabulary • Uses two-word utterances: "shoe off," "baby cry" • Points to body parts on self • Begins to follow simple directions • Begins pretend play using dolls and other objects
2–3 years	• Explosion of vocabulary • Use of pronouns, some prepositions • Three- and four-word combinations • Uses plurals: socks, shoes, balls • Answers simple questions
3–4 years	• Uses most speech sounds; can be understood by others • Expresses ideas and feelings; can relate a short narrative • Uses prepositions, descriptive words, pronouns • Can answer and ask questions • Enjoys playing with language through rhymes and nonsense • Talks to self and uses pretend scenarios
4–5 years	• Follows three-part directions • Has large vocabulary • Knows some opposites; can define objects by use • Uses longer complex sentences with mostly correct grammar • Answers "why" questions • Can converse using turn-taking with peers; beginning to use language appropriately in different social situations
5–6 years	• Expressive vocabulary of approximately 2,200 words; more than twice that receptively • Grammar almost adult-like; speech intelligible and socially useful • Can tell connected narrative with cause and effect
6–8 years	• Can repair conversational breakdown • Shifts from word association to conceptual word meaning • Is developing passive voice and irregular verbs • Is beginning to understand figurative language • Can identify sounds, syllables, words, sentences

8.6 *Early Language Development Milestones*
Adapted from: Owens 2005; Bowen 1998; Berkowitz 2003

Understanding language

Children learn their family's language—or even two or more languages—not from any specialized teaching, but simply by growing up within the social relationships of a family and community. Infants and young children are learning simultaneously to understand what others say to them (**receptive language**) and to verbalize their own needs, feelings, and information (**expressive language**).

Language is a shared system of symbols and rules for expressing concepts. The use of language allows humans to communicate information, ideas, feelings, and needs. Communication and speech are two elements of language development:

- **Communication** is the process of exchanging information and feelings (Owens 2005).
- **Speech** is the oral form of language.
- Spoken language requires us to organize neuromotor responses using the specific sounds (**phonemes**) of the language we speak.

When a baby first babbles and coos in the crib, she is practicing the various sounds she can make that are similar to the sounds she hears. In every culture and region around the world, children learn the shared code of their community's language in a predictable sequence, but as with other areas of development, there are many variations in these patterns. By the end of the first year, most babies have a few words they can use to express meaning to others. As we can see from the milestones of early language development in Figure 8.6, by the age of five, a child is likely to have an impressive expressive and receptive vocabulary. In fact, children continue to add vocabulary and to become more adept at using language during adolescence and throughout adulthood (Owens 2005).

However, language learning is a complex process. It is not only about acquiring new words and connecting them to specific meanings. Social rules about language use differ in different cultures and communities. Young children need to be taught the social communication cues of their communities: for example, how and when to speak to adults, where to direct their gaze, and what kinds of nonverbal gestures and expressions are acceptable.

Bilingualism

Some of the children in Room 205's inclusion kindergarten grew up hearing and learning a language other than English at home. Some of those children were also learning English and came to Room 205 proficient in English and at least one other language. Other ELLs like Lucia, who had not been exposed to English until she began Head Start, learned one language and then another. She, too, is becoming bilingual but is taking a different path. She is emergent bilingual.

All these children's families want them to learn English, but they have different attitudes and beliefs about when and where their children will speak it. Parents, teachers, and the general public have concerns about how bilingualism might affect a child's school progress:

- Could hearing and speaking more than one language interfere with a child's overall language development?
- Or does speaking two languages instead give a child the advantage of two ways of communicating and a deeper understanding of language in general?

In most other parts of the world, people speak more than one language (Tucker 1999). Linguists agree that learning more than one language early in life will not hin-

> Language learning is not only about acquiring new words and connecting them to specific meanings but also about the social rules of language use and how they differ in various cultures and communities.

time with relatives who add to these narratives. Lucia's parents write shopping lists at home, and Lucia accompanies them to the store, often helping them translate labels and signs from English to Spanish. Thus, although Lucia does not have much prior experience with books, she has a strong background in oral language and in some kinds of writing. During their literacy assessment of all the children in Room 205, the teachers learn about and plan how to build on Lucia's oral literacy strengths, some of which they discovered when Lucia's mother spent time with her daughter in the classroom. The teachers will provide access to many kinds of books and other experiences with print to support Lucia's literacy development because, although most children learn to speak just by living in a family and hearing language, they need specific instruction to learn how to read and write. Figure 8.7 displays common early literacy development milestones.

The teachers of Room 205 will spend much of their instructional time in kindergarten

- reading to the children,
- demonstrating writing by recording what the children say,
- giving the children time to write and draw,
- posting messages and signs,
- giving the children access to many books, and
- helping the children learn the early concepts about print that will support their literacy development in first grade and beyond.

With proper instruction, most children learn to read fluently by third grade. But some have more difficulty than others:

> Tony's older brother, Max, had problems with expressive and receptive language as a preschooler and a kindergartner. In second grade, when Max continued to struggle with reading and writing, he was given a full educational and psychological evaluation and was identified as having a learning disability. The special education consultant teacher provided Max with a specialized reading program designed for children with learning disabilities. With this extra help, Max is now making slow but steady progress learning to read.

CHILDREN WITH SPECIAL NEEDS

What does it mean for a child to have special needs?

All children developed in unique patterns, reminding us of Developmental Principle 2, that there is always a range of variation in development. For some children, though, the variation is greater than what we would expect. At first, Tony's family and pediatrician attributed his differences to his fussy temperament and thought he would outgrow his difficult behaviors. Only when Tony started preschool did his teachers and family recognize that his differences were indicative of a specific disability. In contrast, because Amy has Down syndrome, her unique needs were apparent at birth.

To read, children must grasp many concepts and put them to work. For example, children need practice associating what they see in print with what they hear spoken. They must also:

- Understand the **alphabetic principle**—that each letter or letter combination represents a sound or sounds in the English language.
- Develop **phonemic awareness,** the ability to hear and notice the separate sounds in words, which helps them master the alphabetic principle.
- Learn to **decode** words—that is, to figure out what word the letters spell.
- Master **comprehension** (understanding) of what they read and what is read to them.

THOUGHT QUESTION Consider what you know from your own experience of learning to read or watching someone else learn to read. Think of an example to illustrate each of these four terms.

Children with
special needs
are those who
are significantly
different from
most other
children of the
same age, to
the degree that
they need special
services to fully
benefit from
the educational
process and
to reach their
potential.

When Difference Requires Diagnosis

How are we to know when development is within expected ranges? When should we be concerned? Children with special needs are those who are significantly different from most other children of the same age. The degree of that difference is such that these children need special services to fully benefit from the educational process and to reach their potential. (Refer to Chapter 2 for a review of issues surrounding disproportionate representation.) "Significantly different" has been defined as:

- a 33 percent delay in one domain of functioning, or
- a 25 percent delay in two or more domains of functioning.

Thus, a three-year-old child who has the language capabilities of a two-year-old (a 33 percent delay in the language domain) is considered in need of services. So is a four-year-old with the cognitive skills and social development of a three-year-old. It is important to view children **holistically** (looking at the whole child) in determining their needs. For example, although Tony possessed an advanced vocabulary and superior cognitive skills, he was not able to use those abilities in meaningful ways. The frequency of his tantrums, the atypical quality of his play, and his limited interactions indicated his need for special services.

None of the children in Room 205 this year have any physical disabilities, but there is a child named Aliya in a fourth-grade classroom who has **cerebral palsy,** a disability that affects the motor control centers of the brain. Aliya is part of a group of older children who come to Room 205 weekly to read to the kindergartners. Older children benefit from using their skills with younger children, and the younger ones look up to the older children and become motivated to read by having the "big" kids read to them. Although Aliya's speech is somewhat slurred, the children have learned to understand her and enjoy hearing her read their favorite books. Aliya knows that her reading is as valued as the reading of other children her age.

With all children, we may see behaviors that concern us. Lucia's Head Start teachers were initially concerned because she was so quiet. They were perplexed by the amount of time she spent in the house corner by herself, only playing with one doll. When the teachers understood how much Lucia missed the younger sister she had left behind in Guatemala, her behavior made sense. Through observation and conversations with Lucia, the teachers could see that she was developing and benefiting from her time in the program.

Sagal's parents were equally concerned about their daughter, although for different reasons. They worried about her activity level and her seeming disregard for social conventions. However, Sagal used her incredible energy to immerse herself in learning. Other children looked up to her, thanks to her assertiveness. As we keep in mind that some children may need special services to reach their potential, we also must learn to identify and value variation in development that does not require a special intervention.

When children do need special services, the Individuals with Disabilities Education Improvement Act (IDEA) specifies federal regulations that teachers must follow for the protection of children and their families. (See Chapters 2 and 15 for more information about IDEA.)

Universal Design

In their attempts to develop methods that will work for all their students, Ms. Scott and Mr. Aragona draw on the principles of **universal design,** which were derived

As a parent of a child with multiple needs, at first I assumed that all the professionals working with my daughter Angelica had read textbooks about us and understood what we were going through. But then I started to wonder, why did all of them ask me the same painful questions? Didn't they keep charts? It's been fifteen years, and I am still waiting for some of them to cross the bridge to my "lonely island" and understand what it means to be here.

Our story began three days before Angelica was born, when the doctors told us that our baby had **anencephaly,** a condition in which the brain does not fully develop, and would be born dead. I am from Mexico, and my mother raised me to respect and believe doctors, teachers, and priests. We prepared for a baptism and a funeral.

I gave birth to a baby girl whom we named Angelica, and Angelica *didn't* die. They inserted a shunt in her head, and, after nine days in the hospital, we learned that she had Dandy-Walker syndrome and hydrocephalus, both forms of brain malformation. Her head was humongous, and my recovery from a massive classical cesarean section took months.

At the beginning, I sat in my house day after day, waiting for death to come. I did not bond or become attached to Angelica, since that would make it harder for me when she died. For the first seven months of Angelica's life, I could not see my daughter for who she was. In California, hospitals automatically refer babies who have special needs for intervention services; but I did not answer the phone, and all the letters from Early Start piled up on the table. Also, my pediatrician told me to wake Angelica every two hours throughout the day and night to feed her and watch over her.

I was in a twilight zone—still expecting death and exhausted from no sleep. My mother finally said, "Do you know that babies in China like to sleep? Do you know that babies in Europe like to sleep? Angelica is a baby, and babies like to sleep. Please listen to me, and stop waking her up." I began to let her sleep!

One morning when Angelica was seven months old, I woke up depressed and tired but saw her in her crib with an incredible smile, kicking her legs (she couldn't move her arms due to severe hypotonia, or flaccid muscles, in her upper body). I approached her crib and said, "You are seven months old today. I am not a doctor, but I think that you're not going to die. You are not like another child, but you are not going to die, so let's begin again." I'm not sure how this change came about; maybe everything was just too painful.

That day I signed up Angelica for Early Start services. I brought her to a center twice a week for physical therapy, occupational therapy, and early intervention with a special educator. Based on my recent experiences with professoinals, I was skeptical. I would listen without listening. I was just going through the motions. They told me to practice this and she will do that, but in the back of my mind was still, "She'll die."

Sabrina Rotonda Irvin

My first big dream was for Angelica to sit in a wheelchair. Angelica had zero balance, and her head was so big. Then, one day when she was eighteen months old she sat up for ten seconds. I couldn't believe it! Slowly, my perceptions of Angelica—and probably of early intervention, too—began to change. She began to hold onto toys for a short time. I thought, "Well, I don't know how she'll do it, but maybe I'm going to have a real child who'll be able to do—I don't know what, but something!"

Most children develop so quickly that their parents miss stuff. For us, each new step comes so slowly, I have time to catch everything. My new dream was that we would walk together like the others, to the mall, to the supermarket. And, when she was five-and-a-half or six, after practicing for years, she did it. It took her thirteen years to be potty trained. Angelica has never uttered a word, but she communicates with her hands, her eyes, and her body, and now she has a communication device. She works hard and has taught our family about resilience, love, and patience. I have learned that patience is not about an hour or a day, but about a whole life.

I become enraged when people say, "God sent you a special child. You are so lucky." I don't want to be special. I want to be anonymous. My daughter is like a rock star without the fringe benefits.

Many people call children with special needs "angels"; and I resented that, too. But a mother of another child with special needs changed my mind. She made me realize that Angelica never utters a bad word or lies. I receive the purest, most unconditional love.

When I was pregnant, I thought, "In this incredible country, my child will experience what I couldn't afford." But the way she was born, I couldn't come up with another dream for her. That was a disservice to her. She has her own personality, thoughts, and agenda. Now, I keep adjusting my dreams for Angelica to her abilities. I want professionals to understand that I have dreams and to see Angelica as more than a number or a diagnosis on a chart. If I were not a parent with dreams, I would definitely go crazy.

from theories and standards of architecture and product development. Universal designers create accessible spaces and easy-to-use items for everyone regardless of ability (or disability). When you walk into a building with automatic doors or push your grocery cart up a curb cut, you are experiencing universal design. Innovations that make it easier to open jars, reach high spaces, or regulate the sound on your telephone are examples of universal design in products. Within classrooms and other learning environments, universal design principles can meet the needs of a wide range of diverse learners. Universal design is not a "one size fits all" approach but a systematic way of planning that recognizes that people with all kinds of learning differences need a variety of ways to acquire information, to show what they have learned, and to stay engaged in learning activities (Center for Applied Special Technology 2003).

As an example, when the occupational therapist suggested giving Sam some other ways to sit during meeting time, Ms. Scott and Mr. Aragona decided to make those adaptations available for everyone. They realized that many kindergartners had problems sitting and staying engaged during group time. So, instead of everyone sitting cross-legged on the rug, children were encouraged to sit in chairs and against back supports, as needed. The teachers shortened the meeting times, and they introduced physical activities in addition to listening activities to keep children engaged.

The teachers thought systematically about the entire spectrum of learning styles and needs in their classroom. This helped them to **differentiate their instruction,** that is, individualize their teaching and ways of assessing what the children knew. For example, when some ELLs had difficulty replying to questions in English, the teachers had them point to pictures to demonstrate their receptive vocabulary. They encouraged the children to work with manipulatives, draw, and use graphs to show what they knew about math concepts. This approach also worked for many other children who found it difficult to answer the teachers' questions verbally. For children like Sagal, who had advanced skills in all areas, the teachers provided opportunities for extended time in listening, discussion, reading and writing, and working collaboratively with others to explore her many areas of interest in ways that kept her engaged and excited about learning. The teachers knew it was just as important for Sagal to experience challenges and stimulating experiences as it was for any other child.

Universal design is not a "one size fits all" approach.

SUMMARY

Over the first months of kindergarten, Ms. Scott and Mr. Aragona worked hard to make their classroom a safe, supportive, and inviting place for all the children. They systematically observed the children individually and as a group and learned how to work with each child's cognitive, social, emotional, linguistic, and physical strengths to help him or her develop needed skills. They formed relationships with the families, learned about the children's early lives, and began to develop a classroom community that was warm, caring, and respectful of each child. The teachers understood that some children need repetition and many opportunities for success to develop their memory for letters and numbers. Others need practice directing and maintaining their attention and planning how to accomplish a task. Some children need less guidance and seem able to demonstrate what they are learning. Others require creative strategies on the part of their teachers to show what they are learning.

UNDERSTANDING AND APPLYING CHILD DEVELOPMENT PRINCIPLES
What do teachers need to understand about child development, and how do they apply those understandings?

The study of child development tries to determine how children develop over time, what causes growth and change, and what accounts for individual differences. It rests on four principles:

1. Genetic inheritance and experience are intertwined.
2. The sequence of development is both predictable and variable.
3. The course of development can be altered.
4. All children have strengths.

Culture, temperament, and biological and environmental factors influence children's development.

DOMAINS OF DEVELOPMENT
How is knowledge of developmental domains useful to teachers?

Developmental sequences are usually separated into specific domains, or areas, such as the ones we use in this chapter: physical, social-emotional, cognitive, and language and literacy. A child's thinking, language, physical skills, feelings, social interactions, and prior knowledge are intertwined in any activity. Yet when teachers organize their many observations of a child according to separate domains of development, they can see more clearly what they are learning about that child in different areas. Knowing what each domain involves helps teachers to observe children better and to make sense of what they observe.

CHILDREN WITH SPECIAL NEEDS

What does it mean for a child to have special needs?

There is always a range of variation in development, but for some children, the variation is greater than what we would expect. Children with special needs are those who are significantly different from most other children of the same age. The Individuals with Disabilities Education Improvement Act (IDEA) specifies federal regulations that teachers must follow for the protection of children and families who need special services. Universal design creates accessible spaces and easy-to-use items for everyone regardless of ability (or disability).

FURTHER ACTIVITIES

1. Research the different rationales for the increase in autism during the past twenty years, and write out bullet points for a discussion with your classmates to air viewpoints from parents and researchers. (**NAEYC Standard 1: Promoting Child Development and Learning**)

2. Investigate what services your community provides that support young children's development (for example, early intervention, screening, home visits). Present your findings in a chart. (**NAEYC Standard 2: Building Family and Community Relationships**)

3. Visit an early childhood program for children who have special needs or an inclusive early childhood classroom. Arrange to interview a teacher. Ask the teacher how she or he assesses children's development. Find out how the teacher differentiates learning based on assessment. Write up your findings in a short paper. (**NAEYC Standard 3: Observing, Documenting, and Assessing to Support Young Children and Families**)

Observation: The Roots of Practice

Observing and recording children's behavior is the wellspring that nourishes and integrates the dual elements of a teacher's role—"doing" and "reflecting."

Dorothy Cohen and colleagues

nteracting with children—the doing of teaching—keeps teachers busy. No matter how busy they are, though, an equally important part of their job is to observe. Teachers who pay close attention to children and to their own teaching can reflect, make sense of what happens in the room, and continually adjust what they do to what they learn about the children.

Think about the baby gazing at a patch of light whose photograph opens this chapter. Look at her hands and at the position of her body. What words can you use to describe her? What could you learn from your observation of her that could shape your interactions with her?

In this chapter, you will read about how to pay systematic, focused attention to children. We will talk about how teachers record what children do and say, about how teachers carefully consider—on their own, with colleagues, or with the children's families—what they have noticed, and about how teachers act upon what they have learned from their observations.

OBSERVING AND RECORDING

What does it mean to observe and record?

Although most of us observe our surroundings as a matter of course, we always miss something. As you read the observation Natasha wrote about six-month-old Lyric, think about what makes this description different from ordinary observation and therefore useful to a teacher-caregiver:

> Lyric was leaning against the step near a clear tube that had colorful shapes inside. Every time she hit the tube, it rolled away from her, and she reached out for it. I asked her, "Are you trying to get the tube?" She kept reaching out and began to fuss when she couldn't get the tube. I then moved it closer to her. When Lyric grabbed the tube, I said, "Yeah, you got it!" She began smiling and continued to hit the tube. I placed other toys in front of her, but her gaze remained on the tube. She seemed determined to move to get the tube on her own. She was reaching out so hard that she looked as if she was superwoman flying on the floor.

Natasha sets the scene and tells you who was there and what happened. Her descriptive language helps you picture Lyric's efforts; you can imagine how the child might have felt. It's almost as if you were present yourself.

In Natasha's fine-grained, detailed observation, we see a hardworking, determined infant. We gain a sense of how competent and focused Lyric is. If you were her teacher-caregiver and made this observation, you would have some new information about Lyric to help you as you interact with her, provide her with learning materials and experiences, and support her relationships with the people around her. Observing her determination and with a keen sense of her ability to aim her body

Lyric reaches for the toy.

and coordinate her motions, you would think about where to place toys. You would also know which toys seemed to attract her the most. And you would keep observing to see when and how her interests and abilities changed.

Noticing and Describing Details

Opportunities for observations, such as the one of Lyric, occur over and over in the daily life of a classroom. Attention to detail and richness of description make a teaching observation different from just being present with your eyes and ears open. The observer notices tone of voice, quality of movement, and facial expression, along with words and actions.

Had Natasha not recorded her observation, she might have overlooked some of these details. Writing it down prompted her to notice and collect specifics that she might have ignored in the course of the daily life of the classroom.

In her observation, Natasha followed the dictum that we will discuss in more depth later in the chapter: *Describe, don't decide.* Natasha described what she saw Lyric do, but she didn't decide what it meant. She and her colleagues will have lots to discuss when she shares her detailed description with them. Then they can "decide," or interpret the observation, together and plan experiences for Lyric based on their interpretations.

Observations occur in the context of classroom activity and relationships, and those activities and relationships affect what you see when you observe. Moreover, Natasha's observation of Lyric provides a snapshot, but not a full portrait, of her because she continues to grow and develop. Natasha can recall the observation to jog her memory and think about Lyric as she changes over the coming months. Observation can lead you "beyond your expectations or assumptions to see the many dimensions of a child that are revealed over time" (Jablon, Dombro, and Dichtelmiller 2007, 7).

In the scene that follows, Anita is a kindergartner who avoids both conversations with adults and academically oriented activities at her extended day program. Her teacher, Leela, recorded the following interaction:

> "My mother face is brown and me and my dad," Anita comments as she uses the brown paint to color in the faces on her painting. "What about your brother?" I ask. "No," Anita says softly. Her tone suggests slight horror at my suggestion. "My brother not brown. And my sister not brown," she corrects me. "What color are they?" I ask. "White," she answers. "This is all-l-l the snow," continues Anita, as she paints. "I make snow right here in the grass. I make BIG snow!" Her voice is full of excitement.

Leela comments afterward that this observation supports her hunch that Anita enjoys art activities. Anita's posture and facial expressions are relaxed and calm, especially in contrast to Leela's other observations of Anita reading aloud to an adult or answering an adult's questions. Leela suspects that an **open-ended activity,** such as painting, that places no pressure on Anita and for which there are no external expectations, releases Anita to converse freely. Based on several such observations, Leela writes that the confidence Anita exuded while painting "allowed me to see a much more generous . . . side of Anita, and it is this side that I think truly reflects who she is" (Sarathy 2007).

Leela's observation of Anita painting, discussing skin color, and plunging back into her work helps Leela to become and remain attuned to the child, able to read her cues and to get to know her as an individual. Leela's written description helps her to see Anita's "uniqueness, complexity, and integrity" (Carini 2000a, 4).

Natasha's observation of Lyric provides a snapshot of her but is not a full portrait because the observation was one moment in time and Lyric continues to grow and develop.

Watching, Listening, and Analyzing

According to *Webster's New Collegiate Dictionary,* to observe means "to see or sense especially through directed analytic attention" and to "come to realize or know especially through directed analytic attention." **Analytic attention** means clear and focused concentration on unfolding events. The observer takes in information, examines it closely, and then hypothesizes about and interprets that information. Anthropology, sociology, psychology, and medical science are examples of academic disciplines that regularly use analytic attention. In the early childhood classroom, we observe *purposefully*—and are aware of ourselves doing so—rather than randomly taking in information.

When teachers observe in the early childhood classroom, they are "watching to learn" (Jablon, Dombro, and Dichtelmiller 2007, 1). That is, they observe specific actions and interactions that help them get to know and appreciate a child. What teachers learn from observation helps guide how they interact with the child. Regardless of the method, observation follows a pattern (Figure 9.1):

- Collect and record **data,** or information, as **objectively** as you can, that is, without inserting your own opinion.
- Analyze the data in a variety of ways.
- Interpret the data to make sense of them.
- Collect more data and continue the cycle.

Observing need not be a passive activity. When you visit a classroom merely to observe, the staff may ask you not to interact with the children, since you do not have an ongoing relationship with them. However, once you are in a working relationship with children, you can observe while you are involved with them. This takes some practice, but, as you saw in Natasha's and Leela's observations of Lyric and Anita, talking and listening to children (no matter how they communicate) are important aspects of observation. Remembering the details of the interaction and recording them as soon as you can after the event will provide you with valuable information to review later.

The next step after collecting data is to analyze them to make sense of what you have seen. The more explanations you and your colleagues can come up with to explain any child's behavior, the more facets you will see and the more deeply you will understand the behavior. Based on your analyses of the observations, you can then determine what materials and environments to provide and how to interact with the child most thoughtfully.

Paying analytic attention to what a child does can reveal the way he experiences the world. Every child has a unique perspective on the actions going on around him.

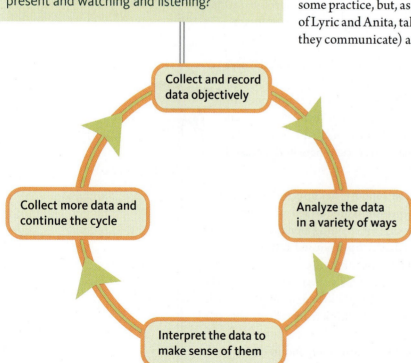

Collect and record data objectively

Analyze the data in a variety of ways

Interpret the data to make sense of them

Collect more data and continue the cycle

9.1 *The Observing Cycle*

(Left) A child standing next to Zoe has this perspective. (Right) But a teacher standing nearby has this perspective of the scene around Zoe.

When you attempt to put yourself in a child's shoes physically or emotionally or intellectually, you gain insight into that child's experience, which can help you form hypotheses about the thoughts and motives behind her behaviors. This insight can help you become attuned to a child who grapples with separation from her family, contends with the classroom and its rules, engages in relationships of all kinds with other children and adults, or rises to the challenges inherent in acquiring new skills. Take, for example, Don's observation:

> I was cleaning the tables after lunch. The toddlers were lying on their cots for nap, and Cristina asked me to read *The Runaway Bunny* to her. I told Cristina that I would read the story to her in a few minutes, and she began to whine.

Don may think it's clear that he will read to Cristina in a little while; however, Cristina may not understand the difference between a few minutes and a few seconds and may protest because she wants immediate attention. She may be tired and have less tolerance for delayed gratification of her wishes than she would at other times in the day. Perhaps she had a difficult time saying goodbye to her grandmother that morning and badly needs adult company now, just as she is about to close her eyes for yet another separation (read more about that in Chapter 11). What if, earlier that morning, Cristina had accidentally knocked over Tony's block building and

> **When you attempt to put yourself in a child's shoes, you gain insight into that child's experience.**

THOUGHT QUESTION To look at a classroom from a child's physical perspective, squat or kneel to child height and look around and up. How does the furniture look from your vantage point? How do pictures high on the walls (if there are any) appear to you now?

When you observe a child, describe what you see and hear rather than how you think the child feels.

made him cry? Maybe other children destroyed her building. When Cristina feels sad and disgruntled, a transition like the one between lunch and nap may be too hard for her without adult support.

Placing his interaction with Cristina into context, Don can try to see her point of view. His analysis may not give him ready answers but may provide some insight into Cristina's experience and lead him to temper his reaction to her demands. Don may decide to stop cleaning tables and read to Cristina until she falls asleep or is resting peacefully. If he must continue to clean the tables, he can sympathize with Cristina's wishes and talk to her about them as he works nearby, reassuring her with his presence and attention. Viewing the world from both an adult's and a child's perspective will help you gain a better understanding of children's interests, temperaments, and personalities and learn how these intersect to form the child's point of view. Awareness of the child's point of view enriches the analysis of any classroom situation.

THOUGHT QUESTION How does observing and recording a child's behavior help you to look at a situation from the child's point of view?

Describing, Not Deciding

When teachers make judgments while collecting data, personal opinion clouds the data, and the people interpreting the observation later cannot assess the situation fairly. When collecting data, limit yourself to describing the situation. Deciding and interpreting come later.

In the following example, the observer is deciding, not describing:

Markus arrived today at 8:30 a.m. When he entered the room, he was obviously still tired and angry at his mom for bringing him to school. During circle time, Markus got angry at other children and refused to listen to the story. As a result, Jonah (the assistant teacher) had to remove Markus from the circle and take him to the other side of the classroom to calm down. For the rest of the morning, Markus was tired, angry, and couldn't wait to get back home.

A less **subjective** observation—one that tries not to reflect the teacher's perspective and judgments but instead is more **objective** and describes only what has occurred—would be more informative. In this instance the observer describes the same event but avoids deciding what it means:

Markus arrived today at 8:30 a.m. When he entered the room, his eyes were halfway closed, he dragged his feet along the floor, and his mouth stretched into a wide yawn. As his mom turned to leave, Markus screamed at her and clung to her coat. During circle time, Markus began hitting Abby immediately after she sneezed loudly near his ear. Markus turned his body away from the teacher and could no longer see the book. Jonah (the assistant teacher) removed Markus from the circle and took him to the other side of the room, where Markus sucked his thumb and wrapped his arms around Jonah's shoulders. For the rest of the morning, Markus moved more slowly than usual and frequently asked, "How long 'til Mommy comes?"

In the first observation, the observer *decided* that Markus was tired and angry and couldn't wait to go home. Even the words "refused to listen" imply intentions that an observer cannot be sure of. The observer arrived at these conclusions without providing specific, concrete, and descriptive actions of Markus's behavior. The decisions that the observer made shut out the many possible explanations that could help us understand Markus's perspective that morning and that could lead his teachers to react in the best interests of him and the rest of the class.

The second observation *describes* Markus's morning, and the information collected suggests several different hypotheses. Perhaps Markus screamed and clung to his mother because he wanted her to participate in the classroom, or maybe he had not seen her the night before and was missing her deeply. Yet another possibility is that Markus had an ear infection. He was tired when he came in, he clung to his mother, he became agitated when Abby sneezed in his ear, he sucked his thumb (both a comfort measure and a way to relieve ear pressure), and he remained listless throughout the day. This hypothesis would lead you to call his mother to confer about his health and ask about his morning before he arrived at day care. Deciding what is happening while collecting information puts you at risk of misinterpreting the situation.

THOUGHT QUESTION Descriptive observation demands a large vocabulary. Children walk and run, of course, but they walk and run in lots of ways. How many different verbs can you think of that describe how children move? Compare what you have written to your classmates' lists.

Teaching Reflectively

Observations are literally food for thought. They nourish reflection and can help you determine how to adapt your teaching. When teachers reflect on their observations, they can think beyond preconceived ideas to benefit their interactions with children.

Reflection based on observation can help answer some of your questions as you work with children. Manny and Esther are two-year-olds in a half-day class. Since the group only meets twice a week, the children need plenty of time to become aware of and begin working with each other. Their smiles, hugs, and gleeful noises make it obvious to the teacher that Manny and Esther enjoy playing together. But Esther also hits Manny with her hands or with toys at least once each session. The teacher remarks to her assistant that maybe Esther is not yet able to use her words to express her frustrations and thus resorts to hitting. She recognizes that many toddlers hit other children to express their needs and wants because they cannot express their needs verbally.

This is a reasonable guess, given what the teacher knows about toddlers, but it may be inaccurate. Esther might be tired or excited. She might hit Manny when he gets too close to her or when he uses a toy that is important to her. By recording her observations, Esther and Manny's teacher can document the hitting episodes thoroughly, including what occurs before, during, and after them. She can reflect on these observations with the assistant teacher and then, based on their conclusions, change what she does.

Everyone gravitates to some theories over others, and those theories inform our documentation and our reflection, just as our documentation and reflection support one theory or another (Gandini & Goldhaber 2001). When she documents Esther and Manny's behavior, their teacher can focus on the **precursors** of (that is, what led up to) Esther's hitting. Do you remember reading about triggers and stimuli in the section about behaviorism in Chapter 6? This theory posits that a child's action is in reaction to a stimulus. Teachers who take that view might examine their records to try to figure out what stimulated Esther's hitting and then try to remove or reduce that trigger.

When teachers reflect on their observations, they can overcome prejudices and think beyond preconceived ideas to benefit their interactions with children.

Reflection includes wondering about your application of theories and questioning the way you have always taught. For example, Clarence, a second grade teacher, is preparing his class for the state's standardized language arts examination. He uses small mixed-ability reading groups of four or five to encourage the children to work together because he values what children learn from, and with, peers.

However, after observing the students in their reading groups, Clarence notices that some of the higher-level students dominate the groups. The struggling students do not participate unless asked and then talk in barely audible voices; a couple of them visibly tremble when it is their turn to read. These signs lead Clarence to speculate that the struggling students might be embarrassed to read out loud in a group. He wonders if paired reading might be a better approach. His shift to using pairs starts working: the struggling readers seem less embarrassed when paired with only one other student. Clarence observed his students' progress—and lack of it—and reflected on ways he could change his teaching to help his students learn better.

REASONS TO OBSERVE AND RECORD

Why observe and record?

The point to observation, Pat Carini (2000b, 57) writes, is

> not to scrutinize children or even to "figure them out"—and certainly not to change them into someone else. The purpose is simpler and more ordinary: to be more sensitively attuned to who they are and are becoming, so that, recognizing them as persons, we can assist and support their learning better.

Recording your observations helps you remember them so you can use them to become more attuned to and assist in children's learning. If you heard a good joke several weeks ago, you might have vowed not to forget it so you could tell it to others. But when you try to remember it later, you may find vital parts missing, reducing what was hilarious to a boring story. Although you thought you could never forget that joke, your mind is full of so many things that it can be hard to remember anything completely unless you write it down.

Interesting events occur in classrooms all the time, and teachers often feel as if they could never forget one. Yet, something else invariably crowds out the memory. Unless you record an observation that gave you insight into a child's behavior, when you try to remember it two weeks later, you may recall the larger details but forget the smaller, equally important ones. Recording observations helps us remember details. Look at all the details that Micaela included in this observation of Ayana, a new member of a combination kindergarten-first grade:

> Ayana lines up quietly against the wall. She looks around, moving her head back and forth, as her classmates line up around her. Then she slumps down onto the ground. Standing back up again, she leans over and whispers something into her friend's ear. She unzips her backpack and removes her homework folder. Then she pulls her homework out of the folder, grabbing it by the side. She leafs through her homework pages and then sticks the sheets halfway back in the folder. She then hands the homework folder and her purple folder to the teacher with the papers still splayed out of the folder.

Had she not recorded this observation, Micaela might recall her overall impression of Ayana but forget something important, such as the slump of her shoulders. That detail led Micaela to wonder what Ayana's demeanor means. Is Ayana expressing a lack of interest in school, does she feel bad about herself, or is she just tired? Micaela decides to look more closely over time to examine whether Ayana exhibits the same quiet, slouched behavior at other times.

Later in this chapter, we will look at different methods for recording observations. Each method has strengths and drawbacks, and some may be more helpful in certain situations than in others. Although these methods are useful for observing children, just writing down what you see is a great way to help you remember and be able to use your observations in any number of ways.

Another reason for observation is as a tool for understanding diversity (Jablon, Dombro, and Dichtelmiller 2007; Smidt 2005). It can be hard to determine the reasons behind a child's behavior or to figure out ways to support a child's learning and relationships within the group, especially when children and teachers come from different backgrounds. Observation can generate knowledge and understanding that leads to deepened respect for children, their families, and their ways in the world.

Observation can be a tool for drafting respectful "scripts for actions" with children (Gandini and Goldhaber 2001, 124), for becoming an effective decision maker around children, and for making changes in what you do because of what you learn about the children in your care (Jablon, Dombro, and Dichtelmiller 2007). It can help you plan curriculum, communicate with families, and grow professionally.

To Become a Skillful Learning Partner

If we allow them to, children will teach us about themselves (Gandini and Goldhaber 2001) so that we can become more skillful partners in their learning. Young children's growth and development often sneaks up on adults who expect them to be the same as they were yesterday. Observation helps teachers to think constantly about how to change what they do to match children's ever-evolving selves.

Here is how Thea describes Anna, a new student, after lunch, when her kindergarten class has a modified rest period. Anna teaches us about herself through her actions as well as her words, but, as Thea learns, every observation is only part of a growing picture:

> Anna sits quietly on the rug. Her legs are crossed and her hands are resting in her lap. Evan, another student, points to the schedule to explain "Quiet Time" to the class's new student. Anna's eyes move from Evan to her teacher. She turns and looks beside her at Adam, who is beginning to whine. She puts the collar of her cotton shirt in her mouth and chews on it. . . . The children who sit at her table are called to move from the rug to the table spots for "Quiet Time." She gets up quickly and walks immediately to her table, pulls out her chair, and sits down. She sits with one leg tucked under the other and puts her shirt collar back in her mouth. . . . Sascha says something that includes the word "jail" as Anna looks on, her eyes wide. Addressing Sascha and her other tablemate, Edward, Anna says in a whisper, "Silly is a bad word."

Thea sees that Anna watches vigilantly to see what other children do and is quick to follow rules herself, walking immediately to the table. Anna remonstrates with the others when she gets to the table, telling Sascha that silly is a bad word. From her many observations of Anna, Thea sees Anna as composed and well-mannered during classroom activities. Later, though, when Anna greedily grabs a pile of white paper, Thea wonders about other facets of her personality. Putting all her observations together, Thea can think about Anna's learning experience in the classroom in relation to the other children. She can consider how to help this new child become part of the group.

Young children's growth and development often sneaks up on adults who expect them to be the same as they were yesterday.

As Thea kept observing Anna, she got to know her better. Based on her observations, Thea initially pegged Anna as a compliant child, but, over time, she saw how Anna could use her help in relating to other children and learning about her new classroom.

A teacher who is a skilled learning partner shapes the environment to match the child, and observation enables the teacher to do that. For example, an infant with an easy-going temperament might be satisfied with lying on the floor watching the world go by for an extended period, while an infant with a high need for close physical contact might prefer being held while exploring the world. Neither temperament is better than the other. But teachers must take extra precautions to provide warm, responsive attention to children with an easy-going temperament, because they may not immediately communicate their needs. Conversely, infants who express their requirement for constant and close physical contact make it immediately clear to the teacher when they need attention. By observing these infants' temperaments, the teacher can help promote a goodness of fit, a match between the child and the learning environment.

Looking for cues about temperament helps teachers learn about and tailor learning to a child's preferences. A six-year-old who grows up on the Lakota reservation, where early childhood care is shared by several generations, may prefer playing in small groups to playing alone. While genetics may or may not contribute to her desire to play with others, certainly her home environment has something to do with it. A teacher who observes this child in action and learns more about her temperament may not be so quick to judge when the girl hesitates to participate in solitary activities. A preschooler with a "slow-to-warm-up" temperament may not participate fully in circle, and the teacher who notices can better understand the reasons if she is aware of the boy's temperament. The teacher can plan ways to help the child gradually enter into activities in ways that do not provoke his sensitivities. Insights about a child's temperament help teachers appropriately adjust their curriculum, techniques, and environment and can strengthen the teacher-child bond.

To Frame Experiences and Interactions

Precisely and comprehensively recorded observations make an excellent assessment tool on which to base classroom experiences and interactions and to develop curriculum. In early childhood, the environment makes an essential contribution to the curriculum. Your observations can shape it, too.

Observations can help ensure that the curriculum is relevant and respectful of children's life experiences. Imagine moving from the city to teach in the country and planning a preschool study of public transportation. A little observation reveals that your rural students do not have access to a public bus system. While exposing the children to new options is an important goal of early schooling, it makes more sense to listen to the children as they talk about tractors, riding mowers, and trucks and to ask questions to elicit their stories about riding on the tractor with daddy or sitting in the truck with mommy. Once the children share their own experiences and become interested in transportation, the teacher can move on to experiences outside the children's known interests, such as learning about public transportation.

As you will read in Chapter 10, *assessment* shapes early childhood curriculum. Teachers assess

- what children know, can do, and are predisposed to learn and
- how planned or spontaneous activities affect children and their learning.

Observations can help ensure that the curriculum is relevant and respectful of children's life experiences.

Observational records document teachers' ongoing assessment. They are the most regular source of information about children and classroom life. Observations occur in the **natural setting**, the classroom, which makes them a reliable source of information about children, in contrast to a test on a day when a child did not eat breakfast. Of course, teachers have an inexhaustible supply of observational material.

Planning curriculum

Teachers observe in order to guide and adjust their curriculum planning. In early childhood, "curriculum . . . includes everything that happens in the early childhood setting" (Billman and Sherman 2003, 233). Teachers develop the most meaningful curriculum and organize their environments best when they realize what interests the children. For instance, at a campus-based program, the young toddlers' room overlooks the university's loading dock. At first, the teachers bemoaned the dismal view, but the children's actions and words demonstrated that nothing could be more interesting to them than watching trucks arrive and seeing their loads moved to and from the dock. Comparable trucks in the block area and books about trucks and their deliveries began turning the room's location and the teachers' observations of the children's interests into rich toddler curriculum.

In addition to organized and spontaneous activities, curriculum planning includes (but is not limited to) schedules, routines, and defining goals and expectations. Observing helps you adjust your classroom schedule to better meet the needs of the children and staff in your classroom. Your observations will help you analyze the routines, too.

As children participate in daily activities they demonstrate their knowledge and abilities. Observant teachers use this information to develop curriculum.

For example, in a mixed-age group of twos, threes, and fours, the transition from lunch to nap felt chaotic. The teachers observed that a few children finished quickly, used the bathroom, reentered the room, and began jumping on cots, while several others lagged at the table after everyone else had left. All the other children finished lunch at the same time, and the bathroom became overcrowded and noisy.

Analyzing their observations at a staff meeting, the teachers developed a plan. One teacher followed the group that finished lunch first to the bathroom. A second teacher sent more children to the bathroom gradually; and, once the first teacher moved on to the classroom, the second teacher went into the bathroom, reminding children to go back to the room as they were ready. A third teacher stayed with the slowest eaters, cleaning up the lunch area while they finished eating. The transition went smoothly after that.

States, districts, and teachers have goals and expectations for their students. One common goal for first grade students is oral reading with reasonable fluency (NAEYC and IRA 1998). If children are to achieve that goal, the classroom needs a multitude of books in the range of first graders' reading levels. Observing a student's interest in and ability to read a particular text tells a teacher whether that book is too easy or too difficult. Providing children with and helping them select appropriate reading material enables teachers to meet goals and expectations in a way that is less stressful and more realistic for children.

Teachers who work together with a group of children or who teach children of the same age in different classrooms learn a lot when they meet with one another.

Careful, descriptive observations of children enrich these meetings and enable teachers to discuss classroom environments and curriculum more effectively.

Changing the environment

A classroom's physical and social environment affects children's behavior both positively and negatively. Observations can help teachers make that environment a more effective place for children to develop and learn.

Environment is not just the physical space of the classroom. It includes several different aspects of daily life. Classic rating scales (Harms, Clifford, and Cryer 1998, 2005; Harms, Jacobs, and Romano 1995) each contain more than forty items observers use to rate a classroom's environment. Some areas to observe are peer-to-peer interaction, adult-child interaction, caregiving routines, program structure, provisions for children with special needs, and use of physical space. For example, the Early Childhood Environment Rating Scale–Revised (ECERS-R) describes developmentally meaningful interactions for teachers to look for in their classroom (Figure 9.2). One such interaction is whether adults help children develop social skills with peers—for example, helping children to talk through conflicts instead of fighting.

Observation tools such as the ECERS help teachers improve specific aspects of their classroom's environment. For example, if a teacher realizes that she warmly greets most, but perhaps not all, children, her objective might be to greet each child individually as they enter the room. This kind of direction is particularly helpful for new teachers, who may not be sure how to go about improving their classroom's environment. These rating tools guide teachers' observations, providing a framework for analyzing their classroom's environment.

> If a teacher realizes that she warmly greets most, but perhaps not all, children, her objective might be to greet each child individually as they enter the room.

Encouraging Children to Communicate: Rating scale for classroom environment

1	2	3	4	5	6	7
inadequate		minimal		good		excellent

1.1 No activities used by staff with children to encourage them to communicate (Ex. no talking about drawings, dictating stories, sharing ideas at circle time, finger plays, singing songs).

1.2 Very few materials accessible that encourage children to communicate.

3.1 Some activities used by staff with children to encourage them to communicate.

3.2 Some materials accessible to encourage children to communicate.

3.3 Communication activities are generally appropriate for the children in the group.

5.1 Communication activities take place during both free play and group times (Ex. child dictates story about painting; small group discusses trip to store).

5.2 Materials that encourage children to communicate are accessible in a variety of interest centers (Ex. small figures and animals in block area; puppets and flannel board pieces in book area; toys for dramatic play outdoors or indoors).

7.1 Staff balance listening and talking appropriately for age and abilities of children during communication activities (Ex. leave time for children to respond; verbalize for child with limited communication skills).

7.2 Staff link children's spoken communication with written language (Ex. write down what children dictate and read it back to them; help them write note to parents).

9.2 *Encouraging Children to Communicate: Rating scale for classroom environment*
Item from the ECERS-R Language-Reasoning Subscale for Rating Classroom Environment
From: Harms, Clifford, and Cryer 1998

To Communicate with Families and Colleagues

Observing and recording children's behavior also helps teachers prepare for informal and formal communication with children's families. And observational records, and discussions about them, also increase communication within the teaching team and with other professionals who work with the children and their families.

Informal communication with families

Teachers frequently use observations to ground informal discussions about a child's classroom experiences. Generally, these discussions are brief conversations that occur when a child is dropped off or picked up at school. In a preschool classroom, observation notes can help a teacher answer a family's question, "How did my child do in school today?" Instead of responding with "Great!" the teacher can say, "He worked for twenty-five minutes with the cubes. He had a special pattern that he repeated. We saved them so you could see it." Most families appreciate the specificity, and children usually beam with pride as they show family members their work.

Such observations give depth to an informal conversation and help parents feel connected to their child's daily classroom experiences. This connection generally translates to better parent-child communication outside the classroom, which in turn contributes to the child's in-class success.

Informal conversations are just the time for observations that do not raise thorny issues—for example, when a teacher observes a child designing ornate structures in the block area or notices how happy another child becomes after seeing the animals on a class trip to the zoo. Too often, teachers talk to families about their child only when a problem or potential problem arises—for example, when an infant has poor muscle tone, when a three-year-old is still biting others, or when a second grader is not reading. What if, instead, Mary contacted Emil's mother just to let her know about his day? Emil is nearly five and has been diagnosed with cerebral palsy. Although Mary meets regularly with Emil's mother about his individualized education program, she wants to provide ongoing information to the family. Mary would like to share the following observation with Emil's mother:

> Emil was in the block area. He grabbed his walker but couldn't get past a group of children at the art table. I offered to move the chairs, but Emil puffed out his cheeks and walked around the room to the rug, where children had scattered dress-up clothing and hollow blocks. He dropped to a crawling position. Oscar came face to face with Emil, pulled out a harmonica, and began to play. Emil asked Oscar, "Can you get some food for the monster? He really likes food. Get some food. He loves pickles." Holding out a plastic cob of corn, Emil instructed Oscar to cut it in half and to get a pickle. Emil continued to talk as Oscar played his harmonica. When I announced cleanup time, the two boys picked up plastic food, pretended to eat it, dropped it into a basket, and giggled.

Careful observations will help you share children's strengths with their families and learn more about the children in conversation with their families. These seemingly insignificant conversations can be powerful tools for making families feel connected to what happens when their children are away from them. A series of casual remarks about a child's work and interactions builds a picture for families of who their child is in school. Teachers who feel uncomfortable sharing information casually or who cannot find

Too often, teachers talk to families about their child only when a problem or potential problem arises.

THOUGHT QUESTION If you were Mary, how would you use your observation with Emil's mother? Would you give it to her in writing? Would you reword it? Would you give her your interpretation of it? Role-play with a partner, speaking as if you were Mary and your classmate were Emil's mother. Then discuss your reasons for what you have said.

the time or place to do so should look for other ways to share their observations, such as in quick notes home, telephone calls, or email.

Formal communication with families

Several types of formal communication help teachers disclose information to parents and concerned individuals. You will read more about formal communication with parents in Chapter 14. Here we will talk about the kinds of observations that support working together with children's families.

Parent-teacher conferences give teachers the chance to discuss a child's growth, development, strengths, and areas in need of improvement. Such conferences also provide parents with an opportunity to share more with the teacher about a child's home experiences and to discuss any worries they have. Teachers help alleviate parental fear or concerns when they use their observations as a source of positive anecdotal stories about a child. Such stories help parents feel comfortable and enable them to bond with their child's teachers.

THOUGHT QUESTION What observations do you want to have on file to be prepared for a parent-teacher conference?

When discussions turn to more difficult topics, recounting a specific observation can help teachers talk clearly about the situation. Teachers concerned about a child benefit from sharing their observations with the rest of the classroom team, supervisors, and specialists before they broach the subject with the family. And when they speak to the family, it should be in a prearranged meeting where they and the family formally discuss observations that might form the basis for referrals, behavior management, or some other action.

Observational records provide specifics for families to consider instead of generalizations, which can sound like accusations. Rather than telling parents that their child hits other children, a teacher can discuss when and where the child has hit others and can speculate with the parents about the child's reasons for doing it. Observations enable a teacher to tell parents the precise actions that precede the hitting. Then teachers and parents can find ways to reduce this behavior, both in the classroom and at home, by watching for events that typically come before the behavior. They also can agree to share future observations.

Observational records provide specifics for families to consider instead of generalizations, which can sound like accusations.

Another way to provide families with information is through written communication. Although they can be used in any setting, daily-journal notebooks typically help teachers communicate with parents they don't see every day—for instance, in settings where children are bussed to a school far from their home or when children are dropped off by a nanny or babysitter. Teachers jot down notes, observations, and questions and send the notebook home with a child regularly. Parents also write their own responses, notes, and questions in the journal. Teachers keep up the conversation, writing back and forth and sharing their observations of a child with the family. This type of formal communication helps strengthen the bond between home and school, thus benefiting the child.

In infant/toddler programs, in addition to a daily log or wall chart that families can write on when they bring in their baby and can glance over at the end of the day, some teacher-caregivers write a paragraph or two of observations for families to take home. Some family members have commented that they save these notes with other precious documents of their child's babyhood. Working parents, in particular, cherish observations of moments in their children's lives that they feel they are missing.

In addition, teachers turn to their observations when they refer children and families for services that are not available in the classroom. They may also use their observations to determine if a family needs other help, such as social services, financial assistance, emotional support, or nutritional counseling. The referral process might resemble the next example.

October 10th

Dear Marcia and Steve,

I haven't written in the book for a week or two, and wanted to let you know how I see Ben's adjustment. He is engaging in more activities with other children, and appears more open to explore materials that he shunned a few weeks ago. I observed him in free play this morning. Roberta filled me in about the am outing and lunch.

Just following his activities this am tells us a lot. He began to play alone with the beaded structure and soon Jim and Pete joined him. He smiled and moved over, making space for them. The three of them then moved over to the block area and built a simple ramp, placing three rectangular blocks on the bottom. Together, they then added three slanted rectangular blocks on top and voila!

Ben then walked across the room to get a small car and slid it down the ramp repeatedly, clearly demonstrating a goal with a plan to achieve it.

After free play and snack, then circle time, the smaller group went out to the church to see the peacocks and explore the end of the season garden. Ben saw a worm and initiated the word "worm." That made for a great group discussion during lunch, where he became the center of the conversation.

We are all aware of how busy you are with the new baby on its way, but when you have a moment, let me know how things are going for Ben at home.

Best wishes,

Karen

Karen, the special education teacher, uses her observations as the basis of a note to Ben's parents in this journal.

PARENT'S DAILY REPORT

Child's name: Josh

Date: 6/8

Drop off: Dad   Pick up: Mom

Last fed: brought Cheerios and berries

Last slept: woke up 6:30

Any special comments or instructions?

All weekend he was obsessed with the book Everybody Poops (!)

CHILD'S DAILY REPORT

Activities: water play
              Ubblick
              Helped Sue make
              pancakes (w. Peter & Clöe)

Nap: 2 hrs

Eating: Toileting:
ate all his sandwich   dry all day
and juice

General comments:

Josh told everyone about the new fish tank and fish you got over the weekend. He knows how to feed fish and is very proud.
— Martha

Observations also help teachers write quick reports home.

Ms. Johnson, a first grade teacher, has concerns about Joanne. During group discussions, Joanne has difficulty articulating certain speech sounds. Over the past four months, Ms. Johnson has not noticed any improvement. After keeping anecdotal records of Joanne's language, Ms. Johnson decides to use the observations to discuss her concerns with her assistant principal. The assistant principal then uses Ms. Johnson's observations to discuss Joanne with her family. Joanne's mother and stepfather agree that evaluation would be in Joanne's best interest. The assistant principal refers Joanne to a speech therapist for evaluation, and the speech therapist determines that Joanne would benefit from speech therapy.

Ms. Johnson's detailed observations of Joanne's language difficulties are convincing and get Joanne the services she needs. The teacher's observations could just as easily have revealed that Joanne did not need special services. A collection of observations helps teachers go beyond their feelings about a child to think concretely about what a child does and says.

Communication with colleagues

One teacher's observations of a child are useful to all the adults who work with that child. When teachers record observations and read each other's documentation, they can see what someone else has noticed in the course of the busy day that they did not. When a teacher and an assistant teacher in the same classroom look at their observations together, they benefit from each other's information and can share their points of view while at the same time cementing their working relationship.

Keeping in mind guidelines for **confidentiality**—disclosure of information only to those professionals and family members who are authorized to know it—teachers generally share observations with other teaching staff, with supervisors, and sometimes with parents or other primary caregivers. Children's educational records can follow them throughout their schooling, and observations are a vital part of a child's overall academic record. Teacher observations also might be shared with authorities who investigate child abuse and neglect.

Some of the most engrossing staff meetings you attend will involve a discussion of one teacher's observation of a child that attending staff interpret together. When the focus is on an individual child, everyone can contribute. The student teacher, teachers, and director all will have observed the child at one time or another. Their specific roles mean that they bring various perspectives to the discussion. Then, too, their different backgrounds, experience, and professional training will lead them to see different things.

Interpreting a child's behavior is a bit like putting together an unusual puzzle—unusual in that you can assemble it, take it apart again, and reassemble it in many ways. Working with others to put that puzzle together gives you more potential solutions. It also acknowledges everyone's expertise and builds the professional classroom community. Think back to Don's observation of Cristina. A staff meeting about Cristina and her after-lunch transition could help Don see possibilities that would not otherwise occur to him.

To Develop Professionally

Observation challenges teachers to think about what they are doing and then to tailor their teaching practice to fit the children they serve. Observation is part of the informal research in which teachers regularly engage. It is part of their professional development.

Observation is part of the informal research in which teachers regularly engage. It is part of their professional development.

For many, the words *professional growth and development* summon images of conferences, additional college credits, or a promotion. But growth also comes from daily effort. Through observation, you learn which teaching methods work well in your classroom and which may need improvement. Through observation, you begin to see how your habits and beliefs affect the children and other adults in your room. As you observe children and think about what you are learning about them, you will reflect, too, on yourself, your reactions, your previous experiences as a child, and perhaps on your experiences as a parent. You will learn a great deal about yourself. This increasing self-awareness will, in turn, give you more insight into children as well as into your effectiveness as a teacher-caregiver (Jablon, Dombro, and Dichtelmiller 2007).

Observation helps teachers grow in other ways, too. Additional knowledge about a child and children in general can increase your flexibility (Borich 2003) and help you to develop an "attitude of openness" (Jablon, Dombro, and Dichtelmiller 2007, 6). The more you observe individuals and groups of children and the more able you are to look at things from their perspectives, the more accepting and understanding you can become of all children. Knowing them and yourself better can let you listen to children more easily, and it can make your relationships with them increasingly authentic and natural.

In order to grow, teachers must do more than observe children's and their own behavior and consider how these behaviors affect individual children and the classroom as a whole. The next step is for teachers to use their observations to change their own behavior. Constant, consistent observation helps you evolve over time. It also assists you in recognizing how much you have grown as a teacher. In addition, observation makes you aware of how much you *don't* know about children and their families, which keeps you interested in learning more about them (Sowa 1999). Observation makes teaching and caregiving invigorating and thought provoking, and it helps teachers remain engaged in their work.

THE HOW OF OBSERVING AND RECORDING

What is important to observe, and what can guide your observations?

If observing is a special kind of watching and listening, one that enables teachers to analyze what they have observed and take action based on those observations, then how do teachers go about observing? What should teachers observe, and what guidelines should they follow?

First, teachers have a professional responsibility to respect confidentiality. Second, teachers must take their biases into account as they observe, but to do that they must first be aware of those biases. Finally, repeated observation is important. When teachers collect many observations over time, they gain a fuller picture of a child's behavior than any one observation, no matter how rich, can give them. Continuing to observe can keep teachers from jumping to unwarranted conclusions about a child.

What to Observe and Record

Follow your instincts as you decide what and when to observe. Observation is one way to enhance the relationship you have with children, and your feelings are the best guide to what is important (Jablon, Dombro, and Dichtelmiller 2007). Anything that interests or intrigues you about children is worth learning about.

For example, watching how a child uses the housekeeping area gives the teacher a wealth of information about how the child views the world. A child who has dolls

> The more you observe individuals and groups of children and the more able you are to look at things from their perspectives, the more accepting and understanding you can become of all children.

and stuffed animals sit in specific chairs and asks his classmates to do particular household chores may see the world around him in an organized fashion and have a temperament that thrives on schedules and predictability. A child who jumps from activity to activity in the manipulatives area may be investigating the possibilities before settling into constructive play, might have attention issues, or might be bored and need more challenging manipulatives. By observing the child's interactions with the world around her, the teacher begins to develop a fuller sense of the child and can decide how to adjust the classroom environment accordingly.

- When a child plays alone, is he fully invested in solitary play? Is his play self-directed? Does he figure out ways to maintain interest in an activity and to problem-solve?
- How does a child use her body in space? Is she a seven-year-old who frequently trips while walking or a two-year-old who runs up and down stairs with ease? When sitting in a large group, does she sit or lie on top of other students and need to be redirected to keep her body to herself?

These are the types of questions teachers ask themselves to direct their observations.

In most cases, observers need objectives, whether they state them formally or not. Educators who clarify their objectives before beginning to observe can decide more easily which method of observation will be most effective, how much time they will need, and how to prepare to observe. Objectives also help teachers maintain focus during the observation.

A teacher's objective might be to gather developmental information, to understand a burgeoning relationship, or to solve a classroom management problem. An objective might be as simple as observing "to see if Tina is smiling yet" and recording the finding as an answer on a checklist. An adult who does not know much about Tina's play might achieve the objective of learning more about it by keeping a running record of everything Tina does as she lies on a blanket in the middle of the infant room. The teacher's objective determines which observational method to use.

As you verbalize your objectives for observations, remember that everything children do is worth observing. Observe and record children's:

- transitions to the classroom in the morning and how they leave at the end of the day;
- routines—eating, sleeping, hand washing, using the toilet, moving from one activity to another;
- activities and use of materials, both the choices children make and the ways in which they conduct themselves;
- language; and
- interactions with adults and other children.

In the same way, everything you and other adults do is worth observing. Pay close attention to your behavior throughout the day, analyze it, interpret it, and decide what is worth continuing and what you want to change.

Respecting Confidentiality

As you observe and collect information about children, confidentiality is essential. The International Organization for Standardization defines confidentiality as "ensuring that information is accessible only to those authorized to have access"

(KnowledgeLeader 2007). All members of a teaching team have that authorization. They need observations to recognize a child's strengths and areas of concern and to plan curriculum together.

Who else may have access to your observations of children? The answer follows logically from the purposes of observation discussed earlier in this chapter. The teaching team's supervisors, such as principals and directors, have authorization because their job is to support teachers in their interaction with children, in curriculum development, and in growing professionally. Consultants or specialists to whom you refer a child need your observations. You will share observations with family members as examples of their child's behavior, but first you will think about how to word the observations so that family members hear them in the spirit you intend. You also may include observations in a child's portfolio that is passed on to future teachers.

Who is *not* authorized to have access to your observations? You may share them with teachers in other classrooms if they are helping you to think through a situation, as was the case with Michael's teachers in Chapter 6, but not for the sake of idle gossip. Do not share information about a child with another child's family. In particular, do not discuss a referral with other teachers, with other children's parents, or with anyone outside the school community who is not directly involved in the referral process.

Confidentiality is an issue for college students as well as for teachers. Students often are in field placements in their communities or at the college child care program or lab school and in these placements are privy to information about children and families that is meant for professional use only. Sometimes students are tempted to talk outside of class about their observation, for example, of a friend's child, but observations made as a student or as a teacher are confidential. In addition, all discussion of children within the college classroom must remain in that classroom.

Being Aware of and Examining Biases

Everyone has biases for and against people, things, and situations. We are not born with biases, but we acquire them at an early age through interactions with our environment. Since it is impossible to eliminate all biases, a more realistic goal is to be aware of and examine them to try to reduce their effect on your observations and behavior.

Observation can help you understand the motivation behind a child's behavior, if you first take your biases into account to ensure that your analysis is fair. It is natural to like a certain child more than other children when that child seems to understand intuitively what it is we expect from him. Some teachers prefer the child who rarely creates problems in the room, follows rules, and maintains an even temperament. Some teachers are influenced by a child's appearance, preferring a well-groomed child to one whose nose runs all the time. Some teachers are more comfortable working with children of a similar cultural background because of comparable disciplinary styles, lifestyles, and academic expectations. While observation may not directly help teachers recognize their biases, analyzing an observation can help you recognize patterns that may indicate a bias.

THOUGHT QUESTION Tim's father noticed Esther hitting Manny and spoke to you about it. The father is worried that Esther might hit Tim or that Tim will learn to hit other children. What would you say to Tim's dad?

THOUGHT QUESTION What is your bias?

Think for a moment about children with whom you have bonded immediately. What are the characteristics of children you like to work with? What do you think draws you to them?

Now think about a child you find unappealing or difficult to work with. What was it about this child that you found unappealing or difficult? Did the child's behavior remind you of someone or of something in yourself that you don't like?

As teachers, we are not supposed to have favorite students; we are expected to see each child for his or her strengths and abilities. Of course, there are always the "difficult" students—those with whom we struggle because they present behavior that makes it hard for us to do our jobs. Perhaps worse than categorizing students as problematic would be to have a "least favorite" student—someone who, for personal reasons, one simply dislikes. What can you do about someone who just rubs you the wrong way?

I have such a student. She is not one of the attention-demanding ones, nor is she a struggling student. Victoria is a quiet child who follows directions, works well independently, and meets grade-level academic standards. Yet, while I have forged a connection with almost all my students, I cannot seem to find any endearing qualities in Victoria.

What is perhaps most surprising about my reaction is that Victoria comes from a background very similar to my own. In fact, Victoria is the student whose background most resembles mine: she is American-born Chinese. The way Victoria performs well on tasks that demand right answers but loses confidence in open-ended activities, her quiet competitiveness when interacting with peers, the way her parents seem concerned only about the standardized tests, the fact that she plays violin—all this feels so familiar to me.

There are the more subtle behaviors, too: the way Victoria scrutinizes those around her so that she can mimic behavior or gain advantage. The reason I recognize these behaviors is because I engaged in them as a child. As I spent my childhood striving to be "truly American," I constantly studied other children to see what made Americans *American,* and what made the Chinese I knew so *un-American.* Victoria's behaviors confirm the discoveries I made in my personal lifelong study. Whatever the behavior—quiet, outgoing, mean, silly—the American kids' actions seemed to come naturally. Unlike us, American kids didn't have to create themselves, because, in the end, they belonged here; we were the foreigners always striving to find our place. Among non-Asians, Chinese kids (including me) always seemed so self-conscious and out of place, and anything resembling a personality seemed contrived.

If I identify with Victoria's struggle for identity, why would I react to it with such distaste? It would seem, in understanding her position, that I would feel more of a connection to her. Instead, the words that come to mind when I think of Victoria are the ones I always heard my mother use to criticize someone: "Such a selfish girl." "So stubborn." When Victoria refuses to speak during whole-group discussions, even when I carefully offer her "easy" entry points, I am irritated by her "stubbornness." When she demands to play another game during gym because she doesn't like

Elaine Chu

the one we're playing, I think "selfish." Victoria's conduct calls to mind my own childhood behaviors that were labeled selfish and stubborn, so much so that I, too, now see them this way.

When I finally realized that what made Americans truly American was an independence of thought and action, I began to actively cultivate this quality. I still remember the day in high school when a friend asked me why I alway agreed with what everyone said. It was embarrassing to be confronted so directly, but it gave me the determination to change this "defect of character," which happens to be a respected trait in many Eastern societies. It probably wasn't until college—when I learned to think critically and to engage in discourse and debate—that I achieved the qualities so valued in our society. It was really only then that I finally felt American.

If other kids in the class are "following the crowd," I might attribute it to age-appropriate behavior to establish one's identity among one's peers, but when I observe this behavior in Victoria, I am put off by her lack of authenticity. I worked hard to eradicate this in myself, and Victoria brings back the memories of this painful past. Rather than eliciting feelings of compassion for someone who may feel foreign and out of place in her native world, I am instead disgusted by behaviors that I long ago determined were deficits within me.

It turns out that my least favorite student is not Victoria, but me—or the way I used to be. While I may possess a particular understanding of Victoria due to our similar backgrounds, I have projected a great deal of myself onto her for the same reason. The challenge now is to see her for who she is. I have begun to do some observation and recording of Victoria. I hope that the nonjudgmental stance observation demands will allow me a glimpse of who this child is.

I hope that in pursuing an honest examination of these complex, deeply rooted issues, not only will I react less to my personal history, but I will have the opportunity to recreate my own narrative so that I do not need to deny aspects of myself and, in doing so, deny my students.

A teacher might think that a child who has little difficulty in class is not a priority when it comes to observation. However, all children deserve thoughtful attention. A fours teacher named Harold kept a small notebook in his back pocket. When he noticed something he wanted to remember, he jotted it down. At the end of each week, he recorded his observations in the loose-leaf notebooks the class used for observations of children. Then Harold listed the children he had *not* observed that week and determined to observe them the following week. Noticing that Luz was often missing from his list, he tried to figure out what it was that made him overlook her.

Think about the cycle shown in Figure 9.3: Who we are and what we believe affects how we observe. What we observe (as long as we are giving it analytic attention) can affect our understanding of our biases and help us to change them. Glenda Mac Naughton (2003, 203) reminds us that an anti-bias view

> assumes that we can only ever have partial knowledge of the child and that to create socially just and equitable relationships with children requires educators to seek multiple perspectives on the child, including their own.

Subjectivity, the way you see things from your unique position in the world, influences how you observe. In *Fish Is Fish,* a children's book by Leo Lionni, a frog goes out into the world. When he returns to the pond where he grew up with the fish, the frog tells his old friend about what he saw. As the fish listens, he filters the frog's report through his subjective fish lens: the illustrations show the fish imagining birds, cows, and even people equipped with fins, scales, tails, and other fishy characteristics. Each of us does the same: we filter the world through our own lens, adding our respective versions of fins, scales, and tails to whatever we observe.

Our subjectivity even determines what we notice, that is, what we choose to observe in the first place. We don't record everything we see and hear. We can't! We screen out aspects of our environment, record observations based on what is important to us, and are usually unaware of that selection process. Examining one's subjectivity and biases takes effort and reflection, but descriptive observation based on analytic attention is not effective unless teachers are aware of their own perspectives and the effect of those perspectives on their observations of and interactions with children. Thus we strive for diminishing subjectivity, since it is impossible to erase one's point of view completely (Mac Naughton 2003).

To make your subjectivity clear, you can use phrases such as "I think . . ." and "I believe . . ." and "it seems to me . . ." and "the child appears to. . . ." These let your listener or reader know that you understand that your observations and your interpretations of your observations reflect your understandings and are not objective truth.

Observing Continuously over Time

An accumulation of observations over an extended period reveals details and variations you may not have noticed at first.

Who we are and what we believe affects how we observe

What we observe (as long as we are giving it analytic attention) can affect our understanding of our biases

Observation can help us change our biases

9.3 *How Observation Changes Us*

This is because your increasing familiarity with each child helps you to know him better and because a series of observations will reveal patterns of behavior. Take, for instance, Dorothy's summary after several months of observing six-year-old Tom:

> The word *excited* best describes Tom's tone of voice in most situations throughout the school day. When Tom decided to use the wooden kangaroo, he called excitedly across the block area to Gracie and Mia and then told Stew about the kangaroo in the same excited tone. This excitement is also evident in a later observation when, after reading a book about a grandpa with false teeth, Tom exclaimed excitedly that his mom could take out two of her teeth. Another day he told me at least four times in a very excited tone that he was going to play at John's house after school. On yet another occasion, when he wanted Ike to feel the underside of the snake, he blurted excitedly in a high-pitched tone, "Feel right there!" When making a paper box, he said spiritedly and with great enthusiasm, "I still can't believe I made this!" Even when he exhibited uncharacteristically sluggish and dreamy behavior during dismissal one day, he showed a glimmer of his usual excited self as he said "da, da, da, da" while walking in the class line.

You can see that Dorothy is not jumping to a conclusion about Tom. She has lots of evidence, or data, to support her. Her idea of Tom is built from concrete descriptions of his words and behaviors. As she observes him, she looks for patterns that could be meaningful and useful in knowing him as a learner and a member of the classroom community.

However, sometimes patterns of behavior can get in the way of working well with a child, and this is something to watch for. Your observations can help you here, too:

> Len was a sturdily built four-year-old who often pushed his way into spaces, shoving other children out of his way. Once, as an observer was watching a group of children with a teacher at the play dough table, Len approached, and Gloria suddenly began to cry. Another child quickly explained that Len had pushed Gloria, and the teacher began to speak seriously to Len. What the observer noticed, though, was that despite Len's history of pushing, this time he was not the culprit. Len's pattern of behavior led children and teacher alike to stereotype him as someone who pushes. Close observation revealed otherwise.

THE PRACTICALITIES OF OBSERVING AND RECORDING

What do observing and recording look like in action?

Teachers can choose from a variety of ways to record observations. The range enables them to document what they see and hear in the way that best serves their purpose. Likewise, teachers can choose how to **synthesize**, or put together and make sense of, their findings. They also have a variety of strategies for making observing and recording part of their work with children.

Selecting Methods

We describe several of the most popular methods for recording observations in this section. Each method has its strengths and weaknesses, and some are more useful in

An accumulation of observations over an extended period can reveal patterns of behavior.

TABLE 9.1   Methods of Observing

METHOD	TYPE	DESCRIPTION	ADVANTAGES	DISADVANTAGES
Running record	Narrative	A precise description of everything a teacher observes, recorded while the teacher sits and watches	Highly detailed	Time consuming; teacher can't interact while observing
Anecdotal record	Narrative	Short observation, usually written after the fact	Can be done informally and quickly while interacting with children; a series of anecdotals reveals patterns and unexpected behaviors	Can be unsystematic; teachers must pay attention to their subjectivities and biases
Diary/journal	Narrative	Observations and reflections that a teacher records regularly	Comprehensive and ongoing	Time consuming; teachers must pay attention to their subjectivities and biases
Event sampling	Structured	A record of only one type of event each time it occurs	Focusing on an event can help teachers understand when and why it occurs	Provides no information beyond the event in question
Checklist	Structured	Predetermined criteria to watch for and mark off as they occur	Easy to use; helps teachers watch for behaviors they might otherwise overlook	Limits observation to the criteria on the checklist; no descriptive details are available later
Media	Use of media	Video, audio, and photographs of children and their activities and interactions	Depicts the event as it occurred; is attractive; families appreciate receiving copies	Limited to the view and scope the camera operator or audio equipment captures

certain situations than in others. For example, event sampling allows the teacher to pinpoint particular behaviors. Keeping a journal or diary allows the teacher to take in what is happening in a holistic way and then reflect in writing about her sense of what she saw. Knowing something about each of these methods (Table 9.1) helps teachers decide which to choose, depending on the circumstances. Regardless of which method a teacher uses, the overriding goal is to direct analytic attention to the situation and to gain insight into a child's experience.

Narrative records

Narrative records (the first three methods in Table 9.1) require a teacher to write. In a **running record,** the teacher writes down exactly what she sees for a period of time. An **anecdotal record,** like most of the observations you have read in this chapter, describes one event or occurrence and is usually written after the fact. In a **diary** or **journal,** the teacher regularly records what happens and includes his commentary or musings.

A running record is particularly useful when observing within a short time frame because the teacher writes down every action that occurs exactly as it happens. A running record is highly detailed, and a five-minute block of time may be all that's needed to gather significant information. While writing a running record, the

> A running record is particularly useful when observing within a short time frame because the teacher writes down every action that occurs exactly as it happens.

teacher has to focus all his attention on the child or children being observed. Producing a running record takes time, concentration, and practice. It is almost impossible to do while interacting with children.

A student enrolled in an early childhood class has an assignment to observe a three-year-old in a classroom setting. Here is an example of her running record:

> Eleni entered the classroom at 8:19 a.m. She put her coat in her cubby, ambled over to the block area, and sat on the floor, crossing her legs like a pretzel. She picked up two rectangular blocks in her right hand and one square block in her left hand. She looked at the photograph of the Eiffel Tower on the wall, placed the rectangular blocks on the floor in front of her and the square block on the floor beside her, picked up additional rectangular blocks, and began placing rectangular blocks on top of each other, making a tower. She stopped to look at the Eiffel Tower photograph about once every sixty seconds. Mike, John, and Taina were also working in the block area, but Eleni did not talk to them. At 8:31 a.m. she put the blocks back on the shelves, first placing each block on a shape label on the shelf. She then walked to her teacher, pulled the teacher's skirt, and pointed toward the bathroom. The teacher said, "You have to use the bathroom, Eleni?" to which Eleni nodded her head.

What has the student learned about Eleni from this observation? During the time period, Eleni constructed a building based on a photograph. She set a task for herself and completed it. She did not communicate verbally with anyone. However, Eleni demonstrated her receptive language skills when she nodded her head in reply to the teacher's question. Based on this short observation, the student may decide to spend more time observing Eleni's verbal skills. You can imagine that without the directed focus of a running record, adults could overlook Eleni's quiet but directed work and that her simple affirmative nod easily could be lost in a bustling classroom.

Unlike running records, anecdotals are brief written notes. They include the date and time of the observation, who was observed, what the children were doing, and what the children were talking about or communicating about in other ways (Henniger 2005). A teacher may jot down just a few words to remind her of an event and expand the notation when she records it later. Many teachers find anecdotals helpful for figuring out how particular aspects of the classroom curriculum affect individual children or groups of children.

For example, Ms. Brown, a second-grade teacher, is teaching a unit on poetry. During writing time, children work in pairs and write poems about winter. As Ms. Brown walks around the classroom listening and watching, she notices that Franklin and Martha are having a heated debate. Ms. Brown takes some notes on their conversation and writes it up later:

> Franklin and Martha are sitting together working on a poem. Franklin says, "Poems have to rhyme!" Martha responds, "Poems don't have to rhyme! My mom told me that poems are like little stories and they don't have to rhyme." Franklin looks at Martha and raises his hand. When I go over to their table, Franklin asks, "Ms. Brown, don't poems have to rhyme?"

How can this brief incident help Ms. Brown plan her classroom curriculum? After reflecting on her students' interactions, Ms. Brown may decide to expand her poetry unit to include several different styles of poetry, including types that don't rhyme, such as haiku. Ms. Brown could also lead a discussion about poems, asking students to identify their favorite poem and to describe why it is their favorite (be-

Unlike running records, anecdotals are brief written notes that a teacher may jot down at the moment and expand when she records the notation later.

cause it rhymes? because it tells an interesting story?). Ms. Brown might also bring in a guest poet who can talk with the students about different types of poems.

Diaries or journals enable teachers to write narratives about a child or children regularly and repeatedly. They may choose to focus on a particular aspect of a child's behavior, the classroom setting, or even their own reactions to classroom events. A journal provides flexibility because the teacher can take notes during the classroom day and later turn them into a narrative—or she may sit and write as events occur if she has the time. A journal can be time consuming, and many teachers do not have the time to write in one regularly and comprehensively. Journals are by definition subjective, since teachers write from their point of view. They are most helpful if the teacher consistently describes what is happening in the classroom as well as gives personal impressions, reactions, or interpretations of particular situations. A journal entry need not be elaborate or particularly eloquent.

Structured observations

Using any of the three methods we have described so far—running records, anecdotals, and journals/diaries—teachers record information as they see and hear it. Here we discuss two structured observation methods that guide the teacher to look for something specific.

The first, **event sampling,** is the observation and recording of a predetermined event. Teachers choose something to watch for, such as a child's attempts to bite other children, and record each time it happens as it happens. If possible, they include what preceded and followed the episode. Event sampling is useful when teachers want to figure out what causes a certain behavior. It provides them with more details about that behavior, thus reducing or eliminating speculation and helping them find reasons for its occurrence. Teachers often use event sampling to plan ways to reduce or increase the incidence of a particular behavior (North Central Regional Educational Laboratory 2007).

For example, Iris is a second grader with significant cognitive and verbal delays. With the help of an aide, she attends class with typically developing second graders for most of her day. Lately, Iris has tried to bite other children in the classroom. Her aide or her teacher has intervened in most of these attempts, but neither has pinpointed what causes Iris to bite. At first it seemed as if Iris was biting randomly, but her aide and her teacher believe that she is reacting to an event or situation. The teacher decides to record every instance of attempted biting for a week. Whenever Iris tries to bite someone, the teacher immediately records what she can about the events that occurred before and after the incident. The teacher and the aide notice that Iris tries to bite others immediately after she removes her jacket when she comes in from outside. Because Iris has difficulty expressing herself verbally, the teacher and the aide wonder if Iris is too cold to remove her jacket and protests by trying to bite anyone who comes near her. The aide allows Iris to wear her jacket in the classroom after coming in from outside, to see if that changes her biting behavior, and it does, at least for a while. In this instance, event sampling helped a teacher reduce potentially dangerous actions while at the same time protecting Iris's integrity and helping her to be more comfortable in the classroom.

The second structured observation method, **checklists,** can be formal evaluations that measure a child's developmental performance against a set of predetermined criteria (Ahola and Kovacik 2006). They can also be more informal tools teachers create for their own purposes. Checklists are usually easy to use. The same checklist can be used throughout the year to help measure a student's progress in

Checklist for Observing Large Motor Activities

Child	Walks without stumbling		Runs easily		Jumps		Hops on one foot		Skips		Gallops	
	Yes	No	Yes	No	Yes	No	Yes	No	Yes	No	Yes	No

9.4 *Checklist for Observing Large Motor Activities*

social/emotional, physical, cognitive, academic, or other domains. Some curriculum outlines include ready-made checklists that allow teachers to see if students are achieving the intended outcomes of the curriculum or if a child is ready to move on to the next part of the curriculum. For example, a prekindergarten or kindergarten teacher may use a checklist to ascertain if a child has a grasp of letter awareness, **phonemic awareness** (the ability to pay attention to sounds independent of a word's meaning), and/or listening skills when deciding whether the child exhibits traits of reading readiness. A teacher can simply check "yes" or "no" on a checklist; or the checklist may include such evaluations as "achieved this task," "approaching this task," or "does not occur." A teacher might use a checklist she designed herself to guide her classroom planning decisions. For example, a teacher who is curious about which three-year-olds can skip, jump, and hop can construct a checklist like the one in Figure 9.4, check off the children's abilities as she observes them outdoors, and then plan circle games based on her findings.

Checklists are just that, predetermined lists. They can call a teacher's attention to points to observe but rarely include room for teachers to record additional information. Also, checklists may be based on experiences not all children share. For example, a consultant using a checklist to test Josh's speech showed Josh a picture of a ham, which Josh identified as meat, and another of a church, which he called a building. Josh and his family are Jewish and keep kosher. At age three, Josh did not know about hams and churches. Care should be taken that checklists include items that are part of most children's lives. It is crucial that teachers understand the disadvantages and biases of any checklists used in their classroom because many schools use checklists to determine whether children are prepared to take on new academic challenges. (You will read more about assessment, advantage, and bias in Chapter 10.)

Use of media

Many aspects of our daily life are recorded: proud parents photograph and videotape birthday parties, graduations, and even births. Recording instruments can be useful observational tools, too. Teachers may set up a video camera to record the classroom's environment and activity. Some early childhood centers have webcams that allow parents to log on to the Internet to catch a glimpse of their child in action. Photographs provide excellent long-term visual documentation of children engaged in various pursuits, such as going on field trips or participating in small-group projects. Audio recordings document children's conversations and allow teachers to supplement their visual observations with auditory ones. Schools may be able to purchase recording equipment without a large monetary investment, and the quality is typically reliable.

However, video, audio, and photographic recordings all have drawbacks. One difficulty with photographs and video recording is their lack of dimensionality. Live observations are three-dimensional, allowing the observer to fully appraise children's movement within space. The observer can also move about the room as necessary to gain a better understanding of what he is observing. A photograph is two-dimensional, and a video only allows the viewer to see what the camera sees, which is either a stationary view from a tripod or the subjective point of view of the camera operator. Notice how we used the word *viewer* to describe the person watching the video? That is because video does not allow the observer to be a participant. Rather, the observer is a passive viewer, able to see only what the video shows.

Audio recording has limitations as well. It can mislead a listener because it does not provide the full context of a situation. Audio also can be edited so that the listener hears only what the editor considers to be important. To ensure fairness and reliability, video, audio, and photographic recordings should be used only in combination with other documentation.

> To ensure fairness and reliability, video, audio, and photographic recordings should be used only with other documentation.

Analyzing Data

After recording your observations, you need to make sense of them. One way is to read them over many times, sorting them to find patterns of behavior. Another is to write summaries to see what general statements you can make based on them.

THOUGHT QUESTION Which of the observation methods do you think are most likely to work for you? Which will you try first?

Think of a time when you did not understand something a child did. When and where could you have observed to learn more? What methods would have given you information to help you answer the questions you had about the child? Why?

Sorting observations

Like an **ethnographer,** a researcher who studies people in their natural settings, you can reread your observations many times to see what categories emerge from the data. As you do this, you may find that your observations seem to sort themselves neatly into what the child does with other children, alone, and with adults. Once you have organized the observations, you can reread them to see what they tell you now about the child.

Alternatively, you already may have categories in mind. For example, you may want to know about each child's social development, intellectual progress, and physical abilities. You can then sort your records by domain to learn about the child in each of those areas.

Besides enabling you to learn from the data as you place related observations together, sorting your data will help you see what is missing. You may find that you know very little about a child's fine motor skills, for example, and decide you will observe her next at the drawing and writing table.

Writing summaries

Here is Dorothy's summary of many observations of John:

> John is a leader in his first grade class of twenty-eight children. Other children often seek him out when they need help with writing or reading. When the class is on the rug for meetings and lessons, John regularly responds to questions from the teacher and shares his thoughts. When he speaks, his strong, clear, sure tone projects confidence and self-assuredness, and other children are attentive to what he says. John is not afraid to ask questions, to disagree with and question the teacher and other children. Other children have begun to follow his lead.

This teacher generalizes that John is a leader and substantiates that generalization with several examples. Her use of the word *regularly* indicates that she has observed the same behaviors repeatedly.

Preparing such summaries helps teachers pinpoint patterns of behavior. Written for the classroom teacher's use and not for outside readers, the summary gives teachers ideas they can use when they interpret observations (Cohen et al. 2008, 227). When teachers gather together all the observational records on a child over a period of time to summarize them, they are likely to spot trends in the child's behavior, along with changes or unusual occurrences.

Synthesizing Findings

After analyzing the observational data, teachers are ready to make sense of them and use them. Early childhood students often consolidate their observations of children into a child study or a descriptive review of a child. Teachers are less likely to write child studies, but early childhood programs find that descriptive reviews are a productive means for teachers to work together to appreciate and plan for children. Whether or not they use descriptive reviews, teachers often synthesize their findings as they discuss children and curriculum at staff meetings.

Teachers may write summaries of their observations that they intend to send beyond their classroom walls—to give to a parent, to include as part of a letter of reference for a child transferring to a private school, or for a referral for special services. This kind of summary synthesizes observations for an outside reader. It is like a digest of the child's behavior and will probably address specific categories. Unlike the summaries discussed in the previous section, teachers write these summaries with their audience in mind, taking care to keep the reader from misinterpreting any of the behaviors they describe.

Child study

A **child study** is a comprehensive document put together from observations of a child over a period of time. After collecting data in a variety of ways, the writer analyzes them systematically, categorizing them and searching for patterns before writing.

Such a paper allows the reader to learn in-depth details about a child's development in many different domain areas. It may quote anecdotal or running records; notes from home visits; event sampling observations; video, audio, or photographic

Many early childhood programs find that descriptive reviews are a productive means for teachers to work together to appreciate and plan for children.

recordings; journal excerpts; checklists; and/or examples of the child's work within the classroom. Child studies are particularly useful for you as a beginning student of early childhood because, to write one, you must conduct the kind of in-depth investigation you need to perform to understand children.

Descriptive review

A **descriptive review** uses the child's work—her efforts to stand upright and then take steps, her paintings and block buildings, the stories she writes—as a starting point for understanding her. This sort of review originates from appreciation of the child, not from a crisis or a problem to solve.

In a descriptive review, teachers record descriptions of many sorts as well as collect examples of the child's work (which can include photographs of an infant doing the work of trying to sit up, for instance). Then the staff gathers with the child's family to think together about *who* the child is, based on her work and these many descriptions.

Although the teacher presenting the child has thought about the child in advance, the group engages in systematic attempts to understand the child and contributes important additional, perhaps unexpected, understandings. Through the descriptive review, the group gets to know and appreciate the child more deeply and to enhance their own work with that child and all the children (Carini 2000a).

Making Observing and Recording Work

Observation and, especially, recording, demand tools, time, and forethought. Teachers are more likely to accomplish the task of recording if they think in advance about what they need to record and why.

Tools for recording

The tools teachers use to record observations depend on the observation method they are using. They might use a small pad for on-the-spot anecdotal records. They might keep a notebook for running records. A bound journal might work for diary entries, although some teachers keep their diaries on their computers.

Teachers also choose recording tools based on availability and personal preferences. Sticky notes are popular because they are easy to keep in a pocket and then attach to a book shared by the teaching team. Some teachers keep a tiny notebook or several index cards in their back pocket. Then they can drop notes into a child's file or store index cards in card files that have a section for each child. Scrap paper is an inexpensive and tried-and-true alternative.

Some teachers find it helpful to create their own shorthand system for commonly used words, such as NT for naptime or FP for free-play. Others just write exactly what they see happening. It doesn't take much time at the end of the day to insert the notes in children's files. A series of short but regular notes can turn into a long-term record of a child's growth and development.

Having the right tools handy when an observation opportunity arises saves time and ensures that you don't miss a great moment. Keep your pen or pencil handy, and

A child study can capture fine details about a child and describe patterns of behavior that help teachers get to know children better.

Teachers interact with a nine-month-old as they observe and record her behaviors.

be sure to have a watch, perhaps a digital one to note seconds as well as minutes, for running records.

Time and timing

In the best-case scenario, teachers would set aside time for observation daily. However, most cannot anticipate a specific time to observe regularly. Also, spur-of-the-moment observations often yield precious insights. However much time is available, what is most important is that the time be focused primarily on observation. Ten minutes of well-focused observation is more useful than sixty minutes full of distractions.

Within your time constraints, try to observe children at different times during the day to understand how they react to various interactions, activities, and routines. *When* you observe will depend on *what* you hope to learn. Unless your goal is to study the morning separation, observing a toddler who is dealing with separation issues first thing in the morning may not be the wisest choice because the child is still transitioning to life in the toddler room. Similarly, right after an infant wakes up is not the ideal time to observe peer interaction because most infants need time to adjust after sleeping. Keep in mind, however, that preschoolers and elementary school children are active most of the day. Every moment, including transitions when children are between activities, is potentially a rich opportunity to learn through observation.

Tips from teachers

Some teachers don't observe and record children's behavior regularly. You may talk to teachers who say they just remember what children do. Teachers who want to understand the individual children with whom they work, however, do find some way to keep track of what they learn about them.

Ten minutes of well-focused observation is more useful than sixty minutes full of distractions.

Helaine writes on sticky notes during free-play or center time. Her comments are as simple as "July 23, 8:15 a.m., Julie zipped up vest herself" and "March 12, 1:10 p.m., Nothani washed his hands without assistance before going to rest." Sometimes Helaine just sticks her notes in the child's section of the notebook she and her assistant teacher keep. Sometimes she elaborates on her notes.

Caitlin stashes pieces of paper around the room so that she can jot down notes whenever the opportunity arises. Joyce has a notebook nearby that she grabs whenever the three-year-olds don't need her and she sees something she wants to record. Sam tries to observe and record two children's behavior each day. Keeping records takes time, and it can be difficult to learn to do it well and just to do it. As we hope you have seen, though, what you learn about children makes it worth the extra work.

THOUGHT QUESTION Talk to a teacher who has a system for observing and recording children's behavior. How does that teacher record observations? When and how does he or she use those observations?

SUMMARY

OBSERVING AND RECORDING

What does it mean to observe and record?

Observation is a way of watching, listening, and analyzing. When teachers record detailed observations that describe but don't decide, they can take into account children's perspectives and understand the workings of the classroom better.

REASONS TO OBSERVE AND RECORD

Why observe and record?

Observing and recording enables teachers to become skillful learning partners with children. Observation is a critical means of assessment for curriculum development and an important source of information when teachers set up and adapt their environments. When observations are in writing, teachers can use them to communicate with colleagues and children's families in helpful ways and to grow professionally themselves.

THE HOW OF OBSERVING AND RECORDING

What is important to observe, and what can guide your observations?

Teachers' objectives—what they want to know about children—guide their observations. Everything that children do is worth observing: arrival in the morning and departure in the afternoon; routines, such as eating and sleeping; all learning experiences, including the choices children make and their approaches to problem solving; children's language; and their interactions with adults and other children. In addition, all teachers should respect confidentiality, strive to be aware of their personal biases, and remember to collect many observations over time.

THE PRACTICALITIES OF OBSERVING AND RECORDING

What does observing and recording look like in action?

Teachers can choose from among many methods for collecting observational information, enabling them to use the method that best suits the situation. Narrative methods, such as running records, anecdotals, and diaries or journals, give a fuller picture of a child than more structured methods, such as event sampling or checklists; however, narrative records are more time consuming. Media, both audio and visual, can enhance written records, although they are limited by their single focus and dimensionality. To make observation useful, teachers must analyze their observations and synthesize many observations to form a broad picture of each child.

Since observation takes time, all teachers must find the tools and setups that work best for them.

FURTHER ACTIVITIES

1. Observe a child between birth and age eight whom you can see several times. Each time, record anecdotals. Based on these observations, write about an activity that would be respectful, supportive, and challenging for the child. In a short essay describe the activity and explain why you think it is a good match for this child. Refer to your observations in your essay. (**NAECYC Standard 1: Promoting Child Development and Learning**)

2. Watch a video of a child, and record what you see. In a short paper, explain what you learned about the child from your observation. State what questions remain in your mind. In a final paragraph, explain how your systematic observations can positively influence the child's development and learning. (**NAEYC Standard 3: Observing, Documenting, and Assessing to Support Young Children and Families**)

3. After spending time in a classroom, develop a graphic (perhaps a web) that shows what children do there. Create a link from each of four activities in the graphic to an observation of a child engaging in that activity. In a short essay, summarize the graphic and explain how the activities in it promote comprehensive developmental and learning outcomes for all young children. Wherever possible, use your observations to substantiate your claims. (**NAEYC Standard 4: Using Developmentally Effective Approaches to Connect with Children and Families**)

Ss
some

Early Childhood Assessment

The Latin root of the word assessment is *assider*, meaning, to "sit beside."

Larry Braskamp, Muriel Poston, and Jon Wergin

itting beside children literally and figuratively, teachers learn about them in a variety of ways. As you read about the assessment cycle, you will see how assessment can be a part of, not separate from, education and care settings. We will discuss the purposes of assessment, what assessment looks like in different situations, and the tools teachers use to assess children. We will talk about how you can make assessment a daily and natural part of your work with children, but you will also see that assessment is not always an integral part of a program. Instead, as you will read, assessment often is imposed on early care and education settings.

In this chapter, you will meet several children, the families of some of them, and the early childhood professionals who work with them. In one way or another, all are involved in assessment all the time. Their stories will help us to look closely at what assessment is. In each case, we will think about who does the assessing and for what purpose. We will talk about how to do different kinds of assessment. We will consider whose interests it serves to assess children, teachers, or programs and under what circumstances. This chapter will help you learn to evaluate types of assessments and their uses.

THE ROOTS OF ASSESSMENT

What does assessment mean in early childhood settings?

Keep in mind the etymology, or root meaning, of the word *assess* as you read about assessment in action. We begin with Bruce, one of the four/fives in Allison's class:

> Children are playing in various parts of the room, having first practiced writing their names on lined paper and "written" their plans for the afternoon. Bruce wanders between the house area and those children who lie on the rug as they write, but he does not pick up a piece of paper. He watches as the teacher, Allison, speaks to the children individually about their plans and sends them on their way. Allison approaches Bruce and asks him to get some paper. She goes with him and points to the paper as she asks him again to get a piece. He takes one, and together they spell his name aloud. Allison writes his name on the paper in bold letters. He makes a "B," and she tells him it's beautiful. He says, "I can't make an 'r.' I can't do it!" "It's a stick and a sad face," she answers. After much coaxing, Bruce makes an "r" successfully. A steady and observant presence, Allison sits beside him as he writes his whole name. As he finishes, Allison and Bruce gaze at each other and smile.

Allison was teaching, and, at the same time, she was learning about Bruce. Based on her relationship with Bruce and her past and present observations of him, she made a series of decisions and acted on them. She believed he could write the letters of his name, and, with her support, he confirmed her hunch. This slice of her assessment of Bruce included sitting beside him, listening carefully, attuning herself to him, and "understanding the other's perspective before making judgments of quality and integrity" (Braskamp, Poston, and Wergin 1998). Increased understanding of children based on relationships with them is an aim of early childhood assessment.

The ultimate goal of early childhood assessment is to benefit the child (Shepard 1994). In this case, thanks to the actions Allison took based on her assessment of Bruce, he not only wrote his name, he also gained a sense of himself as someone able to do what the other children could and what their teacher had established as a goal for them.

Assessment and Evaluation

Often the terms *assessment* and *evaluation* are used interchangeably, but they have different meanings. Assessment data guide our ongoing work, and evaluation of those data informs our judgments and decisions in a more formal way. **Assessment** refers to the ongoing methods of gathering, analyzing, and interpreting information about children to identify children's strengths and needs, with the goal of improving teaching strategies and children's learning. Assessment is a systematic process. It leads to evaluation that is neither a snap decision nor based on a single incident. Instead, teachers collect and organize numerous observations or pieces of work to assess and then evaluate.

Together, multiple sources of data can confirm or deny a hypothesis. What if a child drew a picture or wrote or dictated a story on a day when he was sick or upset? What if it did not represent his best work for other reasons? A collection of observations or of work over time enables teachers to discern patterns and to note what behavior is consistent, what is an anomaly, and what changes seem to be occurring. The expression "safety in numbers" applies well to gathering data for assessment. And good teaching, at any level, always incorporates ongoing assessment.

Evaluation uses assessment information to make an informed judgment, for instance, about whether children have achieved learning goals teachers have established for them, the relative strengths and weaknesses of the teaching strategies used, or how (or whether) to change those goals and teaching strategies. Here, too, teachers should draw upon multiple sources of data.

> Assessment data guide our ongoing work, and evaluation of those data informs our judgments and decisions in a more formal way.

THOUGHT QUESTION Think about your work in this or another course in your program of study. Which of your contributions during the semester are included in the overall evaluation of your work? Does your instructor utilize multiple sources of data?

Formative and Summative Assessment

Educators distinguish between two types of assessment. One is ongoing and supports the process of the educational activity. The other evaluates the activity after it is finished.

Formative assessment provides feedback *during or before* the completion of a course of study, enabling the student or teacher to identify areas for improvement and make modifications. When your college instructor asks for feedback about the course once or more during the semester, early enough so that she can make changes in response to student feedback, you give her formative assessment.

Summative assessment is the gathering of information *at the conclusion of* a course of study, also with the goal of improving learning. You provide your professor with summative assessment at the end of the semester when you fill out the course feedback form. In this case, the instructor can use the student feedback as she prepares to teach the course the following semester. Or, as Bob Stakes has described it, "When the cook tastes the soup, that's formative; when the guests taste the soup, that's summative" (Stakes, quoted in Scriven 1991, 169).

THE ASSESSMENT CYCLE

What is the assessment cycle?

Early childhood assessment is "[a] systematic procedure for obtaining information from observation, interviews, portfolios, projects, tests, and other sources that can be used to make judgments about characteristics of children or programs" (CCSSO

> "When the cook tastes the soup, that's formative; when the guests taste the soup, that's summative."
> —Bob Stakes

Build a relationship

Gather information through observation

Interpret information and make decisions

Take action while continuing to observe

10.1 *Assessment Cycle within the Context of a Relationship*

THOUGHT QUESTION What are your memories of assessment prior to college? How were your teachers' definitions of *assessment* similar to or different from the definition proposed and illustrated in this chapter?

2007). Assessment is a multistep circular process (Figure 10.1). Think back to Bruce and Allison. Allison's first step in assessment was to build a relationship with Bruce; when she sat next to him, her support contributed to their ongoing relationship. Her second step was gathering information. We saw her do so through an informal observation, but in the time she has known Bruce, she has done more-formal observation, too, using some of the methods you read about in Chapter 9 and has also collected and examined Bruce's work. Allison's third step was to make sense of the information she had collected and decide what to do to further Bruce's learning and development. The final step in the assessment process involves taking action, but that is not the end. Instead, as Allison took action, coaxing, urging, and remaining with Bruce as he wrote his name, she collected more information about what he could do and how he did it. We also saw Bruce and Allison become closer; the interactions of their assessment process nourished their relationship.

The assessment process is **recursive,** meaning that it cycles back to revisit ongoing issues, sometimes to throw new light on a previous situation based on new information. The assessment cycle is part of continually getting to know more about the children and your own work as a teacher. The cycle begins with the relationship, but it does not end with the actions you take. Whatever you do—whatever curriculum you implement, intervention you try, or practice you institute—you will have gathered more information, your relationship with the child will deepen, and you will learn more about the child. And, so the cycle continues. Although you may report certain assessment data periodically (monthly, quarterly, annually), the assessment cycle is part of a teacher's everyday work.

Let's look more closely at how the assessment cycle works in practice. We will see how the steps apply to twenty-month-old Felix Garcia, who was playing with his five-year-old brother, Enrique, when Isabel, a bilingual special educator, visited their home to do an early intervention (EI) assessment.

Building Relationships

Isabel's first contact with the family was a phone call in Spanish with Mrs. Garcia, who is most comfortable speaking in her mother tongue. They agreed that Isabel would visit to do an evaluation to determine if Felix was eligible for EI services. Mrs. Garcia had initiated the process when she mentioned her concern about Felix's language development to his pediatrician. The doctor suggested that she notify the EI program to arrange for an evaluation. Mrs. Garcia spoke to an EI representative on the phone and, later that week, received a call from Rosa, her initial service coordinator. Rosa explained the EI system and talked with Mrs.

Garcia about Felix's development and her concerns. Together, they decided on an evaluation by a special educator and another by a speech and language pathologist.

So, when Isabel arrived for the special education evaluation, she had not yet met the family. She knew that establishing a comfortable personal relationship with Felix and his family was crucial for the success of the assessment process.

When Mrs. Garcia let Isabel into the apartment and showed her to the living room, Isabel greeted the two brothers, who were playing on the carpet and who looked up at her shyly for a moment. Then Enrique continued building garages for his many trucks and cars, and Felix crashed into them with his trucks, cars, hands, and feet.

Isabel did not rush into her relationship with Felix. Instead, she and Mrs. Garcia sat on the couch and chatted in Spanish about Felix and the rest of the family. Isabel asked Mrs. Garcia about her son's birth and early development and also about her family's resources, priorities, and concerns regarding Felix. She knew from his file that Felix had been born four weeks premature and had spent three weeks in the hospital's neonatal intensive care unit (NICU). Mrs. Garcia discussed some of the details of this period and then talked about Felix's early development. Throughout, she stressed her concern that Felix wasn't talking very much. She also mentioned that he was clumsy when he walked or tried to climb things. Isabel asked about the family's history, home country, and culture and learned that they had emigrated from the Dominican Republic five years earlier. Mrs. Garcia explained that while she and her husband were at work, her mother cared for the boys, mostly for Felix, who was not yet in school.

As Isabel learned about Felix and his family, she appreciated the close family connections and support the Garcia family enjoyed. Mrs. Garcia seemed glad to have an open and sympathetic listener, someone who understood child development and her concerns about Felix and who could converse in Spanish. This initial respect and trust laid the groundwork for information gathering and sharing. Isabel's visit also gave the family a first impression of EI, and perhaps reduced their anxieties a bit. In addition, the boys saw their mother talking with Isabel, which sent them a message that Isabel was probably a good person.

Isabel's visit ended with recognition of the relationship that she and the family had established. The next step was that the family would hear from the initial service coordinator, Rosa. As Isabel left, she gave Mrs. Garcia her card and said to call her about any concerns. When Isabel said goodbye to Felix and his family, she even got an unexpected hug from older brother Enrique.

Gathering Information

Throughout her visit, Isabel had gathered information from as many sources as possible and in as many ways as she could. When Mrs. Garcia's mother entered the room and joined in the conversation, the grandmother shared her thoughts about Felix as well. Isabel also asked Mrs. Garcia and her mother about Felix's **self-help skills,** for example, to what extent he participated in getting dressed and undressed, eating, and washing his hands and whether he had some way of letting them know when his diaper was wet or soiled.

Instead of a one-sided series of questions and answers, the three women exchanged information with each other in an easy, natural way. When Isabel inquired how their family used language, she learned that the adults consistently spoke Spanish but that Enrique, who had recently started kindergarten, had begun to speak some English at home. Mrs. Garcia explained that she spoke very little English herself but was "getting better at understanding." She wondered if she should try to speak English to Felix so that he wouldn't have even more trouble with language when he went to school. Isabel encouraged them to continue to speak Spanish at home and explained that a strong foundation in his first language would help Felix learn English *and* give him a better chance of keeping his skills in Spanish.

Then, to learn more about Felix in another way, Isabel asked if she could play with Felix and Enrique. Her observations of Felix at play with his brother would add to what the adults had already told her and would give her a clear idea about Felix's strengths and skills and what he was still learning. And, by playing with the brothers using materials she had brought with her, along with Felix's own toys, she could make sure that specific behaviors that she wanted to observe would occur. Isabel also used a **play-based assessment tool**—an approach that uses play activities with peers or adults in a natural setting to observe a child's behaviors—to help her determine how Felix's skills compared with those of other children his age.

At first Felix was shy, but with help from Enrique and lots of encouragement from Mom and Grandma, Felix began to play with Isabel. She paid careful attention to how he expressed himself and responded to the language around him, how he moved and balanced his body and manipulated objects like cars and foam puzzle pieces, how he solved problems like fitting cups inside each other, how he responded to pegs that were difficult to push into the form boards, and how he reacted to meeting someone new. Isabel was happy to have Enrique beside her because big brother was masterful at keeping Felix smiling and engaging him in whatever task she presented. Isabel also noticed that when he was perched on Grandma's lap, Felix was much more interested in pointing to the pictures she showed him and labeled. She believed that her evolving image of Felix was more accurate because he was able to behave naturally with the people he loved around him.

Before Felix climbed down from Grandma's lap, Isabel asked if she could take a photo of Felix and his family. Mrs. Garcia agreed, and Isabel took two digital photos. When asked to choose which one she would like Isabel to give her the next time they met, Mrs. Garcia chose the one in which Felix was reaching out to hold Enrique's hand. Isabel planned to print the photos as another source of information about Enrique that she could use later to jog her memory about him.

The information gathering did not end with Isabel's visit. The speech pathologist's visit was next. Based on Mrs. Garcia's concerns about how Felix moved and used his body and on her own observations that Felix walked on his toes and demonstrated some difficulty balancing, Isabel recommended that a physical therapist evaluate Felix's motor skills. Mrs. Garcia agreed to this idea.

Interpreting Information and Deciding What to Do

After early childhood educators gather information, they have to figure out what it means before they make decisions based on it. To gain a sense of what the data are telling them, they may summarize what they know, giving the facts educational significance. This search for meaning from isolated pieces of evidence is called **interpretation.** Early childhood educators interpret data and make decisions throughout their work with young children. This reflection helps early childhood educators to develop **hypotheses,** or educated guesses, that they can then test. As you read in Chapter 9, interpretation comes *after* observation.

Isabel's first home visit gave her a sense of the many factors involved in the Garcia family's wishes for Felix's enhanced language development. These were not incidental bits of information. To understand Felix in the context of his family, Isabel and the other professionals with whom she works will go over everything she learned from the visit. Together they will consider and interpret every detail to design Felix's therapy. This comprehensive look at Felix in context will contribute to how successful his therapy will be.

So that she and her colleagues could interpret all the information productively, Isabel made sure that what she knew about Felix was as complete and accurate as possible. Before leaving, she asked Mrs. Garcia if she considered Felix's behavior that afternoon to be typical for him and if there was anything else she would like to share about Felix's skills and development.

Interpretation involves evaluation, or making a judgment. After her visit, Isabel scored the items from the play-based assessment she had done. She reviewed and organized her notes. Then she taped the photos she had taken of Felix and his family to the corner of her laptop and wrote a report on Felix that consolidated and summarized what she had learned from her visit. Writing it helped her to make sense of her interactions with Felix's family members and all she had learned from them.

An important part of assessment is stepping back and taking stock, often in collaboration with others. In addition to organizing her thinking about Felix and his family and enabling her to make recommendations, Isabel's report allowed others to combine their findings with hers. At the end of her visit, Isabel explained to the Garcia family that after receiving the reports from the speech therapist and the physical therapist, she would write a summary in Spanish of the multidisciplinary evaluations and also would call Mrs. Garcia to discuss the results and consider recommendations. The family would be involved in all aspects of the interpretation and decision making to design Felix's early intervention.

Isabel told Mrs. Garcia that if Felix qualified for services, she would hear from her initial service coordinator to schedule and plan for an **Individual Family Service Plan (IFSP)** meeting at which the family and the service providers would work out interventions for Felix. Isabel explained that everyone at the meeting would speak Spanish. They would meet in the Garcia home or in the EI agency's office. Isabel, Rosa, and an EI representative (called the EI official designee) would attend, and Mrs. Garcia was free to bring her husband, her mother, or anyone else she wanted.

Taking Action

Once early childhood educators make decisions about the information they have collected, they are ready to act upon it. **Incorporation** is another name for this step of the assessment process because teachers incorporate, or weave, what they have learned from assessment into their practice with children. As they do, they keep track of what happens and adjust the process as necessary. Here is what incorporation looks like in EI.

The IFSP that Isabel, Rosa, the Garcias, and the EI representative developed led to Felix's participation three times a week in an inclusive bilingual program for children with and without language delays. All the children played together in groups of their own choosing, and the children who did not have language delays were effective models of clear language. Felix's grandmother brought him to the program and continued to provide information to program staff and to pick up ideas to support Felix's language development that she shared with Felix's parents. In addition, a speech therapist visited Felix at home once a week to work with him individually, to give the family additional feedback, and to receive their input.

Throughout these interventions, the assessment cycle continued. Felix and his family developed and enhanced their relationships with the professionals they encountered. They shared insights with, and gleaned information from, the professionals

An important part of assessment is stepping back and taking stock, often in collaboration with others.

in ongoing IFSP meetings and in the course of Felix's group attendance and individual therapy. Professionals and family members continued to review new information, make decisions based on it, and take action accordingly.

THE PURPOSES OF ASSESSMENT

Why do we assess?

We assess so that we can better achieve our goals and objectives for young children. As you saw when you read about the assessment cycle, assessment also helps us to repeatedly reassess those goals and objectives as children and situations constantly change. Once you have data from multiple sources, you can begin to make some evaluative judgments that lead to curricular decisions that shape children's learning.

Evaluative Decisions

It is worth repeating: evaluative judgments should be made based on data from more than one tool. Aside from observations, there are three basic categories of assessments (Figure 10.2).

Performance-based assessments are those in which each child's progress is noted individually; children are not compared with each other. A spelling test that you create based on words the class has been learning is a good example of a performance-based assessment.

Criterion-based assessments allow a child's progress to be viewed individually *or* compared with that of other children using a common set of expectations. Such expectations set the criteria against which the capabilities of children (or teachers or the effectiveness of a program) can be measured. Criteria allow teachers to examine

> Evaluative judgments should be made based on data from more than one tool.

10.2 *Types of Assessments*

Types of Assessments

Performance-based	Criterion-based	Norm-referenced
Assessments based on what a child has been taught or exposed to	Assessments that measure a child's mastery of a specific skill set	Assessments based on a single child's performance on a test or other measure
Each child's performance is looked at individually, not in relation to another's	Each child's performance is compared with a predetermined criterion	Each child's performance is compared with that of a representative sample of children
Examples: Spelling test; portfolio of a child's work	*Example:* Early Childhood Literacy Assessment System	*Example:* Paper and pencil standardized tests

Evaluative decisions

Curricular decisions

PART 3 Knowing All Children "From the Inside Out": The Observation, Assessment, and Teaching Cycle

the performance of a child in their classroom to a preestablished level of skill or mastery. The Early Childhood Literacy Assessment System (ECLAS), which you will read about later in this chapter, is an example of a criterion-based assessment.

Standardized tests are a form of **norm-referenced screening and assessment.** Screening is used to identify potential developmental delays but not to assess development or growth over time. On the other hand, assessment is often used after screening determines that more in-depth analysis of development is needed. Additionally, assessment can be used at the beginning and the end of a child's participation in a program or intervention.

For both screening and assessment, the score of each person is compared with that of a normed test-taker—that is, the average of the scores of a **representative sample,** a group that shares important characteristics with everyone taking the test, in this case, children of a certain age. A single child's performance is compared with that of the sample of children, or **norm group,** on which the test has already been piloted. Comparing one child's score with that of the norm group provides an understanding of how the child performed relative to others in his or her cohort, or group. For the results of a norm-referenced assessment to be meaningful, it is essential to know how closely the child resembles the children in the norm group. Information about the child's performance on a norm-referenced test is usually expressed as a number, a developmental-age equivalent, or a percentile score.

Norm-referenced tests become outdated as their target population shifts and as legislation and guidelines for assessment change, based on what are considered to be best practices in the field. For example, in revising its Fourth Edition, the developers of the Preschool Language Scale, an assessment of various aspects of a child's developing language abilities, adjusted their norm group to reflect the increase in racial, ethnic, and other diversity of the U.S. population and an increase in the percentage of parents who have finished high school.

We need a trustworthy set of developmental expectations when we evaluate children. (Note: Some teachers use the words *expectations, criteria,* and *standards* interchangeably even though they are not identical in meaning.) Although having a set of expectations usually makes sense to teachers, they can find it hard to break the old habit of comparing children with each other instead. Teachers can find themselves using prior experience as a basis for informally assessing children they have just met—even when those children have had opportunities or life experiences very different from those of the children with whom the teachers have worked previously.

On the other side of the spectrum, some teachers of young children think it is unnecessary to evaluate young students at all. They may have had bad experiences with evaluation or worry that evaluation will lead to children being labeled. Also, none of these assessments are intuitive; teachers have to learn how to use the tools.

Evaluative decisions make judgments about children, teachers, and schools, but they cannot stand alone. Evaluative decisions are, however, essential to support curricular decisions.

Curricular Decisions

In curricular decision making, early childhood educators figure out how to integrate assessment into their practice. Teachers use what they learn from the assessment process to decide what and how to teach individual children and groups of children. The purpose of curricular decision making is twofold: assessment of individual children helps teachers to shape curriculum, which, in turn, allows children to take optimal advantage of teaching.

In curricular decision making, early childhood educators use what they learn from the assessment process to decide what and how to teach individual children and groups of children.

You saw how Isabel evaluated Felix's language development and his physical development using a predetermined set of criteria but administered the test in a play-based context. Based on what she learned, Isabel and her colleagues, in consultation with Felix's family, were then able to arrange for services to support Felix's development in the evaluated areas. Such individual assessments of young children are **diagnostic.** That is, they serve as a **screening tool** to identify how early childhood educators can help children to do their best in school and in life.

Basing curricular decision making on assessment enables teachers to develop curriculum that best fits the children. This curriculum may be far-reaching, like the Brooklyn Bridge study you will read about in Chapter 13. It may also be immediate interaction, such as you saw with Allison and Bruce. When Allison made it possible for Bruce to get the paper and write his name, she was scaffolding, a strategy you read about in Chapter 6. Lorrie Shepard (2005, 66) describes assessment as "a dynamic process in which supportive adults or classmates help learners move from what they already know to what they are able to do next, using their zone of proximal development." Assessment helps teachers determine each child's zone of proximal development and scaffold suitably.

Goals and Objectives

The overall purpose of assessment is to ask what children know and do and what they can reasonably do next. You will have goals related to the curriculum—what you plan for children and what happens as those plans unfold. But, as you read in Chapter 8, it is crucial to balance curricular goals with each child's strengths and needs.

Goals are broad. They answer the big question, what do I want the children in my group to know and be able to do? As often as possible, goals should encompass the children's interests. As you will read in Chapter 13, the children in Trish's mixed second and third grade class expressed interest in the Brooklyn Bridge, which was near their school. A broad goal of that classroom for that semester was to study a topic in depth. This large goal related to Trish's ongoing goals for her students' social studies curriculum, which included enhancement of their reading, writing, mathematics, artistic representation, and inquiry skills.

Objectives are more specific, and smaller in scale; by successfully achieving them, learners make progress toward reaching larger goals, too. Trish took her second and third graders to see the bridge from close up and far away. She and the children had numerous meetings at which the children raised many questions. Who built the bridge? What do the people who work on the bridge do? How does the bridge stay up? The questions led the children to meet various learning objectives. For example, to answer the question of how the bridge stays up, the children built a model bridge. That activity addressed the following learning objective:

Children will experiment systematically with materials to discover and understand scientific principles related to span and load.

Unlike with a goal, which is broad and difficult to measure, Trish could observe whether children were experimenting with materials and how systematic they were in doing so. Their discussions and subsequent writing and graphing showed her to what extent they had discovered and understood the scientific principles she hoped they

THOUGHT QUESTION Select a unit in a course you are taking. Formulate the broad goal you think your instructor had for that unit, as well as a few learning objectives that related to the goal.

would learn. The bridge project also demonstrated to Trish how the children met her objectives for them in reading, writing, math, and artistic expression.

The children who met Trish's objectives were a step closer to achieving her larger goal of enhancing their inquiry skills and scientific knowledge. When objectives lead to your overall learning goals, you can determine where the learning is rich and for which children—and also where the learning falls short and, again, for whom.

ASSESSMENT IN A SCHOOL CONTEXT

How do teachers assess children in schools?

We begin this discussion of assessment in schools with Min's public kindergarten (reported first in Genishi and Dyson 2009). Although Min experiences numerous assessment pressures that stem from her district and school's implementation of NCLB, she has found ways to use assessment to learn about children and develop goals and objectives for their growth. To do this, Min keeps her focus on the children, not on the assessment, and finds that certain ways of assessing are more relevant to some children than to others. Despite a requirement to use specific assessment tools, Min is able to be selective. She does not use all ways of assessing all the time, and she uses observation as her primary source of assessment information.

Keeping the Focus on Children

Min assesses all the children in her class, but she also chooses a child to study in depth for the year to learn more about that child and about her own teaching. This year, Min chose Jenny, an ELL evaluated to be at risk for repeating kindergarten.

Min keeps anecdotal records on each child, but they don't tell her everything she needs to know. Jenny's dominant language was Spanish. Min could see from the assessment notes she keeps, in addition to anecdotal records, that Jenny needed work on vocabulary. She made a list of Jenny's vocabulary words in Spanish and in English to see if that could provide insights into possible reasons for Jenny's weak English vocabulary and help her add more elaborate English words. Min's assessment notes were based on competencies that she knows children need to acquire to succeed in her school.

THOUGHT QUESTION Below you can see a sample of Jenny's work that Min studied. Two more samples are on the next pages. What can you learn about Jenny from looking at her work? If you were Min, what learning activities might you plan based on what you are learning about Jenny?

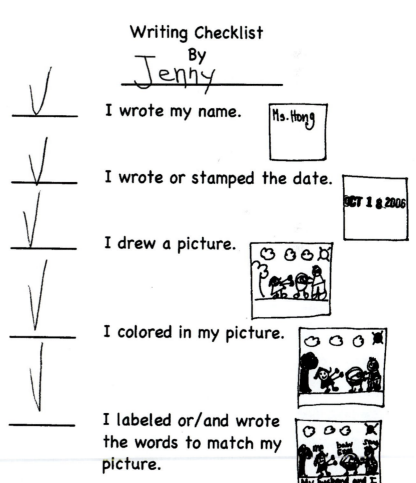

Here and on pgs. 296–297 you see some of Jenny's work: the checklist she used as she completed her writing, her self-portrait, and her story.

Min's close look at what she hoped Jenny would learn in her class and her observations of Jenny over a period of time led her to wonder how her curriculum could help Jenny the most. What was she *not* doing that could help Jenny? She conferred one-on-one with Jenny and began to use those conferences as teaching time to fill in what Jenny needed most. With help from a colleague who observed her working with Jenny, Min came to realize that Jenny benefited when a teacher intervened more than Min usually did. She was used to holding back to allow children to discover answers for themselves, but as Min began to differentiate her instruction by giving Jenny clearer and more specific directions, Jenny began to thrive as a learner.

It takes a teacher a long time to be able to coordinate assessment activities. After fifteen years in the classroom, Min says that she is still working on fitting assessment into the day. She wants to make assessment authentic, not superficial. She struggles to find the time to write anecdotes and other assessments, knowing that they make planning and teaching so much more purposeful.

Since the purpose of assessment is to help children learn, it is not surprising that children and their learning should be its focus. Unfortunately, pressures to assess and achieve results—from the district, from the principal, and from the teachers of the next grade—can divert a teacher's attention away from the children and the curriculum that helps them learn and toward the assessments themselves. Particularly at schools where children have scored poorly on standardized tests in the past, the test itself can become the curriculum. In these situations, children learn test-taking skills and content that teachers know will be on the test instead of working to acquire skills and learn content that grows out of a rich and interesting study or children's ongoing play.

You saw how Isabel assessed Felix's development in the Garcia home, his natural environment, to get to know him at his best when he was most comfortable. In a classroom for older children (which is their natural environment), teachers will learn most reliably about children through their regular activities. The classroom is the best place to learn about children's prior experience and knowledge, what they can do well, what and how they are ripe for learning, and what interests them most.

Observation Is the Foundation of Assessment

How do teachers of young children discover what children are able to do so that they can build on those capabilities to enhance children's learning? They do this primarily through observation, which means "to take notice, to pay attention to what children do and say" (Almy and Genishi 1979, 21). As you learned in Chapter 9, observation is not a clearly defined or scripted activity; it is ongoing, a habit of mind

> **After fifteen years in the classroom, Min says that she is still working on fitting assessment into the day in a way that makes assessment authentic, not superficial.**

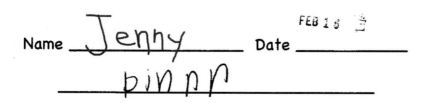

Name _Jenny_____ Date _____
_____pinnr_____

I went to the stor
and bt fod for
pihnr + bt geZ
miK brad and giKn
my mom mad pihnr
and we et pihnr.

and the senses that ingrains itself in the practitioner, always over time. Observant teachers see or hear behaviors and often intuit the "vibes" of each day, perhaps each minute. They observe to learn about children's abilities and behaviors, not to see whether those abilities or behaviors match a checklist from a mandated curriculum or a developmental-stage theory.

As you saw with Min, assessment involves more than simply making observations. Min met with a colleague to discuss her observations and other assessments of Jenny. In Jan's preschool, there are two different types of teacher meetings:

- Each team of teachers shares observations and notes at a daily after-class meeting. This allows them to chart each child's ongoing development and the interests and activities that emerged in that day's class.

- The whole staff also meets every two weeks to discuss curriculum and the environment, and for ongoing teacher education. They even role-play actual classroom situations to gain insight into any problems with children, teachers, and parents.

The teachers find that these collaborative meetings continually challenge them to use assessment conscientiously, to plan better, and to improve their teaching practices. At the root are the teachers' strong relationships with each child and family and with each other. Along with professional assessments and supports as needed, this combination helps these teachers promote each child's optimal development.

Here is an example of how Jan and her colleagues use observations, taken from a note Jan wrote herself on the first day of school (reported first in Genishi and Dyson 2009):

Four-year-old Dominic is playing hockey, flailing his arms and scattering himself about. He has fascinating energy, but it looks as if someone will die. I want to get to know this kid. So I put my clipboard down and draw a hockey court on the sidewalk. Dominic can hardly stop playing to listen to me, but I become a coach and call the hockey team over. I ask the name of the teams, and Dominic says "Superheroes and Power Rangers." Then, I draw an X in the middle of the court. I make a scoreboard for the teams. "Here is where to start," I say. Three boys, including Dominic, play vigorous hockey with only a few reminders to stay in the court. No one gets killed or even hurt. I assess Dominic to have great physical skills, have a big desire to play with others, be interested in literacy by naming his team, and have some difficulty listening to an adult (not unusual for a four-year-old with a lot of energy). I learned a lot about this very interesting boy, and I think I can have fun while getting to know him better.

Jan made this assessment of Dominic through observing him in a natural environment, in this case in the yard, and in the context of play. She knew that children operate at their optimal level of development during play that they have chosen. Even though it was hard for him to listen to a teacher's words, Dominic began to control his movements, was motivated to cooperate with rules, and was interested in being a member of a team with a name.

Jan continued to observe Dominic over the long term and at various times in the day. She organized her observations so that she and her colleagues could make sense of them. To get further input, she also shared her observations at meetings that included the director and other teachers from within and outside her classroom.

Like the teachers at Michael's Head Start, whom you read about in Chapter 6, Jan watched *how* Dominic did what he did instead of looking for specific skills that Dominic might or might not possess. She also gauged how time, place, and other people affected what he did. All of these factors helped the group of teachers to think productively together about Dominic and to calculate what curriculum and teaching strategies would help him emotionally, socially, and intellectually. Jan believes that if she had narrowly focused on skills instead, she and the rest of the teaching team would not have come to know Dominic as a whole and complex person.

Dominic's mother eventually had him tested for sensory integration issues, and he became able to control his movements thanks to exercises that the physical therapist recommended. Jan had confidence in Dominic's success in her class because, having come to know him as well as they did, the teachers and children were eager to help him become more socially appropriate while allowing him to play at what interested him.

ASSESSMENT TOOLS

What assessment tools are available to use with young children?

In this section, we examine a range of ways of assessing that are as fair as possible and provide clear contrasts to standardized tests and narrowly defined curricula. In every case, clear communication—between child and teacher, between parents and teacher, and among colleagues—is an aim.

Shepard (2000) points out that new teachers know plenty about anxiety-producing tests from their own experience as test takers. But, she warns, teachers will create equally unpleasant assessment experiences for the children in their classes unless they have the chance to experiment with authentic and meaningful assessment for themselves. As you go on to read about assessment tools in this section, think about how to get helpful information about children to support their development and learning. Then figure out where you can try out some of these assessment procedures for yourself.

Assessing Children from Birth to Three

Babies are assessed from the moment they are born. Is the new family member a big eight-pound baby girl? Does she look like Grandpa Joe when he started to go bald? More formally, doctors and nurses administer an **Apgar test** (Apgar 1953) to determine the baby's vital signs at birth and at five minutes after birth (Figure 10.3).

Another assessment, the **Brazelton Neonatal Behavioral Assessment Scale** (BNBAS), is not given in most hospitals. However, many experts have advocated translating this research tool into an abbreviated form (Nugent 1999) to demonstrate to parents what babies are capable of in the **neonatal period,** or first month of life. Unlike the Apgar, the BNBAS focuses on the baby's social and interactive abilities as well as his neurological signs (Brazelton and Nugent 1995), producing a richer picture of how a newborn may interact in his environment.

Often, family members want to know whether further assessment or a full evaluation is necessary. The **Ages and Stages Questionnaire** is a screening tool that provides this information for children birth to age four. A family can complete the questionnaire or give the information to a professional in an interview, usually with the infant or toddler present (Squires et al. 2001). The **Ounce Scale** is another assessment tool for very young children that also looks at the infant or toddler within

> Most teachers know plenty about anxiety-producing tests from their own experience as test takers.

	Apgar Scale				
	A	P	G	A	R
SCORE	APPEARANCE (COLOR)	PULSE (HEART RATE)	GRIMACE (REFLEX IRRITABILITY)	ACTIVITY (MUSCLE TONE)	RESPIRATION (RESPIRATORY EFFORT)
0	Blue, pale	Absent	No response	Limp	Absent
1	Body pink, extremities blue	Slow (below 100)	Grimace	Some flexion of extremities	Slow, irregular
2	Completely pink	Rapid (over 100)	Cry	Active motion	Good, strong cry

10.3 *Apgar Scoring*

will

Virginia Apgar

Dr. Apgar was a teacher at a big hospital in New York City. She invented a test named after her called the Apgar Scale. It's a test for babies when they are first born. It measures hart beat, brething, colers, and musles. It lets docters know if babies are O.k. The end

This second grader chose Virginia Apgar for his project on a famous woman.

the context of his or her family. These birth-to-three assessments are best categorized as **functional assessments** (Greenspan 1996) because they are administered within the context of an infant's or a toddler's everyday life, as in the example of Felix. Remember how Felix sat on his grandmother's lap and how his brother played with him and Isabel as she conducted the assessment? With functional assessments, the adult accommodates the child's interests, abilities, and wishes, rather than requiring the child to conform to the constraints of an assessment.

The **Bayley Scale of Infant Development** is the most formal method of gaining an in-depth picture of how a young child is developing and is a good example of a standardized and normed test. It uses a **task-based,** or milestone, method (Dichtelmiller and Ensler 2004). The assessor sits with the child and elicits item after item from her. Infants or junior toddlers are usually in a parent's arms, whereas twos and threes have a caregiver close by. In both task-based and functional assessments of very young children, the goal is to elicit the child's best performance.

Evaluating Three- to Eight-Year-Old Children's Performance and Progress

There is no single way to monitor and evaluate children's development and learning over time. In the twenty-first century, however, performance assessments have increasingly become utilized as a structured way to view preschool and school-age children's growth.

The Early Childhood Literacy Assessment System

The Early Childhood Literacy Assessment System, or ECLAS-2, is designed to help teachers monitor children's progress in literacy from kindergarten through grade three. Not considered a test, ECLAS-2 is typically administered over a two-day period. Teachers working with kindergartners and first graders have the option of using a puppet to engage the student for some of the practice activities and instructions, but not with the assessment itself. This particular assessment covers phonemics, phonics, alphabet recognition, decoding, sight words, reading comprehension, and fluency.

A teacher generally works one-on-one

Assessment is part of this first grade teacher's teaching as she sits beside a child who is deaf.

with a child at a table, while the rest of the class works in small reading groups or at other activities. The teacher usually administers the assessment because the process provides information about the child's learning style that the teacher needs to know to help the child learn best. This assessment experience adds to the teacher's ever-growing knowledge of each child and tells her more than a test score would. The child, in turn, usually enjoys this one-on-one time with the teacher—a typically nonthreatening experience that doesn't compare to taking a test as one child in a large group.

Teachers appreciate having an assessment that follows the child throughout the early years and helps provide a broad picture of learning over time. For many teachers, the ECLAS confirms or disconfirms data they have gathered day by day about their children's work. However, administering the ECLAS one-on-one with children only works in classrooms where children are accustomed to working independently of the teacher alone and with each other for extended periods.

Using standards

More and more states have developed early learning standards for preschoolers. Whether you use state standards or have shared learning goals within the grade level at your school, you will want to see how children are doing in relation to your state's measures of accomplishment. Using a **rubric** (a chart with categories) to break down the learning components of state standards or other learning goals makes it easier to evaluate how a child is moving toward each benchmark or goal. Each category of the rubric separates the objective into measurable bits—cutting with scissors, using a pen, cleaning up one's work—so that you can observe each component of the objective and arrive at a broader and more stable evaluation of the child's work. Figure 10.4 shows an example of a rubric for assessing children's progress toward meeting the objective "Works toward the achievement of group goals."

Teachers also develop their own tools to help children, especially those in the early elementary years, become more aware of their own learning or increase their

4. Most competent
Actively helps identify group goals and works hard to meet them

3. Emergent
Communicates a commitment to group and effectively carries out assigned roles

2. Novice
Communicates a commitment to the group goals but does not carry out assigned roles or tasks

1. Needs significant help
Does not work toward group goals or actively works against them

10.4 *Rubric for Assessing Progress toward Group Goals Objective*

metacognition, their thinking about how they think and learn, which begins to develop around this time. Megan teaches a group of first, second, and third graders in a Montessori school. After the long morning work period, children fill out the Work Recording Sheet in Figure 10.5. This is an assessment tool the children can complete repeatedly and that they, their families, and Megan can review over time.

Case studies

There is also growing interest in the **case study** assessment method, which uses detailed description of a child's learning and of teachers' strategies over time. In one case study (Darling-Hammond and Snyder 2000), Susan Gordon describes Akeem's entry into her third grade public school classroom after he was expelled from another school for violent behavior. As Susan documents when Akeem's various aggressive behaviors occur, she recognizes a correlation between them and new and challenging academic tasks. Her hypothesis is that Akeem's behavior is a screen to "deflect attention from the fact that he cannot read or write with any ease" (531).

Working with colleagues who also get to know Akeem well, Susan develops activities and assignments that capitalize on Akeem's artistic side, and she also teaches him reading strategies that provide him with increasing success in his schoolwork. Over the course of the year, Akeem's classmates begin to respect his artistic skills, and Akeem learns to document his work through reading and writing. His academic skills soon match those of the rest of the class. As the case study follows him throughout grade school, he continues to be interested in and to enjoy his studies and ultimately gains admission to a high school for the arts. Thus, Susan's discovery and support of Akeem's artistic interest and ability was a key to his success as a student and Susan's as a teacher.

Of course, not every case study has such a positive ending, and teachers can learn from missteps as well as from the moments when they get it "right." Whether or not they portray successful learning experiences, case studies document experience over time that teachers can examine for a clearer and more nuanced picture of children's learning. Case studies are also a way to demonstrate your teaching abilities and can be showcased well in your own professional portfolio.

Creating Portfolios of Children's Work

Portfolios are purposeful collections of children's work samples that reveal individual learning and contribute to a comprehensive assessment process. Teachers collect samples of children's work in portfolios for several reasons.

The first reason is pragmatic. The more teachers know about the children they teach, the more effectively they can guide their learning. However, life in early childhood classrooms is busy and demanding. Opportunities to reflect on and think carefully about what children can do and how they think are rare. Portfolios filled with concrete evidence of children's learning afford teachers the luxury of reflecting on and studying children's work during calmer moments when they can notice details about that work and detect patterns that emerge over time.

A second reason for creating portfolios is that they offer children an excellent way to reflect on their own learning. Even children as young as three can learn to look at work they have done, talk about what was easy and what was hard, notice changes over time, and identify what they would like to try next. When children review their portfolios, they often are amazed at their progress. In

THOUGHT QUESTION Think of someone you know well. What details might you include in a case study of that person to show how he or she learned something over time?

Work Recording Sheet Assessment Tool

Work Recording Sheet

Name of child: _____ Date: _____

Name of work: _____

What I did during this work: _____

Something I learned during this work is that: _____

Another thing I learned during this work is that: _____

10.5 *Work Recording Sheet Assessment Tool*

Portfolios are purposeful collections of children's work samples that reveal individual learning and contribute to a comprehensive assessment process.

this way, portfolios boost children's self-confidence as learners. Seeing their work can spark memories about whom they were with or other events that occurred at the time of a painting or story. Thus, a portfolio can promote metacognition, or reflection about what their work is like as a whole, which is one of the important executive functions that develop during children's "five to seven shift."

A third reason for creating portfolios is that they offer families a window into their child's school life. Family members can look at artwork, writing samples, and photographs; read the teacher's written anecdotes of intriguing learning episodes; and even listen to audiotapes or watch video footage of their child engaged in learning. In the portfolio they see the range of learning experiences their child has at school, notice how his work is changing, and read any comments the teacher adds to the work samples. Reviewing such a body of work during parent-teacher conferences sparks rich discussions that can begin with parental observations, not just teacher comments. Given this opportunity, families' appreciation and respect for their child's learning grows significantly. Families also increase their understanding of the curriculum and its purpose, giving them new knowledge to use to help augment their child's learning within the family and community.

Finally, other professionals in the education community may be interested in a child's portfolio. Specialists might wish to examine a child's work as part of an evaluation process to determine the need for extra services. Administrators or supervisors may use portfolios as a way to provide support to a classroom teacher.

Children's portfolios provide rich stores of information that early childhood educators can use in assessing and evaluating children's learning. Figure 10.6 lists a variety of resources for finding out more about portfolio creation and use.

THOUGHT QUESTION Imagine sharing a child's portfolio with his or her parents or other family members. What kinds of questions do you think they would have as they look at the portfolio?

Assembling a portfolio

No single way to organize a portfolio is right or wrong. Some teachers divide the school year into thirds and strive to insert eight to twelve samples during each time period. Others organize portfolios by seasons (fall, winter, spring) or by

Portfolio Resources

Dichtelmiller, Margot L., Judy R. Jablon, Aviva B. Dorfman, Dorothea B. Marsden, and Samuel J. Meisels. 2004. *Work sampling in the classroom: A teacher's manual.* Upper Saddle River, N. J.: Pearson Education (Pearson Early Learning).

Gronlund, Gaye, and Bev Engel. 2001. *Focused portfolios: A complete assessment for the young child.* St. Paul, MN: Redleaf Press.

MacDonald, Sharon. 1997. *The portfolio and its use: A road map for assessment.* Little Rock, AR: Southern Early Childhood Association.

Shores, Elisabeth F., and Cathy Grace. 1998. *The portfolio book: A step-by-step guide for teachers.* Beltsville, MD: Gryphon House.

Wortham, Sue C., Ann Barbour, and Blanche Desjean-Perrotta. 1998. *Portfolio assessment: A handbook for preschool and elementary educators.* Olney, MD: Association for Childhood Education International.

developmental and content areas, such as social studies, art, literacy, and physical development.

Some common portfolio formats include the following:

- Accordion folders with files inside for different types of samples
- Hanging folders with files inside for different types of samples
- Three-ring binders with sections for different types of samples
- Spiral-bound pocket folders holding different types of work samples

Portfolios can also be organized by broad learning goals that are important strands of the teacher's curriculum. Here are some sample goals:

- Expresses ideas through emergent writing and/or dictation
- Uses counting to solve real-life mathematical problems
- Observes and describes the natural and physical world
- Demonstrates understanding of how people work and live together
- Uses art materials to represent experiences

Many teachers also reserve a section of the portfolio for samples of work that children choose to keep for their own reasons.

Since children are one of the primary audiences for portfolios, it makes sense to involve them in as many parts of the portfolio-making process as possible. Building a "portfolio culture" in your classroom boosts children's motivation to learn. Here are some ideas:

- Teach children the word *portfolio,* and make portfolios visible in the classroom.
- Let children decorate and write their name on the outside of their portfolio.
- Set up a work collection system that children can participate in. Have a bin, a large envelope, or a hanging folder with each child's name on it (and perhaps a symbol also, if they are very young) so that children can set aside work that might go into their portfolios later.
- Periodically, take a few minutes to sit with a child and talk about one or two samples. Ask questions like "What do you notice? What part was hard to do?

What happens to a cookie . . .

These are his eyes and that's his tongue + he's saying "Run!"

Number strings

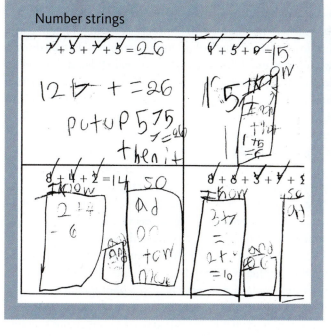

Park ranger interview

Question: How do you get your job?

Answer:

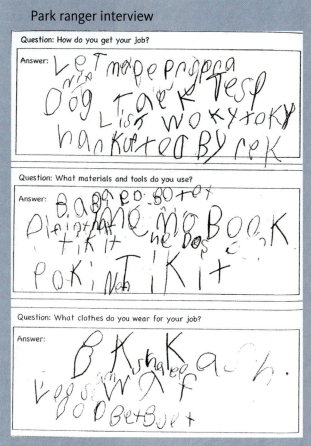

Question: What materials and tools do you use?

Answer:

Question: What clothes do you wear for your job?

Answer:

You might share this second grader's portfolio with the child's family at a parent-teacher conference.

What part was easy? Why are you proud of this?" Record the child's responses, and attach them to the work samples.

To capture and reveal the full range of children's learning in their portfolios, teachers include a variety of **artifacts,** or pieces of work. Obvious artifacts include emerging writing or artwork with a descriptive narrative the child dictates to the teacher. Less obvious and underutilized methods for representing children's learning include sketches or photographs of children's art or block buildings and other three-dimensional work, with explanatory dictation from the child. Audiotapes or video footage of play or conversations and problem solving with other children capture moments with the emotion and affect, not just the words used. Likewise, photographs of any kind, with captions, tell a story of children involved in varied learning experiences such as puzzles, games, math manipulatives, dramatic play, books, fine motor work, gross motor activities, music, sand and water exploration, and cooking. Sometimes, teachers simply write or draw anecdotes based on their observations to describe a child's learning episode.

Because it can be challenging to decide what to put in a portfolio, these sometimes become more like scrapbooks than true portfolios. It is important to keep in mind that portfolios are not intended to show everything a child does at school, but rather to reveal the child as a *learner*. Before inserting a piece of work, ask yourself, "What is the significance of this item? What does it tell me about this child's learning?" Perhaps the child recalled details from a story or tried several different ways to solve a problem or observed an ant on the playground and described how it moved.

Most teachers amass many work samples and then periodically "weed" the collection to select the most appropriate ones for the portfolio. This ensures them of having several samples to select from instead of just one or two. Excessively large portfolios are not useful because few people have time to look through everything in them. A small number of carefully selected pieces of work, with a few thoughtful teacher comments attached to them, will tell more about the child than a thick wad of unorganized and undocumented work samples.

Using portfolios to assess and evaluate children's learning

As with all assessments, teachers must go beyond simply creating portfolios and learn how to use them to inform their curriculum and instruction. Establishing a practice of reviewing two or three portfolios each week will help toward this end.

As you look at a child's work, ask yourself what the portfolio shows you about this child's strengths as a learner. Think about some next small steps this child is ready to take. How can you use her learning strengths to help her take those next steps? Then consider what else you need to learn about this child and how to focus your observations. What kind of work samples should you try to collect next? Since portfolio assessment also follows the assessment cycle, ask yourself what you are learning from the portfolio that will help you to strengthen your relationship with the child.

Rather than evaluating each piece of work in the portfolio, most teachers of young children base their overall, summative evaluations of children on multiple sources: their observations, the portfolio, and any formal assessments that may have been administered. Comments attached to work samples in the portfolio are usually descriptive rather than evaluative. They help other people understand the significance of the work. For example, a note attached to a photograph might say, "Kenny spent twenty minutes building this tower. He used three different kinds of blocks. Note how stable and symmetrical it is. He called it a skyscraper and was able to clearly describe the steps he took to build it."

When created thoughtfully, portfolios can be powerful tools for educators, children, and families—tools to help us see beyond the surface of what a child does and understand how a child learns and thinks. Your efforts to construct portfolios will reward you with deeper knowledge of and insight into the children you teach and, consequently, with the joy of becoming an increasingly effective teacher of young children.

EXTERNALLY IMPOSED ASSESSMENTS

What issues do external assessments raise?

Meaningful early childhood assessment is first and foremost in the interest of the child. No matter who decides that the assessment is necessary and how it will be done,

> Before inserting a piece of work in a child's portfolio ask yourself, "What is the significance of this item? What does it tell me about this child's learning?"

its primary purpose must be to benefit the child. However, different constituencies—teachers, administrators, families, and government officials—may differ in their thinking as to what will benefit children and how to achieve that goal. Here we will examine issues of power, control, responsibility, and accountability that arise in early childhood assessment.

Historical Context

With the increase in academic kindergartens and preschools in the 1980s, widespread testing of young children was not far behind. But as you read in Chapter 5, this was not the first time tests loomed large in educational settings. Influenced by the movement for social efficiency, educational managers in the first part of the twentieth century used factories as a model for making schools productive and learning easy to measure. That push for so-called scientific measurement, along with the behaviorist ideas you read about in Chapter 6, contributed to the development of standardized tests to measure what people at that time believed children should know (Shepard 2000).

Figure 10.7 illustrates how a century ago instruction theory was more in keeping with behaviorist theories of motivation and learning, as well as with emergent ideas about testing children's learning. During the twentieth century, especially in the field of early childhood, constructivist theories, particularly those of Piaget and, later, Vygotsky, became widespread. As a result, over time, the dominant approach to learning and the dominant approach to testing have come to be at odds.

Early Learning Standards

In Chapter 5, we discussed how each society's ideas about what children should learn shapes education in that society. The practice of using standards or goals for learning is growing worldwide, and standards serve as a window into what each

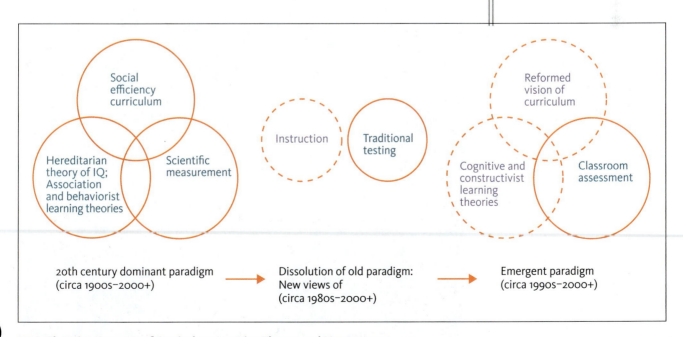

10.7 *Changing Concepts of Curriculum, Learning Theory, and Measurement*
From Shepard 2000, 5

During the first decade of the twenty-first century, more than half the states in the United States developed early learning standards to guide the content of what children in preschool programs should learn.

country, province, or state wants teachers to teach and students to learn. Compared with elementary education, early childhood education came late to state standards, but during the first decade of the twenty-first century, more than half the states in the United States developed **early learning standards** to guide the content of what children in preschool programs should learn.

In the dawn of this new century, Head Start developed the Head Start Child Outcomes Framework (Head Start Bureau 2003), and the second Bush Administration put forth its **Good Start, Grow Smart** initiative. The three aims of Good Start, Grow Smart were

- to improve Head Start,
- to provide educational information to teachers and parents, and
- to encourage the states to develop early learning standards for all preschool learners, with an emphasis on improving children's language and literacy skills.

The Bush Administration also outlined how early learning standards should be in **alignment** with preexisting K–12 standards and be flexible enough to be used in a range of early education and care settings. In this case, being in alignment means fitting into the larger picture of the U. S. education system so that what young children learn in preschool, for example, prepares them for success once they enter school.

Not surprisingly, a study examining how states created their standards found much variance in their quality. Those states that incorporated the greatest depth and breadth of learning issues into their standards produced the highest quality ones (Scott-Little, Kagan and Stebbins Frelow 2005).

Standards for teaching and learning are important, but using standards should not mean standardizing your teaching. Standards, by definition, dictate what teachers should do, at least to some degree. The true challenge is to find creative ways to follow children's interests in your curriculum development and still adhere to mandated standards. True integration of learning standards into a vital child-centered

There are many ways to meet state standards, and programs in different parts of a state can draw on local resources to do so, as shown in this map of Wisconsin.

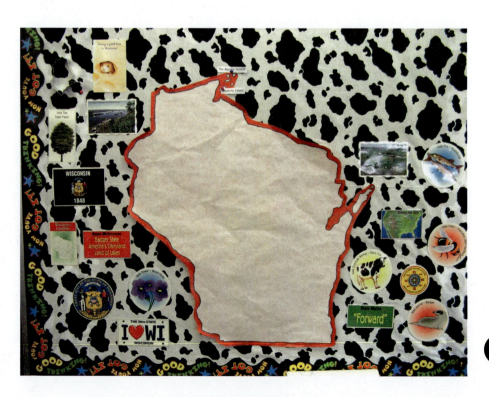

PART 3 Knowing All Children "From the Inside Out": The Observation, Assessment, and Teaching Cycle

curriculum does not mean choosing between them and child-centered curriculum; it means simultaneously attending to both.

Doing integrative curriculum building well means using standards as a guide, not a blueprint. For example, a map of Wisconsin hangs on the wall of third grade classrooms in a school in Milwaukee. Children in one classroom visit farms in the northern part of the state, and children in another class take a trip to a power tools factory near their school. Both classrooms then use the information they learn in those visits to create studies of cheese and power tools, respectively, incorporating reading, the arts, mathematics, and social studies, as shown in the photo. Their learning activities address the Wisconsin early learning performance standards and program standards on the Wisconsin Department of Public Instruction website, among them:

> Early care and education programs in Wisconsin will provide the environment, context, and opportunities for children to develop literacy concepts and skills.

Accountability and Power

Systems of **accountability** are also increasing; these assess a program's success in helping young children learn what the standards have defined they should learn (Scott-Little, Kagan and Stebbins Frelow 2005). When we say that a program is "accountable," we mean that it is accomplishing what it set out to achieve.

Accountability has become important to many parents, school districts, and politicians because, even for young children, learning has become a **high-stakes** issue—that is, a lot is riding on children's becoming successful learners. If we say that children in first grade will learn to read, then we educators and principals, and our districts overall, are accountable for making sure that happens.

Accountability and power are linked. Those in a position to demand accountability have power over those who are accountable to them. This power can result in a school being closed or having its funding withdrawn if the children do not perform in ways that demonstrate the school's successful teaching. Everyone wants schools and teachers to do a good job, but many disagree about how to accomplish this goal. While the increase in testing is intended to create better schools, most early childhood educators maintain that high-stakes testing that has serious consequences will not serve to improve teaching and learning.

Power relations play a role in testing, too. Think back to the last exam you took. Was power one of the emotions you felt? Or did you feel a lack of power? Some people experience an adrenaline surge when they are about to take a test. It is as if the test poses a challenge to which they can rise or offers them an opportunity to show off what they can do. However, most people do not feel powerful when they are tested or evaluated academically. They feel even less powerful if they think they are unprepared, if they have had prior bad experiences with tests or assessments, or if the test or assessment really doesn't measure what they can do.

Systems of accountability are also increasing; these assess a program's success in helping young children learn what the standards have defined they should learn.

Tests and Young Children

Genevive's first graders have just finished taking a standardized test and are eager to talk about their initiation into this school ritual. Genevive explains that the test is required by the school board.

> *Shawnda:* But why would the school board give us such a hard test? We never gave them a hard test.

Genevive: That's a good question for you to ask them. . . . What else might you want to ask them?

Monique: Why did you just give us a hard test? Because some of us don't really think it's good, 'cause me and Maya started to cry. And it was hard for some of us.

Many other children express similar sentiments. Edward J., however, begins to get silly:

Edward J: I would write [to the school board], "Scram, beat it, get lost."

Genevive: But would they know what you mean?

Eugenie: They would get mad.

Genevive: Would that help? . . .

Eugenie: They'd mark it wrong.

And Edward offers a more appropriate sentence:

Edward: That test is hard.

Genevive suggests that the children act on their concerns and write to the school board. She talks to them about how letters are written, and they begin writing their own letters to the school board—in their own handwriting, using their own ways of spelling. Mollie offers Genevive a suggestion:

Mollie: I think that what you should do is when we're done, you should read them 'cause they might not be able to understand them.

Genevive: After I read them, I'll see if they need editing. (Dyson and Genishi 1993, 122–123)

Here we have a group of children who are simultaneously questioners, problem solvers, jokers, readers, beginning writers, as well as test takers, although the test does not address all these aspects of their identities. Writing a letter of protest may be hard for children, too, or at least challenging; but it is a better demonstration of children's abilities than tests are and is a meaningful activity for both children and teachers.

Nonetheless, testing young children has become commonplace. The federal NCLB Act mandates testing beginning in third grade. In the context of norm-based, standardized tests, some children must fall below the norm, or fiftieth percentile of scores. Their schools will receive funding to enable teachers to teach them the needed skills, and at the end of the year the children will take another test to demonstrate how much they have learned. In kindergarten and above, children may take a standardized test three times and may have additional monthly tests tied to the teaching of skills.

Other tests are required for younger children in some states and counties. In the first part of this century, the National Reporting System (NRS) assessed Head Start children's readiness. Representatives of major professional organizations as well as nationally respected educators testified before Congress about the problems inherent in using standardized tests with preschoolers. This strong reaction gave the government pause and the NRS is no longer used, but the question of early testing is not going away.

NAEYC opposes testing young children. The organization asserts that young children, especially those under five, should not be given standardized tests, nor should evaluative judgments about them be made based on such tests.

Young children cannot sit for long periods to do something that is not of their choosing, much less focus with great concentration on something that does not engage them. Second, children this age learn in context, and their learning is tied to

Because young children learn in context and are just developing the ability to generalize, they take ideas at face value and have trouble decontextualizing test questions. Thus, children may attempt to answer questions in ways that link to their own experience but not to the test questions.

George looked at the test. It said:

Rabbits eat:

☐ lettuce

☐ dog food

☐ sandwiches

He raised his hand.

"Rabbits have to eat carrots, or their teeth will get too long and stick into them," he said.

The teacher nodded and smiled, but she put her finger to her lips. George carefully drew in a carrot so the test people would know.

Text and illustrations from *First Grade Takes a Test* (Cohen and Hoban 2006).

that context. They are in the process of developing the ability to generalize. They take ideas at face value and have trouble decontextualizing them to answer a question. Thus, children may attempt to answer questions in ways that link to their own experience but not to the test questions.

In the excerpt above from Miriam Cohen's *First Grade Takes a Test,* a child demonstrates true understanding and is able to apply it in context, but unfortunately his answer will not be marked correct on the test. Rabbits do eat lettuce, it is true; but they also eat carrots. This test question calls for a more limited response than George can comfortably give as a result of his prior experience and knowledge.

Yet another problem with testing young children has to do with the nature of standardized tests themselves. Children's results are ranked by comparing them with those of other children. The ranking does not provide teachers with information about what to teach next or how to teach better. It just shows how a given child performed on a given day. So although a test may indicate that a school's teaching should improve, it offers insufficient guidance as to how.

Finally, though test results are expressed in numbers and seem scientific, people create tests, and people can make errors, including errors of interpretation. As you saw with George's carrot, the test maker's right answer might not be right to the child, to the teacher, or to the person scoring the test. More importantly, test makers may have narrow interpretations of test content in general. For example, many reading tests for young children focus on sound-letter relationships, or phonics, to the exclusion of other ways of thinking about a child's reading level. Multiple sources of information paint a richer learning portrait.

Still, we can learn from this era of testing. The high-stakes tests brought about by NCLB have had some unanticipated effects. At a public school in rural Virginia, the preschool teachers and the early elementary grade teachers now meet regularly to increase their awareness of the content and pedagogy that comes before and after the grade they teach. This kind of collaboration for greater alignment and curricular consistency is a positive effect of high-stakes testing that we hope will continue independent of the testing.

COMMUNICATING ASSESSMENT RESULTS

How can early childhood educators communicate assessment results?

Assessments are only meaningful if they change adults' behavior with children. For this to happen, adults need to discuss assessment data with one another to make sense of it. And they should involve children in assessment whenever possible so that they can take as much responsibility as possible for their own learning.

Reports to Families

When you read about family conferences in Chapter 14, you will see that preparing yourself *and* families for the process is the first step. Parents will be more receptive and eager to participate if you let them know what to expect ahead of time. Letters home at the beginning of the year along with statements during the first curriculum night are opportunities to inform parents about how you assess their children's work and behavior as you discuss the curriculum itself. If you use portfolios, explain the process and perhaps show a few wide-ranging examples from a previous year. Provide families with a list of things to think about during the fall semester: "What have you noticed about Eric's _____ [language, social skills, etc.]. Do you have questions about his progress?" Then, if you begin conferences by asking families what *they* have noticed, they will not be taken off guard. They will have had time to consider their child's behaviors at home and perhaps to discuss them with other family members.

As you think about reporting on a child's progress, consider the whole child—his social-emotional, physical, and cognitive development—just as you do in your teaching. The child's age and the type of program you work in also determine the ways you will report to his family. Grades are typically not used in preschools but are required in most kindergartens and on through the educational system. Many early childhood educators believe that **narrative reporting**, a written description of the child's behaviors, is the most meaningful way to convey information about young children from infant and toddler through the early elementary years, even when grades are also reported. Narrative reports take time and considerable effort, but if you have accumulated evidence and taken careful notes throughout the semester or year, they are less burdensome.

What might you include in such a narrative? As with all assessment, it is crucial to keep the data in context and make sure they are accurate and fair. Working from a positive approach that looks at what children can do and goes on from there, state the child's strengths and areas for improvement, and make recommendations. Provide evidence in the form of concrete examples for every statement. This keeps you "honest" and transforms reports into learning tools for families. Your recommendations can be the basis for conversations with families about activities they can do at home, but keep these short and focused. Two or three items are plenty (McAfee and Leong 2002).

Reports to Colleagues

As Joanne Frantz tells us in her Real Voice, she kept her colleagues abreast of her observations of Allan, and they in turn kept Joanne in the loop even before Allan arrived in her class.

> Many early childhood educators believe that narrative reporting, a written description of the child's behaviors, is the most meaningful way to convey information about young children, even when grades are also reported.

4/5s Mid-year Report

Name: Morgan
Age: 5.2
Teachers: Emily Booth and Joan Campbell

Initial Adjustment

Morgan entered the 4/5s with curiosity and interest. He spent most of his time with teachers during the first weeks of school. Right away, he talked with us, asked questions, and gave hugs. Morgan warmed up more slowly to other children. Once he connected more deeply with Nini and George, his comfort in his new classroom community grew.... He seems happy and engaged in school, sharing stories about his family, his cat, and karate.

Social and Emotional Development

Personable and friendly, Morgan shows a range of emotions and has grown in his ability to speak up for himself. Morgan's connections with teachers helped him adjust to this new school. Though he continues to tell us stories, sit in our laps, and show us work, his friendships have increased in value for him since the beginning of the year. Morgan chats, plays, and works with everyone, especially Nini and George.

At the beginning of the year, Morgan stayed next to a teacher in the yard, watching other children.... At this point in the year, Morgan sometimes takes leadership roles in games. One day he went outside with Nini and George and announced with enthusiasm, "Let's go camping!" They busily built tents and roasted marshmallows.

Morgan sometimes seems tired or engaged in his own inner world of imagination. It may also be an age-typical strategy to avoid something he doesn't want to do, such as help clean up. However, with a clear reminder that everyone helps in our room, he does. Yet Morgan helps others in the room when he sees them in need.... He also checks with someone who is hurt or upset, as when he offered a hurt friend a hug and self-composed songs of comfort.

Cognitive Development and Work with Materials

Morgan has become a more independent worker since the beginning of the year. He works in all areas of the room, most frequently with manipulatives, the sensory table (water first, now sand), and dramatic play. At the start of the year, Morgan moved around to many work areas during one work time. Now, he engages for longer periods with materials before moving on to something new. We'll continue to support his deepening investment in materials.

Morgan also engages in more imaginative dramatic play now. He creates narratives for his block work, such as when he built a home for two horses and then played with them as a parent horse and child horse that got lost and then found. In the dramatic play area, where children assume pretend roles, Morgan contributes more ideas than at the beginning of the year. When he is a chef, he builds in his kitchen and prepares and delivers food to other children. We will continue to encourage his participation in play to further develop his abstract thinking. . . . From early on, Morgan has displayed his understanding of the interconnection between speaking, writing, and reading as communication. He made many signs to let people know about days that school would be closed. He not only used his literacy meaningfully, he also expressed his increased sense of ownership of his classroom.

At this point in the year, Morgan's comments at meetings are usually on topic. He tends to raise his hand, get called on, and then think about what to say but is starting to think first and state his thoughts more succinctly. He also tends to start sentences, stop, restart a few times, and wander to different topics. Though this is challenging for the age group, Morgan shows some development in this area.

Physical Development
Morgan's physical development is age appropriate at all levels. . . . Morgan joyfully uses his gross-motor skills to play outside. He runs, jumps, and climbs on different levels of the climber and uses the ladders, slides, and chain ladder. He does not cross the bars or rings, perhaps because some children who are large for their age, like Morgan, do not yet have the upper body strength. Sometimes Morgan trips or bumps into things, as if he is still growing into his body and developing full coordination and sense of his body in space.

Goals
- We will continue to provide opportunities for Morgan to expand and deepen his social connections in the classroom.
- We will continue to help Morgan speak more succinctly in meetings.
- We will help Morgan further develop his graphomotor skills by encouraging his writing and drawing as well as his work with manipulatives that can strengthen his fingers and hands.

Conference Notes
Morgan and his parents met with Emily and Joan on November 1. In addition to the above:

- We talked about shooting games. Morgan's mother shared her dislike of this kind of play.
- Morgan's mother explained her strategy of playfully "shooting back with love" at home.
- Morgan's parents described their deeper understanding of progressive education and their perception that Morgan is learning about how to learn.

Final Comments
It has been delightful getting to know Morgan and seeing him become more confident and comfortable in class. His warmth and friendliness have been welcome additions to our classroom community. We look forward to his continued growth during the second half of the year.

Portions of a mid-year narrative report about a five-year-old child.

I teach the threes/fours class in a private preschool. We assess our students' learning all the time, but in an informal way. We use careful observation to get a picture of each child's development. We record daily observations of children and share them with co-teachers. This is our style of informal assessment. Allan's story (see also Genishi and Dyson 2009) illustrates how we work on assessment with each other and with families.

Allan was in the twos class before he entered our three/fours. Angela, one of his teachers, alerted me that she thought Allan had a severe language delay and didn't engage with other children. She wondered about possible autism spectrum issues and spoke to Allan's parents frequently about what she saw. She also invited them to observe him. Angela believed that his suburban school district was scheduled to test him over the summer.

Allan attended our summer play camp, and he often "escaped," or tried to escape, from the class. His teachers said that Allan loved to paint at the easel and chase bubbles outside but seemed to be "in his own world" most of the time. They also reported that he rarely spoke.

As school began in September, our classroom team discussed having good communication with both his parents and agreed to document his behavior carefully. We took quick notes on what Allan did and did not do throughout the day. At regular meetings with our director and other teachers, we discussed our observations.

For example, Allan was drawn to two verbal young threes who put on superhero costumes when they first arrived at school. Allan watched and imitated them but rarely spoke. He remembered what costume everyone wore the day before and didn't seem to respond to new plans. If he spoke, he used one word, "Spiderman" or "Batman."

As the fall progressed, I became more concerned about Allan's continued lack of language. He rarely responded to questions we asked him or to other children's comments or questions.

We tried to spend one-on-one time with Allan, and we pointed out what other children were doing during free-play time and invited him to join them. He didn't respond to these cues. I didn't know how else to help him. I told Allan's mom about our concerns. At the end of that fall, Allan was absent from time to time.

As I found out only later, Allan's mom had begun exploring the assessment process for Allan before he entered our class. Although I did not know it at the time, after I spoke to her, she immediately contacted her pediatrician and went ahead with the assessment process. In December, she consulted with a behavioral specialist at the local children's hospital. The specialist asked me and Allan's mom to complete the Gilliam Autism Rating Scale (GARS-2, Gilliam 2006). Based on our ratings, Allan

Joanne Frantz

was diagnosed with pervasive developmental disorder not otherwise specified (PDD-NOS) because his behaviors did not meet the criteria for a specific disorder such as autism. For example, Allan was interested in other children and their superhero games and mimicked sounds they made.

Allan's mom and I did not communicate in December, but on January 1, she wrote me an email about the diagnosis. She said it was hard to write because she "felt Allan was perfect." I understood how hard this was for her, but I also knew that she was angry at us for not helping Allan more in the classroom. I felt we couldn't give Allan as much help as he needed, *and* there were seventeen other children in the class.

Although his parents kept him home in January—I later learned that they did not think our school was a good fit for him—Allan let his parents know that he wanted to return. In February, he was back; and our director, Stephanie; Allan's parents; and I met. Stephanie had developed a good relationship with the family from the previous year when Allan's dad chaired our maintenance committee, and she moderated our discussion.

At this point, Allan's mom became his advocate and coach in our class, sharing what she was learning from a class Allan (and she) had begun to attend at a local center that specializes in "speech and social delays." We, in turn, learned a lot from her. That spring, we had two parent-teacher conferences where we discussed Allan's great progress and future plans.

The following year, Allan returned to our school, attending two days a week and continuing to receive speech and other therapy. The year after, Allan was still at our school, with no special classes, and he will begin in a typical kindergarten when he is six.

We felt that the continuing dialogue between Allan's parents, Stephanie, and me, even through times of anger and miscommunication, allowed a plan for Allan to evolve. As teachers we needed our observations and the discussions among ourselves, the professional diagnosis and strategies from outside therapists, *and* mom's help in the classroom to maximize Allan's progress.

In addition to regular oral communication between colleagues and exchanged written observations, teachers write reports to share with one another and with people outside the school. Reports of any kind should not be too lengthy and should be written in a professional manner with carefully chosen language. Your role in the report should be stated explicitly, for example, "I have been keeping anecdotal notes about Allan's social skills since October."

Often administrators within the school may have a more distant relationship to the classroom than teachers. In Joanne's story, the program director, Stephanie, was able to play a key role with Allan and his family, in part, because of Joanne's written and oral communication to her about Allan throughout the year. She was able to participate in the family meeting on short notice because she had been kept informed all along. This exemplifies why providing clear and periodic written reports is so important. Administrators cannot be in more than one place at a time, so they rely on various information pathways to enable them to play a responsible role in their leadership of a school or program.

Reports sometimes are sent out of the school to help others who will be working with a child. Such reports might go to the child's new school, to a special needs professional, or to a day camp. Communicating with other classrooms, schools, and programs must be done with the kind of professionalism we discussed earlier. However, the recipients of these reports may need background and context information. Sometimes a short summary of that information may be all that is needed to help the reader make better sense of a report. As a professional courtesy, however, always include your contact information in case the reader has any questions. *Information in a child's report is absolutely confidential and is not to be disclosed informally in any setting other than an educational one.*

Teachers may mistakenly assume that a teaching partner within the classroom has the same information they do. Avoiding misunderstandings with teaching partners is an ongoing challenge. Some classrooms have adopted "open notebooks" that all teaching adults in the classroom write in to ensure that key information does not get lost before the next team meeting. This does not preclude the need for ongoing, less formal communication, but it does safeguard against those days when so much is going on that a teacher can forget to mention an important occurrence.

Feedback to Children

Feedback to children happens throughout the day, in individual and group conferences about work, and with periodic progress reports. Such reports can use pictures and simple words but, like all feedback, should be specific. Telling a child that you notice that her story has a beginning, middle, and end and that you like the detail about the way the kitten's fur feels provides concrete information about the ways she is integrating the curriculum. "Drawing a happy face and saying 'OK'" (McAfee and Leong 2002, 201) doesn't help children move forward in their learning. If you say to a child that his work has fewer errors, includes a lot of color, or required a lot of concentration, you will have conveyed more content than telling him "I like your painting" or using the very popular but unhelpful descriptor, "Good job." And, as you have already seen in this chapter, young children can assess themselves, developing a portfolio or filling out a form about a morning activity, as you saw with Megan's children in the Montessori school (see Figure 10.5).

Since the 1960s, the field of early childhood has been aware of the difference between praise and encouragement (Gartrell 2007). Think back to this chapter's discussion about power relationships inherent in testing. It makes sense that in many aspects of classroom life, children are well aware of the not-so-subtle power that teachers have over them. Not only do most young children want to please their teachers, but they can easily mistake a moment of praise (or no praise) as an evaluation of their very being, not just of their drawing, vocabulary words, or story.

And is the child alone in his or her interpretation? Most likely not. Other children, who are not often praised or perhaps not praised for that particular activity, make generalizations about who is good based on what may have been an incidental remark.

Figuring out how to provide encouragement rather than praise seems easy compared with the task of encouraging children when their work is not going well. Here, individual differences in self-esteem and a history of parenting practices can come into play more directly. If a child either receives endless praise at home or, at the other end of the spectrum, can never seem to succeed in the eyes of family members, those experiences will affect a teacher's ability to help a child through problematic work. As with adults, it can help to take a step back, look at the broader picture, and see that there has been progress, just not at the moment.

Then, it is important to help children find patterns in their errors and provide them with strategies to overcome them. Remember Min's work on vocabulary with Jenny: Concentrating on one area to help a child achieve immediate progress can provide some welcome validation and success. Guard against sugarcoating problem issues, as doing so doesn't help children move forward, nor does it help them learn how to deal with criticism, an important ability to acquire and bring to adulthood. Make clear that you are not commenting on the essence of the children's selves, but on their work. Remember, too, that, as with Jenny and Min, the point is to assess and then communicate the results of the assessment in order to help the child learn more and better.

> Not only do most young children want to please their teachers, but they can easily mistake a moment of praise (or no praise) as an evaluation of their very being, not just of their drawing, vocabulary words, or story.

SUMMARY

THE ROOTS OF ASSESSMENT

What does assessment mean in early childhood settings?

Assessment is a systematic, ongoing process of gathering, analyzing, and interpreting information about children to identify their strengths and needs, with the goal of improving teaching strategies and children's learning. Assessment data guide our ongoing work, and evaluation of those data informs our judgments and decisions in a more formal way. Formative assessment is ongoing and supports the process of the educational activity; summative assessment evaluates the activity after it is finished.

THE ASSESSMENT CYCLE

What is the assessment cycle?

The assessment cycle describes a multistep circular process. The first step is to build a relationship with the child. The second step is to gather information formally and informally. The third step is to make sense of that information and decide what to do as a result. The final step is to take action, but that is not the end. Ideally, these actions both nourish the relationship between adult and child and generate additional information. Thus, the cycle continues.

THE PURPOSES OF ASSESSMENT

Why do we assess?

We assess to better achieve our goals and objectives for young children. Based on data from multiple sources collected over time, assessment helps us to reassess those goals and objectives repeatedly as children and situations change. Three types of assessment fulfill different purposes. Performance-based assessments record each child's progress individually; children are not compared with each other. Criterion-based assessments allow a child's progress to be viewed individually *or* compared with that of other children using a common set of expectations. In norm-referenced assessments, each person's score is compared with that of a normed test-taker. Still, the primary purpose of all three types of assessment is to help teachers and other school personnel to make decisions about curriculum for children.

ASSESSMENT IN A SCHOOL CONTEXT
How do teachers assess children in schools?
In schools, as in out-of-school settings, whoever is assessing what children do must maintain focus on the children. It stands to reason, then, that observation is at the foundation of assessment in schools. It takes time to learn to coordinate observation with multiple other sources of assessment, including collaboration with colleagues.

ASSESSMENT TOOLS
What assessment tools are available to use with young children?
The Apgar test determines the baby's vital signs at birth and at five minutes after birth. The Brazelton Neonatal Behavioral Assessment Scale focuses on the baby's social and interactive abilities as well as his or her neurological signs. The Ages and Stages Questionnaire is a screening tool for children birth to age four. The Ounce Scale looks at the infant or toddler within the context of his or her family. The Bayley Scale of Infant Development is the most formal method of gaining an in-depth picture of how a young child is developing and is an example of a standardized and normed test. The ECLAS is an assessment tool designed to help teachers monitor children's progress in literacy from kindergarten through grade three.

Rubrics break down the learning components of state standards or other learning goals and make it easier to evaluate a child's progress toward each benchmark or goal. Teachers may also write case studies that provide detailed descriptions of a child's learning and of teachers' strategies over time. Some teachers develop tools to help children become more aware of their own learning. Portfolios serve that function, too, as purposeful collections of children's works that reveal individual learning to children, teachers, and families and contribute to a comprehensive assessment process.

EXTERNALLY IMPOSED ASSESSMENTS
What issues do external assessments raise?
More than half the states in this country have developed early learning standards, which, by definition, dictate what teachers should do, although standards need not mean standardization. Systems of accountability are also increasing; these assess a program's success in helping young children learn what the standards have defined they should learn. Naturally, those in a position to demand accountability have power over those who are accountable to them. Yet different constituencies—teachers, administrators, families, and government officials—may differ in their thinking as to what will benefit children and what actions will achieve those benefits.

COMMUNICATING ASSESSMENT RESULTS

How can early childhood educators communicate assessment results?

Teachers report the results of their assessments to families in conferences, through letters home, and with portfolios of children's work. Narrative reporting describes children's behaviors and communicates more than a grade on a report card. Teachers also keep one another abreast of their observations and other assessment data. Administrators, too, can do their jobs better when they are fully informed about the children in their programs. Feedback to children occurs throughout the day and should be specific and concrete, recalling that the purpose of assessment and communicating the results of an assessment is to help children learn more and better.

FURTHER ACTIVITIES

1. Contact an agency in your community that provides early intervention, and make an appointment to visit and interview an early interventionist. Prepare a list of questions beforehand about the goals and benefits of EI, and how the agency implements it. Be sure to find out about the tools that early interventionists at this agency use. Ask about their work with families, and learn which professionals are involved in assessment (and how) and in delivery of services. Write up your findings in a short paper. (**NAEYC Standard 3: Observing, Documenting, and Assessing to Support Young Children and Families**)

2. Visit a child care center to learn how assessment is conducted there. Using your notes from this chapter, find out all the ways in which teachers learn about and exchange information about children. Create an assessment web illustrating all of the center's assessment activities and showing how these activities support the relationships between and among teachers, children, and families at this center. In a short essay, explain how and why developmentally effective approaches to teaching and learning and content-rich curriculum result (or do not result) from the center's assessment procedures. (**NAEYC Standard 3: Observing, Documenting, and Assessing to Support Young Children and Families**)

3. Collect three pieces of work from a child between the ages of three and eight. What are some things you notice about each item? Given the strengths and needs demonstrated in them, create a chart listing your goals and objectives for the child. Next to each, describe two learning activities you have created for it. (**NAEYC Standard 4: Using Developmentally Effective Approaches to Connect with Children and Families**)

CHAPTER ELEVEN

Infants, Toddlers, and Two-Year-Olds

From thousands of interactions . . . the child builds an internal working model or representation that says: "This is how my caregiver cares for me. This is how I am."

Carollee Howes

rying to make their way around this new and curious world, infants, toddlers, and two-year-olds crawl, run, jump, snuggle, push, poke, climb, stomp, sing, cry, giggle, and hug. What can early care and education look like for these busy ones? In this chapter, you will read about relationships and other aspects of the environment that support a safe and trusting space for very young children and their families. You will think about how to help infants, toddlers, and two-year-olds feel safe while they are away from their families.

LIFE WITH INFANTS, TODDLERS, AND TWO-YEAR-OLDS

Who are infants, toddlers, and two-year-olds?

Here are three "snapshots" of some under-threes in child care:

> While the teachers are helping the toddler group dress for an outing, Lucy, sixteen months, is busily taking off her clothes. By the time a teacher sees her, she is as bare as a tree in winter.
>
> The group is preparing for a nap. When the teacher removes twenty-one-month-old Sofia's left shoe, Sofia flings herself backward, lies down on the floor, and screams with all her might, "Me! Me!" "Okay, you want to take it off yourself," says the teacher as she puts the shoe back on.
>
> At eight months, Simmi is the youngest in a mixed-age group and is sitting contentedly with a stack of rings in a corner of the room. Luis, thirty months, who plays with Simmi in a brotherly way, comes by to engage him when their teacher hears Luis yell out loudly, "Simmi made a poop. I can smell it!"

As you can see, working with children under age three is a unique learning and growing opportunity for teachers.

A Dynamic Period

Children under three are not "little preschoolers." Where preschoolers have a pretty clear concept of their own "self," infants and toddlers are just forming this idea and depend on their caregivers and teachers for *warm, close relationships* to teach them that they are lovable (Lally 1995, Howes 1998). They need caregivers to provide a secure base (Bowlby 1972), a safe starting point from which they can venture to explore the world. Whereas preschoolers have fairly developed language, infants and toddlers are just starting to use words. Whereas preschoolers are beginning to regulate their emotions, infants and toddlers *continually* need a calm, focused caregiver to help them control themselves and understand their emotional reactions. Instead of telling the toddler "No!" or punishing him for crying and pushing the peas off his plate, the teacher helps him understand what he wants by saying, for example, "You're unhappy because you don't want that food on your plate. I'll move it away." The teacher provides the words that the toddler doesn't yet have.

In this chapter, we will talk about infants (birth to about eleven months), toddlers (eleven to approximately twenty-two months), and two-year-olds (twenty-two to thirty-six months). These children are complicated beings and as different one from the other as pebbles on the beach. Their caregivers learn to appreciate them as they are, *at the moment,* because from one moment to the next they can surprise you. If you kept tabs on one infant or toddler all day long through her varied activities from playtime to naptime, you would be hard-pressed at the end of the day to say, "I've got it! I know her well." The ten-month-old who waved good-bye to Mom with a smile yesterday might erupt in a storm today. The two-year-old who today ate his entire lunch on his own next week might ask to be fed. The toddler who refused to pick up a tossed plaything today might pick it up tomorrow.

Children under three are as changeable as a summer day—thunder and lightning one minute, sunny blue sky the next. During these first three years of life, children's development is so rapid and their changes so dramatic that a caregiver coming in on Monday may gasp at seeing Luca walking when he was still crawling on Friday. Think of it: in the space of only thirty-six months, a child learns to sit, creep, stand, walk, jump, babble, talk, sing, have (and express) preferences, tell strangers apart from family and friends, and understand most language addressed to him.

Not surprisingly, infants' brains grow faster than at any other time after birth. The cerebral cortex, the largest part of our brain—which controls functions such as thinking, memory, language, sensory information, and motor development—*triples* in size during the first year of life (Eliot 1999). Brain growth occurs by means of "wiring" that links nerve cells, or neurons, together, similar to a mass of wires that we would need if all the telephones in the world were linked together. However, as you read in Chapter 3, the "pruning," or shaping of neural connections, that is based on the type and amount of particular experiences a young child has influences how that child's thinking and behaving develops. Thus, how adults

- lovingly care for babies,
- respond to them when they cry, and
- expose them to positive experiences with people, places, and things

directly affects brain growth. Deep, personal, responsive, affectionate connections to both parents and teacher-caregivers are "the primary source of a child's security, self-esteem, self-control, and social skills" (Eliot 1999, 305).

Development Is Bumpy

Children's development doesn't progress in a straight path—it lurches forward and slips back, and then may repeat the process. Also, one aspect of development may not be in synch with other aspects. For example, a toddler may put together a simple puzzle but not walk yet. Often, what looks like a delay may be just a rough patch. And because their world is a sensorimotor one, young children's learning may not always make sense to our adult **categorical** world, where everything has a name and fits in a conceptual system. When a one-year-old uses her first word, "dog," at her aunt's house but looks bewildered by dogs on the street, her parents, too, may be confused. It may take time for the toddler to realize that there is a category of animals called dogs, not just the one at her auntie's house.

Very young children's uneven development can create a challenge for their caregivers and teachers, who are trying to understand them and create environments for them. Moreover, teachers may have difficulty recognizing when a child's development needs special attention. With a developmental issue such as autism, for example, development may proceed without any glitches in the first year. Alternatively, caregivers may notice that the child does not imitate "gestures, sounds, or actions with a toy . . . or engag[e] in back-and-forth vocalizations" (Muratori 2008, 18) as frequently as typically developing children.

Children under three are as changeable as a summer day—thunder and lightning one minute, sunny blue sky the next.

Age	Behavioral Shift
Neonate	Development and early coordination of motor and state systems with the environment
2 months	Brain growth; regulation to day and night schedule ("settling in"); focused attention to human beings; social smile
3—4 months	Social flowering; sophistication of communication; increased vocalization; visual ability close to adult's; "veto power" (Stern 1985), i.e., infant can turn head away to communicate displeasure in an interaction
5—6 months	Reaching out for more social and environmental stimuli, including objects as well as caregivers; anticipates what comes next in a routine
7—9 months	Increased intentionality, movement; increased sense of self and thus, often, attachment to caregivers; joint attention and an early sense of others' minds (intersubjectivity); beginning of symbolic thinking; shows emotional connections to at least one key person in their life
9—12 months	Surge in representational abilities; imitation of some simple gestures; understands simple instructions; may show basic pretend by a year (e.g. cup to mouth)

Caregivers, especially beginners, who have questions or concerns about a child's development are best off working with other professionals and the child's parents to determine if an EI assessment is the next step. Many inclusive programs, those serving children who are developing typically as well as those with delays, such as Early Head Start, have a disabilities coordinator. Including children with developmental delays and/or disabilities in a child care program can enrich all children's experience but requires careful planning and an experienced teaching staff who are knowledgeable about very early development. Figure 11.1 catalogs shifts in behavior typically seen during the first year of life.

Influences on Development

How do those soft, warm infants who love to nestle and stare become independent, self-directed, sometimes-fearful toddlers and two-year-olds who obey as well as defy

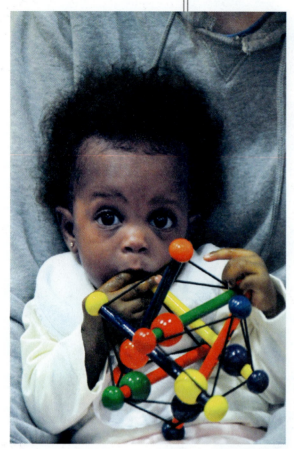

Child care can provide many exciting experiences for infants.

All parents have goals and expectations for their children, but parents sometimes may not be aware of their goals that influence their children's development.

and cuddle as well as resist? Many factors influence how a baby's personality will develop, including the baby's family and culture, the baby's teachers and caregivers, and the baby's own way of reacting to other people and the world.

Families: their cultures and beliefs

The psychiatrist D. W. Winnicott wrote: "There is no such thing as a baby.... If you set out to describe a baby, you will find you are describing a baby and someone. A baby cannot exist alone, but is essentially part of a relationship" (1978, 88). This statement emphasizes how critical a primary person—a parent, grandparent, or relative—is for a baby's development and well-being.

During the first three years of life, infants, toddlers, and two-year-olds focus on finding out who they are and what they can do. They actively absorb everything around them, and what their families and their cultures believe about child rearing and about the world becomes part of who they are.

All parents have goals and expectations for their children (LeVine 1974), but parents sometimes may not be aware of their goals that influence their children's development. For example, one set of parents might want their baby to sleep separately in a crib, while another expects their child to sleep with them during the first years. Whether the families think of these practices as doing so, they teach children early independence or give them a sense of membership in the family—and what children learn reflects what their parents want for them.

Some families believe that babies should become do-it-yourself, independent go-getters who sleep in their own cribs, learn to hold their own bottles, and eventually feed themselves. "The child is perceived to have an identity, rights, and needs, starting at the moment of birth" (Gonzalez-Mena 2005, 114). Other families believe that babies should stay close to the family, be obedient, behave properly, sleep in or near the parents' bed, and be fed by someone up to age two or three. "Children in these cultures are taught to see themselves as part of something larger than themselves; their family, their people" (Gonzalez-Mena 2005, 115). Of course, as Janet Gonzalez-Mena points out, these two points of view—being independent as an individual or having the ability to function as an interdependent group member—are not mutually exclusive. Every culture depends on children's ability to do both, but in some cultures, one or the other can take greater priority. Even within a family, various ideas about what is best for a child may be in competition.

Although the family and community transmit their culture to the child, the child affects the culture as well. Even very young babies bring their preferences for and inclinations toward certain kinds of touch and sounds into their developmental niche. The baby's reactions to what their adults do, such as to the music they play and how loudly they play it, influence the adults' responses to them. One baby may love the stimulation of the sounds, but another may shy away from it, covering her ears. Even if her family reacts negatively to or ignores her behavior, young children are **resilient**—that is, they possess a range of inner strengths to help them recover from experiences that do not fit their preferences and inclinations.

Raising children is an awesome task. Frequently families are mystified about what is best for their children. Some parents may not realize how important they are to their children. For these reasons, any child care community *must* form positive, accepting, and supportive relationships with the families of the infants and toddler/twos in their care. Caregivers sometimes struggle to form such relationships when they don't agree with parents' child-rearing methods. Although parents seldom want to be told what to do, they often welcome a good listener who can help them examine questions about their children's behavior from several perspectives.

Teachers: their cultures and beliefs

In their efforts to form their own identity, infants, toddlers, and two-year-olds are influenced by the goals that their teachers believe are important (Lally 1995). As you saw in Chapter 1, teachers' cultures, personal histories, and identities contribute to the goals they have for children and determine how they interact with children and families.

Some teachers believe that children aged birth to three need, not only attention and loving care, but also clear, flexible guidelines for behavior and predictable routines. These teachers help children to control their environment by offering choices with such questions as, "Do you want milk or water?" "Do you want me to change your diaper now or in a little while?"

Some teachers believe that children aged birth to three require a lot of adult control in addition to loving care. They may worry that children will be spoiled if they don't learn to obey adults. Some teachers believe that management takes precedence over flexibility.

Robin Leavitt (1994) describes a teacher who insisted that a toddler play with shaving cream even though the child did not want to get his hands messy. Perhaps the teacher did not know that many young children can be **sensory defensive,** that is, sensitive to a range of sensory experiences.

We favor observing children's cues, following their lead, and giving them reasonable choices because we want children to build a relationship of trust with a caregiver who provides a model of **responsive care,** a way of caregiving that listens to children and responds to them respectfully. Magda Gerber's Resources for Infant Educators (see http://www.rie.org/), too, is based on principles of respect for young children's ability to begin to learn how to take responsibility for their behavior and to develop confidence in themselves. Children tend to imitate their teacher's responsive care, as the following story demonstrates:

> Maddie (eight months) is seated on a mat playing with a stuffed animal. Suddenly, she begins to cry. Jonas (fourteen months) goes to her, squats down, and offers her the pacifier that is pinned to her shirt. She accepts the pacifier and seems comforted for a few moments. Before long, though, she begins to cry again. Jonas walks to the other side of the room, picks up a ring of plastic keys, and offers it to Maddie. He pats her gently on the back. She quiets, looks into Jonas's eyes, smiles warmly, picks up her stuffed animal, and resumes quiet play. Jonas watches her for a moment and then walks away. The caregiver observing all this smiles quietly.

In giving Maddie attention, Jonas imitates his teacher's responsive care. With her smile, this caregiver demonstrates that she can step back, observe for a few moments, and see the extent to which she is a model of caring behavior for the young children in her care.

The context of group care

What do you think about very young children spending the day away from their parents in a group care setting? As an early childhood educator, your feelings about

Infant/toddler programs are *not* schools, although some of them are now housed in public schools.

center-based care for infants and toddlers and its increasing prevalence are worth examining, even if you are not planning to work with the youngest children. If you will be working with infants and toddlers, clarifying your feelings about their separation from their families will help you to create a safe, homelike, and loving place for the children and a supportive one for families when they reunite with their children each day.

The demand for child care has grown as the workforce has increased and as "school readiness" has filtered into the public domain as a dominant societal goal. But infant/toddler programs are *not* schools, although some of them are now housed in public schools. Infants and toddlers are not ready for academics. Instead, they require simple yet well-thought-out experiences to meet the demands of their rapidly developing minds and bodies.

If you visit several infant/toddler programs, chances are that you will describe each of them differently, for each will have its own culture of care. Some centers exude busy activity, while at others, calm, soft music and the quiet movements of the caregivers give the opposite impression.

THOUGHT QUESTION Infant/toddler caregivers contribute to the culture of the place. Jot down your thoughts about the atmosphere you want to create for the youngest children and the kinds of relationships you want to establish with them and their families.

ATTACHMENT AND SEPARATION ALL DAY LONG

How will you support children's attachments and help them manage separations?

Although attachment to cherished adults is vital throughout our lives, it is *central* in the first three years, promoting self-confidence and curiosity about the world (Bowlby 1969/1982). As you read in Chapter 3, affectionate interpersonal relationships and secure attachments to their parents and caregiver-teachers form the basis for infants' and toddlers' security and their ability to adjust comfortably to child care. Their earliest attachments to their families lay the groundwork for future ones, as well as for the separation process. The adults in the room become the anchors for a young child's day because being away from their attachment persons often causes infants and toddlers to feel frightened or even angry. Recall that infants and young toddlers are remembering their loved ones mostly in sensory, nonetheless powerful, ways. Luckily, humans are adaptable creatures, and those very young children who spend many hours in infant and toddler care apart from the primary people in their lives are an outstanding example.

Program Support for Attachment

The first priority of an early childhood program is to support young children's development and attachments. Child care arrangements support infant/toddler development by *maximizing attachments* and *minimizing transitions* from one group to another (Daniel 1993). In one arrangement, for example, infants and toddler/twos stay together in a mixed-age, family-style group with their caregiving staff for nine months or longer (Howes 1998; NAEYC 2005). This structure ensures both continuity of care—stability across the care and education experience—and secure attachments. The age range from five or six months to three years helps children engage with one another naturally, as they do in families, and is ideal for programs that include children with disabilities.

In a mixed-age group, eight-month-old Mei-Mei crawls to the couch and pulls on it to stand. Two-year-old Alex exclaims, "Hey! Hey! Mei-Mei standing up!"

Alex has a feeling about himself as a "big boy" and can exult in the baby's achievement. Caregivers working in mixed-age groups, too, enjoy both the rewards of providing intimate care for two or three infants as well as engaging with mobile, talking toddlers and two-year-olds (Theilheimer 1993).

In contrast, a "school model" that groups children according to age–babies in one room, one-year-olds in another, and two-year-olds in yet another—may require children to move from one group to another before they or their families are ready. When infants begin to walk, for example, they move to the toddler group. However, transitions are stressful for both children and teachers because they disrupt attachments. Babies' departure for a toddler group affects their caregivers, who miss them and the experience of following their development. These transitions also affect parents, who must disconnect from familiar caregivers. To counteract these disruptions, some centers enact a continuity of care model in which the teachers stay with the same children for their entire three years in a center.

This form of looping (see Chapter 7) has its supporters as well as those who don't approve of such continuity. Detractors may find annual transitions more familiar than the mixed-age group approach. Also, separate infant and toddler groups may meet the needs of caregivers who prefer one age or the other. Clearly, teachers who move to the next developmental grouping with children get to know them in extraordinary ways. However, sometimes parents want their children to experience different adults.

With program support, the caregiving adults, through their attachment to the babies, help children and families adapt to a new environment with its new people. When caregiver-teachers do all they can to make group care a pleasurable experience, they minimize the stress that very young children might feel.

Given the primacy of the caregiving role, what can teachers do to help young children feel secure during a long day in care? You learned in Chapter 3 how important it is for children, especially the youngest, to have a sense of continuity and predictability. Consistent routines and rituals go a long way toward giving children some control over their potentially difficult transition to daily care. Knowing that every day, for example, singing time follows playtime helps mediate stress for young children, fostering both a sense of autonomy and a connection to others. Every day in care, children make a transition from the place they know best to an environment that is not their home. Help from teacher-caregivers and children's families eases that transition.

Children have no choice about whether or when their parents come and go, but if they have a routine for saying good-bye, they can at least predict what will happen next. Take a look at Jonnia Jackson's Real Voice to see the routine she established to help Nikkia say good-bye to her mom. Jonnia thought and rethought that routine to make it work for

Knowing that, every day, singing time follows playtime helps mediate stress for young children, fostering both a sense of autonomy and a connection to others.

One of the most important elements in an infant/toddler program is you and your relationships with the children.

Jonnia R. Jackson

I worked as an infant/toddler teacher in a program that focused a lot on children's social and emotional needs, and part of that focus involved learning how to help children and parents have good separations at the beginning of the day. I thought I understood what that meant until one year I had a two-year-old girl in my class, Nikkia, who seemed to challenge everything I thought I knew.

When Nikkia started in the program, she would run away or ignore her mother whenever her mother tried to say good-bye. Soon after her mother left the room, Nikkia became very unfocused, just wandering around the room, or she would start throwing things. So I worked with Nikkia and her mother to create a good-bye ritual to help Nikkia gain some control over the separation. The routine involved me carrying Nikkia from the classroom to the door of the main office with her mom. She gave her mom a hug and a kiss from my arms and waved good-bye to her at the office door. Then I took Nikkia to the window that looked out onto the sidewalk in front of our building, and she watched her mom wave one last time. When her mom turned away, we stayed at the window, watching her until she was out of sight. Through all of this Nikkia showed very little expression, except on occasion she would hit the window, which she also did without expression. I then carried her back to the classroom, telling her all the things we were going to do all day and that her mom would be back. But no matter what I offered her, she couldn't get engaged in any activity, and she would often throw things and run away. I knew I was doing the separation routine in a way that made sense, but nothing in her behavior seemed to change.

Then one day in talking to colleagues about Nikkia's reactions to her good-byes, I realized that even though she was going through the good-bye ritual, she was still running away. But now instead of physically running away, it was like she was running into herself and not allowing herself to feel sad or angry while her mother was there. This also made me realize that even though I talked to her about how her mommy would come back, how her mommy would miss her, and what we were going to do

all day, I never really connected with her about her feelings. The next day, after sharing my thoughts with her mother and warning her that the good-bye might be harder at first, I talked to Nikkia about her feelings as part of the ritual. Without my having to say much, she started to cry during the good-bye. Even though the crying helped, it turned out that that wasn't the only thing missing from the ritual. As I stood at the window with Nikkia watching her mother walk down the street, something made me stay at the window with her longer than usual. I noticed that, even though her mother was out of sight, Nikkia was still watching, not with a distant, expressionless look like she usually had, but with a very serious look. After a few minutes she turned to me and held her arms out. I picked her up, and we walked back to the room, and instead of wanting to get down, Nikkia still held on tight. I sat on the couch with her, and she picked up a book, which I read to her. Then she slid off my lap and joined some other children who were busy playing with play dough at the table. As I watched her for the first time really engaged in her play, I realized that even though I had created the ritual to give her a sense of control over the separation, I had always decided when the good-bye was over, not Nikkia. Now I know not only how important it is to have a good separation, but that having a good separation sometimes means so much more than just saying good-bye or even having a good-bye ritual.

Nikkia. Notice, too, how Jonnia collaborated with Nikkia's mother to create continuity with home.

Different rituals will ease transitions for different children, and some children need a routine more than others. Sometimes, too, children surprise their caregivers by apparently adjusting to a program and then bursting into tears a few weeks later. While at first they didn't need a ritual or extra support of any kind to say good-bye, now they do.

to parents when they talk about the meaning that a transitional object has for them and their child will learn about the family and be able to synchronize their treatment of the child with the family's ways.

Not all teachers feel as Lin does about security objects. Some require that children leave them at home or store them in a cubby until the end of the day. Directors and teachers may also disagree, which challenges teachers to take a stand on behalf of young children's attachment. The teacher might consider presenting her beliefs to the director by citing a reliable resource (Jalongo 1987; Balaban 2006) that gives expert opinion about transitional objects.

THE DAY WITH INFANTS, TODDLERS, AND TWO-YEAR-OLDS

What takes place during a day at a program for infants, toddlers, and twos?

A full day with infants and toddlers is filled with ups and downs, loud dramas, and quiet moments. Children play and learn, use a wide range of materials in a variety of ways, and interact with many people. Their rapidly developing skills make each day exciting for them and for the acute observer of their changes. Their teachers must be flexible planners, well-prepared with activities that they are nevertheless ready to forgo should children's interests and energy lead them in another direction.

Playing and Learning

Infants and toddlers learn about the world, other people, and themselves through play. Play is the primary vehicle for making friends (and sometimes, "enemies"). It includes exploration, social interaction, make-believe, and many ways children can joyfully try out what their bodies can do. Long ago, social psychologist Dr. Lawrence Frank wrote that through play a child "learns what no one can teach him" (1974, 17).

Most children concentrate on self-selected play tasks. Although generally young children do not need a teacher to tell them what to do, they do need a teacher's support and help when they are frustrated or at loose ends in a play situation. Illness or a serious developmental disability or delay may change the nature of a child's play. Teachers need to take an active, co-playing role, particularly with infants and toddlers who have special needs, because they may lack some skills needed for exploratory and social play (Doctoroff 1996). For example, a toddler with motor planning difficulty will need guidance in stacking cardboard blocks or turning the handle of a jack-in-the-box to make it pop up. A two-year-old with a language delay will need help joining and interacting with the children who are "cooking" dinner in the play kitchen.

The driving force behind the integrity and professionalism of any infant/toddler program is the teacher's belief that play is essential for children's

A toddler with motor planning difficulty will need guidance in stacking cardboard blocks or turning the handle of a jack-in-the-box to make it pop up.

Toddlers are just beginning to take on roles in their dramatic play.

growth, development, happiness, and intellect. Infant/toddler teachers and caregivers promote and support play when they observe the children's interests; they select sturdy, easy-to-clean, and safe playthings that appeal to children of varied ages. Uncluttered, safe space lets children move about and make-believe. Playthings arranged attractively on low shelves enable children to make their own choices. Large blocks of unrushed time and a daily variety of unstructured sensory materials such as water, play dough, or crayons allow for experimenting and exploring. Most important, adults who possess an encouraging, flexible, and responsive attitude (Hitz and Driscoll 1988) nourish children's play. It is always the adult's role to help infants, toddlers, and two-year-olds get along with one another and to offer them a welcoming lap or encircling arm when play becomes overwhelming.

Exploring nonstructured materials

Infants and toddlers use their sensorimotor capacities to find out about the world when they look, taste, touch, smell, and move about. Materials such as paper, crayons, paint, water, clay, sand, blocks, and teacher-made play dough directly address very young children's natural way of learning. According to James Greenman (2005, 99), "So much of young children's learning is sensory-motor based and requires hands-on experiences. Pounding on play dough or smearing paint is not only therapeutic and fun but exactly the kind of learning that teaches children how the material world works."

Items such as play dough or paint are called open, or **nonstructured, materials** because there is no right or wrong way to use them, as there is with closed, or **structured, materials,** such as shape sorters or puzzles. For example, a child can roll, squeeze, or pinch play dough. Harriet Cuffaro (1991, 64) describes nonstructured materials as the "textbooks of early childhood classrooms . . . [the] tools with which children give form to and express their understanding of the world."

Very young children enjoy the experience of art materials and are less interested than older children in the outcome.

When a material is set out on a table, a child can choose to play or not:

With Toby and Cerise (both twenty-seven months), the teacher makes a batch of "goop" or "gak" (see Figure 11.2 for the recipe) in a large bowl. When the mixture congeals, Cerise plays with it for a few minutes, then leaves to wrap up a small doll in a blanket. Toby almost dives into the bowl, plunging his hands deep into the goop, lifting it, pulling it, and stretching it with large rapid and repeated movements. He leans on the edge of the table, his feet off the floor. He is grinning and humming to himself as he plays vigorously for ten minutes, until the teacher tells him that lunch is about to arrive. He reluctantly extricates his hands from the smooth and stretchy material.

Although today Cerise was not interested in the goop for long, Toby had a sensory and intellectual experience. He examined the physical properties of the stuff, finding out how thin and thick he could make it. Like any good scientist, he repeated his experiments, throwing his entire self into the process. Toby had a long attention span for the goop. If lunch had not been on its way, he would have played and learned for even longer.

When they paint, young children learn to control their hands and arms. They react with enjoyment to the sight of the colors and how they change with mixing. They become aware of the effect they have on a blank sheet of paper, and feel pride.

Two-year-old Tania is seriously engaged in controlling the red paint and in making a variety of strokes, but she is not interested in the *product*—what her painting looks like. She is in charge of the *process* of her work. Her teacher notes, "Red like your shirt," rather than giving an opinion such as "It's beautiful" or asking, "What is it?" Tania hears from her teacher's comment that the teacher is truly interested in what she is doing and encourages her efforts (Hitz and Driscoll 1988).

Both teachers and children can have fun finding ways to use similar materials differently. On one day, a tub of water with dolls, sponges, and small cakes of soap can engage youngsters for many minutes. On other days, plastic fish and animals or dishes are fun to wash. Cups and containers of different sizes offer opportunities for filling up and dumping out. Small boats float on top, but a cupful of water sinks to the bottom. Water play allows for focus and concentration, hand-eye coordination, investigating the properties of water, and experiencing competence: "Me do it myself!" The water is soothing, and children respond to it on an emotional and intellectual level. This type of play, which involves direct interaction with and learning from

Toddlers are just learning words such as *up*, *down*, *in*, *out*, *under*, *over*, and *through*. They enjoy creating structures in which they can practice those concepts.

Recipe for Goop/Gak

Mix equal parts water and liquid white glue in a bowl. In a different vessel, dissolve two teaspoons borax with one-half cup warm water.

Slowly pour the borax solution into the water-glue mixture, stirring constantly until the material starts to gel. Then set it out for the children. When the children are done playing, clean up right away.

Recipe for Oobleck

Oobleck is a solution of cornstarch and water. Start with a 1:1 water-to-cornstarch ratio. Then you can vary it as you wish.

The interesting aspect of this material is that it hardens slightly in the bowl but becomes drippy when children pick it up in their hands.

11.2 *Recipes for Goop and Oobleck*
Test each of these recipes at home before trying them with children.
These recipes are for use only with children older than two years. Make certain that children do not put the material in their hair or mouths.

Children may play with water for a long time. Do toddlers really have short attention spans?

objects and other children, is an example of how developmental-interaction theory works.

Playing with toys

Infants and toddlers are insatiable—they are interested in everything from house keys to dropping wooden clothespins into a coffee can. Your observations of children's interests and abilities are your most reliable guide for selecting playthings (TRUCE 2006). Some toys encourage make-believe play—dolls of varied ethnicities and objects that resemble real things, such as plastic food and dishes. As their language develops and blossoms, children use it to engage in make-believe together, as well as to learn about each other. Other types of toys help develop small muscles and eye-hand coordination—puzzles with and without knobs, pop-up toys, and balls. Yet other playthings are designed to strengthen large muscles—riding toys and climbing structures.

Toys and playthings come in a wide array of forms. A grown-up's wooden spoon and cooking pot are as valuable for play as many toystore-bought objects. By manipulating objects of different shapes, textures, colors, weights, sizes, and sounds—turning them, lifting them, mouthing them, dropping them, or even sitting on them—infants and toddler/twos begin to experience, first hand, the vast range of the sensory environment. The characteristics of varied objects teach very young children the basics of the world around them. When teacher-caregivers provide many types of interesting and safe objects, they enhance children's creative thinking.

Sasha, eight months, pulls herself up to a toy bin, peers in for several seconds, and pulls out a small egg-shaped shaker. She plops down next to Clara, the student teacher. "Oh, you found a shaker! Shake, shake, shake!" says Clara softly, moving her arm gently up and down. Watching Clara, Sasha begins to move her arm, too. She shakes the egg and smiles when she hears the pebbles moving inside.

Sasha is learning about her own effectiveness and experiencing the joy of self-discovery. Although her object play is entirely exploratory, such play forms the foundation from which more complex object play will develop as she gets older.

As a result of her early infancy object play, two-year-old Valora is motivated to struggle for many minutes to dress a doll. Totally absorbed in her task, she uses her small muscles and focuses intensely. An observer can't tell whether Valora is pretending to be the doll's parent or just wants the challenge of getting the clothes on the doll—or both. When she finally succeeds, she holds the doll in front of her, gazes at it for a moment, then drops it on the floor and walks away. We can guess that her satisfaction lay in accomplishing the task she set for herself.

Toys that are adaptable to a range of skill levels—such as Bristle Blocks and sensory materials, for which there is no correct use—are appropriate for many children with special needs, too.

Toys that are adaptable to a range of skill levels are appropriate for many children with special needs, too. Bristle Blocks, for example, allow for an "infinite number of creations, while being simple enough to provide enjoyment for the child who just wants to stack them, pull them apart, or match the colors" (Klein, Cook, and Richardson-Gibbs 2001). Because there is no right or wrong way to use them, sensory and art materials like felt-tip markers, paint, water, and teacher-made play dough allow pleasurable engagement for *all* young children, regardless of whether they have a disability. The opportunity to use these playthings and materials daily encourages a sense of mastery and gives children the chance to play and communicate with others. For an extensive list of play materials and activities categorized by age, see Bronson (1995) and Miller (2005).

Building with blocks

Toddlers, up to two years, do best with large cardboard blocks. They like to pile them one on top of another and then knock them down, squealing with delight as they do so. Sometimes they build an enclosure or make long rows, getting into or on them and scattering the blocks as they go. This knocking down and building back up is an exercise of autonomy, not a test of adult authority. And cardboard blocks, unlike wood unit blocks, won't hurt anyone when they fall. One toddler teacher arranges cardboard blocks on shelves according to color so that matching at pickup time becomes a game—all the blues on one shelf, the greens on another, the yellows on yet another.

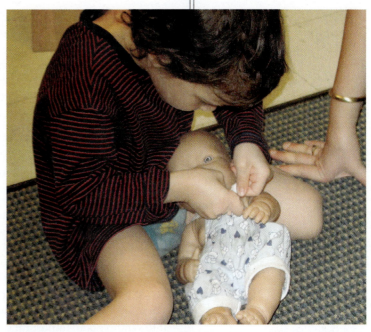

Buttoning a doll's clothes may show caring and develops fine motor control.

Children between two-and-a-half and three years can use wooden unit blocks, which require more supervision. Young children go through stages in using blocks, first carrying them around, then lining them up in rows and towers, and later building enclosures and bridges (Hirsch 1996). Using blocks, children learn physical coordination; balance; mathematics; turn taking and cooperation with others; pride of achievement; and expression of their ideas, imagination, and experiences. They learn rules: blocks are for building, not throwing; walk carefully near another's building to avoid breaking it. Two- to three-year-olds need only four or five different simple shapes to work with. Providing bins of props, such as animal and people figures, small cars, and one-inch colored cubes, may spur dramatic play in the block area and encourage children to make more elaborate buildings.

When they return blocks to the shelf, children learn about classification of shapes—units in one place and double units in another. Setting aside enough space for block building, well away from a trafficked area, is critical—otherwise, buildings get knocked down, blocks get dented, and children get discouraged. Since very young children often have difficulty sharing space, a nearby teacher can help them negotiate as needed.

Making believe and dramatic play

Early **representational thinking,** or the ability to use an object to stand for something else, begins during the first few years of life. As early as eight or nine months, a baby can wave bye-bye and learn, over time, that waving has to do with someone leaving. During the second year of life, young children begin to make-believe. They pretend to sleep, wake up, eat, or go to child care, enacting the everyday events of their lives as eighteen-month-old Liam does when he holds a toy phone on his shoulder and says, "Hi, hi." His toy phone **represents,** or stands for, the real phone. The younger the child, the more play objects need to resemble the real thing. By age two-and-a-half or three, children are more flexible in their thinking and can use a leaf or a block to represent a phone.

By age two, children can play out events in their lives as a way of recalling and understanding them. Play seems to arise spontaneously in most children without any adult prompting. For example:

> Farhad (twenty-three months) pushes a doll stroller around the room, calling "Bye-bye!" and waving to his teacher, Charlie. "Bye," says Charlie. "Where are you going?" "To 'cool,'" Farhad replies.

Farhad might, or might not, actually come to his school in a stroller, but in play, invention often replaces reality.

These two girls play a more complicated scenario that involves the passage of time:

> Yi-Min (twenty months) lies down on a blanket in the "house" corner, saying, "Night, night." Sari (twenty-four months) lies down next to her, covering herself with a blanket. Yi-Min jumps up and says, "Morning!" Sari then jumps up, smiles, and says, "Morning! Now go day care."

As they get older, toddlers pretend that their play objects represent the real item. For example, a plastic cow stands for a real cow and thus is a **symbol.** Making objects into symbols is an important cognitive achievement, because the child is thinking in a new and more complex way.

Talking with children about their make-believe play is a skill worth developing. As Mohan pushes a toy boat around in the water table, Monica talks to him slowly, unobtrusively, and with sensitivity. Her questions, intimately related to Mohan's play, help to build their close relationship. Be sure to watch and listen, as Monica does, before asking children questions. We cannot assume we know what the child is playing.

Play, Friendship, and Interaction

All healthy young children have an inborn, driving motivation to play. At first, infants play with their parents' bodies, faces, and hair. Older infants play with colorful and textured objects like soft stuffed animals, plastic kitchen bowls, and chunky board books. They are interested in seeing and touching other baby "friends." Toddlers and two-year-olds on a playground who have never met before can fall into a play mode with one another without any encouragement from adults. However, when they are together regularly in a group setting, they begin to show preferences for specific playmates.

While relationships are born in play, the basic toddler mode of connecting with peers is imitation. For example, one toddler sings a silly song, fills a basket with dinosaur figures, and dumps them out. Another joins her to do the same thing; at that moment they are "friends."

Adults, however, need to be vigilant and supportive with toddlers because their social skills are raw—conflict is often a form of toddler interaction. Some conflicts arise because toddlers do not understand how a behavior happens.

> **Making objects into symbols is an important cognitive achievement, because the child is thinking in a new and more complex way.**

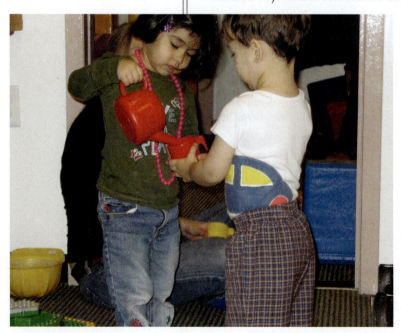
Pouring water for a friend.

Negotiating conflict in play

A young toddler's desire to play often takes the form of grabbing a toy no matter who is using it. Such young children often do not understand the consequences of their actions and don't see another child's point of view. At the moment of grabbing, they are thinking about what *they themselves* want and feel. Over time, however, when an adult explains but does not punish, children learn from the adult's guidance.

The caregiver's role in children's play is to teach **social skills**— that is, the ability to get along with others, for example, how to resolve differences and how to take turns. The teacher mediates between children's impulses and appropriate social behavior. Teachers may find themselves repeating the same words because it is a stretch for an eighteen-month-old to wait her turn.

A conflict also can be an opportunity for children to learn how to stand up for themselves without striking out at others. In a mixed-age group, young toddlers often tread on the territory of two-year-olds, and the teacher must attend to the needs and abilities of both. Here the teacher understands the limits of one-year-old Alex, while at the same time she protects two-year-old Molly's drawing and teaches her some social skills:

A quiet moment alone with a book.

> Alex (thirteen months) toddles over to the easel where Lisa, the teacher, gives him a marker. He goes around to the other side of the easel, where two-and-a-half-year-old Molly, deep in concentration, is drawing. Molly glares at him, grunts, and shoves him just as his outstretched marker makes contact with her drawing. Alex stumbles but moves back to Molly's drawing. Molly yells, "Lisa!" "Coming," says Lisa as she sees Molly watching Alex make a mark on her drawing. "Come here, Alex," Lisa says, "draw with me. Molly wants to draw there by herself. Sit on my lap, and we'll slide to the other side of the easel together. Molly, I'm sorry Alex drew on your picture. Next time, say 'Stop' to him." Alex slides off Lisa's lap and heads toward Molly. "STOP!" Molly yells. Alex backs away. Lisa says, "See, Molly, it worked! Good for you!!"

This incident is a prime example of the self-regulating role that teachers play with children. If this kind of scenario is repeated in one form or another over an entire year, children will begin to try to control their impulses. They gain satisfaction from their increasing autonomy and from feeling some control over their exchanges with peers. They also have a natural desire to please their teachers.

Nothing upsets teachers and parents as much as biting. However, biting always happens *for a reason,* not because a child is naughty. Since it is difficult for toddlers to control their emotions and because they have few words to express those feelings, we can expect toddlers to bite (Kinnell 2008).

When Sue grabs a toy from Ani, Ani screams and bites Sue because she is *angry* and she has no words. The teacher comforts Sue and soothes the bite. She does not punish Ani but wants to help her understand what happened. In a soft voice, she says, "You were angry. You bit Sue. You cannot bite anyone. You can say, 'No! My toy!' but no biting." The teacher may have to repeat this message many more times.

Biting is a challenge for teachers, who must remain calm in order to help toddlers and work with upset parents. Kinnell (2008) asserts that teachers need a developmental perspective and a written policy about biting so that when it occurs, the whole staff acts consistently and parents know what to expect.

Since it is difficult for toddlers to control their emotions and because they have few words to express those feelings, we can expect toddlers to bite. However, biting always happens for a reason.

THOUGHT QUESTION Lucas (twenty months) is pushing a shopping cart full of plastic blocks. Letisha (eighteen months) tries to take the cart. Lucas shrieks. The caregiver gently says to Letisha, "I know you want a turn with the cart, but Lucas is using it right now. I will help you wait." Letisha yells, "No!" and persists in grabbing the cart. The teacher puts Letisha on her lap and says quietly, "Sit here with me until Lucas is finished. I need to keep you and Lucas safe." Letisha starts to cry. "I know, it's hard to wait for something you want," says the teacher. "You will have a turn when Lucas is finished. I promise," and she sings, "Waiting for the cart, we're waiting for the cart." What is Lucas learning? What is Letisha learning? How would you handle this situation?

Newborns make a narrow range of sounds, but they can communicate well to those who pay attention.

About talking

Babies communicate from the moment of birth—not with words but with looks and sounds. The baby in the photograph below, just a few days old, listens intently as his aunt tells him how much she loves him. Although he is not yet making any specific sounds, he does cry—and that is his way of talking. His cry says, "I'm hungry," or "I have a belly ache," or "I want you to pick me up and rock me." Within a month or two, this newborn will begin to coo and gurgle. Because his family responds to his baby talk, he will continue to expand his repertoire with babbles, ahhhs, and sighs. Even though an adult might feel foolish having a conversation with an infant, remember that a child's receptive language develops long before he can say words and influences his expressive language. Through talking, you and the child connect to each other, and the child learns to communicate.

Acquiring the ability to talk and to be understood takes a long time. Some children begin saying distinct words like "Mama," "Dada," "bye-bye," or "uh-oh" by the age of one. Others need a longer period to gear up—and begin uttering single words at eighteen months to two years. Some children put two or even three words together at fifteen or sixteen months, and others do so somewhere around twenty-four months. However, if, by age two, a child has few or no words, teachers must bring this to the program director's attention. The director should make a referral to Early Intervention for a speech evaluation. Toddlers want *and need* to be understood.

People who care for infants and toddler/twos teach literacy when they consistently talk to, listen to, sing to, and read to the children. Through everyday play and routine care interactions with children (but *not* through formal instruction), adults teach vocabulary, listening and attention abilities, and turn taking, all of which are pre-reading skills. Changing a diaper, for example, is an excellent opportunity to talk face-to-face about a painting the child did, the doll he washed, or the truck she filled with sand that day. Sitting at the lunch table with a small group is an opportunity to describe the different foods children are eating, how they came to the center that day, who will pick them up, and who got a boo-boo and now feels better. Your most powerful language and literacy teaching occurs when your words are related *directly* to the child's activity and experience.

As young children become more proficient talkers, they enjoy using language and understand how effective words can be. They also begin to play with words. The girl in the following observation is having fun matching her freely moving body with her made-up words:

Two-year-old Emilia jumps along a path of large outdoor blocks that she has constructed. She jumps and bumps to the end of the path, then turns and goes back the way she came. As she bumps and jumps along, back and forth, on this short path, she chants several times, "A horsey, of coursey, horsey, horsey, horsey."

The big "NO!"

Have you ever wondered why "NO!" and "MINE!" are among toddlers' first words? It is their *declaration of independence*. "Me do it myself!" the toddler asserts as she struggles to tie her shoe and then, frustrated, tosses it across the room. Toddlers often say no to something they really want, so it helps to offer a choice. "Do you want to go outside?" "No!" "Do you want to play on the swing or the slide?" "Want slide." "Well, here we go!"

Toddlers require positive guidance and support, especially when they assert themselves by opposing the caregiver. If adults lose patience and demand obedience, they may end up in a contest of wills that no one wins. The toddler has a tantrum, and the adult seethes. Teacher-caregivers need to try out various ways that do not involve scolding to help toddlers comply with classroom expectations. When teachers see themselves as helpers in redirecting children's behavior, they develop discipline and limit-setting practices that are more positive (and effective) than punishment.

It takes a lot of effort and thinking for teachers to work around a toddler's oppositional behavior instead of confronting it. Here is an example of a teacher who gives a toddler a warning that cleanup time is coming and then helps her put away the doll rather than getting into a conflict with her:

> Two-year-old Safia walks around the room with a purse and a cell phone, saying "Hello, Mommy." Teacher Marissa announces two minutes to cleanup. Despite the signal, Safia puts on a pair of dress-up shoes and continues to walk around repeating "Hello, Mommy." Although everyone is now singing the cleanup song, Safia puts on yet another pair of dress-up shoes. "It's cleanup time, Safia," says Marissa. Safia turns away, clasps the bag and phone close to her body, and shouts, "No!" Seeing a doll lying on the floor, Marissa asks her, "Do you know where this baby doll goes?" "No!" says Safia. Marissa tries another tack, "I think this baby belongs in her bed. Please put the baby to bed—she's so tired." Safia, still holding the bag and the phone, takes the doll and puts it in the crib. "Great! Thanks, Safia," says Marissa, "Now where do the bag and phone go?" Safia puts them on the shelf and walks to the snack table, still wearing the dress-up shoes.

Planned Experiences

Although much that happens in infant/toddler/twos rooms is spontaneous, teacher-caregivers do choose materials to put out, set up activities, and interact with children based on observations of them. If they have materials on hand, know how to set them up, and are ready to change plans in an instant, teachers can offer children rich experiences that are just right for the time. In the following sections we talk about cooking and music activities, examine children's time outdoors, and then discuss scheduling for very young children.

Large blocks allow for rich play scenarios outdoors.

> Your most powerful language and literacy teaching occurs when your words are related *directly* to the child's activity and experience.

THOUGHT QUESTION Marissa didn't argue with Safia, and when she saw that Safia resisted her announcement of cleanup time, she tried another tactic. Finally, she gained Safia's cooperation by engaging her in dramatic play that coincided with cleaning up. What do you think would have happened if the teacher had said, "Clean up *now! This minute!*"?

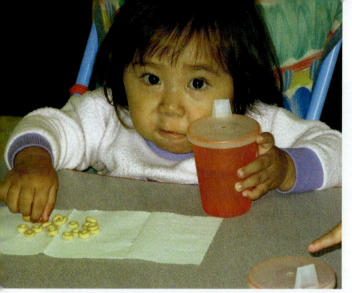
Snack time requires close attention and manual skills.

Cooking is a broad term for making something with real food that may or may not involve heat.

"Who am I?" is answered as, "I am the person who slides down."

Cooking and music

Infant/toddler and twos teachers plan a variety of special experiences for the children in their care. Two good examples are cooking and music.

Cooking is a broad term for making something with real food that may or may not involve heat. Very young children "cook" when they spread jam on a cracker or watch the teacher cut open an apple or a melon to see what is inside and then, of course, eat the fruit. Cooking is also dipping a slice of bread into an egg-and-milk mixture and making French toast in an out-of-reach frying pan or putting pizza sauce and shredded cheese on an English muffin and toasting it in a toaster oven. Cooking in a group of two or three children fosters concentration, cooperation, turn taking, vocabulary, and experience with **transformation** (once it was a bowl of batter, but now it's transformed into pancakes). Taking part in preparing "snack" for the group, like slicing bananas into yogurt, gives toddlers and two-year-olds a sense of satisfaction and pride in their accomplishment.

Even at its simplest, cooking has a series of steps, from gathering the ingredients through eating and cleanup. Each has learning potential, whether it is naming ingredients, coordinating small fingers to manipulate a plastic knife, or tasting something new.

Cooking works best with a small group of children. For example, if everyone has a slice of bread and a small cup of apple butter, no one has to wait for a turn. But if the cooks pass around a bowl to stir, the wait will be too long for more than three children.

With music, on the other hand, everyone singing and dancing together forms strong large-group bonds. When one- and two-year-olds join a group that is singing and moving, they experience the release and joy of physical motion and rhythm together with others. They may participate fully, partially, or not at all. A child might dance and sing all the songs at home for his parents while only watching the action from the sidelines in his care setting. Observant caregivers will learn which children respond to encouragement to join the group and which learn by watching.

At circle time, the group develops its set of favorite songs and musical games. Start the year with a short time together and slowly increase it as the year goes on. Don't forget songs that mention each child's name, like "Hello, Everybody." Include songs that have hand motions, such as "Open Shut Them" and "The Eentsy-Weentsy Spider." To help children regulate their energy, alternate such finger plays with songs that get everyone up and moving. This is the perfect opportunity, too, to introduce songs in different languages.

Outdoor play

Toddlers and two-year-olds as well as crawling babies need both to be safe and to have the leeway to explore their burgeoning physical skills and developing **sense of self.** In outdoor play, the question, "Who am I?" is answered as, "I am the person who slides down."

Outdoor play develops courage and risk taking, companionship, strong muscles, and as-yet-untried abilities. The freedom available outdoors can never be duplicated inside the classroom. Go outdoors every day to dig in the mud, climb the slope, slide, roll balls, run, and feel the joy of the moving air. Go outdoors!

When possible, take short outings with small groups of children within the neighborhood, for example, to buy bananas for snack. For very young children the journey—not the destination—is the goal. With so much to see and talk about, outings are an invaluable part of children's experience and become part of their knowledge base. The cashier becomes more familiar to them each time they go to the store, and, as they return to the center and the big tree just outside it comes into view, the children call out, "The tree, the tree!"

Outings are manageable for the adult and secure for the children when one caregiver goes out with only two or three children, perhaps with a baby under eight months snuggled in a soft baby carrier. Rain need not stop these outings as long as children have proper gear. Besides, the rain provides an experience with wetness that is different from a child's water table experiences. Sometimes, all it takes is a walk around the block to create a change of mood for children and grown-ups alike. For both children and teachers, these small-group outings provide a respite from the intensity of being in one room all day with the entire group.

To schedule or not to schedule

It's 10 o'clock, and the children in the mixed-age infant/toddler room are busy playing, although nine-month-old Danny is asleep in his crib in a separate nook. One by one, the oldest children in the group put down their toys and seat themselves at the table. One caregiver turns to the other and says, "Well, I guess they're telling us it's time for snack, and they're right, too!"

Can these two-year-olds tell time? That's doubtful, but they know that in the routine of their daily schedule, snack follows playtime, and they are finished playing and maybe a little hungry. The predictable sequence of daily activities puts them somewhat in charge of their day.

But Danny is sleeping. He, too, follows a predictable routine, but his routine follows his own rhythms. Young infants are on their own schedules. Gradually, as they live together in a group, they will give up morning naps and follow the same schedule as everyone else. Teachers can phase out children's naps to get them all on the same schedule, but we believe in gathering information from families about their children's schedules and following them. If caregivers can provide the kind of care children know from home, center-based care will be more comfortable and pleasurable.

Thus, many infant/toddler teachers learn flexibility. On the one hand, they have predictable schedules that ensure that children go outdoors and have meals. On the other, they adapt schedules to the children instead of forcing everyone in the group to conform to one schedule.

As for older children, schedules invariably have transition points, times in the day when children are in between activities. The two-year-olds in the earlier example beat the transition by going to the snack table on their own. Most of the time, though, adults must interrupt children to get them ready for the next activity. How adults approach those interruptions reflects the level of respect they have for children and for children's self-directed activities. Warnings such as, "In five minutes we'll be getting ready to go to the yard" alerts children to a transition, even if they don't know what five minutes means. When you speak to children about what is about to happen—for example, when you tell a child you will change her diaper soon instead of removing her wordlessly from the rug—you show respect for the child and whatever she was doing before the diaper change.

Transitions and the waiting that often accompanies them can be easier when children are involved in some way. Dressing takes longer if a child is fully involved in putting on his shoes and jacket,

THOUGHT QUESTION For the past few months, an assistant teacher has worked in a classroom where the lead teacher believes that infants and toddlers need to follow a schedule for naps and outings. When one of the toddlers kept falling asleep in the stroller and it wasn't "naptime," she took the toddler out of the stroller and insisted that he walk. Even though he cried, she told him, "If you sleep now, you won't sleep at naptime" (and the teachers won't get their breaks). If you were the assistant and did not agree with the lead teacher, how might you respond?

Hammocks provide an excellent way to nurture infants individually and help them get to sleep.

but it is worth the extra time because of his sense of participation and accomplishment. When you and several children are waiting for the rest of the group to get ready to go outside, try singing a song together or doing a short finger play to make the transition a meaningful and enjoyable time.

PLANNING SPACE FOR INFANTS, TODDLERS, AND TWO-YEAR-OLDS

What should teacher-caregivers keep in mind as they plan space for infants, toddlers, and twos?

In designing the physical setting for care of infants, toddlers, and twos, consider several factors. The room must not only support children's development but also reduce teachers' stress. This means providing safe, sturdy, child-sized equipment that encourages children's movement and autonomy. It also means organizing the room so that teachers can find what they need when they need it. Last, but not least, setting aside space outside the classroom where teachers can take a comfortable, relaxing break gives them a place to refuel.

Some programs find it helpful to use a rating scale to assess and improve their infant/toddler environment. Teachers can work as a team to examine their settings with the *Infant-Toddler Environment Rating Scale* (*ITERS*) (Harms, Cryer, and Clifford 2003). This instrument is widely used both in research and in early care practice. It covers seven basic elements of the environment: space and furnishings, personal care routines, listening and talking, activities, interaction, program structure, and parents and staff.

By providing both teachers and children with comfort and safety, the setting enhances their interactions (Greenman 2005; Bergen, Reid, and Torelli 2001). An adult-size rocking chair or easy chair allows a child and teacher to sit cozily together in the classroom, and it simultaneously invites parents to visit and be a part of the room. Including a private space—say, a large cardboard box with cutout door and window—enables a child to "get away," because living with a group all day is tiring.

In some programs, infants and toddlers watch television, DVDs, and/or videos to relax or to give the staff a break. Although many parents allow this at home, as you read in Chapter 3, we strongly advise against using these media with children in infant/toddler programs.

Keeping Children Safe

Health and safety concerns are of primary importance. Check for the following health and safety features in the infant/toddler/twos rooms that you visit and work in:

- Look at the cribs to see that
  - bars are no more than 2 3/8 inches apart,
  - railings are at least 26 inches higher than the lowest level of the mattress support,
  - mattresses fit snugly into the cribs,
  - bumper guards protect infants from hard railings,
  - there are no pillows in the cribs (to avoid danger of suffocation), and
  - cribs are not near hot radiators or cold drafts.

> Including a private space, such as a large cardboard box, enables a child to "get away," because living with a group all day is tiring.

- Examine the changing table for sturdiness and to see that it has straps to secure infants. Even though they use the straps, teacher-caregivers must *never turn their backs* on babies while changing their diapers.
- Toys should not:
  - have buttons or small objects that children can pull off and swallow,
  - have sharp edges, or
  - be breakable.
- An infant's bottle should never be propped.
- To protect against environmental hazards:
  - remove poisonous house plants: philodendron, poinsettia, caladium, narcissus, daffodils;
  - cover all electrical outlets;
  - keep matches out of reach. Never smoke in the classroom or yard;
  - conduct regular fire drills;
  - have working smoke alarms and a fire extinguisher;
  - keep all solvents, detergents, and medications out of reach; and
  - do not allow children to tie anything around their necks.

Features of Space

The space and the way it is set up govern what happens in the room. Some rooms lend themselves easily to comfortable arrangements. Others do not. By providing children with both the coziness and the challenges they need, along with access to adults and to each other, as well as the chance to be alone, the space lays the groundwork for a successful experience for children and adults.

Praiseworthy space for infant/toddler/twos care incorporates characteristics of a good home, including:

- the softness of laps, pillows, stuffed animals, and play dough (Prescott 1987);
- choices of playthings and activities;
- objects of different sizes, such as a couch and a rocking chair; and
- small spaces for privacy and a peek-a-boo space.

The colors of the space are fresh and set the tone (red, for example, is overstimulating, while blue is more calming). Shelves and tables are sized for infants and toddlers. The space has varied floor surfaces, both carpeted and hard; natural light from windows; and access to the outdoors. Full-spectrum lighting is healthier than fluorescent (Schreiber 1996). Lack of clutter and lots of storage space enable staff as well as children to find everything. A place for information exchange with parents, such as a whiteboard, a bulletin board, or mailboxes, contributes to ongoing communication with families. In some programs, parents fill out a form each morning when they bring in their children. They note anything that happened at home

THOUGHT QUESTION The lights are low, and soft music is playing as the children wake up. Teachers speak in low voices. On the couch, a teacher reads to a sleepy toddler while rocking an infant in her arms. Done reading, the teacher says, "I'll see you later. I need to give Zaida a bottle now." Holding the six-month-old, she says, "Oh, your bottle is too hot. We'll have to wait a minute for it to cool down." Meanwhile, the toddler has gone with another teacher to help her tape drawing paper on the table. He points to the roll of red tape, saying, "Tape." "You want a piece of red tape," the teacher says. The toddler nods and takes the offered piece of tape.

When everyone is awake, a teacher turns on brighter overhead lights and puts on energetic music. Some toddlers start to dance. In another part of the room, a teacher and a fifteen-month-old are playing catch with a ball. The toddler giggles with every throw; the teacher shares his excitement and then asks, "How many minutes until we change your diaper?" The child holds up two fingers. The teacher, holding up two fingers as well, replies, "Okay, in two minutes."

How would you describe the tone of this room? What did the teachers in this room do to create this atmosphere?

Room size affects children's behavior. Too small a space causes crowding that can lead to aggressive behavior. A too-large, overwhelming space produces disorganized behavior and unfocused running.

the night before or that morning, information about the child's eating and sleeping, and at what time and by whom the child will be picked up. During naptime, the staff writes back to the family about the child's day.

Room size affects children's behavior. Too small a space causes crowding that can lead to aggressive behavior. A too-large, overwhelming space produces disorganized behavior and unfocused running.

To start planning a space, make a short list of what babies and toddlers/twos do. For example, they crawl, sit, jump, climb, read books, play house, dance, eat, sleep, put on and take off clothing, use the toilet, have diaper changes, wash, paint, and build. Then draw a room plan on graph paper and set aside spaces for the following:

- tables for activities and eating,
- room for infants on mats or blankets,
- toy shelves,
- sand/water play,
- house play,
- blocks,
- an easel for painting,
- a soft area for books,
- a dancing and group singing area,
- a diapering area near a sink,
- cubbies for clothing,

11.3 *Setup of a Sample Toddler Room*

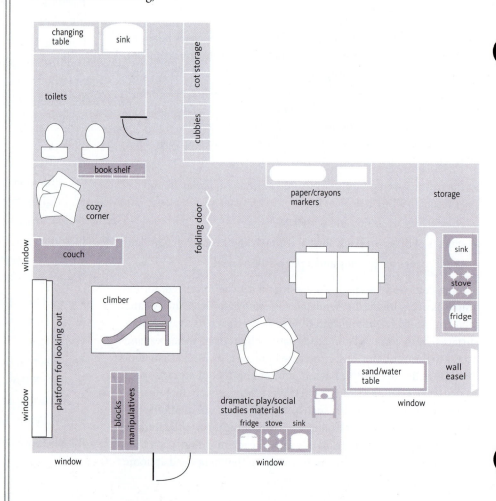

PART 4 Working with Children and Their Families: Applying What We Know

- storage for classroom needs, and
- a parent information exchange area.

Here are a few resources you may find useful:

Curtis, Deb, and Margie Carter. 2003. *Designs for living and learning: Transforming early childhood environments.* St. Paul, MN: Redleaf Press.

Greenman, James. 2005. *Caring spaces, learning places: Children's environments that work.* 2nd ed. Redmond, WA: Exchange Press.

Olds, Anita. 2000. *Child care by design.* New York: McGraw-Hill.

One toddler room

In the toddler room shown in Figure 11.3, most of the floor is tiled, while part of the room is carpeted, providing both a change of texture and a soft place to sit. Windows

AGE GROUP *For further clarification, please also see notes below*	GROUP SIZE									
	6	8	10	12	14	16	18	20	22	24
Infants *(birth to 15 months)*[2]	1:3	1:4								
Toddler/Twos *(12–36 months)*[2]										
12–28 months	1:3	1:4	1:4[3]	1:4						
21–36 months		1:4	1:5	1:6						
Preschool[2]										
2.5–3-year-olds *(30–48 months)*				1:6	1:7	1:8	1:9			
4-year-olds						1:8	1:9	1:10		
5-year-olds						1:8	1:9	1:10		
Kindergarten								1:10	1:11	1:12

NOTES: In a mixed-age preschool class of 2.5-year-olds to 5-year-olds, no more than four children between the ages of 2.5 years and 3 years may be enrolled. The ratios within group size for the predominant age group apply. If infants or toddlers are in a mixed-age group, the ratio for the youngest child applies.

Ratios are to be lowered when one or more children in the group need additional adult assistance to fully participate in the program:

   a. because of ability, language fluency, developmental age or stage, or other factors, or
   b. to meet other requirements of NAEYC Accreditation.

A group or classroom refers to the number of children who are assigned for most of the day to a teacher or a team of teaching staff, and who occupy an individual classroom or well-defined space that prevents intermingling of children from different groups within a larger room or area.

Group sizes as stated are ceilings, regardless of the number of staff.

Ratios and group sizes are always assessed during on-site visits for NAEYC Accreditation. They are not a required criterion. However, experience suggests that programs that exceed the recommended number of children for each teaching staff member and total group sizes will find it more difficult to meet each standard and achieve NAEYC Accreditation. The more these numbers are exceeded, the more difficult it will be to meet each standard.

---

[1] *Includes teachers, assistant teachers/teacher aides.*
[2] *These age ranges purposely overlap. Programs may identify the age group to be used for on-site assessment purposes for groups of children whose ages are included in multiple-age groups.*
[3] *Group sizes of 10 for this age group would require an additional adult.*

From http://www.naeyc.org/academy/criteria/kacher_child_ratios.html

11.4 *Teacher[1]-Child Ratios by Group Size*

let in natural light. Children can climb a few steps to look out the window, and there is a cozy area with pillows. There is a couch next to the bookshelf. There are separate sinks for adults and children, toddler-sized tables and chairs, adult-sized chairs, and a water and sand table. Easels are attached to the wall. Photographs of the children and their families are attached by Velcro to another wall so that children can remove them to carry around. There is a whiteboard for parent-teacher and teacher-parent information exchange.

A space for dramatic play contains a doll bed, several baby dolls of differing skin tones, a few doll-sized blankets, and cardboard blocks. Floppy hats, skirts, and a vest hang on a small clotheshorse. Strollers for dolls and a food market cart are nearby. A basket holds play shoes and purses. Cubbies with hooks for coats and space above for extra clothes contain a photo of the child who uses them. This floor plan provides space for using expressive materials, make-believe play, privacy, books, and movement.

Authoritative source for program planning

States have their own requirements and regulations for the care of infants and toddlers. NAEYC's group size and staff-child ratio (NAEYC 2005) is an excellent guide for structuring an early care program (Figure 11.4). **Low child-to-caregiver ratios**—fewer children per adult—are desirable because they let adults cultivate relationships with children and families more easily. If group size is not ideal, split the group up as much as possible into smaller groups, which produces a less hectic environment and more purposeful interactions between children and adults.

SUMMARY

LIFE WITH INFANTS, TODDLERS, AND TWO-YEAR-OLDS
Who are infants, toddlers, and two-year-olds?

Infants and toddlers are just forming an idea of who they are and depend on their caregivers and teachers for *warm, close relationships* to teach them that they are lovable. They need a calm, focused caregiver to help them control themselves and understand their emotional reactions. Such interactions feed their increasing understanding and use of words. They actively absorb everything around them, and what their families and their cultures believe about child rearing and about the world becomes part of who they are.

ATTACHMENT AND SEPARATION ALL DAY LONG
How will you support children's attachments
and help them manage separations?

Child care arrangements support infant/toddler development by maximizing attachments and minimizing transitions from one group to another. Predictability in the schedule and in the way adults care for the child helps, too; consistent routines and rituals go a long way toward giving children some control over their potentially difficult adjustment to daily care. A child's difficulty saying good-bye is a positive sign that the child is attached to the parent or other significant person who is leaving.

THE DAY WITH INFANTS, TODDLERS, AND TWO-YEAR-OLDS
What takes place during a day at a program for infants, toddlers, and twos?

Although much that happens in infant/toddler/twos rooms is spontaneous, if they have materials on hand, know how to set them up, and are ready to change plans

Low child-to-caregiver ratios—fewer children per adult—are desirable because they let adults cultivate relationships with children and families more easily.

PART 4   Working with Children and Their Families: Applying What We Know

in an instant, teacher-caregivers can offer children rich experiences that are just right for the time. Routines, such as eating and napping, are equally important parts of the day through which infants, toddlers, and twos learn about themselves and others. Infants and toddlers use their sensorimotor capacities to find out about the world when they look, taste, touch, smell, and move about. Thus, items such as play dough or paint, water play or blocks—called open, or nonstructured, materials because there is no right or wrong way to use them—are well-suited to this age group. As time goes on young children will also use closed, or structured, materials, such as shape sorters or puzzles. Although generally young children do not need a teacher to tell them what to do, they do need a teacher's support and help when they are frustrated or at loose ends in a play situation or to help them negotiate their impulses and behave prosocially.

PLANNING SPACE FOR INFANTS, TODDLERS, AND TWO-YEAR-OLDS

What should teacher-caregivers keep in mind as they plan space for infants, toddlers, and twos?

The space and the way it is set up govern what happens in the room. The room must support children's development by providing safe, sturdy, child-sized equipment that encourages children's movement and autonomy. To reduce adults' stress, the room should be organized so that teachers and families can find what they need when they need it. Setting aside space outside the classroom where teachers can take a comfortable, relaxing break gives them a place to refuel.

FURTHER ACTIVITIES

1. Create a PowerPoint or other chart that lists effective approaches, strategies, and tools for positively influencing infant and toddler/twos' development and learning; illustrate each with a photograph from a center you have visited. Present your work to your classmates. (**NAEYC Standard 1: Promoting Child Development and Learning**)

2. Camille won't leave the Big Room, where she and the other toddlers have been climbing, running, and riding wheel toys. Because she doesn't want to stop playing, she throws herself, screaming, to the floor as the others return to their room. You remain with Camille, with instructions to get her back to the room for lunch. Her tantrum makes you tense. In a short paper, describe the positive alternatives to punishment or scolding you could use in response to Camille's behavior. Explain the reasons for your suggestions, referring to parts of this chapter and at least one article. (**NAEYC Standard 4: Using Developmentally Effective Approaches to Connect with Children and Families**)

3. Draw or construct an infant/toddler environment. In a short paper, explain how this infant/toddler/twos' room is homelike, supports attachment and relationships, and is intellectually and physically stimulating for children this age. (**NAEYC Standard 4: Using Developmentally Effective Approaches to Connect with Children and Families**)

4. Develop an annotated bibliography of resources that you will use when you work with infants and toddler/twos. In each annotation, explain how the resource will help you to promote children's learning. (**NAEYC Standard 5: Using Content Knowledge to Build Meaningful Curriculum**)

CHAPTER TWELVE

Preschoolers and Kindergartners

[A] very important fact about healthy children, from the time they begin to walk, is their lively curiosity about everything that goes on around them.

Susan Isaacs

The years from three to six are indeed a time of "lively curiosity"—and enormous growth. While three-year-olds differ significantly from kindergartners, in this chapter we discuss both preschoolers and kindergartners because of the characteristics they share. Preschool and kindergarten children are able to investigate wide-ranging topics, engage in increasingly sophisticated social negotiations, and delight in their growing skills and accomplishments. We begin this chapter with an overview of the developmental changes preschoolers and kindergartners experience and then discuss curriculum—the series of learning experiences that make up the school day—and classrooms for children from three to six.

LIFE WITH PRESCHOOLERS AND KINDERGARTNERS

Who are preschoolers and kindergartners?

> Naptime was over. Four-year-old Melissa wriggled into her snowpants, but Daniel, a young three-year-old, sat dazed. Melissa, who was fascinated by the class's ongoing study of babies, pregnancy, and bodies, noticed that Daniel's belly protruded like a two-year-old's. "Look!" she pointed excitedly. "Daniel has a baby in his uterus."

Melissa's responses to the world around her differed from Daniel's, not just because she was a year older, but also because of her unique personality, interests, skills, and experiences.

Physical Development

From two to five years, children grow much taller. Longer limbs allow children greater leverage, which, along with greater strength and coordination, contributes to the three-year-old's increased motor and movement abilities. Threes also lose their baby fat, although variations occur across children, as you saw with Daniel, who had not yet lost his two-year-old belly.

At three, children may begin to show **hand dominance**—a preference for using one hand over the other. During the preschool years, fine motor skills improve, and many preschoolers competently manipulate large buttons or zippers. Threes usually hold a pencil in a tripod grasp (Allen and Marotz 1999).

Many people expect three-year-olds to control their bladders, and child care programs often require it for entry. This is not realistic for many children, and boys in particular may release urine at night until the age of five. While in some cultures children use the toilet successfully very early, most early childhood educators believe that, besides wanting to learn to use the toilet, a child must be able to:

- control her bladder and sphincter instead of releasing spontaneously,
- be aware of when she needs to urinate or defecate, and
- have the language skills to say that she needs to use the toilet.

In some cultures, adults and older children are physically close to young children almost all the time and become so attuned to their physical and emotional cues that they know when the child needs to urinate and defecate. From early infancy, they place children on the potty or toilet whenever they see or hear those cues.

<aside>
THOUGHT QUESTION As her father drops her off in your classroom, a three-year-old rushes to the easel and grabs a brush with her left hand. Her father tells her to use the other hand, turns to you, and asks you to help him teach his daughter to become right-handed. What additional information might you want from the father? What will you say and do?
</aside>

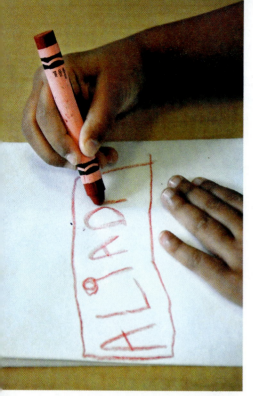

A young child writes, demonstrating a tripod grasp of the crayon.

Beyond walking, children's developing **gross motor,** or large muscle, **skills,** including running, jumping, skipping, and climbing, are difficult to pin down by age. Experts prefer to consider motor patterns, or the combination of a movement's components (Connor, Williamson, and Siepp 1978; Curtis 1982). For example, to begin to walk, babies must be able to shift their weight, have balance, and possess the necessary muscle strength. Children walk before they run, and jumping down comes before jumping up or taking a long jump. Think about what positions a child prefers, what seems to slow him down, and how she uses her joints. Is his whole body behind a thrown ball, or does he just use energy from the elbow down? Sandra Curtis (1982) provides suggestions for observing movement:

1. Focus on the movements themselves, not the outcomes.
2. Try to view movement from several different angles.
3. Notice the efficiency (or nonefficiency) of a child's style of movement.
4. Observe different children playing together doing the same activities.
5. Observe children from different age groups doing the same activity.

Your descriptions of children's movements that accompany a checklist of abilities, such as the one in Chapter 9, Figure 9.4, will help you anticipate new physical developments.

Young children develop purposeful movements using **fine motor skills** with their small muscles, but it often takes time for them to become skilled:

With rounded scissors, Daniel, a young three, works at cutting construction paper. His mouth slowly opens and closes in rhythm with the scissors.

Daniel's mouth opens and closes because he is just emerging from the sensorimotor stage, and one part of his body accompanies another in rhythm. It may take a few years for Daniel to cut paper expertly.

Five-year-olds are at the brink of the most significant changes since their toddler years. Some have already lost their teeth, a physical change that foreshadows other changes to come.

> **Young children develop purposeful movements using fine motor skills with their small muscles, but it often takes time for them to become skilled.**

Learning to use scissors with skill can take a good part of early childhood.

Social-Emotional Development

Three-year-olds still see their parents as superheroes of sorts. Over time, they begin to view adults more realistically as they revel in their innumerable new skills and as their friends become increasingly important to them. Threes, fours, and kindergartners talk incessantly about best friends, and you can expect tearful cries of, "He's not my friend!" Ulterior motives may enter into friendships as children share and trade toys and other objects, and threes find it easier to share, or at least to talk about sharing, than they did a year earlier.

Three-year-olds seem to spend the year realizing what their new physical, intellectual, and social capabilities entail. With more expressive language and newfound independence, many fours have extraordinary zest and energy. A classroom of exuberant four-year-olds can exhaust the adults who work with them, but their creativity is a joy.

You will notice five-year-olds' increased independence and growing sense of empathy for others. Fives who experience a classroom where they can make choices among open-ended activities of interest to them spend time planning projects and dramatic play, which remains important for most kindergartners. When children do not have opportunities to make decisions and solve problems, they do not develop those skills in the same way.

Some young children have best friends; some play with everyone; some play alone most of the time. Others are remote from classmates and gravitate to family members if they are there. Friendships can be fickle, perhaps dependent on who gives whom a toy, or lasting, like the pair who play together all year.

Teachers can cement friendships by talking to children about their friends and also can help children make friends. When the teacher talks to others at the table about what Sara is making, she turns their attention to Sara. When the teacher plays catch with Cyrus and throws the ball to Hiro, he broadens the game to include both boys. The teacher can go with Lamar to ask a group to let the child play, too.

Teachers have a role to play in children's social and emotional development:

"Hey! Look at me!" three-year-old Noam calls to his teacher from the branches of the tree.

After an active morning with blocks, four-year-old Lanie finishes lunch and climbs onto her teacher's lap.

Zach rushes to his kindergarten teacher with, "Guess what? Turtles were on earth two hundred million years ago."

Most children this age want a connection with their teachers and readily approach adults who show interest in them. The level of formality in the classroom and the teacher's personal warmth affect how children seek that connection.

Children who feel close to their teachers are more likely to behave cooperatively (Hyson 2008). When Noam called his teacher's attention to his climbing, she could celebrate his achievement, demand he descend, or both. Noam is more likely to get down from the tree if his teacher acknowledges his skills and then suggests what the three-year-old can do to be safe.

Lanie seems to know that her teacher accepts her independent *and* her dependent behavior. Teachers who take children as they are and show that they care—by

THOUGHT QUESTION Parents who practice elimination communication with their children find that their children gain control and awareness as early as a few months. In place of words, child and parent use cuing sounds to communicate about using the toilet. These parents maintain that their children learn to use the toilet gradually, but no later than other children.

According to the American Academy of Pediatrics, children learn to use the toilet better and faster when they start later rather than earlier. The AAP cites studies indicating that children who begin learning to use a potty or the toilet before eighteen months often are not fully successful until after four years of age. In contrast, children who begin at two years or after tend to use the toilet by age three (Shelov and Hannemann 1998), in part, because brain development occurring between one and two years of age creates and strengthens communication lines between the brain and the anus.

Power, communication, control, resistance, and *support* are words adults use when they talk about toilet learning. A child who uses the toilet conforms to the way grownups in that child's culture behave. What approaches will you take with the children, and what do you want to say to families about toilet learning?

THOUGHT QUESTION Exclusion is the flip side of the sense of belonging. Statements such as "I'm not your friend" and "You can't play" can hurt. How do you think a teacher can help—or can they?

offering a lap or a sincere smile—can help children feel more invested in school (Hyson 2008).

As you can see from Zach's interaction with his kindergarten teacher, children who are involved with their teacher are more likely to be engaged in learning in school (Hyson 2008). When Zach shares an exciting bit of information, his teacher can ask him to elaborate or suggest ways to find out more. If Zach had not rushed to her with his exciting news, that conversation could not occur.

Cognition

By three, children no longer take in the world through their senses alone. They possess more language and symbolic thinking to shape their responses to experiences and are capable of a more sophisticated level of communication. For example, most can now tell a simple story.

As you read in Chapter 6, according to Piaget, children who are predominantly in the preoperational stage of cognitive development rely on what they see rather than on what they figure out. Moving into concrete operations takes time and is a gradual transition. Those truly in the preoperational period rigorously study reality yet are easily swept away by fantasy. One young child proclaimed, "I know Big Bird isn't real. That's just a costume," and then explained, "There's just a plain bird inside" (Gardner 1982, 248).

When children learn big words, adults can't be sure what the words mean to them. When Melissa used "uterus" to describe Daniel's belly, she had the spark of an idea, practiced a new word, and drew upon a fact she had learned—that, before they are born, babies grow in their mother's uterus. Over time, Melissa will assess a situation, such as the size of Daniel's belly, using language and concepts more precisely and accurately than she can at four.

Most children love to play with words, make up rhymes, and experiment with different sounds. They become competent with three-, four-, then five-word sentences, and more, but may play simple word games such as this:

> The kindergarten takes a trip on a city train. As two girls look at the grimy blue tiles in front of them, one chants: "Square, square, square, square."
> Her friend follows suit: "Square, square, square, square."
> They giggle. The second girl begins: "Blue, blue, blue, blue."
> The chant spreads. One girl says "blue," then the other says "square" all the way to the next station.

These children play with language that describes their environment. As Bank Street's founder, Lucy Sprague Mitchell, pointed out:

> Children begin to play with sounds long before words have any meaning to them. . . . Even Piaget . . . suggests that children will soon outgrow the childish pleasures in rhythm and sound qualities and speak sensibly like grownups. And so they do! To Piaget, this dropping of art elements from language is progress, the overcoming of an immaturity. To me it is a tragedy, for to me a child's pleasure in rhythm, sound quality and pattern is the seed from which literature grows. (1953, 281)

Children who don't have spoken language also play with words, as a teacher of threes discovered when she found two deaf children under a slightly moving blanket during naptime. She understood their "whispered" signing: They were supposed to be napping, but instead they were playing with words.

Scribble Stage	Transitions	Preschematic Stage	Schematic Stage
Begins when children first start to use drawing materials	Occur as children move from one stage to the next; the child's work displays elements of the earlier stage along with those of the more advanced stage	Continues through preschool, kindergarten, and first grade	Goes on through the early elementary years
As children begin to make marks on paper, what they draw is more a record of their hand movements. As they see the outcome of their work, instead of randomly moving their hands, they start to make circles and other intentional marks.	As children transition from one stage to the next, an early preschematic drawing, for example, may include scribbles along with more representational drawing.	Now children begin to draw people, animals, and objects. They tend to place them anywhere on the page, and the size of what they draw varies.	Building on their already representational drawing, now children use their drawings to communicate their ideas. They develop their own way of drawing a person. They position what they draw along the bottom of the page.

12.1 *Stages of Drawing*

Although we discuss them separately here, in life the developmental domains work together. For example, children's drawing develops from scribbles to pictographs to more sophisticated representations of their experience (Figure 12.1). At first, children derive pleasure from large movements of the crayon or brush. As they gain more fine motor control and symbolic thinking, they create shapes that eventually take on the rough form of figures (Lowenfeld and Brittain 1987).

WHAT PRESCHOOLERS AND KINDERGARTNERS LEARN AND HOW

What do preschoolers and kindergartners learn, and how do they learn it?

Melissa and other children who were fascinated by a teacher's pregnancy and the prospect of a new baby drew pregnant mothers, visited the nearby hospital's nursery, and made and read books about babies. Melissa made her own sense of the new ideas and vocabulary, recognizing the shape of Daniel's belly and remembering the word

Although we discuss them separately here, in life the developmental domains work together.

uterus for the place where babies grow. Ideally, children, as did Melissa, will think about the curriculum throughout the day. Through their play and investigations, they will acquire knowledge, develop language and literacy skills, and use many media.

Janet Gonzalez-Mena and Anne Stonehouse (2008) contrast **authentic experiences** that have meaning for children against activities that teachers plan to flesh out a theme or project. If the children go apple picking, for example, observe them at the orchard. Back in the classroom, record their discussions, and ask them to sort the photographs you took. Those activities will guide you to extend the experience at the orchard. You may find that children want to cook the apples or taste them raw and compare different types of apples, or you may discover that they are more interested in the apple trees, how they grow, and stories of climbing them.

If, instead, a teacher cut out paper apples and gave children tissue paper to glue on them, the activity would relate to apples but would not enable children to learn more about their experience with apples. It would fill the time and the teacher's plan book but would not contribute to in-depth investigation as authentic experiences do.

Social Studies as Core Curriculum

Social studies, whether teachers call it that or not, is a focal point for content-rich authentic curriculum. Preschoolers and kindergartners are interested in almost every aspect of their environment and will demonstrate and deepen what they know about social studies through their dramatic play. In the following sections, we discuss two essential components of social studies for young children: trips and social justice.

Trips

As with older children, trips enable preschoolers and kindergartners to expand their horizons and investigate topics more fully. Water at the sink and in the water table fascinated so many three-year-olds that their teachers researched the city's fountains and took the children on trips to investigate them. Some four-year-olds on a trip to a local park adopted a tree and visited it weekly to look for changes. A kindergarten took a neighborhood walk on a day when their playground was too wet. They noticed someone asking for money and speculated that he was homeless. Back in the classroom, they pooled their ideas about homelessness, read books about being homeless, and decided to raise money for the nearest homeless shelter.

Trips beyond the classroom can enhance the curriculum or stimulate new curriculum altogether. They can be as local as a walk around the block or as far away as an apple orchard. The whole class can pile on a bus, or a group of three or four children can take clipboards to the school kitchen or into the neighborhood to gather information.

Children and social action

Preschool and kindergarten children eagerly think about how to make change for the better. Whether they champion the cause of a threatened species or stand up for the rights of a discriminated group, most young children care deeply about fairness.

Teachers can supply resources to help children act conscientiously. Vivian Vasquez's (2004) junior kindergarten class was upset that their school excluded them and other young children from what were otherwise schoolwide events. They surveyed their class and other classes and then, at their teacher's suggestion, drew up and signed a petition.

Vasquez (2004) also explains how discussions of children's books led to social action. Beginning with a picture of an amphibian and a child's question of whether it

Preschoolers and kindergartners are interested in almost every aspect of their environment and will demonstrate and deepen what they know about social studies through their dramatic play.

was a frog or a toad, Vasquez and the three-, four-, and five-year-olds in her class embarked on investigations of the animals' environments, new understandings of rain forests, and letter-writing campaigns to protect the forests. Throughout the year, children's discussions led to more discussion, investigation, and action in which children spoke out on such issues as food for vegetarians at school and "who is left out of the books we have in our library" (64).

Many excellent resources can help you implement social justice curriculum, including:

Byrnes, Deborah A., and Gary Kiger, eds. 1992. *Common bonds: Anti-bias teaching in a diverse society.* Wheaton, MD: ACEI Publications.

Derman-Sparks, Louise. 1992. Anti-bias, multicultural curriculum: What is developmentally appropriate? In *Reaching potentials: Appropriate curriculum and assessment for young children,* ed. Sue Bredekamp and Teresa Rosegrant. Washington, DC: National Association for the Education of Young Children.

Derman-Sparks, Louise, and Patricia G. Ramsey. 2006. *What if all the kids are white? Anti-bias multicultural education with young children.* New York: Teachers College Press.

Sparks, Louise Derman, and the ABC Task Force. 1989. *Anti-bias curriculum: Tools for empowering young children.* Washington, DC: National Association for the Education of Young Children.

Williams, Leslie. 2002. *Alerta: A multicultural bilingual approach to teaching young children.* Columbus, OH: Pearson Learning.

Language and Literacy

The NCLB Act of 2001 requires demonstrated academic learning based on standardized test results. This has intensified the debate over academic versus play-based preschool and kindergarten (Blaustein 2005), and some programs have abandoned content-rich curriculum, reduced the time children play, and even use scripted literacy activities. Families and early childhood educators alike feel pressure for children to perform successfully and probably agree that strong academic skills and school success are desirable. Not everyone agrees, however, on how to achieve these goals. Teachers who must follow skill-based curricula may find it hard to create playful, joyful literacy experiences for children, but it is worth the struggle.

As preschoolers and kindergartners hear stories told and books read aloud and play with and delight in language, they develop the skills of readers and writers. Children often use the language of their homes but also mimic what they hear on TV and elsewhere. Some children come to preschool familiar with books; other children get to know books only when they start school. Observing adults and each other and playing with spoken language and books, young children learn about literacy.

Emergent literacy

Emergent literacy refers to children's reading- and writing-related behaviors before they actually read and write. From

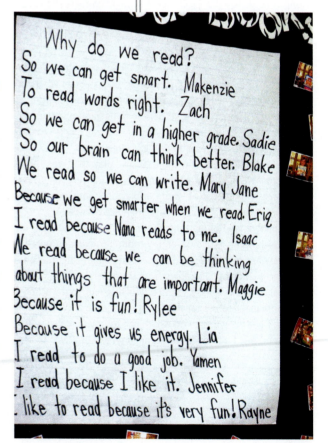

These kindergartners came up with many ideas of what reading means to them.

I've been learning about and teaching young children for more than twenty years—in New York, Florida, and now in Nevada. People ask me why I don't go into administration. They say, "You can't teach kindergarten for the rest of your life." I say, "Watch me!"

My pedagogical roots are in early childhood education. How children learn, appropriate class size, how to observe children, and always keeping in mind what's best for the children—these principles come from my foundation in early childhood education.

A decade ago, I had time to get to know students socially and to take observational notes. I developed curriculum around their thoughts, based on their interests. One year, some students were acting like little cats in the housekeeping area, and soon they drew in the entire class. Cats were so important to the children that they wanted to read about them themselves. Children expressed themselves through their writing and dramatic enactment, and we did art activities. I did research on cats, why cats have whiskers, for example, and I learned about why cats see at night—all these things I'd never thought about. I learned as much as the children did. We brought a cat into our classroom to observe and made a book about it.

This curriculum belonged to the children and went on for a long time. I was the facilitator. I brought in facts—how cats move, for example—and the children were very interested. And I'm not a pet person! I'm allergic to cats, but I still did it. I went out of my comfort zone.

Students in my class who were recent immigrants didn't speak to anyone except during dramatic play as cats. Then they felt comfortable following along, smiling, and participating silently. These students became part of things and practiced English in a safe environment. They began to speak English to their friends even though they wouldn't in a large group.

The cat curriculum and the dramatic play that went along with it created a sense of community. All of us were involved in it. Children had choices of where to play and work, what to do, and everyone was learning through their experiences.

Instilling a love of learning continues to be at the forefront of my teaching style. However, my room has changed over the past few years as the pressure of academic achievement, even in kindergarten, has trickled down from the federal government to the states, to the counties, to the school districts, to the schools, to the principals, to the teachers, to the children and their families. Don't get me wrong. I do what I can for my new generation of learners, but I also incorporate mandated initiatives so that my students can demonstrate their success on future assessments. I assess each child individually and report monthly test results, and I have to use packaged reading curriculum. I have less time to develop authentic curriculum.

Rafael Pena

The reading series we use dictates certain books, but we study winter in January independent of the mandated curriculum. This year, I introduced my students to one of my favorite stories about winter, *The Snowy Day*, by Ezra Jack Keats. We then explored more books by Keats and developed an author study. We talked about how Keats's stories took place in urban settings similar to the one the children live in. We talked about the similarities and differences from story to story. The children really were excited about learning about a single author. It gave them an appreciation for an author, and they spoke to their families about their learning.

I understand that if I don't push academics, these kids won't succeed in school the way school is today. Before, academics were always there, of course, but they weren't my primary emphasis. Now parents are concerned about what their children know and don't know, and they don't want to hear that children learn at their own pace.

My class is still a learning community. We share all our materials and find time to enjoy learning together. And, children still have free-choice time—after all the mandated work is done. They need that time to socialize. They play with manipulatives or reading games. They choose books. I put out new materials regularly, but we have less time for creative activities. They can use the sand table, but not as much as in previous years; and if we have art once a week, we're lucky. We don't have the time or resources. We don't have a family area, but the children create dramatic play space on the big rug we have for large groups. They often play teacher. And they still play cats.

the time they are babies, children are becoming readers and writers. You probably learned the **conventions of literacy,** how to hold a book and turn its pages, for example, when you were quite young. Some conventions, such as reading English from left to right, are part of how print is organized. Children learn these conventions in many ways, including observation, experimentation, and an adult or peer's explanation.

Recognizing the letters and knowing what sounds they make are part of literacy, but to read and write, children also need vocabulary and an understanding of **syntax**—the order in which we string words together—which enable them to comprehend language. Thus, speaking and listening skills are closely connected to reading and writing skills and develop along with them.

Emergent literacy refers to children's reading- and writing-related behaviors before they actually read and write.

Supporting children's language and literacy development

Teachers of young children build upon children's knowledge of oral or spoken language (Strickland 2006). They familiarize children with the sounds, rules, and delights of language and the possibilities that unfold when it is written down.

Teachers create opportunities for children to explore sounds and written language and help them see the connection between the two. They expose children to different sounds and discuss other sounds that come up in conversation. They model literacy when they use an extensive and precise vocabulary and play with language. They read aloud with enthusiasm; often reread children's favorites aloud; and make reading and writing habits explicit, for instance, pointing out words as they read and talking about stories they love. They use print in the classroom to make lists and write reminders, and they transcribe children's language to document activities in charts, in teacher- and child-made books, and in letters, such as Jorge's below:

> Three-year-old Jorge cries inconsolably when his mother leaves. Dale takes him on his lap. After a while, he suggests they write a letter to Jorge's mother. Dale records as Jorge dictates, "Don't go. Come back. I love you." They reread the letter. Jorge slides off Dale's lap, folds the paper, gets a marker, and writes M O M. He puts the letter in his pocket and runs off.

Teachers provide materials that encourage children's language and literacy habits. They have a collection of well-kept, high-quality children's books and rotate a selection at the children's level.

Teachers make writing tools invitingly available in a writing area and as part of curriculum such as an office or a post office in the dramatic play area. They also order or make puppets and enable children to make and play with puppets.

Teachers build children's appreciation of literature. They discuss the ideas in books, ask children to predict what will happen next, and prompt them to extend the narratives they dictate. They listen to children's stories and invite them to act out their stories.

Preschoolers listen to a story and share it in different ways.

Besides reading folktales aloud to the children, Crystal memorizes stories to tell. She makes hand motions and turns to the children as she speaks. She finds that *telling* stories, especially ones that generations have passed down, builds shared enjoyment of the narrative and its language. She is rewarded in the yard, when she sees children standing outside a house built of hollow blocks, shouting, "Who's in Rabbit's house?" a chant from the tale she told the day before.

In addition, teachers scaffold children's learning about oral and written language—that is, they figure out what children know, can do, and like to do and then build on their knowledge, abilities, and interest. Teachers listen carefully as children speak and, with open-ended questions, prompt them to extend their ideas and request clarification. They also give directions that are simple enough to follow but as complicated as the child can manage. They use **decontextualized language**—language that is about times, places, and events that are *not* part of the child's experience at that moment—as well as **contextualized language,** which is about the immediate surroundings.

Some kindergarten classes have readers' workshops and writers' workshops just as first grades do. You will read more about these in Chapter 13. In Anna and Amanda's kindergarten, the children do paired reading during readers' workshop, with clear rules of how to approach reading together.

Children's books

Children's books illuminate universal life experiences—going to sleep at night and fear of the dark, separation and the death of a loved one, friendship, birth of a sibling, growing and changing, and more. In addition, books expose children to people whose lives are different from theirs.

Through books, children experience the formal syntax of written language. Many picture books offer minimal text with sensory images and a rhythmic flow of language that is poetic if not strictly poetry.

Often at story time, quiet descends, and even if children start out sitting in designated places, they inch closer to the teacher. The chapter books that you read aloud to kindergartners, a bit at one sitting, leave them yearning for more. From such times, children come to see the pleasures of reading. Such anticipation is a key ingredient of emergent literacy.

Activities and Materials

Every area of the classroom provides its own challenges and has the potential to engage children. The following sections describe what can happen in those spaces.

Blocks, manipulatives, and dramatic play

Through blocks, manipulatives, and dramatic play, children explore all the major subjects: language, mathematics, science, social studies. Experiences in these three areas activate children's imaginations and creativity and require them to solve problems of their own making.

THOUGHT QUESTION Tara put out her favorite books at the beginning of the year, and now they are in tatters. She doesn't want to replace them, fearing the children will destroy new books, but she worries that the children won't be exposed to books in good condition. What would you advise her to do?

THOUGHT QUESTION Anna tries to hold one side of the book, but Amanda pulls it away, and a struggle ensues. After several seconds, Anna gives up and drops her side of the book but quickly returns her attention to it as Amanda begins to read aloud. Anna says, "I don't think that's right." When Amanda claims that it is, Anna whines, "We didn't figure it out together." Amanda puts the book away in her book bag. What is each child learning about reading and about herself? What challenges does paired reading pose for the kindergarten teacher who wants both children to get the most out of it?

Making stacks or rows (repetition)

Bridging

Making enclosures

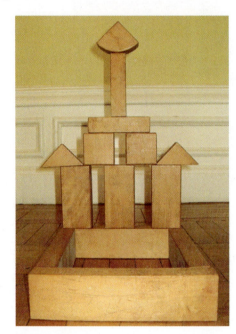

Making patterns

Naming buildings

Building to represent something

12.2 *Development Sequence of Block Building*
No matter how old they are when they begin to play with blocks, children seem to progress through this sequence in block building: making stacks or rows (repetition), bridging, making enclosures, making patterns, naming buildings, building to represent something.

Here you can see how block shapes relate to each other.

THOUGHT QUESTION What if no girls play in your block area? Why is it important for both girls and boys to play with blocks? How will you draw girls into the area?

Children must master one-to-one correspondence to count meaningfully. Otherwise, they chant the numbers 1, 2, 3, 4, and so forth, without matching what they say to the item they are counting.

The wooden **unit block** is a rectangle; half a unit is a square. All the shapes in the set are based in some way on the unit block, so that children using the blocks can feel and see mathematical relationships.

Once they start to build with blocks, children usually make stacks or rows. They then bridge blocks, build enclosures, and create patterns. Eventually they name their buildings and make representational structures, ones that they know from their environment or their reading and that can form the basis of elaborate play (Hirsch 1996).

Children's block building thrives in a large, carefully arranged and maintained space. You encourage children to build when your questions prompt them to think and talk about their constructions. Your drawings or photographs of their buildings and pictures of buildings from their environment will also stimulate their efforts. On trips outside the classroom, you and the children can talk about buildings they see and how they might replicate them with blocks.

Perhaps more than any other material, blocks stimulate children to work together. At first they may simply build next to each other, but soon children as young as three build and rebuild together. They may connect their buildings with roads or bridges, developing intricate play schemes in the process.

Children also arrange and build with **manipulatives,** small toys that require them to use their fine motor skills. As with all forms of play, children have fun and use their imaginations as they do so. In manipulative play, children coordinate hand and eye movements, sharpen their **perception** (their ability to see details), and differentiate between an object and its background (**figure-ground**). They will use all these skills as they learn to read and write.

Much math is embedded in children's work with manipulative materials, too. Figure 12.3 shows the relationship between Lego play and understandings about mathematics that the National Council of Teachers of Mathematics lists for pre-K and kindergartners. For more information, please see the NCTM's website at http://standards.nctm.org/document/chapter4/index.htm.

Catalogs of teaching materials offer many different manipulatives. As you make selections, keep in mind the range of mathematical understandings three- to six-year-olds can gain from each.

Children learn math when they manipulate real objects, too. For example, a neatly set table is clearly organized, establishing relationships and patterns that use mathematical thinking. As children match a placemat to each chair and a plate, fork, cup, and napkin to each placemat, they learn about **one-to-one correspondence,** or matching an item in one set to an item in another. Children must master one-to-one correspondence to count meaningfully. Otherwise, they chant the numbers 1, 2, 3, 4, and so forth, without matching what they say to the item they are counting.

Most preschoolers and kindergartners love board games. You can purchase them or make some that fit your curriculum and the children in your group. A duplicate set of photographs of the children in action, for example, makes a lotto, or matching, game or a set of concentration, or memory, cards. You can create sets of sequence cards with step-by-step photos of children cooking, and children can put them in order to practice their **seriation** skills.

Mathematical Understanding	Lego Activities That Develop the Understanding
Count with understanding and recognize "how many" in sets of objects	As children build with Legos, they see how many they need and how many will fit in the space they have. Children may spontaneously count what they are using.
Sort, classify, and order objects by size, number, and other properties	Children arrange Legos of different shapes, colors, and sizes and make decisions about which to use where.
Recognize, describe, and extend patterns	Children use different colored Legos to create patterns.
Recognize, name, build, draw, compare, and sort two- and three-dimensional shapes	Many Lego pieces are rectangular, but they also include other shapes. As children work together and ask others for pieces, they learn the names, compare and sort shapes, and see how shapes fit together.
Recognize the attributes of length, volume, weight, and area and compare and order objects according to these attributes	Children compare Legos of different lengths as they work with them and see which fit their construction needs.

12.3 *How Children Can Use Legos to Develop Mathematical Understandings*

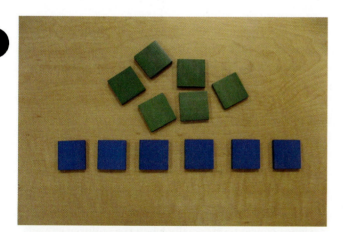

A child who uses one-to-one correspondence matches each number to the object she is counting.

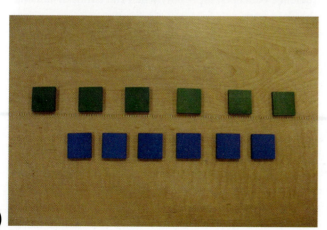

THOUGHT QUESTION How will you set up the dramatic play area? What props belong there: clothing or swatches of material for children to drape? Adult clothes are alluring but can lead to sex-role stereotyping. List the items you want for the dress-up area, and explain your reason for including each item. Will you have miniature adult furniture or hollow blocks for children to build what they need? Miniature furniture is inviting, but children may use their imaginations more fully if they create furniture themselves.

Use of purchased and homemade manipulatives and games along with your thought-provoking questions and comments can help children to meet the NCTM process standards:

- building new mathematical knowledge and thinking flexibly about mathematical ideas,
- conjecturing and supporting their reasoning with clear arguments,
- talking to others about their mathematical thinking,
- seeing mathematical relationships and understanding how mathematical ideas apply in everyday life, and
- using mathematical notations to record their ideas and discoveries.

Children use blocks and manipulatives for dramatic play, too; but in the family area (also called the housekeeping or dramatic play area), children's imaginations and social skills soar as they become whomever they like, however they wish. Here is where children play most freely. You read about dramatic play, its purposes and benefits, in Chapter 4.

In a special area of your room, children play house, put out fires, wait on tables, and sort mail. In an "office" children research through trips and then construct in the classroom, they can practice literacy skills, social studies, and social skills.

Science, sand, and water

Armed with clipboards and flashlights, bands of four-year-olds and their baby brothers and sisters, Head Start teachers, parents, and grandparents fan out into the halls of the museum. They enter an African rain forest exhibit, a spectacular diorama with more than 160 species of flora and fauna and more than 500,000 leaves. They shine their flashlights on each layer, looking for their assigned animals or plants, observing, drawing, and discussing their observations. Back in the classroom, they examine real leaves and millipedes and snakes; draw pictures of what they are seeing; and describe their experience as adults write or help them write in their "field journals."

Throughout their visit and subsequent activities, the children do science. They use scientific language and meet scientists (Wahl 2003). Trips to a natural history museum are ideal for learning science concepts, especially when the children can analyze their findings back in the classroom.

Scientific opportunities abound in the classroom, too. Children observe the plants on the windowsill and the animals in their cages. In the block area, they test engineering principles. A science area has magnets, magnifiers, eyedroppers, mirrors, and other tools for investigations. Children's science books suggest experiments. The sand and water table entices children to stay for a long time. There children explore physics, for example, as they find ways to make water travel from place to place.

Finally, children's outdoor play is full of scientific learning opportunities. A seesaw is a fulcrum and a lever, and a teacher's questions about how children place their weight can prompt children's hypotheses and experimentation.

You can help children record their findings and analyze the information they gather. Your knowledge of science will help you to

THOUGHT QUESTION What if you hated science in school and struggled with math? What can you do to engage children in math and science without passing along your negative feelings?

ask thought-provoking questions, provide helpful vocabulary, and suggest observation strategies.

Music and movement

Music is an auditory experience that begins in the womb. Children perceive music through the ear, body, and soul. When people hear live music, they connect to each other: each person brings meaning to and takes meaning from a musical exchange. Note that young children also sing or hum to themselves. Music aimed at oneself is similar to private speech and can serve to self-regulate attention or emotions.

Even though most children sing, dance, and imitate without instruction, teachers can create opportunities for them to grow with music. Children usually join in with the sounds around them and, when necessary, shut them out. In an early childhood classroom, music is about the here and now: the dance feeling, the jump urge, the desire to sing with friends or alone, and, for some, the decision to watch from a safe distance and try later at home. Betsy Blachly (personal communication) notes that children are attached to individual songs, though not necessarily to the same ones as their peers. "Sometimes they tell me, emphatically, 'I have that song,' just as they say, 'I have a baby sister.'" If you forget their good-bye song, they may sing it anyway. Such a song can serve as a transitional object and connect a child to a feeling he wasn't aware of until the singing started.

Besides offering joy and communication, music, rhythm, and rhyme are learning tools. For example, when children sing songs that switch initial consonants to make nonsense words, they have fun, but they also play with **phonemic awareness,** "the general ability to attend to language's sounds as distinct from its meaning" (Epstein 2007, 24). Children can learn about animals, culture, or numerous other topics through music, including songs in languages other than English. Songs in English teach ELLs words that have meaning and context in a rhythm and melody that are easy to remember. When they sing songs in their language of origin, ELLs experience pride and share their heritage with others.

Musical experiences stimulate change and growth: A child who is usually quiet calls out a word or vocalizes in a song; two children who often taunt each other share a drum. A teacher who only sings in the shower may surprise himself when the children's musical energy is contagious.

Movement goes naturally with music and, like music, is a vehicle for learning. Young children need to use their muscles to develop them well. Moreover, sitting on chairs or even on the floor attending to words and symbols is hard for most of them. Some individuals are especially tuned in to kinesthetic intelligence (Gardner 1982). They pick up visual and verbal information as they exercise their muscles, watching and then enacting the movement (Altman 1992). Teachers can provide opportunities for all children to learn motorically as they support children who learn especially well through moving their bodies.

All children can understand and express their understanding of science, math, or other concepts through movement. Children studying the solar system, for example, can explore the concept of gravity by moving as if they were traveling in space without its pull or on a star that has a stronger gravitational pull than the Earth's. Movement and physical gestures help ELLs, especially, connect to classroom activities, whether the words are in their home language or in English. They understand the word *run* or *skip* by experiencing it with their bodies and thus can connect the meaning to a word in either language.

Finally, regular class exercises can help you as a teacher. Getting the blood circulating through our bodies helps our brains work better. When moving breaks are part

Music aimed at oneself is similar to private speech and can serve to self-regulate attention or emotions.

"Sometimes they tell me, emphatically, 'I have that song,' just as they say, 'I have a baby sister.'"

of your day, you instill important habits in the children that can serve them well as they continue through the higher grades, where they will do more sedentary work.

Art

Children who have easy access to art materials become accustomed to representing their ideas with words and other symbols. Although teachers can find and develop art activities with cute outcomes, we do not consider that art. In fact, those activities work against children's self-expression. In contrast, **open-ended materials** that children can use in many ways, such as markers, paint, and clay, allow the child to decide how to use them and what the outcome will be. Once children have a sense of how the properties of clay differ from those of paint or wooden blocks, they can predict how the materials will respond.

When they draw or paint, children may not have an outcome in mind. If a teacher asks, "What is that?" children may not have an answer. To support young children's creative endeavors, teachers can observe them and their art and comment on the colors, shapes, and lines.

While overstructuring art prevents exploration, too little teacher involvement can lead to children's creating stereotypic images from the culture at large (Gwathmey and Mott 2000). The teacher plays an active role in preparing activities and organizing art materials for children to use as they need them. Aside from painting, you may set up supplies for collage or gluing, printmaking, and play dough—or have them all ready for children to take out. Clay—a natural substance that people dig up and that potters use—is different from play dough and enables children to make stable creations. Clay is harder to manipulate than play dough, and preschoolers are ready to experiment with it. Older preschoolers and kindergartners can use it to represent their ideas.

When you label children's artwork with their names and the date, you can follow a progression in their work. Out of respect for children's work, some teachers only write on the back unless children ask otherwise.

Classroom teachers can cooperate with art teachers—or *atelieristas* in Reggio Emilia–influenced programs—to bring artwork into closer connection with the curriculum. One October, when a kindergarten read about, cooked, ate, and discussed harvest vegetables, they returned from the art room with African masks. The masks were fun, but had the teachers collaborated, the children could have explored the vegetable curriculum more deeply through art or studied African masks together instead.

> While overstructuring art prevents exploration, too little teacher involvement can lead to children's creating stereotypic images from the culture at large.

Technology

Over the past twenty years, early childhood educators have differed about when to introduce computers. Some believe that although computer use can enhance social skills such as sharing, collaborating, and verbal and nonverbal problem solving, young children are not ready for much more than simple drawing programs.

Yet children experience a gratifying sense of competence from the cause and effect of computer use. Push a button or move a mouse, and something happens! Mistakes go away,

Kindergartners with their African masks.

and you begin again. *Technology* literally means "tools" and includes the pencils and scissors in your classroom. Just as children learn to use those tools, they can learn about computers in your classroom whether or not they use them at home.

Research on the use of IBM's KidSmart program in Head Start centers demonstrated that teachers who were thoughtful about blocks, sand, and paint tended to be equally thoughtful about computer use (Nager, Sherman, and Blachman 2003). As with any material or experience, the teacher's insightful comments and probing questions enhance children's computer abilities.

You and the children can use the computer to support your curriculum as you look up information on the Internet and find child-friendly resources on topics of interest. Some games on the computer can challenge children to think in new ways.

These children work together on one computer.

Children can use computers to write stories in print or with digital media. You and the children can make books, presentations, and other classroom materials. Children can communicate with friends and relatives. Computers enable children and teachers to find information that they could never locate otherwise.

Here are some points to consider as you plan computer use in your classroom (Bers 2008):

- Do children make decisions, including design decisions, as they use the computer?
- Does children's work at the computer lead them to reflect on their learning?
- Are children engaged in complex projects at the computer?
- Is the computer work and play flexible enough for children to express themselves and learn about themselves and their community?
- Is computer work interesting enough to engage children for lengths of time?
- Does working on the computer connect children to other people and other ways of thinking and behaving?
- Does computer work enable children to take action?

You can find the International Society for Technology in Education's National Educational Technology Standards (NETS) by searching for "standards" at http://www.iste.org.

Some organizations design Web-based materials for parents to use with their children. For example, the Public Broadcasting System's site has games to spark children's creative thinking and stimulate them to

This robot moves according to directions that a child gives via computer.

strategize. Often children use these programs most productively with a nearby adult to support them.

Robotic manipulatives enable children to build with manipulatives. Then they connect what they have built to the computer and program their construction to interact and respond to some stimulus (Bers 2008).

THOUGHT QUESTION Whether you use robotic manipulatives or use computers in other ways, technology can put you in the position of learner. How do you feel about not knowing all the answers and learning alongside, and even from, the children you teach?

CLASSROOMS FOR PRESCHOOLERS AND KINDERGARTNERS

What characteristics do effective preschool and kindergarten classrooms exhibit?

Much thought goes into an early childhood classroom that enjoys a natural rhythm and where learning seems effortless. Teachers consider what will happen when, where, with whom, and, especially, why. They may record their plans or keep them in their heads. They may develop their own ideas or incorporate someone else's. They may plan time and space alone or together. However they do it, they plan.

Planning Authentic Experiences

According to Gonzalez-Mena and Stonehouse (2008, 8, emphasis in original):

> Planning involves thinking about what you *want* to happen and what you think *will* happen and how to blend the two. You have to be prepared for what you have planned, as well as for what you haven't planned.

Teachers need confidence in their ability to create learning spaces. Then they can relax and interact in meaningful ways throughout the day. Five actions that begin with the letter A will help you to create curriculum *with* the children:

- *Arrange an environment with materials for investigations.* Stock the basics such as clay, paint, scissors, paper, blocks, magnifiers, magnets, dolls, and hats. Children can use these flexible resources as they need them.
- *Acquaint children with the materials and their possibilities.* In one school, children use red paint for a week, and blue or yellow the next week. After exploring each primary color, they use two colors. The children eventually paint with red, yellow, blue, black, and white and mix their own greens and oranges.
- *Attend to details.* Know the children and the content they can investigate, and use that knowledge to match children and curriculum. Read widely to continue your own general education. Become conversant enough with resources to develop curriculum with children on anything from homelessness to horses.
- *Accept that learning happens anytime and everywhere* and be alert to all learning possibilities at all times.
- *Acknowledge that everything children do is worth considering carefully.* A passing interest in earthworms or stones can lead to rich curriculum. And, although you may stop extended play at the sink or calm children when spontaneous word games get too silly, these instances provide a glimpse of children's interests and can spark meaningful planned experiences.

Taking these five actions can't guarantee that you will have a curriculum that works for the children in your class. Take a risk and try out your ideas (Gonzalez-Mena and Stonehouse 2008). Go beyond the familiar and take a chance on the possible (New, Mardell, and Robinson 2005).

No single planning method is right for everyone all the time (Gonzalez-Mena and Stonehouse 2008). Sometimes a principal or director will require you to use a certain format. You will fit your style to their administrative directives, but the real question is: What makes a planning system work for you?

A useful planning system integrates what you learn from your observations and other assessments of children with what they do in your class. It not only draws on your assessments of children's academic skills but also considers their social lives and physical prowess. It starts with who each child is, and families are a great source for this information.

How will you plan for small groups and individuals? Some teachers keep planning charts and write specific experiences and interactions next to each child's name. To facilitate getting to know individuals and groups, some classrooms have small-group time where each teacher works with the same group each day. Teachers then develop relationships with the children and can plan for them as individuals more easily.

A good planning system enables you to be true to what you hope to accomplish in your classroom. As you use it, keep these questions in mind:

- What do you want for the children in general and for each child in particular?
- What do their families want for them?
- How can you make these outcomes occur in your classroom?

Go beyond the familiar and take a chance on the possible.

Emergent curriculum

Emergent curriculum is a plan of activities that arises from the children's interests. The curriculum combines adult goals for children with what children do and say. Consequently, it is constantly up for revision.

At Leech Lake Head Start in north-central Minnesota, the fours classroom takes a spontaneous trip that fits the annual cycle of events of the children's Ojibwe culture. A teacher's adult son, John, has phoned saying that he and five friends are back from netting fish in one of the area's many lakes. Because the teachers have heard children talk about their fathers' and uncles' evening trips to set nets and their early morning trips to haul in the fish-filled nets, they decide to take the children to see the men bring in the fish. The excursion will build on the children's interest in fishing and support their learning about their Ojibwe traditions.

The children pile into the Head Start bus and stream into their teacher's backyard, where John and his friends are removing fish from the nets, then sorting and cleaning them. "It smells!" several children call out. "Are they dead?" a child asks with wide eyes. "Teacher, is this your house?" asks another, curious not about the fish but about the teacher. Another child, whose grandfather is cleaning fish a few yards away, says, "It smells good!"

Some children hang back as others eagerly don blue plastic gloves to touch the fish. John chats with the children as he extracts fish from a net and tosses them into a basin. He shows the children how he sorts the fish, so they can help.

Nearby, one of the children explains the fish's bone structure to everyone within earshot. Another child notices a dark red spot on a fish and asks if it's blood. The teacher touches the spot to see if it will wipe off. When it doesn't, they decide that it

Children arrive with one of their teachers to her backyard, where the just-caught fish are being sorted and cleaned.

The fish drew some children over immediately, but others approached more slowly.

A child watches an elder fillet a fish.

Children observe closely as they hear how larger fish eat smaller fish.

is part of the fin. She picks up the fish and opens its mouth so the children can see the teeth and compare them with their own and each other's. They hold open one fish's mouth and see how the larger fish swallows little minnows.

The visit is not just an opportunity for the children to learn about their culture and the nature around them. The children also express their feelings about power and fear. One child tells others about the daddy fish and the baby fish and which fish will eat the others. Another child is frightened and remains safely in a teacher's arms throughout the visit.

A girl holds a fish proudly.

This child seems intrigued by the fish.

When it's time to return to the center, the teachers encourage the children to say "chi miigwech!" or "huge thanks" in the Ojibwe language. The children pile into their bus. The teachers hold several fish fillets wrapped in paper to cook with the children back at school. They return in time for lunch, during which they have more conversations about the trip.

What curriculum will emerge from this trip? Back at the center, the teachers will web their ideas, not all of which they will implement. Webbing (Figure 12.4) is a way for teachers to record their brainstorming. Then they can revisit their ideas, see how they fit together, see which seem to suit their group best, and plan the intricacies of each.

Integrated curriculum

Integrated curriculum addresses all subjects as children explore a topic. Through a single activity such as printing with fish skeletons, children explore color and design and investigate the structure of a fish's body. As they talk about their prints and the fish bones, they build vocabulary. The precision with which they stamp the print and the care they take to keep the skeleton intact hone their small motor skills.

This activity, in turn, is part of the larger curriculum webbed in Figure 12.4. Children learn math as they compare fish sizes; language as they speak, read, and write about the fish; social studies as they investigate the history of Ojibwe fish netting; science as they classify and discover the habits of different fish; art as they draw, print, create collages, and make fish from clay; and even music as they sing songs about fish.

Children could learn subject matter and accompanying skills through isolated math, language, social studies, science, art, and music activities, but the coherence of the integrated curriculum makes their learning more meaningful (Bredekamp and Rosegrant 1995). Children have different learning styles and strengths, and the integrated curriculum approach capitalizes on that diversity.

The project approach

The **project approach** (Katz and Chard 1989) involves children's serious investigation of a topic of interest to them. Deep respect for children's ability to think lies at

> The coherence of the integrated curriculum makes children's learning more meaningful than learning subject matter and accompanying skills through isolated math, language, social studies, science, art, and music activities.

Telling stories from home about netting fish

Visiting the teacher's home to see the fish that her son and friends just caught

Figuring out how to hold slimy fish

Learning the names of fish caught: walleyes, northern tullaby, perch and bullheads

Touching the fish

Looking closely at the fish

Listing characteristics of fish that make them similar to and different from each other

Watching as adults clean the fish and remove the insides

Comparing different types of fish

FISH NETTING CURRICULUM

Bringing fish back to school to cook

Hosting a visitor to talk about how he nets fish

Printing with the fish skeleton

Visiting a lake

Talking and writing about the fish

Making nets

Reading about fish

Graphing who touched the fish and who didn't, who liked seeing the fish and who didn't

Measuring different fish, comparing sizes, discussing narrow and wide, long and short

THOUGHT QUESTION This example of curriculum is unique to Leech Lake Head Start. What comparable trip might stimulate a meaningful investigation with preschoolers or kindergartners you know? How could you find out? What do the parents at your school do that you and the children could learn more about and that could grow into relevant early childhood curriculum?

the core of this approach. Because children closely examine whatever they are studying, the topic must have many details for them to investigate.

A project has three phases (Katz and Chard 1989):

- *A discussion:* Children contribute what they know about the topic. Unstructured activities, such as dramatic play or painting, help them air their ideas.

- *The project in full swing:* Experiments, field trips, discussions, construction, and expressive activities lead to a deeper investigation of the topic. Children represent what they are learning, generating products that teachers can display for further discussion among the children and with their families.

- *A culminating activity that sums up the project:* A presentation to other children or to families, a classroom museum, or a book the children write and illustrate helps them consolidate what they have learned. Children evaluate the project, and, as you listen to them, you get ideas for future projects.

Working with small groups

In small groups, children can exchange ideas, plan, and solve problems. Children naturally form their own groups, and some kindergarten curricula direct teachers to create groups for activities. In addition to group work on a pattern block challenge or in the block area, various projects lend themselves to small-group work.

One preschool class forms committees that think together about a child whose birthday is near. Together, the birthday committee comes up with the just-right gift or event and often sketches the plans. A child in the class who is autistic posed a particular challenge because the children on his birthday committee did not know him well. With adult support, they thought about what they did know. Recalling that he loved maps, they developed an intricate one leading to a treasure in his cubby.

Scheduling and Predictability

Preschoolers and kindergartners' days have predictable rhythms. Clear schedules let children know what is to come next, yet they should be flexible enough to accommodate moods, weather, and special occasions. Thus, the preschool and kindergarten schedule aims for a balance of predictability, stability, and spontaneity.

The teacher records the birthday committee's ideas.

Blocks of time for activities

Sometimes teachers allocate too short a time for an activity. Give children at least thirty minutes, preferably longer, to be outdoors each day (Council on Physical Education for Children 2000). Plan at least forty-five minutes to an hour for indoor activities, and children will have time to work in more than one area or to focus at length on a project.

Whether you call it playtime, choice time, or work period, let children select from inviting experiences that require them to exercise judgment and control their interactions with the material. Let them choose whether to create patterns with geoboards or to glue boxes together to create a sculpture. These decisions give them practice in making good choices.

To ensure that children make good choices, design your room for open-ended play experiences. Such experiences pose problems that have many possible solutions.

Children need a balance of activities throughout the day. When you have daily outdoor time and extensive indoor play, you balance indoor and outdoor activities, some of which are quiet and others active. Meeting or circle time is a whole-group activity that requires children to focus outside of themselves.

Later, children can work individually or in small groups of their choosing. Some activities afford children less choice than others. When they come in from outside, for example, they *must* remove and hang up their coats, wash their hands, and sit in the circle. In contrast, during work or play time, children can construct a water flow system, make a print at the art table, or write a letter, among other choices. Once you recognize the qualities of various activities, you can allocate time to those that make different demands on children.

Group meetings and classroom community

Group meetings serve many purposes. They remind the attendees of events to come—for example, a trip to the grocery—and enable reflection on events past. Children learn about the latest additions to the classroom, such as new block shapes. Such a meeting (or circle time) also is a chance to reinforce the curriculum, as when a kindergarten

THOUGHT QUESTION Try this: Spend five minutes drawing on a blank piece of paper. Now, take a newspaper advertisement and color it in. What are the challenges of each? What kind of thinking did each require? Keep this comparison in mind as you set up activities for children that will make them use their imaginations and problem-solving skills.

As children put rubber bands on the geoboard's pegs, they create geometric shapes, and abstract concepts such as "area" and "perimeter" become concrete.

class studying winter vegetables passes around acorn squash for everyone to touch, smell, examine, describe, and discuss.

Group meetings can build community. You and the children can raise community issues: what made the hamster sick, what to do about litter in a public playground, or how to make cleanup time go more smoothly. When you listen closely to children's responses, they will be more likely to listen to each other.

Vasquez (2004) writes that children lead meetings in her class. As the rest of the children read books and do other quiet activities each morning, the designated chair moves among them soliciting agenda items for the meeting. Vasquez is an active participant, but the child runs the meeting.

Discussions at meetings stimulate thinking and do not always end with a clear answer to a question. For example, a kindergarten teacher posed the question: Is the whale a mammal? Defining "mammal," the children and their teacher talked about animals that are born alive; that drink their mothers' milk; and that have hair, fur, or whiskers. They decided that whales meet the first two criteria but don't have hair or fur. They debated whether whales have whiskers, perhaps small ones. Finally a child said, "I think two things. First, a whale doesn't have those things. Second, a mammal doesn't have to." Everyone listened carefully, more intent on finding a truth than winning a point. Meeting was over, and the question remained unanswered for the time being.

After such a discussion, the teacher can find books about whales and about mammals in general for the reading area. She can plan a trip to a zoo or an aquarium. She can locate photos and video clips for children to look at over and over. Most important, she can reintroduce the discussion another day after the children have gathered more information.

At a meeting, you can conduct surveys, or children can share their findings from doing them. Through surveys, children gather information that they can depict with graphs. For example, you can find out how children came to school—walking, bus, car, and so forth. During the winter vegetable investigation, children graphed who liked roasted squash seeds, who didn't, and who wouldn't taste them. Most important, children can decide what they want to know and then find out by surveying their peers and others.

Classrooms are cultures that develop as people spend time together. They have traditions that come from daily practice. The sign that lets children know if the science area is open and the chant that you and the children sing as they fold their blankets after nap become part of your classroom culture. You and the children read books, some of which become class favorites. At your group meeting, you and the children enrich your common culture with meeting traditions that make sense to everyone.

Transitions

Throughout the day, teachers ask children to stop what they are doing to do something else. It may be time for lunch, or your group's time to use the yard. Then you must interrupt children to switch, or make a **transition,** to the next activity. When children take off their coats, wash their hands, and, most likely, mill around before their next activity, they are in transition. For smooth transitions, ask yourself what you need to do. Where will you be? Will you sit or stand? How will you coordinate what you do with the other adults in the room to use space and people efficiently? For example, when naptime is over, one adult might wake children and help them fold blankets while another stays near the cubbies to help children put their things away.

You probably know how it feels to want to finish what you are doing while someone urges you to stop. Children may feel this way, too, and the desire to complete a job can foster traits of perseverance and persistence. These are characteristics of productive workers and ones that most of us want children to have. A warning that soon it will be time to stop does not solve the problem, but it helps children manage their own time somewhat.

Routines

Routines are predictable, repeated daily events, such as using the toilet, washing hands, setting the table, eating, cleaning up from meals, and napping. Children and teachers can deepen their relationships with one another during these activities. Children can learn about themselves and their capabilities and gain knowledge and skills. Throughout the day's routines, ask yourself:

- What do I want children to gain from this experience?
- What messages do I think the children are taking away?
- What evidence do I have for my answers?

For example, what will children learn about themselves from the way adults treat toileting in your class? Children's emotions affect how successfully they use the toilet. A three-year-old enrapt at the water table may forget to use the toilet. A kindergartner upset about her parents' fights may have a series of accidents. Sometimes adults become angry when children wet or defecate on themselves, but we believe that children do not have those accidents on purpose. Try to figure out what causes the accidents and to enlist children's help in avoiding them. Respectfully remind children to use the toilet. When no bathroom is attached to the classroom, the children may have to line up down the hall to use the toilet. Imagine how you would feel if you were herded to facilities on someone else's schedule.

Using the toilet involves dressing and undressing. If you tend to value children's independence, guide them to do this themselves. For example, you can button a child's pants at the waist, and encourage her to zip them herself. If you lean more toward interdependence, you might encourage children to help each other in addition to helping them yourself.

Setting the table and eating offer more opportunities for children to learn about themselves. Children who set the table participate in the functioning of the classroom. Preschoolers and kindergartners are capable of many such jobs—which preferably are rotated and listed on a job chart—that contribute to their ownership of the classroom. Try to set up meals so that children can do as much as possible for themselves and each other. Figure out what decisions you can expect them to make, for example, how much rice they want on their plates.

What would you like mealtime to look like in your class? We think snack and lunch can be relaxed and informal, a time for conversation and joking as well as eating. Children can enjoy food *and* one another's company. Small tables, each with no more than six children, encourage conversation and exchange.

What about your role? Once again, try putting yourself in the children's shoes: How would it feel if someone stood near your dinner table and watched while everyone ate? Some advance planning will enable you and the other teachers to sit

For smooth transitions, ask yourself what you need to do. Where will you be? Will you sit or stand? How will you coordinate what you do with the other adults in the room to use space and people efficiently?

THOUGHT QUESTION When you give transitions the same consideration you give other activities, they become a worthwhile time for everyone. Imagine a transition from the children's point of view. How much waiting does the transition require? What can they do while they wait? Sometimes waiting is unavoidable and, since waiting is part of life, doing so comfortably is a skill for children to acquire. How will you teach children to wait with ease? Will you sing with them? Chat? Play word games or Simon Says? Encourage them to help each other to speed the dressing or handwashing process?

Teachers sit with children to enjoy snack time together.

and eat with the children instead of rushing to find more spoons and leaving the children unattended while they eat.

When your routines are clear and you have equipment available, children can take more responsibility. A nearby trash can, for example, enables them to dispose of their garbage, scrape their plates, and put dishes and utensils in a bin to be washed. With ample pathways between lunch tables, children who have finished will not disturb children who are still eating as they leave the table and prepare for rest time.

Although some children badly need midday sleep, not all three-, four-, and five-year-olds sleep during the day. Teachers can create a calm atmosphere by lowering the lights, putting on soft music, and rubbing or patting children's backs, but no one can force someone else to sleep. Naptime can be a battle of wills between teachers and children. Your conviction that rest is healthy and your calm demeanor will help you set the right tone.

You may also tell children that they don't have to sleep, that they can look at a book or play a quiet game. Children who need sleep deserve comfortable space and enough time to rest. Children who don't need to sleep can find ways to accommodate others' needs without sacrificing their own. Whether you use cots or mats for naptime, arrange them so that children are head to foot and not breathing on one another.

The Space

How can you make your classroom noninstitutional, beautiful, and welcoming to families (Greenman 2003)? Beauty is in the eye of the beholder, and a classroom is a shared environment that should reflect your taste and that of the children and their families. A Head Start program for children of migrant workers, all of them from Mexico, had brightly colored furniture, toys, and wall displays. A visiting early childhood professional called it "busy" and "overwhelming" until he learned that the families wanted the bright colors. The environment, like other aspects of the early childhood experience, is a negotiated space that can change over time with input from the children and their families as well as from you and the other teachers.

Balanced environments

Elizabeth Prescott (1984) notes seven dimensions of an early childhood classroom environment. Each is a pair of opposites that the teacher balances.

1. *Softness/hardness:* What surfaces are hard and which are soft? What effect do curtains—they must be nonflammable—have on a window? What message do the hard surfaces give you?

2. *Open/closed:* Which materials can children use in a variety of ways? Which have but one right answer? What benefits do open materials (those with many possible uses or solutions) have? What is the advantage of a puzzle that can be completed only one way?

THOUGHT QUESTION Many preschool and kindergarten programs have one toilet facility for boys and girls. Some people believe that young children should learn about privacy and that separate bathrooms for boys and girls teach them to protect themselves from predators. Other people don't want to impose adult thinking on three- to six-year-olds, who do not see using the toilet as a privacy issue. Young children usually are not embarrassed about their bodies or about natural bodily functions. When boys and girls see each other use the toilet, they can think and talk openly about their bodies. Some adults are uncomfortable with such openness; others believe it is healthy and encourage it. What do you think?

3. *Simple/complex:* How many components do areas and materials have? Materials with a single component are simple; the more components, the more complex. For example, if you put a mound of play dough at each of four places with no tools, children will use the dough with their hands and learn what happens when they pinch and pound it. Once they are familiar with the dough, you can add complexity to their investigations with rollers and other objects.

4. *Intrusion/exclusion:* What private space do children have? Particularly in full-day programs, a child—especially a less outgoing child who needs more personal space—can refuel when he can escape the hubbub of a busy classroom, perhaps in a corner nestled between two pieces of furniture.

5. *High mobility/low mobility:* What spaces are there for high-mobility activities, such as climbing, running, and throwing? How are these activities balanced with those that children do sitting down, such as writing, cutting, and manipulating puzzle pieces?

THOUGHT QUESTION James says, "Tell me not to eat this sandwich because it's poison, okay?" When you comply, he takes a bite, and he and the other children erupt in raucous laughter. The hilarity escalates, and children tumble off their chairs with food in their mouths. How will you enjoy their jokes, take calm pleasure in the meal, *and* prevent children from horsing around to the exclusion of healthy eating? What do you want them to learn about food, about their bodies, about social conventions, and about enjoying time with others?

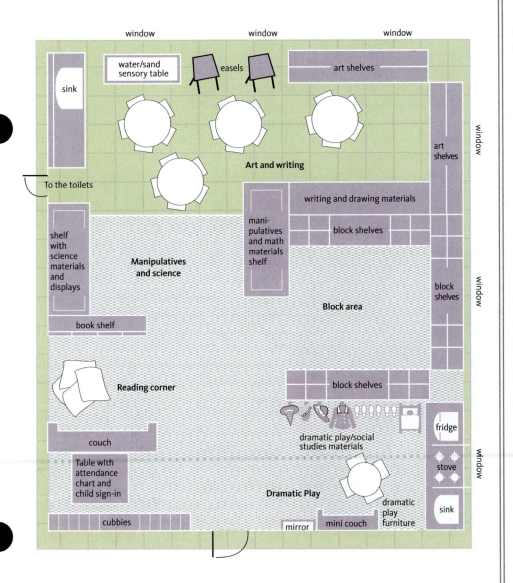

12.5 A Classroom Space for Preschoolers or Kindergartners

When your routines are clear and you have equipment available, children can take more responsibility.

6. *Risk/safety:* What challenges does the space offer? Your comfort with risk will determine how you balance risk and safety for children. Is the tree with low branches off-limits or an opportunity for children to learn about their physical capacities? New, Mardell, and Robinson (2005) point out that what we consider risky is culturally determined and that someone else might not think the same thing is risky at all.

7. *Large-group/individual:* How can your space help children work well with each other *and* as individuals? Children work together better when they aren't crowded together and thus likely to get on each other's nerves. Protected space without distractions (for example, at the woodworking table) enables children to focus on individual projects.

Arranging space

The amount of room you allocate to various activities determines how an area will be used. Consider this example of a cramped block area:

> As Melissa and Cory step back to admire their building and decide whether to change it, Charles's truck zooms toward them and topples their construction. Cory bursts into tears, and Melissa throws the truck at Charles as hard as she can.

How could you make room for Charles's truck and ensure that the girls have enough room to build? Ask the children. They may suggest a separate driving area for trucks and cars, or they may make room for both buildings *and* roads.

How you define spaces in your classroom affects the way people use those spaces. On the one hand, a cozy nook in your library or reading area encourages two or three children to cuddle up with a book. A crib mattress with pillows can serve the same function. A table with four chairs at the writing center establishes a group that is neither too large nor too small for collaborating on writing projects. On the other hand, a too-small dramatic play or family area will lead to the kinds of fights you just read about. A long table that seats ten or more children decreases the amount of interaction children will have with each other no matter what activities take place there. Think about how the bathtub shown here, at the edge of a preschool room, enables a child to separate himself and take a "bath" with some stuffed animals. How you set up your room can promote children's self-regulation.

Traffic patterns determine how children move in a room. Think about which parts of the room children use most and how they go from those areas to other places in the room. Since children need basic blocks—units, doubles, and quads—for almost every building they make, some teachers put those blocks on the right-hand *and* left-hand shelves of the block area to relieve congestion and enable every child to get what she needs. A strip of tape a foot from the block shelves reminds Melissa not to build right next to the shelf, where Jeremy is sure to come for blocks and inadvertently knock down her building.

Simple enclosures can provide a quiet moment for children.

Most early childhood classroom furniture is child sized, so children can reach materials on a shelf and get in and out of chairs easily. Child-sized furniture puts objects at children's eye level and blocks out distractions, while teachers are able to see over the furniture to other areas. That overview of the entire room lets you know what children are doing and where you are needed. Teachers who value children's collaboration want children to see other areas, too, to get ideas from children in other parts of the room. Teachers who value independence want children to move around the room on their own and be able to reach materials.

What can you do to make your room accessible to everyone? For instance, how will the child who is blind make his way around your room? While reevaluating your space and moving furniture as needed is important, you may do less rearranging if a child in your group is visually impaired and has learned the room as it is. If a child in your group uses a wheelchair, you will need wide pathways.

Some materials should be out of children's reach. You, not the children, need access to bottles of concentrated food coloring and the adult scissors. Well-arranged teachers' cabinets give you more time to interact with children because you will spend less time looking for what you need.

THOUGHT QUESTION How teachers allocate and design space sends a message about how children will use the space. Picture a room arranged in each of these three ways:

- Shelving and other furniture are against the walls, some tables are near the shelves, and space is left in the center of the room.
- Tables and chairs fill most of the room.
- Low furniture creates separate spaces, such as a block area.

How might children use each of these arrangements differently? Think about your goals for children. What furniture arrangements reflect your goals?

Outdoor space

Outdoor space, like indoor space, must be safe and challenging for children of different abilities and interests. An accredited program "provides at least 75 square feet of outside play space for each child playing outside at any one time. The total amount of required play space is based on a maximum of one-third of the total center enrollment being outside at one time" (NAEYC Accreditation Standard 9.B.04).

For outdoor space to be safe, children need room to run, climb, ride, or swing (NAEYC Accreditation Criteria for Physical Environment, see http://www.naeyc .org/academy/standards/standard9/standard9B.asp) without colliding with each other. While children need a hard, smooth surface to ride tricycles and pull wagons, in climbing areas they need soft ground cover, whether wood chips or matting (NAEYC Accreditation Standard 9.B.06). Defined spaces will help children use the outdoors safely, and fences or other barriers with a closed gate will keep them from the street and other dangers. The Consumer Product Safety Commission provides a Public Playground Safety Checklist (http://www.cpsc.gov/CPSCPUB/PUBS/327 .html) that you can check to ensure the space you and the children use is safe.

Equipment that is too challenging can be dangerous: for instance, if children climb higher than they can manage. Conversely, equipment that isn't challenging enough can prompt children to use it dangerously. Both boys and girls should use equipment to test their strength and endurance. Appeal to them with

- durable materials kept in good condition,
- structures and experiences that pose many different challenges,
- textures for children who are visually impaired and platforms wide enough for wheelchair access, and
- experiences that engage children's new skills and support skills they already have.

Children can be independent of adults outdoors, yet adults must position themselves near climbing equipment and other areas that need supervision. If your play space has benches, avoid congregating there with other teachers; instead, stay near the equipment with the children. Your presence may draw children into physical activity when they otherwise might be reluctant.

Depending on the weather, children can play with water, paint, and read books outdoors. In warm climates, classrooms may have these activities outdoors all the time, and the outside space becomes an extension of the classroom. No matter what the weather, the outdoors can spur children's dramatic play. Refrigerator boxes that the children paint to support play themes, together with props they create or bring from the classroom, enhance their outdoor dramatic play. Some schools use large wooden crates, sanded and painted a solid color, for the children to build structures for their dramatic play outdoors. Large hollow blocks also enable the children to construct their own outdoor environments.

Criteria for evaluating environments

Children grow and develop, new children enter the group and the dynamic shifts, and seasons and interests change. How will you know when it is time to switch things around? You can start simply and add more elements to your environment as the children change and their interests expand. A colleague can help you rethink your classroom, and you can reciprocate.

Mac Naughton (2003, 199) raises a set of questions that will help you to create classroom space, keeping in mind the children and families who use it. These questions remind us that classroom environments teach children about people, their cultures, and their relationships:

- Do the everyday objects we use reflect the languages and cultures of the children within this group?
- Do we have everyday objects from diverse cultures?
- Do the materials respect and celebrate cultural and racial diversity?
- Do the materials challenge traditional sex-role stereotypes and understandings?
- To what extent do the materials support and respect diverse abilities and ways of being?
- Can children of differing physical abilities move around the space easily?
- Can children of differing physical abilities participate in a range of activities?
- Can children of differing abilities and ages easily see and touch display areas?
- Can all children in the group—irrespective of their cultural background—recognize their own cultures in the materials and staff they encounter?

SUMMARY

LIFE WITH PRESCHOOLERS AND KINDERGARTNERS
Who are preschoolers and kindergartners?

The years of three to six are a time of enormous growth. Longer limbs allow children greater leverage, along with their increased strength and coordination. At this age, children develop purposeful movements using fine motor skills, too, but it often takes time for them to become skilled. Experts who observe young children prefer to consider motor patterns or the combination of a movement's components rather than how children perform isolated skills, because this knowledge helps us know how to help the child develop further.

Three-year-olds seem to spend the year realizing what their new physical, intellectual, and social capabilities entail. With more expressive language and newfound

---

Children can be independent of adults outdoors, yet adults must position themselves near climbing equipment and other areas that need supervision.

independence, many fours have extraordinary zest and energy, and friendships become increasingly important to most of them. Five-year-olds usually exhibit increased independence and a growing sense of empathy for others. In contrast to themselves just a few months ago, preschoolers and kindergartners possess more language and symbolic thinking that shapes their responses to experiences, and they are capable of a more sophisticated level of communication.

WHAT PRESCHOOLERS AND KINDERGARTNERS LEARN AND HOW
What do preschoolers and kindergartners learn, and how do they learn it?
Through their play and social studies investigations, enhanced by trips and discussions, preschoolers and kindergartners acquire knowledge, develop language and literacy skills, and use many media. Preschoolers and kindergartners are interested in almost every aspect of their environment and, when confronted with authentic problems, think eagerly about how to make change for the better.

From the time they are babies, children are becoming readers and writers. Children learn the conventions of literacy in many ways, including observation, experimentation, and an adult or peer's explanation. To read and write, children also need vocabulary and an understanding of syntax. Thus, speaking and listening skills are closely connected to reading and writing skills and develop along with them. Children learn these skills when teachers listen carefully to them as they speak and, with open-ended questions, request clarification and prompt them to extend their ideas. Teachers of young children familiarize them with the sounds, rules, and delights of language and the possibilities that unfold when it is written down. They create opportunities for children to explore sounds and written language, helping them see the connection between the two. The classroom contains well-kept, high-quality children's books, and teachers rotate a selection at the children's level.

Through blocks, manipulatives, and dramatic play, children explore all the major subjects: language, mathematics, science, social studies. Experiences in these three areas activate children's imaginations and creativity and require them to solve problems of their own making. As they use blocks, they see mathematical relationships, represent the world using three dimensions, and negotiate with each other. Manipulatives are small toys that enable children to explore many mathematical concepts. Through dramatic play, children develop narratives that they enact, usually with one another, and use play symbols of their own making.

Scientific opportunities abound for preschoolers and kindergartners. They can experiment with plants and observe classroom animals. They can test engineering principles as they build with blocks and explore physical properties when they use magnets, magnifiers, eyedroppers, or mirrors and when they play with sand or water. The playground, too, is full of scientific learning opportunities as children slide, swing, and test what their bodies can do.

Music helps children to connect with the group and to regulate their attention and emotions. It offers joy, communication, and an opportunity to rhyme, play with sounds, learn new words, and create patterns. Movement promotes children's physical and emotional development and can be an alternative way to explore curriculum topics. Both music and movement are important ways for emergent bilinguals to engage in the curriculum and to learn English.

Art enables children to represent their ideas and express themselves with a variety of materials. Open-ended materials, such as markers, paint, and clay, allow the child to decide how to use them and what the outcome will be.

Computers, like any other medium, depend on the teacher's careful consideration of how children will use them in the classroom. Use of technology can lead to collaboration and verbal and nonverbal problem solving and offer children a gratifying sense of competence.

CLASSROOMS FOR PRESCHOOLERS AND KINDERGARTNERS
What characteristics do effective preschool and kindergarten classrooms exhibit?

Classrooms for preschoolers and kindergartners require planning and foresight along with the flexibility to adjust plans and rearrange space depending on the children, the curriculum, and even the weather. A useful planning system integrates what you learn from observations and other assessments with what the children do in your class. Webbing is an appropriate planning tool for emergent curriculum that arises from children's interests and develops as children enact it; webbing is also useful for planning integrated curriculum in general and the Project Approach in particular. Teachers also use charts that track individual children's interests or plan small-group activities. Routines and transitions may not require written plans, but they still warrant planning.

The preschool and kindergarten schedule aims for a balance of predictability, stability, and spontaneity. Large blocks of time give children the opportunity to work in different areas or to focus at length on a project. Inviting choices of materials give children experience making decisions. A schedule that balances activities enables children to work both outdoors and indoors, at quiet and active endeavors, and individually and in both small and large groups. Group meetings build a sense of community as children plan, reflect back on what they have done, work on curriculum, and solve problems together.

How teachers arrange the space determines how that space will be used. When safe materials are within children's reach and furniture is child sized, the children have more control over what happens in the space. Ideally, teachers arrange space with materials for investigations, acquaint children with the materials and their possibilities, attend to details, accept that learning happens anytime and everywhere, and acknowledge that everything children do is worth considering carefully. They balance softness and hardness; open and closed materials; simple and complex areas and materials; places for play with other places to be alone; and space for high and low mobility, for risk and safety, and for large groups and individuals. They consider children who have disabilities and make the space accessible to them. Outdoor space, too, must be simultaneously safe and challenging for all children. To adapt space to the children, who grow and develop constantly, teachers regularly reevaluate their use of outdoor and indoor space.

FURTHER ACTIVITIES

1. Observe at a preschool or kindergarten during a group discussion or meeting. Take notes to capture as much as you can of what each child says. You may want to observe the same class more than once, to have your choice of discussions to document. In a short paper, transcribe the discussion and analyze it. To what degree and in what ways did this discussion positively influence children's development and learning? Give reasons for each point you make. (**NAEYC Standard 3: Observing, Documenting, and Assessing to Support Young Children and Families**)

2. Think of a child you know or have observed who is three, four, or five. Describe the child to a classmate. Have your classmate describe a child to you. Imagine that the two children you have described to each other are in the same class. What curriculum ideas do you have for them? Create a web, like the fish netting web in Figure 12.4, with ideas for experiences the children could have as part of this curriculum. Choose one activity from your web and, in a short paper, explain

   a. why you consider it a good one for these children, and

   b. what you would need to learn in order to design, implement, and evaluate this experience. (**NAEYC Standard 4: Using Developmentally Effective Approaches to Connect with Children and Families**)

3. Choose to work on math, science, social studies, art, music, or science. Browse catalogs and the Internet to find the materials you want to have to make sure the children in your preschool or kindergarten classroom have everything they need for that content area. Then build a model of one or more areas, equipping it fully. Check what you have built against what you read in the section in this chapter on space. Take a digital photo of your construction. (**NAEYC Standard 5: Using Content Knowledge to Build Meaningful Curriculum**)

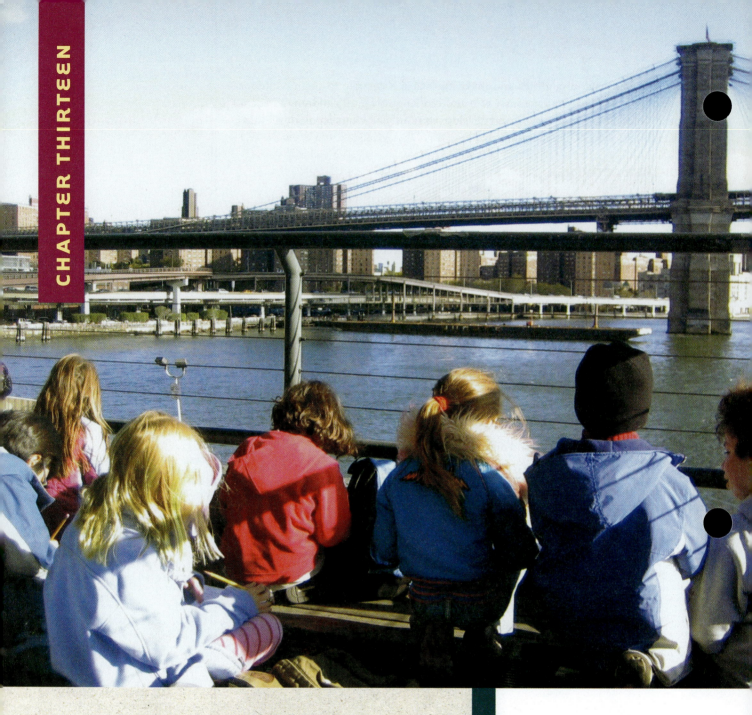

CHAPTER THIRTEEN

First, Second, and Third Graders

. . . Education—a leading out—and learning cannot occur without the engagement of both teacher and learner.

Carol Anne Wien

Just as do younger children, those in the first three elementary grades learn when they are engaged in what they are learning and when the teacher is involved in it, too. They learn about written language, mathematical relationships, and especially about the social and natural worlds. In this chapter, you will read about how teachers respond to the ways children grow and change in the early elementary years and how they plan the curriculum and schedule and set up classrooms to maximize children's learning.

We will visit some classrooms for first, second, and third graders, beginning with Trish's second/third grade at a public school in New York City's Lower Manhattan. In this class, **social studies**—investigation of the human environment—was the central focus of the children's school day. Through their social studies curriculum, they learned a great deal of science and math and became increasingly fluent readers and writers.

The class walks across the Brooklyn Bridge together on their field trip.

On a walking trip, Trish and her class explored the Brooklyn Bridge. Going toward Brooklyn and back to Manhattan several times, they examined the geography of the city from different vantage points. They wrapped their arms around the cables to feel the vibrations and simultaneously got a sense of the cables' size.

The children set up interview stations on the bridge with signs inviting passersby to talk to them. They took notes and charted where walkers began their trips, where they were going, and why they were walking across the bridge. They even spoke to one of the bridge high cable workers.

Back in the classroom, a variety of activities helped the students think about the aesthetic and functional aspects of the bridge and understand how it was constructed. When Trish sent home ideas for more experiments, families got involved, and children returned with stories and photographs of what they had tried. Although gaining an understanding of how suspension bridges are constructed was difficult, the children eventually succeeded.

College students who visited Trish's class wondered how the children would do on the standardized tests that spring. They learned that the school had a record of high scores, at least in part because the children developed and used academic skills rigorously as they studied topics that interested them.

LIFE WITH FIRST, SECOND, AND THIRD GRADERS

Who are first, second, and third graders?

Between the ages of five and eight, children all over the world, across time and cultures, undergo significant physical, cognitive, and social-emotional changes. Since the middle of the past century, developmental psychologists have referred to this period as the five-to-seven shift (Sameroff and Haith 1996) because it occurs at approximately those ages. This is also the time when families, teachers, and communities begin to change what they expect of children. The nature of children's new responsibilities may vary,

Two children work together on their trip sheet.

A child interviews a cable worker, recording his findings on his trip sheet.

The nature of children's new responsibilities during the five-to-seven shift may vary across cultures, but altered expectations both mirror and fuel children's increasing abilities in all areas.

but altered expectations both mirror and fuel most children's increasing abilities in all areas.

Paul, age six, holds his four-year-old brother's hand as they prepare to cross the street. Paul does not talk or watch his brother but looks up and down the street in each direction. A car stops for them. The driver waves them on, and the brothers dash across the street. When they reach the other side, Paul, smiling, turns and waves back.

Is Paul old enough to cross the street without an adult? Some people would think not, but he rises to the responsibilities his family has given him, and this accomplishment becomes part of his growing identity. In other homes, children his age care for animals or do household chores. In yet others, they work alongside the adults of the family, for instance, selling fruit at the market. And in still others, families consider them too young to take on any responsibilities.

Physical and Cognitive Changes

From five to eight, children's bodies change dramatically, a source of pride for both families and children. Healthy children experience a growth spurt and gain strength, agility, and endurance. Their legs become longer, and permanent adult teeth replace their baby ones. Their fine motor control also improves, giving them greater mastery over tools of all kinds.

Tremendous changes in children's reasoning abilities also appear during these years. Unseen but significant are the neurobiological changes. Think back to what you learned in Chapter 3 about the connective synapses in the brain. There's less pruning of connections during the five-to-seven shift than in the first few years of life, yet connections that have been used repeatedly become stronger and more stable, while less-used ones continue to wither away. And, increased and more complex communication between the frontal and prefrontal cortex of the brain and other brain regions also seems to bear some relationship to these children's new mental abilities.

Some of the more pronounced changes during this time are in children's ability to organize and manage information: their executive functions (Pianta, Cox, and Snow 2007). Think of the skills an executive uses, and you can see how this term pertains to children's increasing ability to manage ideas, information, and their own behavior. In Trish's second/third grade classroom, the children conducted experiments to investigate stress and load on the bridge. They collaborated, conducted repeated trials, recorded their results, and kept track of their findings. Had they been in kindergarten, their guesses and subsequent actions probably would have been more random and less reasoned. But as second/third graders, they placed two unit blocks upright six inches apart, laid paper across the blocks, and tested how many cubes fit on the paper before it collapsed. Working in groups and keeping systematic records, they folded paper in different ways. Finally, they discovered that if they made accordion folds, the paper could hold *hundreds* of cubes. They also found that beams are weaker than arches and illustrated their findings to accompany their written explanations.

Sometimes teachers have to listen hard to what six-, seven-, and eight-year-olds are saying to figure out what they mean because children's thinking may not follow the same track as the teacher's. A first grade teacher showed children cards with one-syllable words such as *not*, *pot*, and *lot*. When she said *cot*, a child sitting on the edge of the group mumbled, "Is that like got caught?" Some teachers might assume the child was talking and not paying attention, especially since he sat only half-facing the teacher, but listening to him revealed that he was paying attention and thinking about the words, perhaps beyond the scope of the teacher's lesson of the moment.

Another change you may see in these early elementary years is in children's **attentional abilities,** such as the ability to shut out extraneous information or to focus on the more immediate aspects of a cognitive task. The first grader in the nearby photograph uses his body to zero in on his book. He retains his concentration, screening out the potential distraction of the reading group meeting nearby and the children at the next table working together on a word puzzle.

Children can now pay attention longer and engage in more sophisticated problem solving than when they were younger. This is the period when, according to Piaget, children move into **concrete operations** and are able to think through problems more easily than before. The children in Trish's class, for example, built an accurate model of the suspension bridge out of box cardboard, string, and glue, complete with anchorages to secure the main cables. It was a challenge, but they did it, calling upon the engineering knowledge they had gained from experiments, their reading, and firsthand observations. Imagine the problems they had to solve so that the model would stand and how diligently they worked on the project for extended periods over many days.

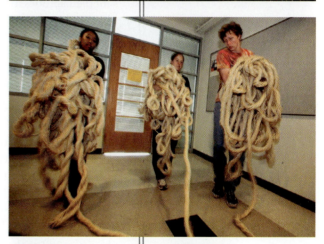

First, second, and third graders' memory capabilities increase, as does their metacognition. When children can reflect on their own thinking, they can find strategies for learning and remembering. They may look for clues to help themselves remember the spellings of irregular English words, for example, and enjoy tricks or prompts they learn from their teacher or other children. Both increased memory and metacognition are significant markers in the development of children's thinking. They can better understand the difference, for example, between internal and external cues and will use an external cue such as leaving new socks next to the bed at night to remember to wear them to school the next morning.

While five- to eight-year-olds still enjoy learning discrete facts, as they did as preschoolers who proudly shared information about dinosaurs, now they tend to pull ideas together and grasp the structural frameworks for what they know and want to learn. Children in a first grade class who are learning about newspapers, for example, will use words such as *column, editorial, reporter, interview,* and *layout,* but they also make sense of them and know how the words relate to each other as they create their own newspaper.

These Massachusetts Institute of Technology graduate students are engaging in a project similar to that of Trish's second and third graders at the beginning of the chapter: learning firsthand about how bridges hold weight.

This child uses his body to screen out the distractions of nearby workgroups, displaying his developing attentional and self-regulatory abilities.

These changes in cognitive abilities pave the way for children's increased interest in the world and how things work. Their interests and abilities allow for new richness in curriculum—for example, observing patterns as a basis of mathematical relationships or exhibiting a readiness for geographical thinking in social studies. What Lucy Sprague Mitchell (1934/2001, 4) wrote about the geographer applies to the child in the early grades, who

> does more than collect factual data.... He sees the bearing of one fact upon another fact and thereby produces something different from and added to the two separated facts—a relationship.

More than in previous years, children are ready for grown-ups to help them observe relationships, see patterns, and discover the world about which they are so eager to learn.

Social-Emotional Changes

The cognitive changes children are undergoing affect their social-emotional development, which in turn influences their cognitive development. Increasingly, school-age children can represent their abilities in more complex ways and create mental maps of ideas and categories (Fischer 1980). They are more likely to group their abilities, often with a positive evaluative edge, such as "I'm good at kickball and baseball, and I'm a great dancer, too." In contrast, preschoolers might describe themselves more simply and somewhat randomly, with "I can jump rope," "I live with my mother and little brother," and "I like popsicles." However, as you read in Chapter 3, early elementary schoolers who experience consistent failure and/or harsh criticism or abuse may say, instead, "I'm no good at anything" (Harter 1996).

School, with its focus on new skills, becomes an avenue for the development of "grown-up" abilities that lead to a sense of "industry" (Erikson 1964) and the development of an integrated social and cognitive self. As Erikson (1959) said, "I am what I learn." But school becomes much more. *How,* not just *what,* children learn becomes part of their identity, including a sense of what kind of learners they will become (Sameroff and Haith 1996). Relationships are at the heart of the elementary school classroom just as they are with younger children.

With children's increased interest in events, skills, and other people, their social world expands, and they edge away from family and move closer to their peers. The world at large increasingly influences their developing self-concept. They take in what others expect—not just peers, teachers, and family, but the media as well—and begin to measure themselves against various standards. Becoming a member, joining a sports team, belonging to an after-school club, or participating in a religious group can promote a sense of belonging.

Children now spend more time together with slightly less adult supervision. The social skills they developed as preschoolers form the basis for more sophisticated interactions with one or more children. Individual children face the challenge of **self-regulating** their needs and feelings when the group makes a decision with which they disagree. As you read in Chapter 4, their increasing interest in games with rules

School, with its focus on new skills, leads to a sense of "industry" and the development of an integrated social and cognitive self.

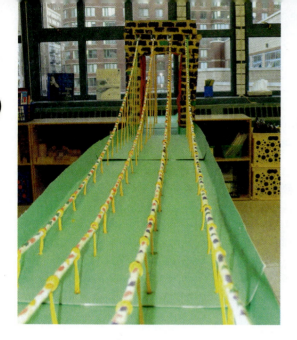

This model of the Brooklyn Bridge deck (left) and the supporting cables (right) demonstrates some of what Trish's grades two/three children learned in their bridge study.

also helps children regulate themselves for longer periods and with greater numbers of playmates (Hartup 1984).

Teachers often are not there when some children wield power over others and include only their favorites of the moment. A group of teachers at an after-school program in an affluent community in Seattle (Pelo and Pelojoaquin 2006) struggled with what to do when the children's Lego play resulted in a microcosm of a political system. Certain children had the power to obtain and dispense valued goods in the form of "cool" Lego pieces, the special pieces in any Lego set. They came to control all work with Legos and excluded some children.

How do teachers decide when and how to step in and how to highlight the issues so that children think about them on their own? Children may not take in, or may even shut out, what adults tell them about being fair to others. The children in the after-school program drew pictures about power and thought about this difficult topic in a dimension other than the verbal. Experiential activities, in which children play games that illustrate unfairness, also can bring home its essence. However, these games can have unforeseen effects. Children may find it difficult to remember that the game is just a simulation to learn how other people feel. The thoughtful adult guidance that children need to confront questions of power and fairness requires teachers to consider the complexity of such issues for themselves; raise them with questions that children can answer; and continue watching, listening, and participating in discussions with the children accordingly.

THOUGHT QUESTION What early experiences contributed to your sense of yourself as a learner? What do your experiences make you want to do as a teacher of early elementary schoolers?

WHAT CHILDREN LEARN IN THE EARLY GRADES

What do children learn in the early grades, and how do they learn it?

In this section, we discuss the subject areas of the early elementary curriculum. The first is social studies because of the richness of curricula such as Trish's. We then look at the language and literacy learning that is a vital part of first, second, and third grades, including self-expression through the arts. We end the section with math and science.

Viewed from farther away, this class's undertaking is impressive in its scope and execution.

Through social studies, children and their teachers explore the web of relationships that underlies daily life.

Social Studies

Trish put social studies at the core of the curriculum, and the bridge study allowed the children to acquire and use the skills and knowledge of the standard second and third grade curricula. Since children often worked in groups and individually, Trish could **differentiate instruction,** that is, create learning opportunities for different children according to their experience, knowledge, and skills.

Through social studies, children and their teachers explore the web of relationships that underlies daily life. These connections often are not apparent to children and can be invisible to adults as well. A child who says, "You may get your milk from a cow, but I get mine from the store" hasn't thought about where the store gets it. When children trace the sources of the food they eat, they can begin to comprehend the interdependency that sustains them and their communities, and they can investigate and question the logic and order of the world around them. Such a study, which involves reading, writing, calculations, science experiments, and artistic representations, provides a way for the children to integrate, or fit together, what they are learning. Through discussions with one another, the children also simultaneously build their social environment and learn about their classroom community.

Contact with the larger community

When children actually or metaphorically venture out of their classroom and into the community, the social studies curriculum parallels their movement outward into the world and supports their growing ability to construct a bigger picture from separate pieces of information. When children can go behind the scenes to probe what has become familiar and is taken for granted, the curriculum feeds their interest in how things work.

To understand more about where their food comes from, a first grade class visited a wholesale fruit, vegetable, meat, and fish market. There they interviewed a trucker and were fascinated by the inside of his truck, where he slept and made dinner. They found a willing partner in their education: the trucker subsequently sent the children postcards, and, on a map in their classroom, the children followed his truck's progress across the country. From the trucker's personal account, the children gained a sense of how their food is grown

Only after my first year of teaching was completed did I allow myself to accept how successful it had been. The following September, my incoming parents seemed to be expecting something extraordinary. I felt too new for such high expectations on their part.

It didn't take long to realize that this would be a very different year. Unlike my first-year group, these children came charging into the room and seemed oblivious to my efforts to create order. However, by slowly and carefully proceeding the same way I had the year before, I managed to achieve order and get some productive work done. Yet the whole tone was different. By keeping the lid secured tightly, I was able to get these second-year children to do some of the same activities and routines as my previous-year's group, but the experience lacked luster. As the year progressed, the situation became more and more difficult. I was ashamed, and I felt like a fraud.

It was a parent who helped me see the year, the children, and myself differently. During the spring progress report conferences, this parent told me she was Iroquois, with some Scottish background. She wanted to talk to my class about changes in clothing styles of the American Indians, a topic of great interest to her. Clothing styles seemed like the last thing these first and second graders would be interested in. I was also concerned that they would show their lack of interest and, worse, act out as they had already done with some visitors. Still, I agreed to let her speak.

From the time she entered the class and sat among us, I noticed a different kind of attention from the children. She began her talk by holding up a doll of an Indian and asking how it was different from her. The children responded: "She's brown and you're white." "She has straight hair and yours is curly." To this last comment, she laughed and said she had a permanent. Her son said, "She made her dress, and you bought yours." She said yes and then told the children that despite their differences, she and the doll were the same in one important way: "We both have Indian blood." She then related the story of how she grew up on a reservation with her grandmother. Being the youngest female child in the family, she became the repository of their stories and their crafts. She explained how her grandmother built her own home, without a single nail, all with wooden pegs. She described her grandmother's beadwork and showed us samples: first, a necklace that was similar in style to those created before the time of Columbus. She passed the necklace around and told us that her grandmother, like all of her ancestors, inserted one bead that threw off the pattern. It was an error, done intentionally to show that she was not perfect and still had a lot to learn. If the pattern were perfect, she would be ready to die. As the children admired

American Indian dolls and a teachable comment

the intricate necklace, they all looked for and claimed to find the error. They asked if she, too, put an error into her work, and she responded, "My work has many errors, and unlike my grandmother's, they are not intentional."

So this was what she meant by changes in clothing style! She left the beadwork and a book with us to display, thanked us, and left.

When we talked about her visit, the children's responses were alive and substantive. They wrote about her visit in ways they had never done before. Perhaps for the first time, my class and I had truly shared an experience. Also for the first time, I had stepped outside my role and seen these children differently. I had lived with them for almost a full school year, but now I wondered if I really knew them. Had I taken the time to discover what propelled them, what their needs were? They had lived in the shadow of my previous class, and I had judged their work by that standard. When the methods that had been so successful with my first class didn't go over well with these children, I had judged them to be deficient. Now I began to consider how I could have changed things to meet their particular needs: the daily schedule, the room arrangement, the topics we studied, how I grouped them, and, ultimately, my expectations. In my graduate preparation, I had learned that we are always teaching the individuals in front of us, that who they are and the curriculum are not separate entities, but it was only through the experience of that parent's visit that those ideas became real to me.

The fact that it was a parent visit was significant, and this parent had conveyed something to the children that was extremely important to her, that was, in a very real sense, an essential aspect of her being. It was profoundly personal, and the children reacted in a profoundly personal way.

Although it was a long time ago, I often think back to that year and those children: it was the most difficult experience I was ever to encounter as a teacher—but it was also the most important.

far away, is transported to their city, and is distributed to the store where they and their families buy it.

Some workers, like this trucker, appreciate children's interest in their work and gladly participate in the children's educational experience. Then the curriculum enables children to see things from another person's perspective. At the same time, the vocabulary children learn, the reading and writing they do, and the information they acquire can meet state standards for first, second, or third grade. For example, California's English–language arts content standards stipulate that first graders should be able to "[m]atch oral words to printed words" (California State Board of Education 1997, 14). The first graders you just read about dictated the story of their trip to the wholesale market to their teacher, who recorded it on a chart that they read and reread.

Finding meaningful curriculum

Trips take us away from our familiar surroundings to study the interaction between people and their world and open doors to learning. Teachers who are knowledgeable about the school's neighborhood can find meaningful social studies curriculum on trips just outside the school doors. Still, a walking trip is not always possible. Some schools are on or near busy streets, and others are in dangerous neighborhoods.

In one school where outside walks were not an option, a first grade teacher found curriculum when she read aloud parts of the school newspaper published by children in the upper grades. The first graders asked who wrote the articles and discussed what they wanted to know about the newspaper. After a visit by upper-grade reporters, the first graders contributed an article to the newspaper about their class's guinea pigs. They continued to learn about newspapers—the parent newsletter, their community newspaper, and even the city paper. The school had funds for one bus trip per class, and the children visited the town's newspaper, where they saw the production process. Then the first graders started their own newspaper, featuring news from other classes and their own.

This newspaper study has many of the characteristics of core social studies curriculum:

- The children's investigation started small and evolved into a larger study.
- The children used traditional social science research techniques, such as observations and interviews.
- The children met standards for math, writing, and reading skills in a real context; for example, they considered size and proportions as they laid out their class newspaper.
- The curriculum extended over a period of months.
- The class went outside their classroom to learn from the real world, in this case using their single trip of the year to support their curriculum.
- The study involved planning and learning on the teacher's part.

Children's discussion

Children put social studies into action when they listen to each other on the rug or in another space that accommodates the whole class. Trish considers discussion a way to "glue the group together."

She planned a discussion for the children as they prepared for a celebration of the bridge study and explained, "I just wanted them to decide something together. . . . I wanted them to look in each others' faces."

Here is an example of how first graders in Jenna's class changed the tenor of their classroom community through thoughtful discussion:

> From the day Jahnathan entered the class, children complained that he broke "long-established rules, the rights and wrongs that held the playground world together for the children" (Laslocky 2005, 27). His behavior on the playground and his stumbling academic work made him an outsider. In a class meeting, Jenna finally asked the children, "Why do people bother to be nice to each other?" Jenna writes that it was "the first honest question I'd ever asked—the first time I wasn't trying to orchestrate order or compassion, the first time I wasn't in some way addressing misbehavior, thinking that I could somehow manage it. . . . [S]omehow the ball had been tossed into the children's court. It was up to them to carry the conversation forward—and they owned that responsibility whole-heartedly" (30). After that discussion, the children and even adults in the school began to recognize Jahnathan's helpfulness. Gradually, children became kinder toward him, and he reciprocated.

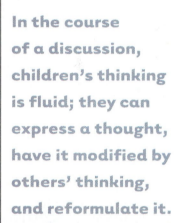

While Jenna's heartfelt question and the children's forthright answers were no instant cure to the problems in their class, they created a forum for thinking aloud about a shared issue. Children who participate in discussions like these inevitably encounter, think about, and confront other peoples' perspectives.

Both Jenna and Trish respect children's ability to think about classroom relationships and about curriculum. In both classrooms, children expressed their thinking and built on it with others. In the course of a discussion, children's thinking is fluid; they can express a thought, have it modified by others' thinking, and reformulate it. One child's insights can help everyone else think more deeply. Children also get to know each other better. As for teachers, class discussions help them learn what children know and the best way to monitor their ongoing language development—which is particularly important for the ELLs in the class.

In the course of a discussion, children's thinking is fluid; they can express a thought, have it modified by others' thinking, and reformulate it.

Language and Literacy

Oral language lays the foundation for written language; thus, discussions should be part of any literacy program. Throughout the United States, state language arts standards for first through third grades refer to children's growing ability to read fluently and their increasing proficiency as writers. The teacher's role in this process is "discovering what writers and readers need and providing plenty of it in a predictable setting" (Atwell 1998, 90).

Learning to read

As you enter first, second, and third grade classrooms, you will see teachers who inspire children to want to read and who teach them reading strategies. Children

Teachers provide a "predictable setting" for blossoming readers.

A child enjoys some quiet reading time.

This boy focuses on the task of choosing a book.

may read alone, in pairs, in groups, or as a whole class. You may see classroom libraries from which children can choose books at different readers' levels. Children may play games with words or fill in worksheets. You may hear children discussing books or see them writing about stories they have read. You may watch a teacher read aloud. You may see a mini-lesson that takes ten minutes or observe a two-hour literacy block that has sporadic breaks so the children can move around.

Some teachers must follow a reading curriculum using specific texts or must schedule **reader's workshop,** a program in which children

- select books to read independently;
- read books that the teacher introduces to them in small groups;
- participate in mini-lessons in which the teacher introduces strategies: for example, how to use cues from meaning, from the structure of a sentence, and from the letters themselves;
- have individual conferences with their teacher; and
- learn strategies through **guided reading,** a session in which the teacher helps a group of children apply strategies to a text they read together.

Whether they follow a curriculum or develop their own, teachers who understand the complexity of reading can think about the many factors that influence the reading process: memory, attention, anxiety, risk taking, oral language use, comprehension of speech, sociocultural differences, and how young children learn. As you read the following vignette, notice how this teacher used what she knew about the reading process and about each child.

Toward the end of the first-grade year, despite Joan's rich and varied reading program, four children applied phonics skills inconsistently and recognized just a few sight words. Joan was determined to find a way for each of them to experience the pleasure of reading a book on his or her own. She knew the method had to be active, pleasurable, and different.

Joan created a special reading group for the four of them. She told them that they would learn a number of new words and that when they did so, they would read their first book completely on their own. She chose *Go, Dog. Go!*, an early reader with a controlled vocabulary, repetitive sentence structure, and, most of all, a story that is catchy, silly, and full of action. Knowing the children, she knew they would love the dogs.

First Joan introduced the story as a read-aloud. For the next three weeks, she reinforced the vocabulary; the children formed the words with letter and word cards, matching games, board games, sentence strips, and manipulative materials that she created for them. The extensive practice helped them to recognize the words and grow familiar with the book's sentence structure, and they had a lot of fun.

Joan knew they were ready when they began suggesting different ways to use the materials. In the fourth week, thanks to PTA-generated funds, she handed each child a fresh copy of *Go, Dog. Go!* and a bookmark with dog stickers on it. The children were silent at this important moment. Without instruction, they opened their books and took turns reading aloud. Once they had read the book through, Alex said, "Let's read it again." This time they read it together. When they finished the second reading, they screamed with delight and started rereading it on their own. All of them took the book home to read to their parents.

The next morning, Alex's mother told Joan that Alex had read the book to her, his father, and his sister and had insisted on carrying the book with him when they went to a restaurant. As they waited for a table, Alex's parents realized that he was sitting on a bar stool reading *Go, Dog. Go!* to the headwaiter.

Joan made these four children a priority and used what she knew about beginning readers and about these children's behavior, learning styles, and interests to create learning games and activities. These offered playful and active practice that reinforced the book's vocabulary and sentence structure before the children read it (see Pinnell and Fountas 1998, 2007). Joan helped the children acquire the necessary skills and gave them the time they needed for success. Only then did she give them the book.

Most of the children in Joan's class learned to read using the main instructional approaches in a "balanced approach." A balanced approach is "not simply a random combination of strategies" but a thoughtful consideration of what specific ways will help the individuals in a class learn best (Morrow 2005, 16). The four children who did not learn to read as quickly stimulated Joan to think even more deeply about how they would learn best and to develop a plan based on their individual needs.

P. D. Eastman's *Go, Dog. Go!* appeals to most early elementary–age children.

Experiencing literature

The cognitive psychologist Jerome Bruner was once asked why young children would want to learn to read, since they are already vital, active explorers and experimenters, fully capable of learning about the world without the printed word. His answer was, "Stories."

Children want to live in the world of stories and have them as their own. Just as adults do, children enjoy finding themselves and their experiences in books. They also revel in the new and different. They take pleasure in the qualities of language, such as rhyme and rhythm. And they are drawn to the human connection established when books are read aloud to them in a full class, in small groups, and individually.

Why read aloud to children whose reading skills are emerging? James Britton (1970) suggests three reasons:

- A classroom that functions as a community shares pleasurable experiences such as story times, which become common memories and part of the classroom culture. Watch children's faces and bodies as they listen to a story together, and listen to their comments to see what stories mean to them as individuals and as a group.

- Children who are read to learn to *listen,* to take in the artful use of language of many picture books. Books whose reading levels are beyond what children can read on their own may not be beyond their thinking abilities. Hearing thoughtfully selected stories exposes children to a wide and rich range of vocabulary and sentence structure and enables them to build a sense of story. When such books are routinely read aloud to them, they begin to internalize the book's language and use it in their play, their writing, and their lives.

- Stories children hear read aloud extend their personal experiences to include those of the characters in the story. With their growing curiosity, children are ever experiencing the newness of things. Nonfiction read aloud, for example, can

> A balanced approach to reading is "not simply a random combination of strategies" but a thoughtful consideration of what specific ways will help the individuals in a class learn best.

enhance children's natural curiosity, answer their questions, and nourish their sense of wonder.

THOUGHT QUESTION In some classrooms, children study genres, or types of books, such as memoirs, nonfiction, or poetry. They do author studies, reading several books by a single author. They learn about protagonists and antagonists and dissect plots. Some people believe that analyzing literature is unnecessary, tedious, and spoils children's experience with books. Others feel it engages them, helps them to enjoy books, and teaches skills. How might you use children's literature with first, second, and third graders? How will you enable them to attend to stories for longer periods, follow story lines, and gain vocabulary and reference points? How will you share the joy and pure aesthetics of children's literature with the children you will teach?

Self-expression

Writing, one form of self-expression, looks different in different classrooms. When children investigate a social studies topic, they write as they do research, keep track of findings, and prepare documentation to show what they have learned. For example, one year the children in Trish's class wrote the story of the bridge as if each of them were one of the original bridge workers. Their writing revealed that they remembered only certain aspects of the bridge's construction and confused the chronology, so Trish began to wonder what the historical dimension of the study actually meant to them. She noted that, in contrast to their fuzzy sense of the bridge's history, the activities the children did themselves remained vivid and meaningful to them. Trish decided that when she repeated this study with a future class, instead of writing the entire story of the bridge, each child would research and write about a single event or topic—for instance, caisson disease, which bridge workers suffered after toiling deep under the river in the watertight caissons to establish a foundation for the bridge towers.

In a class where time is set aside specifically for writing, you might see a **writer's workshop.** In this example (adapted from Ray 2001), children are spread out in all parts of the room, working in different ways:

- Two children sketch illustrations for their story.
- A teacher conferences with a child, listening as he reads his writing aloud.
- A group of children take notes as they read.
- A child reads his writing aloud to other children.
- Children sit beside each other and revise their work.
- Two children write at computers.
- A group reads the first chapter of a book to see how the author solved problems they encounter in their own writing.
- An aide takes dictation from a child whose disability makes the physical act of writing difficult for her.
- Some children chat with each other for the first part of the workshop but eventually sit in different parts of the room and begin writing.

In another classroom, you'll see a list of spelling words on the board that the children copy into their notebooks. In a third, a child's writing is projected on a screen as she points out a sentence that needed elaboration and tells the class how she developed the idea further. In yet another room, every child has an identical page that starts with a partial sentence and has room for the child to complete the sentence and write about the book the teacher has just read aloud. In Trish's class, the children created a two-dimensional bridge of poems they wrote about the physical elements of the bridge. After they read "Things to Do If You Are a Subway" by the adult poet Bobbi Katz, teams of three children composed poems as if they themselves were the caissons, the towers, the anchorages, the cables, the suspenders, the diagonal stays, and the roadway. Although each class has different strategies and emphases, all the teach-

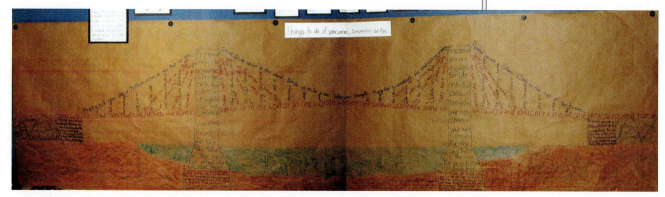

Trish's second/third graders created this poetry bridge as part of the bridge curriculum.

ers want children to express well-developed ideas clearly; and all teach the rules of English grammar, capitalization, and punctuation.

Self-expression also includes the ways in which children draw, paint, sculpt, work with clay and textiles, and engage in music, drama, and movement to demonstrate what they experience, think, and learn. A specialist can coordinate art projects with the class curriculum. But whether or not the school has an art program, classroom teachers can bring the arts into the classroom to support the curriculum.

In addition to writing, the children in Trish's class used a variety of media in their bridge study. Their drawings helped clarify their thinking about different types of bridges and their ability to bear load. As the children used tempera paint, they explored color, form, and design, looked more closely at the patterns within the bridge, and ultimately diverged from realistic images of the bridge. The model they built was actually a sculpture through which the children both learned about the bridge and demonstrated their knowledge of it. The children also drew two pictures of themselves—one of their fronts, another of their backs—that had to match when pasted together. Trish reduced the figures with a photocopier to produce paper dolls the right size to "walk" on the bridge model at the Celebration of the Bridge, to which the children invited their families. These expressive activities took the class beyond the everyday experience of the bridge to an aesthetic experience. During any one of them, the room hummed with the productive sound of children thinking aloud and exchanging ideas and then went still as they worked intently.

Materials challenge children differently from a math question or reading a new book. For example, when children shape the human figure with clay, they learn and master techniques for making arms and legs that won't fall off and that don't topple their figure. They work out how to dry large clay pieces without getting cracks. While they resort to trial and error, they are more likely to have a plan and to keep track of what works and what doesn't than they were last year or the year before. Most six-year-olds enjoy the sensory aspect of materials much as they did when they were younger, but now they are also able to use materials to make their own creations and solve problems that arise as they work.

Blocks are a multifaceted and flexible artistic medium for first through third graders. They can use them

Children painted these bridge details.

Whether or not the school has an art program, classroom teachers can bring the arts into the classroom to support the curriculum.

Math is active; verbs describe it best: explore, conjecture, hypothesize, discover, invent, prove, apply, and generalize.

to build and rebuild, unlike with other materials, where a stroke of paint is more of a commitment to the final product. Children look at their buildings from various angles, reconfigure them, or choose to build other things. Children can build creatively, almost whimsically, but they also may use blocks for precise representation. By the middle of the year, for example, the children in Trish's class had used most of their blocks for caissons and anchorages and for the towers of the suspension bridge. Their block building was curriculum directed.

The block area is also a place where children can engage in dramatic play. Six-year-olds are drawn to dramatic play, just as younger children are, but now they seem more able to take on another's perspective. Younger children adopt a role in the dress-up area and become whoever they are pretending to be, but older ones can use block people to create a world in which they assume the attributes and points of view of different figures simultaneously.

Like blocks, painting externalizes what children are thinking. Paint has a sensual quality, and children enjoy its physical aspects as much as they value what they can make paint do. And, so it is with most art forms.

Math and Science

Mathematics enables children to think about relationships in the physical world and provides a symbol system for recording those relationships. Studying science allows children to explore the physical world, experiment with it, and draw initial conclusions about how it works. When Trish's class experimented with load on a bridge, they explored and recorded mathematical and scientific concepts and relationships, and excitement mounted. Everyone—families included—got involved.

Foundations for mathematical thinking

First through third graders learn about mathematical relationships, about how to represent them, and about mathematical reasoning (National Council of Teachers of Mathematics [NCTM] 2000–2004). Math consists of more than facts to memorize. It is active; verbs describe it best: explore, conjecture, hypothesize, discover, invent, prove, apply, and generalize (see http://www.bankstreetcorner.com/math.shtml). As children investigate math concepts, they use vocabulary and syntax that may be new to some native speakers and to ELLs. Thus, teaching math includes teaching language and giving children time to take in new ideas and the labels for them.

Children in the early elementary years gain increasing fluency using whole numbers, geometry, and measurement. For example, first graders come to understand the order of the numbers and how the amount of one whole number compares with the amount of another. They learn to solve problems using whole numbers and can group numbers by tens. In second grade, children continue to order numbers and solve problems with them, but now they understand multi-digit numbers and place value. Third graders understand that a fraction is part of a whole. Now they compare, order, and solve problems with fractions as well as with whole numbers. Number lines and other models help them to identify equivalent fractions (see the NCTM focal points at http://www.nctm.org/standards/focalpoints).

Creative teachers who understand math themselves can develop a rich math program in which children think on their own, as did the child who created this poster—Hal Melnick, Bank Street College

Throughout the early elementary years, children sort and classify and learn to create and identify patterns. They come to recognize, compare, and draw or build two- and three-dimensional shapes and learn about how shapes can combine to make new shapes. When children use **manipulative materials,** objects they can move and touch, abstract mathematical concepts can become concrete. Teach-

A child can create an a-b-a, a-b-a pattern with fruit, as here, with store-bought manipulatives, or with found objects.

ers purchase manipulatives or collect them, for example, saving bottle caps to use as counters. **Computer manipulatives,** objects children can move on the computer, also support their understandings of quantity when they can connect them to the mathematical ideas that the manipulatives illustrate or represent (Clements 1999).

A teacher's thought-provoking questions enable children to observe mathematical relationships in action. Besides seeing the relationships between numbers, between operations, and among objects, children begin to recognize the connections among mathematical ideas of all sorts, including pre-algebra, for example, when a child has identified her pattern as a-b-a, a-b-a. . . .

Elementary schoolers use symbols—numerals, signs, and other traditional mathematical symbols as well as symbols of their own devising—to represent mathematical thinking. They can collect data and represent their findings through graphs and through less conventional depictions.

Importantly, elementary school children enter the world of mathematical thinking. They estimate, predict, solve problems, and communicate their thinking in print, drawings, and orally. As they do, they organize, consolidate, and support their ideas.

Procedural and conceptual knowledge

When someone knows what steps to take to solve a math problem but doesn't know why to take them, he has **procedural knowledge.** In contrast, someone who has **conceptual knowledge** understands the relationships at work in a math problem (Van de Walle 2004). What the problem *means* is more important than just solving it and recording the answer. A child who can explain and justify the answer to other children has conceptual knowledge as well as procedural knowledge:

> At a morning meeting, one child in a mixed first/second grade class remarked that the class restaurant was making a lot of money that the children could use for trips. When the children totaled their receipts after a week, they found they had earned $153.65, including tips. Marisa said that $50 more would bring their total to $200. John announced that they needed $57 to make $200. Kimberly said that $153 plus $7 equals $160. With $160, you need only $40 to get to $200. So you need $47 to get to $200.

All the children accepted Kimberly's answer, perhaps able to follow her logic more easily than if their teacher had explained the math to them. Their teacher listened carefully, interested in the different ways children solved the problem. Math—famous for one right answer—actually provides an opportunity for teachers to differentiate learning and enable children to learn concepts and solve problems in the ways that make the most sense to them.

Kimberly sounded as if she enjoyed thinking about the problem she solved. According to John Van de Walle, when children use conceptual knowledge, math becomes fun for them as well as easier to learn. When a math problem is more like a puzzle than a chore, children *want* to solve it, they are **intrinsically motivated** to do so. They see math as a web of related ideas instead of a series of isolated questions to answer, facts to memorize, and steps to follow. But how do children gain conceptual knowledge? The more math teachers know and the more they know about teaching math, the better equipped they are to guide children to conceptual knowledge (NCTM 2000–2004).

As with teaching in general, teachers who have opportunities to meet with other teachers to think together about their students' math work will be better able to analyze how they teach math. Together, they can consider the mathematical thinking that goes on daily and look at the big picture of how children are learning and thinking about math.

Thinking mathematically

Mathematical learning occurs in at least four ways in the early grades. When teachers use all four approaches, children can grapple with mathematical ideas in different ways and with a variety of materials, and thereby cement their mathematical understandings.

First, math is part of daily life. Making math a way of thinking all day long can help children gain a broader understanding of mathematical concepts. When children vote during class meetings, they participate in a democratic activity and compare, count, consider ratios, and add and subtract. When they keep track of classroom materials, they take responsibility for collective belongings and sort, count, add, and subtract. Constance Kamii (1985) urges teachers to watch for mathematical opportunities in the daily life of the classroom and not worry about wasting time when they arise. This can be a challenge, as the following example demonstrates:

On Wednesday, during morning calendar time, a first grade teacher noted Miguel's birthday party on the class calendar. As she wrote, several children began to argue. Was it three days until the Saturday party or four? The teacher noticed the disruption but not its essence. She quieted them and continued the ritual of recording the number of days they had been in school so far that year.

It is hard to notice everything children bring up, especially during group times when so much is going on. Yet, teachers who are comfortable with a group of children, who can recognize mathematical conversation when it happens, and who value spontaneous learning opportunities can relax, listen to the children, and seize learning moments as they occur.

Second, math is part of any study the class engages in over time. You saw how the first and second graders' restaurant study provided the opportunity for a math discussion. And the bridge study gave Trish's second and third graders chances to count, measure, explore symmetry, and apply engineering principles.

Third, teachers provide systematic instruction that addresses all the aspects of mathematics in the National Council of Teachers of Mathematics standards for first through third grade (NCTM 2000-2004). Many resources help teachers set up activities for children that lead them to understand mathematical concepts. The websites in Figure 13.1 offer a start.

Resources for helping children understand mathematical concepts

AAA Math: *http://www.aaamath.com/*

Center for Innovation in Education: *http://www.center.edu/index.shtml*

Equals and Family Math: *http://www.lhs.berkeley.edu/equals/index.html*

House of Math Word Problems for Children: *http://www.mathstories.com/*

I love that teaching idea: *http://ilovethatteachingidea.com/ideas/subj_math.htm*

Internet4classrooms: *http://internet4classrooms.com/math_elem_index.htm*

Math Solutions: *http://www.mathsolutions.com/*

TERC: *http://www.terc.edu/ourwork/elementarymath.html*

Fourth, children play games that engage them in calculation, strategy, and estimation. Teachers can create games that incorporate concepts children are learning. Children can play commercial games, too, that require them to think mathematically. And teachers can play games with the whole class as well. Here is an example:

> Third grade teacher Grace wrote, "What's my rule?" on the board. She drew a grid (Figure 13.2) and pointed to an empty box. Tiffany raised her hand, and Grace recorded her answer. The third graders wriggled in excitement as their silent teacher recorded only correct responses and created new grids with greater challenges.

Once a teacher starts thinking mathematically herself, she can see the mathematics in all kinds of situations, including games children play outdoors during recess.

Science education

Some common themes ground the science teaching standards for all grades (National Committee on Science Education Standards 1996):

■ Science learning is **inquiry-based,** with activities structured so that children seek answers to real questions. Children are active learners who use hands-on materials to explore scientific phenomena. Whether they use eyedroppers to see how

What's my rule?		
3	→	9
5	→	15
7	→	

13.2 *What's My Rule? Chart*

Many classroom games help children learn math concepts.

many drops of water fit on a penny or experiment with batteries and bulbs to create a circuit, they are scientists at work. In addition to using the materials, they anticipate what will happen and record both their predictions and the results.

- The teacher's role in science learning is to guide and facilitate student learning, not to demonstrate or transmit information. The teacher sets the stage for learning and then provokes children's thinking as they work. Scientific investigation revolves around questions, but all questions are not equally good (Elstgeest 2001). Good questions are those children can answer and those that don't require lengthy adult explanations. Such questions encourage children to observe, to compare, to measure and count, to try something different, and to think about what would happen if.

- Assessment of teaching and of children's learning shapes the science curriculum. Throughout scientific investigations, teachers keep careful track to assess what children are learning and to plan how to deepen and extend their understanding of science concepts.

- Teachers develop stimulating environments and provide materials that provoke children's interest in scientific phenomena. They gather and organize supplies and equipment for children to use as they investigate color, sound, electricity, water, and motion, as well as rocks, plants, and animals.

- Science is learned within a community of children who investigate and exchange information about their findings. During scientific investigations, teachers interact with children individually and in groups, mindful that, just as with mathematics, children who talk about their findings with each other will think about them more thoroughly and understand them better. When the class is already a community of learners, it can easily become a scientific community, for example, as children discuss what happened when they launched the parachutes they made of plastic bags, string, and a weight.

- A school science program has an overall plan and direction. In addition to planning specific explorations, teachers have a sense of their class's larger science curriculum, keeping in mind the continuum of what children have investigated and how that fits with what they will do next.

Scientific investigation revolves around questions, but all questions are not equally good ones.

THOUGHT QUESTION What does a child have to know and be able to do to play "What's My Rule?" Look back at the theories in Chapter 6. Which of them can help you explain why some third graders will struggle with the game, while others will quickly rise to its challenges?

PLANNING CURRICULUM

How do teachers plan curriculum for the primary grades?

Figure 13.3 illustrates one of numerous teacher cycles reinforcing the notion that children learn best when they own the learning. The teacher is ever-present in the early elementary classroom but does not need to direct learning with an iron hand. Teachers who give children real choices find that they invariably rise to the occasion.

The more the elementary school teacher does behind the scenes, the more choices he can provide and the freer he is to interact with and observe children. The teacher who

- prepares activities in advance,
- schedules time thoughtfully, and
- organizes space and materials

can spend the school day teaching and learning. For example, when Trish first investigated the Brooklyn Bridge with a class, she didn't know all she does now. Consulting a wide range of sources—adult books, the Internet, maps, and children's books—she learned about the bridge's significance to New York City, the process of its building, and the physical principles involved in its design and construction. She collected books at a range of reading levels to use for the study. She planned the classroom schedule to allow large blocks of time for trips and related activities to deepen children's learning about the bridge. Throughout their study, children read and wrote, measured and calculated, and learned social studies and science. They represented their experiences and the knowledge they gained from it with blocks and a variety of art media.

Ways to Plan

Whether you keep a plan book, use commercial sheets or school-generated forms, or write in your own notebook or journal, recording your plans can help you:

- clarify your thinking about day-to-day curriculum,
- stay organized,
- keep track of your thinking as you plan,
- make sure you don't forget anything, such as materials for an activity, and
- let others who work with you know what you and the children are doing. (For example, your plan book will enable a substitute to do what you would have done with the children.)

Collaborative planning makes a teaching team more effective and inspires teachers, even when they do not teach together. A team can support its members to teach reading, writing, and math through exciting curriculum.

Traditional lesson plans

The traditional **lesson plan** is a format used to think through a single activity. It has three

Planning Curriculum Cycle

Understanding the intellectual, political, social, and emotional content of what you teach

Teacher-Child interactions in the Early Elementary Grades

Assessing what occurs and planning the next steps

Planning ways for children to contend with that content for themselves

13.3 *Early Elementary Curriculum Planning Cycle*

This child uses mathematical skills as he measures a cable in the bridge curriculum.

Lesson Plan Format

Preliminary Considerations	The Lesson	Evaluation
Purpose and significance Why teach this lesson? What will children get from it? **Continuity** How does the lesson connect with previous learning? How can it connect to what will follow? **Preparation** What general knowledge do you need? How will you acquire it? What do you need to know about the children? How will you find out? What materials will you need? How will you organize them? **Logistics** (related to fulfilling the purpose of the lesson) Time duration? Why? Where sit? Why? How sit? Facing each other, etc.? Why? Where will you be? Why? If it is a class activity, will you circulate, spend time at each table?	How will you begin? Why? What questions will you ask? Why? What responses do you hope for? What responses do you anticipate given your knowledge of the children? What might children have difficulty with? How will you address this? Will you record the responses on a chart? How? Why? What activity will children do? Writing? Drawing? How can you state the instructions simply and clearly? Who might have difficulty with the activity? How might you help them? How will you end the lesson? Why?	Revisit your original purpose for the lesson. How did children respond? (Be specific, e.g., body language.) Did it go as anticipated? Why or why not? With what did children have difficulty? Why? What responses added new dimensions to the topic? How might this knowledge influence future planning? Who had difficulty? Why? How might this influence future planning? Describe anything that happened that you didn't anticipate. How do you account for it? What lesson or activity will follow-up or continue the topic addressed in the lesson? Did you fulfill your purpose for this lesson? To what extent? How do you account for this?

13.4 *Lesson Plan Format*

parts: *preliminary considerations,* the *lesson,* and the *evaluation.* You think about preliminary considerations as you begin planning. This section includes both the reasons for whatever you will be doing and the details of your preparation. The lesson refers to the activity itself, how you begin or introduce it, what questions you will ask, whether to record children's responses, how to do the activity, and how you will end it. Evaluation involves reflecting on the lesson afterwards and recording your observations of the children and your own reactions. When you use this lesson in the future and as you continue planning activities, you can refer to your notes on children's responses and unexpected occurrences. Together, these three parts of the plan enable you to make an activity fit with everything else the children are learning. After you answer the questions in the lesson plan in Figure 13.4, you will be able to conduct the lesson more knowledgeably.

Weekly plans

A weekly planning sheet (Figure 13.5) lets you map your schedule, with space to insert what your class is doing each day at different times. You can include what you anticipate will happen during work on a long-term project, what stories you will read aloud, what math concepts you will address, and so forth. You can even write reminders for yourself about arrival and dismissal.

A weekly plan does not give the level of detail of a lesson plan, but its overview of the week can help you maintain a balance of activities. The plan also can aid you in estimating how much work on an investigation or study you and the children can accomplish in a week.

Weekly Plan	Monday	Tuesday	Wednesday	Thursday	Friday
8:40—arrival					
9:00—meeting					
9:20—projects					
10:00—writing					
11:00—reading & story					
12:00—lunch/yard					
1:00—special					
1:45—arts					
2:15—math					
3:10—home					

Webbing

Unlike a lesson plan, a web does not give details about activities, nor does it indicate the timing of different activities as a weekly plan does. Instead, a web illustrates how various activities or lessons relate to each other and to what you intend the children to learn. Webs, such as the one in Figure 13.6 for Trish's Brooklyn Bridge curriculum, can both inspire and document your thinking about studies that the class will do over a period of time.

Planning the Schedule

Teachers take a lot into account when they plan their daily schedule. They decide the order of activities and the amount of time they can or want to spend on each. They plan the day's flow, how it will begin and end, and how children will move from one activity or subject to the next throughout the day. At best, they plan time outdoors as well as indoors.

Scheduling the day

Knowing the order of the day gives children a sense of what to expect. A predictable sequence of events, posted where they can read it, helps them feel more in control of their day. When you put the time next to the topic, learning to read the clock takes on added appeal.

Trish's class spent a lot of time on the Brooklyn Bridge curriculum and did much of that work in the morning when they and Trish were fresh. Trish devoted so much time to this social studies investigation because she knew that it would generate meaningful and complex learning opportunities that would engage her class thoroughly. Trish's daily schedule (Figure 13.7) included both a block of time to study bridges and a substantial period of writing time. The children also had outdoor time, both structured and unstructured. While the second graders learned math, the third graders got ready for a standardized test they would take in a month.

THOUGHT QUESTION How could each of the three planning devices—the traditional lesson plan, a weekly plan, and webbing—help you as a teacher? As a student in an early elementary classroom, why might it help you to see your cooperating teacher's plans?

THOUGHT QUESTION Within the constraints of the school's response to standards and testing, how children spend their class time indicates what experiences the teacher believes children should have in school. What do you consider most important for children to learn in the early elementary years? How would that influence the amount of time you would try to devote to each subject and activity?

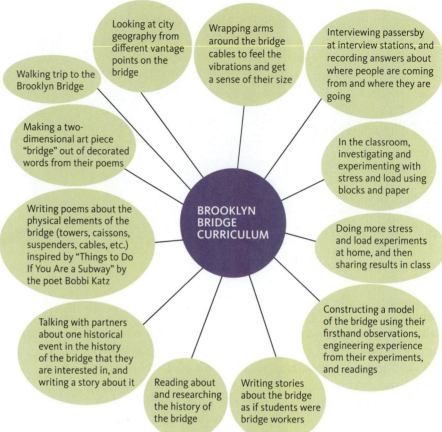

BROOKLYN BRIDGE CURRICULUM

- Walking trip to the Brooklyn Bridge
- Looking at city geography from different vantage points on the bridge
- Wrapping arms around the bridge cables to feel the vibrations and get a sense of their size
- Interviewing passersby at interview stations, and recording answers about where people are coming from and where they are going
- Making a two-dimensional art piece "bridge" out of decorated words from their poems
- In the classroom, investigating and experimenting with stress and load using blocks and paper
- Writing poems about the physical elements of the bridge (towers, caissons, suspenders, cables, etc.) inspired by "Things to Do If You Are a Subway" by the poet Bobbi Katz
- Doing more stress and load experiments at home, and then sharing results in class
- Talking with partners about one historical event in the history of the bridge that they are interested in, and writing a story about it
- Constructing a model of the bridge using their firsthand observations, engineering experience from their experiments, and readings
- Reading about and researching the history of the bridge
- Writing stories about the bridge as if students were bridge workers

Planning the curriculum alongside the state standards for each subject area enables a teacher like Trish to meet these standards through meaningful curriculum.

In Trish's class, the bridge experiments with blocks, paper, and cubes took nearly an hour, including recording and discussing the findings. Children had time to think, explore, experiment, make mistakes, work on those mistakes, get sidetracked, and come back to task. Planning the curriculum alongside the state standards for each subject area enables a teacher like Trish to meet these standards through meaningful curriculum.

If fertile blocks of time are important for in-depth study, why do so many teachers plan bits of time for different activities? Sometimes teachers have to follow a schedule that does not allow them the flexibility they need to devote a long time to children's work. You may have to work within such constraints, doing what you can to give children as long as possible for activities you feel deserve more time. Other teachers schedule a series of activities in short spurts because they are afraid the children will lose interest. But if the curriculum is engaging enough, the children will remain focused.

Daily transitions

Transitions, switching from one activity or mode of working to another, occur throughout the day. The biggest transitions are arrival and dismissal, but all through the day children must switch from one activity to another.

Different teachers begin the day differently. In some schools, children line up on the playground or in the cafeteria, where their teacher

Trish's Daily Schedule

Arrival — 8:40 a.m.
Meeting and poem — 9:00 a.m.
Bridges — drawing and model — 9:20 a.m.
Writing — 10:00 a.m.
Story/Snack — 11:00 a.m.
Yard/Lunch — 11:55 a.m.
Physical education — 1:00 p.m.
Music — 1:45 p.m.
Math and Test fix-ups — 2:15 p.m.
Home — 3:10 p.m.

meets them and leads them to the classroom. In others, parents bring their children to the room, or children come in on their own. However the children arrive, the teacher has to figure out how to help them make the transition to school and gear up for the day's work.

In many classrooms, morning group time includes rituals such as calendar math, so children can see and use mathematics in their daily lives. The calendar activities reveal patterns—a far-reaching mathematical concept—and reinforce the important mathematical phenomenon of the many ways there are to express the same amount. For example, in many classrooms, every day the teacher chooses a child to put a stick in a plastic bag. Each stick represents a day of school. When a bag fills with ten sticks, the class starts a new bag. If children sit for a long sequence of calendar activities, however, they can get bored, especially if one child works at the calendar while some watch and others can't see. When teachers notice this happening, they can adjust the schedule and its activities accordingly.

As with younger children, elementary schoolers have various activities throughout the day, and teachers plan the transitions between them. For instance, after children have worked individually on math, they put away their notebooks before going to the gym. If they all go to the shelf at the same time, chaos will ensue. One teacher handles this and other transitions by having the children look at the patterns on their sneaker soles. Those with zigzag soles are the first to line up.

Recasting transitions and other routine tasks in the form of a game readily engages children. They respond positively to challenge, playfulness, suspense, and competition. As you read earlier, early elementary schoolers are moving from their own, somewhat flexible rules to externally imposed game rules that can't be bent as easily. The following example shows how socially developed rules do not make sense to some children, while game rules do:

> In a school that requires children to be quiet as they walk through the halls, a second grade teacher introduced a game to enable her class to follow the rule. They played a silent red-light/green-light game as they went through the halls. The children enjoyed the game and complied with the school rules at the same time.

The power of play can help teachers and children manage transitions well.

How the day ends is, in a sense, the biggest transition of all. Without the teacher's careful planning and an eye on the clock, the day's end can come in a rush, without time to put work away or tie up loose ends. Before they leave, children organize their notebooks, including any homework for the next day. They pick up papers and straighten up the classroom. They may put chairs on top of desks to make the room easier to clean. There may be last-minute jobs to do, such as watering plants or feeding fish. The teacher might have the entire class play a game that has short rounds, so the game can end when it's time to leave. Or the day can close with a carefully timed story that the teacher reads

THOUGHT QUESTION What advantages and disadvantages do you see to each of these ways of starting the day?

- In a combined first and second grade, children stream into the room, chat with each other and the teacher, arrange their belongings, and begin writing and drawing informally.

- In a second grade, games are on the tables as children drift into the room with their parents. Children show their parents the previous day's work, play games, put away homework, and chat with each other and their teachers before starting the day with a discussion in the large-group area.

- In a first grade, the teacher has written a "Do Now" on the blackboard. Every child has a worksheet on which to practice penmanship or reinforce a recently learned phonics or math skill. After a short time for the "Do Now" activity, the group gathers for a morning meeting. The children read the "morning message" prepared by the teacher that tells them what they will do for the rest of the day.

- In a first/second grade, the teacher has the children start the day by singing together for about fifteen minutes. Then she directs the children's energy to the work of the day.

- In a third grade classroom, the day begins with announcements over the public address system and a mandated half-hour vocabulary lesson. As soon as that is done, children gather on the rug to talk about what they did at home over the weekend or the night before and about the school day ahead.

THOUGHT QUESTION Although adult rules can seem arbitrary to first through third graders, the students are often interested in creating rules, following them, breaking them, and applying them to others. They may follow rules just because they are rules or disregard them without thinking about the reasons behind the rules. What will you do if children do not follow rules? Why?

Teachers have to remain aware of all group configurations because a child who speaks with convincing authority but less knowledge can mislead other children.

aloud. Or the teacher can ask the children to reflect on their day and plan the work they will continue tomorrow—a peaceful and calming endeavor.

A balance of activities

As teachers plan the day, they consider how much of the time children work individually, in small groups of their own choosing, in small groups of the teacher's choosing, and as a whole class. Everyone needs some of each, since each has different advantages. Children working individually can focus on activities that are just right for them—and, perhaps, for no one else. In small groups, children can exchange ideas, see other people's points of view, and enlarge their own as they argue and develop their positions. In large groups, guided by the teacher, children can experience an even wider range of perspectives. In each configuration, teachers have to remain engaged because, for example, a child in a small group who speaks with convincing authority but less knowledge can mislead other children (Tudge 1990).

While children spend most of the school day indoors, fresh air and exercise are essential to good health. Children can put more effort into activities requiring intense concentration if they also participate in activities they find relaxing and energizing. Dramatic play during outdoor time enhances children's language and imaginations as it cements social relationships. Many children are more independent outdoors than at any other time, and, outside, teachers can get to know children in a new way.

Some principals, concerned that children will not perform well enough on tests, have cut back recess to use that time for academics instead. However, the National Association of Early Childhood Specialists in State Departments of Education (NAECS/SDE 2007) asserts that recess supports children's emotional, social, and even intellectual growth and should not be sacrificed. NAEYC's 1998 position statement on *The Value of School Recess and Outdoor Play* puts it this way:

> Our society has become increasingly complex, but there remains a need for every child to feel the sun and wind on his cheek and engage in self-paced play. Children's attempts to make their way across monkey bars, negotiate the hopscotch course, play jacks, or toss a football require intricate behaviors of planning, balance, and strength—traits we want to encourage in children. Ignoring the developmental functions of unstructured outdoor play denies children the opportunity to expand their imaginations beyond the constraints of the classroom.

Using Space

A tiny portable classroom sits in a dusty yard outside the main public school building. The room has barely enough space for twenty-eight second graders, their desks, and the teacher. A chalkboard covers one wall. Along two walls are shelves of books, math materials, and realistic animal puppets the children have made. To one side of the room are a rug and a chart stand. Any free wall space displays children's work and charts related to the curriculum.

Throughout the day, the children move their desks to fit each activity. The school has a mandated phonics program teachers must follow for the first half-hour each morning. With desks facing front, the teacher, Beth, stands at the blackboard and conducts a lesson on the consonant blends *gr, br, dr,* and *tr.*

Once the lesson is over, the second graders push the desks to one wall and gather on the rug near the chart that says "Morning News." Beth records the children's news: the birth of a sibling and what happened at yesterday's ballgame. She reminds them about an upcoming trip and then explains the small-group work that will follow their meeting. The children then reconfigure the room, forming tables of four or five desks pushed together. The children know what group they are in and what activity their group will do.

As Beth's class demonstrates, teachers and children can be resourceful, turning a difficult space into an environment for productive learning. The space and the school's mandated curriculum frame, but don't limit, what Beth and her class can do. In the first few months of school, Beth taught the children how to create and participate in the spaces they need for individual and small-group work, group time, and structured lessons.

Beth found ways to have room for the activities she believes help children learn. For example, she and the children created an area on the rug where they could face each other for open discussion. As she planned how to use the space throughout the day, she asked herself these questions:

- What do I believe children need room for?
- What kind of space will lead children to do different kinds of thoughtful work?
- What activities require a small, confined, perhaps private or semiprivate space?
- How many spaces do I want for small groups to meet and work?
- Where will the whole group meet?
- What materials will children use throughout the day?
- What should they be able to reach without teacher assistance?
- What should be stored away?

Even with her space constraints, Beth paid attention to children's experience in the room. Before school, she squatted to children's eye level to see the room the way they did. She tried not to have cramped spaces because conflicts arise when children crowd each other. She placed materials strategically and taught children where to find what they need. After the first few weeks, most of the children knew where to get their writing journals and their math notebooks, where to put work in progress, and where to leave work for Beth to review.

Different people organize materials differently. How much stuff do you want in your room, and how will you organize it? When does clutter prevent children from reading their environment, from understanding how their classroom works, or from making thoughtful choices in it? When is too little material not stimulating enough? Ask, "What purpose does this item or display serve?" And, periodically, ask, "Is it still important?" No

> The space and the school's mandated curriculum frame, but don't limit, what a teacher and her class can do.

Storage boxes make it easy for children to organize the materials they use daily.

This elementary school classroom is set up for children to get right to work.

THOUGHT QUESTION As you visit schools, notice what teachers post on their classroom walls and in the halls. Some display commercial materials. Others post photographs, perhaps from the school's neighborhood, that are relevant to the curriculum and that raise questions for children. Photographs from the community and beyond—for example, of workers whom the children have met—bring people from various cultures, of both genders, and with and without special needs into the classroom (De Gaetano, Williams, and Volk 1997). Some teachers post children's artwork and writing. As you look at classrooms, which displays seem most meaningful to you? Why?

matter what your personal preference as a teacher may be, consider what adds to or detracts from children's ability and desire to use classroom materials productively.

Personal space

Children need room for their work and personal items. Some teachers set up boxes or trays where they can keep these. Others assign children desks. Some classes have a coat closet; others have separate cubbies for each child. In every case, thoughtfully created personal space helps children keep track of their belongings.

Children may value personal space, since so much of the classroom is communal. Personal space can be particularly important to children who live in a shelter or in cramped accommodations, who share a room with siblings, or whose families are migrant workers because they may not have personal space at home. Make sure children have adequate room for their books, papers, and belongings; that the space is labeled; that children have time to take care of it; and that it remains well organized.

Materials and equipment

A classroom needs two categories of materials and equipment— capital expenditures and expendables. Both capital expenditures and expendables can be **generative,** that is, they can have no right answer and can enable children to think creatively.

Every school invests in **capital expenditures,** in desks or tables and chairs, in rugs, in shelving, and in learning materials such as unit blocks, base-ten blocks, and Cuisenaire rods. Since principals sometimes ask teachers to select these items, many teachers keep a wish list of what to buy when funds are available. Purchasing high-quality items shows respect for children and saves money, too, because quality materials last a long time.

A first grade teacher so clearly articulated what and how children learn from blocks that she convinced her principal to buy some. Gradually the block area grew, and the children represented their social studies investigations of grocery stores and the post office, of the airport, and of a farm they visited. The principal saw how the blocks familiarized the children with the mathematical concepts of size, length, shape, addition, and even multiplication and how they promoted cooperative work. He supported the teacher's additional requests, and eventually half the room was devoted to the block area.

Expendables are materials that children use up, such as paint, paper, and markers. As we have just noted, high-quality supplies can inspire children's best work; but with expendables, children often can use inexpensive or even free items just as effectively as store-bought or costly ones. All these materials should enable children to express their thinking, to experiment, to consolidate and synthesize their thinking, and to externalize it to share it with others.

Generative materials, such as the blocks, cubes, and paper the children used when they studied the Brooklyn Bridge, have seemingly limitless learning potential. Well-kept generative materials provoke children's thinking and also enable them to express their ideas. Children are attracted to fresh paper, neatly arranged art materials, and complete games stored on well-organized shelves; however, dried-out markers and games missing crucial pieces distract them from their work. When shelves become messy, teachers can create new spaces, for example, by providing a box for cut paper to use for collage.

In a print-noisy room, one with an overabundance of print, children may tune out important messages or have trouble focusing.

Print Rich, Not Print Noisy

How do teachers create an environment for literacy? Look carefully at a room full of print. Is it print rich or print noisy? In a print-rich room, the print on display is meaningful to the children. Beginning readers and writers, especially, need simplicity for clarity. A teacher might start the year with very little print on the walls, generate print with the children as the year goes on, and remove charts when they no longer have meaning. Children live in a world of meaningful print, such as street signs, food labels, and newspapers, that they and their teachers can use within the curriculum. In a print-noisy room, one with an overabundance of print, children may tune out important messages or have trouble focusing. For some children with special needs, too much stimulation makes it hard to concentrate and even to read.

As you can see, the classroom environment itself is a learning experience. It teaches children about organization and categorization, about what is important to learn, and about how the teacher believes children learn.

Children also need space to read in a relaxed fashion, as in this couch area in a third grade public school classroom.

SUMMARY

LIFE WITH FIRST, SECOND, AND THIRD GRADERS
Who are first, second, and third graders?

Physically, first, second, and third graders experience a growth spurt and gain strength, endurance, and agility. Their reasoning abilities, capacity to organize and manage information, and attentional abilities increase. Metacognitive abilities enable them to think about how to prompt their memories and what helps them learn. They are more likely to add an evaluative component to their descriptions of themselves, and how they learn becomes part of their identities. Relationships—sometimes fraught with exclusion and power plays—are at the heart of the elementary school classroom, just as they were with younger children.

WHAT CHILDREN LEARN IN THE EARLY GRADES
What do children learn in the early grades, and how do they learn it?

With social studies at the core of the curriculum, children acquire and use the skills and knowledge of the standard first, second, and third grade curricula in a real context. Core social studies curriculum typically starts small and evolves into a larger study that extends over several months. Children use traditional social science research techniques, such as observations and interviews. The curriculum takes children outside their classroom to learn from the real world and involves planning and learning on the teacher's part. Group discussion enables the children to get ideas from each other and deepen their understanding of the curriculum and their classroom community.

Learning to read involves both acquiring reading strategies and wanting to learn to read and requires a teacher's thoughtful consideration of how to help the individuals in a class learn best. Memory, attention, anxiety, risk taking, oral language use, comprehension of speech, sociocultural differences, and how young children learn all influence the reading process. Learning games and activities help children gain the necessary skills to read a book. Engagement with children's literature—individually and as a class—inspires children to want to read. Writing includes learning the mechanics of penmanship and spelling and, most important, putting thoughts down on paper. Encouraging self-expression also includes using the arts to enable children to represent what they are learning.

First through third graders learn about mathematical relationships, about how to represent them, and about mathematical reasoning. In a rich math program, children explore, conjecture, hypothesize, discover, invent, prove, apply, and generalize. Math involves a new vocabulary and syntax. Children deserve time to absorb new ideas and the labels for them so that they gain conceptual—not just procedural—knowledge. Opportunities for mathematical learning arise in the course of the daily life of the classroom, they will be part of any sufficiently complex study, they are addressed through systematic instruction in math, and they abound in group games that children play on their own or as a group with their teacher. Science, too, is inquiry based, so children seek answers to real questions, exchanging findings with a community of peers and a teacher who facilitates investigations and asks thought-provoking questions.

PLANNING CURRICULUM
How do teachers plan curriculum for the primary grades?

The early elementary school curriculum planning cycle begins with the teacher's understanding of the intellectual, political, social, and emotional content of the subject matter. It then extends to planning ways for children to contend with that content for themselves, assessing what occurs, and returning to the beginning of the cycle to further understand the content and do more planning. Recording plans helps teachers to clarify their thinking, stay organized, and communicate with others. Teachers use traditional lesson plans that detail all the elements of the activity, weekly plans that afford an overview of the week's activities with much less detail but that indicate what will happen when, and webs that demonstrate all the elements of a curriculum without details or timing.

As with younger children, knowing the order of the day helps early elementary schoolers know what to expect. Devoting large blocks of time to a study early in the day enables children to get the most out of that work. Transitions, beginnings, and endings need planning for these older children just as for younger ones. Children in the early elementary grades, too, need a balance of activities, including outdoor time, just as younger children do.

Elementary school teachers often have no choice about their classroom space, although they do decide how to use it. As they do, their central questions are who the children are, what they will be learning, and how. They make sure that children have personal space for their books, papers, and belongings. They choose high-quality, generative material and equipment that prompt children to think creatively. The print on their walls is meaningful to the children because the classroom environment itself is a learning experience. It teaches children about organization and categorization, about what is important to learn, and about how their teacher believes children learn.

FURTHER ACTIVITIES

1. Choose a topic that will interest first, second, or third graders. Explain why you think it will interest them, referring to this chapter, Chapter 6, Chapter 8, and other sources. Research the topic, developing a list of websites, children's books, and professional articles and books on it to distribute to your class. (**NAEYC Standard 1: Promoting Child Development and Learning**)

2. In a few paragraphs, describe a child who is struggling to learn to read, to get along with other children, to conform to classroom rules, or who is facing another challenge. Then design an activity to respond to that situation, and answer all the questions in the lesson plan format (see Figure 13.4). (**NAEYC Standard 4: Using Developmentally Effective Approaches to Connect with Children and Families**)

3. Visit a first, second, or third grade classroom. Record what you see on the walls, how the space is arranged, and the schedule of the day. Take notes as you observe the children and teacher. Sort your notes into these categories: social studies, language arts, mathematics, science, and the arts. For each category, explain why you included those materials and activities you did and what you think children are learning in that subject area. Then describe what you think this teacher has to know to be able to teach that subject matter. (**NAEYC Standard 5: Using Content Knowledge to Build Meaningful Curriculum**)

CHAPTER FOURTEEN

Partnering with Twenty-First-Century Families

I think it's important as a teacher to . . . believe in the strength of family as people who live together, work together to raise kids, in whatever sort of combination.

Cathy, a public school kindergarten teacher

n this chapter, we look closely at the wide range of family configurations, at the lenses through which early childhood educators view families, and at ways to work with families within early childhood programs. As you strive toward a deeper knowledge of families and yourself, you will read about how to communicate with *all* families in your early childhood program, whatever their configurations, as Cathy notes on the opening page of this chapter. We use the more inclusive word *families* more often than the word *parents* because children's guardians or the adults closest to and responsible for them may not be their legal parents and because others besides parents are involved in children's well-being.

Families are composed of unique individuals. To get to know families, early childhood educators first must examine their own assumptions and biases and listen carefully to what family members communicate about themselves and their children. Then, there is much to learn.

SOME BACKGROUND AND DEFINITIONS

How do partnerships with families differ from parent education and family involvement?

In so many ways, our work with children brings us into contact with their families. Families create the cultures in which children live and will continue to live long beyond their time in an early childhood class or group. Families know their children best and have valuable information and insights to offer. Thus, building a strong home-school connection is an integral part of our work. However, it has not always been that way.

Historical Roots of Family Involvement

The precursors of family involvement in early childhood education were evident throughout our nation's history, as early as the nineteenth century with the opening of the first kindergartens in the United States, which provided educational sessions and activities for mothers. Over time, these groups evolved into the *Parent Teacher Association* (PTA), which has been a major force in public schools since that time.

Even with these strong beginnings, it took the civil rights movement and other advocacy movements of the 1960s and 1970s to involve families more directly in their children's early education. In 1960, the *American Council of Parent Cooperatives* was founded to exchange information about preschool education. The most significant boost for the family involvement movement occurred in 1965, when Congress funded *Head Start*, with strong family involvement components. Scores of advocacy groups have sprung up since (Table 14.1). Yet the challenge remains to involve more families and schools in authentic partnerships that promote social integration and strengthen democratic participation in addition to benefiting children.

Defining the Terms: Family Involvement, Partnerships, and Parent Education

Teachers can interact with families in many ways, and most use several approaches. Glenda Mac Naughton (2003) describes three types of relationships:

- Teachers teach families how to care for and teach their children. In this type of relationship, teachers assume the expert role, while parents are more passive.

To get to know families, early childhood educators first must examine their own assumptions and biases and listen carefully to what family members communicate about themselves and their children. Then, there is much to learn.

THOUGHT QUESTION Think about your upbringing. Who was in your family when you were growing up? What was your relationship like with the person or people who raised you? Who is in your family now? What influences the way you think about families?

As you reflect, try to remember as much as you can about your childhood, and question why you remember what you do. Talk about your childhood with someone else who is studying to become an early childhood professional or with one of your supervising teachers. Questioning each other can extend both of your memories and help you connect them to your current beliefs. It can reveal ways in which you are similar to and different from others and what meaning that might have for your professional relationships.

■ Early childhood educators try to involve families in the program. They schedule program activities based on the program's way of caring for and teaching children.

■ Teachers and families collaborate on equal terms, honoring and respecting both teachers' and parents' knowledge.

Teachers share their knowledge with families, and, often, parents ask teachers for advice. Yet, when teachers act as experts and family members are more like clients, they are not on equal footing and cannot establish a collaborative relationship on behalf of the child. Instead, we encourage you to work toward family involvement, and, better yet, partnerships with families.

How does family involvement differ from a partnership? Using a **family involvement** approach, teachers encourage families to participate in various aspects of the program, such as attending PTA meetings or volunteering in the classroom. **Partnership,** MacNaughton's third category of parent involvement, involves working together on an equal basis toward a common goal (Swap 1993, Rockwell, Andre, and Hawley 1996). In a partnership you can still use your knowledge and expertise: it is *how* you use it that makes for partnership.

Parent Education and Family Support Programs

Parent education programs attempt to teach the many new skills involved in raising children. Parents are generally most receptive to this teaching when they identify the need, suggest the topics, and participate in the planning. Parent education includes discussion groups and classes, usually with accompanying written information. Culturally sensitive parent education is respectful of a range of acceptable parenting behaviors.

Some parents, such as those accused of child abuse or prospective foster parents, are required to take parenting classes as a condition of their children's remaining with them. Historically, parent education programs have been targeted to low-income parents of color. In general, this model of parent education has focused on the parents' deficits rather than on their strengths (Powell 1989).

Parents who recognized the mutual support that they could offer one another, with or without professional assistance, initiated the **family support** movement. Family support programs focus less on learning specific parenting skills than parent education programs do. Rather, families appreciate the opportunity to meet together in support groups for single parents, families of children with learning disabilities, and other affinity groupings.

Some early childhood professionals discover that they would rather work with families than with children and use their knowledge and expertise about early childhood to support family members raising children. Some family support programs are government sponsored; others are run by nonprofit or for-profit social service agencies. Services can include:

■ Parent education workshops
■ Drop-in play programs
■ Home visiting

Parents are generally most receptive to parent education when they identify the need, suggest the topics, and participate in the planning.

TABLE 14.1 Resources: Parent Information and Advocacy Groups

GROUP	URL	FOCUS/CONTENT
AARP	http://www.aarp.org/grandparents	Information for grandparents
All Kinds of Minds	http://www.allkindsofminds.org/index_families.aspx	Information about learning disabilities, including a "parent tool kit," for parents of elementary school children
American Academy of Pediatrics	http://www.aap.org	Comprehensive information on a range of children's health issues
American Library Association	http://www.ala.org/parentspage	Websites for kids and parents, teachers and caregivers
Association of Family and Conciliation Courts	http://www.afccnet.org/resources/resources_parents.asp	Resources for divorcing or divorced parents
Centers for Disease Control and Prevention (CDC)	http://www.cdc.gov.mill1.sjlibrary.org/ncbddd/child/default.htm	Child development information and "positive parenting" tips; information on developmental screenings and ADHD
Children, Youth and Families Education and Research Network	http://www.cyfernet.org/	Articles and research on a variety of topics
Families and Work Institute	http://www.familiesandwork.org/	Ideas for working parents
FPG Child Development Institute	http://www.fpg.unc.edu/index.cfm	Child development articles and resources, with a focus on children with special needs
Invest in Kids	http://www.investinkids.ca	Development and parenting tips
Just in Time Parenting	http://www.extension.org/parenting	Infant and toddler parenting issues
LD Online	http://www.ldonline.org/	Information for parents, caregivers, and teachers on ADHD and other learning disabilities
National Association for the Education of Young Children	http://www.naeyc.org	Information for both teachers and families on a wide range of topics
National Child Care Information Center	http://nccic.acf.hhs.gov/user/parents.html#information	Articles on quality child care for children
National Parent Teacher Association (PTA)	http://pta.org	Encourages parental involvement in schools
New York University Child Study Center	http://www.aboutourkids.org	Information about physical and mental disorders and general parenting issues
One Tough Job	http://www.onetoughjob.org/	Advice on raising infants to 18-year-olds
Parents as Teachers	www.parentsasteachers.org	Useful parenting tips, plus information for professionals
Parents without Partners	http://www.parentswithoutpartners.org/	Support for single parents
Scholastic	http://scholastic.com/	Information on literacy activities and child development issues
Sesame Workshop	http://www.sesameworkshop.org/	Advice for parents and caregivers; stories and games for kids
Talaris Research Institute	http://www.talaris.org	Articles and videos on child-rearing and parenting tips
Talking with Kids	www.talkingwithkids.org	How to talk to kids about difficult topics
Teacher/Pathfinder	http://teacherpathfinder.org/Parent/drparent.html	Parenting resources: infants through high school age
Tufts University Child and Family Web Guide	http://www.cfw.tufts.edu/	Websites and downloadable articles on parenting, education, child development, and health
Zero to Three	www.zerotothree.org	Information on child rearing and child development issues for parents and teachers

Members of this parent group, for Hmong parents who are deaf, enjoy a light moment. They meet together while their toddlers and two-year-olds have a play group.

A child from the Hmong community signs with her caregiver while in the play group.

- Child abuse prevention
- Counseling
- Information and resources for families

The parent support class shown here meets twice a week. This program works with deaf Hmong parents while their young children are in a toddler/twos group. United after both sessions are finished, the parents, children, and teachers sing and play together briefly before the morning program ends.

Children enjoy working with Play-Doh during their group before being reunited with their families for a good-bye song.

BENEFITS AND CHALLENGES OF TEACHER–FAMILY PARTNERSHIPS

What are the benefits and challenges of teacher-family partnerships?

When teachers reach out to families to establish trusting relationships, families and teachers can work together as partners. Families can contribute their own deep knowledge of their children, sharing information and observations that can help teachers form a more complete picture of a child. Families also are a link to the community surrounding the program, which is particularly important when teachers do not live in the neighborhoods in which they teach (Comer and Haynes 1991).

Classroom life is more meaningful for children when early childhood educators include children's home interests and experiences and when children's families participate in classroom activities. Families can play an important role in ensuring that a program provides culturally diverse experiences for children (Carreón, Drake, and Barton 2005; Swadener 2000). Mick Coleman (1997, 17) clarifies the goal, assumptions, and shared purpose of family-school partnerships in Figure 14.1.

Benefits for Children

Families are the most significant people in young children's lives, and home life is the primary source of their learning. Families possess funds of knowledge (Moll et al. 1991) that include subtle and not-so-subtle ways of being, ranging from language and culture to personal tendencies and preferences. Early childhood educators who

THOUGHT QUESTION Spend a few hours walking around the neighborhood of the early childhood program where you work or go to school. Try to notice things that you may have missed in the rush of your daily life. Record the contact information of a few programs, services, or friendly merchants you might find useful for your work with children and their families.

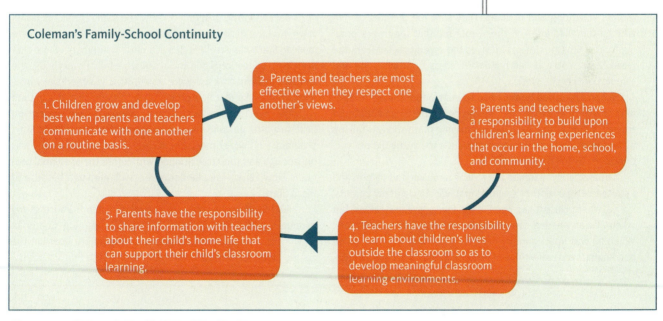

Coleman's Family-School Continuity

1. Children grow and develop best when parents and teachers communicate with one another on a routine basis.

2. Parents and teachers are most effective when they respect one another's views.

3. Parents and teachers have a responsibility to build upon children's learning experiences that occur in the home, school, and community.

4. Teachers have the responsibility to learn about children's lives outside the classroom so as to develop meaningful classroom learning environments.

5. Parents have the responsibility to share information with teachers about their child's home life that can support their child's classroom learning.

Figure 14.1 *Coleman's Family-School Continuity*
The goal is to establish family-school continuity by providing mutually supportive and inviting environments that challenge children to learn and practice positive life skills. This goal is based upon the assumptions above.
From: Coleman 1997, 17

At the time of my deployment to Iraq, I was a single soldier with a one-year-old baby boy, Ellisjah. At that time I was in the Active Guard/Reserve assigned to the 1123rd Transportation Company, Blytheville, Arkansas. Our unit was alerted at 6 p.m. on February 10, 2003, and in less than 72 hours, we were headed for Baghdad. I had only two days to get everything ready. I gave my parents complete guardianship for Ellisjah's health care and education. I left my child, my home, and my bills in my mom's care and was gone for approximately eighteen months. After three months of training, we were in Iraq for 410 days. I know the number to the day.

At my request, my mom enrolled Ellisjah in Early Head Start. He attended Head Start on the college campus where my mom was an instructor. I recommended Head Start because of my familiarity with the program. I was a Head Start teacher for the Mississippi County, Arkansas Economic Opportunity Commission (MCAEOC) Program from 1998 through 2000. I knew it was what I wanted for Ellisjah although I had no opportunity to enroll him myself.

While I was gone, I wrote him every day, letters and postcards, and I would call when I could so he would know my voice. I sent back pictures of me in uniform, and the teachers posted them in the Head Start classroom. Ellisjah knew who I was, but he didn't know our relationship. My parents were "Mom" and "Dad." They were actively involved in the Head Start program. They went to parent conferences. The teachers made home visits to them.

While deployed, I received two care packages from the Head Start program. They sent more, but I never received them. The first was a parent packet with Ellisjah's handprints and his attempts at writing and drawing. They sent me pictures of him with all the children. And they wrote me that they were praying for me. On Christmas, I received the second packet from the Head Start center. It had handmade cards from everyone and samples of Ellisjah's work.

When I returned home, I had to reintroduce myself to Ellisjah as his mother. When I left, he was on the bottle and not toilet trained. When I came back, he was turning three and was talking in sentences and potty trained. Needless to say, he did not recognize me as the nurturer.

I immediately assumed the role of caregiver and parent, and I started being a mother again. At first, we stayed at my parents' house, where Ellisjah had been living. I wasn't really jealous, but when Ellisjah needed something, he naturally ran to my mom. When he was upset and my mom held him and when he called her "Mom," I did feel a tinge of jealousy. I said, "We have a house.

We're going home. He's going to have to get used to me being his mother."

It was rough at first. Ellisjah didn't sleep as well. But we were able to become mother and son again. I have my own business, so my schedule allowed me to spend solid quality time with him during the day.

Through it all, Head Start has been a support system for our family. It's been the most consistent

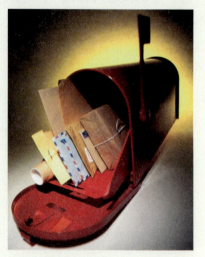

Letters and child care during a time of war

thing in Ellisjah's life since age one. Head Start offered numerous support programs and opportunities for my parents and me to partner with them for a happy, healthy child.

Since it was April when I came home, I was there for the end-of-year activities. I invited the class to take a tour of my unit, and the children got to see the big trucks we used in Iraq. I volunteered in the classroom and became a member of the Policy Council. I knew the importance of parent involvement. For a successful program you need collaboration. I wanted Ellisjah to see me as an active Head Start mom.

I believe in the program. I know the staff. This is my home town. And, we're co-laborers for a cause. I knew the level of care in Head Start was excellent. It's a family environment where children learn educational and social skills. It's full of everybody. The children in Ellisjah's class were Asian, African American, white, and Latino. I like that he's grown up with them all and is in tune with the diversity that exists among people. I have since given birth to a little girl, and she is actively enrolled in the Head Start program. I initially enrolled her in Early Head Start when she was old enough and then transitioned with her to the preschool program. Now Ellisjah is in kindergarten, well prepared because of Head Start.

Head Start and I continue our relationship because of my daughter, Jelisa, who attends the NIBCO Learning Center in Blytheville. I serve as the president for the parent board at the center. I look forward to a rewarding future with this program.

can draw upon these funds of knowledge can care for and educate children in ways that make sense to and are comfortable for children. Infants and toddlers, in particular, rely on the adults in their lives to take care of their most basic needs and to communicate with one another to meet those needs in a consistent manner (Brazelton 1984). Continuity between home and school and strong relationships between families and teachers maximize children's learning at all ages.

Research studies indicate a link between parent involvement during early childhood and a child's later educational accomplishments (Rockwell, Andre, and Hawley 1996). The benefits appear to be greater the earlier the parent involvement begins and in programs that offer multiple types of, and frequent opportunities for, family participation (Powell 1989).

Benefits and Challenges for Families

Organizations ranging from NAEYC to the national PTA recognize the benefits of family involvement in children's educational lives (Rockwell, Andre, and Hawley 1996). Families can feel isolated raising their children and may welcome opportunities to connect with other adults and learn more about children. Relationships with early childhood programs can relieve some of the stress in families' lives. Often, families can learn new strategies or ways of being with their child as they observe or hear about how their child interacts in a group setting where relationships differ from those at home. Research indicates that a positive connection with teachers can raise parents' confidence (Powell 1989).

However, relationships with teachers can be emotionally fraught for various reasons. Some families worry that their child will feel closer to the teacher or that the teacher will know more about their child than they do. Teachers can address these feelings and let family members know that they do not want to usurp the parental role (Katz 2000).

Families may steer away from contact with the school or program for other reasons, such as the need to work or to care for other family members. Some feel guilty about not spending enough time with their children. Others may have had unpleasant experiences that left them distrustful of schools. In some cultures, parents expect to defer to teachers' expertise (Valdez 1996) and are bewildered when the teacher wants their opinions. Cultural or socioeconomic disparities between parents and teachers can make it challenging to establish respectful relationships. More often than not, however, parents are grateful for what you contribute to their children's learning and development.

Benefits and Challenges for Teachers

Remember Sal Vascellero's Real Voice in Chapter 13? Sal unexpectedly learned about curriculum and about his class when he welcomed a mother into his room. Families are a child's first teacher and can put their child's development into a context. Perhaps one of the children in your class was never shy before this year. How would you find out that information on your own?

Beyond the teacher and the classroom, the school or program benefits from the richness of cultural traditions and the range of skills that families bring to family-school partnerships. Family members have a lot to offer in decision-making roles on parent-teacher committees and boards and, at times, in shared leadership.

THOUGHT QUESTION What might you do as a teacher (perhaps unknowingly) that could make a family member feel that you are encroaching on his or her parental role? What could you do to correct that perception?

Families may steer away from contact with the school or program for other reasons, such as the need to work or to care for other family members.

Many beginning teachers express discomfort about working with family members, and this is natural. After all, most people don't decide to become early childhood teachers because they love working with adults! Teachers, too, may have multiple personal responsibilities and little time for communicating with parents beyond the school day. Teachers may be reluctant to work with parents who appear distant, resistant, or hostile. Sometimes, being younger or having less experience with children than a family member can make you feel insecure. Alternatively, you might feel put on the spot as the "expert." In a partnership, however, a teacher and a family member are both secure enough to share their knowledge and thinking with one another.

New teachers often feel unnerved when anyone observes their work with children—most people don't like the fishbowl feeling—and are particularly unsettled when parents are in the classroom. Some feel anxious during parent-teacher conferences. The more you get to know parents as individuals, however, the less you may feel this way. Think back to what you learned about mentalizing abilities in Chapter 6 as you read the following story:

> Four-year-old Olivia's teachers hesitated to tell her mother that Olivia had wet her pants again for fear that Olivia's mother would punish her harshly, as she had before. Olivia was still upset when her mother came to pick her up. The teachers made time to sit down with Olivia's mother to listen to how she felt about Olivia's accidents and to ask her how she thought Olivia might have felt when this accident happened.

These teachers went beyond explaining to Olivia's mother why they hoped she would not punish Olivia. They reached out to help Olivia's mother imagine her child's feelings or mental state. They were not doing therapy, but they helped a parent put herself in her child's emotional shoes. Asking parents to think about the possible reasons for their child's behavior can be more helpful than providing advice that may not be grounded in the family context.

Few if any teacher preparation programs provide direct experiences with families. Although fieldwork students are rarely in a position to relay information to families or to discuss problems with them, as a student you can spend time with families, interview family members for course assignments, and observe carefully to expand your knowledge about family partnerships while you learn about children and early childhood education.

FAMILY DIVERSITIES

What factors contribute to families' different situations?

What do we mean when we say "family"? In this book, we mean the people who surround the child, usually at home, and who love and care for the child. Someone may be part of a child's family without being biologically or legally related to the child. We cannot represent every type of family here. Rather, we strive for ways to think about the wide diversity of families in which the children in your program may live, with the goal of not making assumptions about any family.

Like teaching, being in a family is all about relationships. Before thinking about the specifics of a family's situation, consider that becoming a parent is something which, "by definition, changes an individual through relations with others" (Shanok 1990, 1). The person

Home visits can develop intimacy between families and teachers. This teacher and parent discuss a child's toilet learning progress in the moment!

who is called a parent is not always the one who is involved in the daily role or intimacy of caregiving.

What do we need to know about a child's family in order to understand the child and her daily needs? Various factors contribute to every family's situation. These include adult work issues; languages spoken in the home; income levels; family mobility; family members present in or absent from the home; and health, disability, and housing. Most teachers start the school year with only superficial knowledge about each child's family, and families can change over the course of a year, often just as you think you have come to know them. Whether temporary or not, circumstances based on these factors will likely affect a child's persona in the classroom. The details of each family's situation are unique, and children and families attach individualized meaning to circumstances (Katz 2000).

The increasing complexity of contemporary family life has a pervasive impact on parent connections to early childhood programs (Wasow 2000). Families who face ongoing stresses may have little time or energy to talk with teachers or participate in program activities. Other family members may be so available—to accompany the class on every trip, for example—that they seem to log as many classroom hours as part-time teachers. Teachers and programs need to be responsive to the realities of all families' lives, regardless of the amount or quality of their school participation.

Ethnicity, "Race," and Socioeconomic Class

Many American families face inequities and prejudice due to their race, ethnicity, and/or socioeconomic class. Throughout the history of the United States, African Americans have experienced **institutional racism,** discrimination entrenched in societal structures such as government, schools, and health care. African Americans also experience cultural and individual racism based on claims of the superiority of one group over another (Derman-Sparks and Phillips 1997). Immigrant families face increased bigotry due to attitudes about immigration and efforts to reform immigration policy (Hardy 2007). Especially since 2001, Muslim families, or those perceived to be Muslim, often face discrimination (Mubarak 2006).

Parents of color often encounter discrimination at work and in other settings. Consequently, some may be distrustful of early childhood programs, which may remind them of other situations in which they may not have been treated respectfully. Early childhood educators can work against racism together with the families and children in their programs and schools. Together, the adults can unlearn "patterns of racist thoughts and actions" (Derman-Sparks and Phillips 1997, 23). Among other activities, they can become aware of their respective identities in a racist society, examine interracial encounters they have had, and explore ways of fighting institutionalized racism.

With increased interethnic marriage and childbearing and transracial adoption, there are more children and families of mixed ethnicity (Wardle and Cruz-Janzen 2003). Parents and children in multiethnic families face decisions about how to define and describe themselves as well as confusion or misunderstandings about their ethnicity when they interact with the outside world (Tatum 2003;

Like teaching, being a parent changes who you are through your relations with others.

THOUGHT QUESTION Doris, a mother serving a five-year prison sentence, is still her three children's parent. During Doris's incarceration, however, Doris's mother does the daily caregiving. She is the one who has day-to-day relationships with the children's teachers, with other children and their parents, and with the children themselves. If you were the teacher or caregiver for one of Doris's children, how might you honor both Doris and Doris's mother?

THOUGHT QUESTION The media gave widespread coverage to a serious racial incident among adults at your school. Parents, teachers, and community members are discussing the incident in many venues, but you haven't heard your second graders talking about the incident. Should you raise the issue in morning meeting? What will guide your thinking? How would you include families?

Figure 14.2 *Selected Multiracial Children's Books*

Selected Multiracial Children's Books

Adoff, Arnold. 1973/2004. *Black is brown is tan.* New York: HarperCollins.

Bang, Molly. 1996. *Goose.* New York: Scholastic. (Especially for preschoolers)

Gillespie, Peggy, and Gigi Kaeser. 1994. Of many colors: *Portraits of multiracial families.* Amherst: University of Massachusetts Press.

Kissinger, Katie, and Werhner Krutein. 1997. *All the colors we are. Todos los colores de piel.* The story of how we get our skin color. St. Paul, MN: Red Leaf Press.

Van Gulden and Bartels-Rabb 1995). Early childhood educators can learn from family members how to support the child's identity as a multiracial individual and can share resources and information with the family. Books (Figure 14.2) are a wonderful way to introduce diverse familiesinto any classroom.

Socioeconomic status is perhaps the greatest determinant of a U.S. family's life experiences (*The New York Times* and Keller 2005). Certainly, that status plays a large role in determining which early childhood programs are available to children and families. Families' socioeconomic status shapes their values and beliefs about child rearing and schooling (Lareau 2003). Instead of assuming that families understand school customs and procedures, take the time to be explicit about school expectations. Such clarity helps all families (Delpit 1995). Teachers who have not faced similar experiences may not be aware of the extent to which families may feel alienated, marginalized, and disempowered (Mac Naughton 2003; Sturm 1997). Program staff members who listen carefully and with respect will find it easier to build relationships with families who may be distrustful of the program for whatever reason.

> **Socioeconomic status is perhaps the greatest determinant of a U.S. family's life experiences.**

Linguistic Diversity and Culture

A program whose staff reflects the linguistic diversity of the families can communicate both orally and in writing in the language the family understands best. But in settings of great diversity, that is not always possible. In that case, centers and schools can reach into the community for cultural and language interpreters. Often, parents who do not speak the same language(s) as the teachers will bring someone to school with them who does. Whenever possible, this is preferable to making young children function in this adult role.

A starting point for an authentic school-family partnership is the understanding that no language is superior to another. Teachers communicate their appreciation of language in general and of the families' linguistic heritages in particular when they learn key phrases in children's home languages or, better yet, attempt to gain some proficiency in the languages of the families with whom they work. At one program, a father provided a list of twenty Portuguese words that the staff tacked next to the sink so that they could help two-year-old Manuela feel more comfortable as she made the transition from home to center.

THOUGHT QUESTION List at least five beliefs and practices that your family holds about eating, bedtime, education and school, behavior, and discipline. Find a partner in class who differs in at least one family practice, and share your perspectives about the significance of the practice in your families.

During their parent group, newcomer families created this poster expressing their reasons for wanting to learn English.

Throughout this book we emphasize that the tremendous heterogeneity among human beings requires us to refrain from making assumptions. Even so, members of any culture do share beliefs and practices. The extent to which families express those beliefs and practices depends on many factors, such as their degree of acculturation and how long they have been in the United States.

Fathers

Until recently, research on parenting focused predominantly on mothers. A host of factors, however, including the need for two breadwinners, has caused fathers to play more complex and diverse roles. Rather than discussing "father absence," researchers now investigate the roles that men do play in children's lives. One study, for example, has shown that of the young children who do not have regular contact with their biological fathers, approximately one-third to one-half (by maternal report) do have an ongoing relationship with a man who plays a fatherly role (Black, Dubowitz, and Starr 1999).

Fathers' roles are changing. Many fathers now are responsible for dropping their young children off at child care centers and elementary schools, and, according to 2005 data, approximately 143,000 men in the United States are stay-at-home

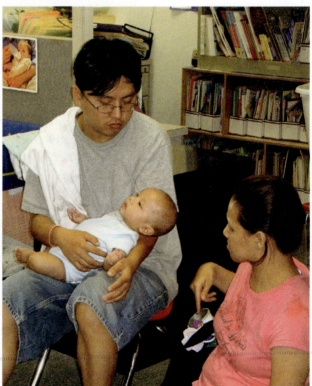

Greater numbers of men are taking on caregiving roles, providing us with a richer and more diverse concept of nurturance.

fathers (U.S. Census Bureau 2006). Given these new roles and responsibilities, Jason Downer (2007, 330) asks, "What is the contemporary definition of father?" and documents three categories:

- Cohabiting fathers—fathers who live in the family
- Nonresidential biological fathers—fathers who don't live in the family
- Social fathers—men who have fathering roles with children

These categories point to the variety of ways that children experience men in their lives, sometimes, as with children in blended families, in more than one way.

Family Configurations

Family configuration refers to the structural makeup of the family—in other words, to the people who are integral parts of the family. Labels that identify these configurations include nuclear and extended families; single-parent households (including parents who have separated or divorced); adoptive and foster families; and **blended families,** in which biologically unrelated children live together with their parents and stepparents as a family. Any family can fit more than one category, family configurations change over time, and each configuration has different meanings for a given family.

Our best route as early childhood professionals is to find out how families define themselves and to respect their self-definitions (Wardle and Cruz-Janzen 2003). For example, a mother who has recently separated from her husband may view her family as a two-parent one, while a mother whose husband is temporarily absent during military service may define herself as a single parent. Some children in blended families call their new parent mommy or daddy, while others use the new parent's first name. Thus, the circumstances (as the parent(s) and child describe them), how they affect the child, how the family functions, and how they view their functioning are more important than a label.

You may not meet everyone whom the child considers a family member. Some families may be guarded about sharing information because of social taboos or legal ramifications. A lesbian mother may be reluctant to reveal that the woman who picks up her child is her life partner. An immigrant family with undocumented members might not be forthcoming about certain of its family members. And some families simply don't share what they believe to be private information.

Nuclear families and extended families

During the middle of the twentieth century, the nuclear family, comprised of two parents and their children, was popularized in various media and came to be considered the norm. According to 2004 Census data, 70 percent of U.S. children still live with two parents (Kreider 2007). Although the two-parent family is not as common as in previous decades, it remains the standard to which many young children may consciously or unconsciously compare themselves (Heilman 2008). When two parents are in synch with each other and provide a loving home to a child, a nuclear family offers security for children's development—but so can other family configurations.

Many of today's children's great-grandparents grew up in **extended families,** living with various relatives as well as with their parents. This may still be the case for some children, and for some of them, grandparents and others play even more of a parental role than they did in the past. Despite the support that extended families can provide, interactions with them can be stressful for parents, for example, when they disagree about child rearing or do not have enough space.

> Some families may be guarded about sharing information because of social taboos or legal ramifications, so you may not meet everyone whom the child considers a family member.

Finally, today many grandparents live far away from their adult children and grandchildren. They may be in another country or in the family's hometown, while the young family lives in a city. Loss of roots and family ties can weigh heavily on young families. When extended family members are not immediately available, a family may seek your advice about children's developmental issues.

Single-parent households and divorce

Some adults today choose to raise a child alone, and others are single as the result of separation, divorce, or death of a spouse. Whatever the reason, a substantial number of the children in your class could be from single-parent homes. In 2005, approximately 22 million children, or about one-third of all children in the United States, lived with a single parent (Shore 2005).

When parents are separating or divorcing, you may be in a delicate position, not wanting to be perceived as forming an alliance with one parent over the other. As you read in Chapter 3, any loss is serious and should not be glossed over, least of all with children. The significant number of children from divorced families today makes divorce less of a stigma than it was fifty years ago, but younger children still feel guilty: they fear having caused the problems between their parents—and, as they mature, often feel responsible for the superhuman task of reuniting their parents.

Giving some thought to the stresses involved in single-parent child rearing, even with help from family or friends, can help you think of ways to be supportive of single parents. As with any family, begin by asking how you can be helpful. Arranging transportation to and from the program might be the biggest challenge for one family, whereas helping the children keep their homework and book bags straight might be at the top of the list for a single mother of three. In situations of separation and divorce, clarify both parents' roles, including who is, and who is not, allowed to pick up the child every day. Figure 14.3 suggests some ways of helping parents (particularly single parents), but keep in mind that you cannot be all things to all parents.

Grandparents continue to provide support for developing families—sometimes via the Internet, but especially when they live close by, as with this extended family.

Lesbian- and gay-headed families

All children and all families face the challenge of integrating their family experience with the expectations and values of the wider society (Tasker and Golombek 1997). The wider the disparity between societal norms and the family experience, the harder this integration can be. For many families, including lesbian- and gay-headed families, early care and education represents the first step as a family into public society.

A child portrays her single-parent family.

Suggestions for Supporting Single, Separated, and Divorced Parents

1. Simplify the communication process: find out whether, for example, email, a phone call, or a note home is the best approach.

2. Find out which adults currently live in the child's household.

3. Inquire about visitation schedules. What does the family want you to know about the transitions between homes?

4. Determine your school's policy about child care during back-to-school night. If child care is not possible, help a group of parents who live near each other provide child care for each other.

5. Collaborate with working parents to devise ways for them to visit the classroom.

6. If there are many single-parent families in your school or center, find ways for them to support each other.

Figure 14.3 *Suggestions for Supporting Parents*

For many families, including lesbian- and gay-headed families, early care and education represents the first step as a family into public society.

As families take this step, their child's teacher needs language to use with children and other families. Most young children tend to be forgiving of difference. "Two mommies" or "two daddies" sounds like fun to most young children from heterosexual families. However, using the word *lesbian* or *gay* early on provides a foundational understanding about two people of the same sex who love each other. Teachers and children can later draw on such understandings, which is crucial in schools where children may face an onslaught of homophobic terms on the playground as early as first grade.

The early childhood years are a good time to help children understand that many family structures exist. One teacher remarked that, during circle time when a child asked how Kyle was born with two mothers and no dad, she wished she could call an 800 number to find out how to respond (Casper and Schultz 1999). One way to address subjects like these is to include family visits in the curriculum. Kyle's moms are the best ones to explain how Kyle came to be and would only volunteer what they are comfortable saying. At the same time, you need to consider ahead of time what difficult questions children might ask, so that you can prepare yourself to respond to "surprise" questions. You and your director or principal can discuss school policies on topics that some families may consider controversial. Letting families know at the outset the kinds of issues you plan to address during the year helps them anticipate questions at home and gives them the chance to discuss their questions with you individually.

Sometimes children themselves disclose the family structure. When teachers make it clear (at curriculum night, in letters home, through the curriculum itself) that the school welcomes all families, families of all kinds are more likely to be open about who they are and what they want for their children.

A group of children painted this portrait of a two-mother family.

Adoptive and foster families

In the United States alone, approximately 1.5 million children live in adoptive families (Evan Donaldson Adoption Institute 2008), and more than 500,000 children live with foster care families (American Academy of Child and Adolescent Psychiatry 2005). Children are adopted through public (child welfare systems) or private agencies, and both systems help children move into kinship settings with extended family members when the child's immediate parents are not able or not alive to care for them. Foster care is organized through the child welfare system, and children in foster care and their foster families usually receive services and support.

Some adoptions are domestic; others are international. Any adoption may be transracial. Stepparents may legally adopt their children depending on family circumstances, and in the past twenty years, second-parent adoptions have become a method for non-birth parents in lesbian- and gay-headed households to become legal guardians of their children.

Many people think that children begin to seek their roots only in early adolescence, but adoption and foster care, like other issues, are issues that grow with the child. Sensitivity to children's and parents' feelings about these situations is crucial. Checking with parents before giving family-related assignments demonstrates your awareness of adoption and foster care issues and shows that you are considering *all* the families in your classroom. Asking children to bring in stories of themselves as babies or family histories can wreak havoc in some homes and make some adopted children anxious. For a sampling of the rich body of children's literature on adoption and what it means to be adopted, see Figure 14.4.

THOUGHT QUESTION Imagine that you work in a second grade classroom where, to your knowledge, no children come from lesbian- or gay-headed households. Nevertheless, from time to time you circulate a few books about children with gay parents. You notice that Lance repeatedly returns to these books. When you mention it to him, Lance tells you that his father, whom you assumed to be a heterosexual single father, is gay. How would you respond to Lance? What else, if anything, might you do?

Resources on Adoption

Literature for Children 	Caines, Jeanette, and Steven Kellogg. 1984. *Abby.* New York: Harper Trophy. (includes sibling relationships)
	Colabucci, Lesley, and Matthew D. Conley. 2008. What makes a family? Representations of adoption in children's literature. In *Other kinds of families: Embracing diversity in schools,* ed. Tammy Turner-Vorbeck and Monica Miller Marsh, 139–159. New York: Teachers College Press.
	Kitze, Carrie A. 2003. *I don't have your eyes.* Illus. Rob Williams. Warren, NJ: EMK Press. (young children questioning why they don't look like their adoptive parents)
	Koehler, Phoebe. 1990. *The day we met you.* New York: Simon and Schuster. (for very young children)
	Schreck, Karen H. 2001. *Lucy's family tree.* Illus. Stephen Gassler III. Gardiner, ME: Tilbury House. (best for children of primary school age)
	Turner, Ann. 1990. *Through moon and stars and night skies.* New York: Harper Trophy. (a book about international adoption—best for young children)
Electronic Sources of Information, Support, and Statistics for Parents and Teachers	Center for Adoption Research: http://www.umassmed.edu/adoption/index.aspx Child Welfare Information Gateway: http://www.childwelfare.gov/adoption/ ECAP Collaborative: http://ecap.crc.uiuc.edu/ Evan B. Donaldson Adoption Institute: http://www.adoptioninstitute.org/index.php Future of Children: http://www.futureofchildren.org/ 

Figure 14.4 *Resources on Adoption*

KNOWING ABOUT FAMILIES

What do early childhood educators need to know about families?

Some early childhood professionals believe that family configurations and situations are none of their business. Indeed, teachers don't need to know everything that happens in a family. But many family configurations and situations have direct or indirect impact on children. In these cases, teachers can work with the child more responsively if they understand the child's home life. When you gather information or when a family member reveals personal information:

- respect the family member's right to privacy,
- use tact and discretion,
- maintain confidentiality and share information about families only with professionals who need it to do their jobs.

Early childhood educators perpetually face the tension between respecting privacy and soliciting information in an effort to establish a closer relationship with family members (Katz 2000).

THOUGHT QUESTION Imagine that you told a good friend at work something private about your life. How would you feel if you found out that your friend violated your trust and told others at work about this private issue?

Will This Information Help My Work with Children?

Do you need to know the family's circumstances to know the child more deeply, and to care for and teach the child better? To answer this question, try to distinguish between what you are curious about and *would like* to know and what you *need* to know.

Usually the age of the child affects the need to know. For instance, moving to a new home (with a new toilet!) will affect a toddler who is potty training differently than it will a first or second grader, who might be upset about leaving friends. Parents can help teachers determine whether family situations such as a move are relevant to the child's life in the early childhood program.

Most teachers gather family information through conversation with parents or from a form parents fill out when the child enters the class or program that asks questions such as, "Who are the important people in the child's life?" or "Has anything happened recently that might affect the child's life at school?" Parents who are uncomfortable with face-to-face interactions or who don't speak the same language as the teacher may prefer completing a written form. Others may prefer talking to writing.

Finding Optimal Distance

Discerning appropriate professional boundaries can be tricky. For instance, what about babysitting for a child in the program over the weekend? In some instances, these are personal decisions; in others, program policies frame and limit teacher interactions with family members (Lawrence-Lightfoot 2003; Rockwell, Andre, and Hawley 1996).

The notion of **optimal distance** (Foley 1994) offers guidance for weighing personal decisions about professional boundaries. Finding optimal distance means aiming to be neither too close (pals) nor too distant (cold and unsharing), but rather finding a reasonable balance.

Because we all bring our previous experiences with us, parents or teachers may overreact to an issue that recalls something from their past. Such powerful feelings are often unconscious and not immediately apparent to the individual. When you

Finding optimal distance means aiming to be neither too close nor too distant, but rather finding a reasonable balance.

have strong feelings about a situation with a child or family, consider possible interfering influences. Recognizing such feelings and thinking about how they might affect your actions in this setting is challenging. Revisit Elaine's Real Voice in Chapter 9 to review how a teacher sorted through her past to identify how her own history clouded her view of a child.

Recognizing and Building on Family Strengths

Today, early childhood educators can honor ways of raising children that differ from white middle-class parenting practices; however, the field of early childhood education has a long history of creating programs intended to compensate for family "disadvantages" or "deprivations." Aimed primarily at low-income families, these programs assumed that children in these families were "at risk" (Swadener 2000) without emphasizing that families always have "promise" as well. By instead taking an open approach and exchanging information and views with families, early childhood educators can honor the strengths of all families.

ESTABLISHING RELATIONSHIPS WITH FAMILIES

How do early childhood educators establish relationships with families?

In their interactions with families, early childhood professionals discuss major life events such as birth, death, parental relationships, and separations. They delight in children's many achievements and seek explanations when children behave in ways that are difficult to understand. Some specific approaches can help early childhood educators to develop relationships with families that are founded on trust.

Building Trust

If family members or teachers feel misunderstood, unheard, or disrespected, they can't trust one another. Establishing trusting relationships requires hard work and time, but without trust, there can be no authentic connection between family members and teachers (Casper and Schultz 1999; Lawrence-Lightfoot 2003; Stern 2003).

Relationships between early childhood professionals and families develop through hundreds of small interactions. These relationships evolve as parents and teachers greet one another in the morning or evening, send notes between home and school, and sit across from one another at parent-teacher conferences. That makes all of these interactions worthy of your close attention, no matter how insignificant they may seem. For instance, the sensitivity with which a teacher greets a harried mother every morning can be just as important as the way in which she presents her observations of the child's behavior during a parent-teacher conference.

THOUGHT QUESTION Imagine that you have much in common with the mother of a child in your class. You are about the same age, you are both single parents, and you enjoy the same music and sports. You have to work hard in the mornings at drop-off to give equal attention to the other family members in the classroom. One day this mother invites you to a concert of a singer you have always wanted to hear perform. What should you think about before you respond?

THOUGHT QUESTION Seven-year-old Pedro's mother, Marisela, is a young single parent. She brings Pedro to school in the morning but is usually in a hurry. When it is time for parent-teacher conferences, she always has to check with her job first. Pedro's grandmother picks him up at school, holding a baby she watches. His grandmother doesn't speak English, and Marisela has told you that Pedro sleeps at his grandmother's house at least one or two nights a week when she has evening classes. What else do you need to know about Marisela and Pedro to avoid characterizing Pedro's life in terms of "deficits" instead of in a way that includes his family's strengths?

Our individual
personalities
affect our
communication
style, but
guidelines
make for better
practice and can
assist teachers
in everyday
interactions with
parents.

Approaches to Working with Families

As we all know, communication is at the heart of relationships. Communication with a family member is an intricate dance that varies with each individual. Different situations also call for different approaches. Still, some principles apply to all interactions with families, whether written or oral. Note that *respect* and *trust* are central to all of these principles.

- Respect a family's beliefs, values, and attitudes about child rearing and learning, yet be honest about communicating your own.
- Honor family members' perspectives on the child. Let the family know that you welcome information about the child that will be helpful to you in the classroom.
- Respect a family's choices and decisions about the child, and, whenever possible, make decisions about the child's school life in a collaborative manner.
- Avoid assumptions or judgments about the family, their feelings, and their responses.

Our individual personalities affect our communication style, but certain guidelines make for better practice and can assist teachers in everyday interactions with parents, as well as in particular ones, such as parent-teacher conferences. As you gain more experience with families and take further coursework, you will develop your own personal communication style.

Teachers may already include in their ways of speaking and listening some approaches that demonstrate respect for families, but they may need to learn or practice others. Consider whether you:

- express interest in and caring about situations that affect individual family members or the family as a whole—for example, recovery from an illness;
- are sensitive to culturally based communication styles—for example, limited eye contact or not shaking hands;
- remain aware of the parents' perspective—for example, understand that parents are partial to their own children and sometimes hold unrealistic ideas about a child's talents or accomplishments or the amount of attention a teacher can give to one child;
- are responsive to parents' reactions—for example, the intensity of a parent's feelings about the child and fear or anxiety about problems;
- control any personal reactions that may create conflict with parents—for example, defensiveness or attempts to prove your expertise.

Whether presenting curriculum at a back-to-school night or informally interacting with parents at a potluck dinner, teachers need to listen closely and articulate their positions well. In the following sections we cover two time-tested communication approaches: active listening and third space. While you also can implement them or their underlying principles with both children and colleagues, they are particularly helpful for work with families.

Active listening
Verbal communication is a back-and-forth dance of speaking and listening, accompanied by nonverbal gestures. Using **active listening,** a teacher

- concentrates on what the family member says;
- takes in and thinks about what she hears and sees;
- communicates nonverbally that she is listening;
- maintains eye contact, nods, and may murmur "uh huh" to acknowledge that she is focusing on what the family member is saying;
- takes into consideration what she knows about the parent and child and recent observations of the child's behavior;
- examines how her biases or assumptions might shape her interpretations of the parent's statements;
- asks for clarification whenever she is unsure of the family member's meaning;
- restates or paraphrases what the parent said to check her understanding;
- asks clarifying questions and draws out additional information; and
- summarizes what she has heard.

As he meets with a parent, this teacher uses active listening to make sure they communicate well. When problems arise that seem impossible to resolve, he uses third space.

Active listening is a powerful way to convey caring and respect for the other person's point of view (Rockwell, Andre, and Hawley 1996). It does not require an immediate response to what the family member tells or asks you. You can always say, "I have to think about that. Can I get back to you later this week?"

Third space

When two perspectives seem to be contradictory or irreconcilable, **third space** offers a way to step back, consider alternatives, and rekindle communication (Barrera and Corso 2003). Ideally, this approach allows the participants in a dialogue to go beyond their differences, to create a new space in which differences are complementary rather than divisive. Third space can be a **habit of mind**—a regular way of approaching many situations, not only those of conflict.

Isaura Barrera and Robert Corso (2003) recommend these third-space considerations:

- Avoid the natural inclination to focus on solutions or resolutions.
- Listen and observe without judgment.
- Identify specific tension points.
- Recognize that one perspective doesn't need to be wrong for another to be right.
- Shift the conversation's focus to equalize participation.
- Explore how contradictory behaviors or perspectives could be complementary.
- Trust the possibility of options that honor diversity.

Consider how Becca, a teacher in an infant-toddler program at a high school, created a third space with Alice and Michael, the first-time teen parents of 21-month-old James:

THOUGHT QUESTION In class, choose a partner, and take turns telling each other a five-minute story about your lives. After you have told your story, have your partner share what she heard, without injecting her thoughts or feelings about the story's content. How difficult is it for you to listen actively? What might you do to improve your listening skills?

Early in the year, Becca noticed that James had motor and speech delays, did not relate well to other children, and clung to teachers during transitions. Becca shared her observations and concerns with the mental health consultant and the director, and they agreed that James should be evaluated. When Becca proposed the evaluation to James's parents, Michael replied, "There's nothing wrong with my son, and we're not taking him to any doctor."

Over the next few weeks, Becca invited Alice to visit before her 10 a.m. class. Although Michael had given Becca the cold shoulder, as Alice spent more time at the program, she began to see that her son functioned at a different level from many of the other children in the room. She, too, became concerned and tried to talk to Michael, but he refused to discuss the subject. Finally, in December, Becca and her director asked Alice and Michael to plan for a lot of time to talk at the mid-year parent conference.

Becca began by saying that there was no one right or wrong solution, and that they might leave the meeting with *no* solution. This was a time for everyone to think together and share what they knew about James.

After Becca and Alice spoke about James, Michael was quiet for a few minutes. Usually a man of few words, Michael now let out a long string of fears about his son. He talked about his younger brother, Gavin, who had been placed in "Special Ed" at an early age, and how other children had made fun of him. An avid athlete, Michael had tears in his eyes as he asked, "Will James and I do hoops together?" Alice reached across and took Michael's hand. Everyone sat in silence for some time. The director noted that a developmental assessment was not a life sentence but a way to find out if James had developmental issues and, if so, to learn what could help him. Everyone made an appointment to meet again the following week at the same time, shook hands, and thanked each other.

INTERACTIONS WITH FAMILIES

How do early childhood educators and families interact with each other?

Teachers connect with family members in different ways. In some cases, program policy dictates the kinds of interactions that teachers have with families. For instance, some programs encourage parents to spend time in classrooms, while others establish a central drop-off point, such as a play yard, and limit parent participation in the classroom. Likewise, some programs require regular written communication with parents, while others prohibit teachers from giving email addresses or cell phone numbers to parents. As teachers develop their own methods and styles of interacting with families, they balance their personality and comfort level, program policy, the cultural norms of the families in the class, and the needs and personalities of individual parents.

Beginning the School Year

The start of a new school year is a transition for everyone. Most programs establish procedures to orient children and families and to help children adjust to a new class. Families, too, have to adjust to changes in routines and expectations for their children. Teachers may feel nervous about meeting new children and families. What follows are ways to help everyone adjust as well as possible.

Home visits bridge the worlds of home and school. Some teachers relish home visits for the closeness they generate with families and children. Others resist making home visits, perhaps for lack of transportation or because of discomfort at entering an unfamiliar neighborhood. For these and other reasons, some teachers make home visits in pairs. The family and child get to know the team, and one teacher can interact with the child while the second chats with the family. Although home visits are time-consuming, they offer a glimpse into a child's family life that can cement the bond between teacher and child and between the teacher and the family. Home visits are more common in programs that serve infants and toddlers and in Head Start, but they are beneficial in any early childhood setting.

Short school or classroom visits familiarize children and families with new teachers and classroom routines. Some programs encourage parents to bring children for a visit right after they are accepted, or even before, to assess the fit between program and child. Children may have trouble separating from parents, particularly if this is their first program experience, and so teachers usually invite a family member to stay. When children move on to a new class, the transition can go more smoothly if the family and child can spend time in the new classroom with the new teacher. Remember that with regular visits between rooms, children may have an easier time with a transition than their parents!

Phase-in periods gradually introduce children to a new classroom. Some early childhood programs structure the phase-in period so that all children spend a short amount of time at school, often with only a portion of the class. Other programs individualize phase-in for each family. For instance, a family member or other familiar caregiver stays with the child at the program, gradually leaving for longer and longer periods of time. Teachers often use highly individualized methods to support each child and family in this process (Balaban 2006).

During the phase-in period, teachers learn about the child's and parent's styles and about cultural factors that influence the parent's caregiving. Teachers also observe how long it takes for the family to adapt to leaving the child at school, and they assess situational factors that affect the parent's ability to spend time at school. This technique recognizes that adjustments to new situations take time, for both children and parents.

A beneficial side effect of phase-in periods is that family members get to know the teachers and program better when they spend time helping their children acclimate to the new setting. Children can sense their family's satisfaction and comfort with their new out-of-home surroundings. A family's appreciation of that environment and the adults in it usually contributes to children's trust in the teachers and in the program as well.

Back-to-School Nights

Back-to-school, or curriculum, nights provide an opportunity for families to meet teachers and the other families and to learn about the program more formally.

Home visits allow the teacher to see children in their home environment, and children feel a special closeness as they share their prized possessions with their teacher.

Home visits offer a glimpse into a child's family life that can cement the bond between teacher and child and between the teacher and the family.

Typically, teachers present information about the curriculum, classroom routines, and expectations for children and families. Visuals, such as photographs or a slide show of all the children, can help explain classroom goals to parents.

Some teachers feel nervous about talking to a large group and being "on display." Parents, too, might be nervous about attending a formal school meeting or speaking, especially in a group. Some teachers run back-to-school nights in an informal and social manner, so that teachers and parents can get to know one another in a relaxed way. Other schools and centers set up children's activities for families to investigate and discuss what children learn.

Parent-Teacher Conferences

Almost all programs have regularly scheduled parent-teacher conferences, usually twice during the school year, in which teachers interact one-on-one with families. Sara Lawrence-Lightfoot (2003) suggests numerous ways in which teachers can make these conferences meaningful. For instance,

- Start by asking what is on the parent's mind or what the parent has observed about the child's participation in school or his behavior at home.
- Share pieces of a child's writing or drawing to demonstrate her capabilities and approach to work; highlight her strengths, even if there are substantial problems to address.
- Include children in parent-teacher conferences because they are in the best position to bridge the worlds of home and school; children's views are worthy of respect, too.

Consider this parent-teacher conference between Melanie, a first grade teacher, and six-year-old Isaiah's parents, Joy and Derek:

Melanie was eager for this opportunity to discuss Isaiah's disruptive behavior. When Joy and Derek arrived for the first parent-teacher conference of the year, Melanie immediately told them stories about Isaiah's behavior and its negative impact on the other children. At the end of the twenty-minute conference, she had not mentioned one positive thing about Isaiah, nor had she talked about his reading, writing, playing, or any other school experiences. Derek sat stone-faced, and Joy looked silently at her lap.

Derek and Joy's reaction startled and annoyed Melanie. She assumed that they were avoiding dealing with Isaiah's behavior. Then Derek angrily said he couldn't think about Isaiah's behavior right now because for the next two weeks he would be away caring for his dying mother. Suddenly Melanie realized that the parents had other things on their minds. She reacted with sympathy to Derek's situation, saying, "Of course, how can you think about Isaiah's behavior at school at a time like this!" As Joy and Derek got up to leave, she remembered that she hadn't shown them Isaiah's reading log. She felt miserable about ruining any possibility of a relationship with Derek and Joy.

Melanie apologized for monopolizing the conversation, admitted that they had gotten off to a bad start, and suggested that they meet again. She joked that next time Derek and Joy could do all of the talking, and, in a more serious tone, asked about Isaiah's behavior at home. She was pleased to hear how well Isaiah and his cousin played together. Melanie invited Derek and Joy to take home Isaiah's reading log. As they said their good-byes, they all said that they looked forward to a more balanced conversation about Isaiah.

Melanie's meeting with Isaiah's parents illustrates how the parent-teacher conference presents an opportunity for teachers to talk *and* to listen. Active listening and third space offer ways for teachers to communicate effectively during conferences.

Community Gatherings

Informal social events are often the most comfortable school situations for parents. Celebrations or potluck dinners offer families opportunities to get to know other families and teachers without any pressure to discuss children's behavior, curriculum, or other school-related topics. Social gatherings can honor diversity when families share food, music, and customs from one another's culture. When family members are comfortable at social gatherings, they are more likely to connect to the program in other ways, too.

When you plan social gatherings, be sensitive to parents' needs. For instance, parents who work or go to school can probably attend social gatherings only in the evening or on weekends. Most parents of young children will need child care, so either include children in the event or provide child care at school during it. Culturally sensitive early childhood programs schedule events, serve food, and conduct activities taking into account families' religious and cultural observances to ensure that everyone is as comfortable as possible.

Encouraging Families to Volunteer

When family members work with children in the classroom or help out in other ways, they are likely to feel more positive about and trusting of the program. Families whose child-rearing practices and beliefs are similar to those of the program staff are likely to feel the most comfortable in the program and to volunteer readily. Teachers can find ways to make other families at home in the classroom, too.

Volunteering in the classroom

Once family volunteers become familiar with the classroom routines, they begin to understand the teacher's role and goals better (Epstein 2001), and teachers get to know the family better. Family members bring new interests and skills and provide additional adult interactions with children. Parents (like other volunteers) generally want to be engaged in meaningful activities other than sweeping floors or setting up snacks. Parents have vast funds of knowledge (Moll et al. 1991) that they can share with children and teachers. Over time, these positive interactions can engender mutual trust.

Some families don't want to share skills or information, and teachers must respect parents' decisions. Consider how Marianna, a day care center teacher, approached Manuel's parents, Henry and Robert, about visiting the classroom and speaking to the group. The class was studying different kinds of families, and Marianna wanted Henry and Robert to talk about their family. She saw the possibility of the children's discussing gay parents, adoption, and transracial families.

Henry was always in a hurry when he dropped off Manuel, but one morning Marianna intercepted him to ask if he and Robert could visit the class next week. She barely had a chance to explain the purpose of the visit before Henry snapped, "We're not freaks, and you're not going to make us look like we are!" He rushed out the door. He later emailed Marianna to apologize, but he still declined her invitations to visit the class.

Culturally sensitive early childhood programs schedule events taking into account families' religious and cultural observances to ensure that everyone is as comfortable as possible.

Marianna realized that she had skipped steps in establishing a trusting relationship with Henry. For instance, they had not spoken much about Manuel's infancy, and Marianna had made assumptions about the circumstances of his adoption. Henry had never spent time in the classroom. Marianna decided not to pursue having him speak to the class about the family. Instead she replied with an invitation to visit the class informally when he had a chance. She hoped that as Henry got to know her better, he would share information about Manuel's adoption. She also hoped to discover some of his interests that he could share with the class. She considered how she might be more sensitive in asking parents to talk about their families with the class.

Volunteering for the program

Families can support programs in many ways, from helping with office work or constructing shelves to planning major fundraising or social events. Parents can be active members of parent-teacher associations or governing boards. Some program structures, such as parent cooperatives, require extensive volunteering and offer parents a voice in decision making. Parents may feel flattered when a teacher or director asks them to share their skills, but they also may feel put upon. Teachers and program staff need to be sensitive to parents' other obligations or feelings about the program that may limit their ability or willingness to volunteer.

INFORMATION SHARING BETWEEN TEACHERS AND FAMILIES

How do teachers and families share information with each other?

Sharing information is the most fundamental way in which parents and teachers work together in the best interest of the child. When teachers know what is happening in the child's home life, they can better understand some of the child's behavior and make necessary adjustments in teaching and caring for him. When parents know about the child's school life, they too can better understand the child's overall behavior and support his experiences in school with similar routines at home. The age of the child determines, to some extent, the need for consistency between home and school. In the case of infants and toddlers, for whom the basic needs of eating, sleeping, and elimination are an essential part of each day, teachers share information about the length of a nap or success using the toilet, and parents share information about new foods or disruptions in home routines. As children get older, parents and teachers exchange information about social and academic learning experiences. Parents can tell teachers about play-dates with friends or a new interest in frogs, and teachers can tell parents about books read or accomplishments in block building.

Teacher-Initiated Information Exchange

Teachers often seize the moment when they see parents at the beginning or end of the day, hurriedly asking a question or sharing a piece of information. This can be efficient, but unless both the teacher and the parent can shift attention easily, it may be stressful. Many parents and teachers prefer to communicate outside of school hours. A phone call or an email message is usually sufficient to convey information, but a face-to-face meeting can be scheduled if parents and teachers need in-depth conversation or follow-up. In cases where the information to be shared is complicated or may upset the parent, an in-person meeting is preferable, as you will see in the later section on addressing serious issues.

The age of the child determines, to some extent, the need for consistency between home and school.

Families may appreciate unexpected contact with teachers. Harry had no trouble saying good-bye to his mother, Janet, in the morning, but Janet hated leaving her three-year-old and rushing off to work. One day, the teacher, Chantal, waited an hour to be sure Janet had time to settle in at her job and then called to let her know what Harry was doing. "He's gluing cardboard boxes together and making a huge sculpture," Chantal reported. "We're saving it to show you." After several of these calls, Janet and Chantal developed a close working relationship that initially had seemed impossible, given the pressure of Janet's work schedule.

On the other hand, Sandra did not have to be at work until 9:30 and always arrived with 25-month-old Edward at 8:45. On several occasions, Khadijah, the early morning teacher, invited Sandra to join her, Edward, and two other children at the play dough table. Khadijah pointed out Edward's motor skills and heard from Sandra about Edward's early morning routine with his father. Their exchange was relaxed, pleasant, and informative but neither private nor uninterrupted, as other children and their families kept arriving and Khadijah greeted them. This period of time in which Sandra both spoke about and learned about her child also served to enhance her relationship with Khadijah.

Parent-Initiated Information Exchange

The same general principles apply to parent-initiated sharing and requesting of information. If you have strong preferences of particular times to communicate, be explicit with parents about them. For instance, many teachers are too busy with the children to converse with families during the school day or even on arrival. Some teachers prefer to have a note or an email message to give them time to think about whatever the family would like to discuss. Others would rather have a phone conversation. Some teachers protect their evening hours by limiting the times when they will receive phone calls, or they guard their privacy by not giving out their cell phone numbers or email addresses. Many schools set up email accounts so that teacher-parent communication can be separate from teachers' personal lives.

Parent-teacher meetings allow parents to express their pride and concerns, and teachers learn more about the goals of the families whose children they teach.

Sharing School Information with the Whole Group of Parents

Teachers strengthen parents' connections to programs when they regularly share information about what the children are doing. They use many methods to do this, including print or email newsletters, notices posted on doors or bulletin boards, displays of children's work, and photo/text documentation of activities. Some programs mandate particular ways of sharing information. For instance, teachers may be required to send home weekly newsletters or to display particular kinds of work on bulletin boards. Reggio Emilio–influenced programs often use extensive photo/text documentation to share classroom activities or class trips with parents. In order to honor a range of communication styles among parents, teachers use a combination of visual, written, and verbal methods.

ADDRESSING SERIOUS ISSUES

What should teachers remember when they raise concerns with parents?

Sometimes teachers or families are concerned about issues that go beyond simple information sharing—issues that call for serious attention and problem solving. For instance, when a child bites other children every day at school, the situation must be treated as more than an isolated incident. The teacher and parents need to share their observations of the child's behavior, explore possible explanations for the biting, and seek solutions. Since interpretations and attitudes about children's behavior are heavily influenced by cultural background, teachers and parents may have different reactions. For instance, a teacher may be quite alarmed by a child's failure to make eye contact during conversation, while this may be normal in the family's culture.

Teachers should encourage parents to report any significant changes in home life that are likely to affect the child's experience in school. For example, a teacher will better understand a child's sudden inability to focus on academic work if she knows that the father was recently hospitalized after a car accident.

Many serious issues can be challenging to discuss, and teachers or parents may shy away from initiating these conversations. Once the topic has been raised, parents may have a difficult time facing the situation and may be in denial about the problem. Teachers themselves may be resistant to getting involved in conversations about the family's personal life and may dismiss the connection to the child's experience in school. However, as the child care professional, the teacher is responsible for keeping the lines of communication open, no matter how challenging that might be.

Collaborating with Other Professionals

Sometimes the best way to address a troublesome situation is in collaboration with other program staff or with staff from outside agencies. Input from other professionals can help a teacher to determine the severity of an issue before raising it with the parents. If a program has a social worker, psychologist, nurse, learning specialist, or other specialists, they can join meetings with families to help explain issues and to problem-solve. If a teacher suspects abuse or neglect, the expertise and perhaps the presence of other professionals can help her raise questions and follow through with the next steps. If the school doesn't have these professionals on staff, teachers can contact outside agencies.

Input from other professionals can help a teacher to determine the severity of an issue before raising it with the parents.

In some situations, other professionals already are involved in children's and families' lives. For instance, a child with a hearing loss might be working with an audiologist, a speech and language pathologist, and other health professionals. Preschool children who have been diagnosed with special needs often work with a special education itinerant teacher (SEIT) who spends time in the classroom, as well as with other specialists such as occupational therapists. Any important decisions about the child should include input from these professionals, and ideally they should participate in school meetings with parents.

Referrals to Community Agencies and Other Helping Professionals

Some family situations are beyond the scope of the teacher's expertise. Each teacher has to determine his own level of involvement in family situations. Setting limits can be painful when a family seems desperately in need of help, but a teacher may not have enough training to be of real assistance, and sometimes involvement drains time and energy from the classroom as a whole.

Teachers usually feel better about limiting their involvement in family situations if they can refer family members to community agencies or other helping professionals. Some schools maintain lists of these organizations to assist families with housing, health care, counseling, and other needs. Many communities have agencies that operate information and referral services for general or specialized kinds of support. Get to know the community in which your program is located and keep your own list of services that families have used successfully.

SUMMARY

SOME BACKGROUND AND DEFINITIONS
How do partnerships with families differ from parent education and family involvement?
From the start of the kindergarten in the nineteenth century through the advent of Head Start in the middle of the twentieth, programs have tried to educate families about their children and involve them in their children's early education. Partnerships with families differ from both of these approaches because, in a partnership, teachers and families collaborate on equal terms. The program staff members are not the experts, and the program's way of teaching and interacting with children is not the only way. Instead, everyone honors and respects both teachers' and parents' knowledge.

BENEFITS AND CHALLENGES OF TEACHER-FAMILY PARTNERSHIPS
What are the benefits and challenges of teacher-family partnerships?
In a partnership, families can contribute their own deep knowledge of their children to help teachers form a more complete picture of the child. Then they can care for and educate children in ways that make the most sense for the children. Partnerships can link the program to its community and can capitalize on family members' various skills. Families, too, feel less isolated and more confident when they connect with other adults and learn with them about raising their children.

However, some parents worry that their children will become more attached to their teachers than to their family. The need to work or to care for other family members, guilt over not spending more time with their children, or prior unpleasant school experiences may steer families away from relationships with their children's center or school. In some cultures parents expect to defer to the teacher's expertise. Teachers, too, may feel uncomfortable when families observe them or may feel defensive when they sense criticism. Moreover, they may feel unprepared to work with adults.

FAMILY DIVERSITIES

What factors contribute to families' different situations?

A family consists of those people who surround the child, usually at home, and who love and care for the child. Teachers cannot know about every type of family situation; instead, they can learn from each family how it defines itself without making assumptions about any family. Various factors contribute to every family's situation. These include adult work issues; languages spoken in the home; income levels; family mobility; family members present in or absent from the home; discrimination the family has experienced; immigration status; and health, disability, and housing. Families' cultural traditions contribute to their beliefs about child rearing and education. These beliefs, in turn, shape family diversity, as do families' configurations. Men and women have different roles in different families. In some families, extended-family members play active roles, while in others they do not. The many possible family configurations include single parents, adoptive and foster families, blended families, and same-sex parents—and any family can fit more than one category.

KNOWING ABOUT FAMILIES

What do early childhood educators need to know about families?

Teachers don't need to know everything that happens in a family, but many family configurations and situations have direct or indirect impact on children. To test whether information is important for you to have, ask these questions:

- Will this information help my work with children?
- Does asking for the information cross a boundary, or does it respect optimal distance?
- Am I responding to a deep-seated feeling of my own that is causing me to over-react to a situation with a child and family?
- Does seeking this information recognize and build on family strengths?

ESTABLISHING RELATIONSHIPS WITH FAMILIES

How do early childhood educators establish relationships with families?

Relationships between early childhood professionals and families develop through hundreds of small interactions. Trust, essential for authentic connections between family members and their children's teachers and caregivers, develops when early childhood educators respect a family's beliefs, values, and attitudes about child rearing and learning, yet are honest about communicating their own. Such open communication expresses caring; is culturally sensitive; avoids assumptions or judgments about families, their feelings, and their responses; and lets families know that teachers welcome information about children that is helpful in the classroom. When teachers and families make decisions about children's school life in a collaborative manner, families will feel that teachers respect their choices and decisions about their children. Active listening and third space are two approaches that teachers use to build such relationships.

INTERACTIONS WITH FAMILIES

How do early childhood educators and families interact with each other?

Many families interact with their child's teacher or caregiver for the first time during home visits, short school visits, or phase-in periods that orient children and families and help children adjust to a new class. Teachers and parents also interact during scheduled meetings, such as back-to-school nights and parent-teacher conferences. Social gatherings are less formal ways for families and teachers to interact, as is the daily contact that many family members have with the teaching staff. When family members volunteer in the classroom or in other ways for the program, they gain knowledge of the room and school and the people who work there.

INFORMATION SHARING BETWEEN TEACHERS AND FAMILIES
How do teachers and families share information with each other?
Both teachers and families may initiate exchanges of information. Teachers contact families to make appointments, inform them of events, convey concerns, and also reassure them that their children are doing well. They use phone calls, newsletters, notices, and displays of children's work. Families, too, approach teachers during the school day or after hours, through email, or by phone.

ADDRESSING SERIOUS ISSUES
What should teachers remember when they raise concerns with parents?
Sometimes teachers or families are concerned about issues that go beyond simple information sharing—issues that call for serious attention and problem solving. As the child care professional, the teacher is responsible for keeping the lines of communication open, no matter how challenging that might be. Teachers should encourage parents to report any significant changes in home life that are likely to affect the child's experience in school. Sometimes discussing a troublesome situation in collaboration with other program staff or with staff from outside agencies can help teachers to determine the severity of an issue before they raise it with a family. When a situation is beyond the scope of a teacher's expertise, teachers can refer families to an outside resource. Many teachers keep lists of referral services that families have used successfully.

FURTHER ACTIVITIES

1. Design and create a family information form. Consider what information to include and how to ask for it in ways that are culturally sensitive and accessible to all parents, including those who are non-English speakers or minimally literate. Write a one-page commentary that explains your rationale for various items and how you phrased them. (**NAEYC Standard 2: Building Family and Community Relationships**)

2. Think of a child you know or about whom you have read in this book or elsewhere. Fully describe him or her to one or two partners whom you've enlisted to play the role of the child's family. Write a script for yourself that includes an opening comment to the family; questions or comments that invite the family to share information, ideas, and concerns; and a closing comment that encourages further communication. Prepare yourself to demonstrate that you use systematic observations, documentation, and other effective assessment strategies in a responsible way. Make sure your actions will illustrate your partnership with the family. Find someone to videotape or use digital audiotape as you and your partner(s) act out the family-teacher conference. You may choose to ask additional classmates to join the conference as other professionals (your director or related service providers). Write a brief essay describing your conference and how it follows the guidelines in this chapter. (**NAEYC Standard 3: Observing, Documenting, and Assessing to Support Young Children and Families**)

3. Imagine that you are a first-year head teacher of four-year-olds. In your school, the traditional curriculum topic is families, but all teachers create the curriculum themselves. Using your knowledge of four-year-olds and some of the ideas in this chapter, list questions to ask families. Note what other research you would do before designing learning activities. (**NAEYC Standard 4: Using Developmentally Effective Approaches to Connect with Children and Families**)

CHAPTER FIFTEEN

Policy Issues and Early Childhood Practice

Whether we are engaged in personal advocacy, public policy advocacy, or private-sector advocacy, it is important that all of us who touch the lives of children do all we can to educate the American public about the needs of children and the social and moral responsibility of our society to care for children.

Adele Robinson and Deborah Stark

What is policy, and why does it make a difference for children, families, and you? Most policies that affect your work with young children are made by people far from the classroom and far from the world in which children and families live. In this chapter, we explore the history of early childhood education policy, the arenas in which policy plays out, and ways in which you can develop connections between early childhood settings and policy.

POLICY

What is policy?

Bruce is a poet and book lover who teaches first grade in an urban public school system. A member of an adult literacy task force, Bruce knows that many adults were bored by the books they read in school. He and his colleagues are concerned about the poor quality of the books in their school, but the principal is reluctant to approach the school board about purchasing new ones. Bruce decides to go directly to the school board. He researches the state allotment for books, and he invites a colleague to testify about the importance of interesting and relevant materials in the classroom. Bruce himself presents testimony about the problems with his school's dated books.

The school board claims there is no money for new books, but the board's president agrees to look into how the board spent its state allotment that year. On learning of this, the district superintendent calls Bruce's principal to express his concern about Bruce's activism. The principal tells Bruce he supports his actions, but he warns Bruce about the dangers of future testimony. Although Bruce is upset by his principal's reaction, he is pleased to learn that a group of activist parents who read his testimony later spoke at a school board meeting about the need for new science and social studies textbooks (Fennimore 1989).

Bruce understood the importance of good books to children's learning. He was also willing to defend his view and **lobby**—try to influence policy makers—for change. The school superintendent saw Bruce's action as unprofessional, out of line. The principal was caught in between. The parents supported Bruce. But in the end, the school board and Bruce may have had different ideas about how to allocate its money.

Merriam-Webster's definition of **policy** as a "course or method of action . . . to guide and determine present and future decisions" sounds straightforward. To develop a plan for influencing policy, you must identify the problem, consider what to do to fix it, and make decisions about how to take action. You must also know who sets the policy or policies you want to influence. But policy is dynamic and interactive, and conflicting views about how to implement change along with the different values that participants hold (Taylor et al. 1997, 15) complicate the process of policy making.

Both the private and public sectors conceive of, debate, and enact policies. Corporations, religious institutions, and even your own social groups have rules, regulations, and established ways of interacting, achieving goals, and making change. In the public arena, the "state," or the government, through the legislature, governor, and departments and agencies, establishes policy and develops methods of accountability to make sure that policies work. But policies often begin with ordinary people. In the past half-century, policies in the social arena, including education, have performed the function of "marshalling and managing public calls for change, giving them form and direction" (Taylor et al. 1997, 2).

> **Policy is a course of action that helps to guide and determine present and future decisions.**

Policy making on the federal, or national, level is a complex process, involving legislative and judicial task forces, committees, conferences, and lobbying. Head Start, which you read about in Chapters 5 and 7, is an example of a federal program that grew out of antipoverty policy in the 1960s. The NCLB Act of 2001 is another federal initiative, one in a long line of attempts to reform our public education system. Federal support of education in general—and early care and education in particular—has traveled a long road paved with conflicts about the role, responsibility, and extent of authority of the federal government (Kaestle 2001, Stoney, Mitchell, and Warner 2006, Zigler and Gilman 1996).

States are also a major force in general education policy making. Public elementary schools are state funded, as are preschool programs that are part of statewide initiatives, including universal prekindergarten. States also provide aid to local school budgets and regulate curriculum content and teacher certification (Kaestle 2001). State boards of education set policy for the selection of school reform methods, assessment, teacher licensure requirements, and textbooks (Robinson and Stark 2002). In recent decades, states have assumed a much more expansive role in early childhood education policy, providing services for children and families prior to elementary school (Frank Porter Graham [FPG] Child Development Institute 2004).

On the local level, your school board is key to education policy making. School boards set policy for public elementary schools and also oversee state-funded prekindergarten programs. Their list of responsibilities is long, reflecting the historic trend toward giving communities more responsibility for education (Kaestle 2001).

School boards coordinate with community-based organizations to support family literacy, children's mental and physical health, and before- and after-school programs. They also weigh in on budgetary issues, including money for full-day kindergarten and plans for reducing class size. Finally, school boards play a role in teacher training in literacy, promotion and grade retention, selecting assessment instruments, and choosing textbooks, as you saw with Bruce (Robinson and Stark 2002). Local communities also help create and enforce regulations for early care and education settings that are outside of the public education system.

On the local level, school boards set policy for public elementary schools and also oversee state-funded prekindergarten programs.

THOUGHT QUESTION What kinds of rules, regulations, and policies have you noticed in the classrooms where you have observed or work? Make a list and think about these policies. Which ones seem to make sense? Which ones do you think have helped to make positive change?

HISTORY OF EARLY CHILDHOOD EDUCATION POLICY

What are the highlights of the history of early childhood education policy?

Today, early childhood education is high on the policy agenda. From Congress to state legislatures to city councils, early learning and the lives of children and families are the subjects of much discussion and debate. A growing number of states are setting up children's cabinets and early learning commissions. States are supporting efforts to promote quality, school readiness, and universal prekindergarten—free, voluntary education for all four- (and some three-) year-olds. States are also struggling with the challenges of school reform initiatives, notably NCLB. Such intense interest is welcome; while new voices have complicated the dynamic, they have also made policy making more vibrant, according to veteran advocate Joan Lombardi (personal communication). A brief look at the history of early childhood initiatives over the past century reveals a number of factors at play in the development of policy.

Attitudes about the Role of the Family in the Early Years

Emily and Luigi are five-year-old cousins who live in low-income communities with large immigrant populations. Both children attend public school. Emily, who lives in a suburb of Los Angeles, just entered kindergarten; previously, she had been at home with her mother, who ran an informal family child care program. Luigi lives in central Paris, where he has attended an *école maternelle,* or preschool, since he was three. Luigi's mother, Dawn, claims that his experience in preschool has nurtured her son's intellectual curiosity and that he has made more progress in his learning than cousin Emily has. Dawn talks enthusiastically about the friends Luigi has made, his social skills, his growing confidence, and how easily he now speaks French and English. Dawn says that Luigi's education is one of her major reasons for remaining in France (Newman and Peer 2002).

Many other nations provide publicly funded, universal (available to all) support for families in the early care and education of their young children. In most of the developed world, expectant mothers, and fathers too, can count on generous paid leaves when their babies are born (Figure 15.1). Among countries belonging to the Organisation for Economic Co-operation and Development (OECD), Belgium, for example, offers fifteen weeks of paid maternity leave, with 55 percent replacement of income. The Netherlands guarantees sixteen weeks with 100 percent replacement, and the Czech Republic, twenty-eight weeks, at a rate of 69 percent replacement (Kamerman 2000). In France, where Luigi lives, free schooling is available for all children; almost all three-, four-, and five-year-olds and 35 percent of two-year-olds attend high-quality preschool (Newman and Peer 2002). In Denmark, legislation mandates public authorities "to make available the required number of day care facilities for children and young people" (cited in Kamerman and Kahn 1994, 11).

Percentage of Income Paid in Selected Countries during Maternity Leave

Legend:
- Belgium (15 weeks)
- Netherlands (16 weeks)
- Czech Republic (28 weeks)

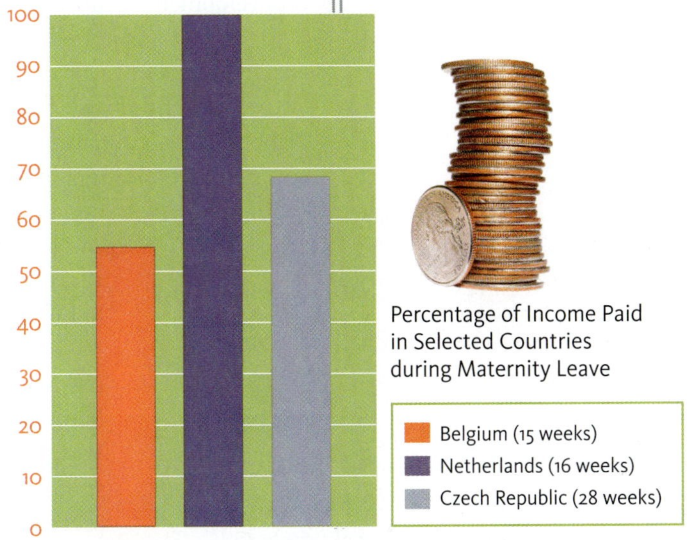

Figure 15.1 *Percentage of Income Paid in Selected Countries during Maternity Leave*
From: Kamerman 2000

Danish local municipalities, called *kommunes,* meet this need through a combination of family child care homes, center-based programs, and generous public funding. The Danes show us that child care regulated and subsidized by the government with universal access is possible.

The United States, on the other hand, historically has left families to their own devices. The United States has long considered child rearing a private matter, and public policy has reflected its citizens' ambivalence about the government's role (Stoney, Mitchell, and Warner 2006; Zigler and Gilman 1996).

Recent polls confirm that people in the United States support the idea of public investment in young children. However, conflicting points of view about the **primacy of parents**—whether parents should take primary responsibility for raising their children—together with ambivalence about mothers working and belief in the value of work and self-sufficiency complicate the policy debate. While people in the United States endorse government *financial* support—in the form of the Family and

> The United States has long considered child rearing a private matter, and public policy has reflected its citizens' ambivalence about the government's role.

THOUGHT QUESTION Do you think parents should be able to stay home with their children? If so, until what age? Why?

Do you think the government should support families and children? If so, how and why?

Medical Leave Act or the Child Development Block Grant (which helps subsidize child care for low-income families), they remain skeptical of intensive government involvement in family issues (Sylvester 2001).

Early Care versus Education/ Targeted versus Universal

Conflicts about what is best for children have informed and shaped early education public policy since its inception. This has often led to *reactions* to "problems," instead of to *proactive,* coherent policies that support young children and families (Zigler and Gilman 1996).

Early initiatives addressed the need for **custodial care,** or out-of-home care that met only minimal standards and was not designed to nurture children's growth and development. Custodial child care took the children of working mothers off the streets but was not educational. These efforts reflected and served to reinforce the dichotomy between *care* and *education,* which you read about in Chapter 7.

Early efforts also targeted a particular group, such as orphans and children of the working poor, rather than being universally available. In most cases, such early care and education programs segregated families and children who could not otherwise afford them from children whose families could pay. Funding only a portion of the U.S. population of children is, of course, much less expensive than universal early childhood education. This separation by income level has persisted.

In the eyes of many early childhood experts and advocates, *reactive* policy making has perpetuated a "hodge-podge of center- and home-based care and education programs" (Stoney, Mitchell, and Warner 2006, 102) that vary greatly in structure, quality, content, sponsorship, and funding sources. This kind of policy making has prevented the development of a cohesive system of high-quality early care and education for all (Bowman, Donovan, and Burns 2001).

A list of twentieth-century federal initiatives highlights these tensions. A 1909 White House Conference on Children, for example, identified the need for noninstitutional care for neglected children and advocated family support measures, but the federal government did nothing. Custodial care for orphans, foster children, and children of the poor and working poor remained mostly private. During the Depression and World War II, the federal government abandoned its hands-off policy and supported the Works Progress Administration Nursery Schools. Under the New Deal, these schools served only a small percentage of the country's children, but they provided them with educational and social services and relied on teachers from the university-based nursery movement (Bellm and Whitebook 2006). The Lanham Act of 1940 established child care centers in "war impact areas" from 1942 through 1946 for women who worked in the defense industry while the men were at war. They provided subsidies for children from all income levels and promoted child development (Cohen 1996). While these initiatives offered a vision of the blending of care and education, they were limited and temporary.

THOUGHT QUESTION In Portland, Oregon, during World War II, the Kaiser Shipyards hired child development experts to design centers for the infants, toddlers, and preschoolers of women who worked in the shipyards. These centers had child-sized furniture, picture books, and other materials suited to children. Teachers had college degrees and received higher salaries than they had in preschools and than those the mothers earned in the shipyards; Kaiser didn't want to lose teachers to better paying jobs. The centers were near where the mothers worked and even provided dinners that they could take home at the end of the day. Kaiser supported the centers until the end of the war, when they closed (Hurwitz 1998; Kirp 2007).

How did these centers combine care *and* education? How do care and education fit together in an early childhood program you have visited?

Social, Economic, and Health Status of Children

In the 1960s, policy making reflected the government's interest in early childhood education as a means of addressing child and family poverty (Table 15.1). Head Start and the Even Start Family Literacy Program were both created in 1965 as part of President Johnson's War on Poverty. At the same time, the Elementary and Secondary Education Act (ESEA) established Title I funding for early childhood education and support services for children living in poverty. The **deficit model,** which held that early childhood education was needed to eliminate the disadvantages, or deficits, that poverty creates for children (Haskins 2004; Stegelin 2004), drove these programs and continues to underlie them today. This approach can lose sight of children's and families' strengths and overlooks the richness different cultural backgrounds have to offer.

Another White House Conference on Children in 1970 highlighted the lack of child care as a growing national problem. The resulting legislation, the Comprehensive Child Development Act, called for federally supported child care centers and even proposed comprehensive universal care; but it was vetoed by President Nixon. Attempts in the late 1970s to introduce child care legislation died quickly (Zigler and Gilman 1996). The federal government, however, had become active on another front during this time, and the passage of the Individuals with Disabilities Education Act (IDEA) in 1975 marked a new commitment to serving children with special needs.

In the late 1980s, welfare reform set the stage for a new focus on child care legislation (Cohen 1996), as many welfare recipients, including mothers of preschoolers, were required to participate in education, training, and work. The Family Support Act (FSA), passed in 1988, guaranteed child care for participating families and provided subsidies for one year after parents left welfare. FSA paved the way for the Child Development Block Grant, in 1990, which provided subsidies to low-income families.

Recent decades have been marked by a stronger policy focus on child development and education. A number of landmark reports in the 1980s—including *Education: The First Sixty Months* (1987), by the National Governors Association, and *Right from the Start* (1988), by the National Association of State Boards of Education—highlighted the importance of early childhood education. The 100th Congress introduced more than a hundred bills in support of children and families (Stegelin 2004). *Starting Points: Meeting the Needs of Our Youngest Children,* a report released by the Carnegie Corporation in 1994, highlighted a "quiet crisis." Significant numbers of U.S. children under the age of three, the report revealed, were suffering from inadequate prenatal care, fragmented families, substandard child care, poverty, and insufficient attention to their intellectual development.

By the dawn of the twenty-first century, "child development and social policy" had "come of age" (Hall, Kagan, and Zigler 1996, 4). State involvement in early childhood policy making was intensifying—a trend that had been growing for some time. New partners emerged on the local level, as businesses and others in the private sector began to take a more active role in issues affecting the welfare of their communities' youngest citizens.

> The passage of the Individuals with Disabilities Education Act (IDEA) in 1975 marked a new commitment by the federal government to serve children with special needs.

WHY POLICY MAKERS ARE INTERESTED IN EARLY CHILDHOOD EDUCATION

Why are policy makers interested in early childhood education?

In recent decades, an explosion of research on child development and the benefits of early childhood education has shown that high-quality early care and education

TABLE 15.1	Federal Legislation and Programs That Influence Young Children's Education
LEGISLATION/PROGRAM	**SUMMARY**
Elementary and Secondary Education Act (ESEA)/Title I	Enacted in 1965, ESEA is the primary source of federal aid to K–12 education, with particular support, through Title I, for children living in poverty. Title I funding, which does not include separate funding for preschool services, goes directly to school districts. Local educational agencies allocate their Title I funds for early childhood services. Title VII of the Act promotes educational excellence by awarding competitive grants directly to school districts serving ELLs. ESEA is the template for all subsequent federal legislation in support of education reform, including Goals 2000: Educate America Act of 1994; the Bilingual Education Act of 1994; and the NCLB Act of 2001.
Head Start	Head Start, established in 1965, is administered by the Department of Health and Human Services. It is the largest federal program with early childhood development as its primary mission. Head Start provides comprehensive services, including education, health, and nutrition, to low-income children with the goal of preparing them for kindergarten. Early Head Start was established in 1994 to serve children younger than three.
Even Start Family Literacy Program	The Even Start Family Literacy Program, first funded under ESEA/Title I in 1965, provides education and related services to parents without high school diplomas and their young children. Services include basic academic instruction and parenting skills training for adults, early childhood education for their children through age seven (age eight, in collaboration with Title I), along with child care and/or transportation.
Individuals with Disabilities Education Act (IDEA)	Enacted in 1975, IDEA authorizes federal funding for special education and related services and sets out principles for provision of these services. Principles include the following: that states and school districts provide a free, appropriate public education to all children with disabilities between the ages of three and twenty-one; that each child has an individual education program; and that children with disabilities, whenever possible, be educated with children who are not disabled.
Child Care and Development Block Grant (CCDBG)	CCDBG, established in 1990, is the primary federal grant program supporting low-income families with child care needs. Administered by the Department of Health and Human Services, it provides states with block grants to be used to provide low-income families with child care subsidies.
Early Learning Opportunities Act (ELOA)	Administered by the Administration for Children and Families, the ELOA was enacted in 2001 and provides grants to communities to enhance the cognitive, physical, social, and emotional development of children under five.
No Child Left Behind (NCLB) Act	NCLB, enacted in 2001, reauthorized ESEA and considerably expanded federal influence by increasing the accountability of public schools and public school systems for improving educational outcomes for all children, especially those living in poverty. States are required to implement standards-based assessments; to determine adequate yearly progress (AYP) for schools and districts; and to raise standards of teacher qualifications.
Early Reading First	Authorized by Title I, as part of the NCLB Act in 2001, this initiative provides competitive grants to local education agencies and other public and private organizations to provide preschool children, particularly those from low-income families, with exposure to language- and literature-rich environments. The initiative also supports professional training and the integration of scientifically based instruction material on reading into programs serving preschoolers.
Good Start, Grow Smart	The early education component of NCLB, Good Start, Grow Smart was launched in 2002 to improve school readiness for young children in all types of early care and education settings. The goals of this initiative are supported through the quality provisions of CCDBG, which require states to use a portion of the funding they receive to improve the quality of early care and education programs.

From: McCallion 2004; Jones et al. 2004; OpenCRS 2007; Martinez-Beck and Zaslow 2006

can significantly and positively influence children's development (FPG Child Development Institute 2004) Child development experts point to a growing understanding among professionals, parents, and the society at large about the value of responsive early care and education (Bowman, Donovan, and Burns 2001). Recently, the research of neuroscientists has helped to strengthen this understanding.

The Power of Brain Research

Knowledge about the brain's complex network and its relation to children's emotional, social, and cognitive growth has reinforced and built on much of what we already know about early care and education. Most importantly from a policy perspective, brain research has provided scientific evidence of the enormous growth that takes place in the first years of life and of the effects that early experiences have on children's future development and capacity to learn.

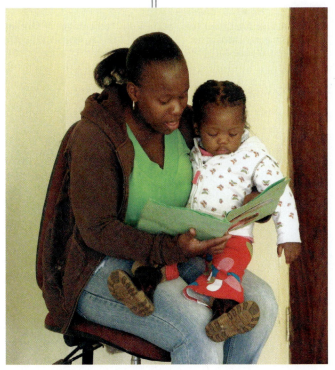

Reading to and with a child early in life is the kind of interaction that fosters neural connections as well as attachment.

Attention to the work of neuroscientists first surfaced in the fields of child development and early education. In recent decades, however, brain research findings have made their way into the public arena and the minds of policy makers. In 1996, the Families and Work Institute, a nonprofit research organization, convened a conference on brain development in young children. Out of this conference came *Rethinking the Brain: New Insights into Early Development* (Shore 1997), an overview of neuroscientists' findings and the challenges and opportunities they present to parents, early childhood educators, and policy makers.

The federal government joined the chorus with a White House Conference, "Early Childhood Development and Learning: What New Research on the Brain Tells Us about Our Youngest Children," described as "a call to action to all members of society . . . to use this information to strengthen America's families" (White House Conference 1997). Subsequent reports by the National Academy of Sciences synthesized the research findings and made policy recommendations. *Eager to Learn: Educating Our Preschoolers* (Bowman, Donovan, and Burns 2001) and *From Neurons to Neighborhoods: The Science of Early Childhood Development* (Shonkoff and Phillips 2000) provided further evidence and information, enhancing policy makers' understanding of child development and suggesting potential areas for action.

Changing Families

Historically, people in the United States have been ambivalent about mothers working and conflicted about delegating the care and education of their children to others. But statistics show that today the majority of mothers of our nation's young children are working. Fifty-eight percent of married mothers and 63 percent of unmarried mothers with children under the age of six are employed (U.S. Department of Labor 2006). Nearly three-quarters of children under age five whose parents work are cared for by someone else (Sonenstein et al. 2002). Twenty-eight percent are in center-based early care and education settings, 27 percent are cared for by a relative,

Statistics show that today the majority of mothers of our nation's young children are working.

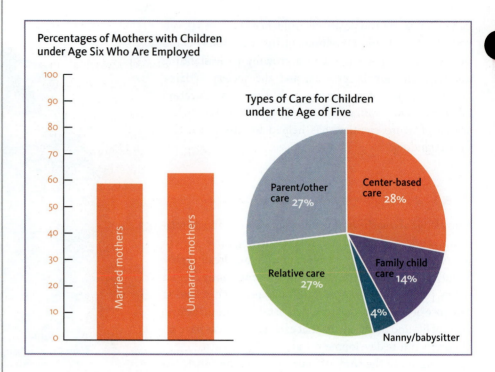

Figure 15.2 *How U.S. Children under Age Five Are Cared For*
U.S. Department of Labor 2006;
Sonenstein et al. 2002

Percentages of Mothers with Children under Age Six Who Are Employed

Married mothers

Unmarried mothers

Types of Care for Children under the Age of Five

Parent/other care 27%

Center-based care 28%

Relative care 27%

Family child care 14%

4%

Nanny/babysitter

14 percent are in family child care, and 4 percent are cared for by babysitters or nannies (Figure 15.2).

In 2002, almost 90 percent of the 9.8 million preschoolers of employed mothers and 30 percent of the 8.2 million preschoolers of mothers not in the workforce were in some form of early care and education program or setting (Sonenstein et al. 2002). Think about what this means. You are, or will be, working with some of these millions of children as well as their mothers, fathers, grandmothers, and others. As you have already seen, twenty-first-century families are an enormously diverse lot, with a wide variety of cultural, economic, religious, and personal backgrounds. All these families need a safe place for their children while they are at work, as well as a rich educational environment that will prepare their children for success in school and life. How do we meet families' demands for early care and education? With such varying needs and a patchwork quilt of arrangements, how do we ensure quality in children's early care and education?

The Achievement Gap and School Readiness

The growing gap in achievement between students with economic and educational advantages and those who must struggle for a decent education has given these questions greater urgency. Academic challenges such as **grade retention,** or repeating a grade; referrals for behavior problems; and placement in special education classes are much more common among children who live in poverty (Ochshorn 2001). In addition, as you read in Chapter 2, racism and other forms of discrimination place people of color at greater risk of being poor. Today, for example, the average African American or Hispanic high school student achieves only at the level of the lowest quarter of white students. Black and Hispanic students are also much more likely than white students to drop out, and less likely to graduate from high school, acquire a college degree, and earn a middle-class living (Education Commission of the States Education Policy Issue Site 2009). Here is how this situation looks in the daily life of one school district:

> The new superintendent is worried. NCLB has set a time by which all students in his district are required to reach proficiency in reading, writing, and mathematics. He is not at all sure that his students can reach this goal. Like many of his colleagues around the country, his options for making improvements will narrow as the deadline draws near, particularly since students from poor families, those with learning disabilities, and new immigrants must also reach the 100-percent-proficiency target. He claims that two of his five schools failed to make adequate progress because special education students and ELLs did not have the time they needed to meet their targets.

The superintendent and the district will be penalized if their schools do not show adequate progress on standardized tests. However, the children are the ones who ultimately suffer from what they do not have time to learn, from the pressure the tests place on them, and from school personnel's seeing them—the children—as an obstacle to the school's success.

The achievement gap has long concerned policy makers and has driven much of education reform in recent decades. It has also brought attention to **school readiness**—the skills that are basic to learning to read, write, do math, and other school subjects—and ultimately, to early childhood education. A national survey of kindergarten teachers in the late 1990s, for example, reported that 46 percent found that at least half of the children in their classrooms had trouble following directions, a key readiness skill (Rouse, Brooks-Gunn, and McLanahan 2005).

Children's earliest experiences may differ depending on their social class. Poor children are less likely to see their family members reading or using computers and less likely to have children's books at home. Adults who read aloud to them are more likely to point out letters or colors than to discuss the story (Rothstein 2004). These different situations foster different skills, with the result that as many as two-thirds of children in poor urban areas may be inadequately prepared for the way teachers expect them to acquire skills in elementary school settings (Ochshorn 2001). Although early care and education can bridge early experiences and elementary school expectations, only a small proportion of the children who would benefit most have access to good early childhood programs (Rouse, Brooks-Gunn, and McLanahan 2005).

The United States has a long history of policy efforts to address school failure; in the past few decades, these efforts have increasingly focused on young children. In the early 1990s, school readiness was endorsed by all state governors as their top education priority and embodied in the Goals 2000: Educate America Act of 1994. That law identified access to high-quality preschool as one of three means of achieving readiness. The other two were support for parents as their children's first teachers and assurance that all children would receive appropriate nutrition and health care (Ochshorn 2001). A decade later, Congress enacted NCLB, which zeroed in on early literacy as a means of fostering school readiness through the Early Reading First and Even Start Family Literacy programs.

NCLB rests on four pillars (U.S. Department of Education 2004):

- *Stronger accountability*—schools must demonstrate that children are learning. Report cards of annual yearly progress inform parents how the school is doing.
- *More freedom for states and communities*—states and communities spend federal money on schools as they see fit and determine tests to measure if schools are performing well.

As many as two-thirds of children in poor urban areas may be inadequately prepared for the way teachers expect them to acquire skills in elementary school settings.

- *Proven education methods*—schools use teaching methods shown to work based on scientific evidence.
- *More choices for parents*—when schools do not perform well for two consecutive years, parents have the right to transfer their children to a higher-performing school and their children can receive tutoring.

These four pillars suggest that U.S. society values all children's success; local control of schooling; educational approaches that work; and consumer—in this case, parental—control of the product. Although many in the United States share these values, educational experts see serious flaws in NCLB and its implementation.

NCLB's reliance on testing to demonstrate achievement has narrowed the curriculum in schools across the country. Since schools can lose their right to operate if their children do not do well on tests, teachers devote time that could be spent on curriculum to test preparation instead. Schools in Florida set aside seven weeks of the school year to prepare for testing (Diane Ravitch, personal communication) because to do well on tests, children need practice in test taking.

> In a second grade classroom, the children spent half an hour doing math problems they had done before, but this time they used the format and rules they would encounter on the standardized math test. Their teacher normally encouraged them to show their work, but now she asked them to solve the problem on a separate sheet they would discard so that stray marks from their calculations would not count as wrong answers on their test sheet.

While review does not hurt children, this exercise confused the second graders, who were accustomed to showing their work. Moreover, the anxiety that tests produce for parents, teachers, and children subtract from any pleasure the learning environment might create.

State and community control means localities can tailor educational policy to their needs. However, in the case of NCLB, local control results in different measures of success in different states, creating the "proficiency illusion" (Cronin et al. 2007). A child whose test scores satisfy standards in one state could cross the state line and be deemed below par or not proficient in the second state.

Early Reading First, a part of NCLB, was intended to focus on all areas of development. The emphasis, however, is on early literacy, to ensure that children are prepared for the rigors of elementary school. This shift in the program's focus illustrates the anxiety about children's future school success that NCLB has generated, one that promotes formal instruction for young children instead of engaging them in meaningful learning experiences.

Schools judged to be in need of improvement face a "cascade of consequences" (Rebell and Wolff 2008, 134) that punishes them instead of building their capacity to teach. Over the course of five years, a school that fails to make adequate yearly progress for two consecutive years must take a series of steps. Families whose children attend the school can choose to send their children elsewhere; their children are entitled to extra instruction; the school has a short period of time to develop a plan to correct problems; and the district may end up restructuring the school.

Critics of NCLB point out its overemphasis on standardized testing, its limited view of education, and the lack of funding and support to carry out its stated goals. They note that in the time that NCLB has been in effect, gains in student test scores have decreased. NCLB illustrates the complexity of attempting to put societal goals into practice.

WHY EARLY CHILDHOOD PROFESSIONALS SHOULD BE INVOLVED IN POLICY

Why should early childhood professionals be involved in policy?

Children cannot vote or speak to policy makers for themselves. They need the adults in their lives to speak on their behalf, and certainly early childhood educators are knowledgeable about the issues that affect children and families. Although the public and policy makers are increasingly aware of how important the early years are, every child still does not have a good early childhood. Stories of early childhood educators' personal experiences can have a powerful effect on policy makers. It is up to early childhood advocates to recount their experiences to policy makers and the public so that they come to understand what communities and states need to develop high-quality systems of early care and education (Robinson and Stark 2002).

Those who work directly with children may not realize how qualified they are to influence policy. Everything about your life in the classroom is affected by policy: the salary you earn, which children can afford to attend, the equipment and materials your program can purchase, the curriculum, even the building you work in. No one knows these needs better than you. Just sharing your knowledge and professional experience contributes to policy. You also can explain how children's issues connect to larger social concerns (early childhood education lays the foundation for an educated workforce, for example); engage parents as more active partners; and reach out to public school leaders, health care providers, business leaders, and community organizations.

You might ask: who am I to try to influence legislators and policy makers? Policy can feel intimidating, something to be left to the "experts." You are not alone. Stacie Goffin and Joan Lombardi lay out five barriers to individual participation in policy development:

> Because children cannot vote or speak to policy makers for themselves, they need knowledgeable adults in their lives, such as early childhood educators, to speak on their behalf.

These children are in a care and education program that joins their families in voicing concerns to policy makers.

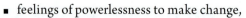

THOUGHT QUESTION Take a moment to think about how you can influence policy. What you choose to do will depend on your personal style and comfort level.

- What local and state agencies fund your program and set policies for other schools, child care centers, and family child care homes in your community?
- What kinds of interactions do you have with these agencies?

All communities have advocates for children.

- Who are the people in your community who support high-quality early care and education?
- How might you reach out to them?

- feelings of powerlessness to make change,
- ignorance of government regulations,
- fear of the political process,
- lack of confidence in your own expertise, and
- lack of time (Stegelin 2004).

Sometimes the issues confronting early childhood education can seem overwhelming. Think about the following example of how one teacher became an advocate:

> Maria is an assistant teacher in the toddler class in a Buffalo, New York, child care center. She holds a Child Development Associate (CDA) credential and is working toward an associate's degree. Maria loves her work. She is eager to pursue further education to build her skills and expand her professional options, but as a full-time worker and single mom, her time is limited. As an early childhood teacher, her salary is low. She will need student loans to continue, and she worries about paying them off.

> The director of Maria's center, a long-time advocate, is active in a statewide group that promotes high-quality early care and education. The coalition has declared an "Early Childhood Workforce Development Day" for advocates to travel to the state capital. There they will meet with members of the Senate and Assembly Higher Education Committees, who are considering bills to grant student loan forgiveness awards of up to $25,000 for individuals who agree to continue working in the child care field (Winning Beginning NY: http://winning beginningny.org/2009).

> Maria wants to take a stand on this important issue that affects her so directly, but she can't travel to the capital. Instead, after putting her son to bed, she logs on to the group's website and registers as an "E-Advocate." She clicks on "Take Action Now" and sees a screen with a letter to state legislators urging support of loan forgiveness (Figure 15.3). With a flick of her wrist and tap of her fingers, Maria adds her voice to the chorus of support for the loan forgiveness legislation. She forwards the link to her friends and colleagues.

Maria didn't think she had the power to change her situation until her director informed her about plans to lobby legislators for a new policy of loan forgiveness. She also could have learned about the action from a newsletter or website. Although Maria didn't have the time to participate and may have lacked confidence, too, she found another way to make her voice heard. Generally, advocates can participate in a variety of ways.

Advocates speak out regularly on a number of issues that affect the lives of children, families, and the teachers who work with them. The quality of early childhood programs, credentials, compensation, access to professional development, and what actually happens in the classroom are interrelated issues about which the public and policy makers need to be informed.

Quality of Early Childhood Programs

Advocacy for high-quality early childhood programming—based on research applied thoughtfully to local situations—calls for more than just increasing the

Figure 15.3 *Loan Forgiveness Letter to Legislators*
From: Winning Beginning NY

Loan Forgiveness Letter to New York State Legislators

As you know, early childhood teachers are underpaid and often without health insurance or retirement benefits. Still, these dedicated professionals want to pursue higher education so that they are better qualified to teach our children.

The Assembly and the Senate recently introduced bills (A.6759/S.4378) that support loan forgiveness for early childhood professionals. Passage of these companion bills would be a huge step toward creating high-quality early learning programs for children.

A.6759/S.4378 would grant student loan forgiveness awards of up to a total of $25,000 for individuals who agree to continue employment in the child care field. Right now, both bills sit in their respective Higher Education Committees. I urge you to help move these bills out of committee and onto the floor for a vote!

Research shows that qualified teachers are the key to ensuring positive educational outcomes for children. Yet many early childhood teachers have little or no formal education in early childhood development. For many, it's because they can't afford that training and education. The field pays very poorly, making it hard to pursue higher education. In fact, many dedicated teachers are leaving the field because they cannot afford to stay.

Loan forgiveness is a great way to encourage and support them. New York State supports other professionals, including lawyers and doctors. Math, science, and special education teachers receive loan forgiveness under a federal program. Why not support the individuals who care for and teach our youngest children every day? Given the research that shows how important the first five years of life are, and how important it is to have qualified teachers in the classrooms, it's time for New York State to support the teachers who work with young children.

We need to have qualified teachers in early childhood programs, to make sure our children enter school ready to succeed. Please support moving A.6759/S.4378 out of committee and to the floor for a vote before the end of the legislative session.

Thank you.

---

quantity of programs for children. Rather, it is the quality of those programs that determines children's experience in them. Researchers measure quality in a number of ways. First, they look at what is known as **process quality.** This involves the interactions, activities, and overall learning opportunities in the classroom as well as the health and safety routines. Second, they consider **structural quality,** which includes group size, the ratio of staff to children, and the education and training of the teachers and staff (Espinosa 2002).

But what does high-quality early childhood education look like? How can Maria make her work with children be of higher quality? NAEYC has helped to shape ideas about quality through its principles of developmentally appropriate practice, as you read in Chapter 1. According to NAEYC (Copple and Bredekamp 2009), rich early childhood experiences are built on:

- stable, positive relationships between teachers and children,
- well-equipped settings,

- ongoing and responsive communication,
- a diverse and integrated curriculum, and
- strong family involvement.

Research also shows that smaller group size, a ratio of children to adults that allows for attention to each child's needs, and adequate preparation and break times for teachers contribute to quality. In high-quality settings, teachers and staff usually have higher levels of education, specialized training in child development, and opportunities for professional development.

Credentials of Early Childhood Professionals

Although many researchers regard teacher education and training as essential for quality, policies that outline requirements vary enormously across the country. Some states require no professional experience at all for early childhood educators, others mandate a CDA credential or an associate's degree, while still others require a bachelor's degree. Regulations that vary according to program—Head Start, public school, community-based preschool and child care centers, and family child care homes—further complicate the picture (FPG Child Development Institute 2004).

In recent years, calls for raising Head Start educational requirements have accelerated. In 2006, 72 percent of Head Start teachers had associate's degrees. With each federal reauthorization of Head Start, the bar has been raised even higher, with associate's degrees proposed for all Head Start teachers, as well as substantial percentages of BAs or advanced degrees. A growing number of states have also been strengthening their licensing regulations. As of 2006, 16 states required at least one head teacher, child care associate, or supervisor to have more training, experience, and/or skills than other staff (LeMoine 2006).

The proliferation of state preschool programs has generated a big push for early childhood teachers to have four-year degrees. As of 2002, only 50 percent of those teaching three- and four-year olds had a bachelor's degree. Almost 90 percent of early childhood teachers with BAs could be found in public school prekindergarten programs; in for-profit child care settings, less than 40 percent of teachers have BAs (FPG Child Development Institute 2004). Missing from this picture are the many early childhood practitioners in nonprofit, community-based settings and family child care homes who live in states with few or minimal requirements for training.

A growing number of states now require that teachers in at least one of their state-financed prekindergarten programs have a bachelor's degree (Jacobson 2007). This policy has stirred lively debate. As you saw earlier, policies are dynamic and ever-changing, and they are complicated by differing views on which approaches are best. For example, some in the field are concerned that higher educational standards will be a burden to current members of the workforce. Darlene Ragozzine, a former kindergarten teacher and Head Start director and an advocate in Connecticut, says that people in her state spend an average of five years on AA degrees. She worries about limited funds for professional development and education for those who are trying to advance in the field (personal communication).

In fact, most experts in the field now embrace the idea of the bachelor's degree as a baseline credential for preschool teachers. A solid body of research shows that in

THOUGHT QUESTION Amanda teaches in a universal prekindergarten classroom in a public school. She develops close relationships with children and families but emphasizes the materials and activities in her room that create a high-quality setting. Her friend, Zoe, is a family child care provider. Zoe cares about materials, too, but prides herself on the relationships she has with the children and their families. Amanda and Zoe respect each other's work and see many similarities in their approaches, yet they measure the quality of their work differently. What do you think makes an environment a high-quality one? How do your ideas compare with established definitions of quality?

addition to other personal qualities, **habits of mind** (knowing how to approach an intellectual problem), higher levels of education, and credentials are positively associated with classroom quality. Specialization in early childhood education is also important. Although some researchers have questioned the direct link between levels of education, major, and credentials and children's outcomes (Early et al. 2006), many studies have shown that children educated by teachers with a bachelor's degree and specialized training in child development and early education are more sociable, use language in a more sophisticated way, and perform at higher levels on cognitive tasks than children taught by less-qualified teachers (Bowman, Donovan, and Burns 2001). Many early childhood experts also believe that teachers need higher levels of education to be able to connect new scientific research about how children learn with their teaching practice (Goffin and Washington 2007).

Compensation of Early Childhood Professionals

Compensation, or what workers are paid, is a huge challenge for the early childhood field. As Marcy Whitebook points out, the field has almost tripled in size since the late 1970s without significant increases in wages (Bellm and Whitebook 2006, 6). This lack of progress, Whitebook claims, comes from confusion about the purpose and nature of early care and education: Is it just custodial, or does it promote children's development and learning? "Fundamentally, public policy has not created higher expectations for this workforce overall," she notes, "because policymakers have remained stuck" between these two views.

As a result, the bottom line for early care and education teachers is pretty dismal, as shown in Figure 15.4. The workforce, mostly women, better-educated than the general population and with many practitioners of color, is marked by the highest concentration of poverty wages of any U.S. industry (Center for the Child Care

> Research shows that in addition to other personal qualities, habits of mind, higher levels of education, and credentials are positively associated with classroom quality.

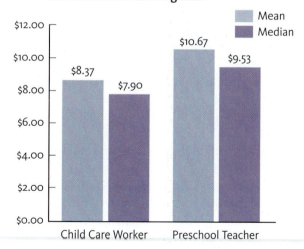

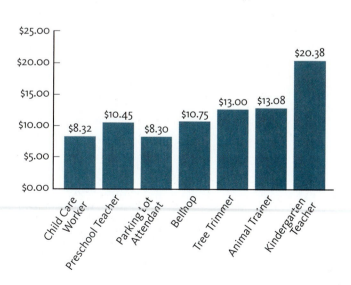

Figure 15.4 *Compensation for Early Childhood Educators*
From: Center for the Child Care Workforce 2004, 7
"Child care worker" and "preschool teacher" are job titles defined by the Bureau of Labor Statistics.

THOUGHT QUESTION Are you discouraged by these numbers? You're not alone. The low pay of early childhood teachers is due to many factors, including the historic division between care and education and the fact that the work of caregiving—work most often done by women—is undervalued. In recent decades, early childhood teachers in schools, at home, from Head Start, and other organizations have worked, through the Worthy Wage Campaign (http://www. ccw.org/about_history.html), to change this perception and to improve compensation and work environments for the early care and education workforce. In addition to these grassroots efforts (efforts that originate in communities), state policy makers have begun to wrestle with this issue, developing initiatives that link higher levels of education with increases in compensation. Later in this chapter, you will see some of these strategies. Go to the Worthy Wage Campaign website and find other resources related to compensation. What can you do to advocate for better pay for early care and education professionals?

Workforce n.d.). Child care workers and preschool teachers are job titles defined by the Bureau of Labor Statistics, which collects wage data in its annual Occupational Employment Statistics survey. Mean or average annual wages for early childhood teachers in 2006 were $18,820 for child care workers and $25,900 for preschool teachers (U.S. Department of Labor 2006). These wages are among the lowest of the almost 800 occupations tracked. Service station and locker room attendants earn more, as do people who repair bicycles. In addition, teachers outside of the public school system or Head Start are much less likely to have benefits such as sick leave, a pension plan, or health insurance (Lowenstein et al. 2004).

Not surprisingly, early childhood **teacher turnover,** teachers leaving for other jobs, is rampant. In 2000, the Washington State Governor's Commission on Early Learning found that wages had remained below $8 an hour for more than a decade, that half of their licensed child care centers provided no benefits to their teaching staff, and that turnover among early childhood professionals in the state exceeded 40 percent (Burbank and Wiefek 2001). In that same year, a longitudinal study of three California communities found a turnover rate of around 30 percent, which has long been cited as the average for early childhood staff (Whitebook et al. 2001). Turnover is not only challenging for teachers and employees, it compromises quality. As you have seen in earlier chapters, young children thrive in the context of secure, stable relationships. Staff turnover undermines those relationships and wastes programs' ongoing investment in training and professional development.

Access to Professional Development

Professional development and compensation are inextricably linked and are essential to raising quality. However, access to opportunities varies across programs and locales. If you are a Head Start teacher, for example, you are likely to participate in more training than your colleagues teaching in prekindergarten, child care, and family child care programs (Kagan et al. 2006).

A growing number of states are adopting policies to create professional development systems or improve those already in place. Still, in many areas, community and four-year colleges, as well as universities and other training institutions, offer little help to students. You may find it difficult to determine exactly which courses you will need to earn a degree and qualify for higher-level positions in the field. Or you may have trouble getting academic credit and transferring that credit. Footing the bill for your training can also be a challenge. But if you live in North Carolina or Nebraska, for example, you can take advantage of a scholarship program that helps cover the costs of higher education or training (Center for the Child Care Workforce n.d.). If you live in one of the states where this policy has not yet taken hold, you will have to be more creative to find the resources you need.

If English is not your first language, you may need extra support to complete your education and training. People throughout the United States today—both children and their early childhood teachers—speak dozens of languages! In some instances, materials and training are available in languages other than English; and some colleges offer intensive English as a Second Language courses to prepare students to take early childhood classes in English. NAEYC has advocated for pre-service and in-service training for non-English speakers, but many communities do not meet this need (NAEYC 1995).

What Happens in the Early Childhood Classroom

In an early-childhood-center kindergarten class in one of Nashville's most challenged communities, the children are learning about their world. Their core curriculum of social studies has always focused on the neighborhood. Under new standards created by the state of Tennessee, however, the children are required to know, not merely the locations of their local landmarks, stores, and parks, but those of the continents of the world, which they learn through song.

What does your classroom look like? How much training are you required to have? How do your children learn, and what do they need to know? Whether you are working with three-year-olds in a child care center, infants in a family child care home, or second graders in your local public school, regulations, or standards, will partly determine how you answer those questions.

Except for Head Start, a federal initiative, most early childhood programs are regulated by state and local governments through licensing and registration. Regulations help ensure that children are physically safe, that their environment is clean and well maintained, that infection is controlled, and that children's healthy development is not compromised. These standards establish a baseline, or what has been called the "necessary level of quality" (Morgan 1996). Group size, child-staff ratios, and staff qualifications and training—critical elements of quality—are all regulated.

In the past decade, a growing number of states have revised their regulations. They have lowered child-staff ratios, established group size requirements (especially for infants), and increased teacher education and training requirements (Ochshorn et al. 2004). In 2002, for example, twenty-two states required ratios of 10:1 for three-year-olds; thirty-three states regulated group size for three- and four-year-olds; twenty-two states mandated pre-service training for teachers; and thirty-six states required annual ongoing training for group family child care providers. Some states also are linking their regulations to quality through star-rating systems like those used for hotels and restaurants. In a quality rating system (QRS), programs receive funding and support to go through the assessment process and are awarded a number of stars depending on how well they meet the standards. All QRS are composed of (Child Care Bureau 2007):

- standards that establish a range from minimal licensing requirements to the rigors of accreditation;
- monitoring that determines whether the program meets the standards and at what level;
- training, mentoring, and technical assistance to support programs;
- incentives such as a higher reimbursement rate per child for highly rated centers; and
- a marketing tool that informs families that the state recognizes the center for its quality.

Today many early childhood programs are affected by program standards that measure children's social and academic progress. With continued concern about school

Most early childhood programs are regulated by state and local governments through licensing and regulations that help ensure that children are physically safe, that infection is controlled, and that children's healthy development is not compromised.

readiness and increased spending for preschool programs, such standards are becoming more common (Jacobson 2002).

The 2002 Good Start, Grow Smart initiative asked states to develop voluntary guidelines on literacy, language, prereading, and numeracy activities for children ages three to five that aligned with their K–12 standards. Today, every state has developed and published such guidelines. In addition, many are working on guidelines for infants and toddlers, which cover children from birth through age three (National Infant and Toddler Child Care Initiative 2007).

At the same time, standardized testing at earlier ages and benchmarks for adequate yearly progress by public schools—requirements of NCLB—have placed greater demands on early childhood education. Like other regulations, these standards vary greatly across the states. Some outline general expectations for programs and the kinds of opportunities they must offer children. Others are more specific in what they require that children be able to do. Some focus on basic knowledge; others, on more complex cognitive skills; and there are those that emphasize social development and nurturing positive attitudes toward learning (Spicer 2002). Depending on where you live and work, you will be guided and influenced by these standards.

THOUGHT QUESTION What do you think about early learning standards? How might they be helpful or harmful, and what is their impact on young children?

WORKING FOR CHANGE ON THE STATE LEVEL

What does working for change on the state level involve?

As you have seen, states play a major role in early childhood policy making—setting standards, determining credentials, and outlining assessment practices. Some are working on comprehensive statewide system reforms for early care and education, while others are tackling parts of the system, such as compensation and training, or launching a universal prekindergarten initiative. Whatever the level of activity, these are exciting times for the field, with many opportunities for advocacy and shaping policy.

Early Learning Systems Initiatives

Shakira and Enoelia work with three-year-olds in a large multiservice city agency. Shakira is the lead teacher in a Head Start classroom; Enoelia is an assistant teacher in a child care classroom. Their classrooms share a common calendar, they participate in joint training, and the parents of children in both classrooms sit on one committee that addresses the needs of all the children. The Head Start and child care classrooms in the agency's early childhood program have agreed to be known as "The Children's Center," a decision that helps create a feeling of unity and shared purpose among the teachers, families, and children. But Head Start and child care have different contracts; different unions represent their employees; and different agencies in the city and on the federal level fund the programs. Attitudes about each of the programs also die hard. Some staff believe that child care teachers are not as well educated as Head Start teachers. Others think that Head Start parents care less than other parents about their children's education. Collaboration helps to dispel some of these myths, but the process is long and hard (David, Ochshorn, and Mitchell 1996).

Calls for collaborative statewide efforts on behalf of children go back decades. Sharon Lynn Kagan once compared the early care and education community to an "amoeba," reforming itself "with each new piece of legislation" (1992, 39). Policy makers, as you saw earlier, have tended to *react* to problems, passing laws that fund and establish separate programs rather than creating integrated systems to ensure collaboration among the many agencies that serve children and families. States have developed separate systems for health, education, child care, and child welfare, for example. But each system addresses only some of the early learning needs of young children. Fortunately, this situation is changing.

In recent years, a growing number of states have begun to build **early learning systems.** States may already provide services to promote the following: children's health and nutrition; competent and confident parenting; constant, stable, and appropriate supervision; guidance and instruction; safe and supportive communities; and schools that are ready for children. An early learning system enables these services to work together (Bruner 2004).

Building such a system requires a much more comprehensive vision than policy makers have historically held. States approach this work in different ways. One may start by creating a task force or commission to identify the needs of young learners and develop plans for addressing them. Another may expand existing programs—home visiting, early literacy, child care, preschool, transition to kindergarten programs. Yet another might set up a governance body, such as a cabinet, under the governor's leadership, with representatives from all the state agencies that serve children and families (Bruner 2004).

North Carolina is the mother of early learning systems–building. Through Smart Start, established in 1993, the state has worked to build a comprehensive early childhood system with partnerships at the state and local levels. The North Carolina Partnership for Children (NCPC) was established at the state level, and twelve local partnerships were begun in eighteen counties. All Smart Start funds pass through the NCPC, the state-level partnership, which works closely with the local partnerships (Coffman, Wright, and Bruner 2006). This structure helps to build an effective system because

- local partnerships have the authority to make decisions that are responsive to their communities' needs; they're not beholden to state policies that may not work for them.
- local partners are better able to finance the projects or programs in their communities because they helped create them.
- local communities serve as laboratories, helping to ensure statewide quality.

All the local partnerships include representatives from health, social service, mental health, K–12 education, county and city government, child care, business, faith-based organizations, and parents. As of 2006, more than eighty local partnerships had been established and were serving North Carolina's one hundred counties (Coffman, Wright, and Bruner 2006).

In North Carolina, local child care providers embraced the state's five-star licensing system because they already were meeting its high standards. When the state raised its standards again, providers felt confident they could meet them thanks to their partnerships with local agencies (Coffman, Wright, and Bruner 2006).

Policy makers have tended to react *to problems, passing laws that fund and establish separate programs rather than creating integrated systems to ensure collaboration among the many agencies that serve children and families.*

THOUGHT QUESTION What do you know about your state? Table 15.2 lists national organizations that focus on early care and education. Some have state affiliates, and many have information and links to early childhood initiatives in your area. Some organizations also keep track of states' progress in early care and education policies. For example, the National Institute for Early Education Research publishes the annual *State Preschool Yearbook*, a profile of state-funded prekindergarten programs across the country.

TABLE 15.2	National Advocacy Organizations with an Early Care and Education Focus

ORGANIZATION	URL
American Academy of Pediatrics	http://www.aap.org
Center for the Child Care Workforce	http://www.ccw.org
Children's Defense Fund	http://www.childrensdefense.org
Early Care and Education Collaborative	http://www.earlycare.org
Education Commission of the States	http://www.ecs.org
National Association for the Education of Young Children	http://www.naeyc.org
National Association for Family Child Care	http://www.nafcc.org
National Association of Child Advocates	http://www.childadvocacy.org
National Association of Child Care Resource and Referral Agencies	http://www.naccra.org
National Black Child Development Institute	http://www.nbcdi.org
National Center for Early Development and Learning	http://www.fpg.unc.edu/~ncedl
National Child Care Information Center	http://www.nccic.org
National Coalition for Campus Children's Centers	http://www.campuschildren.org
National Head Start Association	http://www.nhsa.org
National Institute for Early Education Research	http://www.nieer.org
National Institute on Early Childhood Development and Education	http://www.ed.gov/offices/OERI/ECI
National Network for Child Care	http://www.nncc.org
National Prekindergarten Center, Frank Porter Graham Child Development Institute	http://www.fpg.uncl.edu/~npc
Pre-K Now	http://www.preknow.org
Zero to Three	http://www.zerotothree.org

School Readiness Initiatives

Four-year-old Miranda spends a lot of time in the block corner. She and her friend Luna build factories, houses, and furniture for the "people" of their community. The two girls are busy working when their teacher gives everyone a five-minute warning for the group meeting. When they hear their teacher's voice, Miranda and Luna start cleaning up and are soon ready to join the group. Lucas has wandered aimlessly all morning. He stopped to work on a puzzle but quickly put it down. He then took a book about dinosaurs from the shelf but soon left it on the floor. After all of the children are gathered for the group meeting, Lucas is still wandering. The teacher gently takes him by the hand and brings him next to her in the group meeting.

All children come to school with different skills. Some children are focused—able to follow directions, take turns, share, and participate in classroom tasks with enthusiasm. Others have trouble controlling their impulses, are distracted, and shy away from work with their peers. How children manage tasks influences their experience of school and can profoundly affect their attitudes and outcomes as they move through the elementary school years.

Pressured by demands for accountability and greater equality of achievement, state lawmakers have focused their attention on school readiness. Recently, seventeen states (Arizona, Arkansas, California, Colorado, Connecticut, Kansas, Ken-

PART 5 Linking to Home and Community

tucky, Maine, Massachusetts, Missouri, New Hampshire, New Jersey, Ohio, Rhode Island, Vermont, Virginia, and Wisconsin) participated in a three-year national school readiness initiative. (See Figure 15.5.) The goal of this initiative was to develop **indicators,** or measures of progress, that could be used to track children's school readiness over time. As in Charles Bruner's early learning system, these states agreed that efforts to improve school readiness should be holistic. They should address children's readiness for school, school's readiness for children, and the capacity of families and communities to provide developmental opportunities for their young children. They came up with an equation: Ready Services + Ready Schools = Children Ready for School (Rhode Island KIDS COUNT 2005).

The states identified five indicators for "Ready Children":

- physical well-being and motor development;
- social and emotional development;
- approaches to learning;
- language development; and
- cognition and general knowledge.

States approach the indicators differently. For example, Missouri tracks the percentage of children entering kindergarten who "almost always use language to communicate ideas, feelings, and questions and to solve problems." Massachusetts, on the other hand, tracks those children entering kindergarten whose native language is not English but who are learning English.

This kind of information is critical for your local and state legislators. They need a clear picture of what conditions exist, what needs to be done, and how much it will cost to make the necessary changes. They also need evidence of progress over time to justify the money and time invested.

Readiness raises many questions. Merely defining it is tough, and measuring it is even tougher. Surveys of teachers and parents show that parents focus on children's

Pressured by demands for accountability and greater equality of achievement, state lawmakers have focused their attention on school readiness.

Participants in the National School Readiness Indicators Initiative

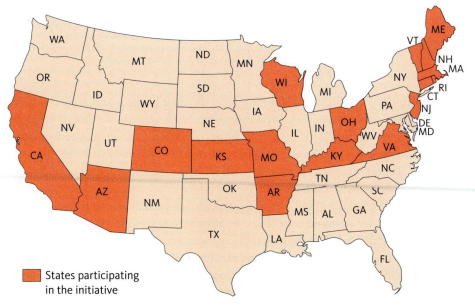

States participating in the initiative

Figure 15.5 *Participants in the National School Readiness Indicators Initiative*
Rhode Island KIDS COUNT 2005

THOUGHT QUESTION Many of the states you just read about look not only at children's readiness for school, but at schools' readiness for children. They also take into consideration the opportunities that children have had within their families and communities. How do *you* think readiness should be defined and measured?

academic skills, while teachers are more concerned with children's social readiness. Each child is different and brings different things to school; there is no one-size-fits-all list of readiness skills (Graue 2006). With NCLB, "[y]oung children today are expected to enter kindergarten classrooms with increasingly advanced skills" (Blaustein 2005, 2).

State Prekindergarten Initiatives

State-funded preschool and prekindergarten programs multiplied as school readiness moved to the top of the policy agenda. Today, a rapidly growing number of states offer a variety of pre-K programs, including Head Start and preschool for children with disabilities. Some states still do not provide funding for the education of children between the ages of three and five, except for those with disabilities (FPG Child Development Institute 2004). In the 2006–2007 program year, thirty-eight states enrolled more than a million children in their pre-K programs. Nearly two-thirds of these children were served in public schools; the others, in private child care, Head Start, and other settings. Total spending reached an all-time high of more than $3.7 billion (Barnett et al. 2007).

The development of state-funded preschool education—described as a "long and winding road" (Barnett et al. 2007)—has been closely watched and studied by the early childhood and policy communities. If you are a preschool teacher working in child care or Head Start, for instance, you may worry about the impact of publicly funded preschool on your program's enrollment. The disparity between your salary and that of colleagues doing the same work in public school may concern you as well. Finally, once you become part of the public education system, you are more likely to think about standards, assessment, and accountability in a larger and more demanding context because the requirements of NCLB have "trickled down" to the early elementary grades and preschool.

The drive toward school readiness continues, and, as one report on state initiatives for four-year-olds aptly concluded, "It is hard to find observers of the current scene who would not predict that by the year . . . 2020 each of the 50 states will have an organized pre-kindergarten program in operation. But the manner by which this will be done is not clear" (Gallagher, Clayton, and Heinemeier 2001, 20).

Professional Development and Compensation Initiatives

Opportunities for professional development are often limited, and access to those that do exist is not always easy, even though teacher training and education are essential to high-quality early care and education. Compensation, too, is a problem that has haunted the field for decades and continues to be a major concern. In recognition of the importance of teacher quality, retention, and compensation, states are stepping up to the plate and developing initiatives to address these issues. Some focus on training and licensing, while others create professional development systems.

In Oregon, for example, a 1999 law established a statewide child care provider training program. A 2001 law in Texas mandated that six hours of required annual training for child care staff and directors include the following topics: child development, guidance and discipline, age-appropriate curriculum, and teacher-child interactions. Colorado, through a state income tax checkoff established by the legislature, generated $312,716 in quality improvement grants in 2002–2003. This money went to a variety of child care programs as grants to help teachers attend national trainings, take college coursework, and pursue accreditation (Lowenstein et al. 2004).

Several states have made progress on licensing. If you work in a state-licensed, publicly funded child care center in California, you are required to have a child development permit. The California Commission on Teacher Credentialing administers permits for assistants, associate teachers, teachers, master teachers, site supervisors, and program directors. Education and experience requirements are specified for each level. In 2000, Illinois created a Director credential to establish professional standards in management and leadership for center-based early childhood administrators. Also in 2000, New Jersey legislation established the Commission on Early Childhood Education to advise the state on appropriate staff credentials and standards for early childhood educators and programs.

A number of initiatives link education and compensation. As with Smart Start, North Carolina has been a leader in this arena. In 1990, the state inaugurated the Teacher Education and Compensation Helps (T.E.A.C.H.) project, which offers continuing education scholarships for people working in regulated child care centers and homes; and many other states have since followed suit. T.E.A.C.H. participants must complete a certain amount of education—for which they receive either a salary increase or a bonus—and must stay in their program or the field for a minimum of six months (Center for the Child Care Workforce n.d.).

Connecticut has been a pioneer in professional development system–building. Through Connecticut Charts-A-Course (CCAC), the state departments of Education and Social Services support both career development and program improvement by promoting accreditation standards. Members of CCAC have access to professional development programs, scholarships for training and education, and career counseling. In addition, CCAC's Accreditation Facilitation Project supports early care and school-age programs seeking accreditation (Connecticut Charts-A-Course).

PROFESSIONAL AND NATIONAL ORGANIZATIONS AND AGENCIES

What role can professional and national organizations and agencies play for advocates?

Darlene Ragozzine, who heads Connecticut Charts-A-Course, sees advocacy as an integral part of professional development. "You've got to be comfortable being an advocate," she believes. "This is part of your responsibility, in the same way that you make sure the environment is clean and safe, that you listen to children, that you provide stimulating experiences." Veteran advocate Jerry Stermer, of Illinois Voices for Children, has declared that "every child in America deserves to live in a state where groups are working on policy and monitoring it" (personal communication).

Fortunately, you have a lot of support to help you fulfill that responsibility to children. Today, hundreds of community, state, and national organizations, coalitions, foundations, partnerships, and agencies advocate for children and help shape policies to ensure their well-being. They set guidelines for healthy child development. They research and evaluate early childhood programs. They provide financial support for initiatives that serve children and families. They lobby for legislation that will raise the bar for quality. Since 1973, the Children's Defense Fund (CDF), founded and still run by Marian Wright Edelman, has been on the front lines of

My path to early childhood advocacy was a bit indirect. I was born and raised in Illinois in a neighborhood where there were lots of children of different ages. I especially liked being involved with the little kids.

In college, I majored in family services, and I started my career in individual and family counseling. Through my work in mental health services, I eventually began to meet others in the community who were working on early care and education.

By the early 1990s, I was involved with a number of local committees here in Fayetteville. I worked with the United Way, where I learned about funding and accountability. I also served on the board of the Department of Social Services. I learned a lot about the child care world in those meetings. When North Carolina inaugurated its groundbreaking early childhood initiative, Smart Start, in 1993, I was on the front lines. In 1994, I served on a local task force charged with assessing the needs of the child care resource and referral agencies in the community. And in 1996, I applied for the position of director of the Cumberland County Partnership.

The partnership was the first of twelve to be established under North Carolina's statewide early childhood initiative. The community was ready. We worked with parents to forge connections between them and the schools. We created a center in an old church where parents and children could work together on homework.

As required by Smart Start, the partnership involved a good cross-section of the community. United Way, the partnership's "midwife," brought us funding and also helped build a board and set up the structure of the nonprofit organization under whose direction the work would take place. We had law enforcement people, grassroots community leaders, the mayor, the public schools, and businesses. Once we were up and running, community-based and faith-based child care providers were involved.

Our partnership members visit the policy makers at the capitol in Raleigh, and we also bring the legislators to see actual child care centers, which makes the biggest difference. Last year, we visited with a new representative, an older gentleman whose business is agriculture. We sat down and told him about Smart Start. "I'm worried that they don't have enough time to just play," he told us, after we finished our presentation. His granddaughter attends a faith-based program in his small rural community. I said to him, "If they're doing it right, she's playing 99 percent of the time and learning all the way." We then took him to visit a pre-K classroom in a public school. He was so engaging with the children, and the teachers were just fantastic. He was there for

Eva Hansen

an hour. It was a wonderful classroom, and he was able to see it, touch it, and feel it.

The same goes for our partnership members—including parents from the Head Start policy council and military child development centers. When they go to Raleigh, they get to see, touch, and feel where policy is made. They walk into the General Assembly room and see the legislators' desks and the podium from which the President Pro Tempore, or leader of the state senate, speaks. This is where they actually get to meet and talk with the people who make policy. All this helps to connect the dots.

The partnership, in fact, has had a significant role in changing people's view of the child care industry from a "mom-and-pop" operation to a profession. We have faith-based and private center directors who have been in the field for thirty to forty years. On our board, we have two director-owners. One of them started out in the military—she goes to Raleigh for our visits with legislators, and she's always the one who writes the letters. As a director-owner, she also sees the business side, and she'll bring up difficult stuff—how do you make a buck, the struggle with different funding sources, and all the accountability. She also does a lot of informal talking with other board and committees and in the community. She'll be standing in the grocery store line or at her grandson's soccer game and she'll be talking about quality and the importance of early care and education. It's these conversations in the parking lot, in the grocery store, and out on the field that really matter!

Harnessing this passion is the core of my work for the Cumberland County Partnership. There was a conversation one day, not long ago, in the van on the way home from a visit to Raleigh. Everyone was fired up by the day's events. After we did our usual debriefing, the parents asked: How are we going to know we made an impact? And what are our next steps? These questions are at the very heart of advocacy work.

advocacy, nationally and in the states. CDF files lawsuits on behalf of children, issues many publications tracking children's well-being, lobbies Congress, and has mobilized action across the country for the Child Care Now! and Healthy Child campaigns (http://www.childrensdefense.org).

Organizations working on behalf of children also provide fact sheets, reports, legislative updates, position papers, and newsletters through flourishing advocacy networks online. A good example is the joint position statement on *Early Learning Standards* issued by NAEYC and the National Association of Early Childhood Specialists in State Departments of Education (NAECS/SDE). (You can find the full text on NAEYC's website: http://www.naeyc.org/about/positions/learning_standards.asp.)

Throughout this and other chapters, you have had a glimpse of what advocacy work involves. You can begin your own explorations using the list of Web resources in Table 15.2. But these sources are just the tip of the iceberg. Keep in mind Eva Hansen's comment in this chapter's Real Voice about "those conversations in the parking lot, in the grocery store, and out on the field." Discussions on the fly with coworkers, families, and other members of the community often spark further connections to the world "out there," the place where policies are debated and created, where young children's education and many other aspects of their lives are determined. It is up to each of us to forge the connection between the classroom and policy.

SUMMARY

POLICY

What is policy?

Early care and education policy consists of the rules and regulations that affect how the business of early childhood education is conducted. Policy is created and implemented at the national, state, and local levels. Both the public and the private sectors enact policies.

HISTORY OF EARLY CHILDHOOD EDUCATION POLICY

What are the highlights of the history of early childhood education policy?

At the start of the twentieth century, care for orphans, foster children, and children of the poor and working poor remained mostly private. Early policy initiatives addressed the need for custodial care for these children, and many policy initiatives have continued to serve only targeted groups. During the Depression and World War II, the federal government supported the Works Progress Administration Nursery Schools that served a small percentage of the country's children. The Lanham Act of 1940 established child care centers in "war impact areas" from 1942 through 1946. In 1965, President Johnson's War on Poverty initiated Head Start and the Even Start Family Literacy Program as well as the Elementary and Secondary Education Act (ESEA) that established Title I funding for early childhood education and support services for children living in poverty. Enacted in 1975, the Individuals with Disabilities Education Act (IDEA) authorized federal funding for special education and related services and set out principles for provision of these services. The Child Care Development Block Grant (CCDBG), established in 1990, is the primary federal grant program supporting low-income families with child care needs. Administered by the Administration for Children and Families, the Early Learning Opportunities

Act (ELOA) was enacted in 2001 and provides grants to communities to enhance the cognitive, physical, social, and emotional development of children under five. NCLB, enacted in 2001, reauthorized ESEA and considerably expanded federal influence by increasing the accountability of public schools and public school systems for improving educational outcomes for all children, especially those living in poverty.

WHY POLICY MAKERS ARE INTERESTED IN EARLY CHILDHOOD EDUCATION
Why are policy makers interested in early childhood education?
Brain research has provided scientific evidence of the enormous growth that takes place in the first years of life and the effects that early experiences have on children's future development and capacity to learn. These findings, in combination with the large number of children in early childhood settings today, have convinced many policy makers of the importance of early care and education. Moreover, the achievement gap has brought attention to school readiness and, ultimately, to early childhood education.

WHY EARLY CHILDHOOD PROFESSIONALS SHOULD BE INVOLVED IN POLICY
Why should early childhood professionals be involved in policy?
Children need the adults in their lives to speak on their behalf, and early childhood educators are knowledgeable about the issues that affect children and families. They have personal stories to tell that can have a powerful impact on policy makers. They have daily contact with families and can mobilize them to join forces on behalf of children. Nonetheless, early childhood educators can feel powerless, be ignorant of government regulations, fear the political process, and/or lack confidence. They also do not have much time. Still, with websites and email, early childhood educators can more easily become informed and take action quickly. Five issues that are important to early childhood educators and about which they can speak authoritatively are quality of programming, credentialing, compensation, access to professional development, and rules and regulations affecting the daily life of their classrooms.

WORKING FOR CHANGE ON THE STATE LEVEL
What does working for change on the state level involve?
Advocates have many opportunities for advocacy and shaping policy at the state level. As states build coherent systems of a variety of services for children and families, advocates can share a more comprehensive vision than policy makers have historically held. As state lawmakers work on readiness initiatives, advocates can provide them with a clear picture of what conditions exist, what needs to be done, and how much it will cost to make the necessary changes, as well as with evidence of progress over time to justify the money and time invested. Both the early childhood and policy communities have been watching and studying the development of state-funded preschool education. Finally, in recognition of the importance of teacher quality, retention, and compensation, states are stepping up to the plate and developing initiatives to address these issues. Here, too, the voices of early childhood educators must be heard.

PROFESSIONAL AND NATIONAL ORGANIZATIONS AND AGENCIES
What role can professional and national organizations and agencies play for advocates?
Hundreds of community, state, and national organizations, coalitions, foundations, partnerships, and agencies advocate for children, providing local advocates with information and opportunities for action. These organizations help shape policies to ensure young children's well-being, set guidelines for healthy child development, and research and evaluate early childhood programs. They provide financial sup-

port for initiatives that serve children and families and lobby for legislation that will raise the bar for quality. Organizations working on behalf of children also make fact sheets, reports, legislative updates, position papers, and newsletters available through flourishing advocacy networks online. With their help, you, too, can forge the connection between classroom and policy.

FURTHER ACTIVITIES

1. Draft a letter to a local newspaper, to one of your state or local officials, or to the board of a program or school for children that explains what you know about young children's characteristics and needs and the multiple interacting influences on children's development and learning. Connect what you say about children to policies you would like to see that person or group enact. (**NAEYC Standard 1: Promoting Child Development and Learning**)

2. Read local newspapers and the websites of local organizations, and talk with teachers and families in your community to find out what issues are most important to them. Find out who else is already working on these issues, and determine the next steps that you and families at a program or school could take together. Document your research, and write up an action plan. Begin to implement it. Record the results. (**NAEYC Standard 2: Building Family and Community Relationships**)

3. In a group of three or four, write a sixty-second public service announcement (PSA) about quality in early childhood education. Research the topic carefully to include what you consider the most important points. Record the PSA on audiotape or as a video. (**NAEYC Standard 6: Becoming a Professional**)

Appendix A

NAEYC CODE OF ETHICAL CONDUCT

Preamble

NAEYC recognizes that those who work with young children face many daily decisions that have moral and ethical implications. The NAEYC Code of Ethical Conduct offers guidelines for responsible behavior and sets forth a common basis for resolving the principal ethical dilemmas encountered in early childhood care and education. The Statement of Commitment is not part of the Code but is a personal acknowledgement of an individual's willingness to embrace the distinctive values and moral obligations of the field of early childhood care and education.

The primary focus of the Code is on daily practice with children and their families in programs for children from birth through 8 years of age, such as infant/toddler programs, preschool and prekindergarten programs, child care centers, hospital and child life settings, family child care homes, kindergartens, and primary classrooms. When the issues involve young children, then these provisions also apply to specialists who do not work directly with children, including program administrators, parent educators, early childhood adult educators, and officials with responsibility for program monitoring and licensing. (Note: See also the "Code of Ethical Conduct: Supplement for Early Childhood Adult Educators," online at www.naeyc.org/about/positions/pdf/ethics04.pdf.)

Core values

Standards of ethical behavior in early childhood care and education are based on commitment to the following core values that are deeply rooted in the history of the field of early childhood care and education. We have made a commitment to

- Appreciate childhood as a unique and valuable stage of the human life cycle
- Base our work on knowledge of how children develop and learn
- Appreciate and support the bond between the child and family
- Recognize that children are best understood and supported in the context of family, culture, community, and society

- Respect the dignity, worth, and uniqueness of each individual (child, family member, and colleague)
- Respect diversity in children, families, and colleagues
- Recognize that children and adults achieve their full potential in the context of relationships that are based on trust and respect

Conceptual framework

The Code sets forth a framework of professional responsibilities in four sections. Each section addresses an area of professional relationships: (1) with children, (2) with families, (3) among colleagues, and (4) with the community and society. Each section includes an introduction to the primary responsibilities of the early childhood practitioner in that context. The introduction is followed by a set of ideals (I) that reflect exemplary professional practice and by a set of principles (P) describing practices that are required, prohibited, or permitted.

The ideals reflect the aspirations of practitioners. The principles guide conduct and assist practitioners in resolving ethical dilemmas. Both ideals and principles are intended to direct practitioners to those questions which, when responsibly answered, can provide the basis for conscientious decision making. While the Code provides specific direction for addressing some ethical dilemmas, many others will require the practitioner to combine the guidance of the Code with professional judgment.

The ideals and principles in this Code present a shared framework of professional responsibility that affirms our commitment to the core values of our field. The Code publicly acknowledges the responsibilities that we in the field have assumed, and in so doing supports ethical behavior in our work. Practitioners who face situations with ethical dimensions are urged to seek guidance in the applicable parts of this Code and in the spirit that informs the whole.

Often "the right answer"—the best ethical course of action to take—is not obvious. There may be no readily apparent, positive way to handle a situation. When one important value contradicts another, we face an ethical dilemma. When we face a dilemma, it is our professional responsibility to consult the Code and all relevant parties to find the most ethical resolution.

Section I

Ethical Responsibilities to Children

Childhood is a unique and valuable stage in the human life cycle. Our paramount responsibility is to provide care and education in settings that are safe, healthy, nurturing, and responsive for each child. We are committed to supporting children's development and learning; respecting individual differences; and helping children learn to live, play, and work cooperatively. We are also committed to promoting children's self-awareness, competence, self-worth, resiliency, and physical well-being.

Ideals

I-1.1—To be familiar with the knowledge base of early childhood care and education and to stay informed through continuing education and training.

I-1.2—To base program practices upon current knowledge and research in the field of early childhood education, child development, and related disciplines, as well as on particular knowledge of each child.

I-1.3—To recognize and respect the unique qualities, abilities, and potential of each child.

I-1.4—To appreciate the vulnerability of children and their dependence on adults.

I-1.5—To create and maintain safe and healthy settings that foster children's social, emotional, cognitive, and physical development and that respect their dignity and their contributions.

I-1.6—To use assessment instruments and strategies that are appropriate for the children to be assessed, that are used only for the purposes for which they were designed, and that have the potential to benefit children.

I-1.7—To use assessment information to understand and support children's development and learning, to support instruction, and to identify children who may need additional services.

I-1.8—To support the right of each child to play and learn in an inclusive environment that meets the needs of children with and without disabilities.

I-1.9—To advocate for and ensure that all children, including those with special needs, have access to the support services needed to be successful.

I-1.10—To ensure that each child's culture, language, ethnicity, and family structure are recognized and valued in the program.

I-1.11—To provide all children with experiences in a language that they know, as well as support children in maintaining the use of their home language and in learning English.

I-1.12—To work with families to provide a safe and smooth transition as children and families move from one program to the next.

Principles

P-1.1—Above all, we shall not harm children. We shall not participate in practices that are emotionally damaging, physically harmful, disrespectful, degrading, dangerous, exploitative, or intimidating to children. *This principle has precedence over all others in this Code.*

P-1.2—We shall care for and educate children in positive emotional and social environments that are cognitively stimulating and that support each child's culture, language, ethnicity, and family structure.

P-1.3—We shall not participate in practices that discriminate against children by denying benefits, giving special advantages, or excluding them from programs or activities on the basis of their sex, race, national origin, religious beliefs, medical condition, disability, or the marital status/family structure, sexual orientation, or religious beliefs or other affiliations of their families. (Aspects of this principle do not apply in programs that have a lawful mandate to provide services to a particular population of children.)

P-1.4—We shall involve all those with relevant knowledge (including families and staff) in decisions concerning a child, as appropriate, ensuring confidentiality of sensitive information.

P-1.5—We shall use appropriate assessment systems, which include multiple sources of information, to provide information on children's learning and development.

P-1.6—We shall strive to ensure that decisions such as those related to enrollment, retention, or assignment to special education services, will be based on multiple sources of information and will never be based on a single assessment, such as a test score or a single observation.

P-1.7—We shall strive to build individual relationships with each child; make individualized adaptations in teaching strategies, learning environments, and curricula; and consult with the family so that each child benefits from the program. If after such efforts have been exhausted, the current placement does not meet a child's needs, or the child is seriously jeopardizing the ability of other children to benefit from the program, we shall collaborate with the child's family and appropriate specialists to determine the additional services needed and/or the placement option(s) most likely to ensure the child's success. (Aspects of this principle may not apply in programs that have a lawful mandate to provide services to a particular population of children.)

P-1.8—We shall be familiar with the risk factors for and symptoms of child abuse and neglect, including physical, sexual, verbal, and emotional abuse and physical, emotional, educational, and medical neglect. We shall know and follow state laws and community procedures that protect children against abuse and neglect.

P-1.9—When we have reasonable cause to suspect child abuse or neglect, we shall report it to the appropriate community agency and follow up to ensure that appropriate action has been taken. When appropriate, parents or guardians will be informed that the referral will be or has been made.

P-1.10—When another person tells us of his or her suspicion that a child is being abused or neglected, we shall assist that person in taking appropriate action in order to protect the child.

P-1.11—When we become aware of a practice or situation that endangers the health, safety, or well-being of children, we have an ethical responsibility to protect children or inform parents and/or others who can.

Section II

Ethical Responsibilities to Families

Families are of primary importance in children's development. Because the family and the early childhood practitioner have a common interest in the child's well-being, we acknowledge a primary responsibility to bring about communication, cooperation, and collaboration between the home and early childhood program in ways that enhance the child's development.

Ideals

I-2.1—To be familiar with the knowledge base related to working effectively with families and to stay informed through continuing education and training.

I-2.2—To develop relationships of mutual trust and create partnerships with the families we serve.

I-2.3—To welcome all family members and encourage them to participate in the program.

I-2.4—To listen to families, acknowledge and build upon their strengths and competencies, and learn from families as we support them in their task of nurturing children.

I-2.5—To respect the dignity and preferences of each family and to make an effort to learn about its structure, culture, language, customs, and beliefs.

I-2.6—To acknowledge families' childrearing values and their right to make decisions for their children.

I-2.7—To share information about each child's education and development with families and to help them understand and appreciate the current knowledge base of the early childhood profession.

I-2.8—To help family members enhance their understanding of their children and support the continuing development of their skills as parents.

I-2.9—To participate in building support networks for families by providing them with opportunities to interact with program staff, other families, community resources, and professional services.

Principles

P-2.1—We shall not deny family members access to their child's classroom or program setting unless access is denied by court order or other legal restriction.

P-2.2—We shall inform families of program philosophy, policies, curriculum, assessment system, and personnel qualifications, and explain why we teach as we do—which should be in accordance with our ethical responsibilities to children (see Section I).

P-2.3—We shall inform families of and, when appropriate, involve them in policy decisions.

P-2.4—We shall involve the family in significant decisions affecting their child.

P-2.5—We shall make every effort to communicate effectively with all families in a language that they understand. We shall use community resources for translation and interpretation when we do not have sufficient resources in our own programs.

P-2.6—As families share information with us about their children and families, we shall consider this information to plan and implement the program.

P-2.7—We shall inform families about the nature and purpose of the program's child assessments and how data about their child will be used.

P-2.8—We shall treat child assessment information confidentially and share this information only when there is a legitimate need for it.

P-2.9—We shall inform the family of injuries and incidents involving their child, of risks such as exposures to communicable diseases that might result in infection, and of occurrences that might result in emotional stress.

P-2.10—Families shall be fully informed of any proposed research projects involving their children and shall have the opportunity to give or withhold consent without penalty. We shall not permit or participate in research that could in any way hinder the education, development, or well-being of children.

P-2.11—We shall not engage in or support exploitation of families. We shall not use our relationship with a family for private advantage or personal gain, or enter into relationships with family members that might impair our effectiveness working with their children.

P-2.12—We shall develop written policies for the protection of confidentiality and the disclosure of children's records. These policy documents shall be made available to all program personnel and families. Disclosure of children's records beyond family members, program personnel, and consultants having an obligation of confidentiality shall require familial consent (except in cases of abuse or neglect).

P-2.13—We shall maintain confidentiality and shall respect the family's right to privacy, refraining from disclosure of confidential information and intrusion into family life. However, when we have reason to believe that a child's welfare is at risk, it is permissible to share confidential information with agencies, as well as with individuals who have legal responsibility for intervening in the child's interest.

P-2.14—In cases where family members are in conflict with one another, we shall work openly, sharing our observations of the child, to help all parties involved make informed decisions. We shall refrain from becoming an advocate for one party.

P-2.15—We shall be familiar with and appropriately refer families to community resources and professional support services. After a referral has been made, we shall follow up to ensure that services have been appropriately provided.

Section III

Ethical Responsibilities to Colleagues

In a caring, cooperative workplace, human dignity is respected, professional satisfaction is promoted, and positive relationships are developed and sustained. Based upon our core values, our primary responsibility to colleagues is to establish and maintain settings and relationships that support productive work and meet professional needs. The same ideals that apply to children also apply as we interact with adults in the workplace.

A—Responsibilities to co-workers
Ideals

I-3A.1—To establish and maintain relationships of respect, trust, confidentiality, collaboration, and cooperation with co-workers.

I-3A.2—To share resources with co-workers, collaborating to ensure that the best possible early childhood care and education program is provided.

I-3A.3—To support co-workers in meeting their professional needs and in their professional development.

I-3A.4—To accord co-workers due recognition of professional achievement.

Principles

P-3A.1—We shall recognize the contributions of colleagues to our program and not participate in practices that diminish their reputations or impair their effectiveness in working with children and families.

P-3A.2—When we have concerns about the professional behavior of a co-worker, we shall first let that person know of our concern in a way that shows respect for personal dignity and for the diversity to be found among staff members, and then attempt to resolve the matter collegially and in a confidential manner.

P-3A.3—We shall exercise care in expressing views regarding the personal attributes or professional conduct of co-workers. Statements should be based on firsthand knowledge, not hearsay, and relevant to the interests of children and programs.

P-3A.4—We shall not participate in practices that discriminate against a co-worker because of sex, race, national origin, religious beliefs or other affiliations, age, marital status/family structure, disability, or sexual orientation.

B—Responsibilities to employers
Ideals

I-3B.1—To assist the program in providing the highest quality of service.

I-3B.2—To do nothing that diminishes the reputation of the program in which we work unless it is violating laws and regulations designed to protect children or is violating the provisions of this Code.

Principles

P-3B.1—We shall follow all program policies. When we do not agree with program policies, we shall attempt to effect change through constructive action within the organization.

P-3B.2—We shall speak or act on behalf of an organization only when authorized. We shall take care to acknowledge when we are speaking for the organization and when we are expressing a personal judgment.

P-3B.3—We shall not violate laws or regulations designed to protect children and shall take appropriate action consistent with this Code when aware of such violations.

P-3B.4—If we have concerns about a colleague's behavior, and children's well-being is not at risk, we may address the concern with that individual. If children are at risk or the situation does not improve after it has been brought to the colleague's attention, we shall report the colleague's unethical or incompetent behavior to an appropriate authority.

P-3B.5—When we have a concern about circumstances or conditions that impact the quality of care and education within the program, we shall inform the program's administration or, when necessary, other appropriate authorities.

C—Responsibilities to employees
Ideals

I-3C.1—To promote safe and healthy working conditions and policies that foster mutual respect, cooperation, collaboration, competence, well-being, confidentiality, and self-esteem in staff members.

I-3C.2—To create and maintain a climate of trust and candor that will enable staff to speak and act in the best interests of children, families, and the field of early childhood care and education.

I-3C.3—To strive to secure adequate and equitable compensation (salary and benefits) for those who work with or on behalf of young children.

I-3C.4—To encourage and support continual development of employees in becoming more skilled and knowledgeable practitioners.

Principles

P-3C.1—In decisions concerning children and programs, we shall draw upon the education, training, experience, and expertise of staff members.

P-3C.2—We shall provide staff members with safe and supportive working conditions that honor confidences and permit them to carry out their responsibilities through fair performance evaluation, written grievance procedures, constructive feedback, and opportunities for continuing professional development and advancement.

P-3C.3—We shall develop and maintain comprehensive written personnel policies that define program standards. These policies shall be given to new staff members and shall be available and easily accessible for review by all staff members.

P-3C.4—We shall inform employees whose performance does not meet program expectations of areas of concern and, when possible, assist in improving their performance.

P-3C.5—We shall conduct employee dismissals for just cause, in accordance with all applicable laws and regulations. We shall inform employees who are dismissed of the reasons for their termination. When a dismissal is for cause, justification must be based on evidence of inadequate or inappropriate behavior that is accurately documented, current, and available for the employee to review.

P-3C.6—In making evaluations and recommendations, we shall make judgments based on fact and relevant to the interests of children and programs.

P-3C.7—We shall make hiring, retention, termination, and promotion decisions based solely on a person's competence, record of accomplishment, ability to carry out the responsibilities of the position, and professional preparation specific to the developmental levels of children in his/her care.

P-3C.8—We shall not make hiring, retention, termination, and promotion decisions based on an individual's sex, race, national origin, religious beliefs or other affiliations, age, marital status/family structure, disability, or sexual orientation. We shall be familiar with and observe laws and regulations that pertain to employment discrimination. (Aspects of this principle do not apply to programs that have a lawful mandate to determine eligibility based on one or more of the criteria identified above.)

P-3C.9—We shall maintain confidentiality in dealing with issues related to an employee's job performance and shall respect an employee's right to privacy regarding personal issues.

Section IV

Ethical Responsibilities to Community and Society

Early childhood programs operate within the context of their immediate community made up of families and other institutions concerned with children's welfare. Our responsibilities to the community are to provide programs that meet the diverse needs of families, to cooperate with agencies and professions that share the responsibility for children, to assist families in gaining access to those agencies and allied professionals, and to assist in the development of community programs that are needed but not currently available. As individuals, we acknowledge our responsibility to provide the best possible programs of care and education for children and to conduct ourselves with honesty and integrity. Because of our specialized expertise in early childhood development and education and because the larger society shares responsibility for the welfare and protection of young children, we acknowledge a collective obligation to advocate for the best interests of children within early childhood programs and in the larger community and to serve as a voice for young children everywhere. The ideals and principles in this section are presented to distinguish between those that pertain to the work of the individual early childhood educator and those that more typically are engaged in collectively on behalf of the best interests of children—with the understanding that individual early childhood educators have a shared responsibility for addressing the ideals and principles that are identified as "collective."

Ideal (Individual)

I-4.1—To provide the community with high-quality early childhood care and education programs and services.

Ideals (Collective)

I-4.2—To promote cooperation among professionals and agencies and interdisciplinary collaboration among professions concerned with addressing issues in the health, education, and well-being of young children, their families, and their early childhood educators.

I-4.3—To work through education, research, and advocacy toward an environmentally safe world in which all children receive health care, food, and shelter; are nurtured; and live free from violence in their home and their communities.

I-4.4—To work through education, research, and advocacy toward a society in which all young children have access to high-quality early care and education programs.

I-4.5—To work to ensure that appropriate assessment systems, which include multiple sources of information, are used for purposes that benefit children.

I-4.6—To promote knowledge and understanding of young children and their needs. To work toward greater societal acknowledgment of children's rights and greater social acceptance of responsibility for the well-being of all children.

I-4.7—To support policies and laws that promote the well-being of children and families, and to work to change those that impair their well-being. To participate in developing policies and laws that are needed, and to cooperate with other individuals and groups in these efforts.

I-4.8—To further the professional development of the field of early childhood care and education and to

strengthen its commitment to realizing its core values as reflected in this Code.

Principles (Individual)

P-4.1—We shall communicate openly and truthfully about the nature and extent of services that we provide.

P-4.2—We shall apply for, accept, and work in positions for which we are personally well-suited and professionally qualified. We shall not offer services that we do not have the competence, qualifications, or resources to provide.

P-4.3—We shall carefully check references and shall not hire or recommend for employment any person whose competence, qualifications, or character makes him or her unsuited for the position.

P-4.4—We shall be objective and accurate in reporting the knowledge upon which we base our program practices.

P-4.5—We shall be knowledgeable about the appropriate use of assessment strategies and instruments and interpret results accurately to families.

P-4.6—We shall be familiar with laws and regulations that serve to protect the children in our programs and be vigilant in ensuring that these laws and regulations are followed.

P-4.7—When we become aware of a practice or situation that endangers the health, safety, or well-being of children, we have an ethical responsibility to protect children or inform parents and/or others who can.

P-4.8—We shall not participate in practices that are in violation of laws and regulations that protect the children in our programs.

P-4.9—When we have evidence that an early childhood program is violating laws or regulations protecting children, we shall report the violation to appropriate authorities who can be expected to remedy the situation.

P-4.10—When a program violates or requires its employees to violate this Code, it is permissible, after fair assessment of the evidence, to disclose the identity of that program.

Principles (Collective)

P-4.11—When policies are enacted for purposes that do not benefit children, we have a collective responsibility to work to change these practices.

P-4.12—When we have evidence that an agency that provides services intended to ensure children's well-being is failing to meet its obligations, we acknowledge a collective ethical responsibility to report the problem to appropriate authorities or to the public. We shall be vigilant in our follow-up until the situation is resolved.

P-4.13—When a child protection agency fails to provide adequate protection for abused or neglected children, we acknowledge a collective ethical responsibility to work toward the improvement of these services.

The National Association for the Education of Young Children (NAEYC) is a nonprofit corporation, tax exempt under Section 501(c)(3) of the Internal Revenue Code, dedicated to acting on behalf of the needs and interests of young children. The NAEYC Code of Ethical Conduct (Code) has been developed in furtherance of NAEYC's nonprofit and tax exempt purposes. The information contained in the Code is intended to provide early childhood educators with guidelines for working with children from birth through age 8.

An individual's or program's use, reference to, or review of the Code does not guarantee compliance with NAEYC Early Childhood Program Standards and Accreditation Performance Criteria and program accreditation procedures. It is recommended that the Code be used as guidance in connection with implementation of the NAEYC Program Standards, but such use is not a substitute for diligent review and application of the NAEYC Program Standards.

NAEYC has taken reasonable measures to develop the Code in a fair, reasonable, open, unbiased, and objective manner, based on currently available data. However, further research or developments may change the current state of knowledge. Neither NAEYC nor its officers, directors, members, employees, or agents will be liable for any loss, damage, or claim with respect to any liabilities, including direct, special, indirect, or consequential damages incurred in connection with the Code or reliance on the information presented.

Appendix B

CONVENTION ON THE RIGHTS OF THE CHILD

ADOPTED AND OPENED FOR SIGNATURE, RATIFICATION AND ACCESSION BY THE UNITED NATIONS' GENERAL ASSEMBLY RESOLUTION 44/25 OF 20 NOVEMBER 1989

Preamble

The States Parties to the present Convention,

Considering that, in accordance with the principles proclaimed in the Charter of the United Nations, recognition of the inherent dignity and of the equal and inalienable rights of all members of the human family is the foundation of freedom, justice and peace in the world,

Bearing in mind that the peoples of the United Nations have, in the Charter, reaffirmed their faith in fundamental human rights and in the dignity and worth of the human person, and have determined to promote social progress and better standards of life in larger freedom,

Recognizing that the United Nations has, in the Universal Declaration of Human Rights and in the International Covenants on Human Rights, proclaimed and agreed that everyone is entitled to all the rights and freedoms set forth therein, without distinction of any kind, such as race, colour, sex, language, religion, political or other opinion, national or social origin, property, birth or other status,

Recalling that, in the Universal Declaration of Human Rights, the United Nations has proclaimed that childhood is entitled to special care and assistance,

Convinced that the family, as the fundamental group of society and the natural environment for the growth and well-being of all its members and particularly children, should be afforded the necessary protection and assistance so that it can fully assume its responsibilities within the community,

Recognizing that the child, for the full and harmonious development of his or her personality, should grow up in a family environment, in an atmosphere of happiness, love and understanding,

Considering that the child should be fully prepared to live an individual life in society, and brought up in the spirit of the ideals proclaimed in the Charter of the United Nations, and in particular in the spirit of peace, dignity, tolerance, freedom, equality and solidarity,

Bearing in mind that the need to extend particular care to the child has been stated in the Geneva Declaration of the Rights of the Child of 1924 and in the Declaration of the Rights of the Child adopted by the General Assembly on 20 November 1959 and recognized in the Universal Declaration of Human Rights, in the International Covenant on Civil and Political Rights (in particular in articles 23 and 24), in the International Covenant on Economic, Social and Cultural Rights (in particular in article 10) and in the statutes and relevant instruments of specialized agencies and international organizations concerned with the welfare of children,

Bearing in mind that, as indicated in the Declaration of the Rights of the Child, "the child, by reason of his physical and mental immaturity, needs special safeguards and care, including appropriate legal protection, before as well as after birth",

Recalling the provisions of the Declaration on Social and Legal Principles relating to the Protection and Welfare of Children, with Special Reference to Foster Placement and Adoption Nationally and Internationally; the United Nations Standard Minimum Rules for the Administration of Juvenile Justice (The Beijing Rules); and the Declaration on the Protection of Women and Children in Emergency and Armed Conflict, Recognizing that, in all countries in the world, there are children living in exceptionally difficult conditions, and that such children need special consideration,

Taking due account of the importance of the traditions and cultural values of each people for the protection and harmonious development of the child, Recognizing the importance of international co-operation for improving the living conditions of children in every country, in particular in the developing countries,

Have agreed as follows:

PART I

Article 1

For the purposes of the present Convention, a child means every human being below the age of eighteen years unless under the law applicable to the child, majority is attained earlier.

Article 2

1. States Parties shall respect and ensure the rights set forth in the present Convention to each child within their jurisdiction without discrimination of any kind, irrespective of the child's or his or her parent's or legal guardian's race, colour, sex, language, religion, political or other opinion, national, ethnic or social origin, property, disability, birth or other status.
2. States Parties shall take all appropriate measures to ensure that the child is protected against all forms of discrimination or punishment on the basis of the status, activities, expressed opinions, or beliefs of the child's parents, legal guardians, or family members.

Article 3

1. In all actions concerning children, whether undertaken by public or private social welfare institutions, courts of law, administrative authorities or legislative bodies, the best interests of the child shall be a primary consideration.
2. States Parties undertake to ensure the child such protection and care as is necessary for his or her well-being, taking into account the rights and duties of his or her parents, legal guardians, or other individuals legally responsible for him or her, and, to this end, shall take all appropriate legislative and administrative measures.
3. States Parties shall ensure that the institutions, services and facilities responsible for the care or protection of children shall conform with the standards established by competent authorities, particularly in the areas of safety, health, in the number and suitability of their staff, as well as competent supervision.

Article 4

States Parties shall undertake all appropriate legislative, administrative, and other measures for the implementation of the rights recognized in the present Convention. With regard to economic, social and cultural rights, States Parties shall undertake such measures to the maximum extent of their available resources and, where needed, within the framework of international co-operation.

Article 5

States Parties shall respect the responsibilities, rights and duties of parents or, where applicable, the members of the extended family or community as provided for by local custom, legal guardians or other persons legally responsible for the child, to provide, in a manner consistent with the evolving capacities of the child, appropriate direction and guidance in the exercise by the child of the rights recognized in the present Convention.

Article 6

1. States Parties recognize that every child has the inherent right to life.
2. States Parties shall ensure to the maximum extent possible the survival and development of the child.

Article 7

1. The child shall be registered immediately after birth and shall have the right from birth to a name, the right to acquire a nationality and, as far as possible, the right to know and be cared for by his or her parents.
2. States Parties shall ensure the implementation of these rights in accordance with their national law and their obligations under the relevant international instruments in this field, in particular where the child would otherwise be stateless.

Article 8

1. States Parties undertake to respect the right of the child to preserve his or her identity, including nationality, name and family relations as recognized by law without unlawful interference.
2. Where a child is illegally deprived of some or all of the elements of his or her identity, States Parties shall provide appropriate assistance and protection, with a view to re-establishing speedily his or her identity.

Article 9

1. States Parties shall ensure that a child shall not be separated from his or her parents against their will, except when competent authorities subject to judicial review determine, in accordance with applicable law and procedures, that such separation is necessary for the best interests of the child. Such determination

may be necessary in a particular case such as one involving abuse or neglect of the child by the parents, or one where the parents are living separately and a decision must be made as to the child's place of residence.

2. In any proceedings pursuant to paragraph 1 of the present article, all interested parties shall be given an opportunity to participate in the proceedings and make their views known.

3. States Parties shall respect the right of the child who is separated from one or both parents to maintain personal relations and direct contact with both parents on a regular basis, except if it is contrary to the child's best interests.

4. Where such separation results from any action initiated by a State Party, such as the detention, imprisonment, exile, deportation or death (including death arising from any cause while the person is in the custody of the State) of one or both parents or of the child, that State Party shall, upon request, provide the parents, the child or, if appropriate, another member of the family with the essential information concerning the whereabouts of the absent member(s) of the family unless the provision of the information would be detrimental to the well-being of the child. States Parties shall further ensure that the submission of such a request shall of itself entail no adverse consequences for the person(s) concerned.

Article 10

1. In accordance with the obligation of States Parties under article 9, paragraph 1, applications by a child or his or her parents to enter or leave a State Party for the purpose of family reunification shall be dealt with by States Parties in a positive, humane and expeditious manner. States Parties shall further ensure that the submission of such a request shall entail no adverse consequences for the applicants and for the members of their family.

2. A child whose parents reside in different States shall have the right to maintain on a regular basis, save in exceptional circumstances personal relations and direct contacts with both parents. Towards that end and in accordance with the obligation of States Parties under article 9, paragraph 1, States Parties shall respect the right of the child and his or her parents to leave any country, including their own, and to enter their own country. The right to leave any country shall be subject only to such restrictions as are prescribed by law and which are necessary to protect the national

security, public order (ordre public), public health or morals or the rights and freedoms of others and are consistent with the other rights recognized in the present Convention.

Article 11

1. States Parties shall take measures to combat the illicit transfer and non-return of children abroad.

2. To this end, States Parties shall promote the conclusion of bilateral or multilateral agreements or accession to existing agreements.

Article 12

1. States Parties shall assure to the child who is capable of forming his or her own views the right to express those views freely in all matters affecting the child, the views of the child being given due weight in accordance with the age and maturity of the child.

2. For this purpose, the child shall in particular be provided the opportunity to be heard in any judicial and administrative proceedings affecting the child, either directly, or through a representative or an appropriate body, in a manner consistent with the procedural rules of national law.

Article 13

1. The child shall have the right to freedom of expression; this right shall include freedom to seek, receive and impart information and ideas of all kinds, regardless of frontiers, either orally, in writing or in print, in the form of art, or through any other media of the child's choice.

2. The exercise of this right may be subject to certain restrictions, but these shall only be such as are provided by law and are necessary:

   (a) For respect of the rights or reputations of others; or

   (b) For the protection of national security or of public order (ordre public), or of public health or morals.

Article 14

1. States Parties shall respect the right of the child to freedom of thought, conscience and religion.

2. States Parties shall respect the rights and duties of the parents and, when applicable, legal guardians, to provide direction to the child in the exercise of his or her right in a manner consistent with the evolving capacities of the child.

3. Freedom to manifest one's religion or beliefs may be subject only to such limitations as are prescribed by law and are necessary to protect public safety, order, health or morals, or the fundamental rights and freedoms of others.

Article 15

1. States Parties recognize the rights of the child to freedom of association and to freedom of peaceful assembly.
2. No restrictions may be placed on the exercise of these rights other than those imposed in conformity with the law and which are necessary in a democratic society in the interests of national security or public safety, public order (ordre public), the protection of public health or morals or the protection of the rights and freedoms of others.

Article 16

1. No child shall be subjected to arbitrary or unlawful interference with his or her privacy, family, or correspondence, nor to unlawful attacks on his or her honour and reputation.
2. The child has the right to the protection of the law against such interference or attacks.

Article 17

States Parties recognize the important function performed by the mass media and shall ensure that the child has access to information and material from a diversity of national and international sources, especially those aimed at the promotion of his or her social, spiritual and moral well-being and physical and mental health.

To this end, States Parties shall:

(a) Encourage the mass media to disseminate information and material of social and cultural benefit to the child and in accordance with the spirit of article 29;

(b) Encourage international co-operation in the production, exchange and dissemination of such information and material from a diversity of cultural, national and international sources;

(c) Encourage the production and dissemination of children's books;

(d) Encourage the mass media to have particular regard to the linguistic needs of the child who belongs to a minority group or who is indigenous;

(e) Encourage the development of appropriate guidelines for the protection of the child from informa-

tion and material injurious to his or her well-being, bearing in mind the provisions of articles 13 and 18.

Article 18

1. States Parties shall use their best efforts to ensure recognition of the principle that both parents have common responsibilities for the upbringing and development of the child. Parents or, as the case may be, legal guardians, have the primary responsibility for the upbringing and development of the child. The best interests of the child will be their basic concern.
2. For the purpose of guaranteeing and promoting the rights set forth in the present Convention, States Parties shall render appropriate assistance to parents and legal guardians in the performance of their child-rearing responsibilities and shall ensure the development of institutions, facilities and services for the care of children.
3. States Parties shall take all appropriate measures to ensure that children of working parents have the right to benefit from child-care services and facilities for which they are eligible.

Article 19

1. States Parties shall take all appropriate legislative, administrative, social and educational measures to protect the child from all forms of physical or mental violence, injury or abuse, neglect or negligent treatment, maltreatment or exploitation, including sexual abuse, while in the care of parent(s), legal guardian(s) or any other person who has the care of the child.
2. Such protective measures should, as appropriate, include effective procedures for the establishment of social programmes to provide necessary support for the child and for those who have the care of the child, as well as for other forms of prevention and for identification, reporting, referral, investigation, treatment and follow-up of instances of child maltreatment described heretofore, and, as appropriate, for judicial involvement.

Article 20

1. A child temporarily or permanently deprived of his or her family environment, or in whose own best interests cannot be allowed to remain in that environment, shall be entitled to special protection and assistance provided by the State.
2. States Parties shall in accordance with their national laws ensure alternative care for such a child.

3. Such care could include, inter alia, foster placement, kafalah of Islamic law, adoption or if necessary placement in suitable institutions for the care of children. When considering solutions, due regard shall be paid to the desirability of continuity in a child's upbringing and to the child's ethnic, religious, cultural and linguistic background.

Article 21

States Parties that recognize and/or permit the system of adoption shall ensure that the best interests of the child shall be the paramount consideration and they shall:

(a) Ensure that the adoption of a child is authorized only by competent authorities who determine, in accordance with applicable law and procedures and on the basis of all pertinent and reliable information, that the adoption is permissible in view of the child's status concerning parents, relatives and legal guardians and that, if required, the persons concerned have given their informed consent to the adoption on the basis of such counselling as may be necessary;

(b) Recognize that inter-country adoption may be considered as an alternative means of child's care, if the child cannot be placed in a foster or an adoptive family or cannot in any suitable manner be cared for in the child's country of origin;

(c) Ensure that the child concerned by inter-country adoption enjoys safeguards and standards equivalent to those existing in the case of national adoption;

(d) Take all appropriate measures to ensure that, in inter-country adoption, the placement does not result in improper financial gain for those involved in it;

(e) Promote, where appropriate, the objectives of the present article by concluding bilateral or multilateral arrangements or agreements, and endeavour, within this framework, to ensure that the placement of the child in another country is carried out by competent authorities or organs.

Article 22

1. States Parties shall take appropriate measures to ensure that a child who is seeking refugee status or who is considered a refugee in accordance with applicable international or domestic law and procedures shall, whether unaccompanied or accompanied by his or her parents or by any other person, receive appropriate protection and humanitarian assistance in the enjoyment of applicable rights set forth in the present Convention and in other international human rights or humanitarian instruments to which the said States are Parties.

2. For this purpose, States Parties shall provide, as they consider appropriate, co-operation in any efforts by the United Nations and other competent intergovernmental organizations or non-governmental organizations co-operating with the United Nations to protect and assist such a child and to trace the parents or other members of the family of any refugee child in order to obtain information necessary for reunification with his or her family. In cases where no parents or other members of the family can be found, the child shall be accorded the same protection as any other child permanently or temporarily deprived of his or her family environment for any reason, as set forth in the present Convention.

Article 23

1. States Parties recognize that a mentally or physically disabled child should enjoy a full and decent life, in conditions which ensure dignity, promote self-reliance and facilitate the child's active participation in the community.

2. States Parties recognize the right of the disabled child to special care and shall encourage and ensure the extension, subject to available resources, to the eligible child and those responsible for his or her care, of assistance for which application is made and which is appropriate to the child's condition and to the circumstances of the parents or others caring for the child.

3. Recognizing the special needs of a disabled child, assistance extended in accordance with paragraph 2 of the present article shall be provided free of charge, whenever possible, taking into account the financial resources of the parents or others caring for the child, and shall be designed to ensure that the disabled child has effective access to and receives education, training, health care services, rehabilitation services, preparation for employment and recreation opportunities in a manner conducive to the child's achieving the fullest possible social integration and individual development, including his or her cultural and spiritual development.

4. States Parties shall promote, in the spirit of international cooperation, the exchange of appropriate

information in the field of preventive health care and of medical, psychological and functional treatment of disabled children, including dissemination of and access to information concerning methods of rehabilitation, education and vocational services, with the aim of enabling States Parties to improve their capabilities and skills and to widen their experience in these areas. In this regard, particular account shall be taken of the needs of developing countries.

Article 24

1. States Parties recognize the right of the child to the enjoyment of the highest attainable standard of health and to facilities for the treatment of illness and rehabilitation of health. States Parties shall strive to ensure that no child is deprived of his or her right of access to such health care services.

2. States Parties shall pursue full implementation of this right and, in particular, shall take appropriate measures:

   (a) To diminish infant and child mortality;

   (b) To ensure the provision of necessary medical assistance and health care to all children with emphasis on the development of primary health care;

   (c) To combat disease and malnutrition, including within the framework of primary health care, through, inter alia, the application of readily available technology and through the provision of adequate nutritious foods and clean drinking-water, taking into consideration the dangers and risks of environmental pollution;

   (d) To ensure appropriate pre-natal and post-natal health care for mothers;

   (e) To ensure that all segments of society, in particular parents and children, are informed, have access to education and are supported in the use of basic knowledge of child health and nutrition, the advantages of breastfeeding, hygiene and environmental sanitation and the prevention of accidents;

   (f) To develop preventive health care, guidance for parents and family planning education and services.

3. States Parties shall take all effective and appropriate measures with a view to abolishing traditional practices prejudicial to the health of children.

4. States Parties undertake to promote and encourage international co-operation with a view to achieving progressively the full realization of the right recognized in the present article. In this regard, particular

account shall be taken of the needs of developing countries.

Article 25

States Parties recognize the right of a child who has been placed by the competent authorities for the purposes of care, protection or treatment of his or her physical or mental health, to a periodic review of the treatment provided to the child and all other circumstances relevant to his or her placement.

Article 26

1. States Parties shall recognize for every child the right to benefit from social security, including social insurance, and shall take the necessary measures to achieve the full realization of this right in accordance with their national law.

2. The benefits should, where appropriate, be granted, taking into account the resources and the circumstances of the child and persons having responsibility for the maintenance of the child, as well as any other consideration relevant to an application for benefits made by or on behalf of the child.

Article 27

1. States Parties recognize the right of every child to a standard of living adequate for the child's physical, mental, spiritual, moral and social development.

2. The parent(s) or others responsible for the child have the primary responsibility to secure, within their abilities and financial capacities, the conditions of living necessary for the child's development.

3. States Parties, in accordance with national conditions and within their means, shall take appropriate measures to assist parents and others responsible for the child to implement this right and shall in case of need provide material assistance and support programmes, particularly with regard to nutrition, clothing and housing.

4. States Parties shall take all appropriate measures to secure the recovery of maintenance for the child from the parents or other persons having financial responsibility for the child, both within the State Party and from abroad. In particular, where the person having financial responsibility for the child lives in a State different from that of the child, States Parties shall promote the accession to international agreements or the conclusion of such agreements, as well as the making of other appropriate arrangements.

Article 28

1. States Parties recognize the right of the child to education, and with a view to achieving this right progressively and on the basis of equal opportunity, they shall, in particular:
   (a) Make primary education compulsory and available free to all;
   (b) Encourage the development of different forms of secondary education, including general and vocational education, make them available and accessible to every child, and take appropriate measures such as the introduction of free education and offering financial assistance in case of need;
   (c) Make higher education accessible to all on the basis of capacity by every appropriate means;
   (d) Make educational and vocational information and guidance available and accessible to all children;
   (e) Take measures to encourage regular attendance at schools and the reduction of drop-out rates.
2. States Parties shall take all appropriate measures to ensure that school discipline is administered in a manner consistent with the child's human dignity and in conformity with the present Convention.
3. States Parties shall promote and encourage international cooperation in matters relating to education, in particular with a view to contributing to the elimination of ignorance and illiteracy throughout the world and facilitating access to scientific and technical knowledge and modern teaching methods. In this regard, particular account shall be taken of the needs of developing countries.

Article 29

1. States Parties agree that the education of the child shall be directed to:
   (a) The development of the child's personality, talents and mental and physical abilities to their fullest potential;
   (b) The development of respect for human rights and fundamental freedoms, and for the principles enshrined in the Charter of the United Nations;
   (c) The development of respect for the child's parents, his or her own cultural identity, language and values, for the national values of the country in which the child is living, the country from which he or she may originate, and for civilizations different from his or her own;
   (d) The preparation of the child for responsible life in a free society, in the spirit of understanding, peace, tolerance, equality of sexes, and friendship among all peoples, ethnic, national and religious groups and persons of indigenous origin;
   (e) The development of respect for the natural environment.
2. No part of the present article or article 28 shall be construed so as to interfere with the liberty of individuals and bodies to establish and direct educational institutions, subject always to the observance of the principle set forth in paragraph 1 of the present article and to the requirements that the education given in such institutions shall conform to such minimum standards as may be laid down by the State.

Article 30

In those States in which ethnic, religious or linguistic minorities or persons of indigenous origin exist, a child belonging to such a minority or who is indigenous shall not be denied the right, in community with other members of his or her group, to enjoy his or her own culture, to profess and practise his or her own religion, or to use his or her own language.

Article 31

1. States Parties recognize the right of the child to rest and leisure, to engage in play and recreational activities appropriate to the age of the child and to participate freely in cultural life and the arts.
2. States Parties shall respect and promote the right of the child to participate fully in cultural and artistic life and shall encourage the provision of appropriate and equal opportunities for cultural, artistic, recreational and leisure activity.

Article 32

1. States Parties recognize the right of the child to be protected from economic exploitation and from performing any work that is likely to be hazardous or to interfere with the child's education, or to be harmful to the child's health or physical, mental, spiritual, moral or social development.
2. States Parties shall take legislative, administrative, social and educational measures to ensure the implementation of the present article. To this end, and having regard to the relevant provisions of other international instruments, States Parties shall in particular:

(a) Provide for a minimum age or minimum ages for admission to employment;

(b) Provide for appropriate regulation of the hours and conditions of employment;

(c) Provide for appropriate penalties or other sanctions to ensure the effective enforcement of the present article.

Article 33

States Parties shall take all appropriate measures, including legislative, administrative, social and educational measures, to protect children from the illicit use of narcotic drugs and psychotropic substances as defined in the relevant international treaties, and to prevent the use of children in the illicit production and trafficking of such substances.

Article 34

States Parties undertake to protect the child from all forms of sexual exploitation and sexual abuse. For these purposes, States Parties shall in particular take all appropriate national, bilateral and multilateral measures to prevent:

(a) The inducement or coercion of a child to engage in any unlawful sexual activity;

(b) The exploitative use of children in prostitution or other unlawful sexual practices;

(c) The exploitative use of children in pornographic performances and materials.

Article 35

States Parties shall take all appropriate national, bilateral and multilateral measures to prevent the abduction of, the sale of or traffic in children for any purpose or in any form.

Article 36

States Parties shall protect the child against all other forms of exploitation prejudicial to any aspects of the child's welfare.

Article 37

States Parties shall ensure that:

(a) No child shall be subjected to torture or other cruel, inhuman or degrading treatment or punishment. Neither capital punishment nor life imprisonment without possibility of release shall be imposed for offences committed by persons below eighteen years of age;

(b) No child shall be deprived of his or her liberty unlawfully or arbitrarily. The arrest, detention or imprisonment of a child shall be in conformity with the law and shall be used only as a measure of last resort and for the shortest appropriate period of time;

(c) Every child deprived of liberty shall be treated with humanity and respect for the inherent dignity of the human person, and in a manner which takes into account the needs of persons of his or her age. In particular, every child deprived of liberty shall be separated from adults unless it is considered in the child's best interest not to do so and shall have the right to maintain contact with his or her family through correspondence and visits, save in exceptional circumstances;

(d) Every child deprived of his or her liberty shall have the right to prompt access to legal and other appropriate assistance, as well as the right to challenge the legality of the deprivation of his or her liberty before a court or other competent, independent and impartial authority, and to a prompt decision on any such action.

Article 38

1. States Parties undertake to respect and to ensure respect for rules of international humanitarian law applicable to them in armed conflicts which are relevant to the child.

2. States Parties shall take all feasible measures to ensure that persons who have not attained the age of fifteen years do not take a direct part in hostilities.

3. States Parties shall refrain from recruiting any person who has not attained the age of fifteen years into their armed forces. In recruiting among those persons who have attained the age of fifteen years but who have not attained the age of eighteen years, States Parties shall endeavour to give priority to those who are oldest.

4. In accordance with their obligations under international humanitarian law to protect the civilian population in armed conflicts, States Parties shall take all feasible measures to ensure protection and care of children who are affected by an armed conflict.

Article 39

States Parties shall take all appropriate measures to promote physical and psychological recovery and social reintegration of a child victim of: any form of neglect, exploitation, or abuse; torture or any other form of cruel, inhuman or degrading treatment or punishment; or armed conflicts. Such recovery and reintegration shall take place in an environment which fosters the health, self-respect and dignity of the child.

Article 40

1. States Parties recognize the right of every child alleged as, accused of, or recognized as having infringed the penal law to be treated in a manner consistent with the promotion of the child's sense of dignity and worth, which reinforces the child's respect for the human rights and fundamental freedoms of others and which takes into account the child's age and the desirability of promoting the child's reintegration and the child's assuming a constructive role in society.

2. To this end, and having regard to the relevant provisions of international instruments, States Parties shall, in particular, ensure that:

   (a) No child shall be alleged as, be accused of, or recognized as having infringed the penal law by reason of acts or omissions that were not prohibited by national or international law at the time they were committed;

   (b) Every child alleged as or accused of having infringed the penal law has at least the following guarantees:

      (i) To be presumed innocent until proven guilty according to law;

      (ii) To be informed promptly and directly of the charges against him or her, and, if appropriate, through his or her parents or legal guardians, and to have legal or other appropriate assistance in the preparation and presentation of his or her defence;

      (iii) To have the matter determined without delay by a competent, independent and impartial authority or judicial body in a fair hearing according to law, in the presence of legal or other appropriate assistance and, unless it is considered not to be in the best interest of the child, in particular, taking into account his or her age or situation, his or her parents or legal guardians;

      (iv) Not to be compelled to give testimony or to confess guilt; to examine or have examined adverse witnesses and to obtain the participation and examination of witnesses on his or her behalf under conditions of equality;

      (v) If considered to have infringed the penal law, to have this decision and any measures imposed in consequence thereof reviewed by a higher competent, independent and impartial authority or judicial body according to law;

      (vi) To have the free assistance of an interpreter if the child cannot understand or speak the language used;

      (vii) To have his or her privacy fully respected at all stages of the proceedings.

3. States Parties shall seek to promote the establishment of laws, procedures, authorities and institutions specifically applicable to children alleged as, accused of, or recognized as having infringed the penal law, and, in particular:

   (a) The establishment of a minimum age below which children shall be presumed not to have the capacity to infringe the penal law;

   (b) Whenever appropriate and desirable, measures for dealing with such children without resorting to judicial proceedings, providing that human rights and legal safeguards are fully respected.

4. A variety of dispositions, such as care, guidance and supervision orders; counselling; probation; foster care; education and vocational training programmes and other alternatives to institutional care shall be available to ensure that children are dealt with in a manner appropriate to their well-being and proportionate both to their circumstances and the offence.

Article 41

Nothing in the present Convention shall affect any provisions which are more conducive to the realization of the rights of the child and which may be contained in:

   (a) The law of a State party; or

   (b) International law in force for that State.

References

A

Ahola, Debra, and Abbe Kovacik. 2006. *Observing and understanding child development: A child study manual.* Clifton Park, NY: Thomson Delmar Learning.

Ainsworth, Mary S., Mary C. Blehar, Everett Waters, and Sally Wall. 1978. *Patterns of attachment.* Hillsdale, NJ: Erlbaum.

Allen, Eileen K., and Lynn R. Marotz. 1999. *Developmental profiles: Pre-birth through age eight.* 3rd ed. Albany, NY: Delmar.

Almy, Millie, and Celia Genishi. 1979. *Ways of studying children.* New York: Teachers College Press.

Alridge, Derrick P. 2008. *The educational thought of W.E.B. DuBois: An intellectual history.* New York: Teachers College Press.

Altman, Roberta. 1992. Movement in early childhood. In *Explorations with young children: A curriculum guide from the Bank Street College of Education,* ed. Ann Mitchell and Judy David, 229–240. Beltsville, MD: Gryphon House.

American Academy of Child and Adolescent Psychiatry. 2005. *Facts for families: Foster care.* No. 64. http://www.aacap.org/cs/root/facts_for_families/foster_care (accessed June 18, 2008).

American Academy of Pediatrics. Bright futures: Health care professionals' tools and resources. http://brightfutures.aap.org/ (accessed March 2, 2008).

American Council on Education. 2007. *Fact sheet on higher education: Summary of higher education institutions.* Rev. February 2007. http://www.acenet.edu/AM/Template.cfm?Section=InfoCenter (click Demographics).

Anderson, Daniel R., and Tiffany Tempek. 2005. Television and very young children. *American Behavioral Scientist* 48 (5): 505–522.

Anderson, Kristin. 1994. Unpublished journal excerpt. Bank Street College of Education, New York.

Anderson, Steven G., Dawn M. Ramsburg, and Jeff Scott. 2005. *Illinois study of license-exempt child care: Final report.* Urbana-Champaign: University of Illinois at Urbana-Champaign.

Antler, Joyce. 1987. *Lucy Sprague Mitchell: The making of a modern woman.* New Haven, CT: Yale University Press.

Apgar, Virginia. 1953. A proposal for a new method of evaluation of the newborn infant. *Current Research in Anesthesia and Analgesia* 32 (4): 260–267.

Ashton-Warner, Sylvia. 1963. *Teacher.* New York: Simon and Schuster.

Atwell, Nancie. 1998. *In the middle: New understandings about writing, reading, and learning.* 2nd ed. Portsmouth, NH: Heinemann.

Ayers, William. 2004. *Teaching the personal and the political: Essays on hope and justice.* New York: Teachers College Press.

B

Balaban, Nancy. 2006. *Everyday goodbyes: Starting school and early care—A guide to the separation process.* New York: Teachers College Press.

Ball, Deborah Loewenberg, and Francesca M. Forzani. 2008. What makes education research "educational"? *Educational Researcher* 36 (9): 529–540.

Bandura, Albert. 1976. *Social learning theory.* Englewood Cliffs, NJ: Prentice-Hall.

Barbarin, Oscar A., and Linda M. Richter. 2001. *Mandela's children: Growing up in post-apartheid South Africa.* New York: Routledge.

Barkley, R. A. 1997. Inhibition, sustained attention, and executive functions: Constructing a unifying theory of ADHD. *Psychological Bulletin* 121:65–94.

Barnett, Rosalind C., and Caryl Rivers. 1996. *She works, he works: How two-income families are happier, healthier, and better off.* San Francisco: Harper.

Barnett, W. Steven, Jason T. Hustedt, Allison H. Friedman, Judi Stevenson Boyd, and Pat Ainsworth. 2007. *The state of preschool 2007.* Rutgers, NJ: National Institute for Early Education Research.

Baron-Cohen, Simon. 1995. *Mindblindness: An essay on autism and theory of mind.* Cambridge, MA: MIT Press.

Barrera, Isaura, and Robert M. Corso. 2003. *Skilled dialogue: Strategies for responding to cultural diversity in early childhood.* Baltimore, MD: Brookes.

Beatty, Barbara. 1995. *Preschool education in America.* New Haven, CT: Yale University Press.

Beck, Aaron T. 1976. *Cognitive therapy and emotional disorder.* New York: International Universities Press.

Belden, Jack. 1949. *China shakes the world.* New York: Monthly Review Press.

Bellin, Harvey F., and Dorothy G. Singer. 2006. "My magic story car": Video-based play intervention to strengthen emergent literacy of at-risk preschoolers. In *Play = learning: How play motivates and enhances children's cognitive and social-emotional growth,* ed. Dorothy Singer, Roberta Michnick Golinkoff, and Kathy Hirsh-Pasek, 101–123. New York: Oxford University Press.

Bellm, Dan, and Marcy Whitebook. 2006. *Roots of decline: How government policy has de-educated teachers of young children.* Berkeley: Center for the Study of Child Care Employment, Institute for Industrial Relations, University of California at Berkeley.

Bereiter, Carl. 1988 (March 14). This week's citation classic. *Current Contents* 11:18.

Bergen, Doris, Rebecca Reid, and Louis Torelli. 2001. *Educating and caring for very young children: The infant/toddler curriculum.* New York: Teachers College Press.

Berk, Laura, Trisha Mann, and Amy Ogan. 2006. "Make believe play": Wellspring for development of self regulation. In *Play = learning: How play motivates and enhances children's cognitive and social-emotional growth,* ed. Dorothy Singer, Roberta Michnick Golinkoff, and Kathy Hirsh-Pasek, 74–100. New York: Oxford University Press.

Berkowitz, Nancy. 2003. Course handout. Bank Street College of Education, New York, NY.

Berman, Paul, and Milbrey Wallin McLaughlin. 1978. *Federal programs supporting educational change.* Vol. 8, *Implementing and sustaining innovations.* Santa Monica, CA: Rand.

Bernard van Leer Foundation. 2007. *Realizing the right to education in multiple contexts: The interplay of universal rights and cultural relativism.* Online Outreach Paper 2. The Hague, The Netherlands: Bernard van Leer Foundation. http://www.bernardvanleer.org/publication_store/publication_store_publications/realising_the_right_to_education_in_multiple_contexts/file.

Bernhardt, Judith L. 2000. A primary caregiving system for infants and toddlers: Best for everyone involved. *Young Children* 55 (2): 74–80.

Bers, Marina Umaschi. 2008. *Blocks to robots: Learning with technology in the early childhood classroom.* New York: Teachers College Press.

Bialystock, Ellen. 2001. *Bilingualism in development: Language, literacy and cognition.* Cambridge, UK: Cambridge University Press.

Bigler, Rebecca S., and Lynn Liben. 1993. A cognitive-developmental approach to racial stereotyping and reconstructive memory in Euro-American children. *Child Development* 64 (5, October): 1507–1518.

Billman, Jean, and Janice Sherman. 2003. *Observation and participation in early childhood settings: A practicum guide.* 2nd ed. New York: Allyn and Bacon.

Bjorklund, David F. 2005. *Children's thinking: Cognitive development and individual differences.* 4th ed. Belmont, CA: Thomson/Wadsworth.

Black, Maureen M., Howard Dubowitz, and R. H. Starr. 1999. African American fathers in low income, urban families: Development, behavior, and home environment of their three-year-old children. *Child Development* 70:967–978.

Blades, Joan, and Kristin Rowe-Finkbeiner. 2006. *The motherhood manifesto: What America's moms want—and what to do about it.* New York: Nation Books.

Blaustein, Mari. 2005a. The basics of learning readiness. *Beyond the Journal.* http://journal.naeyc.org/btj/200507/01/Blaustein.asp.

———. 2005b. See, hear, touch: The basics of learning readiness. *Beyond the Journal: Young Children on the Web,* July, 1–10. http://www.journal.naeyc.org/btj/200507/01Blaustein.asp.

Borich, Gary D. 2003. *Observation skills for effective teaching.* 4th ed. Upper Saddle River, NJ: Merrill Prentice-Hall.

Boswell, Tracy. 2003. Campus child care centers. ERIC Digest, ERIC Clearinghouse on Higher Education. http://www.ericdigests.org/2005-2/child-care.html.

Boushey, Heather, and Joseph Wright. 2004. *Working moms and child care.* Washington, DC: Center for Economic and Policy Research.

Bowen, Caroline. 1998. Speech and language development in infants and young children. http://www.speech-language-therapy.com/devel1.htm.

Bowlby, John. 1969/1982. *Attachment and loss.* Vol. 1, *Attachment.* New York: Basic Books.

———. 1972. *Attachment and loss.* Vol. 2, *Separation, anxiety and anger.* New York: Basic Books.

Bowman, Barbara. 2006. Resilience: Preparing children for school. In *School readiness and social-emotional development: Perspectives on cultural diversity,* ed. Barbara Bowman and Evelyn K. Moore, 49–57. Washington, DC: National Black Child Development Institute.

Bowman, Barbara T., M. Suzanne Donovan, and M. Susan Burns. 2001. *Eager to learn: Educating our preschoolers.* Washington, DC: National Academies Press.

Brandon, Richard. 2005. *Enhancing family, friend and neighbor child care: The case for public engagement.* Seattle: University of Washington, Human Services Policy Institute.

Bransford, John. 2001. Thoughts on adaptive expertise. http://www.vanth.org/docs/AdaptiveExpertise.pdf.

Bransford, John D., ed. 2000. *How people learn: Brain, mind, experience, and school.* Washington, DC: National Academies Press.

Braskamp, Larry A., Muriel Poston, and Jon Wergin. 1998. Accreditation: "Sitting beside" or "standing over"? *The CHEA Chronicle* 1, 4. http://www.chea.org/Chronicle/vol1/no4/index.html.

Brazelton, T. Berry. 1984. Cementing family relationships. In *The infants we care for,* ed. Laura Dittman, 9–20. Washington, DC: National Association for the Education of Young Children.

———. 1994. *Touchpoints: Your child's emotional and behavioral development.* New York: Da Capo Press.

Brazelton, T. Berry, and Stanley Greenspan. 2000. *The irreducible needs of children: What every child must have to grow, learn, and flourish.* Cambridge, MA: Da Capo Books.

Brazelton, T. Berry, and J. Kevin Nugent. 1995. *Neonatal behavioral assessment scale.* 3rd ed. London: Cambridge University Press.

Bredekamp, Sue. 1986. *Developmentally appropriate practice.* Washington, DC: National Association for the Education of Young Children.

Bredekamp, Sue, and Carol Copple. 1997. *Developmentally appropriate practice, revised.* Washington, DC: National Association for the Education of Young Children.

Bredekamp, Sue, and Teresa Rosegrant. 1995. Transforming curriculum organization. In *Reaching potentials: Transforming early childhood curriculum and assessment,* vol. 2, ed. Sue Bredekamp and Teresa Rosegrant, 167–176. Washington, DC: National Association for the Education of Young Children.

Britton, James. 1970. *Language and learning.* Coral Gables, FL: University of Miami Press.

Bromer, Juliet, and Julia R. Henly. 2002. Policy initiatives for the informal child care sector. *Poverty Research News* 6 (1): 15–16.

Bronfenbrenner, Urie. 1979. *The ecology of human development.* Cambridge, MA: Harvard University Press.

Bronson, Martha. 1995. *The right stuff for children birth to 8: Selecting play materials to support development.* Washington, DC: National Association for the Education of Young Children.

Bronson, Martha B. 2000. *Self-regulation in early childhood: Nature and nurture.* New York: Guilford Press.

Bruner, Charles. 2004. *Building an early learning system: The ABCs of planning and governance structures.* Des Moines, IA: State Early Childhood Policy Technical Assistance Network.

Bundy, Anita, Sheila Lane, and Elizabeth Murray. 2002. *Sensory integration: Theory and practice.* 2nd ed. Philadelphia: F. A. Davis.

Burbank, John R., and Nancy Wiefek. 2001 (April 24). *Washington State early childhood education career development ladder.* Economic Opportunity Institute. http://www.eoionline.org/ECE-PolicyBrief2001.htm.

Butler, Christopher. 2002. *Postmodernism: A very short introduction.* New York: Oxford University Press.

Buysse, Virginia, and Patricia W. Wesley, eds. 2006. *Evidence-based practice in the early childhood field.* Washington, DC: Zero to Three Press.

C

California State Board of Education. 1997. *English-language arts content standards for California public schools: Kindergarten through grade twelve.* http://www.cde.ca.gov/be/st/ss/documents/elacontentstnds.pdf.

Cancelmo, Joseph, and Carol Bandini. 1999. *Child care for love or money? A guide to navigating the parent-caregiver relationship.* Northvale, NJ: Jason Aronson.

Carey, Benedict. 2007. This is your life (and how you tell it). *New York Times,* May 22. http://www.nytimes.com/2007/05/22/health/psychology/22narr.html?pagewanted=1 (retrieved January 31, 2008).

———. 2008. Study finds prior trauma raised children's 9/11 risk. *New York Times,* February 5, F6.

Carini, Patricia F. 2000a. Introduction: A page from the prospect album. In *From another angle: Children's strengths and school standards,* ed. Margaret Himley, with Patricia Carini, 1–7. New York: Teachers College Press.

———. 2000b. A letter to parents and teachers on some ways of looking at and reflecting on children. In *From another angle: Children's strengths and school standards,* ed. Margaret Himley, with Patricia Carini, 56–64. New York: Teachers College Press.

Carlson, Vivian, Xin Feng, and Robin L. Harwood. 2004. The "ideal baby": A look at the intersection of temperament and culture. *Zero to Three* 24 (4): 22–28.

Carnegie Corporation of New York. 1994. *Starting points: Meeting the needs of our youngest children* (abridged version). New York: Carnegie Corporation of New York. http://www.carnegie.org/starting_points/index.html.

Carreón, Gustavo Perez, Corey Drake, and Angela Calabrese Barton. 2005. The importance of presence: Immigrant parents' school engagement experiences. *American Educational Research Journal* 42 (3): 465–498.

Carter, Dorothy. 1998. *Bye, Mis' Lela.* New York: Farrar, Straus and Giroux.

Case, Robbie. 1991. *The mind's staircase: Exploring the conceptual underpinnings of children's thought and knowledge.* Hillsdale, NJ: Erlbaum.

Casper, Virginia, and Steven B. Schultz. 1999. *Gay parents, straight schools: Building communication and trust.* New York: Teachers College Press.

Cassidy, Jude, and Phillip R. Shaver, eds. 1999. *Handbook of attachment: Theory, research and clinical application.* New York: Guilford Press.

Cazden, Courtney. 1988. *Classroom discourse: The language of teaching and learning.* Portsmouth, NH: Heinemann.

Center for Applied Special Technology (CAST). 2003. *Summary of universal design for learning concepts.* http://www.cast.org/udl.

Center for Home Visiting. 1998. University of North Carolina. http://www.unc.edu/~uncchv/.

Center for the Child Care Workforce. 2004. *Current data on the salaries and benefits of the U.S. early childhood education workforce.* Washington, DC: American Federation of Teachers Educational Foundation. http://www.ccw.org/pubs/2004Compendium.pdf.

———. n.d. *State and local initiatives: Scholarship programs.* http://www.ccw.org/policy_state_data.html.

Chaiklin, Seth. 2003. The zone of proximal development in Vygotsky's analysis of learning and instruction. In *Vygotsky's educational theory in cultural context,* ed. Alex Kozulin et al., 39–64. New York: Cambridge University Press.

Cheah, Charisa S. L., Larry J. Nelson, and Kenneth H. Rubin. 2001. Nonsocial play as a risk factor in social emotional development. In *Children in play, story and school,* ed. Artin Gonçu and Elisa Klein, 39–71. New York: Guilford Press.

Chess, Stella, and Alexander Thomas. 1996. *Temperament: Theory and practice.* New York: Bruner Mazel.

Child Care Bureau. 2007. Systemic approaches to improving quality of care. *Child Care Bulletin* 32:1.

———. n.d. What congregations should know about federal funding for child care. http://www.acf.hhs.gov/programs/ccb/providers/faithbased.pdf.

Child Welfare League of America, National Data Analysis System. n.d. http://ndas.cwla.org/data_stats/access/predefined/home.asp?MainTopicID=1.

Christie, James F. 1991. Psychological research on play: Connections with early literacy development. In *Play and early literacy development,* ed. James F. Christie, 27–45. Albany, NY: SUNY Press.

———. 1998. Play: A medium for emergent literacy development. In *Play from birth to twelve: Contexts, perspectives, and meanings,* ed. Doris Fromberg and Doris Bergen, 50–55. New York: Garland.

Clandinin, D. Jean, and F. Michael Connelly. 1995. *Teachers' professional knowledge landscapes.* New York: Teachers College Press.

Clark, Kenneth B., Isidor Chein, and Stuart W. Cook. 1994. The effects of segregation and the consequences of desegregation: A (September 1952) Social Science Statement in the *Brown v. Board of Education of Topeka* Supreme Court case. *American Psychologist* 59 (6): 496–501.

Clarke-Stewart, Allison, and Virginia D. Allhusen. 2005. *What we know about childcare.* Cambridge, MA: Harvard University Press.

Clements, Douglas H. 1999. Concrete manipulatives, concrete ideas. *Contemporary Ideas in Early Childhood* 1 (1): 45–60.

Coffman, Julia, Michelle Stover Wright, and Charles Bruner. 2006. *Beyond parallel play: Emerging state and community planning roles in building early learning.* Des Moines, IA: State Early Childhood Policy Technical Assistance Network.

Cohen, Abby J. 1996. A brief history of federal financing for child care in the United States. *The Future of Children* 6 (2): 26–40.

Cohen, Dorothy, Virginia Stern, Nancy Balaban, and Nancy Gropper. 2008. *Observing and recording the behavior of young children.* 5th ed. New York: Teachers College Press.

Cohen, Miriam, and Lillian Hoban. 2006. *First grade takes a test.* New York: Bantam/Doubleday.

Cohen, Sally Solomon. 2001. *Championing child care.* New York: Columbia University Press.

Colabucci, Lesley, and Matthew D. Conley. 2008. What makes a family? Representations of adoption in children's literature. In *Other kinds of families: Embracing diversity in schools*, ed. Tammy Turner-Vorbeck and Monica Miller Marsh, 139–159. New York: Teachers College Press.

Cole, Michael, Sheila Cole, and Cynthia Lightfoot. 2005. *The development of children*. 5th ed. New York: Worth.

Coleman, Mick. 1997. Families and schools: In search of common ground. *Young Children* 52 (5): 14–21.

Comer, James P., and Norris M. Haynes. 1991. Parent involvement in schools: An ecological approach. *Elementary School Journal* 91:271–278.

Connecticut Charts-A-Course. *What is CCAC?* http://www.ctcharts-a-course.org.

Connelly, Rachel, Deborah S. DeGraff, and Rachel A. Willis. 2004. *Kids at work: The value of employer-sponsored on-site child care centers*. Kalamazoo, MI: W. E. Upjohn Institute for Employment Research.

Connolly, Paul. 1998. *Racism, gender identities and young children: Social relations in a multi-ethnic, inner-city primary school*. New York: Routledge.

Connor, Frances P., Gordon G. Williamson, and John M. Siepp. 1978. *Program guide for infants and toddlers with neuromotor and other developmental disabilities*. New York: Teachers College Press.

Consultative Group on Early Childhood Care and Development. 1996. Definitions of quality in ECCD. *Coordinators' Notebook No. 18*. The Consultative Group Secretariat. http://www.ecdgroup.com/issue_18_quality.asp.

Cookson, Clive. 2008. Poverty mars formation of infant brains. *Financial Times of London* 01:39.

Coontz, E. Kim. n.d. *Best kept secret: Cooperative preschool programs*. Davis: University of California, Center for Cooperatives.

Copple, Carol, and Sue Bredekamp. 2008. Professional development: Getting clear about developmentally appropriate practice. *Young Children* 63 (1): 54–55.

———. 2009. *Developmentally appropriate practice in early childhood programs serving children from birth through age eight*. Washington, DC: National Association for the Education of Young Children.

Council of Chief State School Officers (CCSSO). 2007. The words we use: A glossary of terms for early childhood education standards and assessment. http://www.ccsso.org/projects/SCASS/projects/early_childhood_education_assessment_consortium/publications_and_products/2842.cfm#Definition.

Council on Physical Education for Children. 2000. *Appropriate practices in movement programs for children 3–5: A position statement of the National Association of Sport and Physical Education*. Oxon Hill, MD: AAHPERD Publications.

Counts, George S. 1978. *Dare the school build a new social order?* Carbondale: Southern Illinois University Press.

Crawford, James, and Stephen Krashen. 2007. *English language learners in American classrooms: 101 questions 101 answers*. New York: Scholastic.

Cremin, Lawrence A. 1962. *The transformation of the school*. New York: Harper and Row.

Crittenden, Ann. 2001. *The price of motherhood: Why the most important job in the world is still the least valued*. New York: Holt.

Cronin, John, Michael Dahlin, Deborah Adkins, and G. Gage Kingsbury. 2007. *The proficiency illusion*. Washington, DC: Thomas B. Fordham Institute.

Cross, William T. 1991. *Shades of black: Diversity in African-American identity*. Philadelphia, PA: Temple University Press.

Cuffaro, Harriet K. 1991. A view of materials as the texts of the early childhood curriculum. In *Issues

in early childhood curriculum*, vol. 2 of *Yearbook in early childhood curriculum*, ed. Bernard Spodek and Olivia N. Saracho, 64–85. New York: Teachers College Press.

———. 1995. *Experimenting with the world: John Dewey and the early childhood classroom*. New York: Teachers College Press.

Curtis, Sandra R. 1982. *The joy of movement in early childhood*. New York: Teachers College Press.

Cummins, James. 1986. Empowering minority students: A framework for intervention. *Harvard Educational Review* 56:18–36.

D

Daniel, Jerlean E. 1993. Infants to toddlers: Qualities of effective transitions. *Young Children* 48 (6): 16–21.

Dansky, Jeffrey L. 1980. Make-believe: A mediator of the relationship between play and associative fluency. *Child Development* 51:576–579.

Darling-Hammond, Linda, and Jon Snyder. 2000. Authentic assessment of teaching in context. *Teaching and Teacher Education* 16 (5): 523–545.

David, Judy, Susan Ochshorn, and Anne Mitchell. 1996. *An assessment of the integrated early childhood program in three settlement houses*. New York: United Neighborhood Houses of New York.

Davies, Bronwyn. 1998. The politics of category membership. In *Gender in early childhood,* ed. N. Yelland, 131–148. London: Routledge.

Davis, Kiri. 2005. A girl like me. YouTube. http://www.youtube.com/watch?v=Wk_x7s3QiYk.

De Gaetano, Yvonne, Leslie R. Williams, and Dinah Volk. 1997. *Kaleidoscope: A multicultural approach for the primary school classroom*. Upper Saddle River, NJ: Prentice-Hall.

Delpit, Lisa. 1995. *Other people's children: Cultural conflict in the classroom*. New York: New Press.

Derman-Sparks, Louise, and the ABC Task Force. 1989. *Anti-bias curriculum: Tools for empowering young children*. Washington, DC: National Association for the Education of Young Children.

Derman-Sparks, Louise, and Carol Brunson Phillips. 1997. *Teaching/learning anti-racism: A developmental approach*. New York: Teachers College Press.

Derman-Sparks, Louise, and Patricia G. Ramsey. 2006. *What if all the kids are white? Anti-bias multicultural education with young children and families*. New York: Teachers College Press.

DeVries, Rheta, and Lawrence Kohlberg. 1987. *Constructivist early education: Overview and comparison with other programs*. Washington, DC: National Association for the Education of Young Children.

Dewey, John. 1910/1933. *How we think*. Buffalo, NY: Prometheus Books.

———. 1915/2001. *The school and society*. 3rd ed. New York: Dover.

———. 1916/1985. *Democracy and education*. In *The middle works of John Dewey*, vol. 9, *1899–1924*, 93. Carbondale: Southern Illinois University Press.

———. 1938/1997. *Experience and education*. New York: Touchstone.

Dichtelmiller, Margo L., and Laura Ensler. 2004. Infant/toddler assessment: One program's experience. *Beyond the Journal: Young Children on the Web*. January. http://www.journal.naeyc.org/btj/200401/dichtel.asp.

Dickinson, David K., and Patton O. Tabors. 2001. *Beginning literacy with language: Young children learning at home and school*. Baltimore, MD: Brookes.

Doctoroff, Sandra. 1996. Supporting social pretend play in young children with disabilities. *Early Child Development and Care* 119:27–38.

Downer, Jason. 2007. Father involvement during early childhood. In *School readiness and the transition to kindergarten in an era of accountability*, ed. Robert C. Pianta, Martha J. Cox, and Kyle L. Snow, 329–354. Baltimore, MD: Brooks.

Drucker, Jan. 1994. "Constructing metaphors": The role of symbolization in the treatment of children. In *Children at play*, ed. Arietta Slade and Dennie Palmer Wolf, 62–80. New York: Oxford University Press.

Duckworth, Eleanor. 2001. *"Tell me more": Listening to learners explain*. New York: Teachers College Press.

Dyson, Anne Haas, and Celia Genishi. 1994.*The need for story: Cultural diversity in classroom and community*. Urbana, IL: National Council of Teachers of English.

E

Early, D. M., Donna M. Bryant, Robert C. Pianta, Richard M. Clifford, Margaret R. Burchinal, Sharon Ritchie, Carollee Howes, and Oscar Barbarin. 2006. Are teachers' education, major, and credentials related to classroom quality and children's academic gains in pre-kindergarten? *Early Childhood Research Quarterly* 23:174–195.

Early Childhood Matters. 2001. The Convention on the Rights of the Child and Young Children. No. 98. Bernard van Leer Foundation. http://www.ecdgroup.com/Convention_on-the-rights-of-the-child.asp.

Education Commission of the States. 2008. http://www.ecs.org/html/issue.asp?issueid=77 (accessed January 3, 2009).

Education Commission of the States Education Policy Issue Site. 2009. *Closing the achievement gap*. http://www.ecs.org/html/issue.asp?issueID=194.

Educational Development Corporation. 2007 (September). A helping hand. http://main.edc.org/newsroom/features/early-intervention.asp.

Edwards, Carolyn, George Forman, and Leila Gandini, eds. 1996. *The hundred languages of children*. Norwood, NJ: Ablex.

Edwards, Paul, editor in chief. 1972. *The encyclopedia of philosophy*. Vol. 7. New York: Macmillan.

Egan, Kieran. 2007. Imagination, past and present. In *Teaching and learning outside the box: Inspiring imagination across the curriculum*, ed. Kieran Egan, Maureen Stout, and Keiichi Takaya, 3–20. New York: Teachers College Press.

Eggbeer Linda, Tammy Mann, and Nancy L. Seibel. 2007. Reflective supervision: Past, present and future. *Zero to Three* 28(2): 5–9.

Eisenberg, Nancy, Carol Lynn Martin, and Richard A. Fabes. 1996. Gender development and gender effects. In *Handbook of educational psychology*, ed. David C. Berliner and Robert C. Calfee, 358–396. New York: Macmillan.

Elementary and Middle Schools Technical Assistance Center (EMSTAC). 2007. *Disproportionality: The disproportionate representation of racial and ethnic minorities in special education*. www.emstac.org/registered/topics/disproportionality/intro.htm.

Eliot, Lise. 1999. *What's going on in there? How the brain and mind develop in the first five years of life*. New York: Bantam Books.

Elstgeest, Jos. 2001. The right question at the right time. In *Primary science: Taking the plunge*, ed. Wynne Harlen, 25–35. Portsmouth, NH: Heinemann.

Epstein, Ann S. 2007. *The intentional teacher: Choosing the best strategies for young children's learning.* Washington, DC: National Association for the Education of Young Children.

Epstein, Joyce L. 2001. *School, family and community partnerships: Preparing educators and improving schools.* Boulder, CO: Westview Press.

Erikson, Erik. 1959. *Identity and the life cycle.* New York: International Universities Press.

———. 1963. *Childhood and society.* 2nd ed. New York: W. W. Norton.

Espinosa, Linda M. 2002. High-quality preschool: Why we need it and what it looks like. *Preschool Policy Matters* 1: 1–11.

Evan B. Donaldson Adoption Institute. 2008. *Research: Adoption facts.* http://www.adoption institute.org/research/adoptionfacts.php (accessed June 18, 2008).

F

Fass, Sarah, and Nancy K. Cauthen. 2007. *Who are America's poor children? The official story.* National Center for Children in Poverty. http://www.nccp .org/publications/pub_787.html.

Featherstone, Helen. 2000. "– Pat + Pat = 0": Intellectual play in elementary mathematics. Paper presented at the annual meeting of the American Educational Research Association, New Orleans, April.

Fein, Greta G. 1989. Mind, meaning and affect: Proposals for a theory of pretense. *Developmental Review* 9:345–363.

Fennimore, Beatrice S. 1989. *Child advocacy for early childhood educators.* New York: Teachers College Press.

Field, Tiffany, Maria Hernandez-Reif, Miguel Diego, Larissa Feijo, Vera Yanexy, and Karla Gil. 2004. Massage therapy by parents improves early growth and development. *Infant Behavior and Development* 27 (4): 435–442.

Finn, Lou-Ellen. 2002. Using video to reflect on curriculum. *Educational Leadership* 59 (6): 72–75.

Fischer, Kurt W. 1980. A theory of cognitive development: The control and construction of hierarchies of skill. *Psychological Review* 87 (6, November): 477–531.

Fleet, Alma, and Catherine Patterson. 2001. Professional growth reconceptualized: Early childhood staff searching for meaning. *Early Childhood Research and Practice* 3 (2). http://ecrp.uiuc.edu/ v3n2/fleet.html.

Foley, Gil. 1994. Parent-professional relationships: Finding optimal distance. *Zero to Three* 14 (4): 19–22. Washington, DC: Zero to Three.

Foley, Gilbert M., and Jane D. Hochman. 2006. *Mental health in early intervention: Achieving unity in principles and practice.* Baltimore, MD: Brookes.

Fonagy, Peter, and Mary Target. 2003. *Psychoanalytic theories: Perspectives from developmental psychopathology.* New York: Bruner-Routledge.

Foner, Eric, and John Garraty, eds. 1991. *The reader's companion to American history.* Boston: Houghton Mifflin.

Foucault, Michel. 1988. *Madness and civilization: A history of insanity in an age of reason.* New York: Knopf.

Foundation for Child Development. 2007. http:// www.fcd-us.org/issues_more/issues_more _show.htm?doc_id=463877.

Fraiberg, Selma. 1975. Ghosts in the nursery: A psychoanalytic approach to the problems of impaired infant-mother relationships. *Journal of the American Academy of Child Psychiatry* 14:387–421.

Fraiberg, Selma H., with Edna Edelson and Vivian Shapiro. 1987. Ghosts in the nursery: A psychoanalytic approach to the problems of impaired infant-mother relationships. In *Selected writings of Selma Fraiberg,* ed. L. Fraiberg, 100–136. Columbus: Ohio State University Press.

Frank, Lawrence K. 1974. Play and child development. In *Play: Children's business and a guide to play materials,* ed. Patricia Maloney Markun, 17–19. Washington, DC: Association for Childhood Education International.

Franklin, Margery B. 2000. Meanings of play in the developmental-interaction tradition. In *Revisiting a progressive pedagogy: The developmental interaction approach,* ed. Nancy Nager and Edna K. Shapiro, 47–71. Albany, NY: SUNY Press.

Frank Porter Graham (FPG) Child Development Institute. 2004. *Prekindergarten policy framework.* National Prekindergarten Center. http://www .fpg.unc.edu/~npc/framework.

Freud, Sigmund. 1974a. Three essays on the theory of sexuality. In *The standard edition of the complete psychological works of Sigmund Freud,* vol. 7, 225–245, ed. and trans. James Strachey. London: Hogarth Press.

———. 1974b. The ego and the id. In *The standard edition of the complete psychological works of Sigmund Freud,* vol. 19, 1–60, ed. and trans. James Strachey. London: Hogarth Press.

G

Galinsky, Ellen, and Lois Backon. 2007. *When work works: Making work "work."* New York: Families and Work Institute.

Gallagher, James J., Jenna R. Clayton, and Sarah E. Heinemeier. 2001. *Education for four-year-olds: State initiatives (2001).* Supplement to technical report no. 2 (California and Ohio). Chapel Hill: University of North Carolina, FPG Child Development Center, National Center for Early Development and Learning.

Gallas, Karen. 1994. *The languages of learning: How children talk, write, dance, draw, and sing their understanding of the world.* New York: Teachers College Press.

———. 1995. *Talking their way into science: Hearing children's questions and theories, responding with curricula.* New York: Teachers College Press.

———. 1997. *Sometimes I can be anything: Power, gender, and identity in a primary classroom.* New York: Teachers College Press.

———. 2003. *Imagination and literacy: A teacher's search for the heart of learning.* New York: Teachers College Press.

Gandini, Lella, and Goldhaber, Jeanne. 2001. Traces of childhood: A child's diary. In *Bambini: The Italian approach to infant/toddler care,* ed. Lella Gandini and Carolyn Pope Edwards, 124–145. New York: Teachers College Press.

García, Ofelia, Jo Anne Kleifgen, and Lorraine Falchi. 2008. *From English language learners to emergent bilinguals.* New York: Teachers College Press.

Gardner, Howard. 1982. *Art, mind, and brain: A cognitive approach to creativity.* New York: Basic Books.

———. 1983. *Frames of mind: The theory of multiple intelligences.* New York: Basic Books.

———. 1999. *Intelligence reframed: Multiple intelligences for the 21st century.* New York: Basic Books.

———. 2006. *Multiple intelligences: The theory in practice.* New York: Basic Books.

———. 2008. Wrestling with Jean Piaget, my paragon. *Edge,* January 4, 232. http://www.edge.org/ q2008/q08_1.html#gardner (accessed June 17, 2008).

Garforth, Francis W., ed. 1966. Introduction to *John Locke's Of the conduct of the understanding.* New York: Teachers College Press.

Gartrell, Dan. 2007. Guidance matters. *Young Children,* May, 58–59.

Gauvain, Mary. 2001. *The social context of cognitive development.* New York: Guilford Press.

Gay, Peter, ed. 1964. *John Locke on education.* New York: Teachers College Press.

———. 1989. *Freud: A life for our time.* New York: W. W. Norton.

Genishi, Celia, and Anne Haas Dyson. 2009. *Children, language, and literacy: Diverse learners in diverse times.* New York: Teachers College Press.

Gesell, Arthur. 1940. *The first five years of life.* New York: Harper & Row.

Gilkerson, Linda, and Rebecca Klein, eds. 2008. *Early development and the brain.* Washington, DC: Zero to Three Press.

Gilliam, James E. 2006. *Gilliam autism rating scale* (GARS-2), 2nd ed. Bloomington, MN: Pearson Education.

Gleick, James. 1988. *Chaos: Making a new science.* New York: Penguin.

Goetz-Haver, Susan. 2002. Digital video in teacher education. Presentation at SITE (Society for Information Technology and Teacher Education) 14th International Conference, March 25, Albuquerque, NM.

Goffin, Stacie, and Valora Washington. 2007. *Ready or not: Leadership choices in early care and education.* New York: Teachers College Press.

Goldstein, Lisa. 1997. *Teaching with love: A feminist approach to early childhood education.* New York: Peter Lang.

Gomby, Deanna S., Patti L. Culross, and Richard E. Behrman. 1999. Home visiting: Recent program evaluations—Analysis and recommendations. *The Future of Children* 9 (1): 4–26.

Gonçu, Artin. 1993. Development of intersubjectivity in the dyadic play of preschoolers. *Early Childhood Research Quarterly* 8:99–116.

Gonçu, Artin, and Elisa Klein. 2001. *Children in play, story and school.* New York: Guilford Press.

González, Norma, Luis C. Moll, and Cathy Amanti, eds. 2005. *Funds of knowledge.* Mahwah, NJ: Erlbaum.

Gonzalez-Mena, Janet. 2005. *Diversity in early care and education: Honoring differences.* Rev. ed. New York: McGraw-Hill.

Gonzalez-Mena, Janet, and Anne Stonehouse. 2008. *Making links: A collaborative approach to planning and practice in early childhood programs.* New York: Teachers College Press.

Goosen, Fritz A., and Marinus H. van Ijzendoorn. 1990. Quality of infant's attachment to professional teachers: Relation to infant-parent attachment and daycare characteristics. *Child Development* 61:832–837.

Gordon, Ann, and Kathryn Williams Browne. 1996. *Guiding young children in a diverse society.* Boston: Allyn and Bacon.

Graue, Elizabeth. 2006. The answer is readiness: Now what is the question? *Early Education and Development* 17:43–56.

Greene, Maxine. 1978. *Landscapes of learning.* New York: Teachers College Press.

———. 2000. Imagining futures: The public school and possibility. *Journal of Curriculum Studies* 32 (2): 267–280.

Greenman, Jim. 2003. Beginnings workshop: What kind of place for child care in the 21st century? *Child Care Information Exchange*, November, 38–41.

———. 2005. *Caring spaces, learning places: Children's environments that work.* 2nd ed. Redmond, WA: Exchange Press.

Greenspan, Stanley. 1993. *Playground politics: Understanding the emotional life of your school age child.* Reading, MA: Perseus Books.

———. 1996. Assessing the emotional and social function of infants and young children. In *New visions for the developmental assessment of infants and young children,* ed. Samuel Meisels and Emily Fenichel, 231–236. Washington, DC: Zero to Three.

Grieshaber, Susan, and Gaile Sloan Canella. 2001. *Embracing identities in early childhood: Diversities and possibilities.* New York: Teachers College Press.

Grinder, Elizabeth L., Eunice N. Askov, Eugenio Longoria Saenz, and Jale Aldemir. 2005. Understanding the parent-child interactive literacy component of family literacy: A re-examination of research. *American Reading Forum Online Yearbook* 25. http://americanreadingforum.com/Yearbooks/05_yearbook/html/arf_05_askov.htm.

Grinker, Roy Richard. 2008. What in the world is autism? A cross-cultural perspective. *Zero to Three* 28 (4): 5–10.

Gronlund, Gaye. 2006. *Make early learning standards come alive: Connecting your practice and curriculum to state guidelines.* Washington, DC: National Association for the Education of Young Children.

Gropper, Nancy, and Meryl Froschl. 2000. The role of gender in young children's teasing and bullying behavior. *Equity and Excellence in Education* 33 (1): 48–56.

Groth, Lois A., and Lynn Dietrich Darling. 2001. Playing "inside" stories. In *Children in play, story and school,* ed. Artin Gonçu and Elisa Klein, 220–239. New York: Guilford Press.

Gruber, Frederick C. 1973. *Historical and contemporary philosophies of education.* New York: Crowell.

Gunnar, Megan, and Karina Quevedo. 2007. The neurobiology of stress and development. *Annual Review of Psychology* 58:145–174. Available at Social Science Research Network: http://ssrn.com/abstract=1077362.

Gupta, Amita. 2006. *Early childhood education, postcolonial theory, and teaching practice in India: Balancing Vygotsky and the Veda.* New York: Palgrave Macmillan.

Gutek, Gerald L. 1968. *Pestalozzi and education.* New York: Random House.

———. 1995. *A history of the western educational experience.* 2nd ed. Prospect Heights, IL: Waveland Press.

———. 1997. *Historical and philosophical foundations of education.* Upper Saddle River, NJ: Prentice-Hall.

———. 2006. *American education in a global society.* 2nd ed. Long Grove, IL: Waveland Press.

Guthrie, James W. 2003. *Encyclopedia of education,* 2nd ed., vol. 4, 1134–1135. New York: Thomson Gale.

Gwathmey, Edith, and Anne-Marie Mott. 2000. Visualizing experience. In *Revisiting a progressive pedagogy: The developmental-interaction approach,* ed. Nancy Nager and Edna K. Shapiro, 139–160. Albany, NY: SUNY Press.

H

Hall, Nancy W., Sharon L. Kagan, and Edward F. Zigler. 1996. The changing nature of child and family policy: An overview. In *Children, families and government: Preparing for the 21st century,* ed. Edward F. Zigler, Sharon Lynn Kagan, and Nancy W. Hall, 3–9. Cambridge: Cambridge University Press.

Hammond, Margot, with Marva Wright Banks, Ethel M. Cotton, Evangeline Dent, and Mary Reaves. 2003. On the bridge that we are building. In *Putting the children first: The changing face of Newark's public schools,* 126–139, ed. Jonathan G. Silin and Carol Lippman. New York: Teachers College Press.

Hardy, Lawrence. 2007. Coping with illegal immigrants in school. *Education Digest* 72 (9): 4–6.

Harms, Thelma, Richard M. Clifford, and Debby Cryer. 1998. *The early childhood environmental rating scale–revised (ECERS-R).* New York: Teachers College Press.

———. 2005. *The infant-toddler environmental rating scale–revised (ITERS-R).* New York: Teachers College Press.

Harms, Thelma, Debbie Cryer, and Richard M. Clifford. 2003. *Infant/toddler environment rating scale–R.* New York: Teachers College Press.

Harms, Thelma, Ellen Vineberg Jacobs, and Donna Romano. 1995. *The school-age care environmental rating scale (SACERS).* New York: Teachers College Press.

Haroian, Loretta. 2000. Child sexual development. *Journal of Human Sexuality* 3. www.ejhs.org/volume3/Haroian/body.htm.

Hart, Betty, and Todd R. Risley. 1995. *Meaningful differences in the everyday experiences of young American children.* Baltimore, MD: Brookes.

Harter, Susan. 1996. Developmental changes in self-understanding across the five to seven shift. In *The five to seven year shift: The age of reason and responsibility,* ed. Arnold J. Sameroff and Marshall M. Haith, 207–236. Chicago: University of Chicago Press.

Hartup, Willard W. 1984. The peer context in middle childhood. In *Development during middle childhood,* ed. W. Andrew Collins, 240–282. Washington, DC: National Academies Press.

Harwood, Robin L., Joan G. Miller, and Nydia L. Irizarry. 1995. *Culture and attachment: Perceptions of the child in context.* New York: Guilford Press.

Haskins, Ron. 2004. Competing visions. *Education Next* 4 (1): 27–33. http://www.educationnext.org.

Head Start Bureau. 2003. Head Start Outcomes Framework. www.hsnrc.org/CDI/pdfs/UGCOF.pdf (accessed January 15, 2009).

Healy, Ellen M. 2002. Hard earned knowledge: Using videotaping as a tool in professional development for infant/toddler practitioners. Unpublished master's thesis, Bank Street College of Education, New York, New York.

Heilman, Elizabeth. 2008. Hegemonies and "transgressions" of family: Tales of pride and prejudice. In *Other kinds of families: Embracing diversity in schools,* ed. Tammy Turner-Vorbeck and Monica Miller Marsh, 7–27. New York: Teachers College Press.

Henniger, Michael L. 2005. *Teaching young children and early childhood settings and approaches.* Upper Saddle River, NJ: Merrill Prentice-Hall.

Hernandez, Donald J., Nancy A. Denton, and Suzanne Macartney. 2008. The lives of America's youngest children in immigrant families. *Zero to Three* 29 (2): 8–12.

Hernnstein, Richard J., and Charles Murray. 1994. *The bell curve: Intelligence and class structure in American life.* New York: Free Press.

Hewes, Dorothy W. 1998. *It's the camaraderie: A history of parent cooperative preschools.* Davis: University of California, Center for Cooperatives.

Himley, Martha, with Pat Carini, eds. 2000. *From another angle: Children's strengths and school standards.* New York: Teachers College Press.

Hirsch, Elisabeth S. 1996. *The block book.* 3rd ed. Washington, DC: National Association for the Education of Young Children.

Hitz, Randy, and Amy Driscoll. 1988. Praise or encouragement? New insights into praise: Implications for early childhood teachers. *Young Children* 43 (5): 6–13.

Hodgkinson, Harold "Bud." 2006. *The whole child in a fractured world.* Alexandria, VA: Association for Supervision and Curriculum Development.

Holcomb, Betty. 2006. A diverse system delivers for pre-K: Lessons learned in New York state. *Pre-K Now.* http://www.preknow.org/documents/DiverseDelivery_Jul2006.pdf.

Horn, Wade F. 2002. Statement by Wade F. Horn, PhD., Assistant Secretary for Children and Families, HHS, before the Subcommittee on Social Security and Family Policy of the Committee on Finance and the Subcommittee on Children and Families of the Committee on Health, Education, Labor and Pensions, United States Senate. http://www.hhs.gov/asl/testify/t20020319.html.

Howes, Carollee. 1998. Continuity of care: The importance of infant, toddler, caregiver relationships. *Zero to Three* 18 (6): 7–11.

———. 1999. Attachment relationships in the context of multiple caregivers. In *Handbook of attachment theory and research,* ed. Jude Cassidy and Phillip R. Shaver, 671–687. New York: Guilford Press.

Howes, Carolee, and Sharon Ritchie. 2002. *A matter of trust: Connecting teachers and learners in the early childhood classroom.* New York: Teachers College Press.

Human Services Policy Center. Winter 2006/2007. Fact sheet: Percent of all non-parental child care hours by type of child care. http://www.hspc.org/publications/pdf/2005_Childcare_Arrangements_2007.pdf.

Hurwitz, Sally C. 1998. War nurseries—lessons in quality. *Young Children* 53 (5): 37–39.

Hyson, Marilou. 2008. *Enthusiastic and engaged learners: Approaches to learning in the early childhood classroom.* New York: Teachers College Press.

Hytten, Kathy, and Silvia Cristina Bettez. 2008. Teaching globalization issues to education students: "What's the point?" *Equity and Excellence in Education* 41:168–181.

I–J

Isaacs, Susan. 1929/1968. *The nursery years: The mind of the child from birth to six years.* New York: Schocken Books.

Itard, Jean-Marc Gaspard. 1962. *The wild boy of Aveyron.* Englewood Cliffs, NJ: Prentice-Hall.

Jablon, Judy R., Amy Laura Dombro, and Margo L. Dichtelmiller. 2007. *The power of observation for birth through eight.* 2nd ed. Washington, DC: Teaching Strategies.

Jacobson, Linda. 2002. Defining quality. *Education Week* 21:17.

———. 2007. Scholars split on pre-K teachers with B.A.s. *Education Week* 26 (29): 1, 13. http://www.edweek.org/ew/articles/2007/03/28/29bachelor.h26.html.

Jalongo, Mary Renck. 1987. Do security blankets belong in preschool? *Young Children* 42 (3): 3–8.

———. 2002. Editorial: On behalf of children. *Early Childhood Education Journal* 29 (4): 217–220.

Jensen, Arthur R. 1998. *The g factor: The science of mental ability.* Westport, CT: Greenwood Press.

Jensen, Eric. 1998. *Teaching with the brain in mind.* Alexandria, VA: Association for Supervision and Curriculum Development.

Jones, Elizabeth. 1994. Constructing professional knowledge by telling our stories. In *The early childhood career lattice: Perspectives on professional development,* 126–129, ed. Julienne Johnson and Janet B. McCracken. Washington, DC: National Association for the Education of Young Children.

———. 2007. *Teaching adults revisited: Active learning for early childhood educators.* Washington, DC: National Association for the Education of Young Children.

Jones, Elizabeth, and Renatta Cooper. 2006. *Playing to get smart.* New York: Teachers College Press.

Jones, Nancy Lee, Richard N. Apling, Bonnie F. Mangan, and David P. Smole. 2004. *Individuals with Disabilities Education Act (IDEA): Background and issues.* New York: Nova Science Publishers.

K

Kaestle, Carl F. 2001. Federal aid to education since World War II: Purposes and politics. In *The future of the federal role in elementary and secondary education,* ed. Center on Education Policy. Washington, DC: Center on Education Policy.

Kagan, Sharon Lynn. 1992. Birthing collaborations in early care and education: A polemic of pain and promise. In *Early childhood education: Policy issues for the 1990s,* ed. Dolores A. Stegelin, 31–39. Norwood, NJ: Ablex.

Kagan, Sharon Lynn, and Kristie Kauerz. 2007. Reaching for the whole: Integration and alignment in early education policy. In *School readiness and the transition to kindergarten in the era of accountability,* ed. Robert C. Pianta, Martha J. Cox, and Kyle L. Snow, 11–30. Baltimore, MD: Brookes.

Kagan, Sharon Lynn, Kristie Kauerz, and Kate Tarrant. 2008. *The early care and education teaching workforce at the fulcrum: An agenda for reform.* New York: Teachers College Press.

Kagan, Sharon L., Kate Tarrant, Amy Carson, and Kristie Kauerz. 2006 (November). *The early care and education teaching workforce: At the fulcrum.* Summary report. New York: National Center for Children and Families for Cornerstones for Kids.

Kaiser Permanente, Regional Health Education, Northern California Region. 1994.

Kamerman, Sheila B. 2000. Parental leave policies: An essential ingredient in early childhood education and care policies. *Social Policy Report* 14 (2): 3–15.

Kamerman, Sheila B., and Alfred J. Kahn. 1994. *A welcome for every child: Care, education, and family support for infants and toddlers in Europe.* Arlington, VA: Zero to Three/National Center for Clinical Infant Programs.

Kamii, Constance. 1985. *Young children invent arithmetic: Implications of Piaget's theory.* New York: Teachers College Press.

Karoly, Lynn A., M. Rebecca Kilburn, and Jill S. Cannon. 2005. *Early childhood interventions: Proven results, future promises.* Santa Monica, CA: Rand Corporation.

Katz, Lilian G. 1977. *Talks with teachers.* Washington, DC: National Association for the Education of Young Children.

———. 1985. Dispositions in early childhood education. *ERIC/EECE Bulletin* 18:1–3.

———. 2000. Parenting and teaching in perspective. Paper presented at Parent Child 2000 Conference, London, UK, April.

Katz, Lilian G., and Sylvia Chard. 1989. *Engaging children's minds: The project approach.* Norwood, NJ: Ablex.

Kinnell, G. 2008. *No biting: Policy and practice for toddler programs.* 2nd ed. St. Paul, MN: Redleaf Press.

Kirp, David L. 2007. *The sandbox investment: The preschool movement and kids-first politics.* Cambridge, MA: Harvard University Press.

Klein, M. Diane, Ruth E. Cook, and Ann Marie Richardson-Gibbs. 2001. *Strategies for including children with special needs in early childhood settings.* Albany, NY: Delmar Thomson Learning.

Klein, Naomi. 2007. Disaster capitalism: The new economy of catastrophe. *Harper's,* October, 47–58.

KnowledgeLeader. 2007. British Standard 7799 (ISO 17799). http://www.knowledgeleader.com/KnowledgeLeader/Content.nsf/Web+Content/ChecklistsGuidesBritishStandard7799!Open Document.

Kochanska, Grazyna. 1995. Children's temperament, mother's discipline, and security of attachment: Multiple pathways to emerging internalization. *Child Development* 66:597–615.

Kohlberg, Lawrence. 1966. A cognitive-developmental analysis of children's sex role concepts and attitudes. In *The development of sex difference,* ed. Eleanor E. Maccoby, 82–172. Stanford, CA: Stanford University Press.

Kontos, Susan. 1992. *Family day care: Out of the shadows and into the limelight.* Research monograph of the National Association for the Education of Young Children, vol. 5. Washington, DC: NAEYC.

Koplow, Lesley. 2002. *Creating schools that heal.* New York: Teachers College Press.

———. ed. 2007. *Unsmiling faces: How preschools can heal.* 2nd ed. New York: Teachers College Press.

Kozol, Jonathan. 2007. *Letters to a young teacher.* New York: Crown.

Kramer, Rita. 1988. *Maria Montessori: A biography.* New York: Addison-Wesley.

Krashen, Stephen D. 1994. Bilingual education and second language acquisition theory. In *Schooling and language-minority students: A theoretical framework,* 2nd ed., ed. Bilingual Education Office, 47–75. Los Angeles: California State University, Evaluation Dissemination and Assessment Center.

———. 2003. Principles of language acquisition. In *Explorations in language acquisition and use,* 1–14. Portsmouth, NH: Heinemann.

Kreider, Rose M. 2007. Living arrangements of children: 2004. *Current Population Reports,* 70–114. Washington, DC: U.S. Census Bureau.

L

Lally, Ronald J. 1995. The impact of child care policies and practices on infant/toddler identity formation. *Young Children* 51 (1): 58–67.

Lancy, David F. 2002. Cultural constraints on children's play. In *Conceptual, social-cognitive, and contextual issues in the fields of play,* ed. Jaipaul L. Roopnarine, 53–62. Westport, CT: Ablex.

Lareau, Annette. 2003. *Unequal childhoods: Class, race, and family life.* Berkeley: University of California Press.

Laslocky, Jenna. 2005. From resistance to rebellion, and rebellion to revolution: Notes on transformation in first grade. *Rethinking resistance in schools: Power, politics, and illicit pleasures.* Occasional paper series 14. New York: Bank Street College of Education.

Lawrence-Lightfoot, Sara. 2003. *The essential conversation: What parents and teachers can learn from each other.* New York: Random House.

Layzer, Jean I., and Barbara D. Goodson. 2006. *Care in the home: A description of family child care and the experiences of families and children who use it.* Washington, DC: U.S. Department of Health and Human Services, Administration for Children and Families.

Leavitt, Robin L. 1994. *Power and emotion in infant-toddler day care.* Albany: State University of New York Press.

LeMoine, Sarah (adapter, original methodology developed by Gwen Morgan). 2006. *Center child care licensing requirements: Minimum ECE preservice qualifications and annual ongoing training hours for teachers and master teachers.* Compiled by Sarah LeMoine and Sheri Azer from licensing regulations posted on the National Resource Center for Health and Safety in Child Care and Early Education's website at http://nrc.uchsc.edu. Retrieved from http://nccic.org.

Lerner, Claire, and Amy Laura Dombro. 2000. *Learning and growing together: Understanding and supporting your child's development.* Washington, DC: Zero to Three: National Center for Infants, Toddlers and Their Families.

Levine, Linda. 2000. "Everyone from everywhere is in my class now": What anthropology can offer teachers. In *Revisiting a progressive pedagogy: The developmental-interaction approach,* ed. Nancy Nager and Edna K. Shapiro, 95–113. Albany: State University of New York Press.

Levine, Mel. 2002. *A mind at a time.* New York: Simon and Schuster.

LeVine, Robert A. 1974. Parental goals: A cross-cultural view. *Teachers College Record* 76 (2): 226–239.

Levine, Tarima. 2001. Ways to speak to young children about death and dying. *Educational Update,* May, 26.

Levinger, Leah. 1987. "I want to know why," or tolerance for ambiguity in education. *Thought and Practice* 1 (2): 20–25.

Lieberman, A. F., E. Padron, Patricia Van Horn, and W. M. Harris. 2005. Angels in the nursery: The intergenerational transmission of benevolent parental influences. *Infant Mental Health Journal* 26 (6): 503–520.

Lieberman, Alicia. 1993. *The emotional life of the toddler.* New York: Free Press.

Limber, Susan P., and Maury M. Nation. 1998. Bullying among children and youth. *North Carolina Juvenile Justice Bulletin.* www.ojjdp.ncjrs.org/jjbulletin/9804/bullying2.html (retrieved December 19, 2007).

Litt, Carole J. 1986. Theories of transitional object attachment: An overview. *International Journal of Behavioral Development* 9 (3): 383–399.

Lowenstein, Amy, Susan Ochshorn, Sharon Lynn Kagan, and Bruce Fuller. 2004. The effects of professional development efforts and compensation on quality of early care and education services. *Child Care and Early Education Research and Policy No. 2.* Washington, DC: National Conference of State Legislatures.

Ludwig, David S. 2007. Childhood obesity: The shape of things to come. *New England Journal of Medicine* 357:2325–2327.

M

MacCulloch, Diarmaid. 2005. *The Reformation: A history.* New York: Penguin.

Mac Naughton, Glenda. 2003. Curriculum contexts: Parents and communities. In *Shaping early childhood: Learners, curriculum, and contexts*, ed. Glenda Mac Naughton, 255–281. Maidenhead, Berkshire, England: Open University Press. (citations in Ch. 14)

———, ed. 2003. *Shaping early childhood: Learners, curriculum, and contexts*. Maidenhead, Berkshire, England: Open University Press.

Maeroff, Gene I. 2006. *Building blocks: Making children successful in the early years of school*. New York: Palgrave Macmillan.

Mahler, Margaret S., Fred Pine, and Anni Bergman. 1975. *The psychological birth of the human infant: Symbiosis and individuation*. New York: Basic Books.

Martinez-Beck, Ivelisse, and Martha Zaslow. 2006. The context for critical issues in early childhood professional development. In *Critical issues in early childhood professional development*, ed. Ivelisse Martinez-Beck and Martha Zaslow, 1–16. Baltimore, MD: Brookes.

Maschinot, Beth. 2008. *The changing face of the United States: The influence of culture on early child development*. Washington, DC: Zero to Three Press.

Maslow, Abraham Harold. 1999. *Toward a psychology of being* (rev.). New York: Wiley.

McAfee, Oralie, and Deborah J. Leong. 2002. *Assessing and guiding young children's development and learning*, 3rd ed. Boston: Allyn and Bacon.

McCallion, Gail. 2004. *Early childhood education: Federal policy issues*. CRS Report for Congress. http://digital.library.unt.edu/govdocs/crs/permalink/meta-crs-5864:1.

McKay, John P., Bennett D. Hill, John Buckler, and Patricia B. Ebrey. 2004. *A history of world societies*. 6th ed., vol. 2. Boston: Houghton Mifflin.

McNamee, Abigail, Mia Mercurio, and Jeanne M. Peloso. 2007. Who cares about caring in early childhood teacher education programs? *Journal of Early Childhood Teacher Education* 28 (3): 277–288.

Meier, Daniel R., and Barbara Henderson. 2007. *Learning from young children*. New York: Teachers College Press.

Menville, Edgardo J., and Catherine Tuerk. 2002. A support group for parents of gender nonconforming boys. *American Academy of Child and Adolescent Psychiatry* 41 (8): 1010–1012.

Miller, Karen. 2005. *Simple steps: Activities for infants, toddlers, and two-year-olds*. Upper Saddle River, NJ: Pearson Education.

Mishel, Lawrence, and Richard Rothstein. 2007. Schools as scapegoats. *The American Prospect*. http://www.prospect.org/cs/articles?article=schools_as_scapegoats.

Mitchell, Lucy Sprague. 1934/2001. *Young geographers*. New York: Bank Street College of Education.

———. 1953. *Two lives: The story of Wesley Clair Mitchell and myself*. New York: Simon and Schuster.

Mitchell, Stephen A. 1988. *Relational concepts in psychoanalysis: An integration*. Cambridge, MA: Harvard University Press.

Moll, Luis, Cathy Amanti, Deborah Neff, and Norma Gonzalez. 1991. Funds of knowledge for teaching: Using a qualitative approach to connect homes and classrooms. *Theory into Practice* 31:132–141.

Montessori, Maria. 1964. *The Montessori method*. Trans. and ed. A. E. George. New York: Schocken Books.

Moore, Robert I. 1998. Literacy and the making of heresy. In *Debating the middle ages*, ed. Lester K. Little and Barbara H. Rosenwein, 363–375. Malden, MA, and Oxford, UK: Blackwell.

Morgan, Gwen. 1996. *Regulation and the prevention of harm*. http://www.nara.affiniscape.com/displaycommon.cfm?an=1&subarticlenbr=28.

Morrow, Lesley Mandel. 2005. *Literacy development in the early years: Helping children read and write*. 5th ed. Boston: Allyn & Bacon.

Mubarak, Hadia. 2006. Living as a Muslim American. *Islamic Horizons* 35 (1): 51–52.

Mukhopadhyay, Carol C., Rosemary Henze, and Yolanda T. Moses. 2007. *How real is race? A sourcebook on race, culture and biology*. Lanham, MD: Rowland and Littlefield.

Mumola, Christopher J. 2000. *Incarcerated parents and their children*. Bureau of Justice Statistics. Washington, DC: U.S. Department of Justice.

Muratori, Filippo. 2008. Early indicators of autism spectrum disorders. *Zero to Three* 28 (4): 18–24.

N

Nager, Nancy, and Edna K. Shapiro. 2000. *Revisiting a progressive pedagogy: The developmental-interaction approach*. Albany: State University of New York Press.

———. 2007. *A progressive approach to the education of teachers: Some principles from Bank Street College of Education*. Occasional paper series, 18. New York: Bank Street College of Education.

Nager, Nancy, Patricia Sherman, and Jessica Blachman. 2003. *Learning and playing in the early childhood classroom: The place of computers*. New York: Bank Street College of Education.

National Association for the Education of Young Children (NAEYC). 1995. *Responding to linguistic and cultural diversity: Recommendations for effective early childhood education*. Position statement. http://www.naeyc.org/about/positions/pdf/PSDIV98.pdf.

———. 1996. Teaching children not to be—or not to be victims of—bullies. Early tears are learning years. http://www.naeyc.org/ece/1996/14.pdf#xml=http://naeychq.naeyc.org/texis/search/pdfhi.txt?query=bullying&pr=naeyc&prox=sentence&rorder=750&rprox=500&rdfreq=1000&rwfreq=1000&rlead=1000&sufs=2&order=r&cq=&id=452256a30 (accessed January 15, 2008).

———. 1998. *The value of school recess and outdoor play*. http://www.naeyc.org/ece/1998/08.asp.

———. 2002. *Early learning standards: Creating the conditions for success*. Joint position statement of NAEYC and NAECS/SDE. Washington, DC: NAEYC. http://www.naeyc.org/about/positions/learning_standards.asp.

———. 2005. NAEYC Academy for Early Childhood Program Accreditation. Standard 10: NAEYC Accreditation Criteria for Leadership and Management Standard. http://www.naeyc.org/academy/standards/standard10B.asp.

———. 2008. Proposed joint statement on early childhood inclusion. http://www.dec-sped.org/uploads/docs/about_dec/position_concept_papers/Position%20Statement%20on%20EC%20Inclusion_Field%20review%2011_08.pdf.

National Association for the Education of Young Children (NAEYC) and International Reading Association (IRA). 1998. *Learning to read and write: Developmentally appropriate practices for young children*. A joint position statement of the IRA and the NAEYC. http://www.naeyc.org/about/positions/pdf/PSREAD98.

National Association of Child Care Resource and Referral Agencies. 2007. *We can do better: NACCRRA's ranking of state child care center standards and oversight*. Arlington, VA: NACCRRA.

National Association of Early Childhood Specialists in State Departments of Education (NAECSSDE). 2007. *Recess and the importance of play: A position statement on young children and recess*. http://naecs.crc.uiuc.edu/position/recessplay.html.

National Association of State Boards of Education. 1988. *Right from the start. The report of the NASBE Task Force on Early Childhood Education*. Alexandria, VA: NASBE.

National Bureau of Labor Statistics. 2007. Household data, annual averages. http://www.bls.gov/cps/ (accessed March 1, 2008).

National Center on Education and the Economy. 2007. *Tough choices, tough times: The report of the new Commission on the Skills of the American Workforce*. Washington, DC: Author. http://www.ncee.org.

National Clearinghouse for English Language Acquisition and Language Instruction Educational Programs (NCELA). 2006. How many school-aged English language learners (ELLs) are there in the U.S.? http://www.ncela.gwu.edu/expert/faq/01leps.html.

National Commission on Excellence in Education. (1983). *A nation at risk*. onlinebooks.library.upenn.edu/webbin/book/lookupname?key=National%20Commission%20on%20Excellence%20in%20Education.

National Commission on Teaching and America's Future. 1996. *What matters most: Teaching for America's future*. New York: Author.

National Committee on Science Education Standards and Assessment and National Research Council. 1996. *National science education standards*. Washington, DC: National Academies Press.

National Council of Teachers of Mathematics (NCTM). 2000–2004. Appendix: Table of standards. http://standards.nctm.org/document/chapter4/index.htm.

National Even Start Association. 2007. http://www.evenstart.org/. (Website expired April 3, 2009.)

National Governors Association. 1987. *Education: The first sixty months*. Washington, DC: NGA.

National Head Start Association. 2006. *Top legislative priorities for 2007*. Alexandria, VA: NHSA.

National Infant and Toddler Child Care Initiative at Zero to Three. 2007. *Infant/toddler early learning guidelines*. http://www.nccic.org/itcc/PDFdocs/itelg.pdf.

National Institute of Neurological Disorders and Strokes (NINDS). 2006. *Autism fact sheet*. NIH Publication No. 06-1877. Bethesda, MD: National Institutes of Health, NINDS. http://www.ninds.nih.gov/disorders/autism/detail_autism.htm.

National Research Council. 2000. *From neurons to neighborhoods: The science of early childhood development*. Washington, DC: National Academies Press.

National Scientific Council on the Developing Child. 2005. Excessive stress disrupts the architecture of the brain. Working paper 3. www.developingchild.net/reports.html (accessed September 15, 2006).

Nelson, Charles A., and Charles H. Zeanah. 2007. Orphanages and fostering in Romania. *Science* 318 (5858): 1829.

Nelson, Katherine. 1996. *Language in cognitive development*. New York: Cambridge University Press.

Neuman, Susan B., and Kathleen A. Roskos. 1998. *Children achieving: Best practices in early literacy*. Newark, DE: International Reading Association.

New, Rebecca S., Ben Mardell, and David Robinson. 2005. Early childhood education as risky business: Going beyond what's "safe" to discovering what's possible. *Early Childhood Research and Practice* 7 (2). http://ecrp.uiuc.edu/v7n2/new.html.

Newman, Michelle, and Shanny Peer. 2002. *Equal from the start: Promoting educational opportunity for all preschool children—learning from the French experience*. New York: The French-American Foundation.

New York Times Correspondents and Bill Keller. 2005. *Class matters*. New York: Henry Holt.

Nicolopoulou, Ageliki, Judith McDowell, and Carolyn Brockmeyer. 2006. Narrative play and emergent literacy: Storytelling and story acting meet journal writing. In *Play = learning: How play motivates and enhances children's cognitive and social-emotional growth*, ed. Dorothy Singer, Roberta Michnick Golinkoff, and Kathy Hirsh-Pasek, 124–145. New York: Oxford University Press.

North Central Regional Educational Laboratory. 2007. Methods for observing and recording. http://www.ncrel.org/sdrs/areas/issues/students/earlycld/ea5l141a.htm.

Nugent, J. Kevin. 1999. The BNBAS as a form of intervention: Empirical evidence assessing the strengths and risks of families. In *World Association for Infant Mental Health (WAIMH) handbook of infant mental health*, vol. 3, *Parenting and child care*, ed. Joy D. Osofsky and Hiram E. Fitzgerald. New York: Basic Books.

O

Ochshorn, Susan. 2001. *Partnering for success: Community approaches to early learning*. New York: Child Care Action Campaign.

Ochshorn, Susan, Sharon Lynn Kagan, Judith Carroll, Amy E. Lowenstein, and Bruce Fuller. 2004 (March). *The effects of regulation on the quality of early care and education*. Child Care and Early Education Research and Policy Series. Washington, DC: National Conference of State Legislatures.

O'Connor, Carla, and Sonia D. Fernandez. 2006. Race, class, and disproportionality: Reevaluating the relationship between poverty and special education placement. *Educational Researcher* 35 (6): 6–11.

OpenCRS. 2007. *Early childhood care and education programs in the 110th Congress: Background and funding*. http://opencrs.cdt.org/document/RL33805/.

Orfield, Gary, and Chungmei Lee. 2007. *Historic reversals, accelerating resegregation, and the need for integration strategies*. August. Los Angeles, CA: The Civil Rights Project, UCLA.

Orozco, Felipe. 2008. Unpublished paper for Child Development class, Bank Street College of Education, New York, New York.

Owens, Robert E. 2005. *Language development: An introduction*. 6th ed. Boston: Pearson Education.

P

Paley, Vivian Gussin. 1979. *White teacher*. Cambridge, MA: Harvard University Press.

———. 1981. *Wally's stories: Conversations in the kindergarten*. Cambridge, MA: Harvard University Press.

———. 1991. *The boy who would be a helicopter: The uses of storytelling in the classroom*. Cambridge, MA: Harvard University Press.

———. 1993. *You can't say you can't play*. Cambridge, MA: Harvard University Press.

———. 2000. *The kindness of children*. Cambridge, MA: Harvard University Press.

———. 2004. *A child's work: The importance of fantasy play*. Chicago: University of Chicago Press.

Palmer, Parker. 1998. *The courage to teach: Exploring the inner landscape of a teacher's life*. San Francisco: Jossey-Bass.

Parten, Mildred. 1932. Social participation among preschool children. *Journal of Abnormal and Social Psychology* 27:243–269.

Patterson, Charlotte. 2008. *Infancy and Childhood*, 26. New York: McGraw-Hill.

Pavlov, Ivan. 1927/1960. *Conditioned reflexes: An investigation of the physiological activity of the cerebral cortex*. New York: Dover Press.

Pawl, Jeree. 1995. On supervision. In *Educating and supporting the infant/family work force*, ed. Linda Eggbeer and Emily Fenichel, 21–29. Washington, DC: Zero to Three Press.

Peisner-Feinberg, Ellen S., Margaret R. Burchinal, Richard M. Clifford, Mary L. Culkin, Carolee Howes, Sharon Lynn Kagan, Noreen Yazejian, Patricia Byler, Jean Rustici, and Janice Zelazo. 2000. *The children of the Cost, Quality, and Outcomes Study go to school: Technical report*. Chapel Hill: University of North Carolina at Chapel Hill, Frank Porter Graham Child Development Center.

Pelco, Lynn E., and Evelyn Reed-Victor. 2003. Understanding and supporting differences in child temperament: Strategies for early childhood environments. *Young Exceptional Children* 6 (3): 2–11.

Pelligrini, Anthony D., and Lee Galda. 2001. "I'm so glad I'm glad": The role of emotions and close relationships in children's play and narrative language. In *Children in play, story and school*, ed. Artin Gönçü and Elisa Klein, 204–219. New York: Guilford Press.

Pelligrini, Anthony D., and Robyn Holmes. 2006. The role of recess in primary school. In *Play = learning: How play motivates and enhances children's cognitive and social-emotional growth*, ed. Dorothy Singer, Roberta Michnick Golinkoff, and Kathy Hirsh-Pasek, 36–53. New York: Oxford University Press.

Pelo, Ann, and Kendra Pelojoaquin. 2006. Why we banned Legos: Exploring power, ownership, and equity in an early childhood classroom. *Rethinking Schools* 21(2). http://www.rethinkingschools.org/archive/21_02/lego212.shtml.

Pennsylvania State University. 2001. *Employer options for child care: Effective strategies for recruitment and retention*. http://betterkidcare.psu.edu/Employer_Options.pdf.

Pessah, Isaac N. 2006. *Can exposure to environmental toxicants influence autism susceptibility?* Bethesda, MD: Autism Society of America. http://www.autism-society.org/site/DocServer/EH_exposure_to_toxicants.pdf?docID=4747.

Piaget, Jean. 1952. Piaget. In *The history of psychology in autobiography*, vol. 4, ed. C. Murchison and E. Boring. Worcester, MA: Clark University Press.

Piaget, Jean, and Barbel Inhelder. 1972. *Play, dreams, and imitation in childhood*. New York: Basic Books.

Pianta, Robert C., Martha J. Cox, and Kyle L. Snow. 2007. *School readiness and the transition to kindergarten in the era of accountability*. Baltimore, MD: Brookes.

Pianta, Robert C., and M. W. Struhlman. 2004. Teacher-child relationships and children's success in the first years of school. *School Psychology Review* 33:444–458.

Pinnell, Gay Su, and Irene C. Fountas. 1998. *Word matters*. Portsmouth, NH: Heinemann.

———. 2007. *The continuum of literacy learning, grades K–2: A guide to teaching*. Portsmouth, NH: Heinemann.

Polakow, Valerie. 2007. *Who cares for our children? The child care crisis in the other America*. New York: Teachers College Press.

Poole, Carla, and Virginia Casper. 2006. Supervisors and caregivers consider together the lived experience of the child. Paper presented at the Zero to Three National Training Institute, December 1–3, Albuquerque, NM.

Porter, Toni, and Rena Rice. 2000. *Lessons learned: Strategies for working with kith and kin caregivers*. New York: Bank Street College of Education.

Powell, Douglas R. 1989. *Families and early childhood programs*. Washington, DC: National Association for the Education of Young Children.

Prescott, Elizabeth. 1984. The physical setting in day care. In *Making day care better*, ed. Jim Greenman and Robert W. Fuqua, 44–65. New York: Teachers College Press.

———. 1987. The environment as organizer of intent in child-care settings. In *Spaces for children: The built environment and child development*, ed. Carol Simon Weinstein and Thomas G. David, 73–88. New York: Plenum.

Project New Beginnings. 2000. *Guidelines for classroom practice*. Unpublished manuscript. Bank Street College of Education, New York, New York.

R

Ravitch, Diane. 2007. Get Congress out of the classroom. Op. ed. *New York Times*, October 3, A25.

Ray, Katie Wood, with Lester L. Laminack. 2001. *The writing workshop: Working through the hard parts (and they're all hard parts)*. Urbana, IL: National Council of Teachers of English.

Rebell, Michael A., and Jessica R. Wolff. 2008. *Moving every child ahead: From NCLB hype to meaningful educational opportunity*. New York: Teachers College Press.

Reese, Hayne W., and Willis R. Overton. 1970. Models of development and theories of development. In *Psychoanalysis and contemporary science*, vol. 2, ed. Benjamin B. Rubenstein. New York: Macmillan.

Reynolds, Maynard, Margaret Wang, and Herbert Walberg. 1987. The necessary restructuring of special and regular education. *Exceptional Children* (February) 53 (5): 391–398.

Rhode Island KIDS COUNT. 2005. *School Readiness Indicators Initiative: Indicators selection by state*. http://www.gettingready.org.

Rideout, Victoria, Elizabeth A. Vandewater, and Ellen A. Wartella. 2003. *Zero to six: Electronic media in the lives of infants, toddlers and preschoolers*. Menlo Park, CA: Kaiser Foundation.

Robinson, Adele, and Deborah R. Stark. 2002. *Advocates in action: Making a difference for young children*. Washington, DC: National Association for the Education of Young Children.

Robinson, Clyde C., Genan T. Anderson, Christin L. Porter, Craig H. Hart, and Melissa Wouden-Miller. 2003. Sequential transition patterns of preschoolers' social interactions during child-initiated play: Is parallel-aware play a bidirectional bridge to other play states? *Early Childhood Research Quarterly* 18 (1): 3–21.

Rockwell, Robert E., Linda C. Andre, and Mary K. Hawley. 1996. *Parents and teachers as partners: Issues and challenges.* New York: Harcourt Brace.

Rogers, Carl. 1989. On speaking personally. In *The Carl Rogers reader,* ed. Howard Kirchenbaum and Valerie Land Henderson. Boston: Houghton Mifflin.

Rogers, Carol. 2002. Defining reflection: Another look at John Dewey and reflective thinking. *Teachers College Record* 104 (4): 842–866.

Rogers, Sally, and Justin H. G. Williams, eds. 2006. *Imitation and the social mind: Autism and typical development.* New York: Guilford Press.

Rogoff, Barbara. 2003. *The cultural nature of human development.* New York: Oxford University Press.

Rolnick, Arthur, and Rob Grunewald. 2007. *Early intervention on a large scale.* Federal Reserve Bank of Minneapolis. http://www.minneapolisfed.org/research/studies/earlychild/early_intervention.cfm.

Roopnarine, Jaipaul L., and James Ewald Johnson. 2001. Play and diverse cultures: Implications for early childhood education. In *Early education and care, and reconceptualizing play,* ed. Stuart Reifel and Mac H. Brown, 295–319. Oxford, UK: Elsevier Science.

———. 2005. *Approaches to early childhood education.* 4th ed. Upper Saddle River, NJ: Pearson Merrill Prentice-Hall.

Rosaldo, Renato. 1989. *Culture and truth: The remaking of social analysis.* Boston: Beacon Press.

Rothbaum, Fred, John Weisz, Martha Pott, Kazuo Miyake, and Gilda Morelli. 2000. Attachment and culture: Security in the United States and Japan. *American Psychologist* 55:1093–1104.

Rothstein, Richard. 2004. *Class and schools: Using social, economic, and educational reform to close the black-white achievement gap.* New York: Teachers College Press.

Rouse, Cecilia, Jeanne Brooks-Gunn, and Sara McLanahan. 2005. Introducing the issue. *The Future of Children* 15 (1): 5–14.

Rousseau, Jean-Jacques. 1956. *The Emile of Jean-Jacques Rousseau.* Trans. and ed. William Boyd. New York: Teachers College Press.

Rutter, Michael. 1971. Causes of infantile autism: Some considerations from recent research. *Journal of Autism and Childhood Schizophrenia* 1 (1): 20–32.

Ryan, Sharon, and Susan Grieshaber. 2004. Research in review: It's more than child development: Critical theories, research, and teaching young children. *Young Children* 59 (6): 44–52.

———. 2005. Shifting from developmental to postmodern practices in early childhood teacher education. *Journal of Teacher Education* 56:34–45.

Ryan, Sharon, Mindy Ochsner, and Celia Genishi. 2001. Miss Nelson is missing! Teacher sightings in research on teaching. In *Embracing identities in early childhood education: Diversity and possibility,* 45–59, ed. Susan Grieshaber and Gaile S. Cannella. New York: Teachers College Press.

S

Saarni, Carolyn. 1999. *The development of emotional competence.* New York: Guilford Press.

Salling, Mark. 2007. The role of faith-based organizations in providing social and health services to Cleveland's Ward 17 community. *Planning and Action: The Journal for the Center of Community Solution* 60 (3): 1–6.

Sameroff, Arnold J. 1975. Early influences on development: Fact or fancy? *Merrill-Palmer Quarterly* 21 (4): 267–294.

Sameroff, Arnold J., and Michael J. Chandler. 1975. Reproductive risk and the continuum of caretaking casualty. In *Review of child development research,* vol. 4, ed. Frances D. Horowitz, Mavis Hetherington, Sandra Scarr-Salapatek, and Gerald Siegel. Chicago: University of Chicago Press.

Sameroff, Arnold J., and M. Marshall Haith, eds. 1996. *The five to seven year shift: The age of reason and responsibility.* Chicago: University of Chicago Press.

Samway, Katharine D., and McKeon, Denise. 2007. *Myths and realities: Best practices for English language learners.* 2nd ed. Portsmouth, NH: Heinemann.

Sapolsky, Robert. 1998. *Why zebras don't get ulcers: An updated guide to stress, stress-related disease, and coping.* New York: W. H. Freeman.

Sarathy, Leela. 2007. Observation quoted with permission.

Schön, Donald A. 1983. *The reflective practitioner: How professionals think in action.* New York: Basic Books.

———. 1996. *Educating the reflective practitioner: Toward a new design for teaching and learning in the professions.* San Francisco: Jossey-Bass.

Schreiber, Mary Ellis. 1996. Lighting alternatives: Considerations for child care centers. *Young Children* 51 (4): 11–13.

Schultz, Steven B. 1989. Finding meaning in the resistance of preschool children: Critical theory takes an interpretive look. *Thought and Practice* 2 (1): 4–17.

———. 2005. Finding meaning in the resistance of preschool children: Critical theory takes an interpretive look. In *Rethinking resistance in schools: Power, politics, and illicit pleasures,* ed. Jonathan Silin. Occasional Paper series. New York: Bank Street College of Education.

Schweinhart, Lawrence J., Jeanne E. Montie, Zongping Xiang, W. Steven Barnett, Clive R. Belfield, and Milagros Nores. 2005. *Lifetime effects: The High/Scope Perry Preschool study through age 40.* Ypsilanti, MI: High Scope Press.

Scott-Little, Catherine, Sharon Lynn Kagan, and Victoria Stebbins Frelow. 2005. *Inside the content: The breadth and depth of early learning standards.* SERVE Center at the University of North Carolina at Greensboro. www.serve.org/_downloads/publications/insidecontentfr.pdf (retrieved October 22, 2007).

Scriven, Michael. 1991. Beyond formative and summative evaluation. In *Evaluation and education: A quarter century,* ed. M. W. McLaughlin and D. C. Phillips, 169. Chicago: University of Chicago Press.

Seleti, Juliana. 2007 (March 22). Early childhood trends in South Africa. *Exchange Every Day.* http://www.childcareexchange.com/eed/issue.php?id=1686.

Shanok, Rebecca Shamoon. 1990. Parenthood: A process marking identity and intimacy capacities. *Zero to Three* 11 (2): 1–9.

Shelov, Stephen P., and Robert E. Hannemann, eds. 1998. *Caring for your baby and young child: Birth to age three.* American Academy of Pediatrics. New York: Bantam Books.

Shepard, Lorrie A. 1994. The challenges of assessing young children appropriately. *Phi Delta Kappan* 76:206–212.

———. 2000. The role of assessment in a learning culture. *Educational Researcher* 29:4–14.

———. 2005. Linking formative assessment to scaffolding. *Educational Leadership* 63 (3): 66–70.

Sherin, Miriam Gamoran. 2000. Viewing teaching on videotape. *Educational Leadership* 57 (8): 36–38.

Shonkoff, Jack P., and Deborah Phillips, eds. 2000. *From neurons to neighborhoods: The science of early childhood development.* Washington, DC: National Academies Press.

Shore, Rima. 1997. *Rethinking the brain: New insights into early development.* New York: Families and Work Institute.

———. 2005. *Indicator brief increasing the percentage of children living in two-parent families.* Kids Count data center, Annie E. Casey Foundation. http://www.kidscount.org/sld/auxiliary/briefs/twoparfamupdated.pdf.

Shultz, Bridget. 2004. *2003 data analysis, National Coalition for Campus Children's Centers.* Available free from NCCCC: http://www.campuschildren.org/publications.html.

Shutte, Augustine. 1995. *Philosophy for Africa.* Milwaukee, WI: Marquette University Press.

Siegel, Daniel J. 1999. *The developing mind: Toward a neurobiology of interpersonal experience.* New York: Guilford Press.

Siegel, Marjorie, and Stephanie Lukas. 2008. Room to move: How kindergarteners negotiate literacies and identities in a mandated balanced literacy curriculum. In *Diversities in early childhood education: Rethinking and redoing,* 29–47, ed. Celia Genishi and A. Lin Goodwin. New York: Routledge.

Silin, Jonathan. 1995. *Sex, death and the education of children: Our passion for ignorance in the age of AIDS.* New York: Teachers College Press.

Silin, Jonathan, and Carol Lippman. 2003. *Putting the children first: The changing face of Newark's public schools.* New York: Teachers College Press.

Singer, Dorothy, Roberta Michnick Golinkoff, and Kathy Hirsh-Pasek, eds. 2006. *Play = learning: How play motivates and enhances children's cognitive and social-emotional growth.* New York: Oxford University Press.

Singer, Dorothy G., and Jerome L. Singer. 2005. *Imagination and play in the electronic age.* Cambridge, MA: Harvard University Press.

Skinner, B. F. 1979. *The shaping of a behaviorist.* New York: Knopf.

Slavin, Robert E., and Alan Cheung. 2003. *Effective reading programs for English language learners: A best-evidence synthesis.* http://www.csos.jhu.edu/crespar/techReports/Report66.pdf.

Smidt, Sandra. 2005. *Observing, assessing and planning for children in the early years.* New York: Routledge.

Smilansky, Sara. 1968. *The effects of sociodramatic play on disadvantaged preschool children.* New York: Wiley.

Smilansky, Sara, and Leah Shefatya. 2004. *Facilitating play: A medium for promoting cognitive, socio-emotional and academic development in young children.* Gaithersburg, MD: Psychosocial and Educational Publications.

Smith, L. Glenn, and Joan K. Smith. 1994. *Lives in education: A narrative of people and ideas.* 2nd ed. New York: St. Martin's Press.

Snow, Catherine E., M. Susan Burns, and Peg Griffin, eds. 1998. *Preventing reading difficulties in children.* National Research Council. Washington, DC: National Academies Press.

Snyder, Agnes. 1972. *Dauntless women*. Washington, DC: Association for Childhood Education International.

Snyder, Kathleen, and Sarah Adelman. 2004. *The use of relative care while parents work: Findings from the 1999 national survey of America's families*. Discussion paper 04-09. Washington, DC: Urban Institute.

Sonenstein, Freya L., Gary J. Gates, Stefanie Schmidt, and Natalya Bolshun. 2002. *Primary child care arrangements of employed parents: Findings from the 1999 national survey of America's families*. Occasional paper no. 59. Washington, DC: Urban Institute. http://www.urban.org/uploadedpdf/310487_OP59.pdf.

Sowa, Angela. 1999. Observing the unobservable: The Tavistock Infant Observation Model and its relevance to clinical training. *fort da*, 5, no. 1. www.spdecaracas.com.ve/download/cdt_242.doc.

Sparks, Louise Derman, and the ABC Task Force. 1989. *Anti-bias curriculum: Tools for empowering young children*. Washington, DC: National Association for the Education of Young Children.

Spencer, Margaret Beale, and Carol Markstrom-Adams. 1990. Identity processes among racial and ethnic minority children in America. *Child Development* 61:200–310.

Spicer, Scott. 2002. States try to specify what young children should learn. Quality Counts 2002. *Education Week* 21 (January 10): 17. http://www.edweek.org.

Spohn, Kate. 1994. *Broken umbrellas*. New York: Viking.

Squires, Jane, Diane Bricker, Kay Heo, and Elizabeth Twombly. 2001. Identification of social-emotional problems in young children using a parent-completed screening measure. *Early Childhood Research Quarterly* 16:405–419.

Stegelin, Dolores A. 2004. Introduction. *Early childhood education: Policy issues for the 1990s*, ed. Dolores A. Stegelin. Norwood, NJ: Ablex.

Stern, Barbara. 2003. *In their own voices: Parents and teachers talk about struggling readers*. Unpublished master's thesis, Bank Street College of Education, New York, New York.

Stern, Daniel. 1985. *The interpersonal world of the infant: A view from psychoanalysis and developmental psychology*. New York: Basic Books.

St. Joseph's Women's Health Centre. n.d. *Sharing attachment practices across cultures: Learning from immigrants and refugees*. Funded by Health Canada's National Projects Fund. http://www.attachmentacrosscultures.org/about/about15.htm.

Stoney, Louise, Anne Mitchell, and Mildred E. Warner. 2006. Smarter reform: Moving beyond single-step solutions to an early care and education system. *Community Development: Journal of the Community Development Society* 37 (2, Summer): 101–115.

Stott, Frances. 1997. A view from the classroom: Changing minds. *The Signal (Newsletter of the World Association for Infant Mental Health)* July–September: 6–9.

Strickland, Dorothy S. 2006. Language and literacy in kindergarten. In *K today: Teaching and learning in the kindergarten year*, ed. Dominic F. Gullo, 73–84. Washington, DC: National Association for the Education of Young Children.

Sturm, Connie. 1997. Creating parent-teacher dialogue: Intercultural communication in child care. *Young Children* 52 (5): 34–38.

Sturm, Lynne. 2004. Temperament in early childhood: A primer for the perplexed. *Zero to Three* 24 (4): 4–11.

Sullivan, Harry Stack. 1955. *The interpersonal theory of psychiatry*. New York: W. W. Norton.

Super, Charles M., and Sara Harkness. 1986. The developmental niche: A conceptualization at the interface of child and culture. *International Journal of Behavioral Development* 9:545–566. Online: jbd.sagepub.com/cgi/reprint/9/4/545.

Swadener, Beth Blue. 2000. "At risk" or "at promise"? From deficit constructions of the 'other childhood' to possibilities for authentic alliances with children and families. In *The politics of early childhood education*, ed. Lourdes Diaz Soto, 117–134. New York: Peter Lang.

Swap, Suzanne M. 1993. *Developing home-school partnerships: From concepts to practice*. New York: Teachers College Press.

Sweet, Monica A., and Mark I. Appelbaum. 2004. Is home visiting an effective strategy? A meta-analytic review of home visiting programs for families with young children. *Child Development* 75 (5): 1435–1456.

Sylvester, Kathleen. 2001. Caring for our youngest: Public attitudes in the United States. *Caring for Infants and Toddlers* 11 (1, Spring/Summer). The Future of Children (Princeton/Brookings). http://www.futureofchildren.org/information2826/information_show.htm?doc_id=79351.

T

Tabors, Patton O. 1997. *One child, two languages: A guide for preschool educators of children learning English as a second language*. Baltimore, MD: Brookes.

Takanishi, Ruby, and Kristie Kauerz. 2008. P-K inclusion: Getting serious about a P-16 system. *Phi Delta Kappan* 89 (8): 480–487.

Tasker, Fiona, and Susan Golombek. 1997. *Growing up in a lesbian family: Effects on child development*. New York: Guilford Press.

Tatum, Beverly Daniel. 1997. *Why are all the black kids sitting together in the cafeteria and other conversations about race*. New York: Basic Books.

———. 2003. *"Why are all the black kids sitting together in the cafeteria?": A psychologist explains the development of black identity*. Rev. ed. New York: Basic Books.

Taylor, Sandra, Fazal Rizvi, Bob Lingard, and Miriam Henry. 1997. *Educational policy and the politics of change*. New York: Routledge.

Teachers Resisting Unhealthy Children's Entertainment (TRUCE). 2006. *A guide to playthings*. http://www.truceteachers.org.

Theilheimer, Rachel. 1993. Something for everyone: Benefits of mixed-age grouping for children, parents, and teachers. *Young Children* 48 (5): 82–87.

———. 2006. Molding to the children: Primary caregiving and continuity of care. *Zero to Three* 26 (3): 50–54.

Thelen, Esther, and Karen E. Adolph. 1992. Arnold L. Gesell: The paradox of nature and nurture. *Developmental Psychology* 28 (3): 368–380.

Thelen, Esther, and Linda R. Smith. 2006. Dynamic systems theories. In *Handbook of child psychology*, vol. 1, *Theoretical models of human development*, 6th ed., ed. Richard M. Lerner, 258–312. New York: Wiley.

Thomas, Jane. n.d. *Child care and laboratory schools on campus*. National Coalition for Campus Children's Centers, 5-05. http://www.campuschildren.org/pubs/cclab/cclab1.html.

Thompson, Ross. 2000. The legacy of early attachments. *Child Development* 71 (1): 145–152.

Tobin, Joseph. 2004. The disappearance of the body in early childhood education. In *Knowing bodies, moving minds*, ed. L. Bresler, 111–125. Dordrecht, The Netherlands: Kluwer Academic.

Tobin, Joseph, Yeh Hsueh, and Mayumi Karasawa. 2009. *Preschools in three cultures revisited: China, Japan, and the United States*. Chicago: University of Chicago Press.

Tobin, Joseph J., David Y. H. Wu, and Dana H. Davidson. 1989. *Preschool in three cultures: Japan, China and the United States*. New Haven, CT: Yale University Press.

Tronick, Edward, and Andrew Gianino. 1986. Interactive mismatch and repair: Challenges to the coping infant. *Zero to Three* 6 (3): 1–6.

Tronto, Joan. 2001. An ethic of care. In *Ethics in community based elder care*, 60–68, ed. Martha B. Holstein and Phyllis B. Mitzen. New York: Springer.

Tucker, G. Richard. 1999. *A global perspective on bilingualism and bilingual education*. http://www.cal.org/resources/Digest/digestglobal.html.

Tudge, Jonathan. 1990. Vygotsky, the zone of proximal development, and peer collaboration: Implications for classroom practice. In *Vygotsky and education: Instructional implications and applications of sociohistorical psychology*, ed. Luis C. Moll, 155–172. New York: Cambridge University Press.

U

United Nations, Office of the High Commissioner for Human Rights. 1990. *Convention on the Rights of the Child*. http://www.unhchr.ch/html/menu3/b/k2crc.htm.

U.S. Census Bureau. 2006. *Families and living arrangements: 2005*. Washington, DC: U.S. Department of Commerce. http://www.census.gov/Press-Release/www/releases/archives/families_households/006840.html.

U.S. Department of Education. 2004. *Four pillars of NCLB*. http://www.ed.gov/nclb/overview/intro/4pillars.html.

———. 2008. Questions and answers on the rights of limited-English proficient students. http://www.ed.gov/about/offices/list/ocr/qa-ell.html.

U.S. Department of Labor. 2007. *The Family and Medical Leave Act*. http://www.dol.gov/compliance/laws/comp-fmla.htm.

———, Bureau of Labor Statistics. 2006. *Employment characteristics of families in 2005*. http://www.bls.gov/news.release/famee.nr0.htm.

V

Valdez, Guadalupe. 1996. *Con respeto: Bridging the distance between culturally diverse families and schools*. New York: Teachers College Press.

Van Ausdale, Debra, and Joseph R. Feagin. 2001. *The first r: How children learn race and racism*. Lanham, MD: Rowman and Littlefield.

Van de Walle, John A. 2004. *Elementary and middle school mathematics*. 5th ed. New York: Allyn & Bacon.

Van Gulden, Holly, and Lisa M. Bartels-Rabb. 1995. *Real parents, real children: Parenting the adopted child*. New York: Crossroads.

van Ijzendoorn, Marinus H., and Abraham Sagi. 1999. Cross-cultural patterns of attachment: Universal and contextual dimensions. In *Handbook of attachment: Theory, research, and clinical applications*, ed. Jude Cassidy and Phillip R. Shaver, 713–734. New York: Guilford Press.

Vasquez, Vivian Maria. 2004. *Negotiating critical literacies with young children*. New York: Teachers College Press.

Veneman, Ann M. 2007. Empower women to help children. The state of the world's children. Women and children: The double divide—Gender equality. www.unicef.org/cowc07/press/release.php.

Vygotsky, Lev. 1934 (trans. 1978). *Mind in society: The development of higher psychological processes*. Cambridge, MA: Harvard University Press.

———. 1935/1978. *Mind in society: The development of higher psychological processes*. Cambridge, MA: Harvard University Press.

———. 1978/1935. *Mind in society: The development of higher psychological processes*. Cambridge, MA: Harvard University Press.

———. 1986. *Thought and language*. Cambridge, MA: Harvard University Press.

W

Wahl, Ellen. 2003. American Museum of Natural History: Science and Nature Program for Young Children. In *Urban network: Museums embracing communities*, ed. Jennifer Amdur Spitz and Margaret Thom, 58–66. Chicago: University of Chicago Press.

Wallerstein, Judith, and Joan B. Kelly. 1996. *Surviving the breakup*. New York: Basic Books.

Wardle, Francis, and Marta I. Cruz-Janzen. 2003. *Meeting the needs of multiethnic and multiracial children in schools*. New York: Pearson Education.

Wasow, Eileen. 2000. Families and schools: New lenses, new landscapes. In *Revisiting a progressive pedagogy: The developmental-interaction approach*, edited by Nancy Nager and Edna K. Shapiro, 275–290. New York: State University of New York Press.

Watson, John B. 1913. Psychology as the behaviorist views it. *Psychological Review* 20:158–177.

Watson, Malcolm W., lecturer. 2002. *Theories of human development*, Pt. I, *Two world views—Locke versus Rousseau*. Chantilly, VA: Teaching Company.

Weatherston, Deborah. 2000. The infant mental health specialist. *Zero to Three*. October.

Weber, Evelyn. 1969. *The kindergarten*. New York: Teachers College Press.

———. 1984. *Ideas influencing early childhood education*. New York: Teachers College Press.

Weigand, Barbara, Kate Whitaker, Diane Traylor, Sheri Yeider, and Vivian C. Hyden. 2007. Reflective practice and supervision in child abuse prevention. *Zero to Three* 28 (2): 29–33.

Werner, Emmy S. 1990. Protective factors and individual resilience. In *Handbook of early childhood intervention*, ed. Samuel Meisels and Jack Shonkoff, 97–116. New York: Cambridge University Press.

Werner, Heinz. 1940. *Comparative psychology of mental development*. New York: Harper and Brothers.

Wertsch, J. V., ed. 1985. *Culture, communication and cognition: Vygotskian perspectives*. Cambridge, UK: Cambridge University Press.

WestEd. 2005. *Full-day kindergarten: Expanding learning opportunities*. Policy brief. http://www.wested.org/cs/we/view/rs/771.

Whitebook, Marcy, and Laura Sakai, Emily Gerber, and Carollee Howes. 2001. *Then and now: Changes in child care staffing 1994–2000*. Washington, DC: Center for the Child Care Workforce.

White House Conference on Early Childhood Development and Learning. 1997 (April 17). http://clinton3.nara.gov/WH/New/ECDC/.

Williams, Leslie R., and Doris Pronin Fromberg, eds. 1992. *Encyclopedia of early childhood education*. New York: Garland.

Williams, Leslie R., and Nadjwa L. E. Norton. 2008. Thought-provoking moments in teaching young children: Reflections on social class, sexual orientation and spirituality. In *Diversities in early childhood education: Rethinking and redoing*, ed. Celia Genishi and A. Lin Goodwin, 103–118. New York: Routledge.

Williamson, Gordon, and Marie Anzalone. 2001. *Sensory integration and self-regulation in infants and toddlers: Helping very young children interact with their environment*. Washington, DC: Zero to Three: National Center for Infants, Toddlers, and their Families.

Winnicott, Donald W. 1971/2005. *Playing and reality*. New York: Routledge.

———. 1978. *The child, the family and the outside world*. Harmondsworth, Middlesex, England: Penguin Books.

Winton, Pam. 2006. The evidence-based practice movement and its effect on knowledge utilization. In *Evidence-based practice in the early childhood field*, 71–115, ed. Virginia Buysse and Patricia W. Wesley. Washington, DC: Zero to Three Press.

Winzer, Margaret. 1993 *The history of special education: From isolation to inclusion*. Washington, DC: Gallaudet University Press.

Wolfram, Walt, Carolyn Adger, and Donna Christian. 1999. *Dialects in schools and communities*. Mahwah, NJ: Erlbaum.

World Health Organization Multicentre Growth Reference Study Group. 2006. WHO Motor Development Study: Windows of achievement for six gross motor development milestones. *Acta Paediatrica* Supplement 450:86–95.

Wright, David J., and Lisa M. Montiel. 2008. Understanding faith-based organizations and the law. *Zero to Three* 28 (3): 5–10.

Y–Z

Yettick, Holly. 2003. Brain child: A history of the Head Start program. *Cincinnati Post*, May 21. www.cincypost.com/news/brainchild/news_brain2/headstart.html (accessed August 10, 2007).

Zentalla, Ana Celia, ed. 2005. *Building on strength*. New York: Teachers College Press.

Zigler, Edward F., and Elizabeth Gilman. 1996. Not just any care: Shaping a coherent child care policy. In *Children, families and government: Preparing for the 21st century*, ed. Edward F. Zigler, Sharon Lynn Kagan, and Nancy W. Hall, 94–116. Cambridge: Cambridge University Press.

Zill, Nicholas, Gary Resnick, Kwang Kim, Ruth Hubbell McKey, Cheryl Clark, Shefall Pai-Samant, David Connell, Michael Vaden-Kiernan, Robert O'Brien, and Mary Ann D'Elio. 2001. *Head Start FACES: Longitudinal findings on program performance*. Third progress report. Washington, DC: Administration on Children, Youth, and Families (DHHS), Child Care Bureau.

Glossary

abstract thinking thinking that is independent of here-and-now experience

accommodation Piaget's term for modifying one's cognitive schema to allow for new input

accountability showing that a program is accomplishing what it set out to achieve

acculturate adopt beliefs and practices other than one's own

acculturation the degree to which people adopt beliefs and practices other than their own

action movement with a purpose

active listening concentrating as someone speaks to understand what the person is saying and communicating to the speaker, verbally and nonverbally, that one is listening

acute stressors one-time sources of stress

adaptation learning new ways to relate to the world around oneself

adaptations changes in the environment

advocacy speaking out on behalf of children, lobbying legislators, organizing families and others to take action for children's rights and for funding for children's programs

affect expression of feeling; observable signs of emotion

Ages and Stages Questionnaire a screening tool that provides information about children birth to age four

alignment fitting into the larger picture of the U.S. education system so that what young children learn in preschool, for example, prepares them for success once they enter school

alphabetic principle that each letter or letter combination represents a sound or sounds in the English language

analytic attention clear and focused concentration on unfolding events

anecdotal record a description of one event or occurrence, usually written after the fact

anencephaly a condition in which the brain does not fully develop

anticipatory guidance a technique in which the professional and the parent observe the baby with the family, in real time or on video, to identify the baby's cues, discuss meaningful responses, and predict the baby's behaviors over the coming months

apartheid an all-encompassing system of race-based discrimination, instituted by the white governing elite in South Africa, that lasted from the 1940s until 1994

Apgar test a measure to determine a baby's vital signs at birth and five minutes after birth

architecture (of the brain) the way early experience shapes the brain

articulation agreement a document that establishes how credits from a community college will count toward a bachelor's degree

and, in the case of early childhood programs, toward teacher certification

artifacts pieces of work

assessment ongoing methods of gathering, analyzing, and interpreting information about children to identify their strengths and needs, with the goal of improving teaching strategies and children's learning

assimilation Piaget's term for taking in information that fits with one's already established cognitive schema

atelier studio space in a Reggio Emilia–influenced school

atelierista a teacher-artist, who provides materials and instructs children in the skills they need to produce work that expresses their thinking in a Reggio Emilia–influenced school

attachment a deep emotional tie with a specific person that endures over time and space

attention deficit/hyperactivity disorder (AD/HD) a disorder seen in children who are highly active, are easily distracted by sounds and movement and by visual and tactile stimuli around them, and have trouble stopping or controlling their actions and words

attentional abilities what children must be able to do in order to focus, such as the ability to shut out extraneous information or to focus on the more immediate aspects of a cognitive task

authentic experiences experiences that have meaning for children

autism a disorder marked by challenges to interpersonal communication and a restricted repertoire of repeated behaviors

backup child care centers programs families can use when the primary child care arrangement breaks down, such as when the nanny or the family child care provider is ill or on vacation

Bayley Scale of Infant Development a standardized and normed test for gaining an in-depth picture of how a young child is developing

behaviorists theorists who believe that external influences in the environment determine and shape human behavior

biases tendencies or preferences that can affect behavior

blended families biologically unrelated children living together with their parents and stepparents as a family

Brazelton Neonatal Behavioral Assessment Scale (BNBAS) a research tool that measures neonatal capabilities and individual qualities

Brown v. Board of Education the 1954 Supreme Court ruling that segregated education did not provide equal opportunities for all children

bullying use of negative physical or verbal behavior to wield real or imagined power over another person

burnout reaching the point where one can take no more

capital expenditures purchase of materials, such as furniture, that make up the infrastructure of the classroom and are not frequently replaced

career lattice a system of professional roles that extends in all directions

case study an assessment method based on detailed description of a child's learning and of teachers' strategies over time

categorical world an adult worldview, where everything has a name and fits in a conceptual system

cerebral palsy a disability that affects the motor control centers of the brain

charter schools nonsectarian public schools that an individual or a group establishes with approval and funding from the state but that need not comply with all the regulations that govern public schools

checklists formal or informal evaluations that measure a child's developmental performance against a set of predetermined criteria

child abuse doing something or failing to do something that results in harm to a child or puts a child at risk of harm; can be physical, sexual, or emotional; includes neglect, or not providing for a child's needs

child care continuum the range of child care possibilities, from the most informal to the most formal: from at home with parents to family, friend, and neighbor care to family child care to a child care center or school

child care resource and referral (CCR&R) descriptor for agencies that share their lists of child care centers and criteria for choosing a center with families who contact them, offer training and technical assistance to child care providers, and advocate on behalf of the children and families in their communities

child study a comprehensive document put together from observations of a child over a period of time

chronic stressors ongoing sources of stress

chronosystem a sociopolitical context that changes over time

class the stratification of people by their socioeconomic status

classical conditioning, or learning through association pairing two stimuli in such a manner that one comes to stand for the other

code of ethical conduct a statement of the National Association for the Education of Young Children's (NAEYC's) position on teacher roles and responsibilities

cognition intellectual functioning, including the ability to acquire, store, and make use of information or knowledge (Bjorklund 2005), remembering, symbolic representation, thinking, and intentional control

cognitive behavioral approach an educational method based on the belief that behavior changes as structures of the mind change

cognitive domain the area of development that pertains to how a child thinks; intellectual development

cognitive science a multidisciplinary study of the mind and behavior, and their relationship

communication the process of exchanging information and feelings (Owens 2005)

community of learners relationships that create an environment in which people can learn together

compensation what workers are paid

compensation, quality, affordability trilemma the problem that paying adequate salaries to ensure higher quality costs more than families can afford

comprehension in literacy, children's understanding of what they read and what is read to them

computer manipulatives objects children can move on the computer

conceptual knowledge an understanding of concepts, such as the relationships at work in a math problem

conceptual parameters the boundaries of one's thinking

concrete operations Piaget's third stage, in which children are able to coordinate mental actions into a logical system that leads to greater unity of thinking and the ability to rely less on perception alone

conditioning using a stimulus to achieve a desired reaction that becomes a learned response

confidentiality disclosure of information only to those professionals and family members who are authorized to know it

constructive play play in which children combine and arrange objects to construct something new

constructivist theory a theory that emphasizes the child's active role and maintains that children construct their knowledge primarily through engagement with the world

content knowledge the kinds of deep subject matter knowledge teachers need to succeed

contextualist theory a theory that emphasizes the role of the environment in child development, focusing on the dimensions of the child's experiences with other people, the physical environment, and the social-historical context in which the child lives

contextualized language language that is about the immediate surroundings

continuity of care consistency of adult caregivers over time that helps children develop trusting relationships

continuum of settings and services a range of child care and education options, from inclusive classrooms to self-contained special education classes

custodial care out-of-home care that meets only minimal standards and does not nurture children's growth and development

Convention on the Rights of the Child (CRC) an international agreement to guarantee basic human rights for all children

conventions of literacy unspoken, agreed-upon practices that are involved in reading and writing—how to hold a book and turn its pages, for example

cortisol a hormone that floods the system in response to stress

crisis nursery a program that provides short-term, round-the-clock care for children whose families ask for help

criterion-based assessments measures that use a common set of expectations to view each child's progress individually or to compare it with that of other children

cultural competence the ability to listen and learn about families' perspectives

culture "an intricate dynamic process that shapes and is shaped by how people live and experience their everyday realities" (Williams and Norton 2008, 104)

curriculum the series of learning experiences that makes up the school day

data information that can be analyzed

décalage literally, "out of step"; Piaget's term for the exceptional instances in which a child's development does not concur with the stages through which Piaget maintained that all children pass

decode (words) figure out what word a series of letters spells

deconstruct take apart or unpack to reveal the hidden power relations, contradictions, and paradoxes of what is often accepted as fact

decontextualized language language that is about times, places, and events that are *not* part of the child's experience at that moment

defenses the psychological strategies people use to protect themselves and to cope with reality when anxiety becomes overwhelming

deficit model an approach that holds that early childhood education should address a child's disadvantages rather than focus on the child's strengths

deinstitutionalization the return to their communities in the 1970s of people who had been kept in institutions—primarily individuals with developmental disabilities

dependent care assistance plan an arrangement that allows employees to pay for various services, including child care, with money deducted from their paychecks before taxes

descriptive review a discussion of a child's work that originates from appreciation of the child, not from a crisis or a problem to solve, and that is a starting point for understanding the child

developmental guidance assistance that supports families through their child's ups and downs and helps them become more aware of their child's specific needs; not therapy *per se*

developmental interaction an ever-changing set of ideas and beliefs about the learner, learning, and teaching that is based on a commitment to social justice and that helps teachers understand children by applying child development principles to their observations

developmental milestones sequential changes in children's behaviors that correspond to different ages and developmental levels

developmental niche the physical and social setting in which a child lives, the customs of child care and child rearing, and the psychology of the child's caregivers

diagnostic serving as a screening tool to help early childhood educators identify what they can do to provide children with what they need to do their best in school and in life

dialects variations in a language form that follow a specific set of linguistic rules and are used by a specific community of speakers

diary a place where teachers regularly record what happens and include their commentary or musings; also called a journal

dichotomies two opposing ideas or choices

didactic instructive, as in "didactic materials"

differentiate recognize the subtleties of a concept and the differences between it and similar things

differentiate instruction create learning opportunities for different children according to each child's experience, knowledge, and skills

Direct Instruction a method that Siegfried Engelmann and Carl Bereiter developed as an intervention for preschoolers whom they and others considered disadvantaged, in which teachers provide explicit instruction in vocabulary, general information, and basic skills

discourse interpretations of meaning

disequilibrium literally, "off balance"; times when children may seem fragile and not themselves and when changes may occur suddenly

disorganized unfocused behavior seen in some children; lacking core regulatory abilities

disproportionate representation when the percentage of children from a given demographic group is not the same as the percentage that group represents within the general population

domains areas (of development)

Down syndrome a chromosomal disorder that occurs by chance, includes mental retardation, and affects every aspect of a child's development

dramatic play an interactive and open-ended process in which children invent symbols for ideas, feelings, and issues

drop-in care short-term child care services available at, for example, a gym or a shopping center

dual certification in early childhood and special education earning two licenses simultaneously to prepare to teach children with and without disabilities

dynamic in motion

dynamic systems theory of development the theory that multiple factors influence the timing of and variability in children's growing skills, that no model completely explains a child's development, that there are always unpredictable factors that create change, and that systems find a way to reorganize themselves after the effects of the unpredictable

early intervention (EI) a program that offers a variety of therapeutic and support services to infants, toddlers, and twos with disabilities and to their families

early learning standards guidelines that help to define expectations for children's care and education

early learning systems structures to enable many different services for children and families to work together

eclectic approach an approach that borrows from here and there without a common framework

ecological model Bronfenbrenner's contextualist theory, which maintains that children develop through interactions over time with the people, objects, and symbols in their environment

ego Freud's third part of the self that mediates between the id and the superego

egocentric Piaget's descriptor for young children based on his contention that they do not readily take the perspective of others

egocentric speech Piaget's descriptor for children's speech that is not addressed to anyone and may be difficult for others to understand

elaborate extend and enrich one's understanding of a concept

emergent bilinguals children who are learning English in addition to their native language

emergent curriculum a plan of activities that arises from the children's interests

emergent literacy children's reading- and writing-related behaviors before they actually read and write

empathy identification with and appreciation for another's situation and feelings

empiricism scientific thought based on observable phenomena

English language learners (ELLs) students who speak another language and are learning English but cannot yet participate meaningfully in a school program in English

epistemology the study of the origins of knowledge

ethnicity one's ancestry and country of origin

ethnographer a researcher who studies people in their natural settings

evaluation a process that uses assessment information to make an informed judgment, for instance, about whether children have achieved learning goals teachers have established for them, the relative strengths and weaknesses of the teaching strategies used, or how (or whether) to change those goals and teaching strategies

event sampling observing and recording a predetermined event each time it occurs

executive functions brain function that helps individuals plan and organizes other parts

of the brain to carry out complex cognitive functions and physical actions

exosystem the larger societal context, such as the extended family, neighbors, and the services a family receives occasionally, along with the mass media

expendables materials that children use up, such as paint, paper, and markers

experimental tradition a way of thinking based on scientific processes and empirical evidence

expressive language the ability to verbalize one's own needs, feelings, and information

extended family grandparents, aunts and uncles, cousins, and neighbors who are considered family

facilitate aid, scaffold, and serve a regulating function

faith-based programs child care programs that are associated with religious institutions and that may or may not have religious content as part of their programming

family centered based on the family's needs

family child care paid care and education of children unrelated to the caregiver in the caregiver's home

family configuration structural makeup of the family; the people who are integral parts of the family

family, friend, and neighbor (FFN) care paid or unpaid child care provided by someone the family knows well

family involvement approach encouragement by staff of family participation in various aspects of child care and education programs

family literacy programs programs that work with families to help them increase the time they read aloud to their children and play with their children in ways that focus on language and literacy

family support programs opportunities for families to meet with each other to exchange experiences and skills; may be for single parents, families of children with learning disabilities, or other affinity groupings

faultless instruction an approach used in Direct Instruction that provides a script for teachers designed so that they present learning activities in a progressive sequence from easiest to hardest

figure-ground a perceptual skill that involves differentiating between an object and its background

fine motor development the process of developing the more precise movements of the hand and fingers

fine motor skills how children use their small muscles

formative assessment feedback during or before the completion of a course of study, to enable the student or teacher to identify areas for improvement and make modifications

for-profit child care a business run with the assumption that the owner(s) will make money

full inclusion education of children with special needs solely in general education classrooms

functional assessments assessments that are administered within the context of an infant's or a toddler's everyday life

functional play play that involves actions and the body

gender being male or female

gender constancy understanding that one cannot change one's gender by changing one's appearance or behavior

gender equity support for comparable educational opportunities for girls and boys

gender identity an internal sense of being male or female

gender roles cultural and social attitudes and expectations about what constitutes male and female behavior

generative (materials) materials that have no right answer, encouraging creative thinking in children

genetic epistemologist one who seeks the origins of knowledge and is focused on the nature of knowledge itself

gifts materials Froebel provided for children to help them understand the principles of harmony, unity, and diversity

globalization the development of a seemingly smaller and increasingly interconnected world

goals broad statements that answer the question, What do I want the children in my group to know and be able to do?

Good Start, Grow Smart a G. W. Bush administration initiative to improve Head Start, to provide educational information to teachers and parents, and to encourage the states to develop early learning standards for all preschool learners, with an emphasis on improving children's language and literacy skills

goodness of fit when a self-aware adult recognizes and appreciates the child's temperament and can guide the child within the framework of her or his inborn tendencies

grade retention repetition of a grade by a child

gross motor development the process of using large muscles that support actions to move around in the environment

gross motor skills how children use their large muscles

growth, migration, and differentiation a process through which cells grow, then move to those parts of the brain where they will specialize

guided participation Rogoff's term that explains children's active engagement in culturally structured activities with the support and guidance of attentive adults

guided reading a session in which the teacher helps a group of children apply strategies to a text they read together

habit of mind a disposition toward behaving intelligently when confronted with uncertainty

hand dominance a preference for using one hand over the other

hierarchical progressing from lower to higher levels

high-incidence disabilities the most common disabilities

High/Scope an approach, based on Piaget's ideas, that emphasizes children as active decision makers

high-stakes descriptor for a situation in which a lot is riding on an issue, such as children's becoming successful learners

holistically looking at the whole child

home visits professionals and paraprofessionals visiting families where they live

homeschool when one or more adults in the family instruct children in the school curriculum at home

homologous at the same level

homophobia fear of homosexuality

hundred languages of childhood a term coined by Loris Malaguzzi in Reggio Emilia for the many means of expression children can use to communicate, revisit, and revise their ideas

hypotheses educated guesses

hypotonia a condition in which a child's joints and muscles are overly flexible and loose

id the unsocialized part of the self that tries to do as it pleases and seeks gratification any way it can

identity a person's idea about who she or he is

imitative play schemes children copying, in play, something they have seen in real life

incorporation teachers' weaving of what they have learned from assessment into their practice with children

inclusive classroom a group in which some of the children have disabilities and receive special education services

indicators measures of progress

Individualized Family Service Plan (IFSP) an outline that specialists, caregivers, and the child's family create and reassess together of steps for bringing a baby or toddler as far along as possible in development

inquiry-based descriptor for activities structured so that children seek answers to real questions

institutional racism discrimination based on race that is entrenched in societal structures such as government, schools, and health care

integrated curriculum exploration of a topic through experiences in all subject areas, such as math, social studies, language, art, science, and music

intelligence in the psychological literature, a global capacity that typically includes verbal and mathematical abilities and the capacity to learn and to create novel solutions to complex problems

intentional control a complex skill that includes the ability to inhibit or control action; to direct and continue to pay attention; to shift attention; when necessary, to screen out extraneous stimuli; and to figure out what aspect of a task is most important (Barkley 1997; M. Levine 2002)

intentionality having an objective; purposeful behavior

interdependent expecting others to need help and counting on help from others

internal working model a set of beliefs, goals, expectations, and strategies that an individual holds based on experience with others

internalization children's consolidation of what they learn

internalize make a part of oneself

interpretation the search for meaning from isolated pieces of evidence

intersubjectivity a feeling of mutual understanding people experience when they share their attention and adapt their behavior in order to communicate

intrinsic motivation children's urge to achieve a goal they set themselves or to do something they decide on themselves

job description what someone is hired to do

joint attention a shared focus on an object, person, or event and an awareness of the other person's focus as well as one's own

journal a place where teachers regularly record what happens and include their commentary or musings; also called a diary

kindergarten literally, a "children's garden" in German; developed by Froebel; now refers to the year before children enter first grade

knowledge utilization how individuals generate and use knowledge

lab schools college- or university-based programs where students and faculty can do research on children and learning, observe, do fieldwork, and student-teach

language a shared system of symbols and rules for expressing concepts

language and literacy domain the area of development pertaining to a child's communication skills, both oral and written

latency period the elementary school years, during which, according to Freud, sexuality goes underground

least restrictive environment for children with disabilities, learning and living environments that allow the greatest amount of freedom while still having any needed supports and adaptations

lesson plan a format used to think through a single activity

lobby try to influence policy makers

longitudinal study research that follows the same children over time

looping movement of children from class to class or grade to grade with the same teacher or teachers from the previous class or grade

low child-to-caregiver ratio fewer children per adult teacher-caregiver

low-incidence disabilities disabilities that do not affect a large percentage of children

macrosystem environment that houses the values of the larger culture

magical thinking imagining that one makes something happen by thinking about it

mainstreamed descriptor for an educational approach in which children who have disabilities attend some classes with children who are not diagnosed with disabilities

mandated reporter a professional who, unlike a friend or neighbor who suspects abuse or neglect, *must* contact the local child protective agency or state hotline about suspected mistreatment of a child

manipulative materials objects children can move and touch to make abstract mathematical concepts concrete

manipulatives small toys that require children to use their fine-motor skills

materialist a point of view that argues that the social, economic, and political conditions of people's lives determine their psychologies or mental lives

maturational theory a theory that argues that development results from the natural unfolding of children's biological potential and that all children grow and change in directions specified primarily by their own biological makeup, or genetic code

means-over-end concern with the process instead of an end goal

medical model an approach that treats symptoms instead of the whole person

mentalization, or reflective function the ability to imagine that a person's mental state can explain their behavior

mesosystem the interconnections between the people and organizations in the microsystem, such as those between school and home

metacognition children's thinking about how they think and learn

metaphor literally, to "transfer" meaning from one thing to another that shares both similarities and differences; in play, a theme

microsystem the setting in which children live—for example, their family and all the immediate and daily experiences that take place in the preschool, playground, grocery store, or religious institution they attend

military child care programs for children of military families that the Department of Defense regulates and subsidizes

mixed-age grouping a group or class that includes children of different ages

Montessori Method the educational approach developed by Maria Montessori

motoric routines a series of familiar actions

movement the use of motor skills

multiple intelligences Gardner's theory that there are many capacities that indicate how intelligent a person is

muscle tone limpness or tautness of the muscles

myelinated descriptor for nerve pathways that are surrounded by a type of fatty insulation

nanny an individual who takes care of children in their home

narrative reporting a written description of a child's behaviors

natural setting children's normal setting, such as a classroom or the home; contrasts with an experimental setting

naturalism Rousseau's educational approach, based on the notion that what is natural or untainted by humans is inherently good

nature the specific biological and genetic inheritance from their parents with which all children are born

neonatal period the first month of life

nonsectarian having no religious content; can describe faith-based or other programs

nonstructured, or open, materials materials that children can use however they wish, with no right or wrong way to use them

norm group the sample of children on which a test was piloted

norms unspoken rules that determine acceptable or unacceptable behavior

not-for-profit (nonprofit) child care program run by a private agency that is not designed to generate income beyond the cost of operating it

novelty of experience the unfamiliar

nurture the learned experiences of the world outside the child's body

occupational therapist a professional who promotes coordinated use of small muscles and the senses to accomplish the tasks of everyday life: dressing, eating, playing, cutting, writing

object permanence the knowledge that people and objects still exist even when they are out of sight

objective, objectively without inserting one's own opinion

objectives more specific and smaller in scale than goals; by successfully achieving objectives, learners make progress toward reaching larger goals

occupations physical activities such as sewing, weaving, and gardening that Froebel made part of the kindergarten

on-site child care programming that is at a parent's place of employment or school

one-to-one correspondence ability to pair an item in one set with an item in another set

open-ended activity an experience, such as an art activity, that has many possible outcomes and for which there are no external expectations

open-ended materials materials that children can use in many ways

operant conditioning use of reinforcements to increase or decrease the likelihood of an exhibited behavior

optimal distance neither too close (pals) nor too distant (cold and unsharing), but rather in a reasonable balance

oral phase Freud's term for early infancy, when the baby seeks pleasure through the mouth

Ounce Scale an assessment tool for very young children that looks at the infant or toddler within the context of his or her family

parent education programs professional instruction for families in the many new skills involved in raising children

partnership teachers and parents working together on an equal basis toward a common goal

performance-based assessments measures in which each child's progress is noted individually; children are not compared with each other

PK–3 schools elementary schools that serve children from ages three or four through the third grade and regard all of the classes as a cohesive unit of learning and developmental experiences

parent-child programs groups for families and their children

partial inclusion descriptor for an educational approach in which children receive "push-in" services or are "pulled out" to receive services

pedagogista someone in a Reggio Emilia–influenced school who supports the teachers' work and joins their animated discussions about children and curriculum

perception understanding arrived at through the senses

phase-in periods gradual introduction of children and families to a new classroom

phonemes the specific sounds of the language we speak

phonemic awareness the ability to hear and notice the separate sounds in words, independent of their meaning, which helps children master the alphabetic principle

physical domain the area of development pertaining to how children use their bodies

physical therapist a professional who promotes functional use of large muscles to develop motor skills, locomotion, balance, and range of motion

Plan, Do, Review part of the predictable routine of a High/Scope classroom that involves children's discussing where, with what, and with whom they will play; playing; and then discussing their play afterwards

play-based assessment tool an approach that uses play activities with peers or adults in a natural setting to observe a child's behaviors

play symbols ways to make one thing stand for another in play

play themes the main ideas children develop as they play

policy a course of action that helps to guide and determine present and future decisions

polis city or city-state in ancient Greece; also, community or citizenship

postmodern an approach to knowledge and understanding that is skeptical of all-encompassing theories

practical-life skills abilities needed for daily activities, such as buttoning, pouring juice, and washing dishes

precursors events leading up to something

prepared environment a Montessori classroom that has carefully chosen materials placed on open shelves in order of increasing difficulty from left to right

primacy of parents the question of whether parents should take primary responsibility for raising their children

primary attachment relationships children's most important personal connections

primary caregiving system an arrangement in which each child has one caregiver who gets to know the family and child very well

prior knowledge what a child brings to a learning situation from earlier learning

private speech speech for oneself

privately funded not paid for with public monies; in child care, paid for by parent tuitions and donations and gifts from foundations and corporations

privatization control of public services by private groups

procedural knowledge knowing how to do something but not why the approach works, as, for example, when someone knows what steps to take to solve a math problem but does not know why to take them

process quality the interactions, activities, and overall learning opportunities in the classroom as well as the health and safety routines

project approach children's serious investigation of a topic of interest to them

prone lying on one's belly

proprietary child care for-profit child care, owned by an individual or corporation, run with the assumption that the owner(s) will make money

proprioceptive system a series of receptors located throughout the body that informs individuals where they are in space; the sense of one's own body and muscular contractions

prosocial getting along with others

pruning the falling away of unused synapses, or connections, between cells

psychological home base an emotionally safe place

psychosexual as in Freud's psychosexual stages of development, each stage named for the part of the body that gives most pleasure at that stage

publicly funded receiving monies from the local, state, or federal government

"pull-out" services a learning approach in which children who have disabilities are "pulled out" of the regular classroom to work one-on-one with a specialist or special education teacher in a resource room or other setting

push-down of academic curriculum the pressuring of teachers of young children to teach skills that were once taught only to older children

"push-in" services a learning approach in which special educators work in an inclusive classroom with children who have disabilities

reader's workshop a program in which children participate in a range of reading-related activities independently, with other children, and with their teacher

receptive language the ability to understand what others say

reconceptualizers early childhood educators who look analytically and critically at issues facing young children, their teachers, and their families

recursive cycling back to revisit ongoing issues

redshirting a term taken from college sports that means to hold someone back for a time to give the individual a greater advantage, as in delaying children's entry to kindergarten so that they will be older and possibly more mature than their classmates for the rest of their school years

Reggio Emilia approach a way of thinking about and working with children that is based on a vision of the child as a strong and capable human being; named for the region of Italy in which it was developed

regress go back to earlier behaviors or appear to lose newly acquired ones

reinforcement, reinforcers rewards

relational, or interpersonal, theory theory that assumes that development occurs in the context of relationships with others

reparative healing

representational thinking the ability to use an object to stand for something else

represent stand for

resilience the ability to recover from a hardship

resilient possessing a range of inner strengths that aids recovery from undesirable experiences

resegregation the return of segregated schools

respite care a program that gives families a break, for example, from caring for a child with special health or chronic medical needs

representative sample a group that shares important characteristics with everyone taking a specific test

responsive care a way of caregiving that listens to children and responds to them respectfully

routines predictable, repeated daily events, such as using the toilet, washing hands, setting the table, eating, cleaning up from meals, and napping

rubric a chart with categories

running record a written record by the teacher of exactly what she or he observes for a period of time

scaffolding a Vygotskian term that describes what happens when a more experienced person coaches someone in the process of learning something

school readiness possession of the skills that are basic to learning to read, write, do math, and other school subjects

scientific method hypothesis, experimentation, and objective observation leading to proof or disproof of the hypothesis

screening, screening tool a method used to identify potential developmental delays but not to assess development or growth over time

script scenario from everyday life that children imitate

scripted descriptor for a curriculum that spells out exactly what teachers will say and do at each point in the lesson

self-actualization the capacity to reach one's fullest potential

self-efficacy feeling capable and able to accomplish goals

secure base a safe place from which junior toddlers can venture to explore, moving on from their lap-baby status

self-correcting materials materials, such as a puzzle, that inform children whether they have completed a task correctly

self-help skills abilities that enable individuals to care for themselves—for example, dressing and undressing, eating, washing hands, and toileting

self-regulation the ability to monitor, pace, and control one's emotions and needs; a core ability that involves modulating impulses, exerting self-control, delaying gratification, and following routines and social rules even if one does not feel like it

sense of self an idea of who one is

sensory defensive sensitive to a range of sensory experiences

seriation skills ability to put objects or events in a sequence from first to last

sexual orientation patterns of psychosocial and emotional-erotic attraction to another person; the gender of one's love object in relation to one's own gender

sick child care center a program for children who are too sick to be in a group with other children but well enough to go out

silent period the first stage of second-language acquisition, in which a child absorbs the new language without expressing it

social-emotional domain the area of development pertaining to how a child manages feelings and interacts with others

social context interpersonal surroundings

social learning theory a theory based on the belief that children learn through imitation

social motivator something that stimulates children to interact and brings them into a social world that requires them to negotiate, tolerate frustration, and cooperate with others

social referencing checking the caregiver's or other children's facial expressions to judge the emotional meaning of a situation

social skills the ability to get along with others

social studies investigation of the human environment

sociocultural norms the expectations and behaviors of the culture or subculture in which we live

sociodramatic descriptor for dramatic play involving a social group

sociohistorical giving credence to past and present social relations

special needs disabilities or giftedness that requires adaptations in a child's everyday life and learning

speech the oral form of language

spina bifida a congenital malformation of the spinal column

staff turnover loss of teachers to better-paying work or better working conditions

standard American English (SAE) the form of English used in schools

static still, or not moving

Strange Situation procedure a laboratory procedure developed by Mary Ainsworth for young toddlers (thirteen to eighteen months old) that involves separations and reunions between mother/father, toddler, and a stranger and that calls the attachment system into play

stress response reaction of the body to difficult situations

structured, or closed, materials materials, such as puzzles, that have a right way to work with or complete them

structures of the mind mental representations

structural quality such elements as group size, ratio of staff to children, and education and training of teachers and staff

structuralists theorists who construct complex, tightly woven systems that have internal structures

subjective reflecting one's perspective and judgments

subjectivity seeing things from one's unique position in the world

summative assessment the gathering of information at the conclusion of a course of study with the goal of improving learning

superego conscience

supine lying on one's back

symbol, symbolic representation a mental image, an action, a picture, or a notation that represents something else; the understanding that a mental image, an action, a picture, or a notation can stand for or represent something else

symbolically descriptor for using something, such as play, to express meanings other than the surface meaning of the activity itself

synapses extensions that neurons form to connect to other cells

synaptic exuberance the period during pregnancy and the first few months of life when neurons are making an unusual number of connections

syntax the order in which we string words together

synthesize put together and make sense of, as in "synthesize findings"

systemic approach attempt to create a system that enables joint efforts

systems approach a way of looking at children that takes into account the systems that are part of their makeup and the many contexts that make up the systems of their environments

systems theories ways of looking at development through the lens of parts that make up whole systems, and how the parts mutually interact over time

tabula rasa a blank slate onto which the environment writes

task-based descriptor for measuring milestones the child has reached

taxonomies hierarchical categories, for example, of intelligence

teacher turnover loss of teachers to other jobs

teaching portfolios physical or electronic assemblages of work and reflections that usually include a statement of the teacher's personal philosophy and that document the teacher's learning about children

temperament an individual's basic behavioral style

theory a well-developed set of assumptions or principles that attempts to organize, analyze, predict, or explain specific events, behaviors, or processes

theory of mind the ability to think about one's own and other people's thinking

third space consider other alternatives when two perspectives seem irreconcilable

time-out the practice of isolating a child who has behaved inappropriately

touchpoints periods of frustration and irritability that precede a new development

transacting descriptor for multiple influences that interact with each other over time

transactional model of development Sameroff and Chandler's theory that suggests that *over time* the child grows and changes because of mutual, or transacting, influences

transformation change in form—for example, from salt, flour, and water into play dough

transgendered descriptor for individuals whose gender identity differs from their biological sex

transition the time between activities—for example, when children are finished playing indoors and are on the way to their next activity but are not yet involved in it

transitional object favorite comfort toy or other item to use for self-soothing

transmigrate live in more than one country or, perhaps, go back and forth between one's homeland and the United States

transsexual a person who feels she or he is of the other gender

traumatic play play originating from traumatic experience

tummy time placement of babies on their stomachs, during the day, to promote complementary muscle development; needed because infants spend more time on their backs to prevent sudden infant death syndrome (SIDS)

unit block a rectangular block of specific dimensions on which the other blocks are based

universal access availability of programming to everyone, as in after-school for all

universal design creation of spaces that are accessible to everyone and items that are easy for everyone to use, regardless of ability or disability

universal morality a code of ethics that applies to everyone

universal prekindergarten (UPK) a nationwide effort that aims to provide *all* preschoolaged children with a free, supportive, literacyrich educational environment prior to kindergarten

utopian built on a vision for a new and ideal society

vertically aligned or linked descriptor for a school in which teachers in every grade contribute to a coherent education for the child while the child attends the school

vestibular system balance mechanism located in the inner ear, vision, and throughout the body (in proprioceptive receptors); relates to gravity and registers movement that is self or other initiated

volitional able to move independently without a specific objective

vouchers similar to scholarships; enable families to send their child to either private or public school with money that would otherwise pay for the child's public school education

well related reaching out to others or responding to them in ways they expect

writer's workshop a program in which children participate in a range of writing-related activities independently, with other children, and with their teacher

zone of proximal development what a child can do "through problem solving under adult guidance or in collaboration with more capable peers" (Vygotsky 1978, 1986)

Credits

Index

Child-centered families, 227
Child development
   altering course of, 226
   culture and, 226–227
   domains of, 225, 233–247
   language and literacy and, 242–247
   mutual influences on, 231–233
   nature/nurture dichotomy, 225
   principles of, 224–226
   sequence of, 225–226
   social-emotional development, 238–239
   strengths, development of, 226
   temperament and, 227–230
Child Development Associate (CDA) credential, 198
Child Development Block Grant, 448, 449, 450
Child labor laws, 144
Child neglect, 41
Child Observation Record (COR), 216
Children, Youth and Families Education and
   Research Network, 417
Children's books, 360. *See also* Literature
   on adoption, 429
   multiracial children's books, 424
Children's Defense Fund (CDF), 464, 467, 469
Children's Museum of Indianapolis, 207
Child studies, 144, 280–281
A Child's Work: The Importance of Fantasy Play
   (Paley), 120, 122
Child Welfare Information Gateway, 429
Child Welfare League of America, 41
China, early education in, 131–133
Chinese-speaking children, 49–50
Christian, Donna, 245
Christie, James F., 119
Chronic illness, dealing with, 43
Chronic stressors, 40
Chronosystems, 37
Chu, Elaine, 272
Clandinin, D. Jean, 10
Clark, Kenneth B., 184
Clark, Mamie, 184
Clarke-Stewart, Allison, 199, 200
Classical conditioning, 168
Class issues, 48
Classrooms. *See* Environment
Classroom teams, working with, 25–27
Classroom visits, 435
Clay, working with, 366
Clayton, Jenna R., 466
Clements, Douglas H., 399
Clifford, Richard M., 344
Code of ethical conduct, 7
Coffman, Julia, 463
Cognitive behavioral theory, 169–170
Cognitive development, 239–242
   in first, second, and third graders, 386–388
   intentional control, 241–242
   memory, 240–241
   in preschoolers and kindergartners, 354–355
   symbolic representation, 241
Cognitive science, 168
Cohen, Abby J., 448, 450
Cohen, Dorothy, 253, 280
Cohen, Miriam, 310
Cohen, Sally Solomon, 5
Cold war, 151
Cole, Michael, 76, 79, 225, 237, 240
Cole, Sheila, 76, 79, 225, 237, 240
Coleman, Mick, 419
Collaboration
   classroom teams, collaborative, 26
   serious issues, addressing, 440–441
   on statewide initiatives, 462–463

Colleagues. *See also* Collaboration
   observation and communication with, 268
College child care, 202
Colorblindness, 45
Colors of environment, 345
Comenius, John Amos, 135
Comer, James P., 419
Commitment and care, 3
Common bonds: Anti-bias teaching in a diverse society
   (Byrnes & Kiger), 357
Communication
   and classroom teams, 25
   with colleagues, 268
   about death, 90–91, 92
   defined, 244
   observations and, 265–268
   play and, 97, 109, 119
   of test results, 312–317
   written communications, 266–268
Community
   families and community gatherings, 437
   first, second, and third graders and, 390, 392
   of learners, 178
Community agencies, referrals to, 441
Compensation, 7, 459–460
   initiatives for professional compensation, 466–467
   quality, affordability tri-lemma, 7
Competence and care, 2
Competition
   culture and, 114
   and games with rules, 108
Comprehensive Child Development Act, 450
Computers
   manipulatives, 399
   with preschoolers and kindergartners, 366–368
Conceptual knowledge, 399–400
Conceptual parameters and play, 97
Concrete operations in first, second, and third
   graders, 387
Concrete services for infants, 208
Conditioning, 168
Conferences. *See* Parent-teacher conferences;
   Workshops
Confidentiality
   in child's report, 315
   and colleague communication, 268
   and observations, 270–271
Conflict, 18, 159–160
   and collaboration, 26
   resolution techniques, 86–87
   as toddler interaction, 338–339
Confucius, 132
Conjunctivitis, 42
Connecticut Charts-A-Course (CCAC) program, 467
Connelly, F. Michael, 10
Connelly, Rachel, 202
Connolly, Paul, 56
Connor, Frances P., 352
Consistency, providing, 39–41
Constructive play, 105–106
   adult involvement in, 118–119
Constructivist theories, 172–174
Consultative Group on Early Childhood Care and
   Development, 8
Consumer Product Safety Commission's Public
   Playground Safety Checklist, 379
Content knowledge, 21–22
Contextualist theories, 174–177
   contemporary theories, 176–177
   evaluation of, 177
Contextualized language, 360
Continuity of care, 7, 192–193
   model, 326–327

Continuum
   of care, 193–194
   of settings and services, 54
Convention on the Rights of the Child (CRC), 35
Conventions of literacy, 359
Cook, Ruth E., 336
Cook, Stuart W., 184
Cooking with infants to two-year-olds, 342
Cookson, Clive, 55
Coontz, E. Kim, 192
Cooperative play, 104
Cooperative playgroups, 192
Copple, Carol, 5–6
Corso, Robert, 433
Co-sleeping, 35
Council for Exceptional Children—Division of Early
   Childhood (CEC-DEC), 61
   continuum of settings and services, 54
   inclusion, position on, 53
Council on Physical Education for Children 2000, 373
Counts, George, 147, 149
Cox, Martha J., 386
Crawford, James, 49
Credentials
   California Commission on Teacher
      Credentialing, 467
   professionals, programs for, 458–459
Cremin, Lawrence, 147
Cribs, safety issues for, 344
Crisis nurseries, 203
Criterion-based assessments, 292–293
Critical reflection, 14–17
Critical theory, 8
Critical thinking and bias, 56
Crittenden, Ann, 195
Cronin, John, 454
Cross, William, 184–185
Cruz-Janzen, Marta I., 423, 426
Cryer, Debby, 344
Cues from children, 325
Cuffaro, Harriet K., 83, 145, 334
Culross, Patti L., 210
Cultural competence, 208
Cultural psychology, 176
Culture, 35–36. *See also* Diversity; History
   attachment and, 69–70
   awareness of, 13
   biographies of educators and, 9–14
   and child development, 226–227
   defined, 35
   developmental niche, 37–38
   early intervention programs and, 208
   ecological systems theory and, 37
   family culture, learning, 36
   globalization and, 34–35, 127
   and infants to two-year-olds, 324
   language and, 50
   and motor milestones, 236
   music and, 365
   play and, 114–115
   self-regulation and, 77
   temperament and, 228
Cummins, James, 245
Curiosity
   attachment and, 70
   spirit of, 20–21
Curriculum. *See also* Integrated curriculum
   assessment and decisions on, 293–294
   early learning standards and, 308–309
Curriculum planning
   for first, second, and third graders, 402–408
   lesson plans, 403–404

Internet. *See also* Websites
  and globalization, 34–35
Internet4classrooms, 401
Interpersonal intelligence, 186
Interpersonal theory, 165–166
Interpretation
  in assessment cycle, 209–291
  observation and, 256
Intersubjectivity, 75, 166
Intervention
  and bullying, 83–84
  and conflict resolution, 86
  and play, 119
Intrapersonal intelligence, 186
Intrinsic motivation, 101, 170
Invest in Kids, 417
IQ. *See* Intelligence quotient (IQ)
Irizarry, Nydia L., 70
Irvin, Sabrina Rotonda, 249
Irwin, Elisabeth, 150
Isaacs, Susan, 150–151, 350
Isolation of family care providers, 195
Itard, Jean-Marc Gaspard, 137

J
Jablon, Judy R., 255, 256, 261, 269, 304
Jackson, Jonnia, 327–328
Jacobs, Ellen Vineberg, 264
Jacobson, Linda, 458, 462
Jalongo, Mary Renck, 26, 333
Jensen, Arthur R., 186
Jensen, Eric, 65, 75
Job descriptions, 19
Johnson, Harriet, 98, 148, 149
Johnson, James Ewald, 113, 124, 143, 148, 150, 212, 216
Johnson, Lyndon B., 151, 450
Joint attention, 75
Jones, Elizabeth, 3, 10
Jones, Nancy Lee, 449
Journals for observations, 266–267, 275–277
Just in Time Parenting, 417

K
Kaeser, Gigi, 424
Kaestle, Carl F., 446
Kagan, Sharon Lynn, 7, 191, 192, 308, 450, 460, 463
Kahn, Alfred J., 447
Kaiser child care centers, 448
Kaiser Permanente temperament assessment, 229
Kamerman, Sheila B., 447
Kamii, Constance, 400
Karasawa, Mayumi, 131, 132–133
Karoly, Lynn A., 199
Katz, Bobbi, 396, 406
Katz, Lillian G., 19, 101, 371–372, 421, 423, 430
Kauerz, Kristie, 7, 191, 192, 205
Keats, Ezra Jack, 358
Keller, Bill, 424
Keller, Helen, 141
Kellogg, Steven, 429
Kelly, Joan B., 91
KidSmart program, 367
Kiger, Gary, 357
Kilburn, M. Rebecca, 199
Kindergartens, 204. *See also* Preschoolers and kindergartners
  Froebel, Friedrich and, 139
  full-day kindergartens, 204
  proliferation of, 140–141
  universal prekindergarten (UPK), 7, 199
Kinnell, G., 339
Kirp, David L., 8, 448
Kissinger, Katie, 424

Kith and kin care, 194
Kitze, Carrie A., 429
Kleifgen, Jo Anne, 49
Klein, Elisa, 119
Klein, M. Diane, 336
Klein, Naomi, 57
Klein, Rebecca, 40
Knowledge. *See also* Prior knowledge
  inquiry, spirit of, 20–21
  prior knowledge, 8, 13
  utilization, 21–22
KnowledgeLeader, 271
Kochanska, Grazyna, 80, 228
Koehler, Phoebe, 429
Kohlberg, Lawrence, 119, 181
Kontos, Susan, 195
Koplow, Lesley, 76, 112
Kovacik, Abbe, 277
Kozol, Jonathan, 154
Kramer, Rita, 143
Krashen, Stephen, 49, 50, 75
Kreider, Rose M., 426
Krutein, Werhner, 424

L
Lab schools, 202
Lally, Ronald J., 321
Lancy, David F., 114
Lane, Sheila, 237
Language. *See also* Literacy; Nonverbal language; Vocabulary
  See also ELLs (English language learners)
  bilingualism, 244–245
  and child development, 242–247
  contextualized language/decontextualized language, 360
  defined, 244
  developmental milestones, 243–244
  dialects, 245–246
  and first, second, and third graders, 386–387, 393–398
  linguistic diversity, 424–425
  and preschoolers and kindergartners, 354, 357, 359–360
  supporting development of, 359–360
  symbolic representation and, 241
  verbal and nonverbal language, 87
Lanham Act of 1940, 448
Lareau, Annette, 48, 424
Large muscle skills. *See* Gross motor skills
Laslocky, Jenna, 393
Latency period, 164
Lawrence-Lightfoot, Sara, 430, 431, 436
Layzer, Jean I., 194, 195
LD Online, 417
Lead poisoning, 43–44
Learning through association, 168
Least restrictive environment (LRE), 152–153
Leavitt, Robin, 325
Lee, Chungmei, 56
Leech Lake Head Start, 369–372
Léon, Efrén Michael, 12
Leong, Deborah J., 312, 315
Lerner, Claire, 228
Lesson plans for first, second, and third graders, 403–404
Lessons, 404
Levine, Linda, 33
Levine, Mel, 242
LeVine, Robert A., 29, 324
Levine, Tarima, 91
Levinger, Leah, 14
Lewin, Kurt, 157

Liben, Lynn, 185
Licensing. *See also* Credentials
  programs, 467
  standards, 25
Lieberman, Alicia, 70, 91, 209
Lifetime Effects: The High/Scope Perry Preschool Study through Age 40 (Schweinhart), 216
Lightfoot, Cynthia, 76, 79, 225, 237, 240
Lighting issues, 345
Limber, Susan P., 83
Linguistic diversity, 424–425
Linguistic intelligence, 186
Lionni, Leo, 273
Lippman, Carol, 215
Listening. *See* Active listening
Literacy, 246–247
  balanced approach to, 395
  development milestones, 246–247
  early literacy, 462
  emergent literacy, 357, 359
  environment for, 411
  family literacy programs, 210–211
  and first, second, and third graders, 393–398
  play and, 119
  and preschoolers and kindergartners, 357, 359–360
  supporting development of, 359–360
  symbolic representation and, 241
Literature. *See also* Children's books
  appreciation for, 359–360
  and first, second, and third graders, 395–396
Litt, Carole J., 332
Loan forgiveness letters, 457
Lobbying, 445
Locke, John, 136
Logico-mathematical intelligence, 186
Lombardi, Joan, 446, 455–456
Longitudinal studies, 216
Looping, 192, 327
Louisville Free Kindergarten Association, 147
Low child-to-caregiver ratios, 348
Lowenstein, Amy, 460, 467
Low-incidence disabilities, 55
Low-income children, 48, 55–56
Lucas, Maurice, 46
Lucy's family tree (Schreck), 429
Ludwig, David S., 44
Lukas, Stephanie, 8
Luria, A. R., 174–175
Luther, Martin, 135

M
Macartney, Suzanne, 33
MacCulloch, Diarmaid, 135
MacDonald, Sharon, 304
MacMillan, Margaret, 148
MacMillan, Rachel, 148
Mac Naughton, Glenda, 116, 183, 273, 380, 415–416, 424
Macrosystems, 37
Maeroff, Gene I., 204
Magical thinking, 90
Mahler, Margaret S., 70
Main-effect model, 180
Mainstreaming, 152
Make-believe play. *See* Fantasy play
Malaguzzi, Loris, 216–217
Malting House School for Young Children, 150
Mandarin-speaking children, 49–50
Mandated reporters, 41
Manipulatives
  for dramatic play, 364
  for mathematics, 399
  for preschoolers and kindergartners, 361

Pelojoaquin, Kendra, 389
Peloso, Jeanne M., 2
Peña, Rafael, 358
Perception and manipulatives, 361
Performance
  appraisals, 19
  -based assessments, 292
Perkins Institute for the Blind, 141
Perry Preschool Project, 199, 216
Personal space, room for, 410
Pervasive developmental disorder not otherwise
  specified (PDD-NOS), 316
Pessah, Isaac N., 55
Pestalozzi, Johann Heinrich, 138–139
Phase-in periods, 435
Phillips, Carol Brunson, 13, 56, 423
Phillips, Deborah, 171, 451
Phonemes, 244
Phonemic awareness, 278
  and preschoolers and kindergartners, 365
Photographs for observations, 279
Physical growth
  and development, 225
  in first, second, and third graders, 386–387
  and motor development, 235–238
  in preschoolers and kindergartners, 351–352
Physical therapists, 236–237
Piaget, Jean, 39, 95, 97, 151, 172–174, 176, 183, 216,
  225, 307, 354, 387
Piagetian theory, 172–174
Pianta, Robert C., 75, 386
Pine, Fred, 70
Pinnell, Gay Su, 395
PK–3 schools, 205
Plan, Do, Review process, 216
Planned experiences for infants to two-year-olds,
  341–344
Plasticity of brain, 67
Plato, 133–134
Play, 96. *See also* Constructive play; Disorganized
  play; Dramatic play; Fantasy play; Materials;
  Outdoor play; Toys
  adult involvement in, 118–119
  affective components of, 109–112
  ages of children and, 98
  blocks of time, scheduling, 373
  categories of, 104–108
  Comenius, John Amos on, 135
  communication and, 97, 109, 119
  and culture, 114–115
  debates about, 121, 123
  in democratic society, 120–123
  emotions and, 109
  and exercise, 44
  friendships and, 116, 338–341
  functional play, 105
  games with rules, 108
  and gender, 113
  gun play, 110
  identity issues and, 110–112
  imagination and, 96–97, 121
  of infants to two-year-olds, 98–99, 333–338
  integrative role of, 96
  intrinsic motivation for, 101
  marriage play, 16–17
  mastery and, 110–112
  means-over-end quality of, 101–102
  medical play, 23
  observations about, 270
  and peer relationships, 116
  and power, 112
  in preschool years, 99–100
  in primary grades, 100–101

qualities of, 101–104
respect for, 117–118
roots of, 98–99
rules, freedom from, 102–103
science opportunities and, 364
self-expression and, 103–104
self-regulation and, 109
seriousness about, 12
social change and, 121
specialized interventions, 119
and special needs, 115–116
symbols, 96–97, 103–104
and teacher-child relationships, 116–120
themes, 97
transformation of thought and, 97–98
transitions and, 407–408
traumatic play, 110
Play-based assessment tools, 290
Play therapy, 110
Plowden Report (Britain), 151
Poetry for first, second, and third graders, 396–397
Polakow, Valerie, 191
Policy
  achievement gap and, 452–454
  barriers to individual participation in, 455–456
  brain research and, 451
  conflicts in, 448
  defined, 445–446
  early years, attitudes in, 447–448
  economic status of children, 450
  family changes and, 451–452
  federal legislation and programs, 449
  health status of children, 450
  history of, 446–450
  No Child Left Behind (NCLB) Act of 2001 and, 446
  professionals, involvement of, 455–462
  and quality of early childhood programs, 456–458
  school readiness and, 452–454
  social status of children, 450
  state level change, working for, 462–467
  states and, 446
Polis, 133
Poole, Carla, 17
Porter, Toni, 194
The portfolio and its use: A road map for assessment
  (MacDonald), 304
Portfolio assessment: A handbook for preschool and
  elementary educators (Wortham, Barbour &
  Desjean-Perrotta), 304
The portfolio book: A step-by-step guide for teachers
  (Shores & Grace), 304
Portfolios
  artifacts in, 305–306
  assembling, 303–306
  for assessment, 302–306
  organization formats for, 304
  summative evaluations, 306
  teaching portfolios, 15
Postmodern theories, 183–184
Poston, Muriel, 285, 286
Poverty
  low-income children, 48, 55–56
  War on Poverty, 151–152, 450
  working against, 55–56
Powell, Douglas R., 416, 421
Power
  and accountability, 309
  gun play and, 110
  play and, 110, 112
Practical life skills, 142
Pragmatism, 145
Pratt, Caroline, 98, 149–150, 212
Precursors, 259

Predictability, 331
  and attachment, 71–72
  for preschoolers and kindergartners, 373–376
  providing, 39–41
Pre-encounter stage, 185
Pregnancy
  maternity leave, length of, 447
  and toxins, 65
Prejudices, confronting, 11, 13–14
Prekindergarten initiatives, 466
Pre-K Now, 464
Preliminary considerations for lesson plan, 404
Prepared environment, 212
Preschematic stage in drawing, 355
Preschoolers and kindergartners
  activities for, 360–366
  arrangement of class space, 378–379
  art for, 366
  authentic experiences, planning, 368–373
  balanced environments, creating, 376–378
  blocks, working with, 360–364
  blocks of time, scheduling, 373
  classrooms for, 368–380
  cognition and, 354–355
  community issues, meetings for, 374
  curriculum planning for, 368–370
  dramatic play by, 358, 360
  emergent curriculum, 369–371
  emergent literacy, 357, 359
  emotional development, 352–353
  environment for, 368–380
  evaluating environments, 380
  fine motor skills of, 352
  gross motor skills of, 352
  integrated curriculum for, 371
  job charts for, 375
  language and, 357, 359–360
  learning in, 355–368
  life with, 351–355
  manipulatives for, 361
  materials for, 360–366
  meetings with, 373–374
  movement and, 365
  music and, 365–366
  outdoor space for, 379–380
  physical development, 351–352
  predictability for, 373–376
  project approach for, 371–372
  routines with, 375–376
  scheduling for, 373–376
  science with, 364
  small groups, working with, 372–373
  social action and, 356–357
  social development, 352–353
  social studies with, 356–357
  surveys of, 374
  technology and, 366–368
  transitions with, 374–375
Prescott, Elizabeth, 376–378
Presence of educators, 9
Primacy of parents, 447
Primary attachment relationships, 98
Primary caregiving system, 11, 13
  for infants to two-year-olds, 329–330
Primary grades. *See* First, second, and third graders
Print-noisy rooms, 411
Prior knowledge, 8, 13, 234
  and memory, 240–241
Private child care, 199–200
Private speech, 77
Privatization of education, 56–57
Problem-solving and play, 119
Procedural knowledge, 399–400

ISBN: 978-0-07-748739-3
MHID: 0-07-748739-7

90000

9 780077 487393